A STANDARD GUIDE TO PURE-BRED DOGS

A STANDARD GUIDE TO
PURE~BRED
DOGS

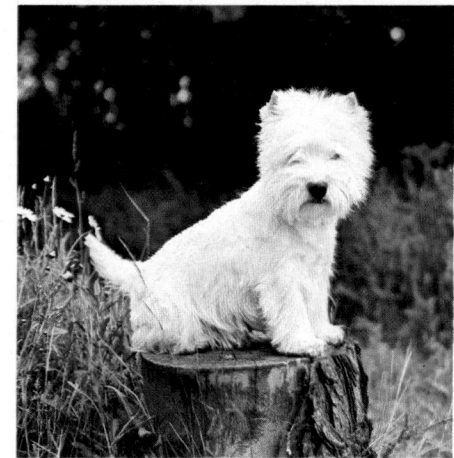

Compiled and Edited by Harry Glover

Published 1977 by Macmillan London Ltd. London and Basingstoke. Associated companies in Delhi, Dublin, Hong Kong, Johannesburg, Lagos, Melbourne, New York, Singapore, Tokyo.

ISBN 0333 227824

Phototypeset in Great Britain by Filmtype Services Limited, Scarborough

Printed by New Interlitho, Italy

The British Standards are reproduced with the kind permission and co-operation of The Kennel Club.

The co-operation of other Kennel Clubs throughout the world is gratefully acknowledged.

We wish to thank the following for permission to reproduce copyright photographs:
Aftenposten, Oslo, pp. 433 bottom, 447 left. *The American Kennel Club*, pp. 40, 63 left, 110, 140 left, 261. *Australian Tourist Board*, p. 416. *Marc Buzzini*, pp. 179, 417 bottom, 418, 420 bottom right, 421 left, 422, 425 right, 427 top, 431, 432 right, 433 top, 434, 435, 437, 438 right, 440, 441, 444 right, 445 left, 447, 448, 449, 451 right, 452 left, 453, 454 right, 455, 456 left, 457, 460 right. *Camera Press*, pp. 63 right, 112. *The Danish Kennel Club*, p. 454 left. *The Finnish Kennel Club*, pp. 419 right, 429 right, 436 right, 444 left. *Fujifotos*, pp. 166, 424 left, 428, 432 left, 458. *Harry Glover*, pp. 7 centre & bottom, 10 bottom, 17 left, top middle of back cover. *The Hungarian Kennel Club*, pp. 422, 460 top left. *Mrs W.H. Mills-de Hoog*, pp. 35, 38. *The Mansell Collection*, pp. 8 centre & bottom, 9 bottom. *Diane Pearce*, pp. 104, 150 right, 174, 180 left, 191, 192, 194, 268, 328, 333, 340 left, 404, 436 left, 445 right. *Photo Researchers Inc*, pp. 42, 61, 65, 110 right, 140 right, 243, 245. *The Polish Kennel Club*, pp. 422, 460 top left. *Paul Popper*, p. 6 top (colour). *Radio Times Hulton Picture Library*, pp. 5, 9 top, 12 bottom. *Ann Roslin-Williams*, pp. 80, 86, 144, 150 left, 274, 295, 336 right, 343, 357, 417 top, 420 left, 424 right, 425 left, 427 bottom, 429 left, 442, 443 right, 451 left, 459, 460 bottom left. *Sally Ann Thompson*, pp. 8 top, 12 top & centre, 14 top, 17 right, 30, 31, 32, 36, 43, 45, 47, 49, 51, 52, 54, 55, 58, 59, 67, 69, 72, 75, 76, 78, 82, 84, 88, 89, 91, 98, 99, 100, 101, 102, 106, 107, 113, 116, 118, 121, 124, 127, 129, 130, 131, 132, 134, 136, 138, 142, 146, 147, 148, 152, 153, 154, 155, 157, 159, 168, 171, 172, 173, 177, 180 right, 183, 185, 187, 188, 190, 196, 198, 200, 201, 202, 204, 205, 206, 207, 208, 210, 211, 213, 215, 216, 217, 219, 221, 222, 224, 225, 227, 229, 232, 233, 234, 235, 238, 240, 242, 246, 247, 248, 258, 263, 265, 267, 270, 271, 276, 279, 280, 281, 283, 284, 286, 287, 289, 290, 293, 297, 299, 301, 304, 306, 308, 310, 311, 313, 315, 317, 319, 326, 330, 332, 334, 335, 336 left, 337, 339, 340 right, 345, 347, 348, 350, 351, 352, 354, 356, 358, 360, 361, 363, 365, 367, 368, 370, 378, 380, 381, 384, 386, 388, 389, 391, 393, 394, 395, 397, 398, 399, 400, 402, 406, 408, 409, 411, 413.

INTRODUCTION

Positive evidence of how man and dog first became associated cannot precisely be established. There are many hypotheses, any of which would make an interesting story. There is early evidence for example in the palaeolithic cave paintings of France and northern Spain and in the paintings and sculptured friezes of Ancient Egypt and Mesopotamia of the dog existing as a domestic animal, but in fact the association must have existed even earlier than that. What evidence we have suggests that early man shared his cave dwellings with dogs. Early cave sites and midden excavations in northern Europe have disclosed remains of canines that clearly lived close to man, though for what exact purpose we do not know. They may have been fellow hunters, joining early man in the chase of game for food. They could possibly have been just scavengers living in close contact with primitive tribes as an easier method of obtaining food than catching it themselves, or they could perhaps have been camp guards. It is likely that they combined any of these, or even all three roles.

The most popular theory concerning the origin of the domestic dog is that it descended from the wolf, or at least one of the wolves, for even they vary from continent to continent. The opponents of that theory, however, point to the vast differences between the various breeds of dog that we have today and maintain that these deny a common ancestry in one animal. Others suggest that several different forms of wild dog, some probably long extinct, played their part in introducing the wide variety of dogs that we now possess and some weight is lent to that theory by the number of wild dogs still in existence, from the Dingo of Australia to the wild dogs of the continent of Africa.

It is not difficult to speculate about how man and dog first became partners. It could have been among the nomadic tribes of Europe, who moved from place to place as the game which was their staple diet moved to avoid the winter snows, or it might have occurred on the continent of America or in the Far East. The association could indeed have developed more or less simultaneously in many parts of the world. It is easy enough to visualise early hunters returning from the

chase with whelps of wild dogs or wolves which they would give to their young to keep them quiet and out of the way. At that primitive stage, sentiment would hardly have been likely to have entered into the relationship, and there would have been no thought of dogs as playthings. The whelps would just have been added to the tribe as one of its possessions.

Wolves and wild dogs are very territorially minded, with tribal customs of their own, and the value of these wild animals as guards around the camp or cave would quickly have been realised, and the step from that to

Below: A scene from an Egyptian fresco at Thebes—an early example of the dog as a domestic animal.

5

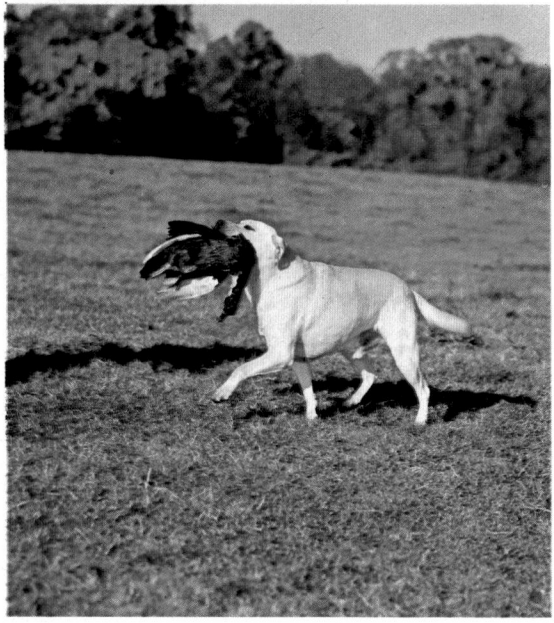

duties as hunters would have been a very short one. Bones of dogs found in Scandinavia prove that dogs and men lived together at least 10,000 years ago and it is likely that the relationship goes back much further. The cave paintings at Altamira (about 12,000 BC) and Lascaux (15,000–10,000 BC) contain representations of dogs, but these are conceived in a generalised way, the dogs being dog-like but with no distinctive features. Subsequent evidence from Ancient Egypt show various dogs of recognizable types, as do the hunting reliefs from Nineveth (7th century BC), where mastiff-like creatures accompany the royal hunt.

By the time of the New Kingdom in Egypt (circa 1570 BC), there were clearly several different breeds of dog in existence, or at least there were sufficient variations to suggest that selective breeding was capable of producing different breeds. Dogs are shown with straight tails or curly tails, with prick ears or pendant ears and with spotted or plain coats. Most of them were hunting dogs or battle dogs and are depicted performing the task for which they had been selected. The heavy, mastiff type of animal is shown in war scenes and the longer-legged sort taking part in the chase. This has led to modern enthusiasts for different breeds laying claim to various paintings or sculptures from the past to prove the antiquity of their own favourite breed. It becomes a little ironical however, when two or more enthusiasts claim the same illustration as proof of ancient ancestry for their own particular choice!

From that time onward, there is little doubt that the many varieties of dog were produced by man's insatiable desire to improve on nature. It is difficult when looking, for example, at a Great Dane and a Pomeranian standing adjacent to one another in the ring, to accept the possibility of a common ancestor. One weighs around five pounds, the other something like thirty times as much, one is eight inches tall, the other thirty. One is small and fluffy, the other huge and smooth-coated, yet somewhere back in time they must have shared common origins. From our knowledge of early man's interest in the dog we can be sure that in the highly sophisticated civilizations of Egypt and the Far East, there were people who spent their time, energy and ingenuity producing animals that had the differences emphasised and fixed. Certainly as civilization spread almost every nation would try to influence the natural development in many species not least in their domesticated dogs, dividing and sub-dividing until the different breeds would be numbered in their hundreds as they are today.

It has been a slow process. Many breeds have emerged and as many have disappeared, and the develop-

Top: The wild dog of Australia, the Dingo. Other wild dogs are still in existence, particularly in Africa.
Centre: Many of the skills learned by the domestic dog are a development of survival instincts.
Bottom: The dog is amenable to command to a degree not often found in other domesticated animals.

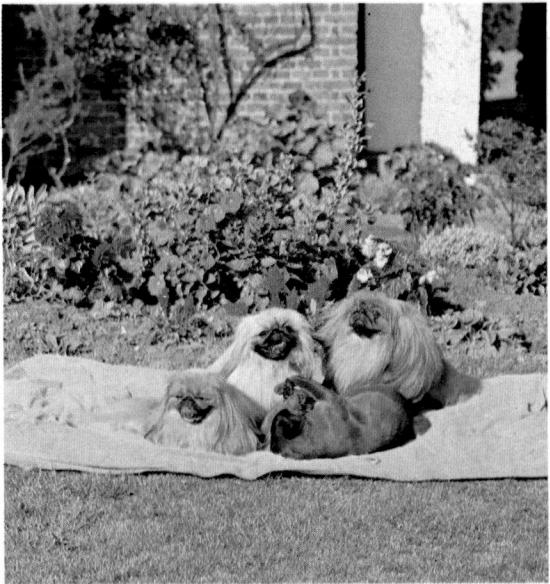

Top: Many of the small dogs from China and Japan were bred purely as toy dogs, at a time when dogs from other parts of the world were going through a very primitive stage in their history.
Centre: A Boar hunt. In the Middle East, sport rather than the arts was considered a suitable pastime for a young man, and this led to the development of a whole race of running dogs, for example the Persian Greyhound, the Saluki and the Afghan.
Bottom: In Spain and Italy particularly, the 'chase' occupied much of a gentleman's time.

ment still goes on. In Britain the Old English White Terrier has gone, as has the Lancashire Heeler, or almost, and other breeds only survived because of the dedication and enthusiasm of a small number of breeders. At the same time the Boxer, the Dobermann and the Norwich Terrier have appeared along with a large number of other breeds and variations.

The domestic dog shares many of the characteristics of the wild members of his race. He will turn round several times before settling down in his bed, will mark his territory by leg-lifting on the local trees and gateposts. He is intelligent, but at the same time has a certain fierceness, and will howl at the moon like the wolf and jackal. Kept in numbers, the domestic dog will establish a 'pecking order' by fighting for supremacy, and the group will thus find itself with a leader as the wolf pack does. There are, however, certain characteristics that are more sophisticated in the domestic dog. The limited vocal noise that the wolf makes has been enlarged and today's domestic dog can express himself much more widely. Any owner can tell by the tone of a bark what it is that has disturbed his dog, and the tone varies from the welcoming back for the children to the hard noise what warns of approaching strangers.

Through his association with man, the domestic dog has developed a whole range of noises with which to express his feelings. He has even been known to mimic, and in one extreme case was taught to say at least two words. He employs many of the movements of submissiveness that can be seen in the wolf and the wild dog when greeting his master, obviously accepting him as the pack leader, but he has added the rather frantic tail wagging, which is not the habit of the wild canines.

Many of the skills learned by the domestic dogg are a development and a sophistication of instincts associated with survival. It is natural for members of the canine race to carry things around in their mouths, and when feeding their young, to transport food to the family lair in this manner. This habit has been used by man as a basis for training a dog to retrieve, which appears to be a clever trick on the part of gundogs, but merely exploits the instinct to pick things up and return with them. The guarding of a territory, instinctive in the wild dogs to preserve the supply of food for the family and to protect it from marauders, develops easily into guarding a home occupied by humans whom he regards as members of his family. The dog's intelligence has made it a simple matter for man to associate certain actions with certain words, and the result is that the dog is amenable to command to a degree that is not often found in other domesticated animals.

As the relationship between man and dog developed, dogs were bred for different functions, and this in itself led not only to the evolution of new breeds, but to a natural grouping of those breeds according to the work that they were to do. Naturally enough this development took place at different speeds in different countries, with the result that some breeds appear in different groups in different countries. The independent growth of civilizations and the lack of communication in the early days led to this, and the apparent anomalies have become so much a part of the history of the dogs of a particular nation that they are difficult to regularise internationally. A typical example of this is the Pomeranian, which appears in Scandinavia as a Spitz breed, in Spain as a companion dog, and in the rest of the world as a toy, in Sweden being shown alongside the Chow Chow, in Spain with the Dalmatian, and in the rest of the world with the Chihuahuas. The manner in which people lived, their relative safety from attack by wild animals or neighbouring tribes, their pursuits and their sports differed widely. In the Far East, where the cultural centres were the emperors' courts, and where women of the household whilst subservient, wielded considerable power, the companion dog became a very important members of the family. The result was that many of the small dogs from China and Japan were bred purely as toy dogs at a time when dogs in other parts of the world were going through a very primitive stage in their history. The Pekingese and the Pug are certainly ancient breeds.

In the Middle East, where the culture was based more on a system of sheikdoms, and where sport rather than the arts was considered a suitable pastime for a young man and where the women took little part in anything apart from the running of the household, coursing dogs were more important. This led to the development of a whole race of running dogs, the Saluki, the Afghan Hound and the Persian Greyhound for example. As with the toys dogs of the Far East, they were much prized and cared for, and their breeding and performance was a matter of considerable pride. In Egypt and the Mediterranian countries generally the dog was not so prized, which is remarkable as he had at one time been an object of worship. There has been some controversy over whether the

Top: Pointer trials. The Pointer is bred for sport in the field, and should look and act the part.
Centre: A hunting-relief of Mastiff-like creatures from the Mound of Kuyunjik, Nineveh.
Bottom: A section from the Bayeux Tapestry, showing Harold hunting. At that time the courts in Britain had a profound influence on dog breeding.

Top: Tsu-Tsi, Dowager Empress of China with her pet.
Companion dogs were popular at the Imperial Court.
Bottom: A statue of the Egyptian dog or jackal God
Anubis, from the Vatican Museum, Rome.

God Anubis was in fact a dog or a Jackal, but which-
ever happens to be the truth the creature was undoubtedly a member of the canine race.

The Western World developed more slowly. At the
time of Confucius China was already well developed
whilst in Britain many of the cultural activities were in
the hands of the Cistercian monks, and America was
still peopled by warring tribes. Britain was divided and
in a constant state of war between the various families.
The Scots were crossing the border from time to time
on their raids, the White Rose and the Red had not
sorted out their own particular problem, and the
Welsh were somewhat unsettled. This meant that the
sort of dog that was needed was a large fearsome animal
not only capable of guarding a castle, but of emerging
from it to go to war when needed. Such a dog was
actually bred in Britain, the ancient Mastiff type,
which, collared with steel spikes went to war every bit
as much as did the man and his horse.

In France and Southern Europe the gentlemen had
yet another idea of what constituted sport, and in Spain
and Italy particularly 'the chase' occupied much of
a gentleman's time. The influence of the running dog
from the Middle East was felt, but was the invention
of gunpowder there was a great change, and a whole
new race of dogs was developed to help the huntsman
with his gun to find and retrieve game. In Spain there
grew up a race of small dogs used to spring game from
coverts, and larger dogs to help discover the whereabouts of animals taking cover, the Pointers. In France
whilst this form of sport was popular enough, the
ancient sport of scent hunting remained important so
that in that country there was yet another race of dogs
bred to use their noses rather than their eyes—pack-
hounds of differing appearance and size yet all with
this well-developed ability to hunt game by its scent.

The difference between races of dogs—it is important at this stage not to use the word 'breed' as the idea
was not to produce finely bred animals whose value
lay in their appearance, but in their ability to perform
the duty for which they were intended—varied with
the game that was indigenous in their country. A much
smaller dog was needed to chase and catch the hare of
Europe than the antelope of Afghanistan, and a much
stronger dog to subdue the wild boar of Germany than
the red deer of Scotland. This led to a fairly early
grouping of dogs on a national basis as well as on a
'use' basis; France produced more scent-hunting dogs,
Spain more gundogs, and the middle European
countries more of the heavy types. It was not in fact
until the advent of dog shows that more concise grouping was arrived at, and even then, with the shows being
small events held in the yard of a hostelry, subdivision
was not needed.

One of the problems associated with research into the history of the dog is that he was so much taken for granted that he rarely gets a mention. He is depicted in drawings, paintings and tapestry, but rarely written about. The battle scenes of the Bayeux Tapestry show dogs, and the early forest laws of the time of William the Conquerer lay down regulations concerning who might and might not own dogs of certain types, but it was not until much later that anyone wrote about dogs as dogs. In the late 15th century Dame Juliana Berner in her book of hunting lists 'divers manners of hounds'.

The courts of Britain had a profound influence on dog breeding at this time. They followed the French in fashion, even adopted the language, and undoubtedly followed their sporting habits. The dog was either something used to take part, and a very active part indeed, in the hunting of game, and was thus tough, hard kept and probably expendable, or was an animal that was the favourite of the ladies of the court, soft and probably overfed, and deeply mourned when it died. There was at that time none of the semi-professional attitude towards dog breeding that is typical of today, and pride in a dog was either pride in performance or the affected pleasure of having a child substitute with none of the attendant responsibilities.

Today's grouping of dogs into a number of fairly similar types, either by appearance or performance has really come about as a matter of convenience. As the numbers of dogs grew under the modern system of registration and shows, it became necessary to subdivide. The process is going on to this day as the Kennel Club in Great Britain has only quite recently divided the Non-Sporting dogs other than the Toys, into the Utility and the Working groups. This pattern has not been followed by other countries, and in many there are far more groups than there are in Britain and the United States of America. Basically the smaller subdivisions are more logical even though perhaps less practical, and the division has been dictated by other factors than registration or exhibition, and it might therefore be easier to consider the various groupings along Scandinavian lines, where the division is more fundamentally to do with purpose.

The invention of gunpowder changed the whole pattern of hunting. Prior to that it was almost entirely a case of chasing game, of driving it into nets, or of treeing, digging or trapping it, and the type of dog needed was fitted to one or the other of those methods. With the advent of the gun, however, game could be dispatched at greater distance and with more certainty, though the advocates of the crossbow might quarrel with that assumption. For the purpose a whole new

Top: English Setters, shown here at a trial.
Centre: The Bloodhound, like most scent hunting dogs, is heavily built, for stamina rather than speed.
Bottom: A foxhound by the nineteenth century painter Archer, from Vero Shaw's Book of the Dog, 1881.
Right: Borzois—from Russia, 'huge and silky'.

race of dogs was needed, dogs that could locate game, that could indicate where it was, and others that could cause it to move, either along the ground in the case of fur, or into the air in the case of feather. Others were needed to recover the game when it had been killed, and even specialists that would retrieve over water.

Within the group of gundogs, came even further divisions. The names Springer, Cocker, Retriever, Setter and Pointer indicate the tasks that these various dogs performed, though there is more than one Springer and a number of Retrievers, some developed in Britain, and others overseas particularly in Spain, Germany and Italy. Old illustrations in such books as The Sportsman's Repository show dogs that are half-way between Spaniel and Setter, and from around the beginning of the 19th century the changes and developments can be followed in words and pictures. Fortunately it was the habit when a gentleman of substance had his portrait painted for posterity, for him to have his dogs included, so that we have more than a fair idea —always allowing for artistic licence—of the appearance of the dogs years ago.

With the spread of wealth, hunting, which was at one time the prerogative of the wealthy landowner, has now become the leisure pursuit of thousands, particularly in America, where the opening of the hunting season sees a great number of men who would normally be seated at their desks, heading for the hills with gun and dog. In Britain too, people of all walks of life now shoot, and have done so for many years, which has meant a tremendous upsurge in the popularity of the gundogs.

Another natural division is the group of dogs that hunt by scent. In many parts of the world they are included in the Hound Group, but they are a natural subdivision as they are built differently and have the gift of a highly developed sense of smell. They do not have the powerful angulation of the running dogs, the group known in some countries as the sight hounds, and they are more heavily built, for stamina rather than speed. Hunting with packs of hounds has been in existence for centuries, particularly in France, where there are still breeds of dog descended from such packs that are not generally known in other countries, such as the Ariegeois and the Bleu de Gascogne, whose names indicate that they originated in small areas of France where they were bred in packs.

In Britain hunting with packs of hounds has always been popular, and now there are probably something over four hundred packs in the country. They too vary from area to area, but there has been a good deal of interchange of drafts of hounds from one pack to another to improve strains, and it is now improbable that anyone can say at a glance where a particular

Top: Wire-haired Dachshunds, supreme as pets.
Centre: Mastiffs, formidable protectors of property.
Bottom: Mosaic pavement from Pompeii, 'Beware of the Dog'—a British idea that impressed the Romans.

hound comes from, though this was once possible. Beagling too is popular, and there are packs of Basset Hounds. Even such unlikely dogs as Sealyhams at one time hunted in packs. In the United States too, pack hunting is extremely popular, and it is almost certain the the number of packs and hounds outnumber by far those in any other country in the world. Careful importation and the expertise that the American people have in the art of livestock breeding have resulted in there being a large number of hounds used in different ways, some still in packs, but some, like the Coonhound used individually.

Unlike the gundogs, the scent hunting group as a whole, with the possible exception of the Beagle and the Basset have never attained popularity as a pet and housedog, as they have certain temperament problems, are somewhat wilful and not easy to train. To any member of this group the scent overrules everything else, and the natural inclination of the dogs to follow their noses does create problems. The other great exception is of course the Dachshund, as whilst it is a scent hunting dog, and is at times used in a pack, it occupies a very special place in the affections of all dog people as being supreme as a pet and a housedog. It could be that its size, and the years that have gone by since it was regularly hunted have blunted its instincts to a certain extent, making it more amenable to domestic restraints than some of the others.

One of the most ancient uses of the dog, was as a guard, which leads to the next type, the Mastiff Group. The Scandinavians do not devote a whole group to these dogs, but they are a natural subdivision widespread all over Europe and even in the Far East. Even before man settled down to till the soil and grow crops, when he was nomadic and moved around and followed his food. The dog must have been a valuable member of the tribe, being territorially minded, attached to the family and seeing the members of it as pack leaders. In his still semi-wild state he would have been a formidable protector of property against the incursions of other tribes and predatory animals.

This guarding instinct was handed down, and in no group more formidably than in the Mastiffs. There is early record of them in places as far apart as Tibet (there is still a Chinese Fighting Dog), and Spain, where there is a Mastin Espanol, and they were all typified by their size. They are large and heavy dogs, and their fierceness, until modern breeding eliminated this, often made them unhandleable. Even to this day examples do occur that cannot be approached, though this is exceptional. When the Romans invaded Britain they found these large heavy dogs which were used as guards and fighting dogs, which impressed them so much that they took some of them back to Rome, where they played their part in the rather sanguine affairs that the Romans called sport.

Modern selective breeding has produced a number of variations on the traditional Mastiff. For example such dogs as the Boxer and the Bulldog are develop-

ments of the original theme, the Boxer being a very modern creation and the other, the Bulldog dating back to the 17th century. During the Second World War the Mastiff virtually disappeared from Britain, and this ancient British dog was only saved from extinction because some had been exported to the United States from where specimens were generously exported back to Britain.

The use of the dog as a worker came fairly late in the development of the race, and has been brought into its present heights in comparatively recent years. There is a history of guarding and herding dogs in many countries, often using what are apparently quite unusual animals, and often the herding dog had to serve in other capacities. A dog like the Afghan Hound for instance was not only a coursing dog, but was also used as a guard, particularly at night, and there is even a suggestion that he too was used for rounding up livestock. The type of herding dog required varied considerably with the sort of terrain they worked in and on the flocks they had to work. This produced mountain dogs such as the Pyrenean, and plains dogs like the Tervueren.

The hills of Scotland and Wales produced a race of dogs which were brilliant herders, the Collies. The original Collie bore little resemblance to the modern show Collie, and was probably more like the Bearded Collie as we know it today, but the work that it did has been continued through various breeds, and the most recent one recognised, the Border Collie is world renowned for its intelligence and hard work. Much of the sheep herding that now goes on throughout the world would have been impossible without the working sheepdog in some form or another, and although the Border Collie is not by any means the only working sheepdog, it forms the bulk of the dogs that are used today in most countries for this work.

Sheepdog trials are an important part of country life, and few of the larger agricultural shows are without these trials as part of the programme in many of the sheep areas of most countries. Whilst the dogs used in say Australia are of many different breeds, working collies and Sheepdogs have been imported to improve the stock and to take part in trials there. The International Sheepdog Society has records of pedigrees of dogs and their performances going back further than those of the Kennel Club of Great Britain, and their requirements for such registration are even stricter than other bodies, the emphasis being on the capability of the animal as a worker only and has nothing to do with appearance.

Britain is the home of the Terrier, and of all the dogs listed in this Group, all but one or two have their origins there. The working terrier has always played a part in the hunting of a pack of hounds, and it was a familiar sight to see small dogs capable of going to ground to turn out the fox, accompanying the hunt, either on foot, or if the journey was likely to be a lengthy one, in special panniers carried by the huntsmen for the purpose. While the noble families had their sport running deer to death and coursing hares and other animals, the working man also had his sport, carried on under much more humble conditions and with none of the ceremony of the chase.

The Terrier was siezed upon as the particular friend of the British working man, and in most of the industrial areas, almost every home would have its Terrier. In the North they were Borders, or one of the Scottish breeds, in the Midlands they would be the Old English White Terrier or a version of the Staffordshire or Manchester Terrier. They were kept as vermin killers, and at the beginning of the 19th century they are mentioned as an essential part of a farmer's livestock for keeping down rats. The name is said to come from the word 'terra' as they were originally intended for unearthing the fox, but they attracted a much wider public by their spirit and sheer dogginess, and became a very important collection of breeds in the latter part of the 19th and the beginning of this century.

Their popularity unfortunately declined over the years, and in most countries their registrations and appearances at shows are getting smaller each year. One or two, the West Highland White and the Staffordshire Bull Terrier have retained their popularity, but for the most part the members of the Group are not so numerous. One of the great countries for Terriers was Ireland, and they had several native terriers, mostly the larger ones that typified a great deal of what was considered the Irish temperament by some people, being sporty, quick, and always prepared to take care of themselves.

From early times there have been dogs that hunted by sight and ran down their prey, for the most part killing the game once it was caught. In Scandinavia these are known as the Vinthundar, 'Wind Hounds' which is a very descriptive name for the Group. They are all the extremely fast, long-legged dogs that have been evolved for the purpose of catching game by running them down rather than by the sheer persistence of the scent-hunting dogs.

In the Far East they were the much prized elegant hounds kept by tribes for sport and for replenishing the larder, the Saluki and the Afghan Hound; in Britain the Greyhound, which is one of Britain's oldest breeds of dog. In Mediterranean countries they were smooth and large, in the colder countries such as Scotland they were rough and large, and in Russia huge and silky. The variations were enormous, but they were all long in the leg, capable of tremendous speed, and had a touch of the killer instinct.

In recent years the members of the Hound Group have largely been denied their right to course, as modern conditions do not lend themselves to this sport. Indeed recently in Britain coursing has come

Top and centre: Norfolk Terriers, at work and at play— sporting dogs for working men.
Bottom: The Afghan, once much prized in the East.

Drab White	Cream	Biscuit	Hare	Fawn
Yellow	Beige	Drab Yellow	Lemon	Light Brown
Light Fawn	Dark Fawn	Isabella	Dead Foliage	Wheaten
Dark Brown	Chestnut	Tan	Sable	Reddish Brown
Orange	Golden	Apricot	Pink	Mauve
Silver	Dark Grey	Grey	Badger Grey	Wolf Grey
Dove Blue	Steel Blue	Slate Blue	Grey Blue	Grey Black
Red	Mahogany	Bronze	Liver	Chocolate

One of the problems constantly encountered in describing coat colour in dogs, is that a word does not adequately describe a colour. There are, for example, so many reds that to say of a certain dog that it is red, probably conveys little of the actual colour of the dog. This chart lists all the major colour names used to describe dogs' coats, and in each case shows the colour.

into disfavour to such an extent that it is likely to cease altogether. Fortunately, however, the breeds that comprise the Group have wonderful temperament and make superb housedogs, and also, the sport of Greyhound racing, which began in America, spread to the rest of the world, and became particularly popular in Britain, has guaranteed the continuance of this particular breed. In recent years other breeds have been tried on the track against the time when coursing became illegal, and have proved themselves to some extent. Oddly enough, Italian Greyhound racing has become popular in Sweden, where the breed is included in this Group, despite the fact that it appears as a toy dog almost everywhere else, and where the proving of a breed for the work that it is supposed to do is an essential part of the philosophy of the sport of dog showing.

For many centuries man has enjoyed the companionship of animals, and pets have become not only part of the everyday life of most families, but have at the same time become big business. There is hardly a household anywhere in the world that does not have its pet or pets, from the domestic cat to the budgerigar and from the goldfish to the alligator and it is natural enough that from man's associationship with the dog should grow up one of the closest relationships between animals and humans. In much the same way as the first dogs were almost incidentally adopted as part of the primitive tribe, so in later years the runts from working and sporting dogs would be adopted as pets by the children and womenfolk of a much more civilized culture.

The result has been a whole number of breeds which are included in the Toy Group. They are mostly typified by their lack of size, their charm and their companionable nature. They are almost all of them too, related to dogs from other groups, the Spaniels, the Terriers and the Running Dogs all having relatives in the group easily recognised as descendants from the original breeds. Constant companionship,

however, has changed their temperament, and environment has played its part, so that whilst an Italian Greyhound will still chase small birds and will kill and eat them given the chance, he is still very much at home on a silk cushion or a counterpane.

Some of the members of the Toy Group have their origins in the courts of Spain and Italy or the Far East. Paintings and drawings of members of the Italian courts show Toy dogs easily recognised for what they are, and the history of the Pekingese is well documented in stories of the early imperial courts of China. There have over the years been attempts to miniaturise breeds in order to produce more small dogs that could be included in the Group, but most of them fortunately have failed, as the Group is well established and has sufficient variety as it stands. New breeds are still being popularised however and appearing for the first time in the showrings of the world. The Lowchen is a typical example of this, as is the Bichon Frise, breeds that went quietly along in their own countries until they were discovered and exploited by the rest of the world.

There is no doubt at all that as the years go by new breeds will be evolved. There is no reason to suppose that man's ingenuity will rest with the Boxer and the Dobermann. There will be other attempts to produce a 'manmade' dog either for a purpose or simply as a challenge. It is not a difficult exercise. Dogs reproduce their kind comparatively quickly, and any determined effort to produce a dog of a given size, colour, proportions and temperament is almost certain to succeed. Such efforts are already being made in many countries, and provided that those who are conducting the experiments have the resources and the patience, any list of breeds of dog will be outdated within a few years.

Left: 'Scotch Deerhounds' from Vero Shaw's Book of the Dog *1881 — long-legged, rough and large.*
Below left: Toy dogs, print by Burton Barber, 1881.
Below right: Italian Greyhounds at play.

NOTE

Group Numbering

In most countries, the Groups of breeds into which dogs are arranged, are numbered. The Groups are known by these numbers as well as by their names, and this numbering is given equal importance with the naming. In Italy for instance the catalogue of a show will be arranged in Group number order. In Belgium the programme of events will indicate which Groups are being judged on a given day, and a judge, when invited to officiate will be informed of the number of the Group in which the breed or breeds that he is to judge, appears. In Australia, where breed standards are often printed in a hard-back edition, the Groups are arranged in number order. In the USA the Groups of breeds are numbered but the numbering is not considered as important as it is in some European countries.

In Britain, none of this happens. Each Group does have a number, but after appearing on the cover of the pamphlet in which the standards are printed, it is never seen again. Catalogues of shows, reports, programmes and invitations to judges, just give the Group its name, and never its number. Thus, in Britain, there is no set order for the Groups.

Standards

The pages which give the official standards also show line illustrations and variations which are our additions and in no way part of the official standard.

The line drawings accompanying the standards have been specially drawn by the author, Harry Glover.

CONTENTS

** Dogs not granted championship
status by the KC(GB)*

PART TWO:
*Breeds recognised by
the Fédération Cynologique
Internationale (FCI)*

PART THREE:
Other Pedigree Breeds

PART FOUR:
Old and Extinct Breeds

PART ONE:
Breeds recognised by the Kennel Club of Great Britain and the American Kennel Club

GUNDOG GROUP: SPORTING BREEDS

Large Munsterlander

Pointer

German Shorthaired Pointer

German Wirehaired Pointer

Curly-coated Retriever

Chesapeake Bay Retriever

Flat-coated Retriever

Labrador Retriever

Golden Retriever

Gordon Setter

English Setter

Irish Setter

American Water Spaniel

Brittany Spaniel

Clumber Spaniel

Cocker Spaniel

American Cocker Spaniel

English
Springer Spaniel

Field Spaniel

Irish Water Spaniel

Sussex Spaniel

Welsh Springer Spaniel

Hungarian Vizsla

Weimaraner

Wirehaired
Pointing Griffon

GUNDOG GROUP: SPORTING BREEDS

The capture of wild animals has been achieved in a variety of ways over the centuries, from the setting of primitive pit traps to today's sophisticated sport of driving game to guns hidden in butts. Animals have been speared, snared, shot with arrows, driven into nets, hauled down by fast dogs, lassoed, tripped by bolas, or even just dug out of the ground, and for many of these methods dogs have been evolved to assist the hunter. With the advent of the sporting gun, the hunting of game became a much more intricate business as the game had to be found before it was scared off by the hunter, and had to be collected when the gun had brought it down. For this purpose a whole Group of dogs was developed, many of which had specific duties in the field, and some were developed as all-purpose gundogs. They all, however, had one thing in common, they existed to help the sportsman armed with a gun when he was out in the field in search of game.

Within the Group there are further divisions according to the specific purposes for which the dog is used. There are those that locate the game, those that put it up so that the sportsman can get a shot at it, and those that retrieve it when it falls. It is, however, not quite as simple as that, as there are other breeds that work under special conditions. There are those that are experts in water, and there is also considerable overlap between duties, some breeds performing at least two tasks well, and others that will perform all the work that a gundog is expected to do. The situation is further complicated by the fact that whilst some of the gundog breeds are normally the property, and under the control of, the man who has the gun, others are kept by gamekeepers, and others by breeders who run their dogs at field trials, and attend shoots, for the purpose of training and using their dogs.

The breeds that locate the game are the Pointers and Setters, and their task is to work in front of the guns when game is being walked up, locating it before it can be seen by the sportsman, and indicating exactly where it is. The Pointers do this by what is called coming to the point, which means that they stand rigidly often with one foot in mid-stride ready to take a further cautious step if it is needed. They carry their tails out in a rigid straight line and the whole dog can thus be used as the sights on a gun to discover the squatting bird or hare. Two such dogs often work together at some distance from one another, which permits the guns to use them as co-ordinates, to discover not only the direction of the game but also its distance. Stories of the powers of these dogs are plentiful.

The Setters perform a similar task, but on discovering the whereabouts of the game do not necessarily stand at the point but sink down, as their name suggests.

The second sub-group is the Spaniels, whose task it is to move the game, either by putting it up in the case of a bird, or forcing it to run in the case of ground game. Spaniels hunt vigorously in front of the guns, but never so far in front as to disturb the game out of gunshot range. They are trained to work within range, to cover the ground by running backwards and forwards, quartering as much ground as possible and using their remarkable noses to put up any game that is lying hidden in the area. They vary a great deal in size and agility, and thus in the speed at which they work, and the sportsman chooses the breed which best suits the country over which he will be hunting and the species of game likely to be encountered.

The third category is those breeds that retrieve the game once it has been killed. These are mostly the larger and stronger dogs, capable of making their way quickly and efficiently through the roughest and most difficult cover. They have wonderful scenting powers, and the ability to mark fallen game, so that a brilliant Retriever can be trusted to watch birds fall, remember where they have come to ground, and fetch them in turn with very little assistance or direction from the gun or the gamekeeper.

Finally there are one or two breeds that have been evolved purely as all-purpose gundogs, dogs that will perform most of the tasks normally undertaken by the three main sub-groups, and one or two specialists such as the Irish Water Spaniel, developed for use in lake and estuary country where protection against wet and cold are essential. When sportsmen are gathered together there is always discussion as to which breed makes the best all-purpose gundog, but like everything else in the world of dogs, this must remain a matter of opinion. What is fact and not conjecture, is that the whole Gundog Group, by virtue of its long association with man and generations of training to obey commands, contains some of the most intelligent and companionable dogs of the whole canine race.

LARGE MUNSTERLANDER

NATIONAL GROUPING		
	Name	Number
KC(GB)	Gundog	2
AKC	—	–
FCI	Gundogs	7

This dog was evolved by a reversal of the more common practice of miniaturisation. The Small Munsterlander was developed at the beginning of this century from old breeds of long-haired hunting dogs common in Westphalia, and as with most breeds that were bred down to size, some large ones were inevitably produced. After a considerable battle the Large Munsterlander Club which had been formed by the supporters of the larger dogs managed to persuade the German Kennel Club to accept the larger dog as a separate breed.

He rapidly gained popularity, and has a number of supporters among the show goers of Germany and Holland where his qualities are appreciated more than they are so far in the rest of the world. In recent years there have been some importations into Britain and since 1971 when the first registrations took place numbers have increased at a remarkable rate, and now he is appearing at most of the major shows. In 1976 thirteen were exhibited in the variety classes under the author as judge at Crufts, and there is no doubt that he will be one of the next breeds to achieve championship status. He is a large, but not heavy dog, having the elegance of the Setters combined with the strength of the Retrievers, and is always black and white in colour. He is a lively dog, and is said to be very spirited and active in the field.

OFFICIAL STANDARD

Characteristics

The Large Munsterlander is a multi-purpose gun-dog, ideal for the rough shooter. He has an excellent nose, staying power, and works equally well on land and in water. A keen worker, easily taught, loyal, affectionate and trustworthy.

General appearance

Alert and energetic, with a strong muscular body, having good movement with drive.

Head and skull

Well proportioned to the body, elongated. Skull sufficiently broad, slightly rounded, with no pronounced occiput. Strong jaw muscles, well formed black nose, wide soft nostrils, slight rise from the nasal bone to the forehead but no pronounced stop. Lips slightly rounded, and well-fitting.

Eyes

Intelligent, medium size, dark brown, not deep set or protruding. No haw showing.

Ears

Broad and set high, lying flat and close to the head, with a rounded tip. Hair on the ears should be long, extending beyond the tip.

Mouth

Strong and sound, with well developed teeth, faultless scissor bite and molars meeting exactly.

Neck

Strong muscular, slightly arched, joining the shoulder and chest smoothly.

Forequarters

Chest, wide and with good depth of brisket. Shoulders laid well back, forelegs straight, pasterns strong.

Body

Firm strong back, short coupled. slightly higher at the shoulder, sloping smoothly towards the croup and tail. Wide well muscled loin. Wide croup. Ribs well sprung, deep and reaching well up to the loins. Taut abdomen, slightly tucked up.

Hindquarters

Hips broad. Well muscled thighs, well turned stifles, hocks well let down. Dew claws should be removed.

Feet

Tight, moderately rounded and well-knuckled with dense hair between the toes; well padded. Nails black and strong.

Gait

Free, long striding springy gait.

Tail

Well set on, in line with the back. Base thick, tapering evenly towards the tip, well feathered. It should be carried horizontally or curved slightly upwards. Docking optional, 1 to 2 cms.

Coat

Hair long and dense, but not curly or coarse. Well feathered on front and hind legs and on tail, more so in dogs than in bitches. The hair must lie short and smooth on the head.

Colour

Head solid black, white blaze, snip or star allowed. Body white with black patches, flecked, ticked, or combination of these.

Weight and size

Height: Dogs approximately 24 inches. Bitches approximately 23 inches. Weight: Dogs approximately 55 to 65 pounds. Bitches approximately 55 pounds.

Faults

Any departure from the foregoing points should be considered a fault and the seriousness of the fault should be in exact proportion to its degree.

Note

Male animals should have two apparently normal testicles fully descended into the scrotum.

AKC VARIATION TO STANDARD

This dog is not granted championship status by the AKC. The above standards are therefore those of the KC(GB).

POINTER

Towards the end of the 17th century and for some time afterwards, the old flintlock gun which took some time to load and to get into position, dictated what type of dog was needed. He had to find the game, indicate its whereabouts, and keep it under observation, until the sportsman was in a position to take a shot. For this purpose the Pointer was developed. There is some difference of opinion as to whether this particular dog was developed first in Spain, in Britain or in other European countries, but there is little doubt that he owes his origin to a mixture of Foxhound, Greyhound and probably Bloodhound. He needed a superb nose, speed over the ground and absolute steadiness, and those breeds were the most likely ones to produce these qualities. It could well be that the development took place simultaneously in several European countries.

The first Pointers of any sort appeared in Britain midway through the 17th century, which was some years before the shooting of birds in flight was a common practice. They were used at this time to locate hares, which were then coursed by the much faster Greyhounds which did not have the ability to

NATIONAL GROUPING		
	Name	Number
KC(GB)	Gundog	2
AKC	Sporting Dogs	1
FCI	Companion Dogs	8

locate the game as the Pointers did. By the end of the 17th century the shooting of game on the wing was in vogue and the Pointer began to come into its own. The old-fashioned Pointer still proved for a long time to lack drive and dash, and up to the end of the 19th century the Foxhound cross was still being resorted to to impart these qualities into the over-cautious Pointer of that time. During that century too the Pointer was repeatedly crossed with various Setters with the idea of improving temperament, as the residue of Greyhound blood together with the Foxhound produced a dog that was over-fierce and had natural killing instincts which needed to be eradicated.

By the middle of the 19th century, the old fashioned Spanish type of Pointer had been left entirely behind and the English Pointer was being accepted as the model of pace, stamina and nerve. By this time sportsmen were shooting with weapons which were self-loaded, and were working their dogs themselves rather than having highly organised teams of beaters, and the sort of dog that could be taken out by one man for a few hours shooting was required. The Pointer was trained to work as one of a pair, and the theory, indeed the practice was for two of these dogs to back one another up to confirm the presence of game and to give a cross-reference as to its exact position. The degree to which they could be thus trained was phenomenal, and endless stories are told of the remarkable performance of individual dogs. This was confirmed by thousands of spectators who witnessed the Pointer that finished in the final six at Crufts some years ago, which for reasons which only it knew, made a superb fix on one of the television cameras.

The modern Pointer is one of the most handsome of the Gundog Group. There is nothing glamorous about him, he has no glowing coat or picturesque colour, but his outline is the epitome of the working gundog at its best, and his conformation is there for everyone to see. He is an upstanding dog with deep chest, straight bone and very lovely body proportions, which, when he is well-muscled up gives him the appearance of a blood horse in full training. He is a show dog with a record of major wins all over the world, and his approach to the show business makes him a delight to handle. His natural ability to freeze in one position and to hold the pose for considerable lengths of time is one of the features of the gundog ring. He is, moreover, not a difficult dog to prepare as he has a short smooth coat that can be given a fine sheen with a little work with a hound glove. Few people look upon the Pointer as a pet, but those who do maintain that he makes a responsive companion and housedog.

OFFICIAL STANDARD

Characteristics
The Pointer should be symmetrical and well built all over. Alert, with the appearance of strength, endurance and speed.

Muzzle: somewhat concave, well defined stop.

Head and skull
The skull should be medium breadth and in proportion to the length of fore-face; the stop well defined, pronounced occipital bone. Nose and eye-rims dark, but may be lighter in the case of a lemon and white-coloured dog. The nostrils wide, soft and moist. The muzzle somewhat concave, and ending on a level with the nostrils, giving a slightly dish-faced appearance. The cheek-bones should not be prominent. Well developed soft lip.

Eyes
The same distance from the occiput as from the nostrils. A slight depression under the eyes, which should be bright and kindly in expression, not bold or staring, and not looking down the nose. The colour of the eyes either hazel or brown according to the colour of the coat.

Mouth
Scissors bite, neither under nor overshot.

Neck
Long, muscular, slightly arched, springing cleanly from the shoulders and free from throatiness.

Ears
The ears should be set on fairly high, and lie close to the head, they should be of medium length, and inclined to be pointed at the tips.

Forequarters
The shoulders long, sloping, and well-laid back. The chest just wide enough for plenty of heart room. The brisket well let down, to a level with the elbows. The forelegs straight and firm, of good oval bone, with the back sinews strong and visible. The knee joint should be flat

Forequarters: shoulders long and sloping. Forelegs: straight and firm.

with the front of the leg, and protrude very little on the inside. Pasterns lengthy, strong and resilient.

Body
Well-sprung ribs, gradually falling away at the loin, which should be strong, muscular and slightly arched. The couplings short. The haunch bones well spaced and prominent, but not above the level of the back. The general outline from head to tail being a series of graceful curves, giving a strong but lissom appearance.

Tail: carried level.

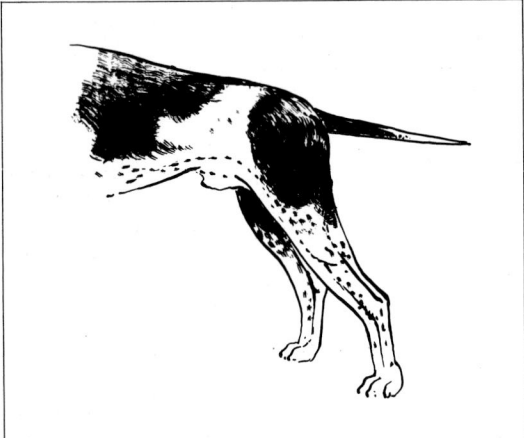

Gradually falling away at the loins, couplings short.

Hindquarters
Well turned stifles. The hock should be well let down, and close to the ground. A good expanse of thigh, which should be very muscular, as should also the second-thighs.

Feet
The feet oval, with well-knit, arched toes, well cushioned underneath.

Tail
The tail of medium length, thick at the root, growing gradually thinner to the point. It should be well covered with close hair, and carried on a level with the back, with no upward curl. With the dog in movement the tail should lash from side to side.

Coat
The coat should be fine, short, hard and evenly distributed, perfectly smooth and straight, with a decided sheen.

Colour
The usual colours are lemon and white, orange and white, liver and white, and black and white. Self colours and tricolours are also correct.

Size
Desirable heights. Dogs 25 to 27 inches. Bitches 24 to 26 inches.

Note
Male animals should have two apparently normal testicles fully descended into the scrotum.

Feet: well knit, arched, well cushioned.

Gait
Smooth, covering plenty of ground with each stride. Driving hind action, elbows neither turning in nor out. Definitely not a hackney action.

AKC VARIATION TO STANDARD
Head: bite even or scissors. *Eyes:* ample size rounded and intense. Dark in contrast with colour, darker the better. *Weight and size:* dogs 25 to 28 inches and 55 to 75 pounds; bitches 23 to 26 inches and 45 to 65 pounds.

GERMAN SHORTHAIRED POINTER

Supporters of almost all gundog breeds will from time to time attempt to convince everyone else that theirs is in fact the best all-round gundog. If there is one breed that has most of the qualities to claim this title, it is without doubt the German Shorthaired Pointer. He is a good pointing dog, a natural retriever on land and water, and an excellent worker with birds. This paragon of all the gundog virtues started off as his name suggests in Germany, being produced from a German pointing dog which was itself probably developed from the old Spanish Pointer. Other blood was introduced from local German hunting dogs of which there were a good many all over Germany and which were used by the German *försteren*. These various *hunde* were descended from the hounds that were popular in France, mostly long in the leg and something of the running type, but with very good noses.

The breed was in existence in the 17th century, though it was probably not the very standardised form that exists today. It was with the establishment of the stud book of the Shorthair Club in 1870 when records started, that it was possible to produce a standard of breed points and abilities. It was this latter which remained uppermost in the minds of the German breeders for many years. The hounds from which the breed descended were not notably obedient and the Spanish Pointer blood did not give the absolute steadiness to command that was desired. The German breeders resorted to the introduction of the English

NATIONAL GROUPING		
	Name	Number
KC(GB)	Gundog	2
AKC	Sporting Dogs	1
FCI	Gundogs	7

Pointer to establish the classical work that was needed, and by selective breeding for obedience, finally around the turn of the century produced what they wanted, a good-looking dog, with a stylish manner of working and the obedience that was required for an all-round gundog.

The German Shorthaired Pointer was recognised in the United States of America in 1930, and some years later the first field trial for the breed was held. This use of the dog in the field has remained a very strong point with German Shorthair Pointer people and trials are now held regularly in many countries. The Shorthair is, however, in the view of many people the ideal one-dog-man's dog. There are large numbers of the breed, beautiful dogs that will never see the inside of a show ring, but will spend their lives doing what they were bred for and leading a very happy life whilst doing it—out with the gun in all weathers. For this purpose he is ideally built, being strongly made with a very robust body, strong limbs and a waterproof coat. He is very tractable, willing, and agile, powerful in performance over all sorts of country and in water, and has tremendous powers of endurance. His nose is excellent and he works just as well at night as he does during the daylight hours, the most severe conditions of snow and ice never deterring him.

As a show dog the German Shorthaired Pointer is excellent, being beautifully behaved, a little suspicious of strangers but very steady with other dogs. He stands well, and is among the soundest of the gundogs, being bred from running hound stock and having the same sort of conformation. As his qualities are becoming recognised his numbers are steadily increasing and over the thirty years since World War II he has become a regular feature of our shows. His temperament is just what is expected of a gundog. He has a high degree of intelligence, and the ability to work out the solutions to problems himself and not to depend on purely repetitive training. He makes a very good watchdog and companion around the house.

OFFICIAL STANDARD

Characteristics

The German Shorthaired Pointer is a dual-purpose Pointer-Retriever and this accounts for his excellence in the field, which requires a very keen nose, perseverance in searching, and enterprise. His style attracts attention; he is equally good on land and in water, is biddable, an extremely keen worker, and very loyal.

General appearance

A noble, steady dog showing power, endurance and speed, giving the immediate impression of an alert and energetic (not nervous) dog whose movements are well co-ordinated. Neither unduly small nor conspicuously large, but of medium size, and like the hunter, 'With a short back stands over plenty of ground'. Grace of outline, clean cut head, sloping long shoulders, deep chest, short back and powerful hindquarters, good bone composition, adequate muscle, well carried tail and taut coat giving a thoroughbred appearance.

Ears: broad, high, hung close.

Ears

Broad and set high; neither too fleshy nor too thin with a short soft coat; hung close to the head, no pronounced fold, rounded at the tip and should reach almost to the corner of the mouth when brought forward.

Mouth

Teeth sound and strong. Molar teeth meeting exactly and the eyeteeth should fit close in a true scissor bite. Neither overshot nor undershot.

Neck

Moderately long, muscular and slightly arched, becoming larger towards the shoulders. Skin should not fit too loosely.

No stop: eyebrow position gives stop effect.

Head and skull

Clean-cut, neither too light nor too heavy, but well proportioned to the body. The skull sufficiently broad and slightly rounded. The furrow between the eyes not so deep, and the occiput not so pronounced as in the English Pointer. The nasal bone rises gradually from nose to forehead (this is more pronounced in the male) and should never possess a definite stop as in the English Pointer, but when viewed from the side there is a well defined stop effect due to the position of the eye-brows. The lips fall away almost vertically from a somewhat protruding nose and continue in a slight curve to the corner of the mouth. Lips well developed but not over hung. Jaws powerful and sufficiently long to enable the dog to pick up and carry game. Dish-face and snipy muzzle are not desirable. Nose solid brown, wide nostrils well opened and soft.

Eyes

Medium size, soft and intelligent, not protruding nor too deep set. Varying in shades of brown to tone with coat. Light eye not desirable. Eyelids should close properly.

Forequarters

Shoulder sloping and very muscular with top of shoulder blades close; upper arm bones between shoulder and elbow long. Elbows well laid back, neither pointing outwards nor inwards. Forelegs straight and lean, sufficiently muscular and strong but not coarse-boned. Pasterns slightly sloping, almost straight but not quite.

Body

Chest must appear deep rather than wide but not out of proportion to the rest of the body; ribs deep and well sprung, never barrel-shaped nor flat as in the hound; back ribs reaching well down to tucked up loins. Chest measurement immediately behind the elbows smaller than that about a handsbreadth behind the elbows, so that the upper arm has freedom of movement. Firm, short back, not arched. The loin wide and slightly arched; the croup wide and sufficiently long, neither too heavy nor too sloping starting on a level with the back and sloping gradually towards the tail. Bones solid and strong not clumsy and porous.

Hindquarters

The hips broad and wide falling slightly towards the tail. Thighs strong and well muscled. Stifles well bent. Hocks square with the body and slightly bent, turning neither in nor out. Pasterns nearly upright.

Feet

Compact, close-knit, round to spoon-shaped, well padded, should turn neither in nor out. Toes well arched and heavily nailed.

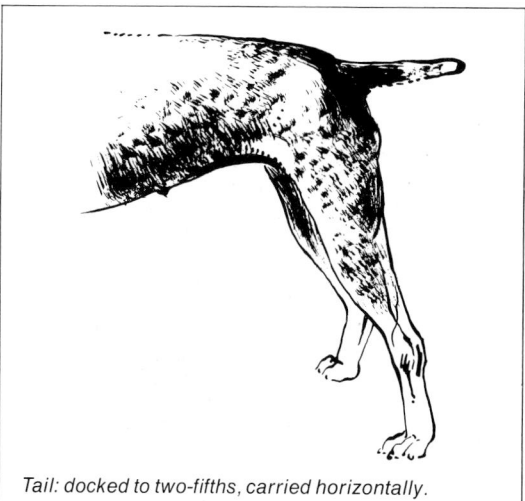

Tail: docked to two-fifths, carried horizontally.

Tail

Starts high and thick growing gradually thinner. Docked to medium length by two-fifths to half its length. When quiet tail should be carried down and when moving horizontally, never held high over the back or bent.

Coat

Skin should not fit loosely or fold. Coat short, flat and coarse to the touch, slightly longer under the tail.

Colour

Solid liver, liver and white spotted, liver and white spotted and ticked, liver and white ticked, black and white.

Weight and size

Dogs 55 to 70 pounds, bitches 45 to 60 pounds. Size: dogs 23 to 25 inches and bitches 21 to 23 inches at the shoulder. Symmetry is most essential.

Faults

Bone structure too clumsy, sway-back, head too large, deep wrinkles in forehead, cone-shaped skull or occiput too prominent. Ears too long, pointed, fleshy or undue

Dish face and snipy muzzle not desirable.

folds. Flesh coloured nose. Eyes too light, too round or too closely set together, eye-lids not closing properly. Wrinkles in neck. Feet or elbows turned inwards or outwards. Soft, sunken or splayed toes; cowhocks, straight hindlegs, or down on pasterns. Tail starting too low, undocked, too thick, curled up or too furry. Tri-coloured.

Faults: tail starting too low, curled up, furry, straight hindlegs, feet turned out.

Note

Male animals should have two apparently normal testicles fully descended into the scrotum.

GERMAN WIREHAIRED POINTER

NATIONAL GROUPING		
	Name	Number
KC(GB)	—	—
AKC	Sporting Dogs	I
FCI	Gundogs	7

In an attempt to produce an all purpose gundog, German fanciers turned to the Pointer type as a promising basis on which to build. Pointers of several sorts were being bred in a good many European countries more or less at the same time, and most of them were retrievers as well. The more sophisticated type of hunting that was to develop later when each type of gundog was used for a specialised purpose, had not yet become fashionable.

There were a number of basic breeds of gundog in Europe, and several of them were other than smooth coated. There were the Braques, probably descended from the now extinct Griffon de Bresse in France, the Spinone of Italy, still in existence as a separate breed, the Poodle Pointer of Germany and the various long and rough-coated gundogs in Britain. Breeders in Germany, having established as their aim the production of a Wirehaired Pointer had a number of breeds to choose from. Beginning with the Short-haired Pointer which was already in existence, they probably used several breeds to develop the one we know as the German Wirehaired Pointer.

Shooting in Germany has always been something of a mixed experience. The country is such that it is possible to switch from pheasant to hare and from duck to buck all in the space of a few hours, and a hardy well-coated dog with enthusiasm, endurance and an adaptability to all sorts of game was needed. In the Wirehaired Pointer just such a dog was produced. Using the best of the existing Pointer blood and introducing that of the Foxhound, the Poodle and the English Pointer the breeders developed a dog that would do all the work of most of the other gundogs, and was staunch enough to stand up to a strenuous day across the roughest country. By the turn of the century the breed was well established, and a club had been formed, the Drahthaar Club. In a few short years he had become such a popular dog that he ousted most of the other gundogs in Germany. He arrived in the United States of America in 1920 and was soon seen as the answer to the all-round gundog there. He has only recently been introduced into Britain where a surfeit of very popular gundogs has probably prevented him from becoming better known, as he is still only shown among the rare breeds.

The German Wirehaired Pointer is, like his near relation the German Shorthaired, a very sturdy and energetic dog. He always gives the impression of enjoying hard work, an enthusiasm that he shares with the *Jäger* with whom he frequently works, as there are few more enthusiastic Sportsmen than the professional German hunter. His coat is one of his most important features and one on which a great deal of emphasis has been placed by the German Club. It lies flat but is long enough and strong enough to protect the body when he is forcing his way through thorn and bramble, and the whiskers around the nose and eyes protects those parts of the dog from injury.

His modern history as a show dog is short as he was accepted for registration for championship in the United States only in 1959, and is insufficiently well-established yet to have made his mark at the highest level. He is, however, a very attractive dog in the ring, his size, outline and colouring making him strikingly different, and there is every chance that he will become a popular show dog. He is intelligent and friendly, and whilst he is not effusive, he stands handling in the ring very well, and will clearly be as good a house dog and companion as any of the other gundogs.

OFFICIAL STANDARD

The German Wirehaired Pointer is a dog that is essentially Pointer in type, of sturdy build, lively manner, and an intelligent, determined expression. In disposition the dog has been described as energetic, rather aloof but not unfriendly.

Head

The *head* is moderately long, the *skull* broad, the occipital bone not too prominent. The *stop* is medium, the *muzzle* fairly long with nasal bone straight and broad, the *lips* a trifle pendulous but close and bearded. The *nose* is dark brown with nostrils wide open, and the *teeth* are strong with scissors bite. The *ears*, rounded but not too broad, hang close to the sides of the head. *Eyes* are brown, medium in size, oval in contour, bright and clear and overhung with bushy eyebrows. Yellow eyes are not desirable. The *neck* is of medium length, slightly arched and devoid of dewlap; in fact, the skin throughout is notably tight to the body.

Head: stop medium, lips close and bearded.

Body and tail

The body is a little longer than it is high, as ten is to nine, with the back short, straight and strong, the entire back line showing a perceptible slope down from withers to croup. The chest is deep and capacious, the ribs well sprung, loins taut and slender, the tuck-up apparent. Hips are broad, with croup nicely rounded and the tail docked, approximately two-fifths of original length.

Legs and feet: shoulders obliquely set and elbows close.

Legs and feet: hind legs moderately angulated, agile.

Legs and feet

Forelegs are straight, with shoulders obliquely set and elbows close. The thighs are strong and muscular. The hind legs are moderately angulated at stifle and hock and as viewed from behind, parallel to each other. Round in outline, the feet are webbed, high arched with toes close, their pads thick and hard, and their nails strong and quite heavy. Leg bones are flat rather than round, and strong, but not so heavy or coarse as to militate against the dog's natural agility.

Coat

The coat is weather-resisting and to some extent water-repellent. The undercoat is dense enough in winter to insulate against the cold but so thin in summer as to be almost invisible. The distinctive outer coat is straight, harsh, wiry and rather flat-lying, from one and one-half to two inches in length; it is long enough to protect against the punishment of rough cover but not so long as to hide the outline. On the lower legs it is shorter and between the toes of softer texture. On the skull it is naturally short and close fitting, while over the shoulders and around the tail it is very dense and heavy. The tail is nicely coated, particularly on the underside, but devoid of feather. These dogs have bushy eyebrows of strong, straight hair and beards and whiskers of medium length.

A short smooth coat, a soft woolly coat, or an excessively long coat is to be severely penalized.

Color

The coat is liver and white, usually either liver and white spotted, liver roan, liver and white spotted with ticking and roaning or sometimes solid liver. The nose is dark brown. The head is brown, sometimes with a white blaze, the ears brown. Any black in the coat is to be severely penalized. Spotted and flesh-colored noses are undesirable and are to be penalized.

Size

Height of dogs should be from 24 to 26 inches at the withers, bitches smaller but not under 22 inches.

Approved 7 February 1959

AKC VARIATION TO STANDARD

This dog is not granted championship status by the KC(GB). The above standards are those of the AKC.

CHESAPEAKE BAY RETRIEVER

NATIONAL GROUPING		
	Name	Number
KC(GB)	—	–
AKC	Sporting Dogs	I
FCI	Gundogs	8

The history of this rather unusual dog is clearly recorded and there is no need to delve into vague references and ancient manuscripts. In 1807 an English ship was wrecked off the coast of Maryland and everyone on board was rescued by the American ship *Canton*. Among the rescued were two puppies, a red dog and a black bitch which were presumed to be Newfoundlands as there was a certain export of these dogs going on at the time. The two were presented to the gentleman who gave hospitality to the rescued sailors and were found to have retrieving ability. As was usual at that time their fame as gundogs spread and they were outcrossed to other dogs being used as sporting dogs in the area, and by 1885 the type had become fixed. Renowned for his powers of retrieving in the cold waters of Chesapeake Bay the dog soon took his name from that stretch of water.

Since that time his sterling qualities as a retriever, especially in water, where he is used extensively to duck, and will retrieve literally hundreds of duck in one day, have endeared him to the waterfowler, and he is now an invaluable ally for the sportsman addicted to that form of shooting. Oddly enough he has never quite achieved the popularity at shows or at field trials that his great ability might warrant. This is probably because he is a rather unglamorous dog, not having the appeal of the Labrador Retriever nor the picturesque qualities of some of the more colourful gundogs, and it is colour which really distinguishes him from all others. He is very much a working animal with no pretence to the more accepted forms of beauty. His appearance is rugged and no attempt has been made over the years to change him into anything else.

He is described as having a coat that varies from dead grass to wet sedge in colour, the actual tone fading in Summer to look like the colour of the dead and shedding coat of the buffalo. It is this coat which is one of the major features of the breed and every effort is being made to retain it, as not only the colour, but also the texture is important. He is used for hunting under the most adverse weather conditions and the natural oiliness of the outer coat and the dense undercoat permit him to swim for long periods in very cold water and remove most of it with one brisk shake when returning to land. He is a well-proportioned dog with a balanced look about him, strong bone and good musculation.

His steadiness to hand makes him a comparatively easy dog to show as he does not suffer normally from nervousness though he can be a little reserved like some of the other gundogs. The breed has made little progress as a show dog outside the United States of America, and is rarely seen at any except the major shows. He is a willing, alert and intelligent dog, very friendly and attached to those that he knows, and always ready to work. They probably make better house dogs than they do kennel dogs, as they are hard and tend to be loners, objecting if other dogs intrude on their territory.

OFFICIAL STANDARD

Head
Skull broad and round with medium stop, nose medium short-muzzle, pointed but not sharp. Lips thin, not pendulous. Ears small, set well up on head, hanging loosely and of medium leather. Eyes medium large, very clear, of yellowish color and wide apart.

Neck
Of medium length with a strong muscular appearance, tapering to shoulders.

Shoulder, chest and body
Shoulders, sloping and should have full liberty of action with plenty of power without any restrictions of movement. Chest strong, deep and wide. Barrel round and deep. Body of medium length, neither cobby nor roached,

but rather approaching hollowness, flanks well tucked up.

Back quarters and stifles
Back quarters should be as high or a trifle higher than the shoulders. They should show fully as much power as the forequarters. There should be no tendency to weakness in either fore or hindquarters. Hindquarters should be especially powerful to supply the driving power for swimming. Back should be short, well-coupled and powerful. Good hindquarters are essential.

Stern: tail medium length, moderate feathering.

Quarters: slightly high. Back: powerful. Coat: tendency to curl on shoulders, back, neck and loins.

Legs, elbows, hocks and feet
Legs should be medium length and straight, showing good bone and muscle, with well-webbed hare feet of good size. The toes well rounded and close, pasterns slightly bent and both pasterns and hocks medium length—the straighter the legs the better. Dewclaws, if any, must be removed from the hind legs. Dewclaws on the forelegs may be removed. A dog with dewclaws on the hind legs must be disqualified.

Stern
Tail should be medium length—varying from: dogs, 12 to 15 inches, and bitches from 11 to 14 inches; medium heavy at base, moderate feathering on stern and tail permissible.

Coat and texture
Coat should be thick and short, nowhere over 1½ inches long, with a dense fine woolly undercoat. Hair on face and legs should be very short and straight with tendency to wave on the shoulders, neck, back and loins only. The curly coat or coat with a tendency to curl not permissible.

Color
Any color varying from a dark brown to a faded tan or deadgrass. Deadgrass takes in any shade of deadgrass, varying from a tan to a dull straw color. White spot on breast and toes permissible, but the smaller the spot the better, solid color being preferred.

Weight
Dogs, 65 to 75 pounds; bitches, 55 to 65 pounds. *Height:* Dogs, 23 to 26 inches; bitches, 21 to 24 inches.

Symmetry and quality
The Chesapeake dog should show a bright and happy disposition and an intelligent expression, with general outlines impressive and denoting a good worker. The dog should be well proportioned, a dog with a good coat and well balanced in other points being preferable to the dog excelling in some but weak in others.
The texture of the dog's coat is very important, as the dog is used for hunting under all sorts of adverse weather conditions, often working in ice and snow. The oil in the harsh outer coat and woolly undercoat is of extreme value in preventing the cold water from reaching the dog's skin and aids in quick drying. A Chesapeake's coat should resist the water in the same way that a duck's feathers do. When he leaves the water and shakes himself, his coat should not hold the water at all, being merely

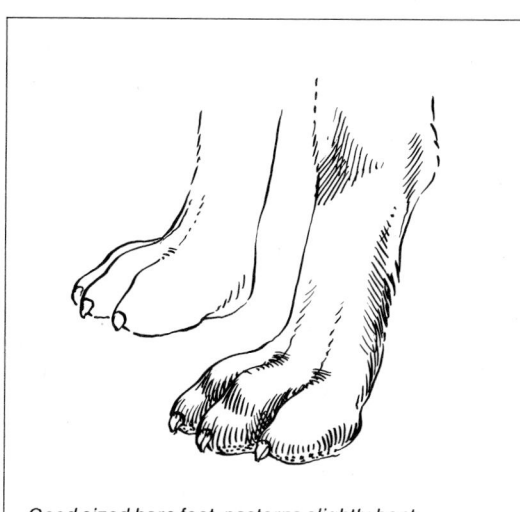

Good sized hare feet, pasterns slightly bent.

moist. Color and coat are extremely important, as the dog is used for duck hunting. The color must be as nearly that of his surroundings as possible and with the fact that dogs are exposed to all kinds of adverse weather conditions, often working in ice and snow, the color of coat and its texture must be given every consideration when judging on the bench or in the ring.

Courage, willingness to work, alertness, nose intelligence, love of water, general quality, and, most of all, disposition, should be given primary consideration in the selection and breeding of the Chesapeake Bay dog.

Measurements of head in inches. Ears: well set, hanging loosely.

APPROXIMATE MEASUREMENTS (in inches)
Length head, nose to occiput ($9\frac{1}{2}$ to 10). Girth at ears (20 to 21). Muzzle below eyes (10 to $10\frac{1}{2}$). Length of ears ($4\frac{1}{2}$

to 5). Width between eyes ($2\frac{1}{2}$ to $2\frac{3}{4}$). Girth neck close to shoulder (20 to 22). Girth of chest to elbows (35 to 36). Girth at flank (24 to 25). Length from occiput to tail base (34 to 35). Girth forearms at shoulders (10 to 10). Girth upper thigh (19 to 20). From root to root of ear, over skull (5 to 6). Occiput to top shoulder blades (9 to $9\frac{1}{2}$). From elbow to elbow over the shoulders (25 to 26).

DISQUALIFICATIONS
Black or liver colored. Dewclaws on hind legs. White on any part of body, except breast, belly or spots on feet. Feathering on tail or legs over $1\frac{3}{4}$ inches long. Undershot, overshot or any deformity. Coat curly or tendency to curl all over body. Specimens unworthy or lacking in breed characteristics.

Approved 9 July 1963

POSITIVE SCALE OF POINTS
Head, incl. lips, ears and eyes (16). Neck (4). Shoulders and body (12). Back quarters and stifles (12). Elbows, legs and feet (12). Color (4). Stern and tail (10). Coat and texture (18). General conformation (12). *Total (100).*

Note: the question of coat and general type of balance takes precedence over any scoring table which could be drawn up.

AKC VARIATION TO STANDARD
This dog is not granted championship status by the KC(GB) therefore the above standards are those of the AKC.

CURLY-COATED RETRIEVER

There existed in Europe some centuries ago a dog known as the Water Dog. He was about the size of a large Spaniel, was mostly black in colour with some white markings, and was covered with close curls. He is presumed by many people to have been the ancestor of the Poodle, and bore a strong resemblance to that other dog that enjoys working in water, the Irish Water Spaniel. There is little doubt that this old breed was also responsible for the Curly-coated Retriever. In fact one old writer carried out an experiment by crossing a Poodle with a Labrador and produced something very like a rather poor Curly-coated Retriever, which led him to the conclusion that through the German Pudel, the old Water Dog had a good deal to do with the ancestry of this breed. At one time the Poodle was shown in curly-coat or at least in cords, which are merely curls left to cling together, and even today, a pet poodle kept in fairly

NATIONAL GROUPING		
	Name	Number
KC(GB)	Gundog	2
AKC	Sporting Dogs	1
FCI	Gundogs	8

short coat will invariably develop curls.

The Curly-coated Retriever is said to have been crossed with the Poodle until well into the 19th century. This could be done without in any way undermining the ability of the breed in the field, as the Poodle was originally a hunting dog, and even today can be trained to perform well in the field. The Curly-coated were at one time one of the more popular of the gundogs and it is interesting that Vero Shaw in 1881 stated that they were beginning to lose ground to the Wavy-coated Retriever, with no mention of today's most popular breeds in the retrieving family. The first were exhibited in 1860 at Birmingham, and before the turn of the century they were being exported to many countries where their capabilities were recognised. New Zealand and Australia took to them and soon after 1900 they began to make their appearance in the United States of America. In spite of his particular qualities as a water dog, he failed to make the progress in either the show ring or the field that some of the other breeds did, and he is now almost relegated to the status of a minority breed in the Gundog Group in Britain.

His principal physical characteristic, his coat, is the one thing that breeders are particularly enthusiastic about preserving. Early writers described the coat in detailed terms, and insisted that each lock should be tightly curled and that they should be close together, anything in the nature of an open coat to be severely penalised. The breed club, first formed in 1896 and reformed in 1933 produced a standard for the breed which re-emphasised this point. This thick curly coat enables him to work through the thickest and most punishing coverts and to spend considerable time in water, where the air trapped forms a good insulation against both wet and cold. He is a strong dog with a depth of chest and tremendously strong hindquarters. His performance in the field makes him a great favourite with gamekeepers in spite of the fact that he has the reputation of being somewhat harder than the other retrievers.

He presents few problems as a show dog, though the search for the perfect coat is constant, a good many tricks of the trade being used to improve and prepare coats. One old expert on the breed was in the habit of stopping at the nearest stretch of fresh water on the way to a show and giving his dogs a swim, allowing them to dry out naturally and trying to disturb the curls as little as possible before entering the ring. He is easily trained, either for the ring or the field, and makes an excellent guard and house dog.

OFFICIAL STANDARD

General appearance
A strong smart upstanding dog showing activity, endurance and intelligence.

Head and skull
Long, well proportioned flat skull, jaws strong and long but not inclined to snipiness. Nose black in the black-coated variety with wide nostrils, coarseness of head to be deprecated.

Ears: rather small, low and close, covered with short curls.

Eyes
Black or brown but not 'gooseberry' coloured, rather large but not too prominent.

Ears
Rather small, set on low, lying close to the head and covered with short curls.

Mouth
Teeth strong and level.

Neck
Should be moderately long, free from throatiness.

Forequarters
Shoulders should be very deep, muscular and well laid back.

Hindquarters
Strong and muscular, hock low to the ground with good bend to stifle and hock.

Body
Well-sprung ribs, good depth of brisket, not too long in the loin, as little tucked-up in flank as possible.

Feet
Round and compact with well-arched toes.

Tail
Moderately short, carried fairly straight and covered with curls, tapering towards the point, gay tail not desirable.

Coat
Should be one mass of crisp small curls all over. This being the main characteristic of the breed should be given great consideration when making judging awards.

Colour
Black or liver.

Weight and size
70 to 80 pounds. Approximately 25 to 27 inches.

Faults
Wide skull, light eyes, curled tail and bad movement.

Note
Male animals should have two apparently normal testicles fully descended into the scrotum.

FLAT-COATED RETRIEVER

NATIONAL GROUPING		
	Name	Number
KC(GB)	Gundog	2
AKC	Sporting Dogs	1
FCI	Gundogs	8

In some ways the Flat-coated Retriever has a strange history, as he was produced from two breeds, the Labrador and the Newfoundland, both of which had their origins in the United States. Yet while he remained virtually unknown in that country he made a name for himself and became quite popular in Britain. The first evidence of the breed is of a dog named Wyndham that was shown at the Birmingham Show in 1860, where he caused something of a sensation. He was new to the dog breeders of Britain in spite of the fact that there was a tremendous interest in Retrievers in general at that time even though their numbers were small. He was christened the Wavy-coated Retriever and the name Flat-coated came later, when it was thought that a wavy coat was not the best for the work that he did in water, something at which he was very adept. It is fairly certain that there had been others before Wyndham, as it was very unlikely that he should be a single one of his type, and much more likely that some experimental breeding had been going on for several generations.

It is fairly certain that the Gordon Setter and the Irish Setter were used later, as the breed had become more elegant and less heavily built than it once was and the coat quality has developed into the fine flat texture that is now so much a feature of the breed. He is an admirable water dog, and this particular quality endeared him to gundog people, as he combined most of the other qualities of the retriever with a constitution that rendered him almost impervious to the effects of long immersion. Later still his popularity was assured, when one of the greatest dog men of all time, S.E. Shirley, founder of the Kennel Club and its Chairman from 1873 until 1899 when he became President, took an interest in the breed and bred, exhibited and worked some of the finest of those times. His portrait hanging in the Board Room of the Kennel Club in London, depicts him with a Flat-coated Retriever.

The breed went into something of a decline as a show dog during the First World War, but was kept alive by the efforts of gamekeepers, many of whom looked upon the Flat-coated Retriever as the finest of all the gundogs. The Flat-coated Retriever Association however did much to revive the breed after 1923 when the club was formed, and since that time representatives of the breed have been seen in ever increasing numbers at the major shows, just on one hundred being exhibited at Crufts in 1977. Fortunately for the working qualities of the breed, they are also being taken up increasingly by those interested in field work.

He is a strong dog, less weighty for his size than the Labrador Retriever, but sturdier than the Irish Setter, and he is remarkably intelligent. His coat, which is his outstanding characteristic is close-lying and dense, and whilst the favourite colour is black, some liver specimens are seen now though they were frowned upon in the early days of the breed. He is a fine show-dog, his intelligent response to environment and circumstances allowing him to deal with the attentions of a judge and the physical contact with people and other dogs with the calm that is part of his nature. His coat, glowing in the sunshine makes him an ideal dog for showing out of doors, where he looks at his best. Temperamentally he is very steady, responsive to attention, and makes a remarkably good guard, as he is very territorially minded.

OFFICIAL STANDARD

General appearance
A bright, active dog of medium size with an intelligent expression, showing power without lumber, and raciness without weediness.

Head and skull
The head should be long and nicely moulded. The skull flat and moderately broad. There should be a depression or stop between the eyes, slight and in no way accentuated, so as to avoid giving either a down or a dish-faced appearance. The nose of a good size, with open nostrils. The jaws should be long and strong, with a capacity of carrying a hare or pheasant.

Body: fore-ribs fairly flat, gradual spring in centre of body.

Jaws: long and strong.

Eyes
Should be of medium size, dark-brown or hazel, with a very intelligent expression (a round, prominent eye is a disfigurement) and they should not be obliquely.placed.

Ears
Should be small and well set-on, close to the side of the head.

Ears: small, well set on.

Neck
The head should be well set in the neck, which latter should be long and free from throatiness, symmetrically set and obliquely placed in shoulders running well into

the back to allow of easily seeking for the trail.

Forequarters
The chest should be deep and fairly broad, with a well-defined brisket, on which the elbows should work cleanly and evenly. The legs are of the greatest importance, the forelegs should be perfectly straight, with bone of good quality carried right down to the feet and when the dog is in full coat the legs should be well feathered.

Body
The fore-ribs should be fairly flat, showing a gradual spring and well-arched in the centre of the body, but rather lighter towards the quarters. Open couplings are to be ruthlessly condemned. The back should be short, square and well ribbed up.

Hindquarters
Should be muscular. The stifle should not be too straight or too bent, and the dog must neither be cow-hocked nor move too widely behind; in fact he must stand and move true on legs and feet all round. The legs should be well feathered.

Feet
Should be round and strong with toes close and well arched, the soles being thick and strong.

Tail
Short, straight and well set on, carried gaily, but never much above the level of the back.

Coat
Should be dense, of fine quality and texture, flat as possible.

Colour
Black or liver.

Weight and Size
Should be between 60 and 70 pounds.

Note
Male animals should have two apparently normal testicles fully descended into the scrotum.

GOLDEN RETRIEVER

Scotland has many native breeds, most of them belonging to the Terrier Group. There are many Scots who would like to lay claim to the Golden Retriever too, but it was in fact more of an accident of geography that resulted in much of the early development of this breed taking place North of the Border. Retrievers in general became popular in Britain during the early part of the 19th century, when, with the growth of wildfowling as a sport, there came the demand for dogs that would work as collectors of game under extreme conditions of wet and cold. The less heavy form of Newfoundland, known at that time as the St. John's Newfoundland had found its way over to Britain from the other side of the Atlantic, and its ability as a water dog was soon realised. This breed was crossed with Setters and Spaniels and produced large strong, intelligent dogs with an affinity to water, the will to work and a soft mouth.

It happened that the early work on the breed was carried out by Lord Tweedmouth. The legend of his having bought a troop of performing Russian dogs from a circus, was exploded by other members of his family. In more recent records it was made clear that the first member of the race was in fact a mutation from Flat-coated Retriever stock, a dog named Nous. He was mated to a small English Retriever, and the line had started. The Tweedmouth dogs were carefully outcrossed to further water-spaniels and some of the Flat-coated Retrievers then known as Wavy-coats, and by the beginning of the 19th century the type and colour was fixed. These yellow Retrievers were recognised as Flat-coats until 1913, when they were registered as a separate variety, called at first Yellow or Golden Retrievers, and eventually Golden Retrievers. The modernity of the breed is best indicated by the fact that in Robert Leighton's very comprehensive work of 1907, it does not get a mention.

Their growth in popularity since those early days has been one of the phenomena of the dog world. In fifty years the number registered in Britain has grown from virtually nothing, to something approaching ten thousand each year, making them one of the most prolific breeds in the Gundog Group. It is not now unusual for them to outnumber both Cockers and Labrador Retrievers at some of the major shows, and one or two quite outstanding dogs have won major honours in recent years.

The Golden Retriever's working qualities are still much exploited and he is seen regularly at field trials, takes part in obedience work and even makes a successful guide dog for the blind. His intelligence is extraordinary and he is one of the few dogs that can work out a problem for himself rather than merely acting on instruction or as the result of repetitive training. As a show dog he has few peers, as he is one of the quietest and best behaved dogs in existence, behaving always in a gentlemanly fashion, at the same time cheerful and never dull. His coat lends itself to preparation and grooming and the minimum amount of shaping and control. His relaxed and quiet behaviour makes it possible to transport several in a car without fuss, and to bench them with confidence.

He is a gentle, sensitive, always responsive dog and is very good with children. His obedience is renowned and his lack of vice recognised throughout the world of dogs. He makes a first class guard and companion.

OFFICIAL STANDARD

General appearance
Should be of a symmetrical, active, powerful dog, a good level mover, sound and well put together, with a kindly expression, not clumsy nor long in the leg.

Head and skull
Broad skull, well set on a clean and muscular neck, muzzle powerful and wide, not weak-jawed, good stop.

Eyes
Dark and set well apart, very kindly in expression, with dark rims.

Ears
Well proportioned, of moderate size, and well set on.

Mouth
Teeth should be sound and strong. Neither overshot nor undershot the lower teeth just behind but touching the upper.

Neck
The neck should be clean and muscular.

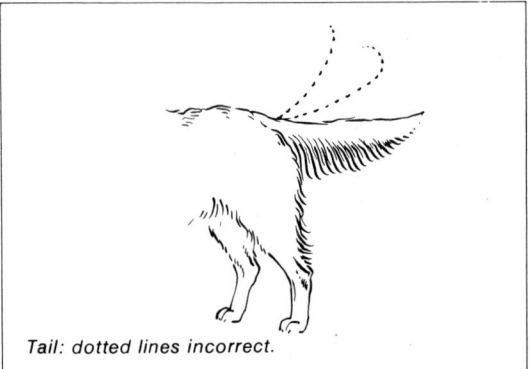

Tail: dotted lines incorrect.

Tail
Should not be carried too gay nor curled at the tip.

Coat
Should be flat or wavy with good feathering, and dense, water-resisting undercoat.

Colour
Any shade of gold or cream, but neither red nor mahogany. The presence of a few white hairs on chest permissible. White collar, feet, toes or blaze should be penalised. Nose should be black.

Weight and size
The average weight in good hard condition should be: dogs, 70 to 80 pounds (32 to 37 kilos); bitches, 60 to 70 pounds (27 to 32 kilos). Height at shoulder: dogs, 22 to 24 inches (55.88 to 60.96 centimetres); bitches, 20 to 22 inches (50.80 to 55.88 centimetres).

Note
Male animals should have two apparently normal testicles fully descended into the scrotum.

Forequarters: shoulders well laid back.

Forequarters
The forelegs should be straight with good bone. Shoulders should be well laid back and long in the blade.

Body
Well-balanced, short coupled, and deep through the heart. Ribs deep and well sprung.

Hindquarters
The loins and legs should be strong and muscular, with good second thighs and well bent stifles. Hocks well let down, not cow-hocked.

Feet
Round and cat-like, not open nor splay.

AKC VARIATION TO STANDARD
Ears: rather short, hanging flat against head with rounded tips slightly below jaw. Forward edge attached well behind and just above eye with rear edge slightly below eye. *Nose:* black or dark brown, though lighter shade in cold weather not serious. Dudley nose (pink without pigmentation) to be faulted. *Neck:* medium long sloping well back into shoulders, untrimmed natural ruff. No throatiness. *Body:* brisket extends to elbows. Loin short, muscular wide and deep, with very little tuck-up. Topline level from withers to croup, whether standing or moving. Croup slopes gently. Slabsidedness, narrow chest, lack of depth in brisket, excessive tuck-up roach or sway back to be faulted. *Disqualification:* deviation from height of more than one inch from standard either way. Abnormal position or direction of eyelashes. *Height and size:* dogs 65 to 75 pounds and 23 to 24 inches; bitches 60 to 70 pounds and $21\frac{1}{2}$ to $22\frac{1}{2}$ inches. Length from breastbone to buttocks slightly greater than height at withers in the ratio 12:11.

LABRADOR RETRIEVER

Few dogs earn their names from a casual remark in a letter. They draw on their country of origin, or the work that they do, or even on the names of those who first bred them. The Labrador Retriever owes his name to a letter written by the Earl of Malmesbury in 1887 in which, in speaking of these dogs he said that he always called his 'Labradors'. The name had the right sort of ring about it and it was adopted for the breed.

Newfoundland was much visited by fishermen and travellers in the early part of the 19th century, and one reported on a small breed of water dog that he had seen there, short-haired, usually black and trained as a retriever by wildfowlers. The Earl of Malmesbury is said to have seen one of these brought over to Britain and found it so attractive that he imported some. The breed gradually died out in Newfoundland where it was virtually taxed out of existence as local fishermen would not pay a heavy dog tax, but it flourished in Britain where its qualities were recognised.

The Labrador Retriever undoubtedly played a part in the development of the at one-time much more popular Flat-coated Retriever, and it is remarkable that he remained a true type as a good deal of inter-breeding must have taken place. It is interesting in this context to note that in the early part of this century, one well known writer was saying he doubted that the Labrador would ever be appreciated by the rank and file and become popular as a show dog. How surprised he would be now to see him one of the best known dogs in the world. Hexham near the Scottish Border was the first Show to schedule the breed, and the Crystal

NATIONAL GROUPING		
	Name	Number
KC(GB)	Gundog	2
AKC	Sporting Dogs	1
FCI	Gundogs	8

Palace, and Crufts soon followed. It is not, however, merely in the show ring that the popularity of the Labrador has grown. He is regularly seen at gundog trials as well as being popular with gamekeepers for day to day work with game, but it is still as a water dog and a wildfowler's companion that he is best known.

At one time almost all Labradors were black, but the yellows have now overtaken the other colours in popularity, and a few chocolates are now appearing in the ring. There was some controversy about which colour was the best for field work, some preferring the blacks which they felt were better workers in water, others the yellows as they were generally more easily seen at work. In fact there is probably little to choose between them, and temperament and ability are more important considerations. The Labrador Retriever must be one of the best all round dogs in the world. In addition to his value as a field dog, and his tremendous popularity as a show dog, he has achieved fame in other directions. He proved a valuable dog in war time, being an excellent mine detector, capable of locating mines by scent even when they were buried at considerable depths. He is a fine police dog, being easily trained in criminal work and as a specialist for sniffing out drugs. In addition most of the dogs trained as guide dogs for the blind are now Labrador bitches.

As a show dog he has attained prominence in recent years over most of the other members of the group, and the number of registrations in the breed in most countries is the highest among the gundogs. He is one of those breeds that in Britain cannot become a full champion until they have received working certificates, and the title of Show Champion has been introduced to cover those that gain certificates but do not qualify. He is a good dog in the ring, being very steady and cheerful, enjoying the company of other dogs and the noise of the crowd. He is not difficult to keep in condition provided that he is given enough exercise to prevent him putting on weight. His temperament is almost ideal, as he is attached to people and places, adopts a sufficiently possessive attitude to property to make a good guard, and is very good with children.

OFFICIAL STANDARD

General appearance
The general appearance of the Labrador should be that of a strongly-built, short-coupled, very active dog, broad in the skull, broad and deep through the chest and ribs, broad and strong over the loins and hindquarters. The coat close, short with dense undercoat and free from feather. The dog must move neither too wide nor too close in front or behind, he must stand and move true all round on legs and feet.

Head: clean cut, jaws powerful.

Head and skull
The skull should be broad with a pronounced stop so that the skull is not in a straight line with the nose. The head should be clean cut without fleshy cheeks. The jaws should be medium length and powerful and free from snipiness. The nose wide and the nostrils well developed.

Fault: snipiness.

Eyes
The eyes of medium size expressing intelligence and good temper, should be brown or hazel.

Ears
Should not be large and heavy and should hang close to the head, and set rather far back.

Neck: powerful, well placed shoulders.

Mouth
Teeth should be sound and strong. The lower teeth just behind but touching the upper.

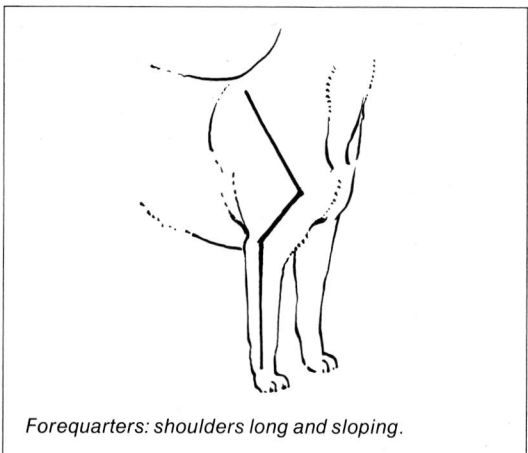
Forequarters: shoulders long and sloping.

Neck
Should be clean, strong and powerful and set into well placed shoulders.

Forequarters
The shoulders should be long and sloping. The forelegs well boned and straight from the shoulder to the ground when viewed from either the front or side. The dog must move neither too wide nor too close in front.

Body
The chest must be of good width and depth with well-sprung ribs. The back should be short coupled.

Hindquarters
The loins must be wide and strong with well-turned stifles; hindquarters well developed and not sloping to the tail. The hocks should be slightly bent and the dog must neither be cow-hocked nor move too wide or too close behind.

Feet
Should be round and compact with well-arched toes and

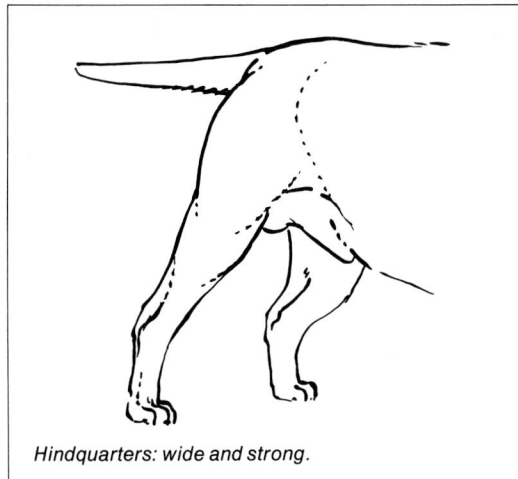

Hindquarters: wide and strong.

well-developed pads.

Tail

The tail is a distinctive feature of the breed; it should be very thick towards the base, gradually tapering towards the tip, of medium length and practically free from any feathering, but clothed thickly all round with the Labrador's short, thick, dense coat, thus giving that peculiar 'rounded' appearance which has been described as the 'Otter' tail. The tail may be carried gaily, but should not curl over the back.

Coat

The coat is another distinctive feature of the breed, it should be short and dense and without wave with a weather-resisting undercoat and should give a fairly hard feeling to the hand.

Colour

The colour is generally black or yellow—but other whole colours are permitted. The coat should be free from any white markings but a small white spot on the chest is allowable. The coat should be of a whole colour and not of a flecked appearance.

Weight and size

Desired height for dogs, 22 to $22\frac{1}{2}$ inches; bitches, $21\frac{1}{2}$ to 22inches.

Faults

Under or overshot mouth; no undercoat; bad action; feathering; snipiness on the head; large or heavy ears; cow-hocked; tail curled over back.

Note

Male animals should have two apparently normal testicles fully descended into the scrotum.

AKC VARIATION TO STANDARD

Head: jaws should be long. *Weight and size:* dogs 60 to 75 pounds and $22\frac{1}{2}$ to $24\frac{1}{2}$ inches at shoulders; bitches 55 to 70 pounds and $21\frac{1}{2}$ to $23\frac{1}{2}$ inches at shoulders.

ENGLISH SETTER

NATIONAL GROUPING		
	Name	Number
KC(GB)	Gundog	2
AKC	Sporting Dogs	1
FCI	Gundogs	8

Even before the days of the shotgun, some of the dogs used to locate the prey were trained to sit when they found the game by nose and eye, and became known as 'sitting' or 'setting' dogs. The English Setter has developed from these dogs. He is essentially European, developed mainly for work on moors or in stubble or roots where his task is to remain motionless when he has located game to give the sportsman the opportunity to see it and dispatch it. His origins probably lie in the Spaniel and the Old Spanish Pointer, and engravings of the Springer and the Setter of 1820 show two dogs with marked similarities. The Springer is lighter and longer in the leg than the modern Spaniel, and the Setter is heavier and shorter than the Setter of today. As their colour and markings are the same they look rather like two examples of the same breed.

The major credit for the development of the modern English Setter undoubtedly belongs to Mr. Edward Laverack who in 1825 obtained a pair from the Rev. Harrison and inbred them until he had fixed the type that he wanted. In 1874 a pair of these dogs was imported into the United States and formed the foundations of the Llewellin line which became the main strain in that country. The Laverack line was so important in the early days of the breed that they were known as Laverack Setters, whilst the Llewellin strain was given

equal prominence and Setter breeders spoke of the two strains almost as if they were separate breeds. The three breeds of Setters, the English, the Irish and the Gordon, almost certainly descended from the same parent stock, but it is remarkable how the popularity of the three breeds has varied. The Irish Setter having gone through a period of doldrums is now one of the most popular of breeds, the Gordon Setter has never achieved a great deal of popularity, whilst the English Setter has made steady progress over the years.

He is one of the dogs that most typifies the English country scene, and many people have an image of the English gentleman, dressed in tweeds, gun under his arm and English Setter by his side, firmly fixed in their minds as part of an idyllic English scene. This is not surprising as he is a very English dog in character. He is gentle and quiet, less exuberant than some of the other gundogs, and with a mild and sweet disposition. He is elegant in appearance yet strongly built with the look of the outdoors about him: he is in fact more hardy and sturdy than his appearance might suggest. The first show of the breed was held in Newcastle-upon-Tyne in 1859 and since that time he has made steady progress as a show dog, culminating in the great win of Supreme Best in Show by Ch. Silbury Soames of Madavale at Crufts in 1964. His elegance of outline, lovely coat and beautiful head make him a superb show dog, and his steadiness in the ring, makes him an easy dog to show. The breed matures late, however, and puppies look very unimpressive alongside some of the faster maturing breeds such as the Terriers, which tends to make them competitive only among other members of their own breed. He is quiet and usually relaxed, well-mannered and most affectionate, and can be completely trusted with children. He settles down to domestic life very easily, and although when out walking he will cover considerable ground enjoying every scent on the air, he is easily trained to return.

OFFICIAL STANDARD

Characteristics
An intensely friendly and quiet-natured dog with a keen game sense.

General appearance
Of medium height, clean in outline, elegant in appearance and movement.

Head and skull
Head should be long and reasonably lean, with a well-defined stop. The skull oval from ear to ear, showing plenty of brain room, and with a well-defined occipital protuberance. The muzzle moderately deep and fairly square; from the stop to the point of the nose should equal the length of skull from occiput to eyes; the nostrils wide and the jaws of nearly equal legth; flews not to be too pendulous; the colour of the nose should be black or liver, according to the colour of the coat.

Forequarters: shoulders well set back. Brisket: good depth. Forearm: big, very muscular.

Head: long, well-defined stop.

Eyes
The eyes should be bright, mild and intelligent, and of a dark hazel colour, the darker the better.

Ears
The ears of moderate length, set on low, and hanging in neat folds close to the cheek; the tip should be velvety, the upper part clothed in fine silky hair.

Mouth
To be level.

Neck
Neck should be rather long, muscular and lean, slightly arched at the crest, and clean cut where it joins the head; towards the shoulder it should be larger and very muscular, not throaty or pendulous below the throat, but elegant in appearance.

Forequarters
The shoulders should be well set back or oblique; the chest should be deep in the brisket, and of good depth and width between the shoulder blades. The forearm big and very muscular, with rounded bone, and the elbow well let down. Pasterns short, muscular, round and straight.

Body
The body should be of moderate length, the back short and level with good round widely-sprung ribs and deep in the back ribs, i.e., well ribbed up.

Hindquarters
The loins should be wide, slightly arched, strong and muscular, with defined second thigh. Stifles well bent and rugged, thighs long from hip to hock.

Feet
The feet should be very close and compact and well protected by hair between the toes.

Tail
The tail should be set on almost in line with the back; medium length, not curly or ropy, to be slightly curved or scimitar-shaped but with no tendency to turn upwards; the flag or feather hanging in long pendant flakes. The feather should not commence at the root, but slightly below, and increase in length to the middle, then gradually taper off towards the end; the hair long, bright, soft and silky, wavy, but not curly.

Coat
The coat from the back of the head in a line with the ears ought to be slightly wavy, long and silky, which should be the case with the coat generally; the breeches and forelegs, nearly down to the feet, should be well feathered.

Tail: slightly curved, hanging feather.

Faulty head: short tapering muzzle, lack of stop, oblique eyes, high ears.

Colour
The colour may be either black and white, lemon and white, liver and white or tricolour—that is black, white and tan; those without heavy patches of colour on the body, but flecked all over, preferred.

Weight and size
Should be: dogs, 60 to 66 pounds, height $25\frac{1}{2}$ to 27 inches. bitches, 56 to 62 pounds, height 24 to $25\frac{1}{2}$ inches.

Faults
Coarse lumpy shoulders; short foreface; tapering to nose; lack of 'stop'; light or obliquely set eyes; high ear placement; loose elbows from bad shoulder placement; flat ribs; too long loin; wide feet; weak pasterns; straight stifles; narrow quarters; gay 'flag'; lightness of bone; mouth undershot or overshot; lacking freedom of action.

Note
Male animals should have two apparently normal testicles fully descended into the scrotum.

AKC VARIATION TO STANDARD
Head: well defined occipital protuberance. *Colour:* blue belton, lemon belton, orange and white, orange belton, liver and white, liver belton and solid white.

GORDON SETTER

Speed in a gundog, and particularly in a Setter, is not all important and this is exemplified in the Gordon Setter, the most heavily built of the three British Setter breeds. In the case of the Gordon, steadiness and brain power have replaced flashiness and he will work on steadily all day, rarely if ever making a mistake. He was developed as the others were by selective breeding from crossing the old fashioned Spaniel with other breeds and was largely a colour separation in the first instance. He was known as the Gordon Setter in his early days as he came to the attention of sportsmen largely through the efforts of the fourth Duke of Gordon, who kept a large kennel of the breed in the latter part of the 18th century. Oddly enough at the turn of the 19th century, he became known as the Black and Tan Setter, as the strain originally kept by the Gordon Castle Kennels was black, tan and white. It was somewhat clumsy and heavy in appearance, and by that time, with the introduction of Irish blood, a more elegant and fashionable dog was being bred.

NATIONAL GROUPING		
	Name	Number
KC(GB)	Gundog	2
AKC	Sporting Dogs	1
FCI	Gundogs	8

When Kennel Club registrations started, the name Gordon Setter was restored, and the formation of a club and the establishment of a standard for the breed ensured its preservation. By 1842 the breed had arrived in the United States of America and by careful further importations from both Britain and Scandinavia the breed has become well established. In recent years the breed went into something of a decline as a show dog, and the numbers of registrations in Britain fell well below the hundred though he still remained popular as a working dog. There is now something of a recovery and the numbers are climbing steadily. It is as a gundog, working in the field that the Gordon Setter has really made his mark, and the efforts of the Gordon Setter Club of America to foster the breed and to organise field trials have done much to preserve those qualities.

It is one of his characteristics that he is ever willing to work, and this has made him a great favourite with the one-dog sportsman who finds him a tireless and co-operative companion. The Gordon Setter breeders and owners have never allowed the sharp division between the show dog and the field dog to develop as it has in so many of the gundog breeds, and most of the dogs are as good in the field as they are on the bench. He is the heavyweight of the Setter trio, is sturdier looking and has a stronger body with a fairly heavy head. He is dignified and even noble in his bearing, and his look is that of a strong dog with stamina rather than a racy type.

He looks well in the ring as his colour is quite dramatic, and the glow that comes on the coat of a healthy dog makes him look quite glamorous when he is mature and well feathered. He suffers from the rather gangling awkward look of the others when a puppy, and he needs understanding for promise rather than polish in his early stages. He is steady though sometimes rather reserved in the ring, and his complete attachment to one person makes him at times shy of strangers. He is intelligent and extremely loyal to the members of the family, taking great pleasure in being a member of a household, and is friendly to those he knows without being effusive.

OFFICIAL STANDARD

General appearance
A stylish dog, built on galloping lines, having a thoroughbred appearance consistent with its build which can be compared to a weight carrying hunter. Must have symmetrical conformation throughout, showing true balance. Strong, fairly short and level back. Shortish tail. Head fairly long, clearly lined and with intelligent expression, clear colours and long flat coat.

Head and skull
Head deep rather than broad, but definitely broader than the muzzle, showing brain room. Skull slightly rounded and broadest between the ears. The head should have a clearly indicated stop and length from occiput to stop should be slightly longer than from stop to nose. Below and above the eyes should be lean and the cheeks as narrow as the leanness of the head allows. The muzzle should be fairly long with almost parallel lines and not pointed, as seen from above or from the side. The flews not pendulous but with clearly indicated lips. Nose big and broad, with open nostrils and black in colour. The muzzle should not be quite as deep as its length.

Eyes
Of fair size, not too deep nor too prominent but sufficiently under the brows to show keen and intelligent expression. Dark brown and bright.

Ears
Set low on the head and lying close to it, of medium size and thin.

Mouth
Must be even and not under nor overshot.

Neck
Long, lean and arched to the head and without any throatiness.

Forequarters
Shoulders should be long and slope well back; with wide flat bone and fairly close at withers; should not be loaded, i.e., too thick, which interferes with liberty of movement. Elbows well let down and showing well under the body, which gives freedom of action. Forelegs big, flat-boned and straight, with strong upright pasterns, well feathered.

Body
Of moderate length, deep in brisket, with ribs well sprung. Deep in back ribs, i.e., well-ribbed up. Loins wide and slightly arched. Chest not too broad.

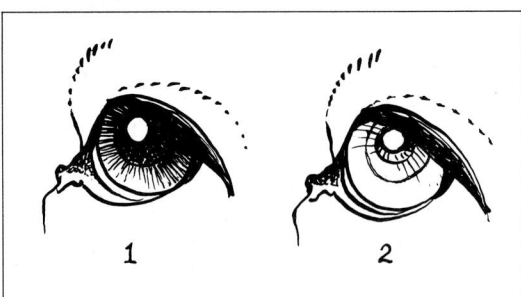

Eyes: (1) dark and bright, (2) too light.

Hindquarters

Hind legs from hip to hock should be long, broad and muscular; hock to heel short and strong, stifles well bent; hocks straight, not inclined either in or out. Pelvis should tend to the horizontal, i.e., opposite of goose rump.

Feet: oval, close knit.

Feet

Oval, with close knit, well-arched toes, with plenty of hair between. Full toe pads and deep heel cushions.

Tail

Fairly short, straight or slightly scimitar shaped and should not reach below the hocks. Carried horizontal or below line of back. Thick at the root tapering to a fine point. The feather or flag which starts near the root should be long and straight, and growing shorter uniformly to the point.

Coat

On the head and front of legs and tips of ears should be short and fine, but on all other parts of the body and legs it ought to be of moderate length, fairly flat and free as possible from curl or wave. The feather on the upper portion of the ears should be long and silky, on the back of the hind legs long and fine; a fair amount of hair on the belly forming a nice fringe which may extend on chest and throat. All feathering to be as flat and straight as possible.

Colour

Deep shining coal-black, with no sign of rustiness, with tan markings of a rich chestnut red, i.e., colour of a ripe horse-chestnut as taken from shell. Tan should be lustrous. Black pencilling allowed on toes and also black streak under jaw. *Tan markings:* two clear spots over the eyes not over threequarters of an inch in diameter. On the sides of the muzzle, the tan should not reach above the base of nose, resembling a stripe around the end of the muzzle from one side to the other. On the throat. Two large, clear spots on the chest. On the inside of the hind legs and inside the thighs showing down the front of the stifle and broadening out to the outside of the hind legs from the hock to the toes. It must, however, not completely eliminate the black on the back of the hind legs. On the forelegs, up to the elbows behind, and to the knees or a little above, in front. Around the vent. A white spot on chest is allowed but the smaller the better.

Tan markings over eyes and on side of muzzle.

Weight and Size

As a guide to size, shoulder height for dogs 26 inches and weight about 65 pounds. Bitches, 24½ inches and weight about 56 pounds. In show condition.

Faults

General Impression: unintelligent appearance. The bloodhound type with heavy and big head and ears and clumsy body; the collie type with pointed muzzle and curved tail. The Head: pointed, snipy, down or upturned muzzle, too small or large mouth. The Eyes: too light in colour, too deep set or too prominent. The Ears: set too high, or unusually broad or heavy. The Neck: thick and short. Shoulders and Back: irregularly formed. The Chest: too broad. The Legs and Feet: crooked legs. Outturned elbows. The toes scattered, flat footed. The Tail: too long, badly carried or hooked at the end. The Coat: curly, like wool, not shining. The Colour: yellow, or straw-coloured tan, or without clearly defined lines between the different colours. White feet. Too much white on the chest. In the black there should be no tan hairs.

Note

Male animals should have two apparently normal testicles fully descended into the scrotum.

AKC VARIATION TO STANDARD

Teeth: should meet in front in scissors bite, with the upper incisors slightly forward of lower incisors. A level bite is not to be considered a fault. *Body:* croup is nearly flat, with only a slight slope to tail-head. *Tail:* tail placement should be judged in its relationship to structure of croup. *Disqualification:* predominantly tan, red or buff dogs which do not have the typical pattern of markings of a Gordon Setter.

IRISH SETTER

NATIONAL GROUPING		
	Name	Number
KC(GB)	Gundog	2
AKC	Sporting Dogs	1
FCI	Gundogs	8

The dog that has raced ahead of the other Setters in popularity is the Irish Setter, his glamour, his association, however tenuous, with the world of field sports and his gay exuberant temperament have endeared him to vast numbers of people throughout the world. His history is fairly obscure, but there is little doubt that he started, as the other Setters did, by careful selective breeding from a number of Spaniels and other Setter types, with perhaps a little Pointer blood thrown in. Suggestions that he began as a cross between the Irish Water Spaniel and the Irish Terrier are pure guesswork as there is no evidence to support the idea. He is known as the Irish Red Setter to many people, who look upon him as a solid all-red dog, but in fact his Irish ancestors were largely red and white and rarely self-coloured.

The solid red dog first appeared in Ireland in the 19th century, and the Earl of Enniskillen had nothing but all-red dogs in his kennels. At the Dublin Show of 1874 there were more classes for red and white setters than for the pure red, and only in 1876 were they classified as merely Irish Setters, when the distinction by colour disappeared. In modern times the only colour that is generally accepted is solid rich chestnut though on both sides of the Atlantic small inconspicuous white markings are not considered a serious fault. The breed is essentially a sporting one, and the fact that the Irish Setter is more suitable to the conditions that exist in Ireland has probably more to do with the way in which the breed has progressed there than any consideration of appearance. In the early days of importation into the United States of America it was his capabilities as a shooting dog that endeared him to so many people and ensured his popularity. In the early days, as now, he was looked upon as a dog that could perform well in the field and look equally well on the bench.

He has the reputation of being flighty and unreliable, but this is almost certainly due to the fact that being such a colourful and glamorous dog he appealed to a great number of people as a pet, and thus got into the wrong hands from the breeders' point of view. There is little doubt that he is a gay and excitable character, and probably needs more careful and consistent training than do some of the other gundogs. However, when he is trained he is a fast and tireless worker in the field, and a steady and reliable companion. In recent years he has achieved great success in the show ring, the number of registrations having quadrupled in most countries, and at most major shows, when a class of the breed is being judged, the ring is full of these striking glossy red dogs.

He is an ideal show dog. He looks the part, is highly intelligent and appreciative of an audience, can be trained to stand and perform with decorum in the ring whatever he happens to be like outside it, is extrovert and an exhibitionist. He enjoys being prepared for show, and his glowing silky coat with the feathering flowing in the breeze on a fully mature dog, pays well for constant brushing, as it contains natural oils and needs no artificial aids. He is a gay dog, full of spirit and usually has a very positive personality. He makes a good family pet and house guard, but it is his value as a shooting dog that really persuades people to own him. He usually develops late, and his training takes more time than does that of some other breeds, but once trained he is very obedient and is a dog of whose appearance any shooting man can be proud.

OFFICIAL STANDARD

General appearance
Must be racy, full of quality, and kindly in expression.

Head and skull
The head should be long and lean, not narrow or snipy, and not coarse at the ears. The skull oval (from ear to ear), having plenty of brain room, and with well-defined occipital protuberance. Brows raised, showing stop. The muzzle moderately deep, and fairly square at end. From the stop to the point of the nose should be long, the nostrils wide, and the jaws of nearly equal length, flews not to be pendulous. The colour of the nose: dark mahogany, or dark walnut, or black.

Eyes
Should be dark hazel or dark brown and ought not to be too large.

Ears
The ears should be of moderate size, fine in texture, set on low, well back; and hanging in a neat fold close to the head.

Mouth
Not over or undershot.

Neck
Should be moderately long, very muscular, but not too thick, slightly arched, free from all tendency to throatiness.

Ears: feather on upper portion, long and silky.

Forequarters
The shoulders to be fine at the points, deep and sloping well back. The chest as deep as possible, rather narrow in front. The fore legs should be straight and sinewy, having plenty of bone, with elbows free, well let down, not inclined either in or out.

Forequarters: shoulders sloping well. Back: chest deep.

Tail: low set, tapering, carried level.

Body
Should be proportionate, the ribs well sprung, leaving plenty of lung room. Loins muscular, slightly arched.

Hindquarters
Should be wide and powerful. The hind legs from hip to hock should be long and muscular; from hock to heel short and strong. The stifle and hock joints well bent, and not inclined either in or out.

Hindquarters:
hip to hock long, hock to heel short and strong.

Feet
Should be small, very firm, toes strong, close together and arched.

Tail
Should be of moderate length, proportionate to the size of the body, set on rather low, strong at root, and tapering to a fine point; to be carried as nearly as possible on a level with or below the back.

Coat and feathering
On the head, front of the legs, and tips of the ears, should be short and fine, but on all other parts of the body and legs it ought to be of moderate length, flat, and as free as possible from curl or wave. The feather on the upper portion of the ears should be long and silky; on the back of fore and hind legs should be long and fine; a fair amount of hair on the belly, forming a nice fringe, which may extend on chest and throat. Feet to be well feathered between the toes. Tail to have a nice fringe of moderately long hair, decreasing in length as it approaches the point. All feathering to be as straight and as flat as possible.

Colour
The colour should be rich chestnut, with no trace whatever of black; white on chest, throat, chin or toes, or a small star on the forehead, or a narrow streak or blaze on the nose or face not to disqualify.

Note
Dog animals should have two apparently normal testicles fully descended into the scrotum.

AKC VARIATION TO STANDARD
Head: teeth meet in a scissors bite in which upper incisors fit closely over lower, or evenly. *Eyes:* somewhat almond shaped, placed rather well apart. *Gait:* at the trot gait is big, very lively, graceful and efficient. Head is held high. Hindquarters drive smoothly and with great power. Forelegs reach well ahead as if to pull in the ground, without giving appearance of a hackney gait. Dog runs as he stands; straight. Seen from front or rear, forelegs, as well as hindlegs below hock joint, move perpendicularly to ground, with some tendency toward a single track as speed increases. But a crossing or weaving of the legs, front or back, is objectionable.

AMERICAN WATER SPANIEL

There is so much similarity between the American Water Spaniel and the Irish Water Spaniel that the idea that the American version developed from an early Irish emigrant is inescapable. He is smaller by a couple of inches than his Irish cousin, is the same colour, and is covered with the same dense curly coat. He differs in the head, and has a plumed tail rather than the partly bare tail of the Irish breed.

There is a possibility that he goes back to the old Water Dog that was the ancestor of many of the curly-coated breeds of gundogs in Europe. The Pilgrim Fathers settled in Massachusetts Bay in 1620, along with their families, possessions, and of course their dogs, which could well have been water dogs. At the time there were three varieties of Water Spaniel in Ireland, the Tweed Water Spaniel, the Northern Water Spaniel and the Southern Water Spaniel. By the 19th century two of these had disappeared, but it is interesting to note that at the beginning of this century there were still old sportsmen in Ireland who spoke of

NATIONAL GROUPING		
	Name	Number
KC(GB)	—	–
AKC	Sporting Dogs	1
FCI	—	–

the Northern Irish Water Spaniels as about twenty inches high and like bad specimens of liver-coloured Retrievers.

It is obviously possible that these rather different dogs could have found their way to the United States during the intervening couple of centuries and have formed the foundation of the present American Water Spaniel. Prior to 1940, when the breed was recognised by the American Kennel Club, he had been essentially a working gundog, and his virtues in that capacity had been much admired. Fortunately he is one of those dogs that has stood the challenge of the show bench without losing any of his prowess. As a retriever he is superb, and it is said that he will watch and mark a number of fallen birds, and then on command go out and retrieve them all in turn, which makes him a very good one-man dog. He is said to have a soft mouth, high intelligence and to be powerful in the water. His coat, as with the Irish Water Spaniel and the Curly-coated Retriever, traps air and remains almost waterproof, as well as protecting him when working through the thick undergrowth. There is very little information about his performance as a show dog, and he is virtually unknown outside the United States. He is, however, reputed to be a very friendly companion and house dog, and in common with so many others in the Group, he is an excellent watchdog and guard.

OFFICIAL STANDARD

General appearance
Medium in size, of sturdy typical spaniel character, curly coat, an active muscular dog, with emphasis placed on proper size and conformation, correct head properties, texture of coat and color. Of amicable disposition; demeanor indicates intelligence, strength and endurance.

Head
Moderate in length, skull rather broad and full, stop moderately defined, but not too pronounced. Forehead covered with short smooth hair and without tuft or topknot. Muzzle of medium length, square and with no inclination to snipiness, jaws strong and of good length, and neither undershot nor overshot, teeth straight and well shaped. Nose sufficiently wide and with well-developed nostrils to insure good scenting power. *Faults:* very flat skull, narrow across the top, long, slender or snipy muzzle.

Eyes
Hazel, brown or of dark tone to harmonize with coat; set well apart. Expression alert, attractive, intelligent. *Fault:* yellow eyes to disqualify.

Ears
Lobular, long and wide, not set too high on head, but

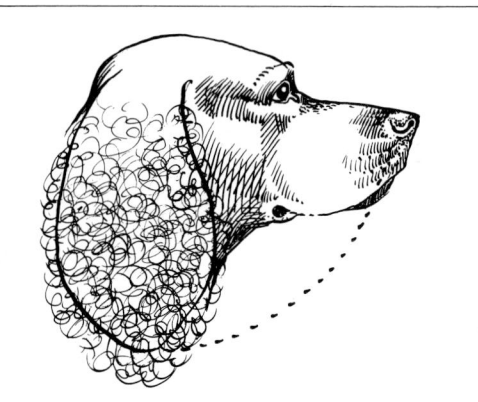

Ears: lobular, long and wide, leather extends to end of nose.

slightly above the eyeline. Leather extending to end of nose and well covered with close curls.

Neck
Round and of medium length, strong and muscular, free of throatiness, set to carry head with dignity, but arch not accentuated.

Body structure
Well developed, sturdily constructed but not too compactly coupled. General outline is a symmetrical relationship of parts. Shoulders sloping, clean and muscular. Strong loins, lightly arched, and well furnished, deep brisket but not excessively broad. Well-sprung ribs. Legs of medium length and well boned, but not so short as to handicap for field work.

Legs and feet: hocks well let down.

Legs and feet
Forelegs powerful and reasonably straight. Hind legs firm with suitably bent stifles and strong hocks well let down. Feet to harmonize with size of dog. Toes closely grouped and well padded. *Fault:* Cowhocks.

Tail
Moderate in length, curved in a slightly rocker shape, carried slightly below level of back; tapered and covered with hair to tip, action lively. *Faults:* rat or shaved tail.

Coat
The coat chould be closely curled or have marcel effect and should be of sufficient density to be of protection against weather, water or punishing cover, yet not coarse. Legs should have medium short, curly feather. *Faults:* coat too straight, soft, fine or tightly kinked.

Color
Solid liver or dark chocolate, a little white on toes or chest permissible.

Height
15 to 18 inches at the shoulder.

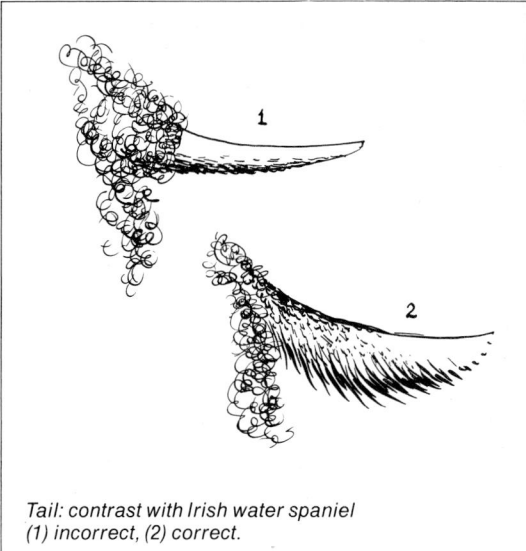

Tail: contrast with Irish water spaniel (1) incorrect, (2) correct.

Weight
Dogs: 28 to 45 pounds; bitches: 25 to 40 pounds.

DISQUALIFICATION
Yellow eyes.

AKC VARIATION TO STANDARD
This dog is not granted championship status by the KC(GB). The above standards are those of the AKC.

BRITTANY SPANIEL

NATIONAL GROUPING		
	Name	Number
KC(GB)	—	—
AKC	Sporting Dogs	1
FCI	Gundogs	7

Great Britain has so many gundogs that it claims as native to the country, though originally in fact none of them were, that gundogs from other countries have failed until recent years to gain a foothold there. The Brittany Spaniel is a typical example of this. He has been popular in Europe for centuries, has become well-established in the United States of America, but is never seen in Britain. He is one of the early French gundogs well established in France and especially in the North as his name would suggest. His ancestors almost certainly came from Spain along with those of many other gundogs, and though many of them finished up in Britain others remained in Europe and have developed along very different lines.

The height of the Brittany Spaniel at the shoulders suggests the Setter rather than the Spaniel, and in general conformation he looks more like the popular conception of one of that family rather than the shorter-legged types that have become popular in Britain. It could well be that it is something to do with the work that by tradition he has had to do, that he has evolved in this way, whilst the Cockers and the Sussex and other British breeds have grown ever shorter in the leg. Even the French, who designed him, do not claim that he is a very good looking dog, but say that he works so well that appearance is relatively unimportant. This has been appreciated in the United States more than anywhere else in the world, and since the breed was first imported into the country its popularity has grown to such an extent that it has become one of the important bird dog breeds there.

The first mention of the tailless Spaniel dates back to about a century ago in Pontou, and resulted from a cross between an imported lemon and white dog and a bitch belonging to an old hunter in the district. A race of dogs resulted that were noted for their work in the field, but by the turn of the century the breed had declined and was revived largely by the efforts of a M. Arthur Enaud. An American club was formed when the breed was first imported into the United States, but declined during the Second World War, to be reformed as the American Brittany Club in 1942. The standard for the breed was then agreed, and the club expressed as one of its aims the desire that the working qualities of the breed should not be subservient to its show career. In this they have succeeded as though the breed has remained an excellent worker, it has also achieved great success on the bench.

His height, and the favourite colour of deep orange and white make him very striking and easily recognised. He is compact but at the same time leggy and very agile, a strong runner, and at home in the water. He has proved himself as an all-round gundog, being easily trained as a retriever as well as a finder of game. His intelligence is unquestionable, and he reacts to human company in a delightfully friendly fashion.

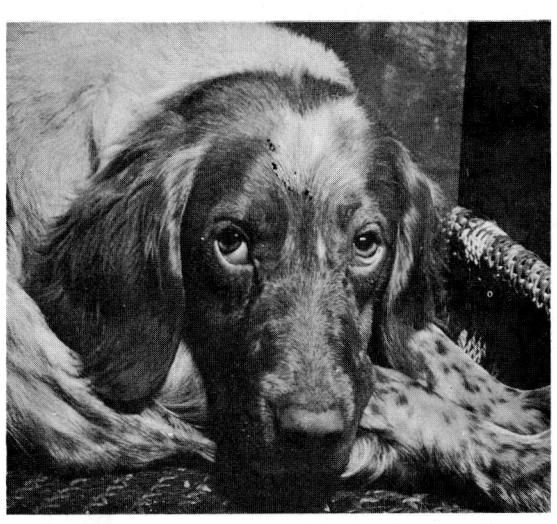

OFFICIAL STANDARD

General appearance

A compact, closely-knit dog of medium size, a leggy spaniel having the appearance, as well as the agility, of a great ground coverer. Strong, vigorous, energetic and quick of movement. Not too light in bone, yet never heavy-boned and cumbersome. Ruggedness, without clumsiness, is a characteristic of the breed. So leggy is he that his height at the withers is the same as the length of his body. He has no tail, or at most, not more than 4 inches.

General description: height equals length.

Weight

Should weigh between 30 and 40 pounds.

Height

$17\frac{1}{2}$ to $20\frac{1}{2}$ inches—measured from the ground at the highest point of the shoulders. Any Brittany Spaniel measuring under $17\frac{1}{2}$ inches or over $20\frac{1}{2}$ inches shall be disqualified from bench-show competition.

Coat

Hair dense, flat or wavy, never curly. Not as fine as in other spaniel breeds, and never silky. Furnishings not profuse. The ears should carry little fringe. Neither the front nor hind legs should carry heavy featherings. *Note:* long, curly, or silky hair is a fault. Any tendency toward excessive feathering should be severely penalized, as undesirable in a sporting dog which must face burrs and heavy cover.

Skin

Fine and fairly loose. (A loose skin rolls with briars and sticks, thus diminishing punctures or tearing. But a skin so loose as to form pouches is undesirable.)

Color

Dark orange and white, or liver and white. Some ticking is desirable, but not so much as to produce belton patterns. Roan patterns or factors of orange or liver shade are permissible. The orange or liver are found in standard parti-color, or piebald patterns. Washed out or faded colors are not desirable. Tri-colors (liver and white with some orange markings) are to be severely faulted. Any black in the coat, or a nose so dark in color as to appear black, shall disqualify.

Skull

Medium length (approximately $4\frac{3}{4}$ inches). Rounded, very slightly wedge-shaped, but evenly made. Width, not quite as wide as the length (about $4\frac{3}{8}$ inches) and never so broad as to appear coarse, or so narrow as to appear racy. Well-defined, but gently sloping stop effect. Median line rather indistinct. The occipital crest only apparent to the touch. Lateral walls well rounded. The Brittany should never be 'apple-headed' and he should never have an indented stop. (All measurements of skull are for a $19\frac{1}{2}$-inch dog.)

Muzzle

Medium length, about two thirds the length of the skull, measuring the muzzle from the tip to the stop, and the skull from the occipital crest to the stop between the eyes. Muzzle should taper gradually in both horizontal and vertical dimensions as it approaches the nostrils. Neither a Roman nose nor a concave curve (dish-face) is desirable. Never broad, heavy, or snipy.

Nose

Nostrils well open to permit deep breathing of air and adequate scenting while at top speed. Tight nostrils should be penalized. Never shiny. Color, fawn, tan, light shades of brown or deep pink. A black nose is a disqualification. A two-tone or butterfly nose should be severely penalized.

Muzzle: medium length, tapering.

Eyes

Well set in head. Well protected from briars by a heavy, expressive eyebrow. A prominent, full or pop eye should be heavily penalized. It is a serious fault in a hunting dog that must face briars. Skull well chiseled under the eyes, so that the lower lid is not pulled back to form a pocket or haw for catching seeds, dirt and weed dust. Judges should check by forcing head down to see if lid falls away from the eye. Preference should be for darker-colored eyes, though lighter shades of amber should not be penalized. Light and mean-looking eyes to be heavily penalized.

Ears: set high. Short and leafy.

Ears

Set high, above the level of the eyes. Short and leafy, rather than pendulous, reaching about half the length of the muzzle. Should lie flat and close to the head, with the tip rounded very slightly. Ears well covered with dense, but relatively short hair, and with little fringe.

Lips

Tight to the muzzle, with the upper lip overlapping the lower jaw only sufficiently to cover under lip. Lips dry so that feathers do not stick. Drooling to receive a heavy penalty. Flews to be penalized.

Teeth

Well-joined incisors. Posterior edge of upper incisors in contact with anterior edge of lower incisors, thus giving a true scissors bite. Overshot or undershot jaw to be penalized heavily.

Neck

Medium length. Not quite permitting the dog to place his nose on the ground without bending his legs. Free from throatiness, though not a serious fault unless accompanied by dewlaps. Strong, without giving the impression of being overmuscled. Well set into sloping shoulders. Never concave or ewe-necked.

Body length

Approximately the same as the height when measured at the withers. Body length is measured from the point of the forechest to the rear of the haunches. A long body should be heavily penalized.

Withers

Shoulder blades should not protrude much. Not too widely set apart with perhaps two thumbs' width or less between the blades. At the withers, the Brittany is slightly higher than at the rump.

Shoulders

Sloping and muscular. Blade and upper arm should form nearly a 90-degree angle when measured from the posterior point of the blade at the withers to the junction of the blade and upper arm, and thence to the point of the elbow nearest the ribs. Straight shoulders do not permit sufficient reach.

Back

Short and straight. Slight slope from highest point of withers to the root of the tail. Never hollow, saddle, sway, or roach-backed. Slight drop from hips to root of tail. Distance from last rib to upper thigh short, about three to four finger widths.

Chest

Deep, reaching the level of the elbow. Neither so wide nor so rounded as to disturb the placement of the shoulder bones and elbows, which causes a paddling movement, and often causes soreness from elbow striking ribs. Ribs well sprung, but adequate heart room provided by depth as well as width. Narrow or slab-sided chests are a fault.

Flanks

Rounded. Fairly full. Not extremely tucked up, nor yet flabby and falling. Loins short and strong. Narrow and weak loins are a fault. In motion the loin should not sway sideways, giving a zigzag motion to the back, wasting energy.

Hindquarters

Broad, strong and muscular, with powerful thighs and well-bent stifles, giving a hip set well into the loin and the marked angulation necessary for a powerful drive when in motion. Fat and falling hindquarters are a fault.

Tail

Naturally tailless, or not over four inches long. (A tail substantially more than 4 inches in length shall disqualify.) Natural or docked. Set on high, actually an extension of the spine at about the same level.

Front legs: pastern slightly bent.

Front legs

Viewed from the front, perpendicular, but not set too wide as in the case of a dog loaded in shoulder. Elbows and feet turning neither in nor out. Viewed from the side, practically perpendicular to the pastern. Pastern slightly bent to give cushion to stride. Not so straight as in terriers. Falling pasterns, however, are a serious fault. Leg bones clean, graceful, but not too fine. An extremely heavy bone is as much a fault as spindly legs. One must look for substance and suppleness. Height to the elbows should approximately equal distance from elbow to withers.

Thighs: well feathered. Hocks: perpendicular.

Hind legs
Stifles well bent. The stifle generally is the term used for knee joint. If the angle made by the upper and lower leg bones is too straight, the dog quite generally lacks drive, since his hind legs cannot drive as far forward at each stride as is desirable. However, the stifle should not be bent as to throw the hock joint far out behind the dog. Since factors not easily seen by the eye may give the dog his proper drive, a Brittany should not be condemned for straight stifle until the judge has checked the dog in motion from the side. When at a trot, the Brittany's hind foot should step into or beyond the print left by the front foot. The stifle joint should not turn out making a cowhock. The cowhock moves the foot out to the side, thus driving out of line, and losing reach at each stride. Thighs well feathered, but not profusely, halfway to the hock. Hocks, that is, the back pasterns, should be moderately short, pointing neither in nor out; perpendicular when viewed from the side. They should be firm when shaken by the judge.

Feet
Should be strong, proportionately smaller than other spaniels, with close-fitting, well-arched toes and thick pads. The Brittany is not 'up on his toes.' Toes not heavily feathered. Flat feet, splayed feet, paper feet, etc., are to be heavily penalized. An ideal foot is halfway between the hare- and cat-foot.

A guide to the judge: the points below indicate only relative values. To be also taken into consideration are type, gait, soundness, spirit, optimum height, body length and general proportions.

SCALE OF POINTS
Head (25). Body (35). Running gear (40). *Total (100).*

DISQUALIFICATIONS
Any Brittany Spaniel measuring under $17\frac{1}{2}$ inches or over $20\frac{1}{2}$ inches. Any black in the coat or a nose so dark in color as to appear black. A tail substantially more than 4 inches in length.

Approved 13 September 1966

AKC VARIATION TO STANDARD
This dog is not granted championship status by the KC(GB). The above standards are those of the AKC.

CLUMBER SPANIEL

NATIONAL GROUPING		
	Name	Number
KC(GB)	Gundog	2
AKC	Sporting Dogs	1
FCI	Gundogs	8

The Spaniel Group of breeds is one of the most numerous and varied in the world of dogs. The division between the Toy Spaniels and the Sporting Spaniels is itself confusing, and the large number of different breeds listed among the sporting members of the Group, the Cocker, Springer and Field for instance, named after the work they are bred to do creates even more problems. There is one breed, however, the Clumber Spaniel that is distinctive not only in appearance, but in name, as it takes its title from a place. Research has so far failed to disclose the origin of the breed beyond the time when the Duc de Noailles presented some of his dogs to the second Duke of Newcastle from whose estate, Clumber Park, the breed took its name. It is probable that the early ancestor of the breed was the old Alpine Spaniel which was crossed with an early form of Basset and even with the Bloodhound, giving it its short legs and heavy head. From Clumber Park the breed spread to surrounding estates and families, and soon became known as a shooting dog.

One of the earliest records of the breed is in a portrait of the second Duke of Newcastle by Francis Wheatley, R.A. at Clumber Park, in which he is depicted seated on a shooting pony with Colonel Litchfield, Mansell, who was his head keeper, and three Spaniels which were believed to have been three of the original draft. The portrait was painted in 1788, almost a hundred years before the breed was first shown in Britain, and before they arrived in the United States of America. It is interesting that whilst the other breeds of Spaniels have changed considerably over the years, the heavyweight of the family has changed hardly at all. The abundance of game in the 18th and 19th centuries meant that a fast-moving Spaniel was not needed, and the better nose, greater efficiency and persistence of the Clumber was more appreciated.

He does in fact have a wonderful nose, considered by many sportsmen the best in the family. He has too, a natural inclination to hunt, tremendous perseverance and stamina, and in spite of his massive build, is considerably agile. He is easily trained, being quieter than some of the other Spaniels, and is very biddable. He also makes a good retriever, and is thus one of the better all-round gundogs. Whilst retaining his popularity among sportsmen, he has never achieved a great deal of fame on the bench since his early days. Although his massive frame and large intelligent looking head give him the look of the aristocratic dog, he has rarely in recent years had major awards at shows. Very few are now registered, under a hundred each year in Britain, and he is hardly seen outside that country and the United States of America. He is not an easy dog to show, as he is somewhat independent in the ring, having the sort of intelligence that causes him to see little point in standing around indoors when he could be hunting through the local countryside. His colour and size, however, make him very spectacular and he is always much admired by spectators, and there is an indication that he is in for something of a revival within the next few years.

He is friendly, affectionate in fact, and makes a very good country companion though he is a little cumbersome indoors.

OFFICIAL STANDARD

General appearance
That of a dog with a thoughtful expression, very massive but active, which moves with a rolling gait characteristic of the breed.

Head and skull
Head large, square and massive, of medium length, broad on top, with a decided occiput; heavy brows with a deep stop; heavy muzzle, with well-developed flew, and level jaw and mouth. Nose square and flesh-coloured.

Eyes
Dark amber, slightly sunk with some haw showing.

Ears
Large, vine-leaf shaped, and well covered with straight hair, and hanging slightly forward, the feather not to extend below the leather.

Forequarters: shoulders strong sloping, muscular.

Head and skull: large, square, massive.

Mouth
Should be level and neither over nor undershot.

Neck
Fairly long, thick and powerful, and well feathered underneath.

Forequarters
Shoulders strong, sloping and muscular; chest deep. Legs short, straight, thick and strong.

Body
Long and heavy, and near the ground, with well-sprung ribs. Back straight, broad and long.

Hindquarters
Very powerful and well developed. Loin powerful, well let down in flank. Hocks low, stifles well bent and set straight.

Feet
Large and round, well covered with hair.

Tail
Set low, well feathered, and carried about level with the back.

Coat
Abundant, close, silky and straight; legs well feathered.

Colour
Plain white, with lemon markings, orange permissible; slight head markings and freckled muzzle, with white body preferred.

Weight and size
Dogs about 55 to 70 pounds; bitches about 45 to 60 pounds.

Note
Male animals should have two apparently normal testicles fully descended into the scrotum.

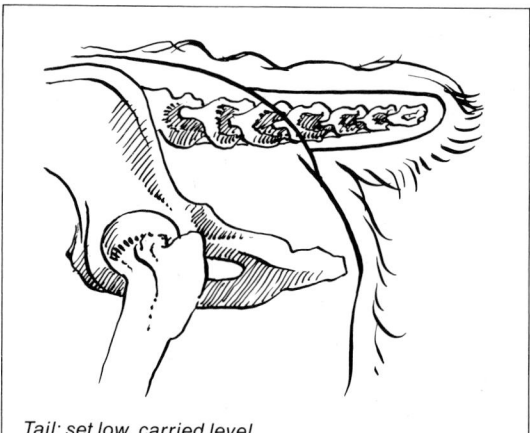
Tail: set low, carried level.

AKC VARIATION TO STANDARD
Weight: dogs 55 to 65 pounds; bitches 35 to 50 pounds.

AMERICAN COCKER SPANIEL

NATIONAL GROUPING		
	Name	Number
KC(GB)	Gundog	2
AKC	Sporting Dogs	1
FCI	Gundogs	8

A further division in the Spaniel family resulted from the importation of the smaller Spaniels into the United States of America, where they developed along quite different lines from those in Britain. This has led to a certain amount of confusion, as whilst the Cocker Spaniel is known in the United States as the English Cocker Spaniel, the dog known there as the Cocker Spaniel is known in other countries as The American Cocker Spaniel. The English Cocker Spaniel Club of America which was formed in 1935 aimed to discourage interbreeding between the two types and in 1946 the Cocker as distinct from the American Cocker was finally recognised. Meanwhile in Britain the Cocker Spaniel was developing, and the American Cocker was not seen on the British show bench until well into the 1960s.

The type developed in the United States is smaller than the British variety, fourteen to fifteen inches as against sixteen to seventeen, and proportionately less heavy. The demands of field work in the United States are different from those in Britain. Birds are on the whole smaller, and quail, which are one of the favourite small game birds in the one country are virtually unknown in the other. In Britain the Cocker is expected to carry pheasant and hare, a task that would prove beyond many of the Cockers on the other side of the Atlantic. Unregistered in Britain until 1968, he has made rapid strides since then, and is fast becoming one of the more popular of the Spaniel family. Apart from the English Cocker and the English Springer he has already overhauled all the other Spaniels and is competing hard even with those, one hundred and sixty-four entries having been made at the Birmingham Show in 1976.

He works in the field by quartering the ground in front of the guns, hunting and putting up game, which he does quickly and efficiently. When the game is flushed he stands still or drops whilst the animal is shot, and then goes in to retrieve on command. This takes a little training, as whilst a Cocker hunts naturally, and will do it all the time, the freezing on a shot is something that is not natural to him and the habit of running in and thus interfering with possible subsequent shots, has to be trained out. Fortunately, he is an easily trained little dog, very biddable and anxious to please. He is a successful showdog, as like his English counterpart, he has natural good manners and an inbuilt willingness to obey commands.

He has the same coat problem as the English dog, and indeed it was only after some heart-searching and an injunction to judges that the British objection to too much coat was finally overcome. Now he is shown with a somewhat reduced volume of coat though still with considerably more than the English Cocker. He poses well in the ring, and covers a great deal of ground for so small a dog stretching out his long neck to produce a very spectacular outline. When moving he goes with such drive that on a dry day he will leave a cloud of dust behind him. Within the last few years there have been one or two dogs that have won at the major shows in Britain, and there is no doubt that this, allied to the fact that he has qualified at field trials, has ensured his future in Britain as a popular gundog.

He is one of the most friendly and affectionate little dogs. One of the features of his character is that he behaves well with children, and is now being shown regularly by youngsters in junior handling classes.

OFFICIAL STANDARD

General appearance

A serviceable-looking dog with a refinedly chiselled head; standing on straight legs and well up at the shoulders; of compact body and wide, muscular quarters. The American Cocker Spaniel's sturdy body, powerful quarters and strong, well-boned legs show him to be a dog capable of considerable speed combined with great endurance. Above all he must be free and merry, sound, well balanced throughout, and in action show a keen inclination to work, equable in temperament with no suggestion of timidity.

Head and skull: well-developed and rounded.

Head and skull

Well developed and rounded with no tendency towards flatness, or pronounced roundness, of the crown (dome). The forehead smooth, i.e. free from wrinkles, the eyebrows and stop clearly defined, the median line distinctly marked and gradually disappearing until lost rather more than halfway up to the crown. The bony structure surrounding the socket of the eye should be well chiselled; there should be no suggestion of fullness under the eyes nor prominence in the cheeks which, like the sides of the muzzle, should present a smooth, clean-cut appearance. To attain a well-proportioned head, which above all should be in balance with the rest of the dog, the distance from the tip of the nose to the stop at a line drawn across the top of the muzzle between the front corners of the eyes, should approximate one-half the distance from the stop at this point up over the crown to the base of the skull. The muzzle should be broad and deep, with square even jaws. The upper lip should be of sufficient depth to cover the lower jaw, presenting a square appearance. The nose of sufficient size to balance the muzzle and foreface, with well-developed nostrils and black in colour in the blacks and black-and-tans; in the reds, buffs, livers, and parti-colours and in the roans it may be black or brown, the darker colouring being preferable.

Mouth

The teeth should be sound and regular and set at right angles to their respective jaws. The relation of the upper teeth to the lower should be that of scissors, with the inner surface of the upper in contact with the outer surface of the lower when the jaws are closed.

Eyes

The eyeballs should be round and full and set in the surrounding tissue to look directly forward and give the eye a slightly almond-shape appearance. The eye should be neither weak nor goggled. The expression should be intelligent, alert, soft and appealing. The colour of the iris should be dark brown to black in the blacks, black and tans, buffs and creams, and in the darker shades of the parti-colours and roans. In the reds, dark hazel; in the livers, parti-colours, and roans of the lighter shades, not lighter than hazel, the darker the better.

Ears

Lobular, set on a line no higher than the lower part of the eye, the feathers fine and extending to the nostrils; well clothed with long, silky, straight or wavy hair.

Neck

The neck sufficiently long to allow the nose to reach the ground easily, muscular and free from pendulous 'throatiness'. It should rise strongly from the shoulders and arch slightly as it tapers to join the head.

Forequarters

The shoulders deep, clean-cut and sloping without protrusion and so set that the upper point of the withers are at an angle which permits a wide spring of rib. Forelegs straight, strongly boned and muscular and set close to the body well under the scapulae. The elbows well let down and turning neither in nor out. The pasterns short and strong.

Body

Its height at the withers should approximate the length

Body height: at withers equals length.

from the withers to the set-on of tail. The chest deep, its lowest point no higher than the elbows, its front sufficiently wide for adequate heart and lung space, yet not so wide as to interfere with straight forward movement of the forelegs. Ribs deep and well-sprung throughout. Body short in the couplings and flank, with its depth at the flank somewhat less than the last rib. Back strong and sloping evenly and slightly downward from the withers to the set-on of tail. Hips wide with quarters well-rounded and muscular. The body should appear short, compact and firmly knit together, giving the impression of strength.

Hindquarters
The hind legs should be strongly boned and muscled with good angulation at the stifle and powerful, clearly defined thighs. The stifle joint should be strong and there should be no slippage in motion or when standing. The hocks should be strong, well let down and when viewed from behind, the hind legs should be parallel when in motion and at rest.

Feet
Feet compact, not spreading, round and firm, with deep, strong, tough pads and hair between the toes; they should turn neither in nor out.

Gait
The American Cocker Spaniel possesses a typical sporting dog gait. Prerequisite to good movement is balance between the fore and hind quarters. He drives with his strong powerful rear quarters and is properly constructed to the shoulder and forelegs so that he can reach forward without constriction in a full stride to counter balance the driving force of the rear. Above all, his gait is co-ordinated, smooth and effortless. The dog must cover ground with his action and excessive animation should never be mistaken for proper gait.

Tail
The docked tail should be set on and carried on a line with the topline of the back, or slightly higher; never straight up like a terrier and never so low as to indicate timidity. When the dog is in motion the action should be merry.

Coat
On the head, short and fine; on the body, medium length, with enough undercoating to give protection. The ears, chest, abdomen and legs should be well feathered, but not so excessively as to hide the American Cocker Spaniel's true lines and movement or affect his appearance and function as a sporting dog. The texture is most important. The coat should be silky, flat or slightly wavy, and of a texture which permits easy care. Excessive or curly or cottony texture coat should be penalised.

Colour
Blacks should be jet black; shadings of brown or liver in the sheen of the coat is not desirable. Black and tan (classified under solid colours) should have definite tan markings on a jet black body. The tan markings should

be distinct and plainly visible and the colour of the tan may be from the lightest cream to the darkest red colour. The amount of tan markings should be restricted to ten per cent or less of the colour of the specimen; tan markings in excess of ten per cent should be penalised. Tan markings which are not readily visible in the ring or the absence of tan markings in any of the specified locations should be penalised. The tan markings should be located as follows:
1. A clear spot over each eye. 2. On the sides of the muzzle and on the cheeks. 3. On the undersides of the ears. 4. On all feet and legs. 5. Under the tail. 6. On the chest, optional, presence or absence should not be penalised. Tan on the muzzle which extends upwards over and joins should be penalised.

Any solid colour other than black should be of uniform shade. Lighter colouring of the feathering is permissible. In all the above solid colours a small amount of white on chest and throat while not desirable, is allowed, but white in any other location should be penalised.

Parti-colours. Two or more definite colours appearing in clearly defined markings are essential. Primary colour which is ninety per cent or more should be penalised; secondary colour or colours which are limited solely to one location should also be penalised. Roans are classified as parti-colours and may be of any of the usual roaning patterns. Tri-colours are any of the above colours combined with tan markings. It is preferable that the tan markings be located in the same pattern as for Black and Tans.

Size
The ideal height at the withers for an adult dog is 15 inches and for an adult bitch 14 inches. Height may vary one-half inch above or below this ideal. A dog whose height exceeds $15\frac{1}{2}$ inches or a bitch whose height exceeds $14\frac{1}{2}$ inches should be penalised. An adult dog whose height is less than $14\frac{1}{2}$ inches or an adult bitch whose height is less than $13\frac{1}{2}$ inches should be penalised. Note: height is determined by a line perpendicular to the ground from the top of the shoulder blades, the dog standing naturally with its forelegs and the lower hind legs parallel to the line of the measurement.

Note
Male animals should have two apparently normal testicles fully descended into the scrotum.

AKC VARIATION TO STANDARD
Colour and markings: in solid colours a small amount of white on chest and throat is to be penalised, and white in any other location shall disqualify. *Black and tan:* tan markings in excess of 10% shall disqualify. *Parti-colours:* primary colour which is more than 90% shall disqualify. *Height:* a dog whose height exceeds $15\frac{1}{2}$ inches or a bitch whose height exceeds $14\frac{1}{2}$ inches shall be disqualified. An adult dog whose height is less than $14\frac{1}{2}$ inches or an adult bitch whose height is less than $13\frac{1}{2}$ inches shall be penalised.

COCKER SPANIEL

The family of Spaniels is one of the largest of the canine race, and certainly one of the oldest. They date back as a Group to the 14th century when they are described as consisting of two sorts, the Land Spaniel and the Water Spaniel. Water Spaniels existed as a separate breed in Britain until well into the 20th century and were shown as small, curly-coated parti-coloured dogs with classes of their own. The Land Spaniels became further divided and whilst some of them became Toys, the others became workers in the field, the smallest of these being called 'Cockers'. There is little dispute about how he got his name. Edwards, writing in 1801 divides the smaller Land Spaniels into two groups, the 'starters' and the 'cockers', the former being used to spring the game when falconry was a popular sport, and the latter to hunt the Woodcock for

NATIONAL GROUPING		
	Name	Number
KC(GB)	Gundog	2
AKC	Sporting Dogs	1
FCI	Gundogs	8

which they were specially trained.

The division into clearly defined breeds took some time, but gradually a distinctive race of dogs emerged, largely in the South West of Britain and in Wales. At first, and indeed well into this century, they had to give pride of place in popular esteem to other Spaniels such as the Sussex and the Field, but they rapidly overtook the other breeds, and by the mid-thirties had become Britain's most popular dog, a position that was held for many years. At first most Cockers were self-coloured, and mainly black, and it was only with the development of the other colours and the roans and black and whites that popularity finally came.

He is highly intelligent, sensitive and affectionate, becoming firmly attached to one family and making a most attractive little house dog. He is amusing, as so many of the Spaniels are, and it is in this respect that his relationship with the Toy Spaniels becomes obvious. This relationship is closer than might at first be suspected, and a team of Toys such as King Charles Spaniels will still hunt, and the larger ones have been known to be trained to retrieve game. The Cocker is a sturdy little dog, hardy, not susceptible to illness, and will live quite happily in kennels, though his favourite place is indoors by a warm fire.

As a show dog he is supreme, and has a long list of major wins to his credit. H. S. Lloyd did much to popularise the breed with his win at Crufts, and his Ware strain remains world famous. He is not the easiest of dogs to prepare for the ring, as whilst his coat appears trouble free, there is always a tendency for him to grow an amount of strong curly coat which is difficult to remove, indicative of his ancestry among the strong-coated Water Spaniels of many years ago. A Cocker Spaniel left in the rough with an uncared-for coat looks very untidy.

He loves country walks and plenty of exercise, and is never happier than when hunting along a hedgerow scenting out small game or chasing a rabbit. He is adaptable, perfectly at home in a farmyard or town flat, in the back of a car or sitting on his owner's knee; and his personal qualities are undoubtedly the reason for his remarkable popularity.

OFFICIAL STANDARD

General appearance
That of a merry sturdy sporting dog. The Cocker Spaniel should be well balanced and compact and should measure about the same from the withers to the ground as from the withers to the root of the tail.

Head and skull
There should be a good square muzzle with a distinct stop which should be mid way between the tip of the nose and the occiput. The skull should be well developed, cleanly chiselled, neither too fine nor too coarse. The cheek bones should not be prominent. The nose should be sufficiently wide to allow for the acute scenting power of this breed.

Ears: lobular, set on low.

Ears
Lobular, set on low, on a level with the eyes, with fine leathers which extend to but not beyond the tip of the nose; well clothed with long silky hair which should be straight.

Mouth
Jaws should be strong and teeth should have a scissor bite.

Neck
Neck should be moderate in length, clean in throat, muscular and neatly set into fine sloping shoulders.

Forequarters
The shoulders should be sloping and fine, the chest well developed and the brisket deep, neither too wide nor too narrow in front. The legs must be well boned, feathered and straight and should be sufficiently short for concentrated power but not too short to interfere with the tremendous exertions expected from this grand little sporting dog.

Good square muzzle, skull well developed, neither fine nor coarse.

Eyes
The eyes should be full but not prominent, brown or dark brown in colour but never light, with a general expression of intelligence and gentleness though decidedly wide awake, bright and merry. The rims should be tight.

Faults: straight shoulder, weak pasterns, light bone, flat ribs.

Body
Body should be immensely strong and compact for the size and weight of the dog. The ribs should be well sprung behind the shoulder blades, the loin short, wide and strong, with a firm topline gently sloping downwards to the tail.

Hindquarters
Hindquarters should be wide, well rounded and very muscular. The legs must be well boned feathered above the hock with a good bend of stifle and short below the hock allowing for plenty of drive.

Feet
Feet should be firm, thickly padded and catlike.

Tail
Tail should be set on slightly lower than the line of the back; it must be merry, carried in line with the back and never cocked up. The tail should not be docked too long nor too short to interfere with its merry action.

Tail: set on slightly lower than back, line carried level.

Coat
Flat and silky in texture, never wiry or wavy, with sufficient feather; not too profuse and never curly.

Colour
Various. In self colours no white is allowed except on the chest.

Gait
There should be true through action both fore and aft, with great drive covering the ground well.

Weight and size
The weight should be about 28 to 32 pounds. The height at the withers should be approximately 15 to $15\frac{1}{2}$ inches for bitches and approximately $15\frac{1}{2}$ to 16 inches for dogs.

Faults
Light bone; straight shoulder; flat ribs; unsound movement; weak hocks; weak pasterns; open or large

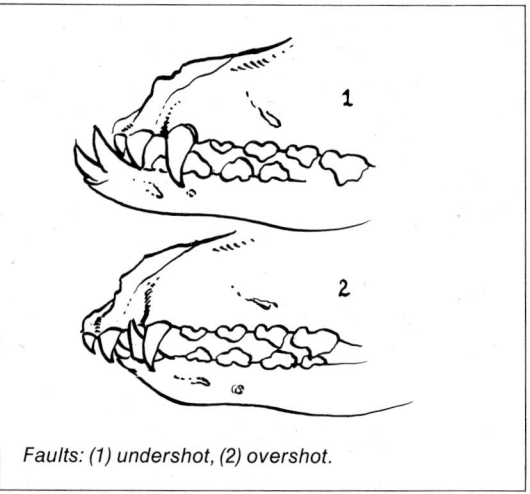

Faults: (1) undershot, (2) overshot.

feet; frown; small beady eyes; undershot or overshot mouth; uncertain or aggressive temperament.

Note
Male animals should have two apparently normal testicles fully descended into the scrotum.

AKC VARIATION TO STANDARD
Coat: flat or slightly wavy. *Weight and size:* dogs 28 to 34 pounds; 16 to 17 inches; bitches 26 to 32 pounds; 15 to 16 inches. *Faults:* muzzle too short or snipy.

ENGLISH SPRINGER SPANIEL

When the Spaniel family divided into the Water Spaniels and the Land Spaniels, the latter further divided into Toys and Working, and the Working Spaniels were allocated different tasks in the field. The smaller ones became the Cockers and the larger and taller ones became the Springers. Their task was to range further than some of the others in the family and to flush or 'spring' the game. He was originally known as the Norfolk Spaniel, though that county can lay no claim to his origins other than the fact that the Duke of Norfolk kept a kennels of the breed. He came from some of the early imported Spaniel stock that produced the other members of the family and helped to produce the Setters, but was not recognised as a separate breed until 1902. The Sporting Spaniel Society was responsible for christening him, as they decided to drop the name Norfolk Spaniel and revert to the much older

NATIONAL GROUPING		
	Name	Number
KC(GB)	Gundog	2
AKC	Sporting Dogs	1
FCI	Gundogs	8

name of Springer, looking after this long legged member of the family partly as a protest at what was going on to make the Field Spaniel so ridiculous a dog. They were determined that the Springer should remain as a sporting Spaniel.

Unfortunately the Springer Spaniel is one of the gundogs that has become sharply divided between the working and the show type, so that a modern show Springer will often stand higher than the twenty inches laid down in the standard, and is a tall rather

75

narrow dog, on the other hand the type most favoured for field work is considerably smaller and is a stockier type with a far less exaggerated head. There are show dogs that perform well in trials, but they are the exception, and there are few dogs of the field type that would win in the show rings of today. In 1924 the English Springer Spaniel Field Trial Association was formed in the United States of America and has as its aim the production of dogs for both the field and the bench, and it could well be that as a result of their efforts greater unity can be achieved in the breed.

He is probably the best dog for the sportsman who wants one dog only, to live in the house, and to do all the work in the field that a single gun requires. He will not point, nor would one expect that he should, but he will do just about everything else. He hunts further and faster than any of the other Spaniels, is an excellent retriever, and a first-class water dog, apparently impervious to wet and cold conditions and a tireless worker in the field with great tenacity and endurance.

As a show dog he is tremendously successful, being adaptable to any sort of condition, shows equally well indoors or outside, is friendly and free from vice in the ring and on the bench, and appears to enjoy being the centre of attention. He is a happy dog, full of character, and always appears interested in what is going on around him. He is easily prepared for show, the minimum amount of straightening up of coat being all

that is required, and he enjoys exercise to such an extent that keeping him in fit muscular show condition presents no problems. His temperament is excellent as he is very friendly, even affectionate with those that he knows, and though normally quiet, makes a very good guard.

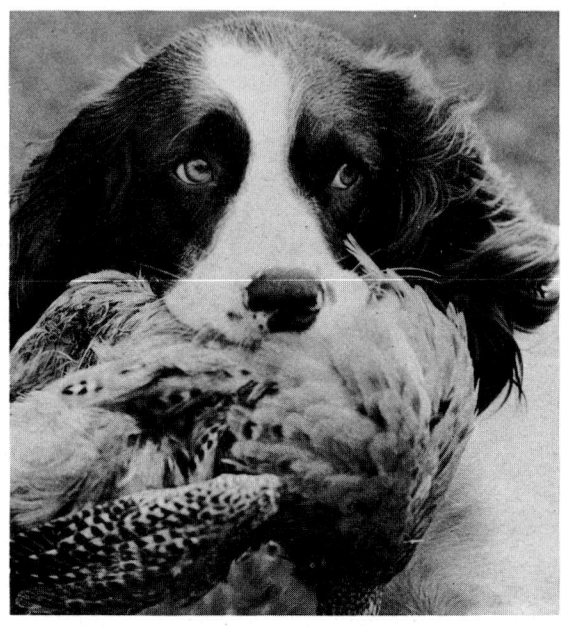

OFFICIAL STANDARD

Characteristics
The English Springer is the oldest of our Sporting Gundogs and the taproot from which all of our sporting land spaniels (Clumbers excepted) have been evolved. It was originally used for the purpose of finding and

Head: skull medium length, and fairly broad and rounded.

springing game for the net, falcon, or greyhound, but at the present time it is used entirely to find, flush, and retrieve game for the gun. The breed is of ancient and pure origin, and should be kept as such. The Springer's gait is strictly his own. His forelegs should swing straight forward from the shoulder, throwing the feet well forward in an easy and free manner, not a paddle nor chopped terrier-like stride. His hocks should drive well under his body, following in a line with his forelegs. At slow movements many Springers have a pacing stride typical of the breed.

General appearance
The general appearance of the modern Springer is that of a symmetrical, compact, strong, upstanding, merry, and active dog, built for endurance and activity. He is the highest on the leg and raciest in build of all British land Spaniels.

Head and skull
The skull should be of medium length and fairly broad and slightly rounded, rising from the foreface, making a brow or stop, divided by a fluting between the eyes gradually dying away along the forehead towards the occiput bone, which should not be peaked. The cheeks should be flat, that is not rounded or full. The foreface should be of proportionate length to the skull, fairly broad and deep without being coarse, well chiselled below the eyes, fairly deep and square in flew, but not exaggerated to such an extent as would interfere with comfort when

Neck: strong, long, free from throatiness.

retrieving. Nostrils well developed, underjaw strong and level mouth, that is neither over nor under shot.

Eyes

The eyes should be neither too full nor too small but of medium size, not prominent nor sunken but well set in (not showing haw) of an alert, kind expression. A mouse-like eye without expression is objectionable, as also is a light eye. The colour should be dark hazel.

Ears

The ears should be lobular in shape, set close to the head, of good length and width, but not exaggerated. The correct set should be in a line with the eye.

Neck

The neck should be strong and muscular, of nice length and free from throatiness, well set in the shoulders, nicely arched and tapering towards the head—this giving great activity and speed. A ewe neck is objectionable.

Forelegs: swing straight forward.

Forequarters

The forelegs should be straight and nicely feathered, elbows set well to body and with proportionate substance to carry the body, strong flexible pasterns.

Body

The body should be strong and of proportionate length, neither too long nor too short, the chest deep and well developed with plenty of heart and lung room, well sprung ribs, loins muscular and strong with slight arch and well coupled, thighs broad and muscular and well developed.

Hindquarters

The hindlegs should be well let down from hip to hocks. Stifles and hocks moderately bent, inclining neither inwards nor outwards. Coarseness of hocks objectionable.

Feet

Feet tight, compact, and well rounded with strong full pads.

Stern: low, well feathered.

Tail

The stern should be low and never carried above the level of the back, well feathered and with a lively action.

Coat

The coat should be close, straight, and weather resisting without being coarse.

Colour

Any recognised Land Spaniel colour is acceptable, but liver and white, black and whate, or either of these colours with tan markings preferred.

Weight and size

The approximate height should be 20 inches. The approximate weight should be 50 pounds.

Note

Male animals should have two apparently normal testicles fully descended into the scrotum.

FIELD SPANIEL

NATIONAL GROUPING		
	Name	Number
KC(GB)	Gundog	2
AKC	Sporting Dogs	1
FCI	Gundogs	8

This is one of those breeds that has suffered the vicissitudes of fortune as the result of man's attempts to conform to fashion rather than considering the work that a gundog was expected to perform. At the turn of the century extremes of selective breeding had produced a race of dogs that looked rather like very heavily built short-legged long-coated Daschshunds. The standard of that time described the breed as long and very low with immensely boned short legs, which was described by Col. Claude Cane in Robert Leighton's book of 1907 as an "absurd craze". The Field Spaniel is one of the older forms of the small Land Spaniel, developed by crossing the Cocker and Springer types, and producing a dog which was in its early days sharply divided into the blacks and the coloureds. At first the blacks were the more important, so much so that they were called Black Spaniels, and it was some time later that the coloured dogs achieved some status.

The craze for a low outline and shorter and shorter legs produced a dog that was useless in the field, and after considerable vogue during the early part of the century, the breed went into such a decline that by the middle sixties the number of registrations at the Kennel Club had shrunk to single figures. In 1879 a dog named Kaffir, a Black Spaniel, looked almost exactly like a modern Field Spaniel, judging from the engraving in Vero Shaw's book of 1881, and it was only in between times that the gross exaggeration took place which almost killed the breed. Fortunately there have always been a few enthusiasts who have been interested in preserving old breeds, and old Spaniel breeds in particular, and it is to them that we owe the fact that the Field Spaniel has survived at all. Now, the breed is again on the increase, and by the judicious use of Cocker crosses either openly or otherwise, a type has evolved which looks like a working Spaniel, yet in its better form is unlike any of the others.

He is stronger, larger and nowadays longer in the leg and more active than the Cocker, and he has a particular manner of working through roots and heavy going, where his ability to spring from the ground and leap from tussock to tussock is of particular value. He has a good nose, can be trained to retrieve, and is a willing and tireless worker. Like all the other members of the family he is a friendly dog, attaches himself to families and households, and makes a good pet and housedog.

OFFICIAL STANDARD

General appearance
That of a well-balanced, noble, upstanding sporting dog; built for activity and endurance; a combination of beauty and utility; of unusual docility.

Head and skull
The head should be characteristic as is that of the Bulldog or the Bloodhound; its very stamp and countenance should at once convey the impression of high breeding, character and nobility; skull well developed, with a distinct occipital protuberance, which gives the character alluded to; not too wide across the muzzle, long and lean, neither snipy nor squarely cut, and in profile curving gradually from nose to throat; lean beneath the eyes, a thickness here gives coarseness to the whole head. The great length of muzzle gives surface for the free development of the olfactory nerve, and thus secures the highest possible scenting powers. Nose, well developed, good with open nostrils.

Eyes
Not too full, but not small, receding or overhung, colour dark hazel or brown, or nearly black, according to the colour of the dog. Grave in expression and showing no haw.

Head and skull: long and lean, neither snipy nor square.

Ears

Moderately long and wide, sufficiently clad with nice Setter-like feather and set low. They should fall in graceful folds, the lower parts curling inwards and backwards.

Ears: moderately long and wide, set low, lower part curling inwards and backwards.

Mouth

Level and strong—neither overshot nor undershot.

Neck

Long, strong and muscular, so as to enable the dog to retrieve his game without undue fatigue.

Forequarters

The shoulders should be long and sloping and well set back, thus giving great activity and speed. The forelegs should be of fairly good length, with straight, clean, flat bone and nicely feathered. Immense bone is not desirable.

Body

Should be of moderate length, well ribbed up to a good strong loin, straight or slightly arched, never slack. The chest, deep and well developed, but not too round and wide. Back and loins very strong and muscular.

Hindquarters

Strong and muscular. The stifles should be moderately bent and not twisted either in or out.

Feet

Not too small; round with short, soft hair between the toes; good, strong pads.

Tail

Well set on and carried low, if possible below the level of the back, in a straight line or with a slight downward inclination, never elevated above the back, and in action always kept low, nicely fringed with wavy feather of silky texture.

Coat: abundant setter-like feather under chest and behind legs.

Coat

Flat or slightly waved, and never curled. Sufficiently dense to resist the weather and not too short. Silky in texture, glossy and refined without duffelness, curliness or wiriness. On the chest, under the belly and behind the legs, there should be abundant feather, but never too much, especially below the hocks, and that of the right sort—viz., Setter-like.

Colour

The Field Spaniel should be a self-coloured dog, viz.: black, liver, golden liver, mahogany red, roan; or any one of these colours with tan over the eyes, on the cheeks, feet and pasterns. Other colours, such as black and white, red or orange and white, etc., while not debarring a dog, is a fault.

Weight and size

From about 35 to 50 pound. Height: about 18 inches to shoulder.

Note

Male animals should have two apparently normal testicles fully descended into the scrotum.

IRISH WATER SPANIEL

NATIONAL GROUPING		
	Name	Number
KC(GB)	Gundog	2
AKC	Sporting Dogs	1
FCI	Gundogs	8

This member of the Spaniel family is very different from all the others, being considerably larger and having a closely curled coat of one colour. There are said to have been two distinct varieties of this breed in Ireland in the early days, the Northern Water Spaniel and the Southern Water Spaniel with somewhere along the line a possible third known as the Tweed Water Spaniel which disappeared somewhere around the middle of the 19th century. The Northern dog was sometimes described as the "Old Brown Irish Retriever" which confuses the issue even further, and fortunately there is now only one Irish Water Spaniel. A certain Mr. Justin McCarthy claimed to have invented the breed in about 1850, but what is more likely is that he acquired specimens of a variety that fitted the description of what he required and interbred them until he had perfected the strain. There is little doubt that the breed owes its origins to the old European Water Dog, which was a Spaniel type, and which was also the ancestor of the Poodle.

It was not until 1862 that the breed attracted much attention in the show ring, when classes were put on at the Birmingham Show, and from that time onwards he became fairly popular, some very good specimens being exhibited between 1880 and 1890. From then to the turn of the century the breed declined and by the middle of this century the registration figures had dropped to an alarming extent and there was even a danger that the breed might not survive. Survive it did,

however, and there is now once more an upsurge in interest and the numbers are steadily increasing. There is no member of the Spaniel family with a more distinctive appearance than the Irish Water Spaniel. He has been described as the clown of the Spaniels, which is no reflection on his intelligence or his behaviour, as in these respects he is anything but. It is merely that his appearance is very unusual with his rather strange shape, his closely curled coat and his somewhat ridiculous tail which starts off looking like a tail and fades away to almost nothing. The Irish Water Spaniel is a first-class water dog as his name would suggest, and is particularly suited to working in his native country of marshes and bogland. He can, and does, work as any other of the Spaniel family, hunting, putting up game, and retrieving, but it is his work with snipe and as a wildfowler that has earned him his reputation. He has a very good nose indeed, a virtually waterproof coat, and tremendous strength and powers of endurance. He is courageous, as indeed any dog needs to be to work tidal waters after duck in the middle of the winter, as he will in the treacherous estuaries of the rivers of Northern Ireland and Scotland. He is highly intelligent and adaptable, easily trained and a great sporting companion.

As a show dog he is only just recovering some of the ground that he lost after the First World War and through to the Second, and more are now seen at shows than have been for some years. He is not an ideal show dog, as his coat is something of a problem. To retain the close curls special care and attention is needed, and some exhibitors maintain that the only way of preserving the quality of the coat at its best is to allow the dog to go for a swim in fresh water just before a show, never bathing in between shows. As the coat is particularly oily which is part of its waterproof character, the result is a dog that often smells like a dog. He makes a very faithful and attentive companion, who enjoys country walks, and is an excellent gundog for the one-dog man.

OFFICIAL STANDARD

Characteristics
The gait, peculiar to the breed, differs from that of any other variety of Spaniel.

General appearance
The Irish Water Spaniel is a gundog bred for work in all types of shooting and particularly suited for wild-fowling. His fitness for this purpose should be evident in his appearance; he is a strongly built, compact dog, intelligent, enduring and eager.

Head and skull
The head should be of good size. The skull high in dome, of good length and width sufficient to allow adequate brain capacity. The muzzle long, strong and somewhat square with a gradual stop. The face should be smooth and the skull covered with long curls in the form of a pronounced topknot growing in a well-defined peak to a point between the eyes. Nose large and well developed, dark liver colour. Withal there should be an impression of fineness.

Eyes
Comparatively small, medium to dark-brown colour, bright and alert.

Ears
Very long and lobe-shaped in the leather, low set, hanging close to the cheeks and covered with long twisted curls of live hair.

Mouth
The jaws should be strong, with a perfect, regular and complete scissor bite, i.e. the upper teeth closely overlapping the lower teeth and set square to the jaws.

Neck
Strongly set into the shoulders, powerful, arching and long enough to carry the head well above the level of the back. The back and sides of the neck should be covered with curls similar to those on the body. The throat should be smooth, the smooth hair forming a V-shaped patch from the back of the lower jaw to the breast bone.

Forequarters
The shoulders should be powerful and sloping. The chest deep and of large girth with ribs so well sprung behind the shoulders as to give a barrel-shaped appearance to the body but with normal width and curvature between the forelegs. The forelegs should be well boned and straight, with arms well let down and carrying the forearm at elbow and knee in a straight line with the point of the shoulder.

Body
Should be of good size. The back short, broad and level, strongly coupled to the hindquarters. The ribs carried well back. The loins deep and wide. The body as a whole being so proportioned as to give a barrel-shaped appearance accentuated by the springing of the ribs.

Hindquarters
Powerful with long well-bent stifles and hocks set low.

Feet
Should be large and somewhat round and spreading; well-covered with hair over and between the toes.

Tail
Peculiar to the breed, should be short and straight, thick at the root and tapering to a fine point. It should be low set, carried straight and below the level of the back; and in length should not reach the hock joint. Three to four inches of the tail at the root should be covered by close curls which stop abruptly, the remainder should be bare or covered by straight fine hairs.

Coat
Should be composed of dense, tight, crisp ringlets free from woolliness. The hair should have a natural oiliness. The forelegs covered with feather in curls or ringlets down to the feet. The feather should be abundant all round, though shorter in front so as only to give a rough appearance. Below the hocks the hindlegs should be smooth in front, but feathered behind down to the feet.

Colour
A rich dark liver having the purplish tint or bloom peculiar to the breed and sometimes referred to as puce-liver.

Weight and size
Height to the shoulders: dogs about 21 to 23 inches. Bitches about 20 to 22 inches.

Note
Male animals should have two apparently normal testicles fully descended into the scrotum.

AKC VARIATION TO STANDARD
Weight and size: dogs 55 to 65 pounds and 22 to 24 inches; bitches 45 to 58 pounds and 21 to 23 inches.

SUSSEX SPANIEL

NATIONAL GROUPING		
	Name	Number
KC(GB)	Gundog	2
AKC	Sporting Dogs	1
FCI	Gundogs	8

This particular member of the Spaniel family is one of the oldest, yet it is difficult to understand why he should have evolved as he has, since he has few of the qualities associated with the working Spaniel, being slower and shorter on the leg than many of the others. The Sportsman's Repository of 1820 speaks of the Spaniels of Sussex as good working dogs and in the same pages mentions the fact that the Toy Spaniels will hunt though they are too small to work all day, being described as delicate and small or 'carpet' Spaniels with exquisite noses that will hunt truly and pleasantly. The juxtaposition of these two pieces of information indicates that at that time although the different breeds of Spaniel were still dividing, there was a race of Spaniels peculiar to Sussex.

One of the principal characteristics of the breed is the rich golden liver colour with the hairs shading to gold at the tips. This colour is said to have originated with one bitch belonging to Dr. Watts which came from the then famous kennels of Mr. Fuller at Rosehill Park. This kennel produced the Rosehill line which on the death of Mr. Fuller in 1847 would have disappeared but for his head keeper who retained a dog and a bitch which kept the strain going. From that time the breed declined, and it was only the efforts of a group of enthusiasts in the 1870s that preserved the breed. Mr. Phineas Bullock who around that time owned the strongest kennel of Field Spaniels, was also successfully showing Sussex, but there is some doubt about the parentage of his big winners as they were believed to be bred from Field Spaniels.

Col. Claude Cane writing in the early years of this century said that he found the breed difficult, as the bitches did not breed freely, the puppies were rather delicate and difficult to rear, and laid this down to excessive inbreeding, which he claimed was almost unavoidable as there were so few specimens left at that time. The same situation almost exists today, as

in Britain only a handful are registered each year. Fortunately they are beginning to find their way into other countries and it will be possible in the future to re-import outcrosses from lines bred in places far distant from their native Sussex. During the early years of this century it was the habit for field trial judges to penalise a Spaniel that gave tongue. Most Sussex Spaniels give tongue when on a scent, and the deep melodious tone of the Sussex is a very pleasing sound and useful in some forms of hunting, especially on fur in heavy undergrowth as the sportsman gets early warning of game.

Owing to his build, the Sussex is a comparatively slow worker, but very conscientious and persevering, being particularly good in heavy coverts, where his strength at a low level and his abundant flat coat enable him to do considerable work without excessive tiring and with no damage to himself. He is a handsome dog and his colour so distinctive that he is much admired in the show ring. He is however rare, and seldom does one make much impression at the higher level at a large show. He shows well enough, as he is a placid individual, easily trained to behave well, and with the sort of temperament that allows him to enjoy the environment of a show without being too demonstrative about it. He is a soft and affectionate companion, makes a very good house dog.

OFFICIAL STANDARD

General appearance
Massive and strongly built. An active, energetic, strong dog, whose characteristic movement is a decided roll, and unlike that of any other Spaniel.

Head and skull
The skull should be wide and show a moderate curve from ear to ear, neither flat nor apple headed, with a centre indentation and a pronounced stop. Brows frowning—occiput decided, but not pointed. Nostrils well developed and liver colour. A well balanced head.

Eyes
Hazel colour, fairly large, not too full, but soft expression and not showing the haw over much.

Ears
Thick, fairly large and lobe shape, set moderately low but above eye level. Should lie closely, hair soft and wavy, but not too profuse.

Mouth
Strong and level, neither over nor undershot, with a scissor bite.

Neck
Long, strong and slightly arched, not carrying the head much above the level of the back. Not much throatiness, but well marked frill.

Forequarters
The shoulders should be sloping and free: arms well boned as well as muscular. Knees large and strong, pasterns short and well boned. Legs rather short and strong, moderately well feathered.

Body
Chest deep and well developed: not too round and wide. Back and loin well developed and muscular both in width

Body: chest deep, deep back ribs.

and depth. The back ribs must be deep. Whole body should be strong and level with no sign of waistiness from aitches to hips.

Hindquarters: thighs strongly boned, not too much bend.

Hindquarters
The thighs must be strongly boned as well as muscular: hocks large and strong, legs rather short and strong with good bone, moderately well feathered. The hind legs should not appear shorter than the fore legs, or be too much bent at the hocks so as to give a settery appearance, which is objectionable. The hind legs should be well feathered above the hocks, but not much hair below the hocks.

Feet
Circular, well padded, well feathered between toes.

Tail
Set low and not carried above level of the back. Free actioned, thickly clothed with hair, but no feather. Docked from 5 to 7 inches.

Coat
Abundant and flat with no tendency to curl and ample under coat for weather resistance.

Colour
Rich golden liver and hair shading to gold at the tips: the gold predominating. Dark liver or puce is objectionable.

Weight and size
Ideal weight: dogs, 45 pounds. Bitches, 40 pounds. Height, 15 to 16 inches.

Note
Male animals should have two apparently normal testicles fully descended into the scrotum.

AKC VARIATION TO STANDARD
Neck: rather short. *Weight:* 35 to 45 pounds.

WELSH SPRINGER SPANIEL

NATIONAL GROUPING		
	Name	Number
KC(GB)	Gundog	2
AKC	Sporting Dogs	1
FCI	Gundogs	8

To the unitiated there appears very little difference between the English and the Welsh Springer, but in fact the differences are quite marked. He is a smaller dog to start with, has shorter ears, and never varies from the dark rich red and white colour. His head too is usually smaller and finer than his English counterpart. He is however a Springer, or as the Welsh sometimes prefer to call him, a 'starter' and there is no doubt that the two breeds share a common origin, though the people of Wales claim that he has been a separate breed for hundreds of years, which would place him before the English Springer. When the claims for the antiquity of the breed were first put forward they were contested by those who maintained that he was merely a cross between the Springer and probably the Clumber which gave him his colour. The fact that he was not officially recognised as a separate breed until 1902 supports the theory that he is a recently developed breed.

There is some evidence that a small Spaniel, somewhere in size between a Cocker and a Springer had been in use as a gundog in Wales for some considerable time before the Welsh Springer emerged. However, when the first really good dogs were shown, around the 1890s, the Welsh exhibitors admitted that they were better than anything previously seen, which suggests that until then these indigenous Spaniels had been a fairly nondescript collection. In 1902 the breed was recognised and a standard produced, with the result that this active little worker was on his way. He is still principally known in Wales, but has now been exported to many other countries of the world, where his ability to withstand extremes of climate has enabled him to become established both as a working dog and on the show bench. His popularity has steadily increased in recent years and registration figures are growing all the time, but it has only been quite recently that one has won really high honours at a major show in Britain.

The Welsh Springer is an active hard-working dog, well suited to the mountainous country of his native Wales, where he will meet with in any one day the extremes of gorse covered hills and mountain torrents, boggy valleys and rocky gorges. He is smaller and more lightly built than the English Springer, with finer bone and a more silky coat, but this does not prevent him from being an excellent water dog, though it would be unwise to subject him to a hard day's work as a wildfowler during the winter. He can be used on all forms of game, and unless he is well-trained, can become somewhat too active, going off on excursions of his own. He is a good hunter and springer of game and can be trained to retrieve more than adequately.

He did have one or two common faults at one time which held him back as a major winner at big shows, but these have been bred out by careful selection, and he is now a very fine sound dog with few faults and no vices. He is easy to show as he trains well and is then steady and fearless in the ring. His preparation is minimal, and he is easily kept fit and in hard condition as he loves exercise and will run all day. His temperament is pleasant as is that of most of the Spaniels, and though at one time some of them were nervous, he is now generally a fairly bold and friendly dog that makes a good pet and housedog as well as a fine sporting companion.

OFFICIAL STANDARD

Characteristics
The 'Welsh Spaniel' or 'Springer' is also known and referred to in Wales as a 'Starter'. He is of very ancient and pure origin, and is a distinct variety.

General appearance
A symmetrical, compact, strong, merry, very active dog; not stilty; obviously built for endurance and hard work. A quick and active mover displaying plenty of push and drive.

Head and skull
Skull proportionate, of moderate length, slightly domed, with clearly defined stop and well chiselled below the eyes. Muzzle of medium length, straight, fairly square; the nostrils well developed and flesh-coloured or dark. A short chubby head is objectionable.

Neck: long, muscular, clean.

Head and skull: moderate length, clear stop, well chiselled.

Eyes
Hazel or dark, medium size, not prominent, nor sunken, nor showing haw.

Ears
Set moderately low and hanging close to the cheeks, comparatively small and gradually narrowing towards the tip and shaped somewhat like a vine leaf, covered with setter-like feathering.

Mouth
The jaws should be strong with a perfect, regular and complete scissor bite, i.e. the upper teeth closely overlapping the lower teeth and set square to the jaws.

Neck
Long and muscular, clean in throat, neatly set into long, sloping shoulders.

Forequarters
Forelegs of medium length, straight, well boned, moderately feathered.

Body
Not long; strong and muscular with deep brisket, well-sprung ribs; length of body should be proportionate to length of leg, and very well balanced; muscular loin slightly arched and well coupled up.

Hindquarters
Strong and muscular, wide and fully developed with deep second thighs. Hind legs, well boned, hocks well let down; stifles moderately bent (neither turned in nor out), moderately feathered.

Feet
Round, with thick pads. Firm and cat-like, not too large or spreading.

Tail
Well set on and low, never carried above the level of the back; lightly feathered and lively in action.

Coat
Straight or flat, and thick, of a nice silky texture, never wiry nor wavy. A curly coat is most objectionable.

Colour
Rich red and white only.

Weight and size
A dog not to exceed 19 inches in height at shoulder and a bitch 18 inches approximately.

Faults
Any departure from the foregoing points should be considered a fault and the seriousness of the fault should be in exact proportion to its degree.

Note
Male animals should have two apparently normal testicles fully descended into the scrotum.

HUNGARIAN VIZSLA

NATIONAL GROUPING		
	Name	Number
KC(GB)	Gundog	2
AKC	Sporting Dogs	1
FCI	Gundogs	7

Hungary has produced several quite remarkable breeds, notable in that they differ greatly from anything known anywhere else in the world. The Puli and the Komondor are two typical examples. This is probably explained by the fact that the country has acted as something of an ecological bridge across Asia and Europe. The Magyars who penetrated into Europe some thousand years ago brought with them their customs, their peoples and undoubtedly their dogs. Not all the dogs of Hungary, however, are as strange as the Puli. The Vizsla is one that more nearly fits the Western World's idea of what a dog should look like, and it is this, together with other valuable qualities that has made it the increasingly popular dog that it is. Writers on the subject of falconry in the middle ages depicted a dog that was certainly the Vizsla type.

The plains of Hungary, largely agricultural, and rich in game were the perfect place in which to develop a gun dog with more than average all round ability, a dog that would work equally well with fur or feather, one that was fast, clever and with the sort of nose that would permit him to discover game in the thick ground cover of crops and high grasslands. The Vizsla was the answer, and he flourished under these conditions. The period between the wars was a difficult time for the Vizsla owners and breeders in Hungary, and by the beginning of the Second World War, the breed had almost disappeared. A small number of enthusiasts, however, refused to allow it to become extinct and kept the breed alive. World War II brought in its wake the Russian occupation of the country, and those who fled to Austria, as many did, took their dogs with them, others went to Italy and Germany, and the breed not only became more widely dispersed, but, what was more important for its continuance, became more widely known.

By 1960 the breed was admitted to the American Kennel Club register, and since that date has climbed the popularity list until it is now well established. Britain was a little slower in recognising the qualities of this very attractive and indeed important breed, but in recent years more and more are being seen at shows, and now that challenge certificates are being offered in the breed it will increase.

He is described in the official Hungarian standard as a medium sized hunting type dog of noble appearance and lean musculation, a description which fits him admirably, as he is an aristocratic and distinguished looking dog, robust but lightly built with a long strong muscular neck and a lean elegant head. His solid colour, rusty gold or dark yellow makes him quite outstanding among his fellow gundogs and his powerful, light and graceful movement helps to make him popular with spectators at shows. It is, however, as a gundog that he is at his best, and in competition with other pointing breeds he has always held his own. His short coat and clean habits, with his quiet and steady temperament make him an excellent housedog.

OFFICIAL STANDARD

Characteristics
The Hungarian Vizsla should be lively and intelligent, obedient but sensitive, very affectionate and easily trained. It was bred for hunting for fur and feather on open ground or in thick cover, pointing and retrieving from both land and water.

General appearance
A medium sized dog of distinguished appearance, robust but not too heavily boned.

Head and skull
The head should be gaunt and noble. The skull should be moderately wide between the ears with a median line down the forehead and a moderate stop. The muzzle

Head: gaunt and noble. Muzzle: long and tapering.

should be a little longer than the skull and although tapering should be well squared at the end. The nostrils should be well developed, broad and wide. The jaws strong and powerful. The lips should cover the jaws completely and should be neither loose nor pendulous. The nose should be brown.

Eyes
Neither deep nor prominent, of medium size, being a shade darker in colour than the coat. The shape of the eyes should be slightly oval and the eyelids should fit tightly. A yellow or black eye is objectionable.

Ears
The ears should be moderately low set, proportionately long with a thin skin and hang down close to the cheeks, should be rounded 'V' shaped not fleshy.

Mouth
Sound white teeth meeting in a scissor bite, full dentition is desirable.

Forequarters
Shoulders should be well laid and muscular, elbows straight pointing neither in nor out, the forearm should be long.

Body: chest deep, prominent breast bone, slight tuck up.

Body
Back should be level, short well muscled, withers high. The chest should be moderately broad and deep with prominent breast bone. The distance from the withers to the lowest part of the chest should be equal to the distance from the chest to the ground. The ribs should be well sprung and the belly should be tight with a slight tuck-up beneath the loin. The croup should be well muscled.

Hindquarters
Should be straight when viewed from the rear, the thighs should be well developed with moderate angulation, the hocks well let down.

Feet
Rounded with toes short, arched and well closed. A cat like foot is desirable, hare foot is objectionable. Nails short, strong and a shade darker in colour than coat, dew claws should be removed.

Gait
Graceful and elegant with a lively trot and ground covering gallop.

Tail
Should be of moderate thickness, rather low set, with one third docked off. Whilst moving should be held horizontally.

Coat
Should be short and straight, dense and coarse and feel greasy to the touch.

Colour
Russet gold. Small white marks on chest and feet, though acceptable, are not desirable.

Weight and size
Optimum weight $48\frac{1}{2}$ to 66 pounds. Height at Withers: dogs $22\frac{1}{2}$ to 25 inches. Bitches 21 to $23\frac{1}{2}$ inches.

Faults
Any departure from the foregoing points should be considered a fault and the seriousness of the fault should be in exact proportion to its degree.

Note
Male animals should have two apparently normal testicles fully descended into the scrotum.

AKC VARIATION TO STANDARD
Neck: strong, smooth, muscular, moderately long, arched and devoid of dewlap. *Height:* dogs 22 to 24 inches; bitches 21 to 23 inches. *Disqualification:* deviation in height of more than 2 inches from standard either way.

WEIMARANER

The number and variety of gundogs emanating from Germany is considerable. It has always been a hunting country, with a wealth of game, both small animals and birds, and a considerable population of deer and boar. Most of the breeds have found their way into other countries including the United States of America, and the one that did so early in its history and with spectacular success is the Weimaraner. He is not an ancient dog, dating back to the 19th century when he was produced from several indigenous German breeds by careful selective breeding. It is almost certain that at least one of the early scent hounds played some part in his ancestry, probably one of the pack hounds of France. In his early days he was known as the Weimar Pointer and is referred to as such in a few lines in Leighton's book of 1907, which may indicate that the Spanish Pointer which is a fairly early breed was used to produce him, as it was to evolve many of the

NATIONAL GROUPING		
	Name	Number
KC(GB)	Gundog	2
AKC	Sporting Dogs	1
FCI	Gundogs	7

other gundogs.

The court of Weimar, which was a great sportsman's court in the early 19th century, sponsored the production of the breed in an attempt to design the perfect all-round gundog, one that would not only hunt the smaller game but would cope with the bigger animals found in the forests of the republic. The result was a big strong fine dog with wonderful nose and great tracking abilities. In the early days the breed was very jealously guarded, matings being carefully considered for the best bloodlines, and litters being ruthlessly culled to produce only the best specimens. The breeders were reluctant to sell, and it was almost impossible for anyone from another country to acquire one of these dogs. In 1929 an American dog breeder, Howard Knight became a member of the German Weimaraner Club, and was permitted to own a couple which he brought back, founded the breed, helped form a club and became its first President.

From that time onwards the breed found considerable favour with American sportsmen, who found in him the answer to the problem of the all-round gundog. There has been for many years a great deal of personal hunting in America. One or two sportsmen with dogs of their own, kept at home, would spend short periods of time in the country enjoying their favourite sport, and in the Weimaraner they found the ideal dog. He was much later finding favour in Britain, not arriving there until the 1950s, but since then he has made great progress. Nicknamed the 'grey ghost' because of his distinctive colour, he soon became popular as a family dog as well as a worker in the field and a show dog, and in the past ten years his numbers have quadrupled.

He is a fine show dog, easily trained and responsive. He has few vices, is easily prepared for the ring, as all that is required is some work with a hound glove to bring out the natural gloss of his short coat, and is reasonably quiet on the bench. He makes a good companion and housedog, and it is this particular quality that has endeared him to so many sportsmen who do not have to face up to the problem of having a shooting dog that is not allowed in the family home.

OFFICIAL STANDARD

Characteristics
In the case of the Weimaraner his hunting ability is the paramount concern and any fault of body or mind which detracts from this ability should be penalised. The dog should display a temperament that is fearless, friendly, protective and obedient.

General appearance
A medium-sized grey dog with light eyes, he should present a picture of great driving power, stamina, alertness and balance. Above all, the dog should indicate ability to work hard in the field. Movement should be effortless and ground-covering and should indicate smooth co-ordination. When seen from the rear, the hind feet should parallel the front feet. When seen from the side, the top line should remain strong and level.

Head and skull
Moderately long and aristocratic, with moderate stop and

Head and skull: moderately long and aristocratic, powerful jaw.

slight median line extending back over the forehead. Rather prominent occipital bone and ears set well back. Measurement from the top of the nose to stop to equal that from the stop to the occipital prominence. The flews should be moderately deep, enclosing a powerful jaw. Foreface perfectly straight, delicate at the nostrils. Skin tightly drawn. Neck clean cut and moderately long. Expression keen, kind and intelligent.

Eyes
Medium-sized in shades of amber or blue-grey, not protruding or too deeply set, placed far enough apart to indicate good disposition and intelligence. When dilated under excitement the eyes may appear almost black.

Ears
Long and lobular, slightly folded and set high. The ear when drawn alongside the jaw should end approximately one inch from the point of the nose.

Mouth
Well-set, strong and even teeth, well developed and proportionate to jaw with correct scissor bite (the upper teeth protruding slightly over the lower teeth). Complete

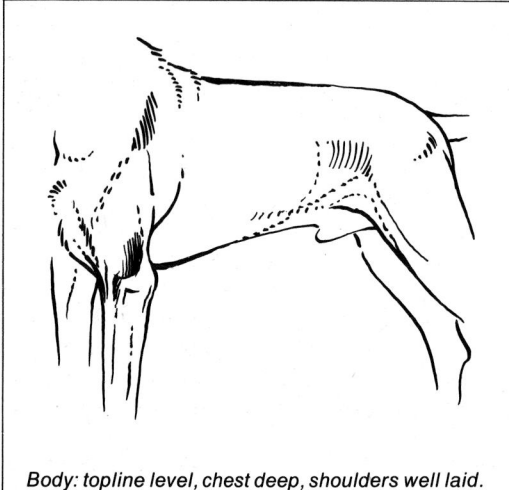

Body: topline level, chest deep, shoulders well laid.

Tail: carried confidently.

dentition is greatly desired. Grey nose, lips and gums of pinkish flesh shade.

Forequarters
Forelegs straight and strong, with measurement from elbow to the ground equalling the distance from the elbow to the top of the withers.

Body
The length of the body from the highest point of the withers to the root of the tail should equal the measurement from the highest point of the withers to the ground. The top line should be level with a slightly sloping croup. The chest should be well developed and deep, shoulders well laid and snug. Ribs well sprung and long. Abdomen firmly held, moderately tucked up flank. The brisket should drop to the elbow.

Hindquarters
Moderately angulated with well turned stifle. The hock joint well let down and turned neither in nor out. Musculation well developed.

Feet
Firm and compact. Toes well arched, pads closed and thick. Nails short and grey or amber in colour. Dew claws allowable only on imported dogs.

Tail
Docked at a point such that the tail remaining shall just cover the scrotum in dogs and the vulva in bitches. The thickness of the tail should be in proportion to the body and it should be carried in a manner expressing confidence and sound temperament. In the Long-haired Weimaraner the tip of the tail should be removed.

Coat
In the long-haired Weimaraner the coat should be from 1 to 2 inches long on the body and somewhat longer on the neck, chest and belly. The tail and the backs of the limbs should be feathered.

Colour
Preferably silver grey, shades of mouse or roe grey are admissible. The colour usually blends to a lighter shade on head and ears. A dark eel stripe frequently occurs along the back. The whole coat gives an appearance of metallic sheen. Small white mark allowable on chest but not on any other part of the body. White spots that have resulted from injuries shall not be penalised. Colour of the long-haired Weimaraner as the short-haired.

Size
Height at withers. Dogs 24 to 27 inches, bitches 22 to 25 inches.

Faults
Shyness or viciousness. Any colour or marking other than specified in this Standard.

Note
Male animals should have two apparently normal testicles fully descended into the scrotum.

AKC VARIATION TO STANDARD
Ears: one inch shorter. *Tail:* docked. At maturity it should measure approximately 6 inches with a tendency to be light rather than heavy and should be carried in a manner expressing confidence and sound temperament. *Disqualifications:* deviation in height of more than 1 inch from standard either way. A distinctly long coat.

WIREHAIRED POINTING GRIFFON

There are some breeds whose history, either because it has been carefully chronicled from very early times as in the case of the Pekingese, or because it is of fairly recent origin, is known in some detail. The Wirehaired Pointing Griffon is one of these. Prior to 1874 the breed did not exist, and it was the decision in that year by Mr. Korthals of Haarlem to produce a new breed that started it. At first the breed was known as the Korthals Griffon, and although the breed is completely unknown now in Britain, it is interesting to note that Mr. Korthals had a fine team, some of which were exhibited in Britain. In fact classes were put on for the breed by the Kennel Club at a show held at Barn Elms in Jubilee Year. On another occasion Mr. Korthals gained the prize for the best sporting dog in the show owned by a foreigner, with one of his Griffons at the Agricultural Hall.

When Mr. Korthals began to collect the dogs with which to conduct his experiments, he purchased a Griffon bitch and proceeded to add to his team short-coated, rough-coated and even smooth breeds of sporting dogs, and all of these are known by name. One litter produced three specimens, Moustache, Querida and Lina that are generally accepted as the

NATIONAL GROUPING		
	Name	Number
KC(GB)	—	–
AKC	Sporting Dogs	I
FCI	Gundogs	7

original ancestors of all the best lines in the breed. Although the breed developed in Holland as the result of work done by a Dutchman, the origins must be accepted as French, as the basic stock from which they were all bred, came in fact from France and the major part of the breeding programme was carried out there. Young Korthals left home and moved to Germany where he continued with his experiments to produce the breed that he was aiming for, and became a well known figure around the field trials, and other sporting activities connected with dogs, in many of the countries of Europe.

The progress of the breed from its early days is well-recorded, but the actual breeds of dog employed remain in some doubt, as Eduard Korthals had fixed ideas of what he wished the breed to be like when he had produced it, and was more interested in the appearance and performance of the dogs that he used than in their breed. He is said to have used French, German and Belgian dogs as various crosses, and in those countries at the end of the 19th century there was a wealth of gundog breeds to choose from. He probably used a mixture of Boulet, Barbet and Griffon and possibly even the Spinone. By the beginning of this century he had fixed the breed, and photographs of dogs in 1907 are remarkably like those of today.

As a working dog he has the reputation of being slow but thorough, and of being intelligent and easily trained. He is shorter on the leg than some of the gundogs, and thus lacks a little elegance. His rough harsh coat, almost bristly, gives him a somewhat unkempt appearance which some find unattractive. He is, however, a strong and vigorous dog, capable of working under extreme conditions. His temperament and intelligence make him a pleasant companion and guard, and there is no reason to suppose that he would be anything other than a very good housedog.

OFFICIAL STANDARD

General appearance
The Wirehaired Griffon is a dog of medium size, fairly short-backed, rather a little low on his legs. He is strongly limbed, everything about him indicating strength and vigor. His coat is harsh like the bristles of a wild boar and his appearance, notwithstanding his short coat, is as unkempt as that of the long-haired Griffon, but on the other hand he has a very intelligent air.

Head
Long, furnished with a harsh coat, forming a mustache and eyebrows, skull long and narrow, muzzle square. *Eyes:* large, open, full of expression, iris yellow or light brown. *Ears:* of medium size, flat or sometimes slightly curled, set rather high, very lightly furnished with hair. *Nose:* always brown.

Hind legs: long thighs.

Head: ears medium sized, set rather high.

Neck
Rather long, no dewlap.

Shoulders
Long, sloping.

Ribs
Slightly rounded.

Forelegs
Very straight, muscular, furnished with rather short wire hair.

Hind legs
Furnished with rather short stiff hair, and thighs long and well developed.

Feet
Round, firm and well formed.

Tail
Carried straight or gaily, furnished with a hard coat without plume, generally cut to a third of its length.

Coat
Hard, dry, stiff, never curly, the undercoat downy.

Color
Steel gray with chestnut splashes, gray white with chestnut splashes, chestnut, dirty white mixed with chestnut, never black.

Height
$21\frac{1}{2}$ to $23\frac{1}{2}$ inches for dogs, and $19\frac{1}{2}$ to $21\frac{1}{2}$ inches for bitches.

AKC VARIATION TO STANDARD
This dog is not granted championship status by the KC(GB). The above standards are those of the AKC.

HOUND GROUP: SPORTING BREEDS

Afghan Hound

Basenji

Basset Hound

Black and Tan Coonhound

Bloodhound

Beagle

Dachshund

Miniature Dachshund

Deerhound

Elkhound

Borzoi

Foxhound

Finnish Spitz

American Foxhound

Greyhound

Harrier

Irish Wolfhound

Ibizan Hound

Otter Hound

Pharaoh Hound

Whippet

Saluki or Gazelle Hound

Rhodesian Ridgeback

HOUND GROUP: SPORTING BREEDS

Long before the invention of the gun, man hunted animals for food and for sport. Even when the bow and arrow had been developed into an efficient hunting weapon, it was virtually useless in certain terrains. In heavy woodland where it is possible to approach close enough without being seen by the quarry, the bow and arrow served, but in open areas the game had to be run down either by sheer speed or steady persistence and stamina. Many breeds of dog evolved for chasing game hundreds and thousands of years ago, which means that the Hound Group has among its breeds some of the oldest in the world.

The Group is large and very diverse including breeds that sight and then run down their game, those that hunt by scent, others that chase, corner the game and bay to call up the hunter, and specialised breeds for hunting large and ferocious animals. There is also a sub-group of smaller dogs that has been developed to go to ground and keep the quarry entertained until it has been dug out. Although the breeds in the Group have for the most part the same sort of temperament, that drives them on to hunt and kill, there is very little overlap of purpose.

The first sub-group, those that hunt by catching and killing their quarry, includes not only some of the most ancient breeds, but also the greatest variety of sizes; from the Irish Wolfhound whose task it was originally to hunt the wolf, wild deer and boar, to the Whippet, one of the youngest breeds, whose quarry is the humble rabbit. They are all built to the same general pattern, with long legs, long necks and very deep briskets, which makes them among the most efficient runners in the animal world. Amongst the oldest breeds are the Saluki and the Afghan Hound which are recorded in ancient Persian manuscripts.

The second category, the ones that hunt by scent, includes most of the pack-hunting dogs, whose task it was to outrun the quarry by sheer persistence and stamina, chasing it until it collapsed through sheer exhaustion or decided to turn and face its pursuers. These dogs are built on heavier lines, with strong legs, deep chests and a very different form of head from the faster breeds. They have large muzzles and noses to allow a greater intake of breath and scent, and are not as streamlined. They are capable of following a scent hours and in some cases days after their quarry has gone.

There is another smaller category which hunts by scent, but which instead of going in to kill when the quarry is cornered, is trained to surround the game, and give tongue, keeping the animal at bay until the hunter arrives to dispatch it. Mostly they hunt the larger animals such as the moose and elk, and the Elkhound is a typical example. Others such as the Black and Tan Coonhound have been evolved to corner their quarry in a tree and give tongue in the same way.

The collection of small low-to-ground Hounds, the Dachshunds, occupies a special position in the Group. The work of the Dachshunds could be described as a mixture of that of the Hounds and the Terriers, in that they hunt by scent, and when their quarry, usually a fox or badger goes to ground, it is their duty to follow it down and engage it until both they and the quarry can be dug out by the hunter. There are in addition one or two specialists in the Group, the Otterhound for instance which is able to scent in water, and the Bloodhound which has the finest scenting powers in the whole canine race but does not kill. There is in addition one breed which will tackle the fiercest game including the big cats, the Rhodesian Ridgeback, which has been known to handle a leopard.

Most dogs in the Hound Group become attached to people, largely because they have enjoyed civilisation for centuries. They have for the most part a well-controlled killer instinct, but many of them have a streak of independence which, under certain circumstances will make them disobedient.

AFGHAN HOUND

In those countries spreading eastwards from the Meditteranean, through Persia and across the north of the land mass of India, coursing has always been the 'sport of kings', or at least ever since tribes had leaders and rulers. In those areas a breed of running dogs developed, varying slightly from country to country, and even from the valleys to the hills. They were called in general terms Eastern Greyhounds, but were given specific names based on the countries or areas of origin. In that area which includes Afghanistan this particular type of dog developed as an extremely fast animal with great stamina, and with a coat to withstand the extreme cold of the hills in which it lived. Early attempts to acquire these dogs from tribesmen failed as they were highly prized and as closely kept as were horses and hawks, and it was in conjunction with both of these that the Afghan Hound was originally used.

Those who first brought these dogs to the West gave them the collective name Afghan Hound, and that name is now applied to a breed that has become popular throughout the world, with a common standard of points, and an accepted appearance. The old tribal names have disappeared in spite of attempts by some people to resurrect them.

The purpose of the dog was to chase game until it became exhausted, and until the sportsman could come up with it and dispatch it. The pattern of the chase was for a hawk to be loosed when an antelope was sighted, to swoop on the head of the animal and delay it so that the Afghan Hound could catch up and detain it until the hunter arrived. The hawks were trained by being flown at stuffed animal heads, and the Afghan Hound was trained to run in on the spot where the hawk swooped. To this day an Afghan Hound will often be seen watching the flight of a bird very closely, and even following it if he happens to be running free.

There is no more glamorous dog in the world than the Afghan Hound. It has a long silky coat, which can be of any colour or mixture of colours, and which grows to a remarkable length. In movement or in a breeze the coat flows beautifully around the contours of the dog, and owners spend considerable time grooming, even when the dog is not being prepared for exhibition, as the result is so rewarding.

As a show dog the Afghan has achieved tremendous popularity and numbers throughout the world, both of registrations and dogs on exhibition, now rival many of the one-time more popular breeds. Increased interest in the dog was due partly to the fact that the worlds of fashion, stage and screen, and professional photography realised the visual potential of so beautiful an animal, and it appeared in the company of beautiful women all over the world.

Temperamentally the dog has certain difficulties. It is a natural pursuer of anything that runs, is very difficult to recall when once it has embarked on a chase, and will kill whatever it happens to catch provided that it is not too big. It is not amenable to discipline, and needs a great deal of exercise, but once these elements are accepted, it has qualities that few other dogs have, and a distinct Eastern personality very different from the dogs of the Western world.

OFFICIAL STANDARD

Characteristics
The Afghan Hound should be dignified and aloof with a certain keen fierceness. The Eastern or Oriental expression is typical of the breed. The Afghan looks at and through one.

General appearance
The gait of the Afghan Hound should be smooth and springy with a style of high order. The whole appearance of the dog should give the impression of strength and dignity combining speed and power. The head must be held proudly.

Head and skull
Skull long, not too narrow with prominent occiput. Foreface long with punishing jaws and slight stop. The skull well balanced and surmounted by a long 'top-knot'. Nose preferably black but liver is no fault in light coloured dogs.

Eyes
Should be dark for preference but golden colour is not debarred. Nearly triangular, slanting slightly upwards from the inner corner to the outer.

Ears
Set low and well back, carried close to the head. Covered with long silky hair.

Mouth
Level.

Neck
Long, strong with proud carriage of the head.

Forequarters
Shoulders long and sloping, well set back, well muscled and strong without being loaded. Forelegs straight and well boned, straight with shoulder, elbows held in.

Ears: set low and well back.

Body
Back level, moderate length, well muscled, the back falling slightly away to the stern. Loin straight, broad and rather short. Hip-bones rather prominent and wide apart. A fair spring of ribs and good depth of chest.

Hindquarters
Powerful, well bent and well turned stifles. Great length between hip and hock with a comparatively short distance between hock and foot. The dew claws may be removed or remain at the discretion of the breeder.

Feet
Forefeet strong and very large both in length and breadth and covered with long thick hair, toes arched. Pasterns long and springy, especially in front and pads well down on the ground. Hindfeet long, but not quite so broad as forefeet, covered with long thick hair.

Hinquarters: well bent.

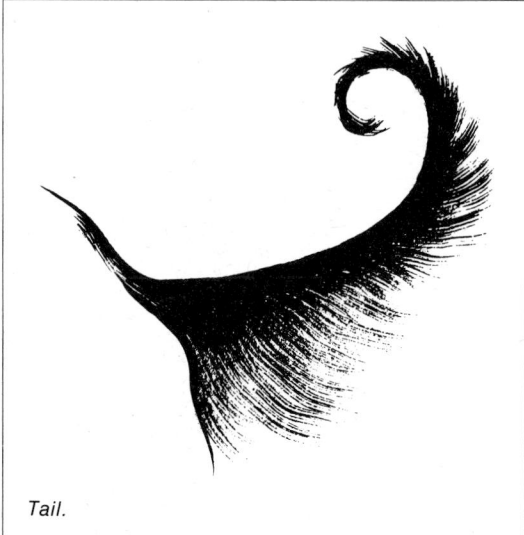

Tail.

the back. Ears and legs well coated. Pasterns can be bare. Coat must be allowed to develop naturally.

Colour
All colours are acceptable.

Weight and size
Ideal height: Dogs 27 to 29 inches. Bitches 2 to 3 inches smaller.

Faults
Any appearance of coarseness. Skull too wide and fore-face too short. Weak underjaw. Large round or full eyes. Neck should never be too short or thick. Back too long or too short.

Note
Male animals should have two apparently normal testicles fully descended into the scrotum.

Tail
Not too short. Set on low with ring at the end. Raised when in action. Sparsely feathered.

Coat
Long and very fine texture on ribs, fore and hind-quarters and flanks. From the shoulder backwards and along the saddle the hair should be short and close in mature dogs. Hair long from the forehead backward, with a distinct silky 'top knot'. On the foreface the hair is short as on

AKC VARIATION TO STANDARD

Neck: arched. *Height:* dog 27 inches; bitches 25 inches. Both plus or minus 1 inch. *Faults:* ewe neck; neck lacking in substance. Overshot or undershot jaw. Roach back; sway back; slack loin; too much width of brisket. Front or back feet thrown outwards or inwards; pads of feet not thick enough; feet too small; any other evidence or weakness in feet; weak or broken down pasterns; too straight in stifle; too long in hock. Lack of short-haired saddle in mature dogs.

BASENJI

The prick-eared ring tailed dogs so often depicted on friezes in ancient Egyptian tombs, have been claimed as the ancestors of a good many breeds, but the strongest claim almost certainly belongs to the Basenji, a breed of dog that has survived on the African continent. It was in the second half of the 19th century that these unusual native dogs began to be commented upon by explorers. They were unusual in that they were small, whereas most hunting dogs are large; that they were of a uniform colour, whilst most native dogs are so mixed that their colour varies considerably; and they did not bark, but merely made a low ululating noise unlike that of any other dog.

The Basenji was used by the natives of the Congo as a pack hunting dog, often wearing a bell to help in location, and controlled by a huntsman sometimes by voice, but even with a whistle in an almost European manner. The pack was used to drive game in to a net, and was so essential a part of the life of a tribe that the

NATIONAL GROUPING		
	Name	Number
KC(GB)	Hound	I
AKC	Hounds	II
FCI	Small Hounds	6

individual dogs were much prized and well cared for.

The first evidence of importation is in 1895 and one was first shown at Crufts in 1937 as an African Bush Dog or Congo Terrier. At the same time there was a pair in the Paris zoo. Little further interest was displayed in the breed until six were imported but unfortunately failed to survive the effects of inoculation against distemper. The final efforts in the mid-thirties were more successful, and the breed became established from stock from Southern Sudan. The numbers have steadily increased since that time, and

101

the Basenji is now a popular little dog.

It combines the qualities of being attached to people and places, with many of the instincts of the hunting dog, and is appreciated by those who are enthusiastic about the breed as a good housedog.

Physically the animal is very attractive, being well-proportioned, having a pleasing expression, slightly quizzical because of the wrinkling between the ears, and with a short silky coat that is pleasant to the touch. It is a friendly dog, and centuries of attachment to the human race have given the Basenji an attitude towards people that is a strange mixture of self-confidence and dependence.

As a show dog the Basenji is much admired for its colour, the reds glowing in the sunlight and the parti-coloured being flashy and showy. It is, however, the showmanship of the dog that most appeals. He will stand like a statue for a considerable time in the ring, and when he moves he does so with all the athleticism of a much bigger dog, flowing round the ring with tremendous style and panache.

The personality of the Basenji is not the easiest to live with if you happen to be another dog. They are very good indeed with people, but have the ingrained habit of the pack dog of scrapping with one another. A pack needs a leader, and leadership is established only by individual combat between contenders. Once the pecking order has been established, and until such time as the leader grows weak or old and loses his place, then generally things are fairly settled. Those Basenji owners who have a number of dogs, either separate them, or allow them to establish their own pecking order.

OFFICIAL STANDARD

Characteristics
The Basenji does not bark but is not mute, its own special noise is a mixture of a chortle and a yodel. It is remarkable for its cleanliness in every way. The wrinkled forehead, tightly curled tail, and legs carried straight forward with a swift, long, tireless, swinging stride, are typical of the breed.

General appearance
The Basenji should be a lightly built, finely boned aristocratic looking animal, high on the leg compared with its length, always poised, alert and intelligent. The wrinkled head, with pricked ears, should be proudly carried on a well-arched neck. The deep brisket should run up into a definite waist and the tail be tightly curled, presenting a picture of a well-balanced dog with a gazelle-like grace.

Head and skull
The skull should be flat, well-chiselled and of medium width, tapering towards the nose, with only a slight stop. The distance from the top of the head to the stop is slightly more than from the stop to the tip of the nose. The side lines of the skull taper gradually towards the mouth, giving a clean-cheeked appearance. Fine and profuse wrinkles should appear on the forehead when the ears are pricked, side wrinkles are desirable but should not be exaggerated into dewlap. Wrinkles are more noticeable in puppies, but, because of lack of shadowing,

are not as noticeable in tri-colours. A black nose is greatly desired.

Eyes
Dark, almond shaped, obliquely set, far-seeing and rather inscrutable in expression.

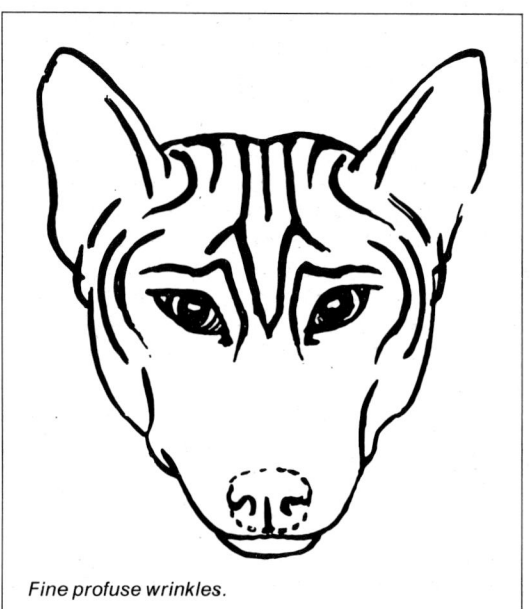

Fine profuse wrinkles.

Ears

Small, pointed, erect and slightly hooded, of fine texture, set well forward on top of the head, the tip of the ear should be nearer the centre of the skull than the outside base.

Mouth

The mouth should be level, with scissors bite, the upper teeth slightly over-lapping and touching the lower teeth.

Neck

Strong and of good length, without thickness, well-crested and slightly full at the base of the throat with a graceful curve accentuating the crest. It should be well-set into laid back shoulders so as to give the head a 'lofty' carriage.

Forequarters

The shoulders must be well laid back, muscular but not loaded. The points of the scapulae should be fairly close at the withers. The elbows should be firmly tucked in against the brisket. When viewed from in front the elbows should be in line with the ribs and the legs should continue in a straight line to the ground giving a narrow front. The forelegs should be straight with fine bone and very long fore-arms. Pasterns should be of good length, straight but flexible.

Forelegs: straight.

Body

Balanced with short, level back. Ribs well sprung, deep and oval. The loin short-coupled and the deep brisket running up into a definite waist.

Hindquarters

Strong and muscular, with hocks well let down, turned neither in nor out, with long second thighs and moderately bent stifles.

Feet

Small, narrow and compact, with deep pads, well-arched toes and short nails.

Tail.

Tail

The tail should be high set with the posterior curve of the buttock extending beyond the root of the tail giving a reachy appearance to the hindquarters. The tail curls tightly over the spine and lies closely to the thigh with a single or double curl.

Coat

Short, sleek and close, very fine. Skin very pliant.

Colour

Pure bright red, or pure black, or black and tan, all with white feet, chest and tail tips. White legs, white blaze and white collar optional.

Size and weight

Ideal heights: dogs 17 inches at shoulder; bitches 16 inches; an inch either way should not penalize an otherwise well-balanced specimen. Ideal weights: dogs 24 pounds, bitches 21 pounds.

Faults

Coarse, domed or peaked skull. Muzzle too long or too broad. Cheekiness. Mouth over-shot or under-shot. Round or light eyes. Ears too low-set or too large. Wide chest, barrel ribs, shelly brisket. Short in the leg, out at elbows, toeing in. Heavy bone, cow hocks, low-set or straight tail, thin flat open feet. Long or heavy coat. Creams, sables, or any other colours than those defined in the Colour paragraph above should be heavily penalised. Poor temperament.

Note

Male animals should have two apparently normal testicles fully descended into the scrotum.

AKC VARIATION TO STANDARD

Weight and size: bitches 22 pounds. Bitches 16 inches and dogs 17 inches long from front chest to farthest point of hindquarters. *Faults:* dewlap.

BASSET HOUND

Prior to the Revolution in France, hunting was an elaborate business, almost a ritual. There were a number of scent Hounds that were regularly hunted in packs by the nobles, and the breeding was as carefully carried out as any modern breeding plan. During the Revolution, hunting was neglected and the packs were dispersed along with the possessions and wealth of the court, and they came into the hands of peasants who used them to help support their families by adding game to a fairly sparse diet.

After the Revolution interest in hunting was revived, but in a different form and using firearms rather than the purer method of merely running the game down. The less wealthy took to hunting on foot and for this purpose they needed a slower dog, still with a wonderful nose, heavy and strong to cope with the conditions under which they worked, but with shorter legs than the traditional pack Hounds of the past. For this purpose the Basset Hound was developed.

Four different versions of the short-legged Hound were produced, the Basset Artésien Normand, the Basset Bleu de Gascogne, the Basset Griffon Vendéen and the Basset Fauve de Bretagne. The Artésien Normand was the one that most nearly resembled the Basset Hound as we know it today throughout the world, being smooth-coated, somewhat similar in head, and roughly the same size and proportions. Everett Millais is presumed by many to be the 'father'

of the modern Basset Hound, as it was he who claimed to have made the first importation from France, though this has been disputed. Certainly he was showing his famous dog 'Model' in 1875, and was deeply involved in early breeding experiments.

Unfortunately numbers in the early days were small, and some of the stock became very inbred and weak until further importations were made. Since those early days the breed has gone from strength to strength, and as the result of tremendous publicity it is one of the most popular breeds of the Hound Group. This is not surprising as the Basset has a most appealing personality, and not just because of his somewhat unusual appearance. He is a sturdy representative of the race, is as friendly as almost all scent-hunting Hounds are, and exceptionally good with children.

He is somewhat wilful, and difficult. He has remarkable scenting powers, will follow a trail that is hours old, and as a result, so thoroughly enjoys what he considers to be his purpose in life that he tends to forget that civilisation has caught up with him and that he is supposed to be an obedient family dog. He makes a first class house dog providing that he can get enough exercise to keep down his weight.

As a show dog the Basset has reached heights that would not at one time have been considered possible. Registration figures have climbed in most countries and there are few climates from temperate North America to tropical Ceylon where this magnificent Hound does not flourish, and where, from time to time, he does not command attention and respect in the show ring. He is amenable, behaves well, and his noble head and distinctive tail carriage always create a favourable impression in competition with other breeds.

OFFICIAL STANDARD

General characteristics

A short-legged hound of considerable substance, well-balanced and full of quality. Action is most important. A smooth free action with forelegs reaching well forward and hind legs showing powerful thrust and the hound moving true both front and rear. Hocks and stifles must not be stiff in movement nor must any toes be dragged.

Wrinkle.

Head and skull

Domed, with some stop and the occipital bone prominent; of medium width at the brow and tapering slightly to the muzzle; the general appearance of the foreface is lean but not snipy. The top of the muzzle nearly parallel with the line from stop to occiput and not much longer than the head from stop to occiput. There may be a moderate amount of wrinkle at the brows and beside the eyes and in any event the skin of the head should be so loose as to wrinkle noticeably when drawn forward or when the head is lowered. The flews of the upper lip overlap the lower substantially.

Ears: set on low.

Nose

Entirely black, except in light-coloured hounds, when it may be brown or liver. Large with well opened nostrils and may protrude a little beyond the lips.

Eyes

Brown, but may shade to hazel in light-coloured hounds, neither prominent nor too deep set. The expression is calm and serious and the red of the lower lid appears, though not excessively.

Ears

Set on low but not excessively so and never above the line of the eye, very long, reaching at least to the end of a muzzle of correct length, narrow throughout their length and curling well inwards; very supple, fine and velvety in texture.

Mouth

The teeth level with a scissors bite although if they meet edge to edge it is not a fault.

Neck

Muscular and fairly long with pronounced dewlap but not exaggerated.

Forelegs: short, powerful and with great bone.

Forequarters

Shoulder-blades well laid back and shoulders not heavy. Forelegs short, powerful and with great bone, the elbows turned neither out nor in but fitting easily against the side. The knees at least slightly crooked inwards but not to so great an extent as to prevent free action or to result in legs touching each other when standing or in action. Knuckling-over is a bad fault. There may be wrinkles of skin between knee and foot.

Body

The breast bone slightly prominent but the chest not narrow or unduly deep; the ribs well-rounded and sprung and carried well back. The back rather broad, level, and with withers and quarters of approximately the same height, though the loins may arch slightly. The back from withers to the inset of the quarters not unduly long.

Knuckling over is a bad fault.

the feet would leave the imprint of a large hound and no unpadded areas in contact with the ground.

Tail
Well set-on, rather long, strong at the base and tapering with a moderate amount of coarse hair underneath. When the hound is moving the stern is carried well up and curves gently sabre-fashion over the back but is never curling or gay.

Coat
Smooth, short and close without being too fine.

Colour
Generally black, white and tan, or lemon and white, but any recognised hound colour is acceptable.

Size
Height 13 to 15 inches.

Faults
Any departure from the above Standard is a fault but the following should particularly be penalised: (a) unsoundness of legs or feet. (b) faulty mouth. (c) lack of balance (i.e. undue exaggeration of any point). (d) lack of typical Basset appearance and expression.

Note
Male animals should have two apparently normal testicles fully descended into the scrotum.

Hindquarters
Full of muscle and standing out well, giving an almost spherical effect when viewing the hound from the rear. Stifles well bent. The hocks as low to the ground as possible and slightly bent under the hound but not turned in or out. They should be placed just under the body when standing naturally. One or two wrinkles of skin may appear between hock and foot and at the rear of the joint a slight pouch resulting from the looseness of the skin.

Feet
Massive, well knuckled-up and padded. The forefeet may point straight ahead or be turned slightly outwards but in every case the hound must stand perfectly true, the weight being borne equally by toes with pads together so that

AKC VARIATION TO STANDARD
Eyes: prominent haw. *Ears:* set far back on the head at base of the skull and in repose appear to be set on neck. *Neck:* well arched. *Forequarters:* distance from deepest point of chest to ground, while it must be adequate to allow free movement when working in the field, is not to be more than one third the total height at withers of an adult. *Tail:* not to be docked. Carried gaily in hound fashion. *Size:* should not exceed 14 inches. *Faults:* cowhocks or bowed legs. *Disqualifications:* height more than 15 inches at highest point of shoulder blades. Knuckled over front legs. Distinctly long coat.

BEAGLE

NATIONAL GROUPING		
	Name	Number
KC(GB)	Hound	I
AKC	Hounds	II
FCI	Small Hounds	6

The highly organised hunt on horseback with large packs of Hounds and a number of hunt staff has become a regional feature of many countries, and being centred around large estates and country houses carried great social weight. However, a need was found for the smaller organisation, attached to schools and colleges or army regiments, which did not have the staff, accommodation or financial resources to maintain a large pack.

The Beagle filled this purpose admirably, and since the 16th century packs of these smaller Hounds have been in existence. They probably started out as small Foxhounds or Harriers, and it is likely that Terrier and even Spaniel blood was introduced to decrease the size whilst retaining the spirit and scenting powers of the larger Hounds. What was wanted was a smaller Hound, shorter in the leg, but not so cumbersome as the Basset, light, easily housed, and not with the rather voracious appetite of the Foxhound. The result is that a very popular small dog has been produced, but that a sport has survived which might otherwise have disappeared.

There are many Beagle packs throughout the world, and every country that enjoys the sport, has organisations to control hunting interests. Associations of Masters of Harriers and Beagles in Great Britain and Ireland, the National Beagle Club of the United States of America are typical examples, and the sport is well established even though it has achieved less publicity than foxhunting.

The breeding of the Beagle down to size continued until a race of Hounds that were under ten inches high at the shoulder became fixed, bred true to type and size, and became known as the Pocket Beagle. This very small Hound was popular up to the First World War, and was exhibited and hunted. They seem to have disappeared after that, though an attempt is being made to reintroduce them.

There was also at one time a rough or hard-coated variety. The rough-coat seems to have disappeared in favour of the popular smooth-coat of today's Hounds.

The popularity of the Beagle as a show dog has become such that in most countries it vies with the most numerous of the Hound Group. It was for a while, the most popular show dog in the United States of America. There are few more attractive sights than a ring full of these small Hounds, all behaving beautifully, and in their rich variety of colours. The Beagle is easily handled even by the youngest child, and is a great favourite with children in the children's handling classes.

The Beagle is a most attractive dog, completely friendly, very attached to particular members of the family, and wonderfully playful. He is, however, somewhat wilful, like so many of the Hounds, and will from time to time go off on his own business from which it is difficult to divert him. One of the most humorous of sights is an owner trying to attract the attention of his Beagle which is fast disappearing, nose in the air, and apparently completely oblivious to all blandishments.

OFFICIAL STANDARD

Characteristics
A merry hound whose essential function is to hunt, primarily hare, by following a scent. Bold with great activity, stamina and determination. Alert, intelligent and of even temperament.

General appearance
A sturdy and compactly-built hound, conveying the impression of quality without coarseness.

Stop: well defined and dividing head equally.

Head and skull
Head fair length, powerful in the dog without being coarse, but finer in the bitch; free from frown and excessive wrinkle. Skull slightly domed, moderately wide, with indication of peak. Stop well defined and dividing length between occiput and tip of nose as equally as possible. Muzzle not snipy, lips reasonably well flewed. Nose broad and nostrils well expanded; preferably black, but less pigmentation permissible in the lighter coloured hounds.

Ears: long, reaching nearly to end of nose when drawn out.

Eyes
Dark brown or hazel, fairly large, not deep set or bulgy, set well apart and with a mild appealing expression.

Ears
Long with round tip, reaching nearly to end of nose when drawn out. Set on low, fine in texture and hanging gracefully close to cheek.

Mouth
Teeth strongly developed. Upper incisors just overlapping and touching outer surface of lower incisors to form scissor bite.

Neck
Sufficiently long to enable hound to come down easily to scent, slightly arched and showing a little dewlap.

Forequarters
Shoulder clean and sloping. Forelegs straight and upright, well under the hound, of good substance, strong, hard and round in bone. Not tapering off to feet. Pasterns short. Elbows firm, turning neither in nor out. Height to elbow about half the hound's height to withers.

Forelegs: well under, height to elbow half height to withers.

Body
Topline straight and level. Chest well let down to below elbow. Ribs well sprung and extending well back. Short between the couplings. Loins powerful and supple, without excessive tuck-up.

Hindquarters
Very muscular about the thighs. Stifles well bent. Hocks firm, well let down and parallel to each other.

Tight foot and hare foot.

Note
Male animals should have two apparently normal testicles fully descended into the scrotum.

Feet
Tight and firm. Well knuckled up and strongly padded. Not hare-footed. Nails short.

Gait
Back level and no roll. Stride free, long-reaching and straight without high action. Hind legs showing drive. Should not move close behind or paddle or plait in front.

Free long-reaching stride.

Tail
Sturdy and of moderate length. Set on high and carried gaily but not curled over back or inclined forward from the root. Well covered with hair, especially on underside.

Coat
Short, dense and weatherproof.

Colour
Any recognised hound colour other than liver. Tip of stern white.

Weight and size
It is desirable that height from ground to withers should neither exceed 16 inches nor fall below 13 inches.

AKC VARIATION TO STANDARD
Two varieties are recognised by the AKC—hounds not exceeding 13 inches in height, and hounds over 13 inches but not exceeding 15 inches in height. *Head and skull:* stop moderately well defined. Lips free from flews. *Colour:* any true hound colour. *Faults:* a very flat skull, narrow across the top; excess of dome, eyes small, sharp and terrier-like, or prominent and protruding; muzzle long, snipy or cut away decidedly below the eyes, or very short. Roman-nosed, or upturned giving a dish-face expression. Ears short, set on high or with a tendency to rise above point of origin. A thick, short, cloddy neck carried on a line with top of shoulders. Throat showing dewlap and folds of skin to a degree termed 'throatiness'. Straight upright shoulders; cowhocks; straight hocks. Lack of muscle power; open feet. Long tail; rat tail. *Disqualification:* any hound measuring more than 15 inches.

BLACK AND TAN COONHOUND

NATIONAL GROUPING		
	Name	Number
KC(GB)	—	—
AKC	Hounds	II
FCI	—	—

The Black and Tan Coonhound, which is peculiar to the United States of America, is one of the newest breeds to be admitted to the American Kennel Club register, only in fact in 1945. It is, however, not only a much older breed than that in America, but is also considerably older in ancestry. It has been suggested that it descends from the Talbot of Britain, through the Bloodhound and Foxhound, but there are other possibilities. The Kerry Beagle is one, as there was certainly some importation of dogs from Ireland into the United States of America, and the small Foxhound of the Ring of Kerry could well lay claim, as it is essentially black and tan. There are breeds in France too, and even in Sweden, where the Hamiltonstövare could have played some part in the early formation of the Coonhound. There were other Coonhounds that were not black and tan, but that particular colour belongs to the line which proved most proficient at the task of hunting the raccoon and the opossum, with the result that the other colours have remained in the background.

The Coonhound is no mere hunting dog in that although he will trail by scent more normal game, he has been specifically bred to hunt the raccoon and opossum which are climbing animals. He has been trained over the years to trail these animals, often by night, as they are both nocturnal in their habits and, when he finally gets them treed, to give voice until the huntsman comes along and dispatches the quarry. Raccoon and opossum hunting is a highly organised sport in the United States of America and Canada, with much of the planning of the activity being in the hands of the United Kennel Club of America rather than the American Kennel Club. The UKCA began the registration of the various types of Coonhounds much earlier than the date of acceptance of the Black and Tan Coonhound by the American Kennel Club,

and hundreds of licensed hunting trials take place annually. The United Kennel Club also holds shows of these hunting dogs in much the same way as the various hunts in Britain hold Hound and Terrier shows in many parts of the country.

The various types of Coonhound resemble breeds of dogs in other countries and it is easy to tell from where they stemmed. The Bluetick, for instance, resembles the Grand Bleu de Gascogne from France, and the Redbone is very close to the red Bloodhound.

The Black and Tan is a powerful, agile and alert dog, with an aggressive and eager expression. Emphasis has at all times been placed on his working qualities even when he is appearing on the show bench. His movement is one of his strong points. He has been evolved to cover the ground very fast even during the hours of darkness, so that he needs a long, powerful rhythmic stride. Black and Tans need, and indeed enjoy a great deal of exercise, and like most of the scent hunting dogs they have a friendly attitude towards humans.

OFFICIAL STANDARD

General appearance

The Black and Tan Coonhound is first and fundamentally a working dog, capable of withstanding the rigors of winter, the heat of summer, and the difficult terrain over which he is called upon to work. Judges are asked by the club sponsoring the breed to place great emphasis upon these facts when evaluating the merits of the dog. The general impression should be that of power, agility, and alertness. His expression should be alert, friendly, eager, and aggressive. He should immediately impress one with his ability to cover the ground with powerful rhythmic strides.

Distinctive marking on head.

Head

The head should be cleanly modeled, with medium stop occurring midway between occiput bone and nose. The head should measure from 9 to 10 inches in dogs and from 8 to 9 inches in bitches. Viewed from the profile, the line of the skull is on a practically parallel plane to the foreface or muzzle. The *skin* should be devoid of folds or excess dewlap. The *flews* should be well developed with typical hound appearance. *Nostrils* well open and always black. *Skull* should tend toward oval outline. *Eyes* should

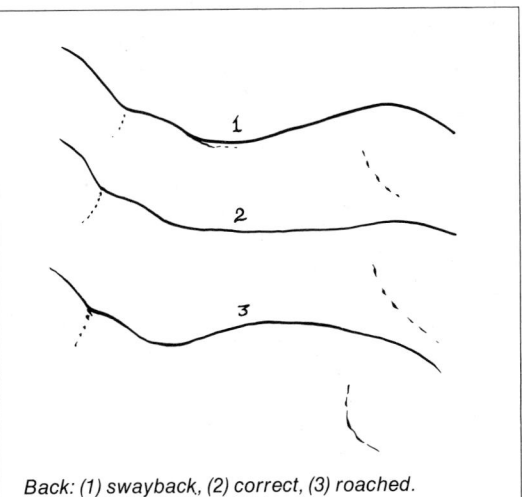

Back: (1) swayback, (2) correct, (3) roached.

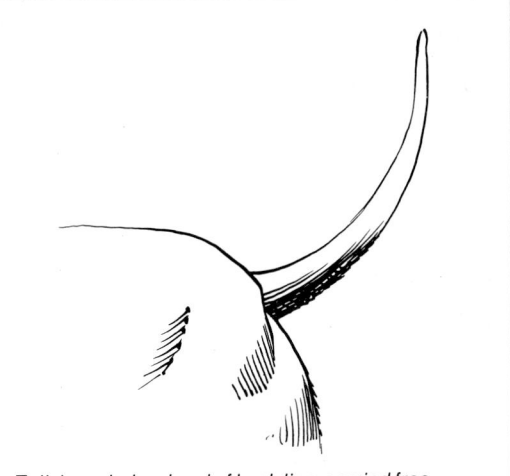

Tail: base below level of back line, carried free.

be from hazel to dark brown in color, almost round and not deeply set. The *ears* should be low set and well back. They should hang in graceful folds giving the dog a majestic appearance. In length they should extend well beyond the tip of the nose. *Teeth* should fit evenly with slightly scissors bite.

Body

Neck, shoulders, and *chest:* the neck should be muscular, sloping, medium length, extending into powerfully

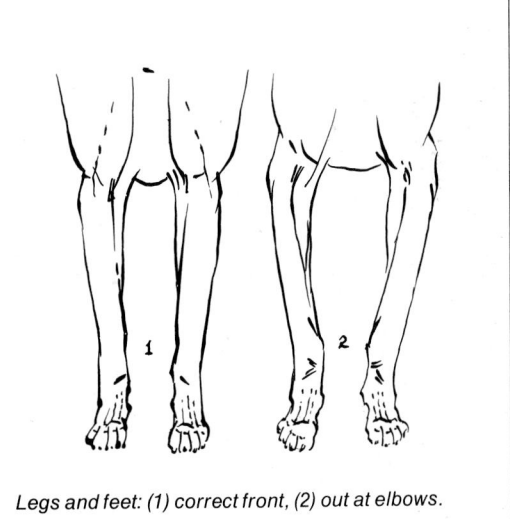

Legs and feet: (1) correct front, (2) out at elbows.

constructed shoulders and deep chest. The dog should possess full, round, well-sprung ribs, avoiding flat-sidedness. *Back and tail:* the back should be level, powerful and strong, with a visible slope from withers to rump. Tail should be strong, with base slightly below level of back line, carried free, and when in action at approximately right angles to back. *Legs and feet:* the forelegs should be straight, with elbows well let down, turning neither in nor out; pasterns strong and erect. Feet should be catlike with compact, well-arched toes and thick strong pads. *Hindquarters:* quarters should be well boned and muscled. From hip to hock long and sinewy, hock to pad short and strong. Stifles and hock well bent and not inclining either in or out. When standing on a level surface the hind feet should set back from under the body, and leg from pad to hock be at right angles to the ground when viewed both from profile and the rear. The stride of the Black and Tan Coonhound should be easy and graceful with plenty of reach in front and drive behind.

Coat and color
The coat should be short but dense to withstand rough going. As the name implies, the color should be coal black, with rich tan markings above eyes, on sides of muzzle, chest, legs and breeching with black pencil markings on toes.

Size
Measured at the shoulder: dogs, 25 to 27 inches; bitches, 23 to 25 inches. Height should be in proportion to general conformation so that dog appears neither leggy nor close to the ground. Dogs oversized should not be penalized when general soundness and proportion are in favor.

Judges should penalize the following defects:
Undersize, elbows out at shoulder, lack of angulation in hindquarters, splay feet, sway- or roach back, flatsidedness, lack pf depth in chest, yellow or light eyes, shyness and nervousness.

Faults
Dewclaws; white on chest or other parts of body is highly undesirable and if it exceeds 1½ inches in diameter should be disqualified.

DISQUALIFICATION
White on chest or other parts of the body if it exceeds 1½ inches in diameter.

Approved 10 July 1945

AKC VARIATION TO STANDARD
This dog is not granted championship status by the KC(GB). The above standards are those of the AKC.

BLOODHOUND

The Bloodhound is an excellent example of mankind's persistence in the search for perfection. Competition between the big estates or the courts of many countries as to who could produce the Hound that could follow the longest or the oldest trail has always been keen. In this work the Bloodhound is supreme, being capable of following a scent for long distances, even when that scent has been laid days before.

The Bloodhound undoubtedly owes its origins to France, along with so many of the scent hunting breeds. The most popular theory is that his ancestor was the St. Hubert Hound, an all black breed supposed to have been brought from the Holy Land, though this, like the reputation that the breed gained at one time for its fierceness is probably a myth. The fact remains that in France the Bloodhound as we know it is still known as the Chien de Saint Hubert.

Owing to the use of the Bloodhound in the fiction of the early part of this century, the dog gained an evil reputation which was ill-fitted to it, as it is the most friendly of creatures. Its association with the capture

NATIONAL GROUPING		
	Name	Number
KC(GB)	Hound	I
AKC	Hounds	II
FCI	Large Hounds	5

of runaway slaves and the putting down of uprisings with the cruelty involved, did not help the Bloodhound's reputation. The hound has been used extensively for tracking possible criminals, and is still called upon by police forces for that purpose from time to time. The fact remains, however, that when the quarry is finally apprehended, the Bloodhound is more likely to lick him than devour him as some novelists would have had us believe.

The Bloodhound is the biggest and the strongest of the scent hunting Hounds, and when on a trail, it needs a very fit person at the other end of a long leash to keep pace with him. He is forceful and positive when tracking, and it takes a great deal to break him off his intended course. His scenting powers are formidable, and this trait is used by owners who run trials for the breed in competition with one another in order to retain this essential quality.

As a showdog the Bloodhound has not achieved a great deal of popularity, as he is a big dog that is not easily transported in numbers to a show, is heavy and not easily handled. One needs to be something of an enthusiast to enjoy showing the breed. In the ring however he is a noble dog, upstanding when he is behaving. He moves up and down the ring with a long, loose, swinging stride that is very deceptive in the manner with which it covers the ground at a remarkable speed.

The Bloodhound is one of the most friendly dogs, wonderful with children on which it tends to fawn, sometimes to the embarrassment of the child, for a kiss from a Bloodhound can be a damp affair. For his size he has a moderate appetite, and is not difficult to feed, though he needs more than average care to keep him in good health, and needs more exercise than some people are prepared to take themselves.

OFFICIAL STANDARD

Characteristics
The Bloodhound possesses in a most marked degree every point and characteristic of those dogs which hunt together by scent (Sagaces). He is very powerful and stands over more ground than is usual with hounds of other breeds. The skin is thin and extremely loose, this being especially noticeable about the head and neck, where it hangs in deep folds. In temperament he is affectionate, neither quarrelsome with companions nor with other dogs. His nature is somewhat reserved and sensitive.

General appearance
The expression is noble and dignified and characterized by solemnity, wisdom and power. The gait is elastic, swinging and free; the stern being carried high scimitar fashion.

Head and skull
The head is narrow in proportion to its length and long in proportion to the body, tapering but slightly from the temples to the muzzle, thus (when viewed from above and in front) having the appearance of being flattened at the sides and of being nearly equal in width throughout its entire length. In profile the upper outline of the skull is nearly in the same plane as that of the foreface. The length from the end of the nose to stop (midway between the eyes) should not be less than that from stop to back or occipital protuberance (peak). The entire length of head from the posterior part of the occipital protuberance to the end of the muzzle should be 12 inches or more in dogs and 11 inches or more in bitches. The skull is long and narrow, with the occipital peak very pronounced. The brows are not prominent although owing to the deep-set eyes they may have that appearance. The foreface is long, deep and of even width throughout, with square outline when seen in profile. The head is furnished with an amount of loose skin, which in nearly every position appears superabundant, but more particularly so when the head is carried low; the skin then falls into loose pendulous ridges and folds, especially over the forehead and sides of the face. The nostrils are large and open. In front the lips fall squarely making a right angle with the upper line of the foreface; whilst behind they form deep hanging flews, and, being continued into the pendant folds of loose skin about the neck, constitute the dewlap, which is very pronounced.

Mouth
A scissor bite with the inner faces of the upper incisors touching the outer faces of the lower incisors.

Head: nearly equal in width throughout length.

Furnished with loose skin.

Eyes: sunk, diamond shape.

Eyes

The eyes are deeply sunk in the orbits, the lids assuming a lozenge or diamond shape, in consequence of the lower lids being dragged down and everted by the heavy flews. The eyes correspond with the general colour of the animal varying from deep hazel to yellow. The hazel colour is however to be preferred, although very seldom seen in liver and tan (red and tan) hounds. The eye should be free from any interference from the eyelashes.

Ears: lower part curling inwards and backwards.

Ears

The ears are thin and soft to the touch, extremely long, set on very low and fall in graceful folds, the lower parts curling inwards and backwards.

Neck

Should be long.

Forequarters

The shoulders muscular and well sloped backwards. The forelegs are straight, large and round in bone with elbows squarely set. The pasterns should be strong.

Hindquarters

The thighs and second thighs (gaskins) are very muscular, the hocks well bent and let down and squarely set.

Feet

Should be strong and well knuckled up.

Body

The ribs are well sprung and the chest well let down between the forelegs forming a deep keel. The back and loins are strong, the latter deep and slightly arched.

Tail

The stern is long and thick tapering to a point, set on high with a moderate amount of hair underneath. It

Tail: carried scimitar fashion.

should be carried scimitar fashion, but not curled over the back or corkscrew at any time.

Colour

The colours are black and tan, liver and tan (red and tan) and red. The darker colours being sometimes interspersed with lighter or badger-coloured hair and sometimes flecked with white. A small amount of white is permissible on chest, feet and tip of stern.

Weight and size

The mean average height of adult dogs is 26 inches, and of bitches 24 inches. Dogs usually vary from 25 to 27 inches and bitches from 23 to 25 inches. The mean average weight of adult dogs in fair condition is 90 pounds and of adult bitches 80 pounds. Dogs attain the weight of 110 pounds and bitches 100 pounds. Hounds of the maximum height and weight are to be preferred providing always that quality, proportion and balance combine.

Note

Male animals should have two apparently normal testicles fully descended into the scrotum.

BORZOI

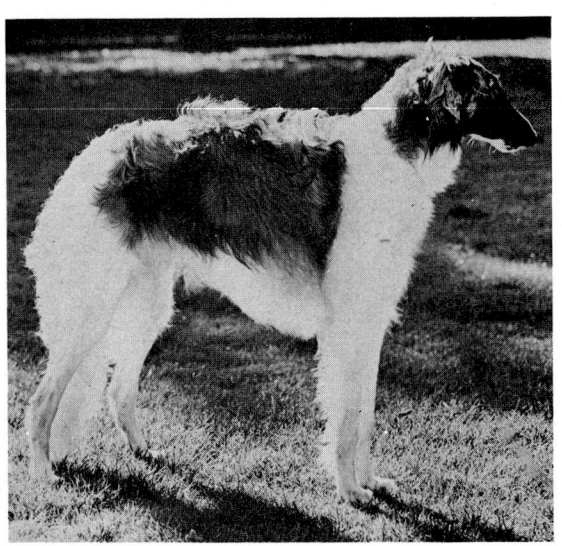

There are breeds of dog that hunt in packs and follow the quarry by sight rather than by scent, in fact in some countries the whole group is known as the Sight Hounds. These breeds are usually distinguishable by their length of leg and neck and their greater elegance. In some countries the courts preferred this type of hunting as it was more spectacular than scent hunting where the pack, the quarry and the kill were often out of sight of the followers. The coursing hounds provided a view from sighting to kill that had all the elements of speed, colour and tragedy that give spice and excitement to the sport.

The Emperors of Russia developed in the Borzoi the most glamorous of all the sight hounds, though owners of other running dogs will disagree. They are the tallest, the most slender and graceful and among the most colourful of the Levriers. Known at one time as the Russian Wolfhound, they were bred in packs with different characteristics, much as Foxhounds were bred elsewhere, but in the present day Borzoi these differences have disappeared. Some of the stories about the fierceness and untrustworthiness of the Borzoi that emanated from Russia in the early days did little to increase the popularity of the breed.

The first Borzoi specimens appeared in the show rings outside Russia in the late 19th century and created something of a sensation, particularly as shortly afterwards a number were presented by the then Czar to Queen Alexandra. As always when any royal household takes an interest in a breed, a degree of popular enthusiasm follows. This graceful hound quickly gained favour, and was soon seen at most of the major shows in both the United States of America and in Great Britain.

The Borzoi as we know it today might be claimed, by those who favour the Greyhound for coursing, to be too narrow in front to carry out the work for which it was originally intended, but that is one of the penalties paid by a breed when it becomes fashionable. The modern Borzoi can run, as it has proved when it has been tried on the running track and in pursuit of the live hare, but it would not compare for toughness with its ancestors that ran wild wolves to ground.

As a show dog this magnificent hound has few peers. Its long silky, often wavy or curly coat repays attention more than does that of other breeds, and as white often predominates, the total effect is most striking. Add to that the fact that it is often the tallest hound in the ring, and almost certainly one of the most graceful, and we have a dog that immediately commands attention both among dog people and the general public. The Borzoi is one of the most graceful of movers in the show ring, carrying himself with great pride, and using his hind legs with a slightly mincing gait.

A Borzoi is far from being the perfect house pet. It is true that one will look most decorative lying on a Turkish rug in front of an Adam fireplace, but the same dog would be completely out of place in a small modern flat. He needs a good deal of exercise to keep him fit, and that exercise must include a certain amount of free running and playing. Without this a Borzoi becomes unfit, probably overweight, and grows somewhat neurotic and unhappy.

OFFICIAL STANDARD

General appearance
A very graceful, aristocratic and elegant dog possessing courage, muscular power, and great speed.

Head and skull
Head, long and lean. Well filled in below the eyes. Measurement equal from the occiput to the inner corner of the eye and from the inner corner of the eye to tip of nose. Skull very slightly domed and narrow, stop not perceptible, inclining to Roman nose. Head fine so that the direction of the bones and principal veins can be clearly seen. Bitches heads should be finer than the dogs. Jaws long, deep and powerful; nose large and black, not pink or brown, nicely rounded, neither cornered nor sharp. Viewed from above the skull should look narrow, converging very gradually to tip of nose.

Eyes
Dark, intelligent, alert and keen. Almond shaped, set obliquely, placed well back but not too far apart. Eye rims dark. Eyes should not be light, round or staring.

Ears
Small and fine in quality; not too far apart. They should be active and responsive; when alert can be erect; when in repose nearly touching at the occiput.

Mouth
Teeth even, neither pig-jawed nor undershot.

Neck
Clean, slightly arched; reasonably long; powerful. Well set on, free from throatiness. Flat at the sides, not round.

Forequarters
Shoulders clean, sloping well back, fine at withers, free from lumpiness. Forelegs, lean and straight. Seen from the front, narrow like blades; from the side, wide at shoulder narrowing down to foot; elbows neither turned in nor out, pasterns strong, flexible and springy.

Body
Chest, great depth of brisket, rather narrow. Ribs well sprung and flexible; neither flat sided nor barrel-shaped; very deep giving heart room and lung play, especially in the case of mature males. (It is from depth of chest rather than breadth that the Borzoi derives its heart room and lung play.) Back, rising in a graceful arch from as near the shoulder as possible with a well balanced fall-away. The arch to be more marked in dogs than bitches. Rather bony, muscular and free from any cavity. Muscles, highly developed and well distributed.

Hindquarters
Loins, broad and very powerful, with plenty of muscular development. Quarters should be wider than shoulders, ensuring stability of stance. Thighs long, well developed with good second thigh. Hind-legs, long, muscular, stifles well bent, hocks broad, clean and well let down.

Feet
Front feet rather long, toes close together; well arched, never flat, neither turning in nor out. Hind feet hare-like, i.e., longer and less arched.

Tail
Long, rather low set. Well feathered, carried low, not gaily. In action may be used as rudder but not rising above level of back. From the level of the hocks may be sickle shaped but not ringed.

Coat
Long and silky (never woolly), or flat, or wavy, or rather curly. Short and smooth on head, ears and front legs; on the neck the frill profuse and rather curly; forelegs and chest well feathered; on hind-quarters and tail, long and profuse feathering.

Weight and size
Height at shoulder; Dogs from 29 inches upwards. Bitches from 27 inches upwards.

Note
Male animals should have two apparently normal testicles fully descended into the scrotum.

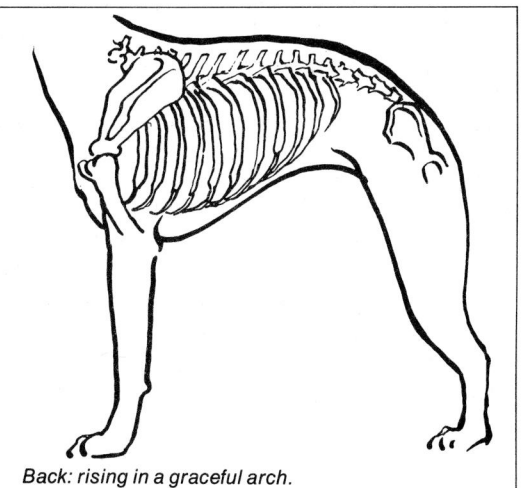

Back: rising in a graceful arch.

AKC VARIATION TO STANDARD
Mouth: missing teeth should be penalised. *Body:* ribs only slightly sprung. *Weight and size:* dogs 75 to 105 pounds; bitches 15 to 20 pounds less. Dogs 28 inches; bitches 26 inches. Dogs and bitches below respective limits should be penalised.

LONG-HAIRED DACHSHUND

There are almost as many styles of hunting with dogs as there are nations that hunt. Sport with dogs varies from laying a pack of hounds on a line to hunt in unison, to chasing one animal with one dog, and from coursing an antelope across the plains, to trying to catch rats under someone's garden shed. For every different form of the hunt, a different dog is needed. The dog that can catch a deer has legs that are too long to allow it to go underground, and a dog that has been built to travel slowly across the fields is incapable of catching a hare.

The forests of Germany have for centuries been the haunt of badgers and foxes, and as the country is completely unsuitable for running these animals down on horseback, some other form of control is needed. The sport of hunting them down to their lairs, sending in dogs to pin them there or pull them out and destroy them, or even digging them out was devised for this purpose. A small, short legged dog with great spirit, the ability to fight in very confined spaces, and the lung room to allow it to breathe under extremely difficult conditions was needed.

The small dog that German sportsmen developed for the purpose was called the Teckel, and it is from this animal that the six varieties of Dachshund that we now know have descended. The original dog was almost certainly the short-coated or smooth variety, and for many years it was this dog that was the most popular; but by careful introduction of other breeds, three varieties of coat and two sizes of each have been developed. The basic Teckel was a shorter smooth coated dog with longer legs than are now fashionable, and it is probable that Spaniel blood was introduced

to give the long coat, and selective breeding has produced the shorter legs and longer bodies that are now seen in our show dogs.

The Longhaired Dachshund is certainly the most glamorous of the family. Often red in colour, he has something of the appearance of a miniature Irish Setter, as he has the same sort of glow on his long silky coat, and his well developed fringes and tail hair give him similar visual appeal. To those who admire him he has lost something of the grotesque character seen in others of the family, whose extremely short legs and long body have a disproportion that many people find very strange, especially those who have not experienced the charm of these little dogs.

As a show dog the Longhaired Dachshund is at the bottom of the poll compared with the remainder of the family, fewer of them being registered and shown that most of the others with the exception perhaps of the Wirehaired variety. This is surprising as some of those that have been shown achieved great success in the hands of enthusiasts and won at major shows.

These little dogs vary tremendously in temperament between one coat or one size and the other, which gives credence to the suggestion that the variations have been brought about by the introduction of blood from other breeds. The Longhaired Dachshund is on the whole less bold, and rather more reserved than the others, though this rarely reaches a stage of nervousness or fear. They are playful enough among friends, and very good with one another and with other dogs, though they are somewhat diffident with strangers and strange animals. There are few breeds that make better housedogs than the Dachshunds, and the Longhaired is no exception. He is a good guard, very territorially minded, makes defensive sounds more in keeping with a much bigger dog, and will defend his own property and family as well as almost any other breed. He is moreover a dog that needs only moderate exercise, and does not have a large appetite which makes him very suitable for modern living conditions.

OFFICIAL STANDARD

Characteristics

The long-haired Dachshund is an old, fixed sub-variety of the 'Teckel', and its history extends back to the beginning of Teckel breeding. The breed is full of character, quick in attack and defence, faithful when properly brought up and very obedient. All the senses are well developed. It has the reputation of being extraordinarily intelligent and easy to train. Its build and temperament fit it to hunt quarry both above and below ground; its eagerness, keen sight and hearing and its sonorous bark make it especially suitable for tracking. In these respects it compares very favourably with any other variety. The thick, soft hair protects it against thorns, enables it to endure both cold and heat and is rain-proof. It is especially suited to water work. In following a trail its highly developed sense of smell stands it in good stead. It is easily trained to retrieve. The long-haired Dachshund can therefore be used in many different ways by the sportsman.

General appearance

Form, colour, size and character similar in all respects to those of the smooth Dachshund, except for the long, soft hair. The form is compact, short-legged and long, but sinewy and well muscled, with bold and defiant head carriage, and intelligent expression. In spite of the shortness of the legs the body should be neither too plump nor so slender as to have a weasel-like appearance. Height at shoulder should be half the length of the body measured

Height: half length of body.

from the breast bone to the set-on of the tail, and the girth of the chest double the height at the shoulder. The length from the tip of the nose to the eyes should be equal to the length from the eyes to the base of the skull. The tail should not touch the ground when at rest, neither should the ears (i.e., the leather) extend beyond the nose when pulled to the front.

Head and skull

Long and conical when seen from above, and in profile, sharp and finely modelled. Skull neither too broad nor too narrow, only slightly arched, without prominent stop. Foreface long and narrow, finely modelled. Lips should be tightly drawn, well covering the lower jaw, neither too heavy nor too sharply cut away, the corners of the mouth slightly marked.

Head: long and conical.

Eyes

Medium in size, oval, set obliquely, clear, expressive and dark in colour.

Ears

Broad and placed, relatively well back, high and well set on lying close to the cheeks, broad and long, nicely feathered and very mobile.

Mouth

Wide, extending back to behind the eyes, furnished with strong teeth which should fit into one another exactly, the inner side of the upper incisors closing on the outer side of the under ones.

Neck

Sufficiently long, muscular, showing no dewlap, slightly arched at the nape, running gracefully into the shoulders, carried well up and forward.

Breast bone: prominent.

Forequarters

Muscular, with deep chest. Shoulders long and broad, set

obliquely, lying firmly on well developed ribs. Muscles hard and plastic. Breast bone prominent, extending so far downward as to show depressions on both sides. Upper arm the same length as the shoulder blade, jointed at right angles to the shoulder, well boned and muscled, set on close to the ribs but moving freely as far as the shoulder blade. Lower arm comparatively short, inclined slightly inwards, solid and well muscled.

Body
Long and well muscled, the back showing oblique shoulders and short and strong pelvic region. Ribs very oval, deep between the fore-legs and extending far back. Loin short, strong and broad. The line of the back only slightly depressed over the shoulders and slightly arched over the loin, with the outline of the belly moderately tucked up.

Hindquarters
Rump round, full, broad, with muscles well modelled and plastic. Pelvis bone not too short, broad, strongly developed and set obliquely. Thigh bone strong, of good length and jointed to the pelvis at right angles. Second thigh short, set at right angles to the upper thigh, well muscled. Hocks set wide apart, strongly bent and, seen from behind, the legs should be straight.

Feet
Broad and large, straight or turned slightly outwards; the hind feet smaller and narrower than the fore. Toes close together and with a distinct arch to each toe. Nails strong. The dog must stand equally on all parts of the foot.

Tail
Set on fairly high, not too long, tapering and without too marked a curve. Not carried too high. Fully feathered.

Tail: set on fairly high, fully feathered.

Coat
Soft and straight or slightly waved, of shining colour. Longer under the neck, the underparts of the body and, particularly, on the ears, behind the legs, where it should develop into abundant feathering, and reach the greatest length on the tail, where it should form a flag. The feathering should extend to the outsides of the ears, where short hair is not desired. Too heavy a coat gives an appearance of undue plumpness and hides the outline. The coat should resemble that of an Irish Setter, giving the dog an appearance of elegance. Too much hair on the feet is ugly and useless.

Colour
Black and tan, dark brown with lighter shadings, dark red, light red, dappled, tiger-marked or brindle. In black and tan, red and dappled dogs the nose and nails should be black, in chocolate they are often brown.

Weight and size
As a rule Long-haired Dachshunds are classified as follows: middle weight up to 17 pounds for bitches and 18 pounds for dogs. Heavy weight over 17 pounds for bitches and over 18 pounds for dogs. The middle-weights are best suited for badger and fox drawing and the heavy-weights for tracking, hunting larger animals and for water work. The last named are also very useful for retrieving rabbits and water fowl.

Note
Male animals should have two apparently normal testicles fully descended into the scrotum.

AKC VARIATION TO STANDARD
The Dachshund is granted championship status by the AKC as one dog with three varieties. Miniature dachshunds are bred in all three coats in the US. They have not been given separate classification by the AKC but are a division of the Open Class for 'under 10 pounds and 12 months old or over'.

Forequarters: forearm—tightly stretched tendons on inside and at back. *Tail:* carried gracefully in prolongation of spine; hair attains here its greatest length and forms a flag. *Colour: one-coloured:* this group includes red (often called tan); red-with-black (heavily sabled) is formally classed as red; red-yellow, yellow, and brindle, with or without a shading of interspersed black hairs. A clean colour is preferable; red is to be considered more desirable than red-yellow or yellow. Dogs strongly shaded with interspersed black hairs belong to this class, and not to other colour groups. A small white spot is admissible, but not desirable. *Two-coloured:* these comprise deep black, chocolate, grey (blue), and white; each with tan markings over eyes, on sides of jaw and underlip, on inner edge of ear, front, breast, inside and behind front legs, on paws and around anus, and from there to about $\frac{1}{3}$ to $\frac{1}{2}$ of length of tail on under side. The most common two coloured is usually called black-and-tan. A small white spot admissible but not desirable. Absence, undue prominence or extreme lightness of tan markings is undesirable. Nose—for grey or white dogs, grey or even flesh colour, but the last named is not desirable in the case of white dogs where black nose and nails are to be preferred. *Dappled:* the colour of the dappled is a clear brownish or greyish colour, or even a white ground, with dark irregular patches of dark-grey, brown, red-yellow or black (large areas of one colour are desirable). Neither light nor dark colour should predominate.

SMOOTH-HAIRED DACHSHUND

The question of which variety of the Dachshund is the oldest and the original type is a matter of some discussion wherever Dachshund people get together. Each will claim the distinction for his own particular favourite, and there is some evidence to support all claims. In Germany, however, which is the native country of the breed, there is no doubt which is the most popular variety. The dogs most commonly seen on the streets of Germany are the Boxer, the German Shepherd Dog, the Doberman Pinscher and the Dachshund, and by far the largest proportion of these Smooth-haired Dachshunds.

The Dachshund, and at that time this meant the Smooth-haired Dachshund became known outside Germany around the middle of the 19th century and soon attracted attention because of his somewhat quaint conformation and his sporting instincts. At that time other countries were accustomed to a dog of what were considered to be more 'normal' proportions. The Terriers and the Gundogs, and even the Toy Dogs were more or less square dogs. To other than German eyes the long bodied Dachshund appeared to be a very strange beast indeed. Nevertheless he soon became quite popular and his numbers increased

NATIONAL GROUPING		
	Name	Number
KC(GB)	Hound	I
AKC	Hounds	II
FCI	Dachshunds	4

as he won his way into the hearts of the dog-loving public of other countries.

During the First World War the Dachshund's popularity went into a decline as anti-German feeling grew, and this most attractive little dog was denigrated in cartoons, stories and even by catcalls in the streets. After the war, the Dachshund returned to popularity on a scale even greater than before, and by the 1950's he was among the most popular dogs in the world.

The Smooth-haired Dachshund has many advantages over other dogs. In the first place he combines the qualities of a hunting dog with those of a family pet and favourite. He is sporting and affectionate, cheerful and friendly yet very protective, and makes a magnificent house guard. Being a small dog he is easily housed and fed, though he is somewhat greedy as a general rule, and with little exercise and feeding that is too rich, he can rapidly become overweight and suffer the spine trouble that affects the breed, and this variety particularly. Properly kept, fed and exercised he remains a very fit, active and sporting dog living to a good age in perfect health.

The show rings of the world have been enriched by the addition of the Dachshund, and of the Smooth-haired particularly, as he is an extremely graceful dog in spite of his lack of height, with a long neck, sweeping lines and proud carriage. His coat too helps, as the smooth quality repays attention, and this little dog can literally be polished to enter the ring. He needs no lotions or special preparations to give his coat this glow, if he is healthy, all that is needed is a good rubbing with a hound glove and he will shine like satin. His colours are attractive, the self-reds and black and tans particularly, and a ring full of Dachshunds in the sunshine is a delightful sight.

His temperament is most attractive. He becomes attached to one person or family very quickly, remains faithful and protective to the members of the family, and succeeds in being affectionate without fawning. Yet all the time he retains much of the instinct of a sporting dog and will enjoy a rabbit chase over the fields and through the thickest undergrowth.

OFFICIAL STANDARD

Characteristics
First and foremost a sporting dog, the Smooth Dachshund is remarkably versatile, being equally adaptable as a house pet; his smooth, close coat is impervious to rain and mud. His temperament and acute intelligence make him the ideal companion for town or country. In the field of sport he is unequalled, combining the scenting powers of a Foxhound with unflinching courage, and will go to ground to fox, otter or badger.

General appearance
Long and low, but with compact and well-muscled body, not crippled, cloddy, or clumsy, with bold defiant carriage of head and intelligent expression.

Head and skull
Long and appearing conical when seen from above, and, from a side view tapering to the point of the muzzle. Stop not pronounced, skull should be slightly arched in profile, appearing neither too broad nor too narrow. Jaw neither too square nor snipy but strong, the lips lightly stretched fairly covering the lower jaw.

Stop: not pronounced.

Eyes
Medium in size, oval, and set obliquely. Dark in colour, except in the case of chocolates, in which they may be lighter; in dapples one or both wall eyes are permissible.

Ears
Broad, of moderate length, and well rounded (not narrow, pointed or folded), relatively well back, high and well set on, lying close to the cheek, very mobile as in all intelligent dogs; when at attention the back of the ear directed forward and outward.

Ears: broad, moderate length.

Mouth
Teeth must be strongly developed. The powerful canine teeth must fit closely. The correct bite is a scissors bite, any deviation being a fault.

Neck
Sufficiently long, muscular, clean, no dewlap, slightly arched in the nape, running in graceful lines into the shoulders, carried well up and forward.

Forequarters
Shoulder blades long, broad and set on sloping, lying firmly on fully-developed ribs, muscles hard and plastic. Chest very oval, with ample room for the heart and lungs, deep and with ribs well sprung out towards the loins, breast-bone very prominent. The front legs should, when viewed from one side, cover the lowest point of the breast-line. Forelegs very short and in proportion to size strong in bone. Upper arm of equal length with, and at right angles to, the shoulder blade; elbows lying close to ribs, but moving freely up to shoulder blades. Lower arm short as compared with other animals, slightly inclined inwards (crook), seen in profile moderately straight; not bending forward or knuckling over (which indicates unsoundness).

Body

Long and muscular, the line of back slightly depressed at shoulders and slightly arched over the loin, which should be short and strong; outline of belly moderately tucked up. What is required is a general levelness of the back, the hindquarters (the rump) not being higher than the shoulders.

Hindquarters

Rump round, full, broad; muscles hard and plastic; hip bone or pelvic bone not too short, broad and strongly developed, set moderately sloping, thigh bones strong, of good length, and joined to pelvis at right-angles; lower thighs short in comparison with other animals; hocks well developed and seen from behind the legs should be straight (not cow-hocked). The dog should not appear higher at the quarters than at shoulders.

Feet

The front feet should be full, broad and close-knit, and straight or very slightly turned outwards, the hind feet smaller and narrower. The toes must be close together with a decided arch to each toe, with strong regularly placed nails and firm pads. The dog must stand true, i.e., equally on all parts of the foot.

Tail

Set on fairly high, strong and tapering, but not too long and not too curved or carried too high.

Coat

Short, dense and smooth, but strong. The hair on the underside of the tail coarse in texture; skin loose and supple, but fitting the dog closely all over, without much wrinkle.

Colour

Any colour other than white (except a white spot on breast). Nose and nails should be black. In red dogs a red nose is permissible but not desirable. In chocolate and dapples the nose may be brown or flesh-coloured. In dapples large spots of colour are undesirable, and the dog should be evenly dappled all over.

Lower arm: short, slightly inclined inwards.

Weight and size

Dogs should not exceed 25 pounds. Bitches should not exceed 23 pounds.

Faults

In general appearance weak or deformed, too high or too low to the ground; ears set on too high or too low, eyes too prominent; muzzle too short or pinched, either undershot or overshot; forelegs too crooked; hare or terrier feet, or flat spread toes (flat-footed); out at elbows; body too much dip behind the shoulders; loins weak or too arched; chest too flat or too short; hindquarters weak or cow-hocked, quarters higher than the shoulders.

Note

Male animals should have two apparently normal testicles fully descended into the scrotum.

Hindquarters: pelvis and thighbone at right angles.

AKC VARIATION TO STANDARD
Tail: brush tail is a fault.

WIRE-HAIRED DACHSHUND

NATIONAL GROUPING		
	Name	Number
KC(GB)	Hound	I
AKC	Hounds	II
FCI	Dachshunds	4

At first sight there seemed to be no need for yet another variety of Dachshund, the smooth coated and the long coated varieties were already in existence, and in those countries outside Germany in two sizes. But they had snags. The smooth coated variety, which is presumed by many to be the earliest form, has a short dense and smooth coat. It is supposed at the same time to be strong, but proved insufficient protection when hunting through gorse and brambles. The longhaired variety on the other hand, whilst having more protection, did tend to lose coat, as do most of the long coated hunting dogs, when hunted through very rough going. It was felt that an even stronger coated dog was needed, with a harsh outer coat as protection from damage, and a dense softer undercoat to keep out the weather. The heavy beard and longer coat around the head came as a bonus.

The first wirehaired versions appeared in Germany towards the end of the 19th century, and were almost certainly the result of crossing the smooth coated variety with one or other of the wirehaired dogs of Germany, probably the Schnauzer. This produced the coat, but increased the leg length so that further crosses were needed to bring this back down again without destroying the quality of the coat. The breed used could well have been the Czesky Terrier from Bohemia, itself a cross between Sealyham and Scottish Terriers, or the Dandie Dinmont. The variety was not known outside Germany until well into this century, but then it soon became quite popular through its ability to work, combined with its temperament which is very like that of the best of the hounds.

It is a keen little dog with an inbuilt desire to hunt, having good scenting powers, a certain obstinacy which gives it persistence, and great courage and stamina. It is a hardy dog, does not suffer from some of the ailments associated with other small varieties,

and is a willing and obedient companion.

As a show dog he has never quite achieved the popularity of the other varieties, largely perhaps because of the variation in coat quality that occurred until recent years. The variety has always been fairly low down in the registration figures, but this may well change, as the type is now more fixed, and the interbreeding that has gone on for a great number of years has now virtually ceased with the result that the overall appearance of the variety is more regular. One or two quite notable dogs that have won the highest honours,

particularly in Britain, have kept interest in the dog alive.

As a house dog there can hardly be any breed of dog more attractive. He is small, compact, takes up very little space and is easy to feed. He is generally rather quiet and unobtrusive about the house. He has too a slightly quizzical expression which makes him attractive to those who like something a little different. He is, moreover, quick and alert as are many of the hounds, and makes an excellent guard and watchdog.

OFFICIAL STANDARD

Characteristics

The Dachshund should be clever, lively, courageous to the point of rashness, sagacious and obedient. He is especially suited for going to ground because of his low build, very strong forequarters and forelegs, long, strong jaw and the immense power of his bite and hold. His loose skin enables him to manoeuvre with ease for attack or defence. His deep, loud bay indicates his position to those working him. He is also well equipped for field work on account of his good nose and sound construction. He can force his way through cover so dense that it would stop even the smallest gundog. Because of his nose, voice, good sight and perseverance he makes a good tracking dog.

General appearance

Low to ground, short legged, the body long but compact and well muscled. The head should be carried boldly and the expression be very intelligent. Despite his short legs, compared with the length of his body, he must not be awkward, cramped, crippled or lacking in substance.

Jaws: strong and long.

Head and skull

Looked at from above or from the side, the head should taper uniformly to the tip of the nose and be clean cut. The skull is only slightly arched, being neither too broad nor too narrow and slopes gradually, without marked stop, to a finely formed, slightly arched muzzle, the nasal bones and cartilage (Septum) being long and narrow. The ridges of the frontal bones are well developed giving prominence to the nerve bosses over the eyes. Jaw has extremely strong bones, is very long and opens very wide. It should not be too square nor yet snipy. The lips are lightly stretched, the corners just marked and the upper lip covers the lower jaw neatly.

Eyes

Oval, medium in size, set obliquely, lustrous and expressive. The colour should be dark except in the case of chocolates, when they may be lighter, and of dapples, when one or both wall eyes are allowed.

Ears: when pulled forward reach halfway between eyes and nose.

Ears

Broad and rounded, the front edge touching the cheek. They are relatively well back and high and are well set on. The length is such that when the ears are pulled forward they reach a point approximately half-way between the eyes and the tip of the nose.

Mouth

The powerful canine teeth fit closely. The correct bite is a scissor bite, any deviation being a fault.

Neck

Sufficiently long, muscular, clean cut, not showing any dewlap, slightly arched in the nape, extending in a graceful line into the shoulders and carried erect.

Forequarters

The shoulder blades are long, broad and placed firmly and obliquely upon a very robust rib cage. The upper arm is the same length as the shoulder blade, set at right angles to it and, like the shoulder blade, is very strong and covered with hard but supple muscles. The upper arm lies close to the ribs but is able to move freely. The forearm is comparatively short, inclined slightly inwards to form the crook, when seen in profile is moderately straight and must not bend forward or knuckle over, a

Upper arm: same length as shoulder blade, at right angles to it.

state which indicates unsoundness. A correctly placed front leg covers the lowest point of the breast bone.

Body

The breast bone is strong and prominent enough to show a dimple at each side. Looked at from the front the thorax should be very oval allowing ample room for the heart and lungs; seen from the side it should intersect the forearm just above the wrist. The top line, very slightly depressed at the shoulders and slightly arched over the loin, is parallel to the ground. The whole trunk should be long, well ribbed up and underneath should merge gradually into the line of a moderately tucked up belly. The rump is full, round and wide with strong and pliant muscles.

Upper thigh: good length. Lower thigh: short.

Hindquarters

The pelvis is strong, set obliquely and not too short. The upper thigh, set at right angles to the pelvis, is strong and of good length, the lower thigh is short, set at right angles to the upper thigh and is well muscled. The hocks are well developed. The legs when seen from behind, are set well apart, straight and parallel to one another.

Feet

The front feet are full, broad in front, straight or turned just a trifle outwards. The four toes forming the foot are compact, well arched and have tough pads. The fifth toe (dewclaw) is usually left on. The nails are strong and short. The dog must stand true and equally on all parts of the foot. The hind feet are smaller and narrower than the forefeet and placed straight. There should be no dewclaw. In all other respects the hind feet and toes are similar to the forefeet and toes.

Tail

Continues line of the spine; is but slightly curved, must not be carried too gaily or reach the ground when at rest.

Coat

With the exception of the jaw, eyebrows and ears, the whole body is covered with a completely even, short, harsh coat and an undercoat. There should be a beard on the chin. The eyebrows are bushy. The hair on the ears is almost smooth.

Colour

All colours are allowed but a white patch on the chest, though not a fault, is not desirable. Except in the case of chocolates, when it may be brown or flesh-coloured, the nose should be black.

Weight and size

It is recommended that dogs should weigh from 20 to 22 pounds and bitches from 18 to 20 pounds.

Faults

Primary faults: an overshot or undershot jaw. Out at elbow. Knuckling over. Toes turned inwards. Splayed feet. Cow hocks. A bad coat. *Secondary faults:* very light eyes. A narrow chest. Breast bone insufficiently prominent. A dip behind the shoulders. A hollow back. A roach back. Rump higher than withers. Weak loins. Excessively drawn up flanks. Bad angulation of forequarters or hindquarters. Legs too long, too close in front, or behind. Toes turned too much outwards. Bowed hind legs. A sluggish, clumsy or waddling gait. Poor muscle. Too long a tail. *Minor faults:* ears too high, too low, sticking out, folded or narrow. Too marked a stop. Head too wide, too narrow or too short. Too pointed or too weak a jaw. Short neck or swan neck. Dewlaps. Goggle eyes. Too short a tail.

Faulty outline: roach back, weak loins, excessively drawn up flanks.

Note

Male animals should have two apparently normal testicles fully descended into the scrotum.

AKC VARIATION TO STANDARD

Tail: robust, as thickly haired as possible, gradually coming to a point, without tuft.

MINIATURE LONG-HAIRED DACHSHUND

NATIONAL GROUPING		
	Name	Number
KC(GB)	Hound	I
AKC	Hounds	II
FCI	Dachshunds	4

Miniaturisation by selective breeding has always been one of man's ambitions, whether he happens to be interested in roses, horses, or dogs, and in many breeds of dog there is a miniature version that closely follows in type and detail the larger relation. Some claim that the standard Longhaired Dachshund developed from the oldest form of the Teckel. Certainly its history parallels that of the smooth variety from early days, and it could well be that the development was a natural division rather than an artificial one, as in many breeds a long coat is found as a sub-variety of the basic animal.

The Miniature Longhaired Dachshund has most of the qualities of the larger variety and it is reasonable to assume that he is just a smaller version of the same dog. In Germany, the country of origin of the Dachshund, division by size has always been accepted in the show ring; and in the field the smaller dogs have often been preferred.

Judging from old photographs, the long coat of some years ago had little of the silky glowing quality that we know today. It was often broken, and rough rather than long, and these little dogs looked rather ragged

as a result. In recent years, by carefully selecting the stock from which future generations were bred, the coat has become a particular feature of the variety, and the dogs are now really attractive. In Germany three colour types were encouraged, the One Coloured, the Two Coloured which was a mixture of any one of two or three colours and tan, and the Dappled which is a splashing of dark irregular spots of grey, brown, tan or black on a background of silvery grey.

The Miniature Longhaired Dachshund is one of the most popular of the six varieties of the breed, it is easily transported, very rewarding to prepare for exhibition and usually gives a very sparkling performance in the ring. He is a sharp little dog, positive in his actions, moves with a certain amount of pride, and can be trained easily to stand perfectly still. He is always a great favourite with those at the ringside, and in competition with the other varieties often carries off the major awards.

The character of the breed is that of a big dog in a small compass, the standard allows a maximum weight of not more than eleven pounds. He is a proud animal, fully aware of the fact that he is much admired, and can dominate a household if he is given the opportunity. With human beings, and particularly with children he is well-mannered and very friendly, which leads to one of his problems. The Miniature Longhaired Dachshund is a sporting dog, a hunter and a hound, but his size and his behaviour often lead people to treat him as a toy.

OFFICIAL STANDARD

Characteristics
The Miniature Dachshund should be gay, alert, bold and highly intelligent. Despite its small size it should be strong, extremely active, hardy and game. Movement should be free and gay. Both fore and hind feet should move straight forward without plaiting or crossing in front and free from any tendency to throw out the hind feet sideways.

General appearance
In conformation the Miniature Dachshund should be in all respects similar to the Dachshund of standard size.

It should be compact, short-legged and long in body, well muscled and strong, with bold and intelligent expression. The body should be neither so plump as to give an impression of cobbiness, nor so slender as to impart a weasel-like appearance. Height at shoulder should be half the length of the body measured from the breast bone to the base of the tail, and the girth of the chest double the height at the shoulder. The length from the tip of the nose to the eyes should equal the length from eyes to base of skull.

Head and skull
Long and conical when seen from above, sharp in profile and finely modelled. Skull neither too broad nor too

narrow, only slightly arched and without prominent stop. Foreface long and narrow, finely modelled. The lips should be tightly drawn but well covering the lower jaw, neither heavy nor too sharply cut away. The corners of the mouth slightly marked.

Eyes

Of medium size, neither prominent nor too deeply set, oval in shape placed obliquely. They should be clear and expressive and dark in colour except in dapples and chocolates, in which wall or light eyes are permissible.

Ears

Broad and placed relatively well back, high and well set on, lying close to the cheeks and very mobile. The leather of the ears when pulled to the front should not extend beyond the tip of the nose.

Mouth

Wide, extending back to behind the eyes. Teeth sound and strong, the inner side of the upper incisors closing on the outer side of the under ones.

Neck

Long and muscular, showing no dewlap, slightly arched at the nape, running cleanly into the shoulders, carried well up, giving the dog an alert, defiant appearance.

Forequarters

Muscular, with deep chest. Shoulder blades should be long and broad, set obliquely and lying firmly on well-developed ribs. The breast bone should be prominent, extending so far forward as to show depressions on both sides. Upper arm equal in length to the shoulder blade, which it should join at an angle of 90 degrees, well boned and muscled, set on close to the ribs but moving freely. Lower arm short, inclined slightly inwards, well boned and free from wrinkle.

Body

Long and well muscled with oblique shoulders and short strong pelvic region. Ribs well-sprung and extending far back. Chest oval, well let down between the forelegs, with the deepest point of the keel level with the wrist-joints. The line of the back level or only slightly depressed over the shoulders and slightly arched over the loin, with the belly moderately tucked up.

Hindquarters

Rump full, round and broad. Pelvis bone not too short, broad, strong and set obliquely. Thigh bone strong, of good length and jointed to the pelvis at an angle of 90 degrees. Second thighs short, set at right angles to the upper thigh and well muscled. Hocks well let down, set wide apart, strongly bent. Seen from behind the legs should be straight, with no tendency for the hocks to turn inwards or outwards.

Feet

Broad and large in proportion to the size of the dog, straight or turned only slightly outwards. The hind feet smaller than the fore. Toes close together and with each toe well

Legs: straight from behind (dotted line, incorrect cow-hocks).

arched. Nails strong. The dog must stand equally on all parts of the foot.

Tail

Set on fairly high, not too long, tapering and without too marked a curve. It should not be carried too high and never curled over the back.

Coat

The coat should be soft and straight or only slightly waved. It is longest under the neck, on the under-parts of the body and behind the legs, where it should form abundant feathering and on the tail where it should form a flag. The outside of the ears should also be well feathered. The coat should be flat, resembling that of an Irish Setter, and should not obscure the outline. Too much hair on the feet is not desired.

Colour

Any colour. No white is permissible except for a small spot on the breast and even this is undesirable. The nose should be black except in dapples and chocolates in which it may be flesh coloured or brown. In all cases the coat colour should be bright and clearly defined. In black and tans the tan should be rich and sharp. Dapples should be free from large unbroken patches, the dappling being evenly distributed over the whole body.

Weight and size

The ideal weight is 10 pounds and it is of the utmost importance that judges should not award a prize to any dog exceeding 11 pounds in weight. Other points being equal the smaller the better, but mere diminutiveness must never take precedence over general type and soundness. Any appearance of weediness or toyishness is to be avoided at all costs.

Faults

Round skull. Round or protruding eyes. Short ears. Shallow chest. Narrowness in front or behind. Short body. Long legs. Splayed feet. Cow hocks. Mouth under or overshot. Nervous or cringing demeanour.

Note

Male animals should have two apparently normal testicles fully descended into the scrotum.

MINIATURE SMOOTH-HAIRED DACHSHUND

NATIONAL GROUPING		
	Name	Number
KC(GB)	Hound	I
AKC	Hounds	II
FCI	Dachshunds	4

The Teckel was used for several different types of hunting in Germany. When it left that country it was given the name Dachshund which implied that it hunted badgers. However, the Teckel was used for chasing other game, and was even sometimes used in packs as a scent dog very much as a Foxhound. He was used on fox and hare, though attacking and dealing with the badger is supposed to have been his primary purpose in life. To this day a Teckel owner in Germany will proudly show photographs of the aftermath of such an underground hunt with the quarry laid out and the Teckels standing proudly by.

Originally the Dachshund was divided by weight in Germany, and the smallest weight, up to twelve pounds, was designated the Toy, which probably gives some clue to the fact that it was not intended that this very small dog should be used to badger. That is not to say that given the opportunity he would not. Even the smallest are very sporting and always ready to hunt anything that moves, especially anything that is covered in fur, even the neighbour's cat.

Outside Germany the Miniature Smoothhaired Dachshund has changed from the rather short heavily built little dog with large ribs and bowed legs, to something much more slender, with a longer neck and straighter legs. The German Teckel owner will rather scornfully say that he doubts very much if this type of dog would go to ground even to the rabbits for which he uses them. The original German version had to conform to a limited measurement round the chest rather than the weight by which we distinguish them, and probably originated by breeding from the small members of a litter from normal sized Dachshunds. Others were probably produced by introducing other breeds of smooth-coated toy dogs.

This particular variety has all the sporting qualities of other Dachshunds, but has additional attributes. He is very self-assured, is lively, gay and dominating, and he is built like a hound. He is very strong and hardy for his size, capable of great exertion for so small a dog, and is determined and persistent in the chase.

It is his air of self-importance which makes him such an excellent show dog. In the ring he is a proud little dog, carrying himself with the complete confidence that he can handle any situation that arises. The result is that the Miniature Smoothhaired Dachshund figures largely among the major awards at shows all over the world, and gains favour with ringsiders as well as with judges everywhere. This keeps him at the top of Dachshund registrations.

This popularity is not surprising and is not limited to the show world, as his temperament is most attractive. He is an affectionate little dog, quick and lively, intelligent and amusing in his antics, and always very sporting and ready for a game, which endears him to children. He is in addition very suited to modern life, fitting into the smallest flat, being easily groomed and fed, and needing only the sort of exercise that can be obtained in games round the garden.

OFFICIAL STANDARD

The Standard of the Dachshund (Miniature Smooth-haired) is identical with the Standard of the Dachshund (Miniature Long-haired) with the following exceptions:

Coat
In Smooths, short, dense and smooth, adequately covering all the parts of the body; coarsest on the under-side of the tail.

Weight and size
The ideal weight is 10 pounds and it is of the utmost importance that judges should not award a prize to any dog exceeding 11 pounds in weight. Other points being equal the smaller the better, but mere diminutiveness must never take precedence over general type and soundness. Any appearance of weediness or toyishness is to be avoided at all costs.

Faults
Woolly or curly coat.

MINIATURE WIRE-HAIRED DACHSHUND

It is probable that the smaller version of the Wire-haired Daschshund was in existence some time before the standard type. Germany divided the sizes somewhat differently from other countries and the early Rabbit Dachshund was probably produced in the wirehaired form for the reasons given in the history of the Wirehaired Dachshund, practical reasons which had nothing to do with appearance. Oddly enough, however, it was the last of the six varieties to be

NATIONAL GROUPING		
	Name	Number
KC(GB)	Hound	I
AKC	Hounds	II
FCI	Dachshunds	4

recognised in Britain, having been given championship status as recently as 1959.

OFFICIAL STANDARD

The standard of the Dachshund (Miniature Wire-haired) is identical with the standard of the Dachshund (Miniature Long-haired) with the following exceptions.

Coat
With the exception of the jaw, eyebrows and ears, the whole body is covered with a completely even, short, harsh coat and undercoat. There should be a beard on the chin. The eyebrows are bushy. The hair on the ears is almost smooth.

Weight and size
The ideal weight is 10 pounds and it is of the utmost importance that judges should not award a prize to any dog exceeding 11 pounds in weight. Other points being equal the smaller the better, but mere dimunitiveness must never take precedence over general type and soundness. Any appearance of weediness or toyishness is to be avoided at all costs.

DEERHOUND

The Greyhound in some form has existed as long as records have been kept, and probably longer. Although the name has become synonymous with the English Greyhound, it was used at one time to describe all the long-legged coursing dogs. In Scotland it evolved in a very special form, now known as the Deerhound, as it was for the purpose of hunting the indigenous deer of Scotland that the breed was developed. Dr. Caius wrote of the family that 'some are smooth skinned and some are curled, the bigger therefore are appointed to hunt the bigger beastes'. Apart from the Elk, there are few members of the deer family larger than the Red Deer of Scotland, and it needed a large, fast and very agile dog to hunt them. It is closely related to the Irish Wolfhound, and there is every likelihood that the two have common ancestors somewhere among the early large running dogs described by Dr. Caius.

The Deerhound has always been associated with the castles of Scotland, and the vision brought to mind by most people when discussing them is of a large marble fireplace with a roaring log fire, a Deerhound or even a couple of Hounds curled up in front of the blaze whilst the laird sips his dram to the music of bagpipes. This is not far from the truth, as at one time only gentry were allowed to own these hounds for fear that

the commoners might use them to poach his lordship's deer, as they undoubtedly would have done. Writers wrote of them and artists drew and painted them. The breed was a great favourite of Landseer's whose drawings and paintings of these dogs in the 19th century depict animals exactly like the ones that we have today.

Like so many of the game chasing dogs, the Deerhound has a dual personality, soft and even sentimental in his attachment to the family to which he belongs, yet an absolute killer when roused to the chase. He has the slightly mincing gait of the perfect running machine, with little of the striding out behind of the working dogs and with a somewhat delicate air. In full flight however he is a different creature, covering the ground with tremendous strides, almost leaps, and conveying his slender frame over rough territory at great speed.

The numbers of the breed are not high, as the Deerhound is a large dog needing a fair amount of food and is at his best on a large estate with acres of grass on which to exercise himself. The numbers have been growing steadily over recent years, however, largely because of the efforts of a few enthusiasts who have shown the breed fearlessly and kept it in front of the public. He is easily prepared for show, having the sort of coat that is natural and does not need a great deal of attention or trimming, and his behaviour in the ring is always gentlemanly.

Temperamentally the breed is most attractive, never boisterous, always obedient and what the running dog people call biddable. He is a lovely dog to own, attaching himself to one person and being extremely faithful. The Deerhound, like most of the running dogs is quiet and trustworthy, and centuries of domestication have developed a creature that enjoys human company and the comforts of the house.

OFFICIAL STANDARD

Head and skull
The head should be broadest at the ears, tapering slightly to the eyes, with the muzzle tapering more decidedly to the nose. The muzzle should be pointed but the lips level. The head should be long, the skull rather flat than round, with a very slight rise over the eyes, but with nothing approaching a stop. The skull should be coated with moderately long hair, which is softer than the rest of the coat. The nose should be black (though in some blue-fawns the colour is blue) and slightly aquiline. In the lighter coloured dogs a black muzzle is preferred. There should be a good moustache or rather silky hair, and a fair beard.

Eyes
The eyes should be dark; generally they are dark-brown or hazel. A very light eye is not liked. The eye is moderately full, with a soft look in repose, but a keen, far-away look when the dog is roused. The rims of the eyelids should be black.

Ears
The ears should be set on high, and, in repose, folded back like the Greyhound's, though raised above the head

Ears: raised above head in excitement.

in excitement without losing the fold, and even in some cases semi-erect. A prick ear is bad. A big thick ear hanging flat to the head, or heavily coated with long hair, is the worst of faults. The ear should be soft, glossy, and like a mouse's coat to the touch, and the smaller it is the better. It should have no long coat or long fringe, but there is often a silky silvery coat on the body of the ear and the tip. Whatever the general colour, the ears should be black or dark-coloured.

Mouth
Teeth level.

Neck
The neck should be long; that is, of the length that befits the Greyhound character of the dog. An over-long neck is not necessary or desirable, for the dog is not required to stoop to his work like a Greyhound, and it must be remembered that the mane, which every good specimen should have, detracts from the apparent length of neck. Moreover, a Deerhound requires a very strong neck to hold a stag. The nape of the neck should be very prominent where the head is set on, and the throat should be clean cut at the angle and prominent.

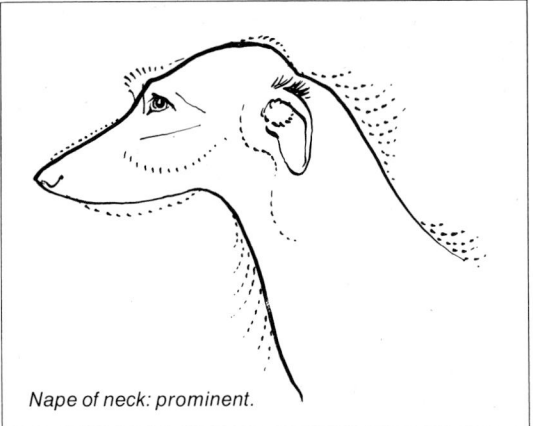

Nape of neck: prominent.

Forequarters
The shoulders should be well sloped, the blade well back and not too much width between them. Loaded and straight shoulders are very bad faults. The forelegs should be straight, broad and flat, a good broad forearm and elbow being desirable.

Body
The body and general formation is that of a Greyhound of larger size and bone. Chest deep rather than broad, but not too narrow and flat-sided. The loin well arched and drooping to the tail. A straight back is not desirable, this formation being unsuitable for going uphill, and very unsightly.

Hindquarters
Drooping, and as broad and powerful as possible, the hips being set wide apart. The hind legs should be well bent at the stifle, with great length from the hip to the hock, which should be broad and flat.

Formation of a greyhound.

Feet
Should be close and compact, with well arranged toes. Nails strong.

Tail
Should be long, thick at the root, tapering, and reaching to within about $1\frac{1}{2}$ inches of the ground. When the dog is still, dropped perfectly straight down, or curved. When in motion it should be curved when excited, in no case to be lifted out of the line of the back. It should be well-covered with hair; on the inside, thick and wiry; on the underside longer, and towards the end a slight fringe is not objectionable. A curl or ring tail is very undesirable.

Tail: when still hanging straight, when moving curved, never over back.

Coat
The hair on the body, neck and quarters should be harsh and wiry, and about three of four inches long; that on the head, breast and belly is much softer. There should be a slight hairy fringe on the inside of the fore and hind legs, but nothing approaching the 'feather' of a Collie. The Deerhound should be a shaggy dog, but not over-coated. A woolly coat is bad. Some good strains have a mixture of silky coat with the hard, which is preferable to a woolly coat; but the proper coat is a thick, close-lying, ragged coat, harsh or crisp to the touch.

Colour
Colour is much a matter of fancy. But there is no manner of doubt that the dark blue-grey is the most preferred because quality tends to follow this colour. Next comes the darker and lighter greys or brindles, the darkest being generally preferred. Yellow and sandy-red or red-fawn, especially with black points, i.e., ears and muzzles, are also in equal estimation, this being the colour of the oldest-known strains, the McNeil and Cheethill Menzies. White is condemned by all the old authorities, but a white chest and white toes, occurring as they do in a great many of the darkest-coloured dogs, are not so greatly objected to, but the less the better, as the Deerhound is a self-coloured dog. A white blaze on the head, or a white collar should be heavily penalised. In other cases, though passable, yet an attempt should be made to get rid of white markings. The less white the better, but a slight white tip to the stern occurs in the best strains.

Weight and size
Should be from 85 to 105 pounds in dogs and from 65 to 80 pounds in bitches. Height of dogs should not be less than 30 inches and bitches 28 inches at the shoulder, respectively.

Faults
Thick ear hanging flat to the head or heavily coated with long hair. Curl or ring tail. Light eye. Straight back. Cow hocks, weak pasterns, straight stifles, splay feet, woolly coat, loaded and straight shoulders, white markings.

Note
Male animals should have two apparently normal testicles fully descended into the scrotum.

AKC VARIATION TO STANDARD
Classified as the Scottish Deerhound by the AKC.
Weight: dogs 85 to 110 pounds; bitches 75 to 95 pounds.
Disqualification: white blaze on head or a white collar.

ELKHOUND

NATIONAL GROUPING		
	Name	Number
KC(GB)	Hound	I
AKC	Hounds	II
FCI	Large Hounds	5

The native deer of Scandinavia is the Elk, a very large and powerful creature indeed, with a menacing head of horns and a weight approaching a thousand pounds. There are few dogs capable of tackling such an animal and pulling it down, though the wolf, hunting in a pack and careless of losses did so when wolves were indigenous to the same country as this large deer. The Elk provided a very welcome addition to food stocks in countries where the winter was long and hard and where the keeping of domestic cattle was far from easy. They had to be hunted through fairly thick forests, often when snow lay on the ground, and through tangled undergrowth that would have dismayed a small weak dog. For the purpose the Scandinavians evolved a number of dogs of very similar build and characteristics, strong, active, with a good voice and a thick coat to protect them against the severe weather.

The basis was a Spitz type of dog that had existed in Scandinavia for centuries, and which is typical of the dogs of the frozen areas of Northern Europe and Asia. The Finnish Spitz and the Samoyed are other examples. In Scandinavia there still exists a much larger version of the Elkhound called the Jamthund or Swedish Elkhound, recognised in Sweden but not elsewhere, and there are at least two other variations still in existence. The dog was originally developed as a hunter, but its other qualities have quickly been recognised and appreciated in most countries, where it makes an excellent guard and housedog. It retains the hunting instinct, and undoubtedly would enjoy a day in the woods, though whether in its smaller form it would still hunt and bay the Elk is another matter.

The coat of the Elkhound is one of its special features, being thick, abundant, coarse and weather resistant, and the extra length of hair around the neck gives it a most distinctive appearance. The dog is one of the stoutest breeds for its size, being very strong in the leg and with great stamina, quite capable of living out of doors in the coldest weathers, and extremely energetic.

As a showdog he has achieved a degree of popularity that does not compare with his Spitz cousins the Samoyed and the Chow Chow, but he has a following because of his tremendous comportment in the ring. The Elkhound is easily trained to stand like a statue even when in close proximity to his fellows, and while on occasions one will give tongue, on the whole when the Elkhounds are being shown things are fairly calm and quiet. There are certain problems in keeping him in good trim as from time to time he sheds his coat, and until this has grown again he loses a great deal of his glamour.

He is a friendly dog, very intelligent and alert, and with a good personality, never being dull and listless and always good company. His voice, which has a bell-like quality, handed down from his forebears who used it in the forests to disclose the whereabouts of the game, is a great deterrent to intruders.

OFFICIAL STANDARD

Characteristics
The Elkhound is a hardy sporting dog of Nordic type of a bold and virile nature, and has good scenting power. Its disposition should be friendly and intelligent, with great energy and independence of character, and without any sign of undue nervousness.

General appearance
It has a compact and proportionately short body, a coat thick and abundant but not bristling, and prick ears; tail tightly curled over back.

Head and skull
Broad between the ears; the forehead and back of the head are slightly arched with a clearly marked but not

Head: broad between the ears, slightly arched nose, not pointed.

large stop. Muzzle moderately long, broader at the base and gradually tapering—whether seen from above or from the side—but not pointed; bridge of the nose straight, jaw strong with lips tightly closed.

Eyes
Not prominent, in colour brown and as dark as possible, giving a frank, fearless and friendly expression.

Ears
Set high, firm and upstanding, height slightly greater than their width at the base, pointed and very mobile.

Neck
Of medium length, firm, muscular and well set up.

Forequarters
Legs firm, straight and powerful with good bone; elbows closely set on.

Body: short, wide, deep.

Body
Short in the couplings; back, wide and straight from neck to stern; chest, wide and deep with well-rounded ribs; loins, muscular; stomach, very little drawn up.

Hindquarters
Hind legs firm strong and powerful, a little but definite bend at stifle and hock, and straight when viewed from behind.

Feet
Compact, oval in shape and not turned outwards; toes, tightly closed; toe nails, firm and strong.

Tail
Set high, tightly curled over the back but not carried on either side; hair, thick and close.

Coat
Thick, abundant, coarse and weather-resisting; short on the head and on the front of the legs; longest on the chest, neck, buttocks, behind the forelegs and on the underside of the tail. It is composed of a longish and coarse top coat, dark at the tips with a light-coloured, soft and woolly undercoat. About the neck and front of the chest the longer coat forms a sort of ruff which, with the pricked ears, the energetic eyes and the curled tail, gives the animal its unique and alert appearance.

Colour
Grey, of various shades with black tips to the long outer coat; lighter on the chest, stomach, legs, and the underside of the tail. Any distinctive variation from the grey colour is most undesirable and too dark or too light colourings should be avoided. Pronounced markings on legs and feet are also not desirable.

Weight and size
For dogs, the ideal height at the shoulder should be $20\frac{1}{2}$ inches (52 centimetres) and for bitches $19\frac{1}{2}$ inches (49 centimetres). Weight approximately 50 pounds (23 kilogrammes) and 43 pounds (20 kilogrammes) respectively.

Note
Male animals should have two apparently normal testicles fully descended into the scrotum.

AKC VARIATION TO STANDARD
Classified as the Norwegian Elkhound by the AKC. *Mouth:* teeth meet in scissors bite. *Body:* distance from forechest to rump equals height at withers. Chest deep and moderately broad; brisket level with points of elbows. *Forequarters:* shoulders sloping. Single dewclaws normally present. *Hindquarters:* without dewclaws. *Weight:* dogs 55 pounds; bitches 48 pounds. *Disqualification:* Any overall colour than grey.

FINNISH SPITZ

NATIONAL GROUPING		
	Name	Number
KC(GB)	Hound	I
AKC	—	–
FCI	Small Hounds	6

Dogs do not recognise national boundaries, and although there has always been a tendency to associate a certain breed with a certain country, there were inevitably areas where bloods and varieties crossed borders. This has led to certain dogs evolving from a mixture of strains. The Finnish Spitz is a typical example of this. This little dog, apart from its colour, which is distinctive, is undoubtedly a mixture of the Spitz types from the Scandinavian countries and certain Russian dogs. The Elkhounds of Norway have always been of more slender build than the Jämthund, and there existed bird hunting dogs in the northern area of the Baltic which were of a similar type to the Finnish Spitz. The Laika too of Russia is a bird-hunting dog so that between the two the evolution of a type such as the Finnish Spitz was almost certain to take place.

The breed was first officially recognised in the latter part of the 19th century and the type became fixed. It was at the turn of this century that the Finnish Spitz was introduced into Britain though it was not until much later that it made any impression on the show scene.

The Spitz is an active, sometimes noisy little dog with a most alert expression and keen look about him. His stand-off stiff coat with a distinct mane especially on the males, allied with his rich bright orange or red colour, gives him a very distinctive appearance. As a show dog he has never achieved great success though one or two enthusiasts have persevered with the breed.

The Finnish Spitz is a friendly little dog as so many of the hunting dogs are. Centuries of dependence on man, and man's dependence on the dog have built up a trusting relationship. Their high-pitched voice and well developed protective instinct make them particularly good guard dogs.

OFFICIAL STANDARD

Characteristics
The Finnish Spitz characteristics are eagerness to hunt, courage and fidelity.

General appearance
Body almost square. Bearing bold. The whole appearance, and particularly eyes, ears and tail, indicates liveliness.

Head and skull
Medium sized and clean cut, forehead slightly arched, stop pronounced. Muzzle narrow and clean cut, seen from above and from the sides evenly tapering. Nose pitch black. Lips tightly closed and thin.

Eyes
Medium sized, lively, preferably dark.

Head: tapering muzzle, pronounced stop.

Ears
Cocked, sharply pointed, fine in texture, exceedingly mobile.

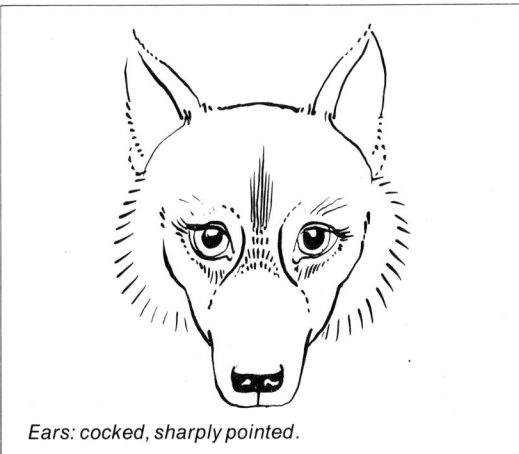

Ears: cocked, sharply pointed.

Neck

Muscular, in males it looks rather short, due to the thick coat, in bitches medium long.

Forequarters

Strong and straight.

Body

Back, straight and strong. Chest, deep. Belly, slightly drawn up.

Back: straight. Chest: deep.

Hindquarters

Strong, hocks comparatively straight.

Feet

Preferably roundish.

Tail

Curves vigorously from its root in an arch, forward, downward and backward, then pressing down against the thigh, with its tip extending to the middle part of the thigh. Extended, the tail vertebrae usually reaches to the hock joint.

Coat

On head and legs, except their back sides, short and close-lying, on the body longish, semi-erect or erect, on the neck and back stiffer. The outer coat on the shoulders, particularly in males, considerably longer and coarser. On the back of the thighs the hair is long and dense, also on the tail. Undercoat short, soft, dense, light in colour.

Colour

On the back reddish-brown or yellowish-red, preferably bright. The hairs on innersides of the ears, cheeks, under the muzzle, on the breast, abdomen, inside the legs, at the back of thighs, under the tail are of a lighter shade. White markings on feet and a narrow white stripe on the breast can be permitted also some black hairs on the lips and sparse separate hairs with black points along the back.

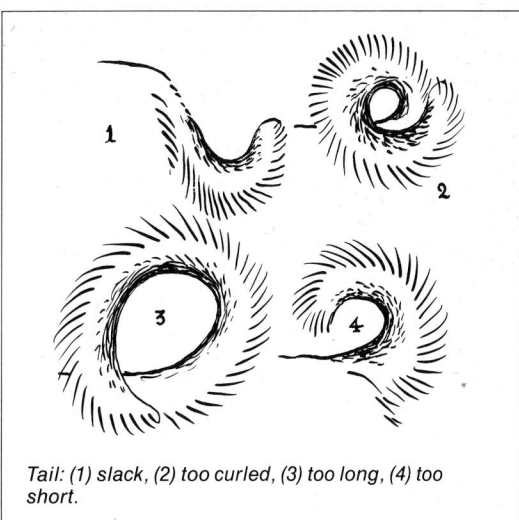

Tail: (1) slack, (2) too curled, (3) too long, (4) too short.

Weight and size

Height at withers and length of body in males $17\frac{1}{2}$ inches, 20 inches; in bitches $15\frac{1}{2}$ inches, 18 inches.

Faults

Fleshy head, coarse muzzle, ears pointing forward at a sharp angle or their tips pointing outwards or towards one another, ears curving backwards or with slack points or with long hairs inside. Yellow or wall-eyes, elbows turned inwards, too weak pastern, slack tail or too excessively curled tail, long, soft or too short, close wavy or curly coat, dirty colour particularly distinctly defined differences between the colours, disfiguring dewclaws.

Note

Male animals should have two apparently normal testicles fully descended into the scrotum.

AKC VARIATION TO STANDARD

This dog is not granted championship status by the AKC.

FOXHOUND

NATIONAL GROUPING		
	Name	Number
KC(GB)	Hound	I
AKC	Hounds	II
FCI	Large Hounds	5

The whole history of sport with dogs is tied up with the hunting of game, with the exception of the breeds that were vermin killers, and those that were used to hunt the fox. While in the view of some people, the fox belongs among the vermin, it has nevertheless been accorded some status as it has long been associated with the sport of horse riding. Few breeds have their history so well documented as the Foxhound. Whilst other breeds depended on the showbench and registration with Kennel Clubs for their records, the Foxhound had its development written down in the history of the various hunts which were spread all over Europe and the United States of America. Even so, the early history of the breed is as much a matter of debate as many other breeds.

As early as 1631 Gervase Markham was writing that 'the best parts of the country bred large hounds, the woodlands and mountains of Cheshire and Lancashire the middle-sized hounds and,' as he so delightfully put it 'other champaigne countreys the light nimble, swift and slender dog'. The light Northern Foxhound is thought to have resulted from the crossing of the old Northern Hound and the Greyhound. Whatever the origins and the differences, the fact remains that very early in the history of Britain and America the Foxhound became well established as the number of packs increased. A complete list of all packs in England alone in 1880, reveals that there were one hundred and forty in existence with an average of some fifty couples per pack which gives an astounding total of seven thousand Hounds.

The Masters of Foxhounds Association has been in existence longer than the Kennel Club. Stud books have been carefully kept and it is possible even to this day to trace the ancestry of the modern Hounds further back than that of any other breed. Hunting became fashionable, with the result that no difficulty was encountered in keeping packs or staffing them as they were supported by wealthy families.

The Foxhound is a friendly creature, calm and almost affectionate. It is one of the sights of the countryside during the winter months to see well-wrapped children making a fuss of the Hounds at a meet, and being fussed over in return. He is a big, squarely built dog with the sort of conformation and build that give him strength and stamina as well as the ability to jump and to crash through thick undergrowth. A pack must be capable of spending the whole day in the field from early morning to late at night, and of running several foxes during that time.

Unfortunately they have never been popular as a showdog, apart from their regular appearance at specific shows arranged for Foxhounds. This is a pity, as they are handsome dogs, very spectacular, and with physical qualities that could well allow them to outshine many of the breeds more frequently shown. It is many years since one appeared at a dog show in Britain.

OFFICIAL STANDARD

Head and skull
Skull broad.

Neck
Long, but not thick. A short-necked hound is deficient in pace.

Forequarters
Shoulders should show quality and no lumber. A shoulder with an excessive amount of fleshy conformation will prevent the hound from running up or down hill at top pace. Legs full of bone right down to the feet, and not tapering off in any way.

Body
Girth should be deep with plenty of heart room. Back broad, and a hound should be well ribbed up; but there should be a fair space between the end of the ribs and the commencement of the hindquarters, otherwise the hound will be deficient in stride and therefore lack pace.

Well ribbed, but fair space between last rib and hindquarters.

Hindquarters
Full, and of great muscular proportions. Hocks should be well let down, and the bone of the hindlegs (as in the forelegs) should continue all the way down to the foot, and not become light under the pastern.

Feet
The toes of the feet should be close together, and not open.

Tail
Should be well put on at the end of good quarters, and these quarters should in no way end abruptly and be of the type that hound-men term 'chopped off behind'. A curly stern, although unsightly, will not be detrimental to the hound's hunting qualities.

Note
Male animals should have two apparently normal testicles fully descended into the scrotum.

AKC VARIATION TO STANDARD

Head: should be of full size, but by no means heavy. Brow pronounced, but not high or sharp. There should be a good length and breadth, sufficient to give in a dog hound a girth in front of the ears of fully 16 inches. The nose should be long ($4\frac{1}{2}$ inches) and wide, with open nostrils. Ears set on low and lying close to the cheeks. Most English hounds are 'rounded' which means that about $1\frac{1}{2}$ inches is taken off the end of the ear. Teeth must meet squarely, either a pig-mouth (overshot) or undershot being a disqualification. *Neck:* must be long and clean, without slightest throatiness, not less than 10 inches from cranium to shoulder. It should taper nicely from shoulders to head, and upper outline should be slightly convex. *Shoulders:* should be long and well clothed with muscle, without being heavy, especially at points. They must be well sloped, and the true arm between front and elbow must be long and muscular, but free from fat or lumber. *Chest and back ribs:* chest should girth over 31 inches in a 24-inch hound, and the back ribs must be very deep. *Back and loin:* must both be very muscular, running into each other without any contraction between them. The couples must be wide, even to raggedness, and topline of back should be absolutely level, the stern well set on and carried gaily but not in any case curved over back like a squirrel's tail. The end should taper to a point and there should be a fringe of hair below. Hindquarters or propellers are required to be very strong, and as endurance is of even greater consequence than speed, straight stifles are preferred to those much bent as in a greyhound. Elbows set quite straight, and neither turned in nor out are a *sine qua non.* They must be well let down by means of the long true arm. *Legs and feet:* legs straight and strong; size of bone at ankle being especially regarded as important. Bone not too large, feet in all cases should be round and catlike, with well-developed knuckles and strong horn. *Colour and coat:* not regarded as very important, so long as the former is a good 'hound colour', and the latter is short, dense, hard, and glossy. Hound colours are black, tan, and white, or any combination of these three, also the various 'pies' compounded of white and the colour of the hare and badger, or yellow, or tan. The symmetry of the Foxhound is of greatest importance, and what is known as 'quality' is highly regarded by all good judges. *Disqualification:* pig-mouth (overshot) or undershot.

AMERICAN FOXHOUND

NATIONAL GROUPING		
	Name	Number
KC(GB)	Hound	—
AKC	Hounds	11
FCI	Large Hounds	5

Hunting has always been a popular sport in the United States of America, and even in the face of increasing urbanisation, the country is so huge that large tracts of it remain unspoilt and rich in game even today. The history of fox hunting goes back almost as far as the history of America to the days of the first settlements. In 1650 Robert Brooke took his pack of hounds with him when he sailed to the Crown Colony and the descendants of these remained in the family for three hundred years or more and formed the basis of the American Foxhound of today. Further importations took place in the middle to late 18th century, some from Britain and others from France. In the early 19th century the Gloucester Foxhunting Club imported some of the best English hounds and then followed further importations from France and Ireland, the latter lending weight to the idea that the Black and Tan Coonhound may have descended from the Kerry Beagle.

The Foxhound in the United States is used for four different purposes and for these four rather different types of Hound are needed. There is the field trial Hound which is run competitively at trials where speed is important. There is the hunting of the fox with the gun, where a slower Hound with a good voice is needed. Trail Hounds or Drag Hounds which are raced on a drag, much as the Fell Hounds of Cumberland are run, are different again, and here speed alone counts. Finally, there is pack hunting where the type is very much the same as in the English Foxhound, where a combination of some speed, great jumping power, a good voice and willingness to hunt in a pack, is needed. As in Britain Hounds have varied considerably from one area to another, but whilst in that country packs have tended to stick to their own type, in the United States of America there has been a move towards greater standardisation.

In Britain Foxhounds are rarely shown, except at Hound shows such as Peterborough, the registration being largely in the hands of the Masters of Foxhounds Association whose stud books go back to the beginning of the 19th century. It is many years now since one was shown at a Kennel Club Show in Britain, and the last group of registrations took place in 1967 when four were registered with the Kennel Club. In the United States things are somewhat different, and the American Foxhound is recognised as a show dog. He is a biggish dog, twenty-two to twenty-five inches, very powerfully built and muscular with a close hard hound coat, and very friendly. Hunts still continue the habit of puppy walking, putting young Hounds out to be reared in the locality of the kennels by hunt supporters, where they live as members of the family, and become as attached and affectionate as any other breed of dog. However, like many other Hounds, they do have a streak of independence and wilfulness, and can become disobedient in later life.

OFFICIAL STANDARD

Head
Skull: should be fairly long, slightly domed at occiput, with cranium broad and full. *Ears:* ears set on moderately low, long, reaching when drawn out nearly, if not quite, to the tip of the nose; fine in texture, fairly broad, with almost entire absence of erectile power—setting close to the head with the forward edge slightly inturning to the cheek—round at tip. *Eyes:* eyes large, set well apart—soft and houndlike—expression gentle and pleading; of a brown or hazel color. *Muzzle:* muzzle of fair length—straight and square-cut—the stop moderately defined. *Defects:* a very flat skull, narrow across the top; excess of dome; eyes small, sharp and terrierlike, or prominent and protruding; muzzle long and snipy, cut away decidedly below the eyes, or very short. Roman-nosed, or upturned giving a dish-face expression. Ears short, set on high, or with a tendency to rise above the point of origin.

(1) correct hindquarters, (2) faulty straight hocks.

Skull: slightly domed. Muzzle: fair length, square cut.

Body
Neck and throat: neck rising free and light from the shoulders, strong in substance yet not loaded, of medium length. The throat clean and free from folds of skin, a slight wrinkle below the angle of the jaw, however, is allowable. *Defects:* a thick, short, cloddy neck carried on a line with the top of the shoulders. Throat showing dewlap and folds of skin to a degree termed 'throatiness.'

Shoulders, chest and ribs
Shoulders sloping—clean, muscular, not heavy or loaded—conveying the idea of freedom of action with activity and strength. Chest should be deep for lung space, narrower in proportion to depth than the English hound—28 inches (*girth*) in a 23-inch hound being good. Well-sprung ribs—back ribs should extend well back—a three-inch flank allowing springiness. *Back and loins:* back moderately long, muscular and strong. Loins broad and slightly arched. *Defects:* very long or swayed or roached back. Flat, narrow loins.

Forelegs and feet
Forelegs: straight, with fair amount of bone. Pasterns short and straight. *Feet:* foxlike. Pad full and hard. Well-arched toes. Strong nails. *Defects:* straight, upright shoulders, chest disproportionately wide or with lack of depth. Flat ribs. Out at elbow. Knees knuckled over forward, or bent backward. Forelegs crooked. Feet long, open or spreading.

Hips, thighs, hind legs and feet
Hips and thighs, strong and muscled, giving abundance of propelling power. Stifles strong and well let down. Hocks firm, symmetrical and moderately bent. Feet close and firm. *Defects:* cowhocks, or straight hocks. Lack of muscle and propelling power. Open feet.

Tail
Set moderately high; carried gaily, but not turned forward over the back; with slight curve; with very slight brush. *Defects:* a long tail, Teapot curve or inclined forward from the root. Rat tail, entire absence of brush.

Coat
A close, hard, hound coat of medium length. *Defects:* a short thin coat, or of a soft quality.

Height
Dogs should not be under 22 or over 25 inches. Bitches should not be under 21 or over 24 inches measured across the back at the point of the withers, the hound standing in a natural position with his feet well under him.

Color
Any color.

Head (20): skull (5), ears (5), eyes (5), muzzle (5). Body (35): neck (5), chest and shoulders (15), back, loins and ribs (15). *Running Gear (35):* forelegs (10), hips, thighs and hind legs (10), feet (15). Coat and Tail (10): coat (5), tail (5). *Total (100).*

AKC VARIATION TO STANDARD
This dog is not granted championship status by the KC(GB). The above standards are those of the AKC.

GREYHOUND

By studying old photographs and prints it can be seen that the modern dog of many breeds, is very different from his forebears. The modern Bulldog looks little like that of a hundred years ago, and the Fox Terrier, especially a Wire Fox Terrier of the turn of the century looks very different from today's. The Greyhound on the other hand has hardly changed at all. Even the name of the dog has its roots in early British history. Today old running-dog men especially in the north of Britain will talk of a 'Greu' which comes from the Saxon word for a running dog. In common with some other breeds, the Greyhound was denied to the commoner at one time in order to prevent him from poaching game and thus spoiling the sport of the wealthier classes. Mention of the dog was made in the time of King Canute, and prior to the signing of the Magna Carta, the destruction of a Greyhound was an extremely serious crime.

Juliana Berners in the 15th century 'Book of St. Albans' describes the Greyhound in detail in a doggerel which has been repeated so often that it is now hackneyed. In the 16th century the coursing of buck by Greyhounds was a regular sport, the buck being driven into an area where they could be watched in comfort by spectators. The buck were pulled down by Greyhounds having been given what was called 'fair law' which means that they had a start. In recent years the Greyhound has been developed along three quite distinct lines, the show dog which is bigger and narrower; the coursing dog which is handier and more agile; and the track Greyhound which was evolved for racing to the artificial hare in the United States and later in Britain; the finest dogs for this purpose being bred in Ireland.

From the earliest days of dog shows the Greyhound has been a popular dog for exhibition, and as the records of the coursing Hounds have been kept in the Greyhound Stud Book since about 1880, so the details of the show Greyhound have been kept, even to their measurements. We even know that a dog named Lauderdale, whelped in 1869 and successfully shown from 1873 to 1880 weighed sixty-seven pounds, so detailed are the records.

The Greyhound has a wonderful temperament, friendly, refined, as gentle with children as he is affectionate with adults. It is remarkable that he has not become more popular as a house pet. His size is against him, though he curls up into a remarkably small space, and is quite wonderfully trainable. The Greyhound is one of the few breeds that takes quite naturally to the lead, obeys commands usually without demur, and is easily handled by a child. It is being well-behaved that makes him such a magnificent show dog. He stands like a statue in the ring, and a parade of these magnificent Hounds in their varied colours, with their coats shining in the sunshine at an outdoor show is a fine sight. In spite of his natural killer instinct, he is among the most sympathetic and even sentimental of dogs, as those who have adopted a Greyhound that has been retired from the track would agree.

OFFICIAL STANDARD

Characteristics
The Greyhound possesses remarkable stamina and endurance, its straight through, long reaching movement enables it to cover ground at great speed.

General appearance
The general appearance of the typical Greyhound is that of a strongly built, upstanding dog of generous proportions, muscular power and symmetrical formation, with a long head and neck, clean well-laid shoulders, deep chest, capacious body, arched loin, powerful quarters, sound legs and feet, and a suppleness of limb, which emphasize in a marked degree its distinctive type and quality.

Head and skull
Long, moderate width, flat skull, slight stop. Jaws, powerful and well chiselled.

Eyes
Bright and intelligent, dark in colour.

Ears
Small, rose-shape, of fine texture.

Mouth
Teeth white and strong. The incisors of the upper jaw clipping those of the lower jaw.

Neck
Long and muscular, elegantly arched, well let into the shoulders.

Neck: long, muscular, elegantly arched.

Forequarters
Shoulders, oblique, well set back, muscular without being loaded, narrow and cleanly defined at the top. Forelegs, long and straight, bone of good substance and quality. Elbows, free and well set under the shoulders. Pasterns, moderate length, slightly sprung. Elbows, pasterns and toes should incline neither outwards nor inwards.

Hocks: inclining neither outwards nor inwards.

Body
Chest, deep and capacious, providing adequate heart room. Ribs, deep, well sprung, and carried well back. Flanks well cut up. Back, rather long, broad and square. Loin, powerful, slightly arched.

Hindquarters
Thighs and second thighs, wide and muscular, showing great propelling power. Stifles, well bent. Hocks, well let down, inclining neither outwards nor inwards. Body and hindquarters features should be of ample proportions and well coupled, enabling adequate ground to be covered when standing.

Feet
Moderate length, with compact well-knuckled toes, strong pads.

Tail
Long, set on rather low, strong at the root, tapering to the point, carried low, slightly curved.

Coat
Fine and close.

Colour
Black, white, red, blue, fawn, fallow, brindle, or any of the colours broken with white.

Height
Ideal height: dogs, 28 to 30 inches; bitches, 27 to 28 inches.

Note
Male animals should have two apparently normal testicles fully descended into the scrotum.

AKC VARIATION TO STANDARD
Head: long and narrow, fairly wide between the ears, scarcely perceptible stop, little or no development of nasal tissues. *Ears:* thrown back and folded, except when excited, when they are semi-pricked. *Tail:* set on low. *Weight:* dogs 65 to 70 pounds; bitches 60 to 65 pounds.

HARRIER

With the exception of Australasia, the hare has a cosmopolitan distribution, being found from the Arctic Circle to the Southern Hemisphere. It has in addition been a favourite food throughout the world since history began, and the hunting of it in one form or another has been in existence for thousands of years. In the Far East, as in many other parts of the world, this consisted of coursing which resulted in the development of breeds that were fast and clever enough to catch him. Certainly hare hunting did go on in ancient Greece with dogs other than those which caught them by sheer speed. The hare was finally caught in a net rather than being run down, and as food rather than sport was the purpose, this is probably excusable.

Though the Harrier looks very much like a small Foxhound, he is a separate breed and should not be confused. There are indications that at one time the tendency was to take small Foxhounds from packs and

NATIONAL GROUPING		
	Name	Number
KC(GB)	—	—
AKC	Hounds	II
FCI	Small Hounds	6

by selective breeding of the smaller specimens, to produce a line of so-called Harriers. The Association of Masters of Harriers however did all possible to prevent this practice, and kept their own stud books of pure bred Hounds.

The first pack of Harriers in Britain was the Penistone pack which was established by Sir Elias de Midhope in 1260. This pack existed for some five hundred years, the Masters being the Wilsons of Broomhead Hall. The pack no longer exists, but it is interesting to note that the hunting of the hare on foot is still popular in the area, and a pack of Beagles still meets regularly there. This hunting of the hare on foot was what led to the popularity of the Harrier as a pack hound as it was not everyone who could, or who wished to ride a horse. Many of the early packs were scratch packs, individual Hounds being owned privately and meeting to hunt, which brought the whole sport within reach of the less wealthy. In the United States of America the Harrier has been known as long as any of the other scent hunting Hounds and has been used for hunting since colonial times. In more recent years he proved a favourite with the drag hunt where his slower pace was found more suitable.

As with the Foxhound there has been no attempt to establish the Harrier as a show dog in Britain. He is never seen on the bench, which is unfortunate, as he is one of the oldest breeds in the country, and now has very little place as a pack hunting Hound. In the United States, however, he is accepted and shown. He is a solidly built little dog, handy in size, well constructed and muscular, and both hardy and active. Those who have had a Foxhound in the house when puppy walking will say how attractive this type of dog can be as a companion, and there is no reason why at some future date the Harrier should not prove as popular as the Beagle.

OFFICIAL STANDARD

The points of the modern Harrier are very similar to those of the English Foxhound. The Harrier, however, is smaller than the English Foxhound and the most popular size is 19 to 21 inches. They should be active, well balanced and full of strength and quality, with shoulders sloping into the muscles of the back, clean and not loaded on the withers or point.

Ribbed well back.

The back level and muscular, and not dipping behind the withers or arching over the loin. The elbow's point set well away from the ribs, running parallel with the body and not turning outwards. Deep, well-sprung ribs, running well back, with plenty of heart room, and a deep chest.

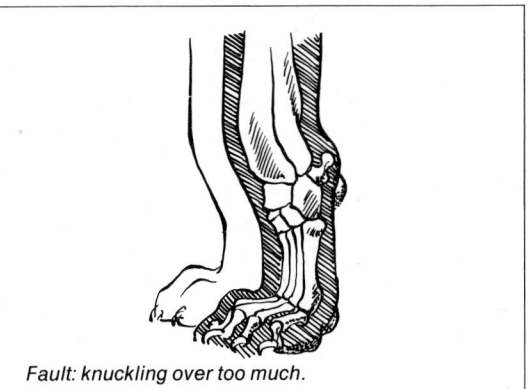

Fault: knuckling over too much.

Round catlike feet, toes turning inwards.

Good straight legs with plenty of bone running well down to the toes, but not overburdened, inclined to knuckle over very slightly but not exaggerated in the slightest degree. Round catlike feet, and close toes turning inwards. Hind legs and hocks stand square, with a good sweep and muscular thigh to take the weight off the body.

Head: well set up on neck of ample length.

The head should be of a medium size with good bold forehead, and plenty of expression; head must be well set up on a neck of ample length, and not heavy; stern should be set well up, long and well controlled.

AKC VARIATION TO STANDARD

This dog is not granted championship status by the KC(GB). The above standards are those of the AKC.

IBIZAN HOUND

NATIONAL GROUPING		
	Name	Number
KC(GB)	Hound	I
AKC	—	—
FCI	Coursing Dogs	IO

This dog is probably the one breed with justifiable claims to great antiquity. Its origins lie in the area of the Mediterranean and particularly in the islands off the coast of Spain, and it is true that ancient drawings and paintings of hunting dogs dating back to Egyptian times depict a type of Hound to which the modern Ibizan Hound bears a remarkable resemblance. A near relative, the Pharaoh Hound can possibly lay equal claim, but the varied colour of the Ibizan is frequently shown in ancient decorations. He was bred as a hunting dog, working by scent as well as sight, though his conformation, the length of his leg and his undoubted speed make it more than likely that he is primarily a sight Hound. Though he was known centuries ago on the islands of Ibiza, Formenters, Majorca and Minorca, he was regularly used on the mainland of the Spanish Peninsula. He is described at the beginning of this century as the Podengo, and was being used for coursing rabbit and hare, but in Andalusia and Estramedura he is said to have been used to catch stag and bear, and to have made an excellent gundog.

In more recent times he has become a popular dog in Spain and in many other countries in southern Europe,

being seen frequently at all the major shows in considerable numbers, and being used as a coursing dog. A small number of breeders have worked hard to maintain the breed over the past couple of decades. It says a good deal for their efforts that the breed that we see today has remained almost exactly like the dogs of centuries ago, when the temptation must have been from time to time to introduce the blood of other running dogs such as the Greyhound or the Saluki to improve speed and performance. They have, however, concentrated on the typical dog of the islands and have succeeded in retaining the erect ears, one of the main characteristics of the dog.

He is a tall Hound, standing around twenty-six inches at the shoulder and very much the running type, with flat sides and long legs. He is less elegant than the Greyhound, and has strong bone, rather larger feet and more bulky joints. His head too is not so long and narrow as some of the other running dogs. He is seen in two coats, the one short and smooth, and the other longer and rather hard. The longer coated variety is rarely seen outside Spain though at shows in Europe it is fairly common. He makes a good show dog though he is sometimes a little restless and impatient. His size and colour make him quite striking, and his preparation is minimal, involving the simplest of cleaning and attention to nails and teeth. He is one of those dogs that looks well as a team, and when a number of them are seen together, standing level, with keen expression and alert ears, they prove very competitive.

His temperament is typical of many of the other running dogs, quiet and steady when relaxed, and very keen when aroused. If he has one fault as a show dog it is that at times he is a little hard in temperament, and can prove somewhat intractable. Although he has the wilfulness of many of the other Hounds, and a streak of independence, he does, however, become very attached to his owner, and is affectionate and faithful.

OFFICIAL STANDARD

Characteristics
A tireless controlled hunter. Retrieves to hand, very kind, rather cautious with strangers, has the ability to jump great heights without take-off run. An agile hound.

General appearance
Tall, narrow, finely built, large erect ears.

Head and Skull
Fine, long, flat skull with prominent occipital bone. Stop not well defined, slightly convex muzzle, the length of which from the eyes to the tip of the nose should be equal to the length from the eyes to the occiput. Nose flesh coloured, should protrude beyond the teeth, jaw very strong and lean.

Eyes
Clear amber, expressive. Almond shaped; not prominent, large or round.

Ears
Large, thin, stiff, highly mobile, erect when dog is alert, in a continuous line with the arch of the neck when viewed in profile; base set on level with the eyes.

Mouth
Perfectly even white teeth; scissor bite; thin lips with no dew-lap.

Neck
Very lean, long, muscular and slightly arched.

Forequarters
Rather steep short shoulder blade, long straight legs, erect pasterns of good length.

Body
Level back sloping slightly from the pinbones to the rump. Long, flat ribcage. Short coupled with well tucked up waist, breast bone very prominent. Depth measured between the bottom of the ribcage and elbow $2\frac{1}{2}$ inches to 3 inches.

Hindquarters
Long, strong, straight and lean, no great angulation, long second thigh, turning neither in nor out.

Feet
Well arched toes, thick pads, light coloured claws. Front feet may turn slightly outwards. Dew claws should not be removed in front. No hind dew claws.

Gait
A suspended trot, which is a long far reaching stride, with a slight hover before placing the foot to the ground.

Tail
Long, thin, low set, reaching well below the hock, when passed between the legs and round the flank should reach the spine; may be carried high when excited but not curled within itself or low over the back.

Coat
Either smooth or rough always hard, close, dense. Longer under the tail and at the back of the legs. Hunting scars should not be penalised.

Colour
White, Chestnut or Lion solid color, or any combination of these.

Weight and size
The Standard in the country of origin varies between 22 inches and 29 inches, but balance is the overriding factor.

Faults
Any departure from the foregoing, the degree of the departure stipulating the seriousness of the fault.

Note
Male animals should have two apparently normal testicles fully descended into the scrotum.

AKC VARIATION TO STANDARD
This dog is not granted championship status by the AKC.

IRISH WOLFHOUND

NATIONAL GROUPING		
	Name	Number
KC(GB)	Hound	I
AKC	Hounds	II
FCI	Coursing Dogs	10

Throughout history dogs have been the subjects of myth and legend, either as in the case of the Lion Dog of China romantic little stories accounting for the character of the Pekingese, or, as in the case of much larger animals living in a country that thrives on legend as Ireland has always done, tales of huge ravening beasts that were capable of giant feats of strength. The Irish Wolfhound gave ample opportunity for such stories, as he is one of the largest dogs in the world, certainly the tallest, and though he is nowadays one of the gentlest of dogs, it could well be that he was not always so. Finn, the hero of one Irish legend had as his companion a dog named Bran which was gifted with magical properties including a deadly poisonous claw and the ability to foretell the future. He was described as a huge black dog, but others such as the one given to Finn by the princess of Iruath were said to be multi-coloured, this one was wearing a gold chain and had the gift of producing gold and silver from its mouth.

Leaving legend behind, however, there is no doubt that large hunting dogs comparable with the modern Irish Wolfhound did exist in Ireland some centuries ago. They were used for the hunting of the Irish wolf and the Irish elk, an exceptionally large version of this member of the deer family said to have stood some six feet at the shoulder. The Romans appreciated him and are said to have imported specimens and used them in arena battles, though there is indication that these were heavier dogs more on the lines of the Mastiff. Bewick in 1792 writes 'The Irish Greyhound is the largest of the dog kind, and its appearance the most beautiful'. By the end of the 19th century the breed had almost disappeared, and there was a good deal of discussion as to whether it should, or even could, be saved. Fortunately, largely by the efforts of one man, the breed was revived. Even though there will always be discussion as to whether this was done by proper means or by the use of crosses, we have been left with one of the greatest and noblest members of the canine race.

The Irish Wolfhound is a huge, impressive, calm and graceful Hound with a most intelligent and understanding expression. He is still very much the running and hunting dog, built for power and speed, though he has come a long way from the apparently rougher more cumbersome animal used for chasing and pulling down wolves in the early days of Irish history.

As a show dog he has few peers, especially in his own group, where his sheer size and magnificence always make him outstanding. There have been one or two kennels in recent years that have campaigned the breed at shows until they have attained world wide recognition, and the numbers have grown steadily as a result. They now appear at shows in almost every country, and some fine dogs have been exported though few these days from Ireland itself.

The temperament of this great dog is wonderful. Gentle and quiet, he is completely friendly and trusting with everyone and even with his own kind, which cannot be said of all breeds. He makes a wonderful guard, his sheer size being sufficient to daunt most intruders, and his bark, when he does give voice, echoes like thunder around the landscape. In spite of his bulk, he is a favourite house dog as his manners and general behaviour are quite impeccable.

OFFICIAL STANDARD

General appearance
The Irish Wolfhound should not be quite so heavy or massive as the Great Dane, but more so than the Deerhound, which in general type he should otherwise resemble. Of great size and commanding appearance, very muscular, strongly though gracefully built, movements easy and active; head and neck carried high; the tail carried with an upward sweep with a slight curve towards the extremity.

Head and skull
Long, the frontal bones of the forehead very slightly raised and very little indentation between the eyes. Skull, not too broad. Muzzle, long and moderately pointed.

Eyes
Dark.

Ears
Small and greyhound-like in carriage.

Neck
Rather long, very strong and muscular, well arched, without dewlap or loose skin about the throat.

Forequarters
Shoulders muscular, giving breadth of chest, set sloping. Elbows well under, turned neither inwards nor outwards. Leg and forearm muscular, and the whole leg strong and quite straight.

Body
Chest, very deep. Breast, wide. Back, rather long than short. Loins arched. Belly well drawn up.

Hindquarters
Muscular thighs and second thighs; long and strong as in the Greyhound, and hocks well let down and turning neither in nor out.

Feet
Moderately large and round, turned neither inwards nor outwards. Toes well arched and closed. Nails very strong and curved.

Coat: rough and hardy.

Tail
Long and slightly curved, of moderate thickness, and well covered with hair.

Coat
Rough and hardy on body, legs and head; especially wiry and long over eyes and under jaw.

Colour
The recognised colours are grey, brindle, red, black, pure white, fawn, or any colour that appears in the Deerhound.

Weight and size
The minimum height and weight of dogs should be 31 inches and 120 pounds; of bitches, 28 inches and 90 pounds. *Anything below this should be heavily penalised.* Great size, including height at shoulder and proportionate length of body, is the desideratum to be aimed at, and it is desired to firmly establish a breed that shall average from 32 to 34 inches in dogs, showing the requisite power, activity, courage and symmetry.

Faults
Too light or heavy a head, too highly arched frontal bone; large ears; ears hanging flat to the face; short neck; full dewlap; too narrow or too broad a chest; sunken, hollow or quite straight back; bent forelegs; overbent fetlocks; twisted feet; spreading toes; too curly a tail; weak hind-quarters and a general want of muscle; too short in body; pink or liver-coloured eyelids; lips and nose any colour other than black; very light eyes.

Note
Male animals should have two apparently normal testicles fully descended into the scrotum.

Feet: moderately large and round, well arched.

AKC VARIATION TO STANDARD
Weight and size: minimum—dogs 32 inches, bitches 30 inches. Dogs 120 pounds; bitches 105 pounds.

OTTER HOUND

NATIONAL GROUPING		
	Name	Number
KC(GB)	—	–
AKC	Hounds	II
FCI	Small Hounds	6

The first mention of the Otter Hound as a specific type of dog comes from the records left by William Twici the huntsman of a pack during the time of Edward II in the 14th century, who writes that they were a rough sort of dog between a Hound and a Terrier. To understand that description better one needs to remember that the Hound to which he was referring was probably something like the Southern Hound, an early form of Foxhound, and the Terrier would be fairly non-descript. Otter hunting never became as popular as fox hunting, largely because in the first place it is a wetter and more uncomfortable pursuit, and secondly because it lacks the glamorous trappings of the fox hunt. During the second half of the 19th century, however, there were upwards of twenty packs in Britain, most of these in the South West and in Wales where the otter was plentiful, and indeed still is.

The origins of the breed are obscure. The Southern Hound and the Harrier have been credited, the Water Spaniel and even the Bulldog have been said by some writers to have played a part in its makeup, but the idea that the breed originated in France is much more credible. A comparison between a painting of the head of a young Griffon de Bresse by Rosa Bonheur in the Wallace Collection and a head study by George Earl of an Otter Hound called Swimmer at the turn of the century, reveals a remarkable similarity. Whilst a photograph of M. Henri Baillet's pack of Griffons Vendéens and Griffons Nivernais of the same period could well be a photograph of a pack of Otterhounds. It was at about the same time, the beginning of this century that the Otterhound first made his appearance in the United States, and in 1907 they were benched for the first time at a show in Claremont. The two first registered were owned by H. S. Wardner who was the first breeder of Otterhounds in the United States where they are still very popular.

The Otterhound's work in the field is remarkable, and he is noted for his fantastic nose and persistence. He is wary in the hunt, will rarely overun a holt, and will stay on the trail through any sort of terrain and through deep fast-running water unwaveringly. Nothing will throw him off the trail, and when he gives tongue seriously, the location of his quarry is certain. He is a big strong noble looking hound in spite of his shaggy coat and somewhat unkempt appearance. He is described by George S. Lowe as requiring the courage of a Bulldog, the strength of a Newfoundland in water, the nose of a Pointer, the sagacity of a Retriever, the stamina of a Foxhound, the patience of a Beagle and the intelligence of a Collie. Praise indeed for a dog that has virtually disappeared in his home country. He is now rarely seen in his original form in Britain, and never on the show bench, whilst oddly enough, such is fashion, the Basset version of his probable ancestor is making rapid headway. The Otterhound makes the most friendly and affectionate of companions and in addition to his prowess in the field, is a remarkably good guard and watch dog.

OFFICIAL STANDARD

General appearance

The Otter Hound is a large, rough-coated, squarely symmetrical hound. The length of a dog's body from withers to base of tail is approximately equal to its height at the withers. However, a bitch is not to be faulted if her length of body is slightly greater than her height. The Otter Hound is amiable and boisterous. It has an extremely sensitive nose, and is inquisitive and persevering in investigating scents. The Otter Hound should be shown on a loose lead. The Otter Hound hunts its quarry on land and water and requires a combination of characteristics unique among hounds—most notably a rough, double coat and webbed feet.

Head

The head is large, fairly narrow, and well covered with hair. The length from tip of nose to occiput is 11 to 12 inches in a hound 26 inches at the withers. This proportion should be maintained in larger and smaller hounds. The *skull* (cranium) is long, fairly narrow under the hair, and only slightly domed. The muzzle is long and square in cross-section with powerful jaws and deep flews. The *stop* is not pronounced. The *nose* is large, dark, and com-

Ears: long, pendulous and folded.

pletely pigmented. The *ears* are long, pendulous, and folded. They are set low and hang close to the head. They are well covered and fringed with hair. The tips of the *ear* leather reach at least to the tip of the nose. The *eyes* are deeply set. The haw shows only slightly. The eyes are dark, but may vary with the color of the hound. The *jaws* are powerful and capable of a crushing grip. A scissors bite is preferred. *Faults:* bite grossly undershot or overshot.

Neck and body

The *neck* looks shorter than it really is because of the abundance of hair on it. The neck blends smoothly into the trunk. The *chest* is deep; the *ribs* extend well toward the rear of the trunk. The *topline* is level. The *tail* is fairly long, reaching at least to the hock. It is well feathered

(covered and fringed with hair). It is carried sickle-fashion (not over the back) when a dog is moving or alert, but may droop when the dog is at rest.

Forequarters

Shoulders clean, powerful, and well-sloped. *Legs* heavy-boned and straight.

Hindquarters

Thighs large and well-muscled. *Legs* moderately angulated. Legs parallel when viewed from the rear. *Feet* large, broad, compact, and well padded, with membranes connecting the toes (web-footed). *Dewclaws*, if any, on the hind legs are generally removed; dewclaws on the forelegs may be removed.

Coat

The rough outer coat is three to six inches long on the back, shorter on the extremities. It must be hard (coarse and crisp). A water-resistant inner coat of short woolly hair is an essential feature of the breed. A naturally stripped coat lacking length and fringes is correct for an Otter Hound that is being worked. A proper hunting coat will show the hard outer coat and woolly undercoat. *Faults:* a soft outer coat is a very serious fault as is a woolly-textured top coat. Lack of undercoat is a serious fault. An outer coat much longer than six inches becomes heavy when wet and is a fault.

Color

Any color or combination of colors is acceptable. The nose should be darkly pigmented, black or liver, depending on the color of the hound.

Gait

The Otter Hound moves freely with forward reach and drive. The gait is smooth and effortless and capable of being maintained for many miles. Otter Hounds single-track at slower speed than light-bodied hounds. Because they do not lift their feet high off the ground, Otter Hounds may shuffle when they walk or move at a slow trot.

Size

Dogs range from 24 to 27 inches at the withers, and weigh from 75 to 115 pounds, depending on the height and condition of the hound. Bitches are 22 to 26 inches at the withers and 65 to 100 pounds. A hound in hard working condition may weigh as much as 15 pounds less than one of the same height that is not being worked. Otter Hounds should not be penalized for being shown in working condition (lean, well-muscled, naturally stripped coat).

Approved 12 October 1971

AKC VARIATION TO STANDARD

This dog is not granted championship status by the KC(GB). The above standards are those of the AKC.

PHARAOH HOUND

NATIONAL GROUPING		
	Name	Number
KC(GB)	Hound	I
AKC	—	—
FCI	Coursing Dogs	10

The rise to popularity of the Pharaoh Hound has been one of the phenomena of the modern dog scene. In 1970 none were registered at the Kennel Club in England, and the breed was hardly known outside Malta. By 1975, the numbers had risen sufficiently for the breed to be granted championship status, and Mr. Hamilton-Renwick who had done so much to further the interests of the breed was judging them at Crufts. The more romantic among enthusiasts for the breed claim it as the most ancient form of dog in the world, and will date it back to some three thousand years BC. They will point to wall paintings on Egyptian tombs and claim that these depict early Pharaoh Hounds. In fact many of the prick-eared canine forms on early Egyptian works depicted the god Anubis, who was actually the Jackal God. The Pharaoh Hound was not the only prick-eared running hunting dog of the Mediterranean area, Italy, Spain and some of the islands can lay equal claim with similar dogs such as the Ibizan Hound. There is little doubt however, that the Pharaoh Hound is a very old breed. It was for a considerable length of time restricted to the island of Malta, and there it was bred true to type. It was at one time considered to be merely a colour variation of the Ibizan Hound, but has now been accepted as a separate breed.

It is probably this matter of colour which has affected the modern history of the dog. The dog now accepted as the Ibizan Hound, which was at one time known as the Podenco Ibicenco, was some years ago preferred as an all-red dog, the parti-coloured being less popular. Once the reds were separated and became a breed in their own right, their rapid rise was assured. The Pharaoh is a beautifully constructed Hound with most attractive body lines, long neck and straight bones, and his glowing reddish tan colour allied to a smooth glossy coat gain him many admirers. He was developed as a hunting dog from the even older dog known as the Egyptian Hound, which was noted for the ability to use his nose as well as his sight. He has retained this ability, and although he is what the Scandinavian countries would term a sight Hound he also has an excellent nose, something denied to the running Hounds proper such as the Greyhound.

As a show dog he has made a tremendous impression in many countries, being exhibited in large numbers in Britain and already being shown at major shows elsewhere. Although he is not yet recognised in the United States, there is little doubt that he will be one of the very popular show dogs of the future. He has the right temperament for the show ring, appearing to enjoy the admiration of the spectators and being in the company of others of his breed. He is steady in the ring, standing well and moving with great power and enjoyment when asked to do so. His coat repays attention as it is short and glossy and needs the minimum of brushing and polishing to look at its best. He is at his best at open-air shows, where when seen in numbers he creates a fine spectacle.

His temperament is most attractive as he is friendly, does not normally show signs of nervousness, is a happy dog and very good with children. He is clean and troublefree around the house, though in common with the other hunting dogs, he does need some exercise. Kept with others in sufficient space he will take exercise naturally, as his nature allows him to play with other dogs without quarrelling.

OFFICIAL STANDARD

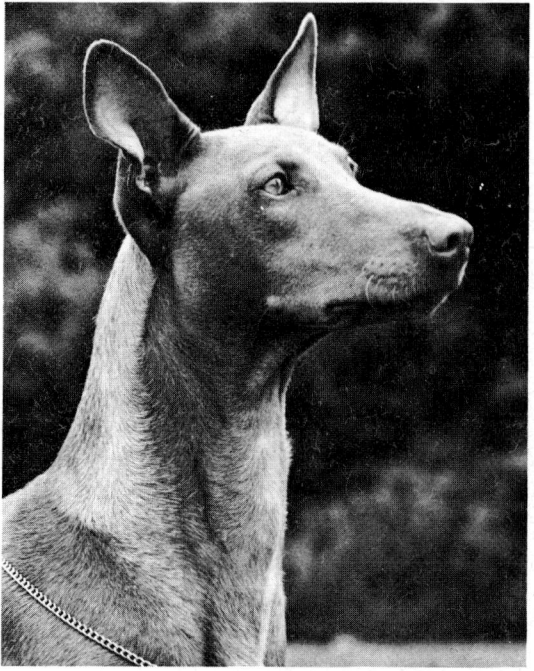

Characteristics
An intelligent, friendly, affectionate, playful and alert breed. An alert keen hunter, the Pharaoh Hound hunts by scent and sight using its large ears to a marked degree when working close.

General appearance
The Pharaoh Hound is medium sized, of noble bearing with clean-cut lines. Graceful yet powerful. Very fast with free easy movement and alert expression.

Head and skull
Skull long, lean and well-chiselled. Foreface slightly longer than the skull. Only slight stop. Top of skull parallel with the foreface, the whole head representing a blunt wedge when viewed in profile and from above.

Eyes
Amber coloured, blending with the coat; oval, moderately deep set, with keen, intelligent expression.

Ears
Medium high set; carried erect when alert, but very mobile; broad at the base, fine and large.

Mouth
Powerful jaws with strong teeth. Scissor bite.

Nose
Flesh coloured only, blending with the coat.

Neck
Long, lean, muscular and slightly arched. Clean throat line.

Forequarters
Shoulders: strong, long and well laid back. *Forelegs:* straight and parallel. Elbows well tucked in. Pasterns strong.

Body
Lithe with almost straight topline. Slight slope down from croup to root of tail. Deep brisket extending down to point of elbow. Ribs well sprung. Moderate cut up. Length of body from breast to haunch bone slightly longer than height at withers.

Hindquarters
Strong and muscular. Moderate bend of stifle. Well developed second thigh. Limbs parallel when viewed from behind.

Feet
Strong, well knuckled and firm, turning neither in nor out. Paws well padded. Dew claws may be removed.

Gait
Free and flowing; the head should be held fairly high and the dog should cover the ground well without any apparent effort. The legs and feet should move in line with the body; any tendency to throw the feet sideways, or a high stepping 'hackney' action is a definite fault.

Tail
Medium set—fairly thick at the base and tapering (whip-like), reaching just below the point of hock in repose. Carried high and curved when the dog is in action. The tail should not be tucked between the legs. A screw tail is a fault.

Coat
Short and glossy, ranging from fine and close to slightly harsh; no feathering.

Colour
Tan or rich tan with white markings allowed as follows: White tip on tail strongly desired. White on chest (called 'The Star'). White on toes. Slim white blaze on centre line of face permissible. Flecking or white other than above undesirable.

Height
Dogs: ideally 56–63 cm (22 to 25 inches). *Bitches:* ideally 53–61 cm (21 to 24 inches). Overall balance must be maintained.

Faults
Any deviation from the foregoing is a fault, hunting blemishes excepted.

Note
Male animals should have two apparently normal testicles fully descended into the scrotum.

AKC VARIATION TO STANDARD
This dog is not granted championship status by the AKC.

RHODESIAN RIDGEBACK

On a farm called 'Valhalla' twenty miles north of Rusape, Rhodesia, there is a rock. The cow, the ox and the dogs depicted in the carving on the rock indicate that the scene is of the burial preparations for a chief, a Hottentot Chief. Hump-backed Zebu cattle and ridged hunting dogs were prize possessions of the Hottentot; the cattle were the forebears of the Afrikander cattle, and the dogs the ancestors of the modern Rhodesian Ridgeback. These dogs were known in Rhodesia a long time before the coming of the white man, though probably the earliest published illustration showing the dog is in 'Livingstone's Missionary Travels in South Africa,' (1857), which clearly shows a dog with a ridge of hair on its back.

It is from this dog that the modern Rhodesian Ridgeback is descended. Undoubtedly there was some crossing with breeds brought in by the early settlers, but the resulting dog was a fine strong hunter that retained the ridge. There is record of dogs being brought to Matabeleland in 1875 and of their being crossed with a hunting pack by a big game hunter

NATIONAL GROUPING		
	Name	Number
KC(GB)	Hound	1
AKC	Hounds	2
FCI	Small Hounds	6

Cornelis van Rooyen and of dogs very like the modern hound being produced. In the 1920's there were a number of different ridged dogs in South Africa, and a meeting was held to compile a standard for the breed. That standard has stood the test of time, with certain minor changes. Since the 1920's the breed and the breed club have gone from strength to strength, and the Rhodesian Ridgeback has been constantly improved.

In the early days the dog was used by big game hunters for the hunting of lion, hence the additional name of 'lion dog', though it is certain that no dog exists that could succeed in a fight with a lion. What the dog did, and probably still does, is to torment the lion by feint attacks in much the same way as the Elkhound worries the Elk, until such time as the hunter can come up with it and shoot it. This means that the dog must have great agility as well as power, as the lion is one of the quickest beasts in spite of its size. He must also be able to run at speed to chase and cut off escaping game. The Rhodesian Ridgeback will, however, attack lesser game than the lion, and this is where the weight of the dog tells, the usual technique being for the dog to charge and knock over the game. He has a good nose and works quite well as a gundog.

As a showdog he is a fine animal, his size and muscularity in the ring giving a great impression of power. He handles well, and a ring full of the breed is usually quiet and well-behaved, though there is a certain amount of suspicion evident between them. When first introduced into Britain this dog was thought to be difficult to handle, but this may well have been due to one or two unfortunate importations,

as it has now settled down and has proved completely tractable.

The Ridgeback becomes very attached to his owner and family, proving an excellent guard, as he will stand no nonsense from strangers, and is very positive in his attention to intruders. Whilst the notice 'Beware of the Dog' rarely prevents anyone from entering property, the notice 'Beware of the Rhodesian Ridgeback' would ensure privacy. His warning is often a low growl rather than a bark, but it is very effective. Judges laying their hands on the dog in the ring will often feel this rumble even if they don't hear it, and whilst it does not mean that the dog is immediately about to attack, it does mean that the dog is wary of the attention being given it. He is still used a great deal as a guard in Southern Africa, being a multi-purpose animal, guarding the property day and night, available for a day's hunting at any time, and always prepared to make a fuss of the children.

OFFICIAL STANDARD

Characteristics
The peculiarity of the breed is the ridge on the back which is formed by the hair growing in the opposite direction to the rest of the coat; the ridge must be regarded as the escutcheon of the breed. The ridge must be clearly defined, tapering and symmetrical. It must start immediately behind the shoulders and continue up to the hip

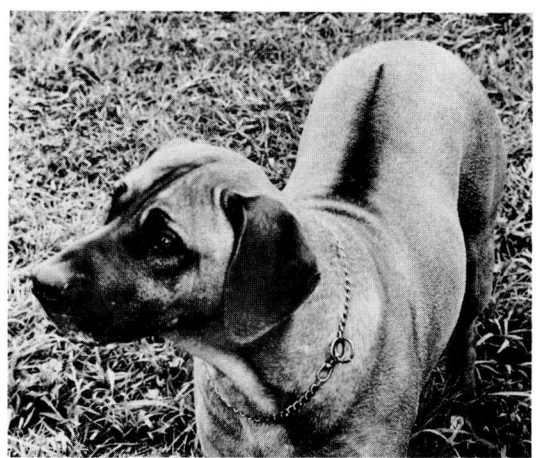

(haunch) bones, and must contain two identical crowns only opposite each other. The lower edges of the crowns must not extend further down the ridge than one-third of the legth of the ridge. Up to two inches is a good average for the width of the ridge.

General appearance
The Ridgeback should represent a strong, muscular and active dog, symmetrical in outline, and capable of great endurance, with a fair amount of speed. Movement should be similar to the Foxhound's gait.

Head and skull
Should be of a fair length, the skull flat and rather broad between the ears and should be free from wrinkles when in repose. The stop should be reasonably well defined, and not in one straight line from the nose to the occiput bone as required in a Bull Terrier. The nose should be black or brown, in keeping with the colour of the dog. No other coloured nose is permissible. A black nose should be accompanied by dark eyes; a brown nose by amber eyes.

Eyes
Should be moderately well apart, and should be round, bright and sparkling, with intelligent expression, their colour harmonising with the colour of the dog.

Ears
Should be set up rather high, of medium size, rather wide at base, and gradually tapering to a rounded point. They should be carried close to the head.

Mouth
The muzzle should be long, deep and powerful, jaws level and strong, with well developed teeth, especially the canines or holders. The lips should be clean, closely fitting the jaws.

Neck
Should be fairly long, strong and free from throatiness.

Forequarters
The shoulders should be sloping, clean and muscular, denoting speed. The forelegs should be perfectly straight, strong and heavy in bone; elbows close to the body.

Body
The chest should not be too wide but very deep and capacious; ribs moderately well sprung, never rounded like barrel-hoops (which would indicate want of speed).

Ears: set rather high, wide at base, tapering.

Tail
Should be strong at the insertion and generally tapering towards the end, free from coarseness. It should not be inserted too high or too low, and should be carried with a slight curve upwards, never curled.

Coat
Should be short and dense, sleek and glossy in appearance but neither woolly nor silky.

Colour
Light wheaten to red wheaten. Head, body, legs and tail should be of a uniform colour. A little white on the chest is permissible but excessive white hairs here, on belly, or above paws should be penalised. White toes are undesirable. Dark muzzle and ears are permissible.

The back powerful, and loins strong, muscular and slightly arched.

Hindquarters
In the hind legs the muscles should be clean, well defined and hocks well down.

Feet
The feet should be compact with well arched toes, round, tough elastic pads, protected by hair between the toes and pads.

Weight and size
The desirable weight is dogs 80 pounds and bitches 70 pounds with a permissible variation of 5 pounds above and below these weights. A mature Ridgeback should be a handsome, upstanding dog; dogs should be of a height of 25 to 27 inches and bitches 24 to 26 inches. Minimum bench standard; dogs 25 inches and bitches 24 inches.

Note
Male animals should have two apparently normal testicles fully descended into the scrotum.

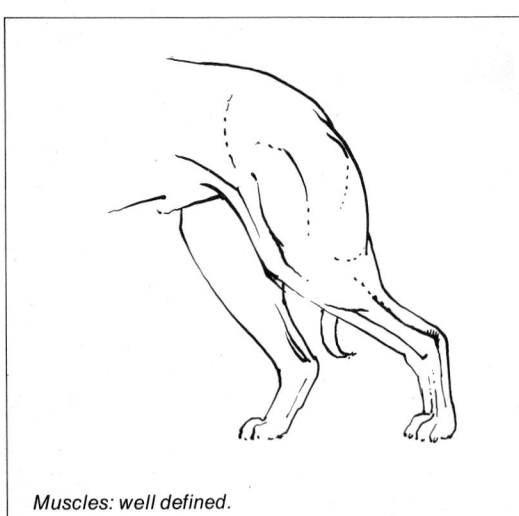

Muscles: well defined.

AKC VARIATION TO STANDARD
Weight: desirable dogs 75 pounds, bitches 65 pounds.

SALUKI (GAZELLE HOUND)

NATIONAL GROUPING		
	Name	Number
KC(GB)	Hound	I
AKC	Hounds	II
FCI	Coursing Dogs	10

This dog is one of the most graceful dogs in the world. As yet another of the Greyhounds, it is the perfectly built running machine with long well angulated legs, great depth of ribs to give it heart and lung room, and a long neck to assist it to pick up game. It remains basically a hunter and a strong dog, capable of moving at high speeds over the roughest of going, picking its way over rocks and through gullies at a speed that would defy most animals. Like the Greyhound proper, its appearance has changed little over the centuries.

As a show dog the Saluki has reached the heights, winning consistently at all the major shows throughout the world, and a mature Saluki in full coat, moving round the ring with long flowing strides and great pride, is a fine sight.

He is a gentle, dignified dog with an attractive attitude towards human beings, being most friendly. He is somewhat aloof at first and does not take quickly to strangers, but once he attaches himself to a person, he does so for life.

When the ice age finally withdrew it moved gradually north. Some of the earliest evidence of man as he exists today was found in the areas that were the first to become fertile and warm, and it was there that the earliest traces of man's association with the canine race were found. Saluki breeders will claim that these early traces, found as cave paintings, show man with his dog, and that dog is a Saluki, or at least a Saluki type. Certainly the dog would have been a long-legged hunting dog, as this is the type that early man would have found useful. Whether it was anything like the Saluki as we know it today, is another matter, as many other breeds have also staked a claim.

The Saluki was, and probably still is, the dog of the Bedouin. Still a nomadic tribesman, the Bedouin needs to hunt to stay alive, as he still lives as his forefathers did, moving from place to place, living off the land and then moving on again when the resources of one area fail him. The dog has always been the prized possession of the tribesmen, being kept very close, even hidden away when strangers are around, and used for the hunt in the early hours of the morning before the heat of the sun. In the early days it was difficult to get a tribesman to part with his dog, as it was considered a member of the family as well as valuable.

As was the Afghan, the Saluki was used in conjunction with a hawk. The hawk was trained to swoop at the head of the game and slow it down until the dog could catch up with it and pull it down. This training was a long and complicated business, and tribes had their Hound attendants and huntsmen whose duty it was to train both bird and dog. Although the Saluki has been known for so long a time, it was not seen in Britain until 1840, and was not recognised by the American Kennel Club until 1927.

OFFICIAL STANDARD

General appearance
The whole appearance of this breed should give an impression of grace and symmetry and of great speed and endurance coupled with strength and activity to enable it to kill gazelle or other quarry over deep sand or rocky mountain. The expression should be dignified and gentle with deep, faithful, farseeing eyes.

Head and skull
Head long and narrow; skull moderately wide between ears, not domed, the stop not pronounced, the whole showing great quality. Nose black or liver.

Eyes
Dark to hazel and bright, large and oval, but not prominent.

Ears
Long and mobile, covered with long silky hair; hanging close to the skull.

Mouth
Teeth strong and level.

Neck
Long, supple and well muscled.

Forequarters
Shoulders sloping and set well back, well muscled without being coarse. The chest deep and moderately narrow. The forelegs straight and long from the elbow to the knee.

Body
Back fairly broad, muscles slightly arched over the loin.

Hindquarter: stifle moderately bent, hocks low.

Hindquarters
Strong, hip bones set wide apart, and stifle moderately bent, hocks low to the ground, showing galloping and jumping power.

Feet: moderate length, strong, supple.

Feet
Of moderate length, toes long, and well arched, not splayed out, but at the same time not cat footed; the whole being strong and supple and well feathered between the toes.

Tail: carried naturally in curve, well feathered.

Tail
Long, set on low and carried naturally in a curve, well feathered on the underside with long silky hair, not bushy.

Coat
Smooth and of a soft silky texture; slight feather on the legs; feather at the back of the thighs; sometimes with slight woolly feather on thigh and shoulders. (In the Smooth variety the points should be the same with the exception of the coat which has not feathering.)

Colour
White, cream, fawn, golden, red, grizzle and tan, tri-colour (white, black and tan), and black and tan, or variations of these colours.

Weight and size
Height should average 23 to 28 inches, bitches proportionately smaller.

Note
Male animals should have two apparently normal testicles fully descended into the scrotum.

WHIPPET

NATIONAL GROUPING		
	Name	Number
KC(GB)	Hound	I
AKC	Hounds	II
FCI	Coursing Dogs	IO

The history of many breeds of dog is shrouded in the obscurity that years of unrecorded progress brings. None more so than the Whippet. From its shape, use and character we can assume a great deal, but much of the early breeding went unrecorded, as it was carried out in areas where more attention was paid to breaking records than to keeping them, and only then to produce running and coursing dogs.

The origin of the name too is obscure. It has been suggested that it came from the word whip, to snap or crack like a whip, and that the sharp quick character of the dog led to the use of the name 'whippet' or little whip. There are however early mentions of a breed of dog that is not recorded pictorially called a Wappit, for example 'sporting dogs out of this question of which doubtless every farmer desires to possess some, the useful pack upon a farm consists of Sheepdogs, Rough Terriers, Vermin Curs and Wappits'. Around the latter part of the 19th century the racing of small dogs over a short straight course was extremely popular among the working classes of the North East of England. The area consisted largely of industrial towns and cities based upon the coalfields, and the miners needed a sport which was not too expensive, and in which they themselves could indulge as owners, whilst satisfying their native desire to keep animals and improve strains.

The Whippet fulfilled all the requirements. He is a small dog, easily housed and fed, and readily becomes a member of the household, living indoors, keeping the children company, and needing the type of exercise that can be given him on quiet walks round the streets and at the odd race or two at the weekend. Originally the dog used in the North East was a type of Terrier, often rough-coated, always long in the leg and very game, enthusiastic about chasing anything that moved,

and prepared to kill at the end of the chase. This itself was important, as an occasional rabbit did not come amiss as a supplement to the often meagre family fare of the hard-working and underpaid underground worker and his family.

When dog shows became popular in England, and it is often suggested that this happened in the first instance in the Newcastle area, the breed rapidly changed to the dog that we now know so well. The smooth coats ousted the roughs, though the latter can still be seen racing in mining areas. The Whippet became a shapely dog, with all the beauty that the swiftest of animals possesses; indeed the Whippet is one of the fastest of all dogs over a short distance, capable of outdistancing even the Greyhound on its initial burst.

The breed has become popular as a show dog throughout the world, largely because of its temperament. The Whippet is among the easiest of dogs to prepare, transport and handle in the ring, even the youngest child being capable of achieving a rapport with one which would be impossible with most breeds. In addition there are few dogs that are as well-behaved in the house, clean in manner and as friendly.

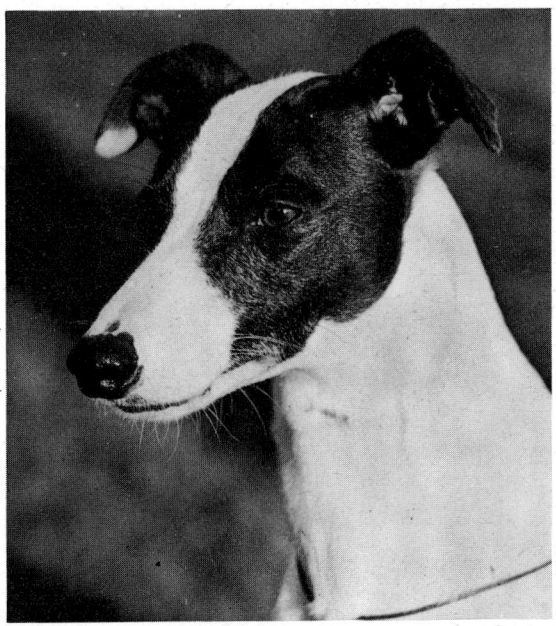

OFFICIAL STANDARD

General appearance
Should convey an impression of beautifully balanced muscular power and strength, combined with great elegance and grace of outline. Symmetry of outline, muscular development and powerful gait are the main considerations; the dog being built for speed and work all forms of exaggeration should be avoided. The dog should possess great freedom of action, the forelegs should be thrown forward and low over the ground like a thoroughbred horse not in a hackney-like action. Hind legs should come well under the body giving a great propelling power, general movement not to look stilted, high stepping or in a short or mincing manner.

Head and skull
Long and lean, flat on top tapering to the muzzle, rather wide between the eyes, the jaws powerful and clean cut, nose black, in blues a bluish colour is permitted and in livers a nose of the same colour and in whites or particolour a butterfly nose is permissible.

Eyes
Bright, expression very alert.

Ears
Rose shaped, small and fine in texture.

Mouth
Level. The teeth in the top jaw fitting closely over the teeth in lower jaw.

Neck
Long and muscular, elegantly arched.

Forequarters
Shoulders oblique and muscular the blades carried up to the spine closely set together at the top. Forelegs straight and upright, front not too wide, pasterns strong with slight spring, elbows well set under the body.

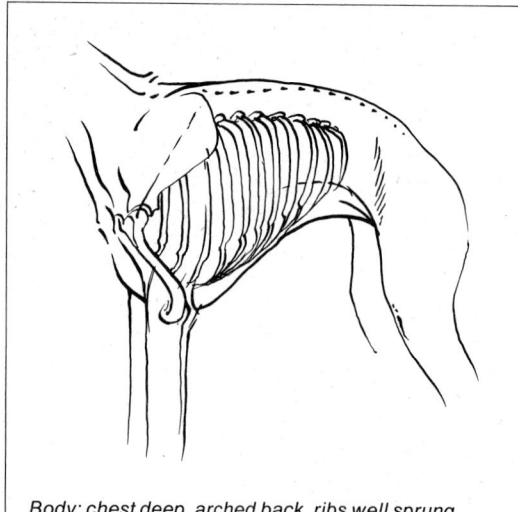

Body: chest deep, arched back, ribs well sprung.

Body
Chest very deep with plenty of heart-room, brisket deep and well defined, back broad, firm, somewhat long and showing definite arch over the loin but not humped, loin giving the impression of strength and power, ribs well sprung; well muscled on back.

Hindquarters
Strong and broad across thighs, stifles well bent, hocks well let down, second thighs strong, the dog then being able to stand over a lot of ground and show great driving power.

Feet
Very neat, well split up between the toes, knuckles highly arched, pads thick and strong.

Tail
No feathering. Long, tapering, when in action carried in a delicate curve upward but not over the back.

Coat
Fine, short, as close as possible in texture.

Colour
Any colour or mixture of colours.

Weight and size
The ideal height for dogs is 18½ inches and for bitches 17½ inches. Judges should use their discretion and not unduly penalise an otherwise good specimen.

Faults
Front and shoulders: weak, sloping or too straight pasterns, pigeon toes, tied elbows, loaded or bossy shoulders wide on top and straight shoulderblades, flat sides. An exaggerated narrow front not to be encouraged. *Head and skull:* appleskull, short fore face or down face. *Ears:* pricked or tulip. *Mouth:* over or undershot. *Neck:* throatiness at the join of neck and jaw, and at base of neck. *Body and hindquarters:* a short coupled or cramped stance, also an exaggerated arch, a Camel or Humped back (the arch starting behind the shoulderblades), a too short or overlong loin. Straight stifles, poor muscular development of thighs and second thighs. *Feet:* splayed, flat or open. *Tail:* gay, ringed or twisted, short or docked. *Coat:* wire or broken coated; a coarse or woolly coat; coarse thick skin.

Note
Male animals should have two apparently normal testicles fully descended into the scrotum.

AKC VARIATION TO STANDARD
Nose: entirely black. *Eyes:* lack of pigmentation around eyelids is undesirable. Yellow or dilute-coloured eyes should be strictly penalised. Both eyes must be same colour. *Size:* ideal—dogs 19 to 22 inches; bitches 18 to 21 inches. *Disqualification:* one half-inch above or below the stated measurements. Blue or china eyes. Undershot. Overshot one quarter of an inch.

WORKING GROUP:
NON-SPORTING BREEDS

Akita

Alaskan Malamute

Alsatian (German Shepherd Dog)

Belgian Shepherd Dog (Malinois)

Belgian Shepherd Dog (Tervueren)

Belgian Shepherd Dog (Groenendael)

Bernese Mountain Dog

Bouvier des Flandres

Boxer

Briard

Bullmastiff

Bearded Collie

Rough Collie

Smooth Collie

Dobermann

Great Dane

Hungarian Puli

Komondor

Kuvasz

Mastiff

Newfoundland

Norwegian Buhund

Old English Sheepdog

Pyrenean Mountain Dog

St. Bernard

Rottweiler

Samoyed

Shetland Sheepdog

Siberian Husky

Cardigan Welsh Corgi

Pembroke Welsh Corgi

WORKING GROUP: NON-SPORTING BREEDS

Since early in the days of dog's association with man, he has been put to work, even if it was only as a guard dog. The group now known as the Working Group has dogs used for a multitude of purposes, from the tiny sheep-herding Shetland Sheepdog to the giant property-guarding Mastiff. Many of the tasks the dogs have learned to undertake are an extension of a natural instinct. The herding dogs for instance are trained to use their instinct to chase anything that runs, and the guard dogs merely exercising on someone else's behalf their natural desire to protect their own territory.

There are those which are essentially guards, those that work as draught animals, originally in sledges and small carts and more recently for sport. There are the herders, and this is probably the largest sub-group, as work with animals has been widespread throughout the world for centuries, and there are a few heelers and cattle dogs. All, however, have one thing in common, they are intelligent enough to be trained, often in very complicated tasks, and with a couple of exceptions, they are large, strong and muscular animals.

When the wild dog first came into contact with early man he would have done so almost certainly as a whelp from a litter of wolves or wild dogs, and partly tamed, his guarding of the area inhabited by the tribe would merely be an extension of his natural defence of his own territory as he exercised it in the wild state. In later years this defensive instinct was encouraged and breeds of dogs were evolved for the purpose, large strong and fierce dogs often used as war dogs and usually of the Mastiff type, though many of the herding dogs doubled as guard dogs, including the home in with the herd as part of their responsibility.

There is a mixed category of hauling dogs in the Group, those that were developed specifically for work in the snow and ice of the Arctic, such as the Huskies and the Samoyed, and others which were used to tow small carts in countries such as Switzerland and the Netherlands. These were used by tradesmen for delivery purposes as an inexpensive alternative to the horse. Though the use of dogs for draught purposes is now banned in most countries, they are still very much in demand as sledge dogs, and are used both seriously and for competitive purposes as racing teams.

By far the largest number of breeds in the Group are those which originally were herding dogs. As man ceased to be nomadic he collected around him herds of beasts that supplied almost everything that he needed, food, drink and clothing. These herds became very precious possessions, and needed to be protected from predatory wild animals as well as kept within the confines of the immediate area of the settlement. For this purpose a wide variety of breeds was evolved to suit both the work and the conditions under which it had to be carried out. In the mountainous country of the Pyrenees a large dog was needed, capable of herding but also of defending against the wolves that existed until recent years. In the less rigorous conditions of Britain the Collie or the Old English Sheepdog were more suitable, whilst in the severe climate of such places as Hungary dogs with protective coats were needed.

Other dogs were evolved for specific purposes. The heelers, the Corgis of Wales for driving cattle by nipping at their heels, and the Rottweilers of Southern Germany which were cattle drovers are typical examples. Subsequently the Collie was developed not just to work as a sheep herder, but to excel in competition, the Border Collie having a world-wide reputation in this field. In those countries where the rearing of sheep is an important industry such as Australia the sheepdog still plays a very important part even in these days of mechanisation, and a considerable degree of specialisation takes place.

The Group includes some of the most popular breeds of dogs in the world, underlining the fact that the process of breeding dogs for exhibition has in no way detracted from their usefulness as workers, as many countries insist on a dog being proved capable of carrying out the task for which it was evolved, before it can gain its full title as a show dog.

AKITA

NATIONAL GROUPING		
	Name	Number
KC(GB)	—	–
AKC	Working Dogs	III
FCI	Guard Dogs	2

The most important dog in Japan is without doubt the Akita. The breed is numerous, is a most trusted member of many families, and has become almost a legend for his combination of courage and kindness. To equate him with the Chow Chow is doing him a disservice even though there is a great deal of re-semblance to that ancient breed. A breed exists on the waterfront of Hong Kong, which guards the godowns and timber yards which is nearer than the smooth Chow Chow is to the Akita, and those who only know the smooth Chow from the version seen in recent years in the Western World probably have a false impression of the original Chow. The Akita is a fairly long-legged version of the chow type with curled tail and pricked ears, and it is more than likely that the two breeds descended from a common ancestor which looked rather like the present day harbour dogs of Hong Kong.

Records place the first development of the breed somewhere in the early part of the 17th century when an exiled nobleman with a keen interest in dogs took up residence in Akita Province. He encouraged the landowners of that province to breed a race of large hunting dogs from which, by selective breeding the Akita resulted. At one time the ownership of the breed was restricted to the aristocracy and the Imperial family, and they became as much a legend in their time as did the Pekingese of China, a special language being evolved for talking with and about them, and dog minders who looked after Akitas wore a special and elaborate costume. In 1927 the Akitainu Hozankai Society of Japan was established to preserve the breed as it had gone into serious decline. The Japanese Government supported the breed and the society to the extent of giving financial support to a dog which by this time had become accepted as something of a national symbol.

He is essentially a hunting dog, strong with a good nose and keen eyesight, and staunch enough to tackle bear and wild boar. He can be trained to retrieve, is a good water dog and is even said to have been used to drive fish into the fisherman's nets. The first to arrive in the United States of America were brought in by the celebrated Helen Keller who was presented with a puppy by the Ministry of Education in Akita in 1937. American servicemen returning from the Far East after the Second World War brought others back with them, and from that time onwards the breed's popularity has grown with remarkable speed in the West. The faithfulness of the breed is exemplified by a dog named Hachiko who continued to arrive at Shibuya station to meet his master for nine years after his owner had died, daily in fact until he himself died in 1934. A statue, erected by public subscription stands on the station to commemorate his devotion. The Akita Club of America was formed in 1956 and the breed is now admitted to register by the American Kennel Club though it remains unshown in Britain.

The whole tradition of the breed has been built around his faithfulness to the family and his loyalty to its members, and though reserved in general behaviour he is very affectionate and thrives on human com-panionship. He makes a very good house dog and pet, and is a first class guard, especially of children and stock.

OFFICIAL STANDARD

General appearance
Large, powerful, alert, with much substance and heavy bone. The broad head, forming a blunt triangle, with deep muzzle, small eyes and erect ears carried forward in line with back of neck, is characteristic of the breed. The large, curled tail, balancing the broad head, is also characteristic of the breed.

Head
Massive but in balance with body; free of wrinkle when at ease. Skull flat between ears and broad; jaws square and powerful with minimal dewlap. Head forms a blunt

Head: massive. Skull: flat between ears.

triangle when viewed from above. *Fault:* narrow or snipy head. *Muzzle:* broad and full. Distance from nose to stop is to distance from stop to occiput as 2 is to 3. *Stop:* well defined, but not too abrupt. A shallow furrow extends well up forehead. *Nose:* broad and black. Liver permitted on white Akitas, but black always preferred. *Disqualification:* butterfly nose or total lack of pigmentation on nose. *Ears:* the ears of the Akita are characteristic of the breed. They are strongly erect and small in relation to rest of head. If ear is folded forward for measuring length, tip will touch upper eye rim. Ears are triangular, slightly rounded at tip, wide at base, set wide on head but not too low, and carried slightly forward over eyes in line with back of neck. *Disqualification:* drop or broken ears. *Eyes:* dark brown, small, deep-set and triangular in shape. Eye rims black and tight. *Lips and Tongue:* lips black and not pendulous; tongue pink. *Teeth:* strong with scissors bite preferred, but level bite acceptable. *Disqualification:* noticeably undershot or overshot.

Neck and body

Neck: thick and muscular; comparatively short, widening gradually toward shoulders. A pronounced crest blends in with base of skull. *Body:* longer than high, as 10 is to 9 in dogs; 11 to 9 in bitches. Chest wide and deep; depth of chest is one-half height of dog at shoulder. Ribs well sprung, brisket well developed. Level back with firmly-muscled loin and moderate tuck-up. Skin pliant but not loose. *Serious faults:* light bone, rangy body.

Body: longer than high as 10:9.

Tail

Large and full, set high and carried over back or against flank in a three-quarter, full, or double curl, always dipping to or below level of back. On a three-quarter curl, tip drops well down flank. Root large and strong. Tail bone reaches hock when let down. Hair coarse, straight and full, with no appearance of a plume. *Disqualification:* sickle or uncurled tail.

Forequarters and hindquarters

Forequarters: shoulders strong and powerful with moderate layback. Forelegs heavy-boned and straight as viewed from front. Angle of pastern 15 degrees forward from vertical. *Faults:* elbows in or out, loose shoulders. *Hindquarters:* width, muscular development and comparable to forequarters. Upper thighs well developed. Stifle moderately bent and hocks well let down, turning neither in nor out. *Dewclaws:* on front legs generally not removed; dewclaws on hind legs generally removed. *Feet:* cat feet, well knuckled up with thick pads. Feet straight ahead.

Coat

Double-coated. Undercoat thick, soft, dense and shorter than outer coat. Outer coat straight, harsh and standing somewhat off body. Hair on head, legs and ears short. Length of hair at withers and rump approximately two inches, which is slightly longer than on rest of body, except tail, where coat is longest and most profuse. *Fault:* Any indication of ruff or feathering.

Color

Any color including white; brindle; or pinto. Colors are brilliant and clear and markings are well balanced, with or without mask or blaze. White Akitas have no mask. Pinto has a white background with large, evenly placed patches covering head and more than one-third of body. Undercoat may be a different color from outer coat.

Gait

Brisk and powerful with strides of moderate length. Back remains strong, firm and level. Rear legs move in line with front legs.

Size

Dogs: 26 to 28 inches at the withers; bitches: 24 to 26 inches. *Disqualification:* dogs under 25 inches; bitches under 23 inches.

DISQUALIFICATIONS
Butterfly nose or total lack of pigmentation on nose. Drop or broken ears. Noticeably undershot or overshot. Sickle or uncurled tail. Dogs under 25 inches: bitches under 23 inches.

Approved 12 December 1972

AKC VARIATION TO STANDARD

This dog is not granted championship status by the KC(GB). The above standards are those of the AKC.

ALASKAN MALAMUTE

NATIONAL GROUPING		
	Name	Number
KC(GB)	—	—
AKC	Working Dogs	III
FCI	Guard Dogs	2

There are four recognised breeds of northern dogs which are used for hauling, the Siberian Husky, the Eskimo Dog, the Samoyed, and the Alaskan Malamute. Of the four, the Samoyed, though still used for exhibition hauling and competitions from time to time, has become so popular as a show breed that he is no longer thought of as belonging to the sledge hauling group. The others are still used, but are being seen more and more frequently in the show ring. The Alaskan Malamute is one of the oldest of the sledge hauling dogs, and was named after the Innuit tribe who were called Mahlemuts and who settled along the shores of Kotzebue Sound in Alaska.

When Alaska was opened up, and the richness of the territory was recognised, there was some intermingling of blood between the native dogs and those brought in by settlers. Sledge racing became popular and many crosses were tried to increase the strength and endurance of the hauling dogs, with the result that in the early part of this century there was considerable decline in the native Arctic sledge dog. The name Husky, often applied to all sledge dogs is unfortunate, as the only breed to which it should apply is the Siberian Husky. Jack London in his novels about the frozen North, for instance, wrote of Huskies when in fact he was almost certainly describing Malamutes. The Siberian Husky and the Eskimo Dog certainly existed, but the hauling dogs weighing eighty pounds, capable of towing heavily loaded sledges over considerable distances under very severe conditions, would certainly be Alaskan Malamutes.

Arctic exploration increased the interest in these powerful dogs that performed incredible feats of endurance under impossible conditions, living rough, subsisting on the absolute minimum of unappetising food, and making travel over frozen snow and ice possible before the days of the aeroplane and the powered sledge. Their prowess was paralleled to that of their human companions, and the stories about their power and abilities made them sound to be more than just dogs. Although the dogs are still used for serious work from time to time, they are now also used for the

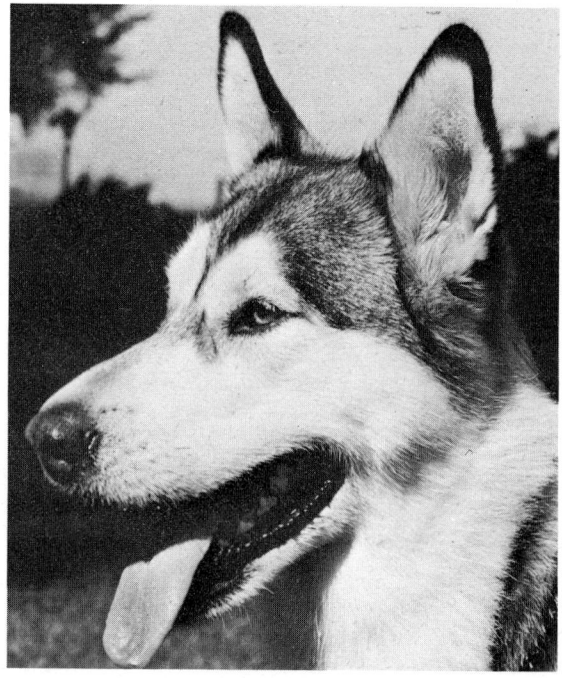

fun of sledge racing. The Samoyed is used for showy teams, but the Alaskan Malamute for the serious competitive long-distance races. A team of six dogs will pull an eight hundred pound load at speeds of up to ten miles per hour for forty or fifty miles a day on a journey that may take days.

The Malamute has not achieved any degree of popularity in the show rings of Europe though specimens have been seen from time to time. Numbers are slowly growing, however, and one or two are now regularly entered in rare breed or unclassified classes. He is a large strong dog, rather positive in his reactions, and this may have had something to do with his lack of popularity as a show dog. He is friendly, becomes attached to people and especially to children, and makes an ideal companion for winter sports.

OFFICIAL STANDARD

General appearance and characteristics

The Alaskan Malamute is a powerful and substantially build dog with a deep chest and strong, compact body, not too short coupled, with a thick, coarse guard coat of sufficient length to protect a dense, woolly undercoat, from 1 to 2 inches in depth when dog is in full coat. Stands well over pads, and this stance gives the appearance of much activity, showing interest and curiosity. The head is broad, ears wedge-shaped and erect when alerted. The muzzle is bulky with only slight diminishing in width and depth from root to nose, not pointed or long, but not stubby. The Malamute moves with a proud carriage, head erect and eyes alert. Face markings are a distinguishing feature. These consist of either cap over head and rest of face solid color, usually grayish white, or face marked with the appearance of a mask. Combinations of cap and mask are not unusual. The tail is plumed and carried over the back, not like a fox brush, or tightly curled, more like a plume waving.

Malamutes are of various colors, but are usually wolfish gray or black and white. Their feet are of the 'snowshoe' type, tight and deep, with well-cushioned pads, giving a firm and compact appearance. Front legs are straight with big bone. Hind legs are broad and powerful, moderately bent at stifles, and without cowhocks. The back is straight, gently sloping from shoulders to hips. The loin should not be so short or tight as to interfere with easy, tireless movement. Endurance and intelligence are shown in body and expression. The eyes have a 'wolf-like' appearance by their position, but the expression is soft and indicates an affectionate disposition.

Temperament

The Alaskan Malamute is an affectionate, friendly dog, not a 'one-man' dog. He is a loyal, devoted companion, playful on invitation, but generally impressive by his dignity after maturity.

Head

The head should indicate a high degree of intelligence, and is broad and powerful as compared with other 'natural' breeds, but should be in proportion to the size of the dog so as not to make the dog appear clumsy or coarse. *Skull:* the skull should be broad between the ears, gradually narrowing to eyes, moderately rounded between ears, flattening on top as it approaches the eyes, rounding off to cheeks, which should be moderately flat. There should be a slight furrow between the eyes, the topline of skull and topline of the muzzle showing but little break downward

Head: showing typical markings.

from a straight line as they join. *Muzzle:* the muzzle should be large and bulky in proportion to size of skull, diminishing but little in width and depth from junction with skull to nose; lips close fitting; nose black; upper and lower jaws broad with large teeth, front teeth meeting with a scissors grip but never overshot or undershot.

Eyes

Brown, almond shaped, moderately large for this shape of eye, set obliquely in skull. Dark eyes preferred.

Ears

The ears should be of medium size, but small in proportion to head. The upper halves of the ears are triangular in shape, slightly rounded at tips, set wide apart on outside back edges of the skull with the lower part of the ear joining the skull on a line with the upper corner of the eye, giving the tips of the ears the appearance, when erect, of standing off from the skull. When erect, the ears point slightly forward, but when the dog is at work the ears are sometimes folded against the skull. High-set ears are a fault.

Neck

The neck should be strong and moderately arched.

Body

The chest should be strong and deep; body should be strong and compactly built but not short coupled. The back should be straight and gently sloping to the hips. The loins should be well muscled and not so short as to interfere with easy, rhythmic movement with powerful drive from the hindquarters. A long loin which weakens the back is also a fault. No excess weight.

Shoulders, legs and feet

Shoulders should be moderately sloping; forelegs heavily boned and muscled, straight to pasterns, which should be short and strong and almost vertical as viewed from the side. The feet should be large and compact, toes, tight-fitting and well arched, pads thick and tough, toenails short and strong. There should be a protective growth of hair between toes. Hind legs must be broad and powerfully muscled through thighs; stifles moderately bent, hock joints broad and strong, moderately bent and well let down. As viewed from behind, the hind legs should not appear bowed in bone, but stand and move true in line with movement of the front legs, and not too close or too wide. The legs of the Malamute must indicate unusual strength and tremendous propelling power. Any indication of unsoundness in legs or feet, standing or moving, is to be considered a serious fault. Dewclaws on the hind legs are undesirable and should be removed shortly after pups are whelped.

Tail: well-furred, carried over back, not tightly curled.

Tail

Moderately set and following the line of the spine at the start, well furred and carried over the back when not working—not tightly curled to rest on back—or short furred and carried like a fox brush, a waving plume appearance instead.

Coat

The Malamute should have a thick, coarse guard coat, not long and soft. The undercoat is dense, from 1 to 2 inches in depth, oily and woolly. The coarse guard coat stands out, and there is thick fur around the neck. The guard coat varies in length, as does the undercoat; however, in general, the coat is moderately short to medium along the sides of the body with the length of the coat increasing somewhat around the shoulders and neck, down the back

and over the rump, as well as in the breeching and plume. Malamutes usually have shorter and less dense coats when shed out during the summer months.

Color and markings

The usual colors range from light gray through the intermediate shadings to black, always with white on under-bodies, parts of legs, feet, and part of mask markings. Markings should be either caplike and/or mask-like on face. A white blaze on forehead and/or collar or spot on nape is attractive and acceptable, but broken color extending over the body in spots or uneven splashings is undesirable. One should distinguish between mantled dogs and splash-coated dogs. The only solid color allowable is the all-white.

Size

There is a natural range in size in the breed. The desirable freighting sizes are:

Dogs: 25 inches at the shoulders—85 pounds.
Bitches: 23 inches at the shoulders—75 pounds.

However, size consideration should not outweigh that of type, proportion, and functional attributes, such as shoulders, chest, legs, feet, and movement. When dogs are judged equal in type, proportion, and functional attributes, the dog nearest the desirable freighting size is to be preferred.

IMPORTANT

In judging Alaskan Malamutes their function as a sledge dog for heavy freighting must be given consideration above all else. The judge must bear in mind that this breed is designed primarily as the working sledge dog of the North for hauling heavy freight, and therefore he should be a heavy-boned, powerfully built, compact dog with sound legs, good feet, deep chest, powerful shoulders, steady, balanced, tireless gait, and the other physical equipment necessary for the efficient performance of his job. He isn't intended as a racing sled dog designed to compete in speed trials with the smaller Northern breeds.

The Malamute as a sledge dog for heavy freighting is designed for strength and endurance and any characteristic of the individual specimen, including temperament, which interferes with the accomplishment of this purpose is to be considered the most serious of faults. Faults under this provision would be splayfootedness, any indication of unsoundness or weakness in legs, cowhocks, bad pasterns, straight shoulders, lack of angulation, stilted gait or any gait which isn't balanced, strong, and steady, ranginess, shallowness, ponderousness, lightness of bone, poor over-all proportion, and similar characteristics.

AKC VARIATION TO STANDARD

This dog is not granted championship status by the KC(GB). The above standards are those of the AKC.

GERMAN SHEPHERD DOG (ALSATIAN)

NATIONAL GROUPING		
	Name	Number
KC(GB)	Working	5
AKC	Working Dogs	III
FCI	Herding Dogs	I

There is no dog in what we now know as the Working Group that has achieved the German Shepherd Dog's popularity and ironically no dog has been more vilified. Its early name, the Alsatian Wolf-Dog would have been enough to guarantee this, but during the First World War, when everything that savoured of Germany was publicly denigrated there was a strong body of opinion against this quite remarkable dog. More recently, as urban attacks on people and especially upon children have increased, and as these attacks have often been carried out by German Shepherd Dogs or dogs very like them, the feeling against the breed has strengthened.

The ancestry of the German Shepherd Dog is fairly well defined. He was developed in Germany around a hundred years ago in an attempt to produce the ideal shepherd dog. It is very unlikely that the breed resulted from crossing wolves with local dogs as has been suggested, and any wolflike character which the dog is incorrectly said to have is most likely due to the vague similarity there is in physical type and colour. The modern dog almost certainly descended from three strains of working dogs in Württemburg, Thuringia and Krone.

The first appearance of a German Shepherd Dog at a show was in 1882 in Hanover and the first specialist club was formed in 1899. Since that time few breeds can have had such care in breeding and recording.

It is one of the most intelligent dogs, being capable of working independently of habit and training. There are many stories of dogs taking naturally to herding and guarding tasks with either no training at all or the absolute minimum. He is probably the best guard in the world, being very forceful and positive and as a result he is much in demand in police and military circles. He is fairly easily trained in apprehending criminals, and police forces throughout the world use the breed for that purpose, the training being carried to a high degree of proficiency, and there is much competition between forces and individual dogs. In addition the German Shepherd Dog is one of the most popular breeds in the world of obedience training.

The German Shepherd Dog's response to training results in a high degree of showmanship, and large numbers of these dogs standing like statues, or gaiting round the ring in their own particular manner is always tremendously popular as a spectacle. They are quiet in the ring, rarely interfering with one another, and their complete understanding of what is going on is shown by their joy and excitement at being released from the tension of the immediate competition.

Some doubt has been cast on the temperamental stability of this dog, largely due to the fact that used as guards in the early days they were discouraged very little from exercising their strength and courage. In recent years there have been many attacks upon people by dogs, sometimes by German Shepherd Dogs, but often by big strong dogs described by unreliable eye-witnesses and the media as the same type when they were probably mongrels or crossbreeds that looked vaguely like them. In fact the temperament of the German Shepherd Dog is no more unreliable than that of any other dog. Correctly trained and housed he will prove every bit as amenable and friendly as a Toy breed or a Gundog. Incorrectly trained, and kept in conditions in which he sees strangers only as intruders to be driven off as in the guarding of dumps and other property, he exercises his strength and natural instincts as he has been encouraged to do.

OFFICIAL STANDARD

Characteristics

The characteristic expression of the Alsatian gives the impression of perpetual vigilance, fidelity, liveliness and watchfulness, alert to every sight and sound, with nothing escaping attention; fearless, but with decided suspiciousness of strangers—as opposed to the immediate friendliness of some breeds. The Alsatian possesses highly developed senses, mentally and temperamentally. He should be strongly individualistic and possess a high standard of intelligence. Three of the most outstanding traits are incorruptibility, discernment and ability to reason.

General appearance

The general appearance of the Alsatian is a well-proportioned dog showing great suppleness of limb, neither massive nor heavy, but at the same time free from any suggestion of weediness. It must not approach the greyhound type. The body is rather long, strongly boned, with plenty of muscle, obviously capable of endurance and speed and of quick and sudden movement. The gait should be supple, smooth and long-reaching, carrying the body along with the minimum of up-and-down movement, entirely free from stiltiness.

Head and skull

The head is proportionate to the size of the body, long, lean and clean cut, broad at the back of the skull, but

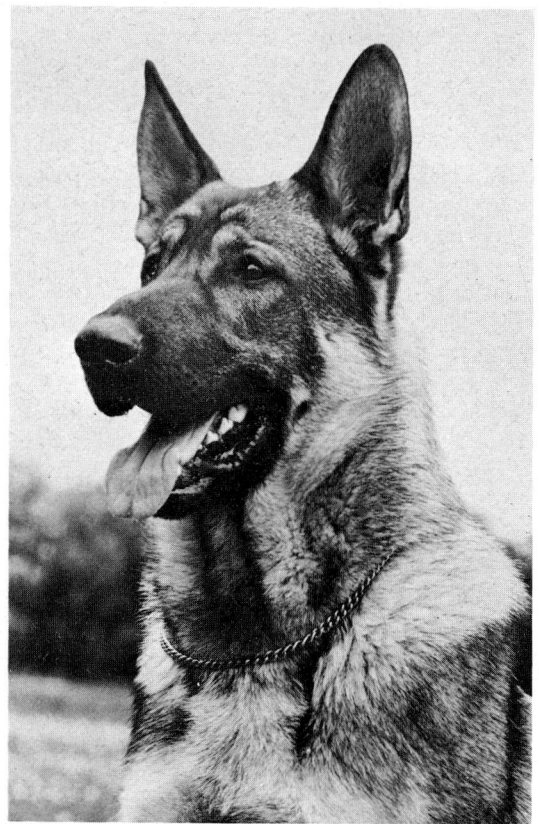

without coarseness, tapering to the nose with only a slight stop between the eyes. The skull is slightly domed and the top of the nose should be parallel to the forehead. The cheeks must not be full or in any way prominent and the whole head, when viewed from the top should be much in the form of a V, well filled in under the eyes. There should be plenty of substance in foreface, with a good depth from top to bottom. The muzzle is strong and long and, while tapering to the nose, it must not be carried to such an extreme as to give the appearance of being overshot. It must not show any weakness, or be snipy or lippy. The lips must be tight fitting and clean. The nose must be black.

Eyes

The eyes are almond-shaped as nearly as possible matching the surrounding coat but darker rather than lighter in shade and placed to look straight forward. They must not be in any way bulging or prominent, and must show a lively, alert and highly intelligent expression.

Ears

The ears should be of moderate size, but rather large than small, broad at the base and pointed at the tips, placed rather high on the skull and carried erect—all adding to the alert expression of the dog as a whole. (It should be noted, in case novice breeders may be misled, that in Alsatian puppies the ears often hang until the age of six months and sometimes longer, becoming erect with the replacement of the milk teeth).

Mouth

The teeth should be sound and strong, gripping with a scissor-like action, the lower incisors just behind, but touching the upper.

Neck

The neck should be strong, fairly long with plenty of muscle, fitting gracefully into the body, joining the head without sharp angles and free from throatiness.

Forequarters

The shoulders should slope well back. The ideal being that a line drawn through the centre of the shoulderblade should form a right-angle with the humerus when the leg is perpendicular to the ground in stance. Upright shoulders are a major fault. They should show plenty of muscle, which is distinct from, and must not be confused with coarse or loaded bone, which is a fault. The shoulder-bone should be clean. The forelegs should be perfectly straight viewed from the front, but the pasterns should show a slight angle with the forearm when regarded from the side, too great an angle denotes weakness and while carrying plenty of bone, it should be of good quality. Anything approaching the massive bone of the Newfoundland, for example, being a decided fault.

Body

The body is muscular, the back is broadish and straight, strongly boned and well developed. The belly shows a waist without being tucked-up. There should be a good depth of brisket or chest, the latter should not be too broad. The sides are flat compared to some breeds, and while the dog must not be barrel ribbed, it must not be so flat as to be actually slabsided. The Alsatian should be quick in movement and speedy but not like a Greyhound in body.

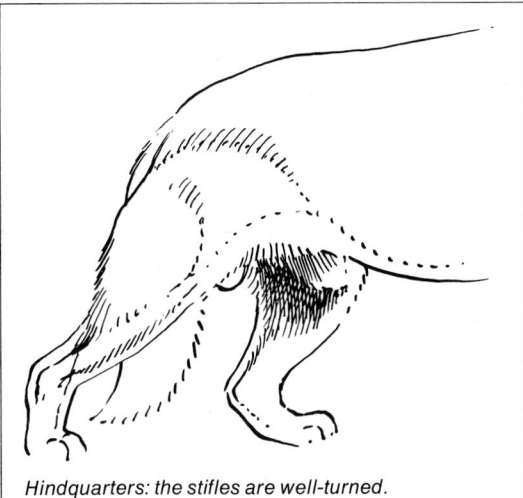

Hindquarters: the stifles are well-turned.

Hindquarters

The hindquarters should show breadth and strength, the loins being broad and strong, the rump rather long and sloping and the legs, when viewed from behind, must be quite straight, without any tendency to cow-hocks, or bow-hocks, which are both extremely serious faults. The stifles are well turned and the hocks strong and well let down. The ability to turn quickly is a necessary asset to the Alsatian, and this can only be if there is a good length of thigh-bone and leg, and by the bending of the hock.

Feet

The feet should be round, the toes strong, slightly arched and held close together. The pads should be firm, the nails short and strong. Dewclaws are neither a fault nor a virtue, but should be removed from the hind legs at 4 to 5 days old, as they are liable to spoil the gait.

Tail

When at rest the tail should hang in a slight curve, and reach at least as far as the hock. During movement and excitement it will be raised, but in no circumstances should the tail be carried past a vertical line drawn through the root.

Coat

The coat is smooth, but it is at the same time a double coat. The under-coat is woolly in texture, thick and close and to it the animal owes its characteristic resistance to cold. The outer-coat is also close, each hair straight, hard, and lying flat, so that it is rain-resisting. Under the body, to behind the legs, the coat is longer and forms near the thigh a mild form of breeching. On the head (including the inside of the ears), to the front of the legs and feet, the hair is short. Along the neck it is longer and thicker, and in winter approaches a form of ruff. A coat either too long or too short is a fault. As an average, the hairs on the back should be from 1 to 2 inches in length.

Colour

The colour of the Alsatian is in itself not important and has no effect on the character of the dog or on its fitness for work and should be a secondary consideration for that reason. All white or near white unless possessing black points are not desirable. The final colour of a young dog can only be ascertained when the outer coat has developed.

Weight and size

The ideal height (measured to the highest point of the shoulder) is 22 to 24 inches for bitches and 24 to 26 inches for dogs. The proportion, of length to height, may vary between 10:9 and 10:8.5.

Faults

A long, narrow, Collie or Borzoi head. A pink or liver-coloured nose. Undershot or overshot mouth. Tail with curl or pronounced hook. The lack of heavy undercoat.

Note

Male animals should have two apparently normal testicles fully descended into the scrotum.

AKC VARIATION TO STANDARD

Eyes: medium size, set a little obliquely. *Feet:* nails dark. *Disqualifications:* cropped or hanging ears. Undershot jaw. Docked tail. White dogs. Dogs with noses not predominantly black. Any dog that attempts to bite judge.

BELGIAN SHEPHERD DOG (GROENENDAEL)

This variety is the black version of the Belgian Sheep-dog and is thus easily distinguished from the other two. For many years he has been shown in the United States of America as the Belgian Sheepdog and has only recently been awarded a separate identity in Britain. When Professor Reul did his study of the herding breeds of Belgium in 1891, he discovered that the long-haired black version was largely limited to one area and tended to breed true. M. Rose of the village of Groenendael had been breeding black long-hairs with considerable success. This had started with a bitch puppy named Petite, which was a long-haired black sport from parents of other colours. After a search he discovered a black male which he acquired, and these two when mated produced the beginnings of the black line which led to almost all of today's dogs.

   The first came to the United States of America in 1907, at which time they were known of but unseen in Britain, where a contemporary book of the time de-scribes them amongst French, German and other Sheepdogs as being of ancient lineage, all having prick

NATIONAL GROUPING		
	Name	Number
KC(GB)	Working	5
AKC	Working Dogs	III
FCI	Herding Dogs	I

ears and bearing a suggestion of the wolf type. Those that were imported into the United States were used as police dogs. The breed soon became popular on both sides of the Atlantic and was appreciated as both a working and show dog some time before the other two Belgian Sheepdogs. In Belgium and indeed in France he has won a great reputation as a herding dog with tremendous versatility, and devotion to duty, and working trials are held regularly to encourage breeders to produce the type of dog that can work in the field and also look well on the show bench.

   The disturbance caused by the Second World War did much to upset the progress of the breed, with none of the advantages that it enjoyed in the First World

War when it gained some recognition as a messenger and guard dog. He is a fairly big dog, but not a heavyweight, in fact he tends towards raciness, being rather slender in body and flexible in movement. He is elegant, proud and upstanding in posture and noted for his free, elegant and ground covering stride. As with the other varieties, the bitch is not nearly as prepossessing as the dog. The Groenendael is noted for his intelligence and his devoted companionship. His long association with humans makes him a very good dog to have in the house, where he settles into a remarkably small space for a large looking dog, is normally very quiet and self-effacing, but an excellent guard when roused who will defend his property to the last. As a show dog he is making many friends in most countries of the world, and is now seen both in the United States and Britain in fairly large numbers at most of the major shows. He makes an excellent show dog as he is amenable to command, takes very little preparation, and looks very imposing in the ring.

OFFICIAL STANDARD

General appearance
A medium-sized dog, well proportioned, intelligent, hardy, and bred to withstand adverse weather. It should be alert and attentive with a lively and enquiring mien.

Characteristics
With its fine proportions and proud carriage of the head, the Belgian Shepherd Dog should convey an impression of that graceful strength which has become the mark of selected representatives of a working breed. In addition to its inborn skill as a sheep-dog, it has a great potential as a guard dog.

Head and skull
The head should be finely chiselled, long, but not excessively so, and gaunt. The skull and muzzle should be roughly equal in length, with at most a slight bias in favour of the muzzle, giving the impression of a balanced whole. The skull should be of medium width in proportion to the length of the head, flattened rather than rounded forehead and centre line not very pronounced; seen in profile it should be parallel to an imaginary line extending the muzzle line. The muzzle should be of medium length tapering gradually towards the nose. The nose should be black with well-flared nostrils. Moderate stop.

Eyes
Of medium size, neither protruding nor sunken, slightly almond-shaped, brownish coloured and preferably dark; black ringed eyelids. Direct, lively and inquiring look. Arches above the eyes not prominent the muzzle finely chiselled under the eyes.

Ears
Distinctly triangular appearance, stiff and erect, set high, of proportionate length, with the external ear well rounded at the base.

Mouth
Wide. Lips thin-textured, very firm, strongly pigmented, not showing the red of the mucous membranes. Cheeks spare, quite flat but well-muscled. Strong, white, regular teeth firmly set in well-developed jaws. Scissor bite, i.e. the incisors of the upper jaw fitting closely over those of the lower jaw, extending slightly beyond them without losing contact with them. Edge to edge bite tolerated.

Neck
Very supple. The neck should be slightly elongated, well-muscled and without dewlap, broadening slightly towards the shoulders. The nape should be very slightly arched.

Forequarters
Strongly boned throughout with wiry and powerful muscle structure. The shoulder blades should be long and oblique, firmly attached, flat, forming an angle with the humerus, so as to enable the elbows to work easily. The forelegs should be long and well-muscled, and should move parallel. The bones joining the feet and pastern joint should be strong and short. Pastern joint clearly defined. Feet round, toes arched and very close together; soles thick and springy with large dark claws.

Body
The body should be powerful without being bulky. The length from the point of the shoulder to the point of the buttocks should be approximately equal to the height at the withers in the case of the male; in the female it may be slightly greater. The chest should not be very broad but deep and low. Ribs should be well sprung. The upper line of the body (back and lumbar region) should be straight, broad and powerfully muscled. The belly should be moderately developed neither drooping nor unduly cut-up, continuing the lower line of the chest in a graceful

Head and skull: finely chiselled, fairly long, moderate stop.

curve. The rump should be very slightly sloping, broad but not excessively so. Male animals should have two apparently normal testicles fully descended into the scrotum.

Hindquarters

The hindquarters should be well muscled and powerful but not bulky. Good, but not excessive, angulation, with hocks close to the ground. Viewed from behind the legs

Hindquarters: powerful but not bulky, good angulation, not excessive.

should be parallel. Dew claws are not permitted. Feet slightly oval, toes arched and very close together; soles thick and springy with large dark claws.

Tail

The tail should be firmly set, strong at the base and of medium length. At rest the dog should carry it hanging down, with the tip slightly bent backwards at the level of the hock; on the move he should lift it, accentuating the curve towards the tip; however it should under no circumstances curl up or bend to one side.

Gait

The movement should be brisk and free, covering the maximum amount of ground, but not necessarily in a straight line.

Coat

The outer coat should be long, straight and abundant. It should not be silky or wiry, the texture should be of medium harshness. The undercoat should be extremely dense. The hair should be shorter on the head, outside of the ears and lower part of the legs. The opening of the ear should be protected by hair. The hair should be especially long and abundant, like a ruff around the neck, particularly in the male. There should be a fringe of long hair down the back of the forearm, long and abundant hair evident on the hindquarters and the tail. The dog should be longer coated than the bitch.

Colour

Black. May be completely black or black with limited white as follows: small to moderate patch or strip on chest, between pads of the feet and on the tips of the hind toes. Frosting (white or grey) on the muzzle.

Skin

Springy but quite taut over the whole body. All external mucous membranes highly pigmented.

Size

The desired height for the dog is 24 to 26 inches and 22 to 24 inches for the bitch.

Faults

Any departure from the foregoing points should be considered a fault and the seriousness of the fault should be in exact proportion to its degree.

AKC VARIATION TO STANDARD

Classified as the Belgian Sheepdog by the AKC.
Head: jaws strong and powerful. *Forelegs:* pasterns medium length, slightly sloped. Bone oval rather than round. *Feet:* nails may be white to match white toe tips. *Size:* dogs 24 to 26 inches, bitches 22 to 24 inches measured at withers. Length, measured from point of breast to point of rump, should equal height. Bitches may be slightly longer. *Disqualifications:* viciousness. Any colour other than black, except white in specified areas. Tail cropped or stump. Dogs under 22½ inches or over 27½ inches. Bitches 20½ inches or over 25½ inches.

BELGIAN SHEPHERD DOG (MALINOIS)

There are three types of Belgian Sheepdogs recognised and registered with other Kennel Clubs and the Malinois is the least well known of the three. The other two are long-coated varieties and seem to have been more readily accepted by the public, possibly because they look rather more striking. It was towards the end of the 19th century that there was a revival of interest in the various sheep herding dogs of different countries, strangely enough at a time when the need for such dogs was declining with greater mechanisation, less droving and greatly increased areas of cultivation for food production purposes. The Belgian sheep herding dogs are very similar in structure, overall size

NATIONAL GROUPING		
	Name	Number
KC(GB)	Working	5
AKC	Working Dogs	III
FCI	Herding Dogs	I

and appearance to the German Shepherd Dog, the Alsatian, and there is little doubt that they shared a common ancestry.

The various dogs used for the herding of sheep in Europe were grouped together under the general term 'Chien de Berger' and the Malinois, to give it its full title should really be called the Chien de Berger Malinois, as it was first developed in the area around Malines. The dogs known as 'chiens de berger' during the last century were of just about every size and type, and so long as they could do the work, were given the title. The result has been a large number of breeds named after their country or place of origin, and many of them are now beginning to make their way on to the show scene. In 1891, Professor Reul made a study of the various types existing in Belgium, and began to sort them out into different breeds. He finally settled for six which could be distinguished one from the other and a group of three which were similar in size and conformation but different in coat and colour. It was these three that the Belgium Kennel Club finally recognised in 1897.

The Malinois first reached the United States of America in 1948, though they were registered and shown simply as Belgian Shepherd Dogs until 1959,

when the three breeds were registered separately. In Britain the interest in the Malinois was delayed, and it is only in very recent years that specimens have been seen at shows and some litters bred.

He is a first class herding and working dog and a fine guard, and was at one time trained for police and army guard duties. Like many of the sheep herding dogs he has a certain reserve, and will not accept strangers without question, but he is at the same time friendly enough with those that he knows. He is a well-built powerful but flexible dog with a short coat of a distinctive fawn to mahogany colour with black tips to some of the hairs, and always a dark mask and ears. He is alert, intelligent and a little suspicious but his years of association with humans means that he quickly becomes one of the family. One of the characteristics of the breed is that the bitches always look smaller and feminine compared with the dogs.

OFFICIAL STANDARD

General appearance
A medium-sized dog, well proportioned, intelligent, hardy, and bred to withstand adverse weather. It should be alert and attentive with a lively and inquiring mien.

Characteristics
With its fine proportions and proud carriage of the head, the Belgian Shepherd Dog should convey an impression of that graceful strength which has become the mark of selected representatives of a working breed. In addition to its inborn skill as a sheep-dog, it has great potential as a guard dog.

Head and skull
The head should be finely chiselled, long, but not excessively so, and gaunt. The skull and muzzle should

Head: clean cut and strong.

be roughly equal in length, with at most a slight bias in favour of the muzzle, giving the impression of a balanced whole. The skull should be of medium width in proportion to the length of the head, flattened rather than rounded forehead and centre line not very pronounced; seen in profile it should be parallel to an imaginary line extending the muzzle line. The muzzle should be of medium length tapering gradually towards the nose. The nose should be black with well-flared nostrils. Moderate stop.

Eyes
Of medium size, neither protruding nor sunken, slightly almond-shaped, brownish coloured and preferably dark, black ringed eyelids. Direct, lively and inquiring look. Arches above the eyes not prominent, the muzzle finely chiselled under the eyes.

Ears
Distinctly triangular appearance, stiff and erect, set high, of proportionate length, with the external ear well rounded at the base.

Mouth
Wide. Lips thin-textured, very firm, strongly pigmented, not showing the red of the mucous membranes. Cheeks spare, quite flat but well-muscled. Strong, white, regular teeth firmly set in well-developed jaws. Scissor bite, i.e. the incisors of the upper jaw fitting closely over those of the lower jaw, extending slightly beyond them without losing contact with them. Edge to edge bite tolerated.

Neck
Very supple. The neck should be slightly elongated, well-muscled and without dewlap, broadening slightly towards the shoulders. The nape should be very slightly arched.

Forequarters
Strongly boned throughout with wiry and powerful muscle structure. The shoulder blades should be long and oblique, firmly attached, flat, forming an angle with

Forequarters: shoulders long and oblique. Legs: straight and strong.

the humerus, so as to enable the elbows to work easily. The forelegs should be long and well-muscled, and should move parallel. The bones joining the feet and pastern joint should be strong and short. Pastern joint clearly defined. Feet round, toes arched and very close together; soles thick and springy with large dark claws.

Body

The body should be powerful without being bulky. The length from the point of the shoulder to the point of the buttocks should be approximately equal to the height at the withers in the case of the dog; in the bitch it may be slightly greater. The chest should not be very broad but deep and low. Ribs should be well sprung. The upper line of the body (back and lumbar region) should be straight, broad and powerfully muscled. The belly should be moderately developed neither drooping nor unduly cut-up, continuing the lower line of the chest in a graceful curve. The rump should be very slightly sloping, broad but not excessively so. Male animals should have two apparently normal testicles fully descended into the scrotum.

Hindquarters

The hindquarters should be well muscled and powerful but not bulky. Good, but not excessive, angulation, with hocks close to the ground. Viewed from behind the legs should be parallel. Dew claws are not permitted. Feet slightly oval, toes arched and very close together; soles thick and springy with large dark claws.

Tail

The tail should be firmly set, strong at the base and of medium length. At rest the dog should carry it hanging down, with the tip slightly bent backwards at the level of the hock; on the move he should lift it, accentuating the curve towards the tip; however it should under no

circumstances curl up or bend to one side.

Gait

The movement should be brisk and free, covering the maximum amount of ground, but not necessarily in a straight line.

Coat

The hair should be very short on the head, the exterior of the ears and the lower parts of the legs. Short on the rest of the body, thicker on the tail and around the neck where it should resemble a ridge or collar, beginning at the base of the ear and extending to the throat. In addition the hindquarters should be fringed with longer hair. The tail should be thick and bushy. The coat should be thick, and of a good firm texture with a wool undercoat.

Colour

Dark fawn with considerable black overlay, washed out fawn or grey is highly undesirable as is patchy black overlay or the total absence of black overlay. Black shading on muzzle and ears desirable.

Skin

Springy but quite taut over the whole body. All external mucous membranes highly pigmented.

Size

The desired height for the dog is 24 to 26 inches and for the bitch 22 to 24 inches.

Faults

Any departure from the foregoing points should be considered a fault and the seriousness of the fault should be in exact proportion to its degree.

Although this dog has been given an interim standard it has not yet been granted championship status by the KC(GB).

AKC VARIATION TO STANDARD

Classified as the Belgian Malinois by the AKC.
Fore and hindquarters: bone oval rather than round. *Feet*: nails may be white to match white toe tips.

BELGIAN SHEPHERD DOG (TERVUEREN)

NATIONAL GROUPING		
	Name	Number
KC(GB)	Working	5
AKC	Working Dogs	III
FCI	Herding Dogs	I

This is the third of the Chiens de Berger Belge to be recognised as a separate breed both in its country of origin and in the rest of the world. At one time they were very much interbred and were all shown as Belgian Shepherd Dogs, but in recent years most countries have only accepted registration of those dogs that have been bred true for a number of generations. As sheep herding declined, breeders of dogs that had been used, often for centuries for that purpose, looked elsewhere for an outlet for their enthusiasm, and dog showing offered a natural alternative. Prior to that time the only requirement for a herding dog was that it could do the work and do it well, and breeding programmes were devised not to produce the best-looking dog, but the best worker. A similar thing happened in Britain with the Border Collie, when breeding was established on the basis of ability and records kept of wins at trials rather than on the bench, with the result that although a magnificent race of working sheepdogs has been produced, few of them are good Border Collie types.

The evolution of the Tervuren was closely linked with that of the Groenendael, and they probably sprang from the same stock. A M. Corbeel of Tervueren owned a pair of sheepdogs with long black-tipped hair that produced a litter of puppies, one of which came into the possession of M. Danhieux who mated her with a black long-haired dog. This mating in turn produced what has been described as the best Tervueren of the 19th century, a dog that became the first

Tervueren champion. In appearance the Tervueren is the same as the Groenendael apart from the colour, so it is natural that colour should become an important factor in the standards of the two breeds. The Groenendael must always be black with white allowed only as a small flash on the forechest, between the pads of the feet and the tips of the rear toes and a slight grizzling on the muzzle and chin. The Tervueren is always a warm mahogany colour with the black overlay typical of the breed; this black tipping being most pronounced on the shoulders, face and ears and the tip of the tail.

The first Tervuerens went to the United States of America in the 1940s but were unregistered, the first registered import being in 1954. In 1959 the breeds were granted separate registers but the progress of the Tervueren has been slow compared with the Groenendael. The same thing is true in Britain, where the breed is only slowly gaining ground. He is particularly suitable for obedience work, and it is probably in this field that he will gain most admirers, as in appearance he is so near to the German Shepherd Dog that many potential owners will prefer the well-established and more popular breed rather than risk having their dog mistaken for a poor specimen of that breed. Like the other Belgian Shepherd Dogs, he is very intelligent, and can be trained for guard duties as well as for normal work with sheep. He makes a very good show dog, as he is noble in outline, upstanding and elegant, and supremely biddable in the ring, willing to please and naturally obedient.

He is watchful and alert, constantly on the move when not relaxing, vigilant with strangers and suspicious without being vicious. With the members of his family he is kind and affectionate, and always desires attention.

OFFICIAL STANDARD

General appearance
A medium-sized dog, well proportioned, intelligent, hardy, and bred to withstand adverse weather. It should be alert and attentive with a lively and enquiring mien.

Characteristics
With its fine proportions and proud carriage of the head, the Belgian Shepherd Dog should convey an impression of that graceful strength which has become the mark of selected representatives of a working breed. In addition to its inborn skill as a sheep-dog, it has a great potential as a guard dog.

Head and skull
The head should be finely chiselled, long, but not excessively so, and gaunt. The skull and muzzle should be roughly equal in length, with at most a slight bias in favour of the muzzle, giving the impression of a balanced whole. The skull should be of medium width in proportion to the length of the head, flattened rather than rounded forehead and centre line not very pronounced; seen in profile it should be parallel to an imaginary line extending the muzzle line. The muzzle should be of medium length tapering gradually towards the nose. The nose should be black with well-flared nostrils. Moderate stop.

Eyes
Of medium size, neither protruding nor sunken, slightly almond-shaped, brownish coloured and preferably dark; black ringed eyelids. Direct, lively and inquiring look. Arches above the eyes not prominent the muzzle finely chiselled under the eyes.

Ears
Distinctly triangular appearance, stiff and erect, set high, of proportionate length, with the external ear well rounded at the base.

Mouth
Wide. Lips thin-textured, very firm, strongly pigmented, not showing the red of the mucous membranes. Cheeks spare, quite flat but well-muscled. Strong, white, regular teeth firmly set in well-developed jaws. Scissor bite, i.e. the incisors of the upper jaw fitting closely over those of the lower jaw, extending slightly beyond them

Head: well-chiselled, long ears erect.

without losing contact with them. Edge to edge bite tolerated.

Neck
Very supple. The neck should be slightly elongated, well-muscled and without dewlap, broadening slightly towards the shoulders. The nape should be very slightly arched.

Forequarters
Strongly boned throughout with wiry and powerful muscle structure. The shoulder blades should be long and oblique, firmly attached, flat, forming an angle with the humerus, so as to enable the elbows to work easily. The forelegs should be long and well-muscled, and should move parallel. The bones joining the feet and pastern joint should be strong and short. Pastern joint clearly defined. Feet round, toes arched and very close together; soles thick and springy with large dark claws.

Body
The body should be powerful without being bulky. The length from the point of the shoulder to the point of the buttocks should be approximately equal to the height at the withers in the case of the dog; in the bitch it may be slightly greater. The chest should not be very broad but deep and low. Ribs should be well sprung. The upper line

Hindquarters: thighs broad and heavily muscled.

of the body (back and lumbar region) should be straight, broad and powerfully muscled. The belly should be moderately developed neither drooping nor unduly cut-up, continuing the lower line of the chest in a graceful curve. The rump should be very slightly sloping, broad but not excessively so. Male animals should have two apparently normal testicles fully descended into the scrotum.

Hindquarters
The hindquarters should be well muscled and powerful but not bulky. Good, but not excessive, angulation, with hocks close to the ground. Viewed from behind the legs should be parallel. Dew claws are not permitted. Feet slightly oval, toes arched and very close together; soles thick and springy with large dark claws.

Tail
The tail should be firmly set, strong at the base and of medium length. At rest the dog should carry it hanging down, with the tip slightly bent backwards at the level of the hock; on the move he should lift it, accentuating the curve towards the tip; however it should under no circumstances curl up or bend to one side.

Gait
The movement should be brisk and free, covering the maximum amount of ground, but not necessarily in a straight line.

Coat
The outer coat should be long, straight and abundant. It should not be silky or wiry, the texture should be of medium harshness. The undercoat should be extremely dense. The hair should be shorter on the head, outside of the ears and lower part of the legs. The opening of the ear should be protected by hair. The hair should be especially long and abundant, like a ruff around the neck, particularly in the dog. There should be a fringe of long hair down the back of the forearm, long and abundant hair evident on the hindquarters and the tail. The dog should be longer coated than the bitch.

Colour
Colour may include all shades of red, fawn and grey with black overlay. The coat should be characteristically double pigmented, wherein the tip of each light coloured hair is blackened. On mature males this blackening should be especially pronounced on the shoulders, back and rib section. The face should have a black mask, not to extend above the line of the eyes, and the ears should be mostly black. The tail should typically have a darker or black tip. Small to moderate white patch or strip permitted on chest, between pads of feet and on the tips of the hind toes. Frosting (white or grey) on the muzzle. Beyond the age of 18 months a washed out colour or colour too black resembling a Groenendael should be considered a fault.

Skin
Springy but quite taut over the whole body. All external mucous membranes highly pigmented.

Size
The desired height for the dog is 24 to 26 inches and for the bitch 22 to 24 inches.

Faults
Any departure from the foregoing points should be considered a fault and the seriousness of the fault should be in exact proportion to its degree.

Although this dog has been given an interim standard it has not yet been granted championship status by the KC(GB).

AKC VARIATION TO STANDARD
Classified as the Belgian Tervueren by the AKC.
Body: top of shoulder blades should be roughly a thumb's width apart. *Feet:* nail colour can vary from black to transparent. *Hindquarters:* stifles clearly defined, with upper shank at right angles to hip bones.

BERNESE MOUNTAIN DOG

This breed is said to have been brought into Switzerland by the invading legions of Rome though this is difficult to prove. He is certainly a very ancient breed, and had been known for generations before he became the draught dog of the weavers of Berne. In this capacity he degenerated as the weavers were little interested in preserving the qualities of a particular breed so long as specimens were produced from time to time that were strong enough to tow a small cart. In 1892, one dog man in Switzerland determined to revive the breed and conducted a search to discover what he considered the correct type of dog with which to commence a breeding programme, and it was only after considerable difficulty that he managed to find sufficient dogs for his purpose. He was joined by other enthusiasts, and in 1907 a breed club was formed and the breed was saved from extinction.

The dog is one of the small group called Sennenhunde, including the Entlebuch which is quite small, and the large Swiss Mountain Dog proper, which form a very ancient group of Swiss national dogs. The only one that is well known outside his own country

NATIONAL GROUPING		
	Name	Number
KC(GB)	Working	5
AKC	Working Dogs	III
FCI	Guard Dogs	2

is the Bernese which also happens to be the only one with a long coat. If one had to place him in one of the old basic categories he would have to go into the Mastiff group, as he bears resemblance only to members of that group. With the basket weavers and cheese makers of Berne he lived very much as a working member of the family, and became the children's pet as well as a worker and guard dog.

In appearance he has been described, perhaps quite accurately as the child's vision of everything that a dog should be. He is large and rounded, warm and woolly. His colour is attractive, his markings distinct and typical, and his construction is in every way that of the average and normal dog. He is very strong and hardy being perfectly happy to live out of doors or in the house, and his coat, which tends towards softness and silkiness always has a fine sheen when he is groomed.

The Bernese Mountain Dog first entered the United States of America and was given recognition in the middle 1930s, and numbers both in that country and in Britain are steadily increasing. He makes a delightful show dog as he is much admired by the general public, who often see in him just the sort of dog that they would like to own. His shining coat and large heavyweight appearance make him a very impressive animal, and as a puppy he is particularly attractive. His temperament is good, and his long association with people gives him instinctive good manners. He is an affectionate and kindly dog, always willing to please and is easily trained to be obedient and trouble free. There is no doubt that he will become one of the important show dogs and companions of future years.

OFFICIAL STANDARD

Characteristics
Self confident, good natured. Aggressiveness must not be tolerated. Slow to mature.

General appearance
Above medium sized, strong working dog, active, alert, well boned, of striking colour.

Head: defined stop, strong muzzle, slight dewlaps.

Head and skull
Strong with flat skull and slightly developed furrow, well defined stop, strong straight muzzle. Lips slightly developed.

Eyes
Dark brown and almond shaped, eyelids tight.

Ears
Medium sized ears, set high, triangular shaped, lying flat in repose, when alert brought slightly forward, and raised at the base.

Mouth
Scissor bite.

Neck
Strong, muscular and medium length.

Forequarters
Shoulders long, strong and well laid back, with the upper arm forming an obtuse angle. Forelegs straight from all sides, with slight slope to the pastern.

Body
Compact rather than long. Ratio height to length 9:10. Broad chest with good depth of brisket reaching at least to the elbow. Well ribbed; strong loins. Back firm and straight. Rump smoothly rounded.

Hindquarters
Quarters broad, strong and well muscled. Stifles well bent. Hocks strong, well let down and turning neither in nor out. Dewclaws should be removed.

Feet
Short, round and compact.

Gait
Stride reaching out well in front, following well through behind, balanced stride in all gaits.

Tail
Bushy, reaching just below the hock. When alert may be carried gaily, but may not curl or be carried over the back.

Coat
Soft and silky with bright natural sheen, long and slightly wavy, but should not curl when mature.

Colour
Jet black, with rich reddish brown on the cheeks, over the eyes, on all four legs and on chest. Slight to medium sized symmetrical white head marking (blaze) and white chest marking (cross), are essential. Preferred but not essential, white paws, white not reaching higher than the pastern, white tip to tail. A few white hairs at nape of neck, and white anal patch undesirable but tolerated.

Weight and size
Dogs: 25 to $27\frac{1}{2}$ inches (64 to 70 centimetres) at the withers, preferred size 26 to $26\frac{3}{4}$ inches (66 to 68 centimetres). Bitches: 23 to 26 inches (58 to 66 centimetres) at the withers, preferred size $23\frac{1}{2}$ to 25 inches (60 to 63 centimetres).

Faults
Any departure from the foregoing points should be considered a fault and the seriousness of the fault should be in exact proportion to its degree.

Note
Male animals should have two apparently normal testicles fully descended into the scrotum.

AKC VARIATION TO STANDARD
Ears: not too pointed at tips and rather short. *Colour:* brown on forelegs must always be between black and white. *Height:* dogs 23 to $27\frac{1}{2}$ inches, bitches 21 to 26 inches at shoulder. *Faults:* ears hanging, as on a hound. Tail cropped or stump. Undershot. White markings anywhere except as specified. Dogs under $22\frac{1}{2}$ or over $27\frac{1}{2}$ inches and females under $20\frac{1}{2}$ or over $25\frac{1}{2}$ inches.

BOUVIER DES FLANDRES

NATIONAL GROUPING		
	Name	Number
KC(GB)	—	—
AKC	Working Dogs	III
FCI	Herding Dogs	I

The word 'bouvier' translated from the French, means cowherd or oxherd which gives a good indication of this breed's original use. The word can also be translated figuratively as 'churl' which the dog certainly is not, as he is a handsome animal of noble bearing, and in recent years of impeccable breeding. The Bouvier des Flandres was first found in the South Western parts of Flanders and in Northern France, where he was being used as a cattle drover by the farmers and butchers. At that time, in the latter part of the 19th century, he was known by a number of rather uncomplimentary names, Koe Hond (cow dog), Toucheur de Boeuf (cattle driver) and Vuilbaard (dirty beard), and his appearance was as varied as his names. The breed appeared in almost every size, though all were fairly large, and in a variety of colours. He appeared on the show bench for the first time at the international show of 1910 when two were shown named Nelly and Even, but there was no standard for the breed until 1912 when a group of interested people encouraged by M. Fontaine, Vice-President of the Club St. Hubert met and formed a society of Bouvier breeders.

From that time onwards the breed made rapid strides, only being halted by World War I, when the area in which the Bouvier des Flandres was mostly concentrated, was devastated. Some dogs however survived, and one, who was the property of the Veterinarian attached to the Belgian army was shown in Antwerp in 1920. Some time later a group of experts and enthusiasts gathered together with some examples of the breed and formulated a revised standard. By the 1930s the breed began to appear in the United States of America. Ch. Marios de Clos de Cerberus was imported after the Second World War and rapidly became an American champion and drew attention to the possibilities of the breed. Since that time, the breed has made steady progress in many countries outside Northern Europe, and is beginning to appear at major shows in Britain.

He is primarily a working dog, and though his shape and coat indicate that he will make a very successful show dog, modern breeders are not losing sight of the fact that he was originally designed for a certain task, and that he must remain capable of doing it. He is a strong dog of tremendous vitality, built along square and robust lines, but extremely fast. In South Africa, where for fun, races are sometimes staged between dogs towing miniature sulkies, jockeyed by children dressed in racing silks, one of the local Bouviers des Flandres is a regular winner. He is easily trained, being intelligent and naturally obedient, and he is one of those dogs which in his native country cannot gain the title of champion without succeeding at working trials.

He makes a very good show dog, being large, impressive, alert and smart. His native obedience makes him easily controlled in the ring despite his size and agility, and his coat is of the quality that repays just a little attention and shaping in the right places. He has a good steady but lively temperament, is an excellent guard and watchdog, being docile with those that he knows but distinctly suspicious of strangers.

OFFICIAL STANDARD

The Bouvier des Flandres is a rough-coated dog of notably rugged appearance as befitting an erstwhile cattle driver and farmers' helper of Flanders, and later an ambulance dog and messenger in World War I. He is a compact-bodied, powerfully built dog of upstanding carriage and alert, intelligent expression.

Head

The head is medium long, with the skull slightly longer than the muzzle. *Skull:* almost flat on top, moderately wide between the ears, and sloping slightly toward the muzzle. The brow is noticeably arched over the eyes. The stop is shallow, and the under-eye fill-in good. *Ears:* rough-coated, set high on the head and cropped to a triangular contour. They stand erect and are carried straight up. *Eyes:* neither protruding nor sunken, the eyes are set a trifle obliquely in the skull and not too far apart. They are of medium size and very nearly oval. Preferred color, a dark nut-brown. Black eyes, although not considered faulty, are less desirable as contributing to a somber expression. Light-colored eyes, and staring or wild expression are faulty. *Muzzle:* wide, deep and well filled out, the width narrowing gradually toward the tip of the nose. Cheeks are clean or flat-sided, the jaws powerful, and the lips dry and tight-fitting. A narrow muzzle, suggestive of weakness, is faulty. *Teeth:* strong and white, with the canines set well apart, the teeth meet in a scissors bite. *Nose:* black and well developed, the nostrils wide open. Across the top the contour is a trifle rounded as opposed to flat. Brown, pink and spotted noses are faulty.

Coat: topknot and beard.

Neck and shoulders

The neck is well rounded, slightly arched, and carried almost upright, its thickness gradually increasing as it fits gracefully into the shoulders. Clean and dry at the throat. The shoulders are long and sloping.

Body

The brisket is deep, extending down at least to the point of the elbows, and of moderate width. *Back:* short, strong and straight. *Loins:* short, taut, and slightly arched in topline, while the rump is broad and square rather than sloping. Ribs are deep and well sprung. As advantageous for breeding purposes, slightly greater length of loin is permissible in bitches.

Tail

Set high, carried up, and docked to about 4 inches.

Legs and feet

The leg bones, although only moderate in girth, are made to appear heavy because of their covering with thick, rough hair. *Forelegs:* straight as viewed from the front or side, with elbows turned neither in nor out. *Hind legs:* hindquarters are firm and well muscled, with large, powerful hams. Legs are strong and sturdy, with hocks well let down and wide apart. They are slightly angulated at stifle and hock joints. Viewed from the back, they are absolutely parallel. *Feet:* round, compact, with toes arched and close. The nails are black, the pads thick and tough.

Coat

Rough, touseled and unkempt in appearance, the coat is capable of withstanding the hardest work in the most inclement weather. *Topcoat:* harsh, rough and wiry, and so thick that when separated by the hand the skin is hardly visible. *Undercoat:* fine and soft in texture, and thicker in winter. On the skull the hair is shorter and almost smooth. On the brows it is longer, thus forming eyebrows. Longer growth on muzzle and underjaw form mustache and beard. On the legs it is thick and rough, on the feet rather short. Soft, silky or woolly topcoats are faulty.

Color

From fawn to black; pepper and salt, gray and brindle. A white star on the chest is allowed. Chocolate brown with white spots is faulty.

Height

Dogs from $23\frac{1}{2}$ to $27\frac{1}{2}$ inches; bitches, a minimum of $22\frac{3}{4}$ inches.

AKC VARIATION TO STANDARD

The dog is not granted championship status by the KC(GB). The above standards are those of the AKC.

BOXER

Many of the breeds of dogs known today have changed very little from their ancestors of hundreds of years ago. The running dogs for instance are much the same now as they were in ancient Persia and medieval England. There are, however, a number of breeds which have been developed by man for specific purposes, which can be considered as manufactured dogs, and the Boxer is one of these. He is a member of the large family of Mastiff type dogs that were spread over most of Europe many centuries ago, but was changed in fairly recent years to an animal with an appearance distinct from any other breed of dog. The basic stock used was a dog called the Bullenbeisser, and around the 1830s German breeders commenced experimenting by crossing these dogs with other breeds including the Bulldog in an attempt to produce what was to be virtually a new breed. By 1895 the breed was well established, being shown at Munich, and from that time it has progressed until it is now not only one of the most popular dogs in Germany, but throughout the world.

The so-called sport of bull-baiting was carried on in Germany in the same way as it was in Britain until public opinion finally put an end to it, and there is no doubt that the German version of the Mastiff type of dog that was used as the basis for the Boxer, was used for this purpose. It is interesting therefore that when the German breeders wanted another dog to cross with their native bull-baiting type, they selected the Bulldog which had been used for the same purpose. There is not a great deal of similarity between the

NATIONAL GROUPING		
	Name	Number
KC(GB)	Working	5
AKC	Working Dogs	III
FCI	Guard Dogs	2

Bulldog and the Boxer, and it is not at all certain what other breeds were used. There is no doubt, however, that the final result had everything that the early breeders set out to achieve, as the animal that they eventually produced, the modern Boxer, is one of the smartest dogs in the world.

Types differ, and each country has worked on the breed to produce a dog that is fashionable in that country. It is a simple matter to differentiate between the Boxers of say Germany, Britain and the United States of America. Attempts are made from time to time to bring the forms of the dog closer together by importing from one country to another, but there remains a tendency for each country to go its own way. The dog generally is a very strong, boisterous and active dog with a very positive personality. It has the muscular development of the Mastiff, the agility of those breeds that needed to avoid the attentions of a furious bull, and the jaws and tenacity of the Bulldog.

There are few breeds that have made the progress of the Boxer as a show dog. Everything about him is expedient for the purpose. He is a big dog, statuesque in proportions with a magnificent presence, and with the sort of coat finish that shines in the sun and glows in artificial light. His behaviour in the ring is usually impeccable and he can be trained easily to stand remarkably still and move with great enthusiasm when the need arises. He allows himself to be handled by a complete stranger without objection knowing full well that he is in complete charge of the situation, and quite capable of handling any emergency.

He is a boisterous dog and yet not one with any vices, which he has proved by his proficiency as a guard and police dog, where fierceness needs to be allied to immediate control. He is a very good house dog, his appearance and positive behaviour deterring any intruder, and whilst it is unlikely that he would savage anyone, he always looks as though he might. He is wonderfully good with children, and though his sheer size and speed of reaction do from time to time cause some trouble, he would never intentionally injure anyone.

OFFICIAL STANDARD

Characteristics

The character of the Boxer is of the greatest importance and demands the most careful attention. He is renowned from olden times for his great love and faithfulness to his master and household, his alertness and fearless courage as a defender and protector. The Boxer is docile but distrustful of strangers. He is bright and friendly in play but brave and determined when roused. His intelligence and willing tractability, his modesty, and cleanliness make him a highly desirable family dog and cheerful companion. He is the soul of honesty and loyalty. He is never false or treacherous even in his old age.

General appearance

The Boxer is a medium sized, sturdy, smooth-haired dog of short square figure and strong limb. The musculation is clean and powerfully developed, and should stand out plastically from under the skin. Movement of the Boxer should be alive with energy. His gait, although firm, is elastic. The stride free and roomy; carriage proud and noble. As a service and guard dog he must combine a considerable degree of elegance with the substance and power essential to his duties; those of an enduring escort dog whether with horse, bicycle or carriage and as a splendid jumper. Only a body whose individual limbs are built to withstand the most strenuous 'mechanical' effort and assembled as a complete and harmonious whole, can respond to such demands. Therefore to be at its highest efficiency, the Boxer must never be plump or heavy. Whilst equipped for great speed, it must not be racy. When judging the Boxer the first thing to be con-

Head and skull: proportions important, sombre expression.

sidered is general appearance, the relation of substance to elegance and the desired relationship of the individual parts of the body to each other. Consideration, too, must be given to colour. After these, the individual parts should be examined for their correct construction and their functions. Special attention should be devoted to the head.

Head and skull

The head imparts to the Boxer a unique individual stamp peculiar to the breed. It must be in perfect proportion to his body; above all it must never be too light. The muzzle is the most distinctive feature. The greatest value is to be placed on its being of correct form and in absolute proportion to the skull.

The beauty of the head depends upon the harmonious proportion between the muzzle and the skull.

From whatever direction the head is viewed, whether from the front, from the top or from the side, the muzzle should always appear in correct relationship to the skull. That means that the head should never appear too small or too large. The length of the muzzle to the whole of the head should be as 1 is to 3.

The head should not show deep wrinkles. Normally wrinkles will spring up on the top of the skull when the dog is alert. Folds are always indicated from the root of the nose running downwards on both sides of the muzzle. The dark mask is confined to the muzzle. It must be in distinct relief to the colour of the head so that the face will not have a 'sombre' expression. The muzzle must be powerfully developed in length, in breadth and in height. It must not be pointed or narrow; short or shallow. Its shape is influenced through the formation of both jaw-bones, the placement of teeth in the jaw-bones, and through the quality of the lips. The top of the skull should be slightly arched. It should not be so short that it is rotund, too flat, or too broad. The occiput should not be too pronounced. The forehead should form a distinct stop with the top line of the muzzle, which should not be forced back into the forehead like that of a Bulldog. Neither should it slope away (downfaced). The tip of the nose should lie somewhat higher than the root of the muzzle. The forehead should show a suggestion of furrow which, however, should never be too deep, especially between the eyes. Corresponding with the powerful set of teeth, the cheeks accordingly should be well developed without protruding from the head with 'too bulgy' an appearance. For preference they should taper into the muzzle in a slight, graceful curve. The nose should be broad and black, very slightly turned up. The nostrils should be broad with a naso-labial line between them. The two jaw-bones should not terminate in a normal perpendicular level in the front but the lower jaw should protrude beyond the upper jaw and bend slightly upwards. The Boxer is normally undershot. The upper jaw should be broad where attached to the skull, and maintain this breadth except for a very slight tapering to the front.

Eyes

The eyes should be dark brown; not too small or protruding; not deep set. They should disclose an expression of energy and intelligence, but should never appear gloomy, threatening or piercing. The eyes must have a dark rim.

Ears

Some American and Continental Boxers are cropped and are ineligible for competition under Kennel Club Regulations. The Boxer's natural ears are defined as: moderate in size (small rather than large), thin to the

Ears: cropped version.

touch, set on wide apart at the highest points of the sides of the skull and lying flat and close to the cheek when in repose. When the dog is alert the ears should fall forward with a definite crease.

Mouth

The canine teeth should be as widely separated as possible. The incisors (6) should all be in one row, with no projection of the middle teeth. In the upper jaw they should be slightly concave. In the lower they should be in a straight line. Both jaws should be very wide in front; bite powerful

and sound, the teeth set in the most normal possible arrangement. The lips complete the formation of the muzzle. The upper lip should be thick and padded and fill out the hollow space in front formed by the projection of the lower jaw and be supported by the fangs of the jaw. These fangs must stand as far apart as possible and be of good length so that the front surface of the muzzle becomes broad and almost square; to form an obtuse (rounded) angle with the top line of the muzzle. The lower edge of the upper lip should rest on the edge of the lower lip. The repandous (bent upward) part of the under-jaw with the lower lip (sometimes called the chin) must not rise above the front of the upper lip. On the other hand it should not disappear under it. It must, however, be plainly perceptible when viewed from the front as well as the side, without protruding and bending upward as in the English Bulldog. The teeth of the under-jaw should not be seen when the mouth is closed, neither should the tongue show when the mouth is closed.

Neck

The neck should be not too thick and short but of ample length, yet strong, round, muscular and clean-cut throughout. There should be a distinctly marked nape and and elegant arch down to the back.

Forequarters

The chest should be deep and reach down to the elbows. The depth of the chest should be half the height of the dog at the withers. The ribs should be well arched but not barrel-shaped. They should extend far to the rear. The loins should be short, close and taut and slightly tucked up. The lower stomach line should blend into an elegant curve to the rear. The shoulders should be long and sloping, close lying but not excessively covered with muscle. The upper arm should be long and form a right-angle to the shoulder-blade. The forelegs when seen from the front should be straight, parallel to each other and have strong, firmly articulated (joined) bones. The elbows should not press too closely to the chest-wall or stand off too far from it. The underarm should be perpendicular, long and firmly muscled. The pastern joint of the foreleg should be clearly defined, but not distended. The pastern should be short, slightly slanting and almost perpendicular to the ground.

Body

The body viewed in profile should be of square appearance. The length of the body from the front of the chest to the rear of the body should equal the height from the ground to the top of the shoulder, giving the Boxer a short-coupled, square profile. The torso rests on trunk-like straight legs with strong bones. The withers should be clearly defined. The whole back should be short, straight, broad, and very muscular.

Hindquarters

The hindquarters should be strongly muscled. The musculation should be hard and stand out plastically through the skin. The thighs should not be narrow and flat but broad and curved. The breech musculation should also be strongly developed. The croup should be slightly sloped, flat arched and broad. The pelvis should be long and, in bitches especially, broad. The upper and lower thighs should be long. The hip and knee joints should have as much angle as possible. In a standing position the knee should reach so far forward that it would meet a vertical line drawn from the hip protuberance to the floor. The hock angle should be about 140 degrees; the lower part of the foot at a slight slope of about 95 to 100 degrees from the hock joint to the floor; that is, not completely vertical. Seen from behind the hind legs should be straight. The hocks should be clean and not distended, supported by powerful rear pads.

Feet
The feet should be small with tightly-arched toes (cat feet) and hard soles. The rear toes should be just a little longer than the front toes, but similar in all other respects.

Tail
The tail attachment should be high. The tail should be docked and carried upwards and should be not more than 2 inches long.

Coat
The coat should be short and shiny, lying smooth and tight to the body.

Colour
The permissible colours are fawn, brindle and fawn in various shades from light yellow to dark deer red. The brindle variety should have black stripes on a golden-yellow or red-brown background. The stripes should be

clearly defined and above all should not be grey or dirty. Stripes that do not cover the whole top of the body are not desirable. White markings are not undesirable, in fact, they are often very attractive in appearance. The black mask is essential but when white stretches over the muzzle, naturally that portion of the black mask disappears. It is not possible to get black toenails with white feet. It is desirable, however, to have an even distribution of head markings.

Weight and size
Dogs: 22 to 24 inches at the withers. Bitches: 21 to 23 inches at the withers. Height above or below these figures not to be encouraged. Dogs around 23 inches should weigh about 66 pounds and bitches of about 22 inches should weigh about 62 pounds.

Faults
Viciousness; treachery; unreliability; lack of temperament; cowardice. Head: a head that is not typical. A plump, bulldoggy appearance. Light bone. Lack of proportion. Bad physical condition. Lack of nobility and expression. 'Sombre' face. Unserviceable bite whether due to disease or to faulty tooth placement. Pinscher or Bulldog head. Showing the teeth or the tongue. A sloping top line of the muzzle. Too pointed or too light a bite (snipy). Eyes: visible conjunctiva (Haw). Light eyes. Ears: flying ears; rose ears; semi-erect or erect ears. Neck: dewlap. Front: too broad and low in front; loose shoulders; chest hanging between the shoulders; hare feet; turned legs and toes. Body: carp (roach) back; sway back; thin, lean back; long narrow, sharp-sunken in loins. Weak union with the croup, hollow flanks; hanging stomach. Hindquarters: a falling off or too arched or narrow croup. A low-set tail; higher in back than in front; steep, stiff or too little angulation of the hindquarters; light thighs; cow-hocks; bow-legs; hind dewclaws; soft hocks, narrow heel, tottering, waddling gait; hare's feet; hindquarters too far under or too far behind. Colour: Boxers with white or black ground colour, or entirely white or black or any other colour than fawn or brindle. (White markings are allowed but must not exceed one-third of the ground colour.)

Note
Male animals should have two apparently normal testicles fully descended into the scrotum.

AKC VARIATION TO STANDARD
Height: dogs 22½ to 25 inches, bitches 21 to 23½ inches. *Disqualifications:* any other colour than fawn or brindle. White markings when present must not exceed ⅓ of the ground colour.

BRIARD

For as long as man has herded sheep and goats there have been long or rough coated sheepdogs. Their distant ancestors are unknown as they date back to the time when nomadic herdsmen moved as the climate changed and food for their animals changed with it. In more recent times, as nations became more stable, breeds developed which were best suited to local conditions. The result was such breeds as the Owtscharka in Russia, the Puli and the Komondor in Hungary and the Shepherd dogs of Germany. Among these different breeds that evolved in Northern Europe, the Briard, or Chien Berger de Brie, to give it its full name, is one of the oldest.

He is found in most parts of France but takes his name from the Province of Brie, and in records of the early part of the 19th century he is referred to as the dog of that area. At one time he was very much the guard dog as well as herder and he was expected to be

NATIONAL GROUPING		
	Name	Number.
KC(GB)	Working	5
AKC	Working Dogs	III
FCI	Herding Dogs	I

capable of tackling wolves if need arose. In later years, however, after the French Revolution and the dividing up of the country into smaller parts, he became a herding dog entrusted with the task of keeping the flocks near to the homestead. He is now found doing this work in almost every part of France, as he is the most numerous of the herding dogs. In 1900 Les Amis du Briard was formed, a society dedicated to the welfare of the breed which wrote at that time a standard still in use today.

He was popular with the French troops during World

War I, and it was at that time that the American troops became acquainted with him. By 1920 the breed was appearing in the United States and made steady progress. In Britain registrations began in 1971, and the breed's popularity increased at such a rate that by 1974 challenge certificates were on offer and by 1975, seventy-nine individual dogs were entered under the author at the Birmingham National Show. One of the most carefully guarded characteristics of the breed is the double dew claw on the hind legs, and breed club publications use this feature as their title.

He is square and strong, extremely muscular and active, and has a coat that will withstand relentless rain. He is seen in a wide range of colours, though principally black and slate grey, and the dogs of the other colours have a coat that can be either plain, or what is called *charbonnée* in which the longer hairs are tipped with black. As a show dog he is a tremendous success, being steady in the ring, easy-going in temperament, and responsive to command. He is easily prepared as apart from brushing the coat needs very little attention, and due to its quality, even looks good when the dog is thoroughly wet at an outdoor show. He is a well-mannered dog, easy to train, and a very good guard, being quiet until roused, when his voice is usually enough to deter intruders.

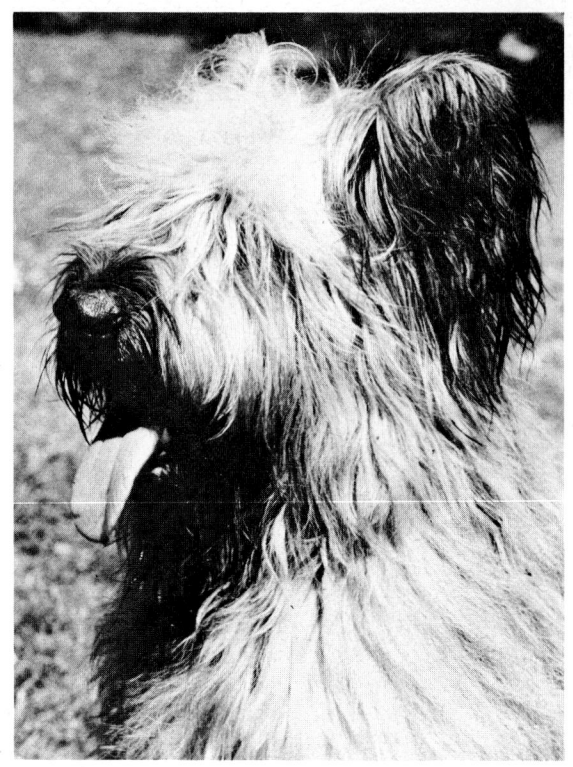

OFFICIAL STANDARD

General appearance
A dog of rugged appearance; supple, muscular and well proportioned, gay and lively.

Head and skull
Head strong, fairly long with well defined stop placed exactly mid-way in the length of the head. The head should carry hair forming moustache, beard and eyebrows which slightly veil the eyes. The muzzle should be neither narrow nor pointed. The nose should be large and square, always black, no matter what colour the dog. The forehead slightly rounded, the skull rectangular in shape.

Mouth
The teeth should be strong, white and well fitting in a scissor bite.

Eyes
Horizontally placed, well opened and rather large, not oblique, dark brown, intelligent and gentle in expression.

Ears
Set on high. The ear should not lie too flat against the side of the head, and the ears should be fairly short. The length of an ear should be equal to, or slightly less than half the length of the head. Covered with long hair.

Neck
Should be well muscled and arching, strong and carried well away from the shoulders.

Forequarters
Should be well angulated and well laid back, the forelegs well muscled with strong bone structure.

Body
The back should be firm and level, the chest broad and well let-down; there should be a very slight slope at the croup.

Hindquarters
Well angulated, with hocks set not too low, but the leg below the hock being not quite vertical. Double dew-claws

Head and skull: strong. Fairly long moustache, beard and eyebrows.

Hindquarters: well angulated, hocks not too low.

on hind legs of the utmost importance.

Feet
Strong and slightly rounded, about mid-way between a cat-foot and a hare-foot. Nails should always be black. Pads should be firm and hard and the toes close together.

Gait
Should be effortless and, when the dog extends himself, should cover a great deal of ground. It should give the impression that the dog is gliding over the ground.

Tail
Long, well covered with hair and with an upward hook at the tip. Carried low and deviating neither to one side nor the other. The bone of the tail should reach at least to the point of the hock.

Coat
Long (not less than 3 inches (7 centimetres) on the body), slightly wavy and very dry.

Colour
All solid colours are correct except those mentioned below. The darker shades are to be preferred. Incorrect colours are: white, chestnut, mahogany and bi-colour. Bi-colour should not be confused with the slightly lighter shadings at the extremities. This slightly lighter colouring is due to the beginnings of uneven pigmentation. This lighter shading should, however, be of the same tone as the rest of the coat, e.g. light fawn on dark fawn, light grey on dark grey. Occasional white hairs through the black coat are acceptable and do not designate a bi-colour.

Size
Dogs 23 to 27 inches (58.42 to 68.58 centimetres). Bitches 22 to 25½ inches (55.88 to 64.77 centimetres). Slight undersize is not to be considered a fault in an animal under eighteen months of age.

Faults
Any departure from the foregoing points shall be considered a fault, and the seriousness with which it shall be regarded is in exact proportion to its degree.

Note
Male animals should have two apparently normal testicles fully descended into the scrotum.

AKC VARIATION TO STANDARD
Head: correct length of a good head, measured from occiput to tip of nose, is about 40% of height of dog at withers. There is no objection to slightly longer head especially if animal tends to longer body line. Width of head, as measured across skull, is slightly less than length of skull from occiput to stop. Viewed from above, from front or in profile, fully-coated silhouette gives impression of two rectangular forms, equal in length but differing in height and width, blending together rather abruptly. Larger rectangle is skull the other muzzle. Occiput is prominent and forehead slightly rounded. Head joins neck at right angles and is held proudly. Head has clean lines, without jowls or excess flesh on sides, or under eyes or temples. *Mouth:* lips black, medium thickness, firm and neatly fitted. *Nose:* nostrils well opened. *Ears:* when cropped should be carried upright and parallel. When alert they should face forward, well open with long hair falling over the opening. Cropped ear should be long, broad at base, tapering gradually to rounded tip. *Forequarters:* shoulder blades are long and sloping forming a 45 degree angle with horizontal. Well muscled pasterns slightly inclined. *Feet:* feet travel straight forward. If rear toes turn out very slightly when hocks and metatarsus are parallel, then position of feet is correct. *Disqualifications:* nose any colour but black. Yellow or spotted eyes. Tail non-existent or cut. Less than two dewclaws on each rear leg. White or spotted coat. White spot on chest exceeding 1 inch diameter. All dogs under minimum size limits.

BULLMASTIFF

NATIONAL GROUPING		
	Name	Number
KC(GB)	Working	5
AKC	Working Dogs	III
FCI	Guard Dogs	2

The original Mastiff of Britain is one of the country's oldest breeds, but its descendant, the Bullmastiff is a comparatively recent development. It was bred by crossing the original Mastiff with other breeds, and probably the Bulldog, which was originally a much longer-legged breed than it is today. The Mastiff type is widespread over most of Europe, from the Neapolitan Mastiff of Italy to the Mountain Dogs of Switzerland. In Britain in the 13th century they were known as Bandogs, and were used principally for guarding property at night. In the middle of the 19th century attempts were made to improve the breed, as its use as a guard ended with increased urbanisation and better policing. Towards the end of the century classes were scheduled for Bullmastiffs belonging to gamekeepers, and clearly a dog of the size and reputed fierceness of the breed would be a useful companion to a gamekeeper at a time when poaching was a favourite country pastime.

There are early literary references to the breed, Buffon in 1791 stated that the cross between a Bulldog and a Mastiff produced a strong large Bulldog, much larger than a Bulldog but more like one of that breed than a Mastiff. In the Field of 1871 there appeared a report of a fight between two lions and Bullmastiffs, but the dogs of these early days were probably casual crosses between the two breeds rather than a serious attempt to produce a new breed. From 1924, when the Kennel Club first recognised the breed, there was a marked improvement, and from 1928, when challenge certificates were first offered, great strides were made and the breed settled down to something approaching the dog that we know today both in appearance and character. It was still much used as a guard dog, being a favourite among country people who needed a big strong dog to deter intruders from making raids on stock, and it was popular as an estate dog, some strains being traceable back to old family estates at the turn of the century.

He is a big strong active dog with a heavy body and very well made limbs which give him an appearance of squareness from every angle, and he should have no tendency towards elegance or legginess. His head, like that of one of his ancestors, the Bulldog, is his main feature, and much store is placed upon its squareness and character. He is supposed to look fierce but at the same time there should be a look of honesty about him so that he always looks trustworthy.

As a show dog he is readily trained, standing well without being set up too rigidly. He easily learns a few simple words of command, and rarely objects to being handled by strangers. He is a tough, likeable dog, has few vices, and whilst at first sight he does not look like the ideal animal to have as a house pet, those that own one rarely lose their love of the breed. He needs a considerable quantity of food to keep him in condition but he is not a fussy eater, subsisting well on any of the normal dog foods. Above all else he is a great guard, his appearance alone being enough to keep most intruders away, and whilst he is not prone to attacking anyone, his sheer weight is often enough to subdue anyone who persists in trespassing.

OFFICIAL STANDARD

Characteristics
The temperament of the Bullmastiff combines high spirits, reliability, activity, endurance and alertness.

General appearance
The Bullmastiff is a powerfully built, symmetrical dog, showing great strength, but not cumbersome.

Head and skull
The skull should be large and square, viewed from every angle, with fair wrinkle when interested, but not when in repose. The circumference of the skull may equal the height of the dog measured at the top of the shoulder; it should be broad and deep with good cheeks. The muzzle short, the distance from the tip of the nose to the stop should be approximately one-third of the length from the tip of the nose to the centre of the occiput, broad under the eyes and nearly parallel in width to the end of the nose; blunt and cut off square, forming a right-angle with the upper line of the face, and at the same time proportionate with the skull. Underjaw broad to the end. Nose broad with widely spreading nostrils when viewed from the front; flat, not pointed or turned up in profile. Flews not pendulous, and not hanging below the level of the bottom of the lower jaw. Stop definite.

Head and skull: skull large and square, muzzle short, underjaw broad.

Eyes
Dark or hazel, and of medium size, set apart the width of the muzzle with furrow between. Light or yellow eyes a fault.

Ears
V-shaped, or folded back, set on wide and high, level with occiput, giving a square appearance to the skull, which is most important. They should be small and deeper in colour than the body, and the point of the ear should be level with the eye when alert. Rose ears to be penalised.

Mouth
Mouth to be level, slight undershot allowed, but not preferred. Canine teeth large and set wide apart, other teeth strong, even and well-placed. Irregularity of teeth a fault.

Neck
Well-arched, moderate length, very muscular and almost equal to the skull in circumference.

Forequarters
Chest, wide and deep, well set down between forelegs, with deep brisket. Shoulders muscular sloping and powerful, not overloaded. Forelegs powerful and straight, well boned and set wide apart, presenting a straight front. Pasterns straight and strong.

Body
Back short and straight, giving a compact carriage, but not so short as to interfere with activity. Roach and sway backs a fault.

Hindquarters
Loins wide and muscular with fair depth of flank. Hindlegs strong and muscular, with well developed second thighs, denoting power and activity, but not cumbersome. Hocks moderately bent. Cow-hocks a fault.

Feet
Not large, with rounded toes, well-arched (cat feet), pads hard. Splay feet a fault.

Tail
Set high, strong at root and tapering, reaching to the hocks, carried straight or curved, but not hound fashion. Crank tails a fault.

Coat
Short and hard, giving weather protection, lying flat to the body. A tendency to long, silky or woolly coats to be penalised.

Colour
Any shade of brindle, fawn or red, but the colour to be pure and clear. A slight white marking on chest permissible but not desirable. Other white markings a fault. A dark muzzle is essential toning off towards the eyes, with dark markings around the eyes, giving expression. Dark toenails desirable.

Weight and size
Dogs should be 25 to 27 inches at shoulder, and 110 to 130 pounds, in weight. Bitches should be 24 to 26 inches at the shoulder and 90 to 110 pounds in weight. It must be borne in mind that size must be proportionate with weight, and soundness and activity is most essential.

Note
Male animals should have two apparently normal testicles fully descended into the scrotum.

AKC VARIATION TO STANDARD
Ears: medium size.

BEARDED COLLIE

NATIONAL GROUPING		
	Name	Number
KC(GB)	Working	5
AKC	—	—
FCI	Herding Dogs	I

There was a time when much of the farming land of Europe was devoted to the raising of sheep and cattle, and particularly of sheep. The urban development that resulted from the industrial revolution changed the pattern and absorbed a great deal of the land. Enclosed farming restricted herding even further and in Britain nowadays, the free ranging of sheep is mostly confined to parts of Scotland and Wales. One of the results of this extensive herding was the development of breeds of dogs that would assist the shepherd in rounding up and controlling the sheep that roamed over the mountains as well as guarding the flocks. A special type of dog was developed for the purpose, known as the working sheepdog, a black and white Collie type, with variations in different areas, but basically a small mostly black and white working dog. In Scotland, and more specifically in Peeblesshire, the dog that was bred for sheep-herding was the Bearded Collie.

He looks something like an Old English Sheepdog though slender, less heavy in body, and much more freedom of choice is permitted in colour, some being similar to the Old English Sheepdog, but others being red, brown or sandy. He was known at one time as the Scottish Bearded or Highland Collie.

It was after the Second World War that the Bearded Collie began its rise to prominence in the show ring. This was largely due to the efforts of Mrs. Willison whose successful search for a mate for her bitch started the Bothkennar line. She campaigned too for recognition for the breed which was finally granted in 1959 and she made up the first champion in the breed which was bred from a son of her original bitch.

The Bearded Collie is not so popular with flockmasters as some of the other breeds, as whilst he is hardy enough, he is temperamentally rather soft, and probably more suited to the gentle task of driving cattle than to using force on a difficult hill ewe with lambs. One of the other problems in the early days was that a Bearded Collie would hunt, and thus become easily diverted from the work that he was supposed to be doing. This was probably due to something deep-rooted in his ancestry dating back to the time when most dogs fulfilled a dual purpose.

As a showdog he is rapidly gaining popularity. The number of registrations have trebled in recent years, and he now vies with some of the once popular gun-dogs and the Dachshunds. At the major shows the breed appears in large numbers, and has recently figured among the top awards for the first time. The Bearded Collie is one of those breeds that really repays attention to coat preparation. The modern Bearded Collie would probably meet with a certain amount of scorn from the working shepherd of a few years ago, who would consider such attention pampering, but there is no doubt that with its coat beautifully brushed out the modern Beardie makes a fine and very competitive spectacle in today's show ring.

Temperamentally he is a delightful dog, being affectionate, always willing to make friends, intelligent and faithful. He is a perfect dog with children, being very well-mannered and gentle, and it is one of the sights of today's shows to see a child handling a Bearded Collie in perfect harmony. The dogs that have won top awards have done so partly because of their demeanour in the ring as they can be trained to stand like a statue and move on command.

OFFICIAL STANDARD

Characteristics
The Bearded Collie should be alert, lively and self confident, good temperament essential.

General appearance
An active dog with long, lean body, and none of the stumpiness of the Bobtail and which though strongly made, shows plenty of daylight under the body and does not look too heavy. The face should have an enquiring expression. Movement should be free and active.

Head and skull
Broad, flat skull with ears set high, fairly long foreface with moderate stop. Nose black except with brown or fawn coats, when brown is permitted.

Eyes
To tone with coat in colour, the eyes to be set rather widely apart, big and bright. Eyebrows arched up and forward, but not long enough to obscure the eyes.

Forequarters: legs straight with good bone.

Ears: medium size, dropping, longish hair, slight lift at base.

Ears
Medium size, drooping with longish hair, slight lift at the base denoting alertness.

Mouth
Teeth large and white, never undershot or overshot.

Neck
Must be fair length, muscular and slightly arched.

Forequarters
Legs straight with good bone, pasterns flexible without weakness, covered with shaggy hair all round.

Body
Fairly long, back level, with flat ribs and strong loins, ribcage both deep and long, shoulders flat, straight front essential.

Hindquarters
Legs muscular at thighs, with well bent stifles and hocks, free from exaggeration.

Feet
Oval in shape, soles well padded, toes arched and close together, well covered with hair including between the pads.

Tail
Set low, should be moderately long with abundant hair or brush, carried low when the dog is quiet, with an upward swirl at the tip, carried gaily when the dog is excited, but not over the back.

Coat
Must be double, the under one soft, furry and close the outer one harsh strong and flat, free from woolliness or any tendency to curl. Sparse hair on the ridge of the nose, slightly longer on the sides just covering the lips. Behind this falls the long beard. A moderate amount of hair under the chin, increasing in length to the chest.

Colour
Slate grey or reddish fawn, black, all shades of grey, brown and sandy, with or without white Collie markings.

Size
Ideal height at the shoulder: dogs, 21 to 22 inches; bitches, 20 to 21 inches.

Note
Male animals should have two apparently normal testicles fully descended into the scrotum.

AKC VARIATION TO STANDARD
This dog is not granted championship status by the AKC.

ROUGH COLLIE

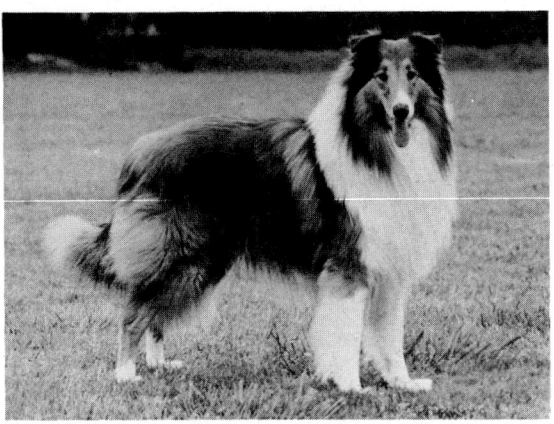

As is the case with a number of breeds there has been a fairly sharp division between the working and the show type of Collie. The working Collie of today is almost exactly like the one of a hundred years ago, whilst the show Collie is very different indeed, and it is unlikely that any show Collie would work sheep as his ancestors did. This divergence began something over a hundred years ago when a number of breeders recognised the potential in the rough-coated working Collie of Scotland, and by selective breeding, improved coat, stature and colouring to produce the magnificent dog that we know today. The breed was originally evolved for sheep herding as with the other Collie types, but today's version was produced almost entirely as a show dog. Queen Victoria took a great interest in the breed which increased its popularity, and around the turn of the century it commanded a very good export market, with prices that would seem high even by today's standards.

The popularity of the Rough Collie has continued, and the registration figures for the breed in Britain are second only to the Alsatian in the working group, whilst in the United States the figures have maintained a high level. As a show dog the Rough Collie has always been a great draw, attracting a ringside audience wherever he appears. This is hardly surprising as the Collie has been developed specifically as a show dog, the head becoming exaggerated by careful selection and the coat quality evolved in the same way. One of the problems has been to produce the perfect small semi-erect ears, and exhibitors go to great lengths to ensure that by care and attention to this feature at an early age, the mature dog has the desired ear.

NATIONAL GROUPING		
	Name	Number
KC(GB)	Working	5
AKC	Working Dogs	III
FCI	Herding Dogs	I

The Rough Collie repays attention and a beautifully groomed dog in full coat is always much admired, whilst a ring full of them, in their subtle colour variations from light gold to silvery blue and black and tan, and in the United States even white, creates a spectacle that everyone admires. He is an easy dog to show, as he enjoys being admired, is attentive in the ring, and always willing to please his handler. Early critics of the direction in which the breed was developing complained that it was becoming too elegant and looking like a thoroughbred than the workhorse that it should resemble. These days this is no longer true, and the breeders have concentrated on producing a less attenuated animal, more compact and with better coupling.

As house pets Rough Collies have always had a following, as they are friendly, yet good guards, and whilst amenable to discipline, they are not easily cowed. They are by nature a dog for the fields and the open country and it is in this environment that they are perhaps at their happiest, but they fit in well to modern more confined living conditions, and are perfectly happy in a small house or apartment provided that they get sufficient exercise. Like all the working dogs they need exercise to prevent overweight, nothing looks worse than a fat Rough Collie.

OFFICIAL STANDARD

Characteristics
To enable the Collie to fulfil a natural bent for sheepdog work, its physical structure should be on the lines of strength and activity, free from cloddiness and without any trace of coarseness. Expression, one of the most important points in considering relative values, is obtained by the perfect balance and combination of skull and foreface; size, shape, colour and placement of eye, correct position and carriage of ears.

General appearance
The Collie should instantly appeal as a dog of great beauty, standing with impassive dignity, with no part out of proportion to the whole.

Head and skull
The head properties are of great importance and must be considered in proportion to the size of the dog. When viewed from the front or the side the head bears a general resemblance to a well-blunted, clean wedge, being smooth in outline. The skull should be flat. The sides should taper gradually and smoothly from the ears to the end of the black nose, without prominent cheek bones or pinched muzzle. Viewed in profile the top of the skull and the top of the muzzle lie in two parallel, straight planes of equal length, divided by a slight, but perceptible 'stop' or break. A mid-point between the inside corners of the eyes, (which is the centre of a correctly placed 'stop') is the centre of balance in length of head. The end of the smooth, well-rounded muzzle is blunt, but not square. The under-jaw is strong, clean cut and the depth of the skull from the brow to the underpart of the jaw, must never be excessive (deep through). Whatever the colour of the dog, the nose must be black.

Eyes
These are a very important feature and give a sweet expression to the dog. They should be of medium size, set somewhat obliquely, of almond shape and of dark brown colour, except in the case of blue merles when the eyes are frequently (one or both, or part of one or both), blue or blue flecked. Expression full of intelligence, with a quick, alert look when listening.

Ears
These should be small and not too close together on top of the skull, nor too much to the side of the head. When in repose they should be carried thrown back, but when on the alert brought forward and carried semi-erect, that is, with approximately two-thirds of the ear standing erect, the top third tipping forward naturally, below the horizontal.

Mouth
The teeth should be of good size, with the lower incisors fitting closely behind the upper incisors; a very slight space not to be regarded as a serious fault.

Neck
The neck should be muscular, powerful, of fair length and well arched.

Forequarters
The shoulders should be sloped and well-angulated. The forelegs should be straight and muscular, neither in nor out at elbows, with a moderate amount of bone.

Body
The body should be a trifle long compared to the height, back firm with a slight rise over the loins; ribs well-sprung, chest deep and fairly broad behind the shoulders.

Hindquarters
The hind legs should be muscular at the thighs, clean and sinewy below, with well bent stifles. Hocks well let-down and powerful.

Feet
These should be oval in shape with soles well padded, toes arched and close together. The hind feet slightly less arched.

Head and skull: well-blunted, clean wedge, skull flat.

White markings.

Gait
Movement is a distinct characteristic of this breed. A sound dog is never out at elbow, yet it moves with its front feet comparatively close together. Plaiting, crossing or rolling are highly undesirable. The hind legs, from the hock joint to the ground, when viewed from the rear, should be parallel. The hind legs should be powerful and full of drive. Viewed from the side the action is smooth. A reasonably long stride is desirable and this should be light and appear quite effortless.

Tail
The tail should be long with the bone reaching at least to the hock joint. To be carried low when the dog is quiet, but with a slight upward swirl at the tip. It may be carried gaily when the dog is excited, but not over the back.

Coat
The coat should fit the outline of the dog and be very dense. The outer coat straight and harsh to the touch, the undercoat soft, furry and very close, so close as to almost hide the skin. The mane and frill should be very abundant; the mask or face, smooth, also the ears at the tips, but they should carry more hair towards the base; the fore-legs well feathered, the hind legs above the hocks profusely so, but smooth below. Hair on the tail very profuse.

Colour
The three recognised colours are sable and white, tricolour and blue merle. *Sable:* any shade from light gold to rich mahogany or shaded sable. Light straw or cream colour is highly undesirable. *Tricolour:* predominantly black with rich tan markings about the legs and head. A rusty tinge in the top coat is highly undesirable. *Blue merle:* predominantly clear, silvery blue, splashed and marbled with black. Rich tan markings to be preferred, but their absence should not be counted as a fault. Large black markings, slate colour, or a rusty tinge either of the top or undercoat are highly undesirable. *White markings:* all the above may carry the typical white Collie markings to a greater or lesser degree. The following markings are favourable—white collar, full or part; white shirt, legs and feet; white tail tip. A blaze may be carried on muzzle or skull or both.

Weight and size
Dogs 22 to 24 inches at shoulder, bitches 20 to 22 inches. Dogs 45 to 65 pounds, bitches 40 to 55 pounds.

Faults
Length of head apparently out of proportion to body; receding skull or unbalanced head to be strongly condemned. Weak, snipy muzzle; domed skull; high peaked occiput, prominent cheek bones; dish-faced or Roman-nosed; under-shot or over-shot mouth; missing teeth; round or light coloured and glassy or staring eyes are highly objectionable. Body flat sided, short or cobby; straight shoulder or stifle; out at elbow; crooked forearms; cow-hocks or straight hocks, large, open or hare feet; feet turned in or out; long, weak pasterns; tail short, kinked or twisted to one side or carried over the back; a soft, silky or wavy coat or insufficient undercoat; prick ears, low-set ears; nervousness.

Note
Male animals should have two apparently normal testicles fully descended into the scrotum.

AKC VARIATION TO STANDARD
The Collie is shown by the AKC under one standard for the two varieties. *Body:* loin is powerful and slightly arched. Croup is sloped to give well rounded finish. *Colour:* four colours include white, and sable and white. *Weight:* dogs 60 to 75 pounds, bitches 50 to 65 pounds.

SMOOTH COLLIE

The standard of the breed says that it is a replica of the Rough Collie in everything except coat. There are many breeds of dog that have a coat difference, the Wire and Smooth Fox Terrier, the variations in the Dachshund, and even in such well-established breeds as the German Shepherd Dog coat differences crop up from time to time. This is sometimes due to variations of climate in the country of origin of the breed, for example, the smooth Chow Chow tends to be found in the south of China whilst the rough-coated variety is found in the north where the weather is colder. This is, however, not true of the Collie, as the two types have developed alongside one another in the same area of Scotland. It has been suggested that the smooth coat resulted from a cross with the Greyhound, but this is improbable and it was more likely to have been just a natural variant.

It is interesting that the Australian Cattle Dog, which undoubtedly was produced from a Collie in the first

NATIONAL GROUPING		
	Name	Number
KC(GB)	Working	5
AKC	Working Dogs	III
FCI	Herding Dogs	I

instance, and indeed has still something of the collie colour variations, is in fact a smooth coated dog. The development of the Smooth Collie as a show dog was largely carried on south of the Border and in the early days both coats were shown in the same classes. It was only later that the two breeds were shown separately, and the smooth coated variety has never competed in numbers with the Rough Collie, less than two per-cent of the collies registered being smooth. It has always been said that though the Smooth Collie is an intelligent dog it is of little use as a worker with sheep, only the odd one being capable of rounding up a flock.

OFFICIAL STANDARD

Characteristics

To enable the Collie to fulfil a natural bent for sheepdog work, its physical structure should be on the lines of strength and activity, free from cloddiness and without any trace of coarseness. Expression, one of the most important points in considering relative values, is obtained by the perfect balance and combination of skull and foreface, size, shape, colour and placement of eye, correct position and carriage of ears. Temperament should be gay and friendly, never nervous nor aggressive.

General appearance

The Collie should instantly appeal as gifted with intelligence, alertness and activity. He should stand with dignity, and his movements, governed by perfect anatomical formation, with no part out of proportion, should be smooth and graceful. He should give the appearance of a dog capable of working.

Head and skull

The head properties are of great importance and must be considered in proportion to the size of the dog. When viewed from both front and profile the head should bear a general resemblance to a well-blunted, clean wedge, being smooth in outline. The skull should be flat. The sides should taper gradually and smoothly from the ears to the end of the black nose, without prominent cheek bones or pinched muzzle. Viewed in profile the top of the skull and the top of the muzzle should lie in two parallel, straight planes of equal length, divided by a slight but perceptible 'stop' or break. A mid-point between the inside corners of the eyes (which is the centre of a correctly placed 'stop') should be the centre of balance in length of head. The end of the smooth, well-rounded muzzle should be blunt, but not square. The underjaw should be strong, clean cut, and the depth of the skull from the brow to the underpart of the jaw should never be excessive (deep through). Whatever the colour of the dog, the nose must be black.

Eyes

Are a very important feature and should give a sweet expression to the dog. They should be of medium size, set somewhat obliquely, of almond shape and of dark brown colour, except in the case of blue merles when one or both eyes may be wall or jewelled. Expression full of intelligence with a quick, alert look when listening.

Ears

Should be moderately large, wider at the base, and placed not too close together nor too much on the side of the head. When in repose they should be carried thrown back, but when on the alert brought forward and carried semi-erect, that is, with approximately two-thirds of the ear standing erect, the top third tipping forward naturally, below the horizontal.

Mouth

The teeth should be of good size, with the lower incisors fitting closely behind the upper incisors; a very slight space not to be regarded as a serious fault.

Neck

Should be muscular, powerful, of fair length and well arched.

Forequarters

The shoulders should be sloped and well angulated. The forelegs should be straight and muscular, neither in nor out at the elbows, with a moderate amount of bone. The forearm somewhat fleshy with pasterns showing flexibility without weakness.

Body

Should be a trifle long compared with the height, back level and firm with a slight rise over the loins; ribs well-sprung; chest deep and fairly broad behind the shoulders.

Hindquarters

The hind legs should be muscular at the thighs, clean and sinewy below, with well bent stifles. Hocks well let-down and powerful. Dog animals should have two apparently normal testicles fully descended into the scrotum.

Feet

Should be oval with soles well padded. Toes arched and close together. Hind feet slightly less arched.

Gait

Movement is a distinct characteristic of the breed. A sound dog is never out at elbow, yet it moves with its front feet comparatively close together. Plaiting, crossing or rolling are highly undesirable. The hind legs, from the hock joint to the ground, when viewed from the rear, should be parallel, powerful and full of drive. Viewed from the side the action should be smooth. A reasonably long stride is desirable and this should be light and appear quite effortless.

Tail

Should be long with the bone reaching at least to the hock joint. To be carried low when the dog is quiet but with a slight upward swirl at the tip. It may be carried gaily when the dog is excited, but never over the back.

Coat

A very important feature of the Smooth Collie is his short, flat top coat of harsh texture, with a very dense undercoat.

Colour

The three recognised colours are: sable and white, tricolour and blue merle. *Sable:* any shade from light gold to rich mahogany or shaded sable. Light straw or cream colour is highly undesirable. *Tricolour:* predominantly black with rich tan markings about the legs and head. A rusty tinge in the top coat is highly undesirable. *Blue merle:* predominantly clear, silvery blue, splashed and marbled with black. Rich tan markings to be preferred but their absence should not be counted as a fault. Large black markings, slate colour or a rusty tinge either on the top or undercoat are highly undesirable. *White markings:* all the above may carry the typical white Collie markings to a greater or lesser degree. The following markings are favourable: white collar, full or part; white front, legs and feet; white tail tip. A blaze may be carried on muzzle or skull or both.

All white or predominantly white is most undesirable.

Weight and size

Dogs 22 to 24 inches at shoulder, bitches 20 to 22 inches at shoulder. Dogs 45 to 65 pounds, bitches 40 to 55 pounds.

Faults

Any departure from the foregoing points should be considered a fault and the seriousness of the fault should be in exact proportion to its degree.

AKC VARIATION TO STANDARD

The Collie is shown by the AKC under one standard for the two varieties. *Body:* loin is powerful and slightly arched. Croup is sloped to give well rounded finish. *Colour:* four colours include white, and sable and white. *Weight:* dogs 60 to 75 pounds, bitches 50 to 65 pounds.

DOBERMANN

It happens to few people that they have a breed of dog named after them to hand down to posterity, but when a man invents and produces a completely new breed as did Louis Dobermann in Germany about the year 1870, it would have been unjust had anything less happened. Herr Dobermann set out with a vision of the sort of dog that he wanted to breed, and beginning with the Rottweiler and the German Pinscher, he produced one of the finest and most popular breeds in the world. He is believed to have introduced into his cross the black and tan English Terrier and one of the shepherd dogs, probably the German Shepherd Dog. In the older books the dog is referred to as a distinctive German Terrier, but there is little of the Terrier look about him now. Originally he was a much coarser dog with a heavier body and a shorter and more rounded head, probably due to the Rottweiler blood. Others after Herr Dobermann, Otto Goeller and Daniel Elmer for instance, did a great deal towards the refinement of the breed and produced a more racy and elegant dog.

The first breed club was founded in 1912, and the breed began to be more widely accepted, finding its way rapidly to other European countries and to the United States and Britain. His qualities as a guard were quickly appreciated and he became a popular dog with the armed forces and police forces of the world. He has never quite achieved the popularity of the German Shepherd Dog for this work, as although he is somewhat lighter, he is tougher and harder to control. In the United States of America he soon

NATIONAL GROUPING		
	Name	Number
KC(GB)	Working	5
AKC	Working Dogs	III
FCI	Guard Dogs	2

became the third most popular dog and other countries followed suit, so that by the middle of the 20th century his fame as a guard, army dog and show dog has spread throughout the world, carrying the name of Herr Dobermann with him.

He is an elegant yet very strong dog, with a powerful body, great strength of limb and tremendous agility. He is fast, has great powers of endurance, and is an ardent worker, all of which make him very popular with the forces, as not only does he do the work that is required of him, but his smart appearance fits him well to the formality and precision of a trained body of men. As a show dog his progress has been amazing, and from small beginnings only a few years ago, he is now seen at shows throughout the world in large numbers. He is as popular in Malaysia as he is in Europe, and as numerous in Australia as he is in Scandinavia. His smart, elegant yet powerful appearance always guarantees him a good audience, and his smooth coat which can be polished until it shines makes him an outstanding dog in mixed company. He usually features among the big winners and the strength of the breed clubs, their enthusiasm and continued work on the breed ensure that this will continue.

At one time his temperament was suspect, and for this reason his use as a police dog declined in those parts of the world where undue force was frowned upon. In America it was recognised at an early stage that this would count against the breed, and his tendency to undue sharpness of reaction was carefully bred out, dogs which showed this trait suffering disqualification. Training programmes were instituted and owners and breeders were encouraged to train their dogs to obedience work, which at one and the same time reduced their aggression and gave them a better public image. In Britain this has not been done to the same extent, and from time to time the Dobermann ring at one of the major shows will explode in fury. Properly trained they become obedient dogs, and within the family circle they are even affectionate, and there can hardly be a better guard dog in the world.

OFFICIAL STANDARD

Characteristics

The Dobermann is a dog of good medium size with a well-set body, muscular and elegant. He has a proud carriage and a bold, alert temperament. His form is compact and tough and owing to his build capable of great speed. His gait is light and elastic. His eyes show intelligence and firmness of character, and he is loyal and obedient. Shyness or viciousness must be heavily penalised.

Head and skull

Has to be proportionate to the body. It must be long, well filled under the eyes and clean cut. Its form seen from above and from the side must resemble a blunt wedge. The upper part of the head should be as flat as possible and free from wrinkle. The top of the skull should be flat with a slight stop, and the muzzle line extend parallel to the top

Head and skull: long, well-filled, clean out.

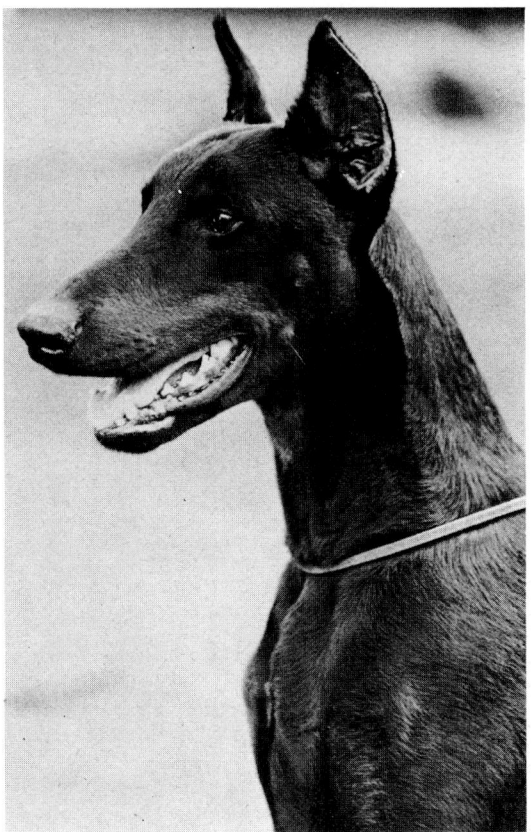

line of the skull. The cheeks must be flat and the lips tight. The nose should be solid black in black dogs, solid dark brown in brown dogs, and solid dark grey in blue dogs. Head out of balance in proportion to body, dish-faced, snipy or cheeky should be penalised.

Eyes

Should be almond-shaped, not round, moderately deep set, not prominent, with vigorous, energetic expression. Iris of uniform colour, ranging from medium to darkest brown in black dogs, the darker shade being the more desirable. In browns or blues the colour of the iris should blend with that of the markings, but not be of lighter hue than that of the markings. Light eyes in black dogs to be discouraged.

Ears

Should be small, neat and set high on the head. Erect or dropped, but erect preferred.

Mouth

Should be very well developed, solid and strong, with a scissor bite. The incisors of the lower jaw must touch the inner face of the incisors of the upper jaw. Overshot or undershot mouths, badly arranged or decayed teeth to be penalised.

Neck

Should be fairly long and lean, carried erect and with considerable nobility, slightly covex and proportionate to the whole shape of the dog. The region of the nape has to be muscular. Dewlap and loose skin are undesirable.

Forequarters

The shoulder blade and upper arm should meet at an angle of 90 degrees. Relative length of shoulder and upper arm should be as one, excess length of upper arm being much less undesirable than excess length of shoulder blade. The legs seen from the front and side, are perfectly straight and parallel to each other from elbow to pastern, muscled and sinewy, with round bone proportionate to body structure. In a normal position and when gaiting, the elbow should lie close to the brisket.

Body

Should be square, height measured vertically from the ground to the highest point of the withers, equalling the length measured horizontally, from the forechest to rear projection of the upper thigh. The back should be short and firm with the topline sloping slightly from the withers to the croup, the bitch needing room to carry litters may be slightly longer to loin. The belly should be fairly well tucked up. Ribs should be deep and well-sprung, reaching to elbow. Long, weak or roach backs to be discouraged.

Hindquarters

Should be parallel to each other and wide enough apart to fit in with a properly built body. The hip bone should fall away from the spinal column at an angle of about 30 degrees. Croup well filled out. The hindquarters should be well developed and muscular, with long bent stifle and their hocks turning neither in nor out. While the dog is at rest, hock to heel should be perpendicular to the ground.

Feet

Fore-feet should be well arched, compact and cat-like, turning neither in nor out. All dew claws to be removed. Long, flat deviating paws and weak pasterns should be penalised. Hindfeet should be well arched, compact and cat-like, turning neither in nor out.

Gait

Should be free, balanced and vigorous with good reach in the forequarters, and a driving power in the hindquarters.

When trotting, there should be a strong rear action drive with rotary motion of hindquarters. Rear and front legs should be thrown neither in nor out. Back should remain strong and firm.

Tail

The tail should be docked at the first or second joint and should appear to be a continuation of the spine, without material drop.

Coat

Should be smooth-haired, short, hard, thick and close lying. Invisible grey undercoat on neck permissible.

Colour

Colours allowed are definite black, brown or blue with rust red markings. Markings must be sharply defined and appearing above each eye and on the muzzle, throat and fore-chest, and on all legs and feet, and below tail. White markings of any kind are highly undesirable.

Weight and size

Ideal height at withers: dogs 27 inches; bitches 25½ inches. Considerable deviation from this ideal to be discouraged.

Faults

Shyness or visciousness must be heavily penalised. Head out of balance in proportion to body, dish-faced, snipy or cheeky should be penalised. Light eyes in black dogs to be discouraged. Overshot or undershot mouths, badly arranged or decayed teeth to be penalised. Dewlap and loose skin are undesirable. Long, weak or roach backs to be discouraged. White markings of any kind are highly undesirable. Hair forming a ridge on the back of the neck and/or along the spine should be classed as a serious fault.

Note

Male animals should have two apparently normal testicles fully descended into the scrotum.

AKC VARIATION TO STANDARD

Head: jaws full and powerful. *Ears:* normally cropped. The upper attachment of ear when held erect is on a level with top of skull. *Feet:* pasterns firm and almost perpendicular to ground. *Colour:* fawns (Isabella). *Height:* (ideal) dogs 27½ inches, bitches 25½ inches. *Disqualifications:* overshot more than $\frac{3}{16}$ inch. Undershot more than $\frac{1}{8}$th inch. Four or more missing teeth.

GREAT DANE

The Mastiff group is one of the oldest and most significant of all the groups of dogs. Amongst its breeds are guard dogs from almost every country in Europe and Asia, and examples of Mastiff type dogs exist in fact and myth in most parts of the world. Zeus is said to have had a golden dog created for him by a smith with miraculous powers and even that dog was a Mastiff. It is difficult to imagine how the large guard dog, often smooth-coated and invariably affectionate with those that it knows but fierce with intruders, developed from the common ancestor of the race *canis domesticus*, but it did, and at a very early stage. One of the finest examples, for sheer size and for the other qualities of the group is the Great Dane. He almost certainly goes back to the ancient Molossus, and to the Alaunt, antique breeds now disappeared, but the progenitors of many of the massive breeds in the world today.

Germany lays claim to having developed the breed in modern times. He was known as the 'Deutsche Dogge' at one time and is still known as the 'Dogo

NATIONAL GROUPING		
	Name	Number
KC(GB)	Working	5
AKC	Working Dogs	III
FCI	Guard Dogs	2

Alemanes' in Spain. In the early days of the breed in Britain he was also known as the German Boarhound, but the name Great Dane eventually became generally used, and it is by that name that he is now known almost everywhere. Denmark had in fact a large dog of the Mastiff type, but more stocky and shorter in the leg than the elegant dog that we know today, and it was certainly Germany that played the major part in developing the breed from the late part of the 19th century. A standard of points was agreed in about 1880, somewhat later in Britain, and adopted in the United States of America.

The first record of a Great Dane being shown in

Britain was in 1878 when one was entered in the stud book as an Ulmer Dogge. This name is a reference to one of the several breeds that were probably used in Germany to produce the breed, along with the Saufinder, Hatzreude and Grosse Dogge, but the history of the modern Great Dane in Britain really started in 1900 when Mrs. Violet Horsfall imported several.

There are few problems about the Great Dane apart from those of feeding and rearing. A dog that will grow from something of the size of a smallish cat to an animal standing over thirty inches high in around six months, needs vast quantities of the very best food at every stage of its growth. He has natural hunting instincts, and very well developed scenting powers. His strength and stamina is such that he will run for miles, swimming rivers and leaping walls on the way, yet at the same time he is remarkably tractable and responsive to commands and can be trained to be quite obedient.

There are few finer dogs in the show ring than the Great Dane. His very size, striking colour and manners in the ring which are usually impeccable, make him one of the favourites with the dog-show-going-public throughout the world. His temperament is excellent, as he is loving and kindly towards people and especially towards children. He is not aggressive, and although he is well able to take care of himself and will eventually lose patience if persistently annoyed, he will not seek trouble. At the same time he is a magnificent guard and watchdog, settles well in a house, and his short coat and clean habits make him easy to groom. He is very much a one-man dog, and will attach himself to one person sometimes even to the point of embarrassment, and for that one person he will do absolutely anything.

OFFICIAL STANDARD

General appearance
The Great Dane should be remarkable in size and very muscular, strongly though elegantly built; the head and neck should be carried high, and the tail in line with the back, or slightly upwards but not curled over the hindquarters. Elegance of outline and grace of form are most essential to a Dane; size is absolutely necessary, but there must be that alertness of expression and briskness of movement without which the Dane character is lost. He should have a look of dash and daring, of being ready to go anywhere and do anything. The action should be lithe, springy and free, the hocks move freely and the head be carried high except when galloping.

Head and skull
The head, taken altogether, should give the idea of great length and strength of jaw. The muzzle or foreface is broad, and the skull proportionately narrow, so that the whole head, when viewed from above and in front, has the appearance of equal breadth throughout. The entire length of head varies with the height of the dog; 13 inches from the tip of the nose to the back of the occiput is a good measurement for a dog of 32 inches at the shoulder. The length from the end of the nose to the point between the eyes should be about equal, or preferably of greater length than from this point to the back of the occiput. The skull should be flat and have a slight indentation running up the centre, the occipital peak not prominent. There should be a decided rise or brow over the eyes but no abrupt stop between them; the face should be well chiselled, well filled in below the eyes with no appearance of being pinched; the foreface long, of equal depth throughout. The cheeks should show as little lumpiness as possible, compatible with strength. The underline of the head, viewed in profile, should run almost in a straight line from the corner of the lip to the corner of the jawbone, allowing for the fold of the lip, but with no loose skin to hang down. The bridge of the nose should be very wide, with a slight ridge where the cartilage joins the bone. (This is a characteristic of the breed.) The nostrils should be large, wide and open, giving a blunt look to the nose. A butterfly or flesh-coloured nose is not objected to in Harlequins. The lips should hang squarely in front, forming a right-angle with the upper line of foreface.

Eyes
Fairly deep set, of medium size and preferably dark. Wall or odd eyes permissible in Harlequins.

Ears
Should be small, set high on the skull and carried slightly erect with the tips falling forward.

Mouth
The teeth should be level and not project one way or the other.

Neck
The neck should be long, well arched, and quite clean and free from loose skin, held well up, well set in the shoulders, and the junction of the head and neck well defined.

Forequarters
The shoulders should be muscular but not loaded, and well sloped back, with the elbows well under the body. The forelegs should be perfectly straight with big bone, which must be flat.

Body: deep well-sprung ribs, belly drawn up showing harlequin pattern.

Body
The body should be very deep, with ribs well sprung and belly well drawn up. The back and loins should be strong, the latter slightly arched.

Hindquarters
The hindquarters and thighs should be extremely muscular giving the idea of great strength and galloping power. The second thigh is long and well developed, the stifle and hock well bent, the hocks set low, turning neither in nor out.

Feet
The feet should be catlike and should not turn in or out. The toes well arched and close, the nails strong and curved. Nails should be black but light nails are permissible in Harlequins.

Tail
The tail should be thick at the root, and taper towards the end, reaching to or just below the hocks. It should be .carried in a straight line level with the back, when the dog is in action, slightly curved towards the end, but in no case should it curl or be carried over the back.

Coat
The hair is short and dense and sleek-looking, and in no case should it incline to roughness.

Colour
(*a*) Brindles must be striped, ground colour from the lightest yellow to the deepest orange, and the stripes must always be black. Eyes and nails preferably dark. (*b*) Fawns, the colour varies from lightest buff to deepest orange, darker shading on the muzzle and the ears and around the eyes are by no means objectionable. Eyes and nails preferably dark. (*c*) Blues, the colour varies from light grey to deepest slate. (*d*) Blacks, black is black. (In all the above colours white is only admissible on the chest and feet, but it is not desirable even there. The nose is always black (except in blues). Eyes and nails preferably dark.) (*e*) Harlequins, pure white underground with preferably black patches (blue patches permitted), having the appearance of being torn. In Harlequins, wall eyes, pink noses or butterfly noses are permissible but are not desirable.

Weight and size
The minimum height of an adult dog over eighteen months must be 30 inches, that of a bitch, 28 inches. Weight, the minimum weight of an adult dog over eighteen months should be 120 pounds, that of a bitch, 100 pounds.

Faults
Cow-hocks. Out at elbows. Straight stifles. Undershot or overshot mouth. Round bone. Snipy muzzle. Straight shoulders. Shelly body. Ring tail.

Note
Dog animals should have two apparently normal testicles fully descended into the scrotum.

AKC VARIATION TO STANDARD
Head: strongly pronounced stop. *Nose:* in case of brindled and single-coloured dogs it must be black. In Harlequins nose should be black. Black spotted nose is permitted and pink nose undesirable. *Teeth:* incisors of lower jaw just touch very slightly bottoms of inner surface of upper incisors. If front teeth bite on top of each other they wear down too rapidly. *Ears:* ears should be high, set not too far apart, medium in size, of moerate thickness, drooping forward close to cheek. Top line of folded ear should be about level with skull. *Forelegs:* seen from front pasterns should slope only very slightly forward. *Hindquarters:* croup must be full slightly drooping and must continue imperceptibly to tailroot. *Colour:* blue Colour must be pure steel blue as far as possible without any tinge of yellow, black or mouse grey. Harlequins—Pure white neck preferred. *Height:* preferred dogs 32 inches, bitches 30 inches.

HUNGARIAN PULI

Fairly wild claims are made for different breeds of dogs concerning their early history, and if all the breeds that laid claim to being depicted on ancient Egyptian carvings and paintings were gathered together, it would be possible to hold a very successful dog show. The Puli is a typical example, attempts having been made to trace him back eight thousand years, to a time when dogs were just dogs, and no particular breeds had established themselves. There is no denying that the Puli is an ancient breed, but it would probably be unwise to go back more than a thousand years to the time when the Magyars migrated into the area now known as Hungary. He was the sheepherding dog of the Magyars, and the smallest of the breeds that they used for this purpose. The others, the Komondor and the Kuvasz almost certainly also existed alongside the Puli, and whilst the larger dogs were used as guards as well as herders, the Puli was probably the daytime herding dog, his darker colour helping in the control of flocks as the sheep would see him more easily. He was probably connected ancestrally with the Tibetan Terrier, a somewhat similar type of dog used for the same purpose, and even today, though the Puli is a much more heavily built dog, there is a good deal of similarity.

The modern history of the Puli dates back to 1751 when Heppe wrote of 'The Hungarian Water Dog' which resembled the Puli. This raises an interesting point, as the Water Dog, described in the Sportsman's Repository of 1820 describes this dog in some detail, and though it speaks of it as a hunting dog, it was almost certainly the ancestor of the Poodle, and has the type of coat, which if allowed to grow would certainly cord as does that of the Puli, and as did that of the Poodle in the early days. Under the Austrian occupa-

tion of Hungary the habits of the country were forcibly changed including the breeds of cattle and sheep that were kept. However, the Hungarian shepherds did their best to preserve the Puli, and persisted with a breeding programme which ensured that the breed remained pure, selecting stock with great care and often travelling great distances to arrange matings.

During the first half of this century there has been considerable concentration on the show qualities of the Puli rather than upon his working ability, though even dogs bred from generations of show stock will work sheep naturally. From 1900 the breeding of the Puli was undertaken as a serious study, scientists and veterinarians joining in the efforts of breeders to retain the purity of the breed. The director of the Zoo in Budapest co-operated and arranged for a part of the Zoo to be devoted to a breeding programme, and the stock produced from this experiment formed the foundation of many of the modern kennels.

The Second World War reduced dog breeding to the minimum in Hungary and the Puli sadly declined, but by one of those odd quirks of fate, the fleeing of the people of Hungary to many other parts of Europe taking with them their dogs, did more to make the Puli generally known than anything else could have done. By the mid-fifties the breed was back to something like its pre-war strength and by the sixties was being regularly shown in its native country and was fairly well-known in other parts of the world. The first had arrived in The United States of America in the 1930s when they were imported primarily as herding dogs, and by 1936 he was recognised as one of the Working Group. He was much slower invading Britain, and has only just begun to gain a foothold. Now, however, he is seen regularly at shows in Britain and in most of the European countries.

He is a sound, solid dog that suffers from very little sickness, is virtually waterproof and very hardy. He is intelligent, alert and very active, takes to obedience work very easily, and makes an excellent property guard.

Although this dog has been given an interim standard it has not yet been granted championship status by the KC(GB).

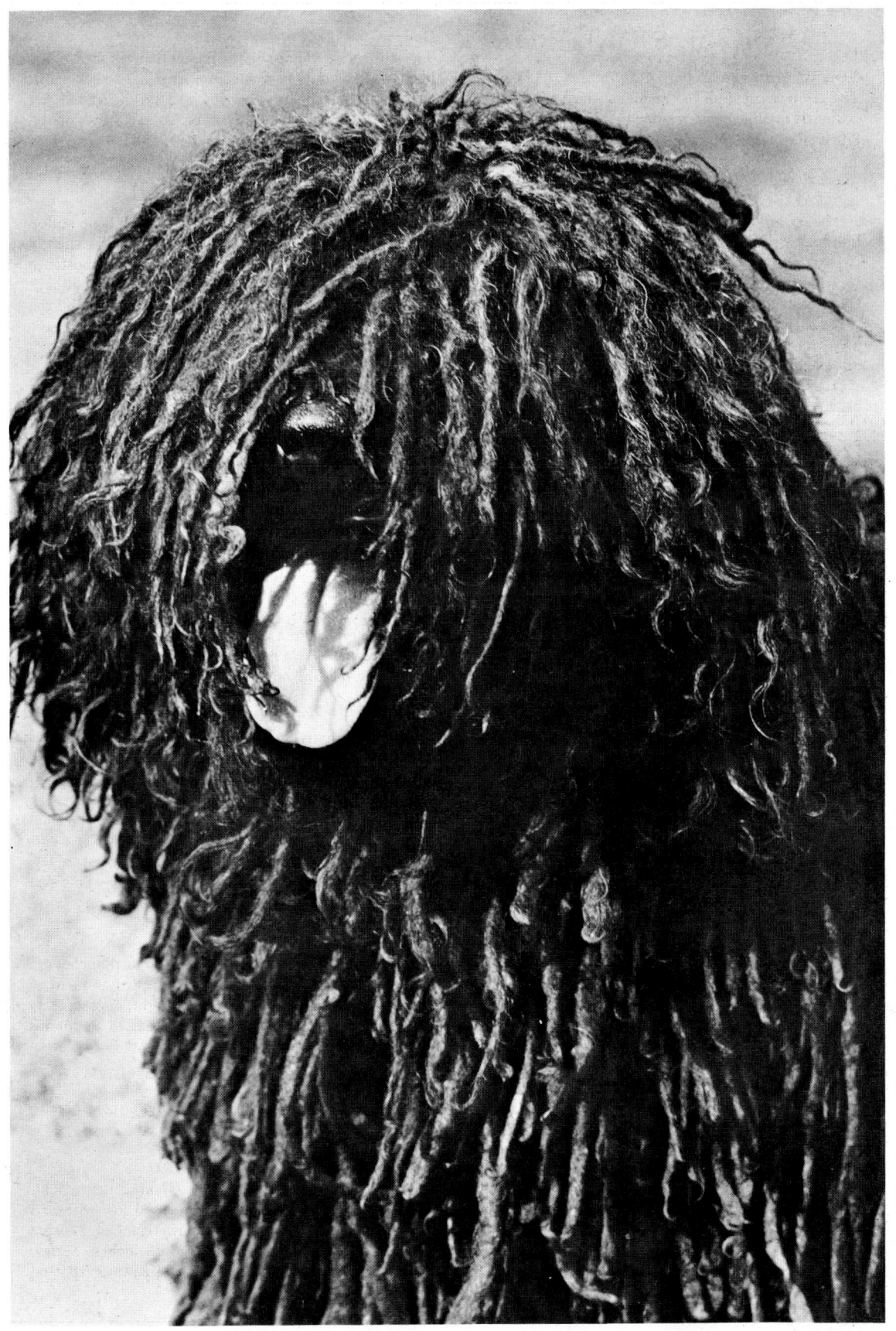

OFFICIAL STANDARD

General appearance
The Hungarian Puli is medium sized, nimble and extremely intelligent. In relation to its size the Hungarian Puli is sturdy and muscular, with good bone. It is not easy to assess the body purely on visual examination, for the whole should be well covered with a long (according to age) profuse corded coat. The long hair overshadows the eyes like an umbrella. Viewed from the side, the Hungarian Puli must present a square figure.

Head and skull
Disregarding the hair, the head should be fine and round, with a slightly domed skull. The muzzle is one third of the length of the head, with well defined stop and straight muzzle, not snipy, but bluntly rounded. The arches of the eye socket should be well defined; nose relatively large and black; eyelids and flews black.

Eyes
Should be of medium size and dark brown.

Ears
Set fairly high 'V' shaped and pendant. Of medium size and covered with long hair. The length of the ears should be about half the length of the head. Ears must not appear noticeable even when alert.

Mouth
Should be regular and strong with scissor bite. The roof of the mouth should be dark.

Neck
The neck should be held at an angle of 45 degrees to the horizontal, of medium length, tight and muscular. When fully coated the neck seems to merge with the body.

Forequarters
The shoulder should be well laid. Elbows tight. The forelegs should be straight and muscular and viewed from any angle should be vertical. The feet should be short, round and tight. The nails black or slate grey. The pads should be full, springy and dark in colour.

Body: relationship of body and coat.

Body
The withers should be slightly higher than the level of the back, which should be of medium length. The loin short, broad and tucked up. The ribs well sprung and barrel shaped. The rump should be short and slightly sloping, but this is not obvious because of the curled tail. The chest is deep and fairly broad.

Hindquarters
Should be strong and well muscled, well bent stifles, hocks set fairly low, and hindfeet (toes) should be slightly longer than the forefeet. Nails strong. The hindstance should be broader than the forestance. Dogs should have two apparently normal testicles fully descended into the scrotum.

Gait
The Hungarian Puli is a short striding dog, the movement should always be nimble, quick and gay.

Tail
Should be of medium length and curled over the back. It should be covered with long hair.

Coat
The correct proportion of top and undercoat creates naturally the desired narrow cords, which are less inclined to become matted. The coat is generally longest on the hindquarters and shortest on the head and feet. Some dogs will grow a floor length coat. A combed coat is as undesirable as is a neglected one. The coat should be corded and matting or felting should be avoided.

Colour
Acceptable colours are black, rusty black, various shades of grey and white. The black sometimes appears weathered and rusty or slightly grey. An intermixture of hair of different colours (white or black) is usually present in the greys, but the overall appearance must be that of a solid colour. A white spot of not more than 2 inches (5 centimetres) in diameter is permissible on the chest, a few white hairs on the feet are also allowable. The whole skin should be well pigmented and slate grey in colour.

Weight and size
Ideal height, dogs usually accepted as 16 to 18 inches (40 to 44 centimetres). Bitches usually accepted as 14 to 16 inches (37 to 41 centimetres). Ideal weight, dogs 29 to 33 pounds (13 to 15 kilogrammes). Bitches 22 to 29 pounds (10 to 13 kilogrammes).

Faults
Any departure from the foregoing should be considered a fault.

AKC VARIATION TO STANDARD
Eyes: deep set and rather large. *Mouth:* flews tight. *Tail:* occasionally born bob-tail. Carried low with end curled up at rest. *Coat:* usually shown combed. *Height:* dogs 17 to 19 inches, bitches 16 to 18 inches. *Serious Faults:* white markings such as white paws or spot on chest.

KOMONDOR

NATIONAL GROUPING		
	Name	Number
KC(GB)	Working	5
AKC	Working Dogs	III
FCI	Herding Dogs	I

Three breeds of dog have traditionally had corded coats, that is, coats that have been encouraged to take on a natural twist and to mat in that position and continue to grow from the base until the whole dog is covered with a mass of long rope-like lengths of hair. The Komondor is one of these, and because of his size and colour, is quite the most spectacular. The earliest record of a dog known as a Komondor dates back to 1555, which leaves no doubt that it is an old established breed. It has been bred virtually without alteration from that time down as a herding and guard dog with the flocks of native sheep in Hungary. It is claimed that he wiped out the wolf in Hungary and that as a result he became a herding rather than a guarding dog, though he probably still fulfils both purposes.

During the 9th century the Magyar tribes entered Hungary bringing with them their dogs, and a breed of sheep known as Racka, which had a strange affinity of appearance with the dogs. They too had masses of curly rather than soft wool and they had the proud appearance of the dog rather than the 'sheepish' appearance normally associated with that animal. The Komondor was the perfect dog for the purpose of guarding these large and somewhat commanding animals, being a very positive dog with a strong personality. Later, in the 12th century smaller sheep were

introduced, and the need for the particular qualities of the breed no longer existed. The Komondor stayed on as a guardian, and the smaller Puli served the purpose of herder to the more amenable smaller sheep.

The Komondor first reached the United States of America around 1933, and was recognised in that country in 1937, but it still remains a rare dog as it does in most countries outside Hungary. In recent years it has been introduced into Britain, where it still creates something of a sensation wherever it is shown. It is shown in Germany, Holland and Switzerland, and some fine examples have been seen in the Italian ring. Like many of the old working breeds, the Komondor is a very intelligent dog, readily trained and an obedient servant when kept under control. His coat is his most obvious point of identification, but that apart he is a big strong working dog with considerable powers of endurance under difficult conditions.

As a show dog he has certain problems, as it is not easy to keep the coat clean and yet at the same time maintain the much admired long cords. At about six months old the process of parting the cords commences, and if this were not continued, the animal would eventually be covered with one solid mat like a coat of armour. Each time that the Komondor is bathed, the coat has to be separated whilst drying, and the cords encouraged to remain as long narrow strips of hair rather than as bunches. The dog is never combed, even as a puppy, and needless to say, never brushed as this is impossible.

He is highly intelligent, and can be trained easily enough to obey simple commands. He needs firmness, and when correctly trained he makes an excellent guard and a pleasing companion. In the United States he is still used for his original purpose, to herd and guard flocks.

OFFICIAL STANDARD

Characteristics

The Komondor is a shepherd's dog of Asiatic origin, an excellent guard, wary of strangers, courageous, faithful and devoted to its master, whom he will defend against any attack. Because of this trait, it was not used for driving the herds, but only for guarding. The Komondor's special task was to protect the herds against wolves, bears, and strange dogs, etc. The Komondor is noted for his imposing strength and courageous manner.

General appearance

A large muscular dog, with plenty of bone and substance. Powerful in conformation.

Head and skull

The head should look somewhat short in comparison to the wide forehead. The skull should be slightly arched when viewed from the side. Stop moderate, muzzle slightly shorter than the length of skull. Broad rather coarse muzzle, not pointed. Nostrils wide. Nose black, though a dark grey or dark brown nose is acceptable but not desirable.

Eyes

Medium sized, not too deeply set, the darker the eye the better; eye rims dark grey or black and close fitting.

Ears

Medium sized and hanging U-shaped. Erect or partially erect ears are incorrect.

Mouth

Powerful jaws, strong teeth. Scissor bite ideal (pincer bite acceptable but not desirable). Lips tight fitting and black. Ideally gums and roof of mouth should be black or dark grey.

Coat: longest at rump and tail, medium length on back.

Neck

Strong, medium length, moderately arched, no dewlap.

Forequarters

Straight, well boned and muscular, viewed from any side the forelegs should be like vertical columns; well laid tight shoulders.

Body

Broad, deep, muscular chest, back level. Rump broad, slightly sloping towards root of tail. The body should be slightly longer than height at withers. Belly tucked up.

Hindquarters

Strong in bone structure and very muscular. Viewed from rear, legs fairly wide apart, parallel, well angulated. Dewclaws should be removed.

Feet

Strong, large and compact, well arched toes. Claws strong, grey or black, toes slightly longer on hindfeet. Pads hard, elastic and dark.

Gait

Light and easy, should move with very long strides.

Tail

Continuation of rump line, should reach down to hocks, slightly curved at tip; when excited, raised in line with body.

Coat

The coat texture should consist of a longer coarse outer coat, which may be wavy or curly, and a softer undercoat. The hair should tend to cling together like tassels, giving a corded appearance, even when combed. When corded, the cords of an adult coat should be strong and heavy and felty to the touch, if neglected will form into large matted 'plates'. Coat should be longest on rump, loins and tail, of medium length on back, shoulders and chest, and shorter on cheeks around eyes, mouth and lower parts of

Head: showing relationship of bone, flesh and coat.

legs. Coat is fairly slow in cording and may not be fully formed before two years of age. Puppy coat should be soft and fluffy, adult coat usually starts appearing 6–9 months of age. Should be presented corded.

Colour
Always white. Ideally the skin should be grey; pink skin is acceptable if no evidence of albinism.

Weight and size
Weight for dogs, about 110 to 135 pounds. Bitches, about 80 to 110 pounds. Dogs, average $31\frac{1}{2}$ inches (80 centimetres), minimum 26 inches (65 centimetres). Bitches, average $27\frac{1}{2}$ inches (70 centimetres), minimum $23\frac{1}{2}$ inches (55 centimetres).

Whilst the average height is given, of the Komondor it can be said that there is no maximum height, but height should always be taken into consideration with the overall picture of the dog, which should be strong, well balanced and give the impression of vast strength.

Faults
Any departure from the foregoing points should be considered a fault and the seriousness of the fault should be in exact proportion to its degree.

Note
Male animals should have two apparently normal testicles fully descended into the scrotum.

Although this dog has been given an interim standard it has not yet been granted championship status by the KC(GB).

AKC VARIATION TO STANDARD
Eyes: Almond shaped. *Size:* minimum—dogs $25\frac{1}{2}$ inches and bitches $23\frac{1}{2}$ inches at withers. *Disqualifications:* blue-white eyes. Colour other than white. Bob-tails. Flesh-coloured nose. Short, smooth hair on head and legs. Failure of coat to cord by two years old.

KUVASZ

NATIONAL GROUPING		
	Name	Number
KC(GB)	—	—
AKC	Working Dogs	III
FCI	Herding Dogs	I

When several breeds of dog develop for roughly the same purpose that eventually look very much alike, it becomes an acceptable theory that all breeds share a common ancestry. The Maremma Sheepdog, the Pyrenean Mountain Dog and the Kuvasz are so generally similar in appearance, that if specimens of all three appear in the ring at the same time, and if the Pyrenean happens to be a reasonably small one, the average spectator will see them all as belonging to the same breed. They are all white, all have the same sort of gait, and all roughly the same sort of coat. Whilst the other two were both herding and guard dogs, the Kuvasz was evolved primarily for the latter duty. His ancestors came from Tibet, via Turkey, to Hungary, and as the court favourite only those who were in favour with the royal family were allowed to own one.

During the late 15th century he was kept by the big estates and had the treatment usually meted out to favourite animals, having a stud book, being carefully guarded and bred, and in turn guarding the person of the King and his family. He was trained for the chase and was capable of handling the large game which was plentiful in his country such as bear and wolf. King Matthias who reigned during the 15th century always had a Kuvasz with him wherever he went. He kept a large kennel at his palace, and with intrigue being a fashionable pursuit, placed more trust in his dogs than in his personal guards. The King developed a large pack for hunting, and it was mainly due to his efforts that the breed not only survived in those early years, but improved, becoming a bigger and stronger dog than he was originally.

In later centuries specimens of the breed came into the hands of commoners, and his value as a herding dog began to be appreciated. It was in the dual role of guard and herder that he made his reputation during the 19th century. Two World Wars, and the subsequent disturbances in Hungary brought about a serious decline in the breed, but fortunately by the 1930s, some had been imported into the United States of America and the future of the breed became assured. The American Kennel Club recognised the breed in 1935, and though the war years halted its progress in its own country, it has steadily gained ground elsewhere. It is seen regularly in most European countries, but not in Britain, where it has as yet failed to capture the public fancy.

He makes a really striking show dog, being large, stately and brilliant white in colour. He is a spirited dog, but very steady in the ring, where his strongly developed sense of curiosity gives him a great deal of interest in what is going on around him, and diverts his attention from possible high-spirited behaviour. Grooming is trouble-free as all that is needed is a constant brushing to remove dead hairs, the coat having a natural luxuriant sheen. His only problems are those that are shared by all large dogs, that he takes up a considerable amount of space and does not lend himself easily to travelling in a box in the back of the car. He is a very intelligent dog, sensitive and not to be dealt with harshly. He is devoted, gentle and patient without being too effusive, has a strongly developed inclination to guard children, and whilst friendly enough, has a natural aversion to making friends quickly with strangers.

OFFICIAL STANDARD

General characteristics
A spirited dog of keen intelligence, determination, courage and curiosity. Very sensitive to praise and blame. Primarily a one-family dog. Devoted, gentle and patient without being overly demonstrative. Always ready to protect loved ones even to the point of self-sacrifice. Extremely strong instinct to protect children. Polite to accepted strangers, but rather suspicious and very discriminating in making new friends. Unexcelled guard, possessing ability to act on his own initiative at just the right moment without instruction. Bold, courageous and fearless. Untiring ability to work and cover rough terrain for long periods of time. Has good scent and has been used to hunt game.

General appearance
A working dog of larger size, sturdily built, well balanced, neither lanky nor cobby. White in color with *no markings*. Medium boned, well muscled, without the slightest hint of bulkiness or lethargy. Impresses the eye with strength and activity combined with light-footedness, moves freely on strong legs. Trunk and limbs form a horizontal rectangle slightly deviated from the square. Slightly inclined croup. Hindquarters are particularly well developed. Any tendency to weakness or lack of substance is a decided fault.

Movement
Easy, free and elastic. Feet travel close to the ground. Hind legs reach far under, meeting or even passing the imprints of the front legs. Moving toward an observer, the front legs do not travel parallel to each other but rather close together at the ground. When viewed from the rear, the hind legs (from the hip joint down) also move close at the ground. As speed increases, the legs gradually angle more inward until the pads are almost single-tracking. Unless excited, the head is carried rather

low at the level of the shoulders. Desired movement cannot be maintained without sufficient angulation and firm slimness of body.

Height
Measured at the withers: dogs, 28 to 30 inches; bitches, 26 to 28 inches.

Weight
Dogs, approximately 100 to 115 pounds; bitches, approximately 70 to 90 pounds.

Color
White.

Head
Proportions are of great importance as the head is considered to be the most beautiful part of the Kuvasz. Length of head measured from tip of nose to occiput is slightly less than half the height of the dog at the withers. Width is half the length of the head. The skull is elongated but not pointed. The stop is defined, never abrupt, raising the forehead gently above the plane of the muzzle. The longitudinal midline of the forehead is pronounced, widening as it slopes to the muzzle. Cheeks flat, bony arches above the eyes. The skin dry, no excess flews.

Muzzle
Length in proportion to the length of the head, top straight, not pointed, underjaw well developed. Inside of the mouth preferably black.

General: slightly longer proportions than high.

Nose

Large, black, nostrils well opened.

Lips

Black, closely covering the teeth. The upper lip covers tightly the upper jaw only. Lower lip tight and not pendulous.

Bite

Dentition full, scissors bite preferred. Level bite acceptable.

Eyes

Almond-shaped, set well apart, somewhat slanted. In profile, the eyes are set slightly below the plane of the muzzle. Lids tight, haws should not show. Dark brown, the darker the better.

Ears

V-shaped, tip is slightly rounded. Rather thick, they are well set back between the level of the eye and the top of the head. When pulled forward the tip of the ear should cover the eye. Looking at the dog face to face, the widest part of the ear is about level to the eye. The inner edge of the ear lies close to the cheek, the outer edge slightly away from the head forming a V. In the relaxed position, the ears should hold their set and are not cast backward. The ears should not protrude above the head.

Neck

Muscular, without dewlap, medium length, arched at the crest.

Forequarters

Shoulders muscular. The scapula and humerus form a right angle, are long and of equal length. Legs are medium boned, straight and well muscled. Elbows neither in nor out. When viewed from the side, the forechest protrudes slightly in front of the shoulders. The joints are dry, hard. Dewclaws on the forelegs should not be removed.

Body

Forechest is well developed, chest deep with long well-sprung ribs reaching almost to the elbows. Shoulders long with withers higher than back. Back is of medium length, straight, firm and quite broad. The loin is short, muscular and tight. The croup well muscled, slightly sloping. The brisket is deep, well developed and runs parallel to the ground. The stomach is well tucked up.

Bone

In proportion to size of body. Medium, hard. Never heavy or coarse.

Hindquarters

The portion behind the hip joint is moderately long producing wide, long and strong muscles of the upper thigh. The femur is long, creating well-bent stifles. Lower thigh is long, dry, well muscled. Metatarsus is short, broad and of great strength. Dewclaws, if any, are removed.

Tail

Carried low, natural length reaching at least to the hocks. In repose it hangs down resting on the body, the end but slightly lifted. In state of excitement, the tail may be elevated to the level of the loin, the tip slightly curved up. Ideally there should not be much difference in the carriage of the tail in state of excitement or in respose.

Feet

Well padded. Pads resilient, black. Feet are closed tight forming round 'cat feet'. The rear paws somewhat longer, some hair between the toes, the less the better. Dark nails are preferred.

Skin

The skin is heavily pigmented. The more slate gray or black pigmentation the better.

Coat

The Kuvasz has a double coat formed by a guard hair and fine undercoat. The texture of the coat is medium coarse. The coat ranges from quite wavy to straight. Distribution follows a definite pattern over the body regardless of coat type. The head, muzzle, ears and paws are covered with short, smooth hair. The neck has a mane that extends to and covers the chest. Coat on the front of the forelegs up to the elbows and the hind legs below the thighs is short and smooth. The backs of the forelegs are feathered to the pastern with hair 2 to 3 inches long. The body and sides of the thighs are covered with a medium length coat. The back of the thighs and the entire tail is covered with hair 4 to 6 inches long. It is natural for the Kuvasz to lose most of the long coat during hot weather. Full luxuriant coat comes in seasonably, depending on climate. Summer coat should not be penalized.

FAULTS

The foregoing description is that of the ideal Kuvasz. Any deviation from the above-described dog must be penalized to the extent of the deviation.

DISQUALIFICATIONS

Overshot bite. Undershot bite. Dogs smaller than 26 inches. Bitches smaller than 24 inches. Any color other than white.

AKC VARIATION TO STANDARD

The dog is not granted championship status by the KC(GB). The above standards are those of the AKC.

MASTIFF

Some breeds have emerged so recently from their countries of origin that information on them is hard to come by, others have been with us so long that books have been written about them as individual breeds. The Mastiff is one of these, the name not only indicating a specific breed of dog, but also a whole Group. Where the dog originated is obscure, but certainly the Mastiff that is now known by that name everywhere in the world was well known in England in Roman times. Records show that an officer was stationed at Winchester for the purpose of collecting and exporting these great dogs to Rome where they probably took part in battles in the Colosseum. Later Dame Juliana Berners, Prioress of Sopwell Nunnery in Hertfordshire wrote of them in the 15th century, and Doctor John Caius mentioned them in his book written in 1576.

In medieval times the Mastiff was a guard dog but was also used for hunting, and farmers living on the outskirts of forests were allowed to keep them only

NATIONAL GROUPING		
	Name	Number
KC(GB)	Working	5
AKC	Working Dogs	III
FCI	Guard Dogs	2

if they had been handicapped by the removal of toes to prevent them from chasing deer. During the Hundred Years War many were taken to France, and the devotion of one to Sir Piers Legh when he was wounded at Agincourt is a familiar story. She watched over him throughout the battle and guarded him against plunderers afterwards, but unfortunately her efforts were in vain as he died on the homeward journey.

In more recent times the story of the breed is equally romantic. During the Second World War owing to the difficulty of keeping dogs of any kind and large dogs as food was so scarce, the breed virtually disappeared from Britain. Fortunately a good many had been exported to the United States of America where the breed remained very much alive, and some were later reimported back into Britain to start up the breed again. Since that time the Mastiff has attained a degree of popularity and is now seen regularly at shows. He is still very much a dog with special rather than general appeal, and fortunately those who own the breed are interested in the preservation of a dog with a long history, so that it is in good hands.

It would be foolish to pretend that the Mastiff is the ideal show dog. He is very large to start with and does not fit easily into today's small cars. Few of them really enjoy showing, and would obviously be happier roaming round some large estate doing a little casual hunting and keeping a careful watch on the gates and fences. Being a fairly rare dog he is not appreciated

by all judges and although he is admired for his sheer size by the general public, few of them would want to take him home to replace their own favourite cuddly pet. Even so he is a magnificent animal when he is standing in the ring, as he has great nobility and the slightly mournful expression of one who regrets past events.

His temperament, as with most of the large dogs, is that of the gentle giant. He has no vice, is absolutely friendly, even embarrassingly so to those to whom he becomes attached, and is one of the most faithful of all dogs. He is quiet and intelligent and rarely uses his immense power in an unfriendly act. As a guard he is supreme, as the instinct to look after his own territory and that of his owner is deeply imbedded in him, and his size and apparent ferocity when aroused are sufficient to deter the boldest of intruders.

OFFICIAL STANDARD

General appearance
Large, massive, powerful, symmetrical and well-knit frame. A combination of grandeur and good nature, courage and docility. The head, in general outline giving a square appearance when viewed from any point. Breadth greatly to be desired, and should be in ratio to length of the whole head and face as 2 to 3. Body, massive, broad, deep, long, powerfully built, on legs wide apart and squarely set. Muscles sharply defined. Size a great desideratum, if combined with quality. Height and substance important if both points are proportionately combined.

Head and skull: nose broad, muzzle short broad under eyes, great depth.

Head and skull
Skull broad between the ears, forehead flat, but wrinkled when attention is excited. Brows (superciliary ridges) slightly raised. Muscles of the temples and cheeks

(temporal and masseter) well developed. Arch across the skull of a rounded, flattened curve, with a depression up the centre of the forehead from the median line between the eyes, to half-way up the sagittal suture. Face or muzzle, short, broad under the eyes, and keeping nearly parallel in width to the end of the nose; truncated, i.e., blunt and cut off squarely, thus forming a right-angle with the upper line of the face, of great depth from the point of the nose to under jaw. Under jaw broad to the end. Nose broad, with widely spreading nostrils when viewed from the front, flat (not pointed or turned up) in profile. Lips diverging at obtuse angles with the septum, and slightly pendulous so as to show a square profile. Length of muzzle to whole head and face as 1 to 3. Circumference of muzzle (measured mid-way between the eyes and nose) to that of the head (measured before the ears) as 3 to 5.

Eyes
Small, wide apart, divided by at least the space of two eyes. The stop between the eyes well marked but not too abrupt. Colour hazel brown, the darker the better, showing no haw.

Ears
Small, thin to the touch, wide apart, set on at the highest points of the sides of the skull, so as to continue the outline across the summit, and lying flat and close to the cheeks when in repose.

Mouth
Canine teeth healthy; powerful and wide apart; incisors level, or the lower projecting beyond the upper but never so much as to become visible when the mouth is closed.

Neck
Slightly arched, moderately long, very muscular, and measuring in circumference about one or two inches less than the skull before the ears.

Forequarters
Shoulder and arm slightly sloping, heavy and muscular. Legs straight, strong, and set wide apart; bones being

Forequarters: heavy muscular, legs straight and strong.

large. Elbows square. Pasterns upright.

Body
Chest wide, deep and well let down between the forelegs. Ribs arched and well rounded. False ribs deep and well set back to the hips. Girth should be one-third more than the height at the shoulder. Back and loins wide and muscular; flat and very wide in a bitch, slightly arched in a dog. Great depth of flanks.

Hindquarters
Broad, wide and muscular, with well-developed second thighs, hocks bent, wide apart, and quite squarely set when standing or walking.

Feet
Large and round. Toes well arched up. Nails black.

Tail
Put on high up, and reaching to the hocks, or a little below them, wide at its root and tapering to the end, hanging straight in repose, but forming a curve with the end pointing upwards, but not over the back, when the dog is excited.

Coat
Short and close-lying, but not too fine over the shoulders, neck and back.

Colour
Apricot or silver, fawn, or dark fawn-brindle. In any case, muzzle, ears and nose should be black with black round the orbits, and extending upwards between them.

Note
Male animals should have two apparently normal testicles fully descended into the scrotum.

AKC VARIATION TO STANDARD
Head: forehead slightly curved. *Ears:* v-shaped, rounded at tips. *Eyes:* medium size. *Body:* reasonable tuck-up. *Forelegs:* pasterns bent only slightly. *Coat:* outer coat moderately coarse. Undercoat dense short, close lying. *Height:* minimum at shoulder, dogs 30 inches, bitches $27\frac{1}{2}$ inches.

NEWFOUNDLAND

NATIONAL GROUPING		
	Name	Number
KC(GB)	Working	5
AKC	Working Dogs	III
FCI	Guard Dogs	2

Some breeds of dogs attract attention by virtue of the romantic stories that have been woven about them (the St. Bernard is a typical example), others because of particular abilities that they possess, such as the Bloodhound, and yet others because they have been portrayed by famous painters, but the Newfoundland has had attention for each of these reasons. Romantic rescue stories have been written about him, most of them true, his ability in water is legendary and the most famous of all animal painters, Sir Edwin Landseer painted him. Yet his origin is far from clear. One authority claims that the Beothuk Indians of Newfoundland had big black water-loving dogs as companions before the advent of the white man. Another reports that Lieut. John Cartwright in his exploration of the island in 1768 remarked that the native Indians did not even have the companionship of dogs to relieve their wretchedness.

There is, however, no doubt that a big black water-loving dog was evolved on the island, and that they were imported into Britain in numbers. There is no doubt too that he was of the Mastiff type, though whether he had evolved independently as such a type in Newfoundland or was originally taken over by early explorers and was a descendant of the Tibetan Mastiff is a moot point. By the 17th century a black and white version had evolved, since named the Landseer after the famous painting 'A distinguished Member of the Humane Society', giving some credence to the idea that the breed was a mixture of imported Mastiff type dogs which could carry coloured bloodlines and a native dog which might have been black. In some countries these black and white dogs are treated as a distinct variety.

By 1860 the breed was being shown. Six appeared at the Birmingham Show of that year and the breed made steady progress, classes at shows filling well, and the character and temperament of the breed gaining it some popularity. Two World Wars, and the difficulty encountered in feeding such large dogs decimated the breed in Britain, but fortunately it remained strong in the United States and Holland, and after the Second World War, when only some ten dogs were left in Britain, reimportations enabled the breed to survive. This was in some measure due to the generosity of the Newfoundland Club of America who presented the secretary of the British Club with a bitch in whelp which produced five puppies. As well as in Britain and the United States the breed is now firmly established in many countries. Australia has quite a number and the Scandinavians have taken a great interest.

The Newfoundland is a big dog, and very much the heavyweight, appearing somewhat lumbering and clumsy in action. It is when he takes to the water, however, that he really comes into his own, swimming with great power and apparently tirelessly, and usually doing it for sheer pleasure. The stories of rescues that he has carried out are endless, and he was a regular member of the crew of fishing boats off the coast of Newfoundland, joining in the work by carrying warps and from time to time affecting a spectacular rescue. As a show dog he is very spectacular too, his sheer size and bulk making him popular with the casual spectator, who enjoys showing a rescue dog to the children.

His temperament is near perfect, as he is one of the most kindly of dogs, very affectionate and becomes deeply attached to the members of a family. He is particularly noted for his care of children, keeping careful watch and placing himself in a position of guard between them and an approaching stranger. His ability in the water and his natural delight in towing things back to land allow those who own one to depend on his watchfulness and capabilities to ensure that the children of the family run no risk of drowning.

OFFICIAL STANDARD

Characteristics
A water dog, used for life-saving; he should have an exceptionally gentle and docile nature.

General appearance
The dog should impress the eye with strength and great activity. He should move freely on his legs with the body swung loosely between them, so that a slight roll in gait should not be objectionable. Bone massive throughout, but not to give a heavy, inactive appearance.

Head and skull
Head should be broad and massive, the occipital bone well developed; there should be no decided stop; the muzzle should be short, clean cut and rather square in shape and covered with short, fine hair.

Hindquarters: strong, tail hanging to below the hocks.

Head and skull: broad and massive, no decided stop. Muzzle: short, clean cut and square.

Eyes
Should be small, of a dark brown colour; rather deeply set, but not showing any haw; should be set rather wide apart.

Ears
Should be small, set well back, square with the skull, lie close to the head, and covered with short hair without a fringe.

Mouth
Should be soft and well covered by the lips, should be neither undershot nor overshot but teeth should be level or scissor bite.

Neck
Should be strong, well set on to shoulders and back.

Forequarters
Legs should be perfectly straight, well covered with muscle, elbows in but well let down; feathered all down.

Body
Should be well ribbed up with broad back and strong muscular loins. Chest should be deep and fairly broad; well covered with hair, but not to such an extent as to form a frill.

Hindquarters
Should be very strong. The legs should have great freedom of action; slightly feathered. Slackness of loins and cow-hocks are a defect. Dew-claws are objectionable and should be removed.

Feet
Should be large and well shaped. Splayed or turned out feet are objectionable.

Tail
Should be of moderate length, reaching down a little below the hocks. It should be of fair thickness and well covered with hair, but not to form a flag. When the dog is standing still and not excited it should hang downwards with a slight curve at the end; but when the dog is in motion it should be carried up, and when he is excited straight out with only a slight curve at the end. Tails with a kink or curled over the back are very objectionable.

Coat
Should be flat and dense, of a coarsish texture and oily nature, and capable of resisting water. If brushed the wrong way it should fall back into its place naturally.

Colour
Dull jet black. A slight tinge of bronze or splash of white on chest and toes is acceptable. Black dogs having only white toes and white chest and white tip of tail should be exhibited in classes provided for black.
Brown. Can be chocolate or bronze. Should in all other respects follow the black except in colour. Splash of white on chest and toes is acceptable. Brown dogs to be exhibited in classes provided for blacks.
White with black markings only—Landseers. For preference black head with narrow blaize, even marked saddle

Weight and size
Size and weight are very desirable so long as symmetry is maintained. A fair average height at the shoulders is 28 inches for a dog and 26 inches for a bitch, and a fair average weight is, respectively: dogs, 140 to 150 pounds. Bitches, 110 to 120 pounds.

Faults
Weak or hollow back, slackness of the loins or cow-hocks. Dewclaws. Splayed or turned-out feet. Tails with a kink in them or curled over the back.

Note
Male animals should have two apparently normal testicles fully descended into the scrotum.

AKC VARIATION TO STANDARD
Head: slightly arched crown. Forehead smooth. Length of muzzle forms definite but not steep stop. Stop to tip of nose is less than from stop to occiput. Nostrils are well developed. *Ears:* triangular with rounded tips. *Body:* croup slopes at angle of about 30 degrees. *Forequarters:* layback of shoulders is about 45 degrees. Upper arm meets shoulder blade at about 90 degrees. Pasterns are slightly sloping. *Hindquarters:* thighs are fairly long, stifles well bent, hocks wide and straight. *Feet:* cat foot, well rounded and tight with firm, arched toes, and webbing present. *Coat:* undercoat is soft and dense. *Disqualifications:* markings other than white on a solid colour dog.

and black rump extending on to tail. Beauty in markings to be taken greatly into consideration. Ticking is not desirable.

The above are the only permitted colours.

NORWEGIAN BUHUND

NATIONAL GROUPING		
	Name	Number
KC(GB)	Working	5
AKC	—	—
FCI	Herding Dogs	I

There is a large group of dogs originating in the northern part of the globe which are classified as Spitz breeds. They occur in several Groups in many countries, from the Pomeranian in the Toy Group in Britain to the Chow Chow in the Utility Group, and the sledge dogs in the Working Group, and the number of such breeds is large enough for them to form a separate Group in Scandinavia. The various members of the Group perform many functions, from towing sledges in the Arctic to keeping madam's feet warm in bed, and even it is said at one time, to serve as food. The Norwegian Buhund, which is included in the Working Group in most countries is one of the typical breeds of the Spitz type. It has the short body, erect ears, curled tail and stand-off coat, all of which are common to the breeds in the Spitz Group in Scandinavia.

The history of the Buhund is rather obscure, though it is certainly Scandinavian in origin, and the name indicates that it was intended as a house guard and possibly a general farm dog. Whilst the most popular colour range seen in the showrings of the world today is between wheaten and red, colour is not important. Black or sable, with or without markings is permissible, which leads to the suggestion that such breeds as the Elkhound or the Jämthund played some part in its ancestry. In recent years the Buhund has been used as a guard and a herding dog, and its alert temperament and ability to move very, very quickly over rough ground seem to suit it to both purposes.

He is a sharp yet friendly dog with great strength for so small an animal. He is intelligent, as all the working dogs are, and he is capable of considerable endurance. His strong coat, excellent conformation and good balance without exaggeration fit him for the arduous work that he is expected to undertake.

The Buhund has never become really popular as a showdog, registrations in Britain rarely exceeding a hundred, and even less at one time. He does, however, make an excellent dog for the show ring, his coat quality, smart expression and sharp ears making him very attractive in the ting. Temperamentally he is very pleasant, being friendly and becoming most attached to one family or one member of the family. His kindly disposition towards children endears him to those who own the breed.

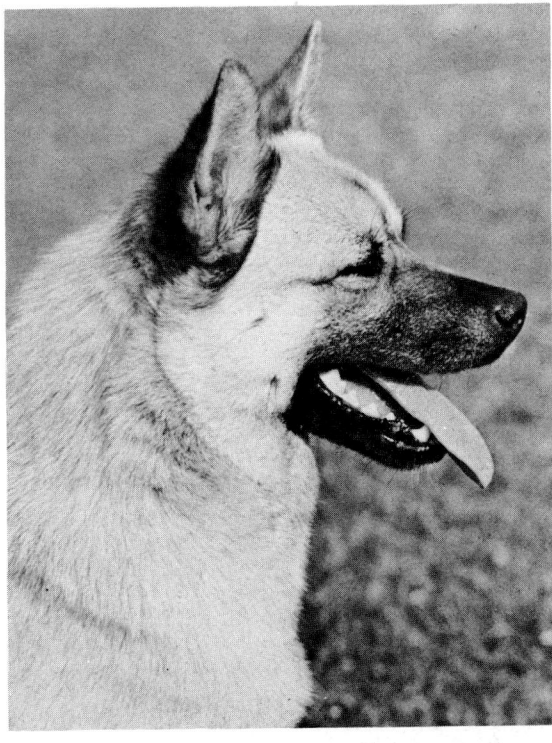

OFFICIAL STANDARD

Characteristics
The Norwegian Buhund should be fearless and brave.

General appearance
The Norwegian Buhund is a typical Spitz dog of under middle size, lightly built, with a short compact body, fairly smooth-lying coat, erect pointed ears, tail carried curled over the back, and with an energetic character.
It is of prime importance that the Buhund should be a well balanced dog, free from all exaggeration and should be capable of the arduous work for which it is bred.

Head and skull
Head lean, light, rather broad between the ears, wedge shaped, narrowing towards the point of the nose. Skull and back of head almost flat; marked but not sharp stop; muzzle of medium length, tapering evenly from above and side, with straight bridge; lips tightly closed.

Forequarters: legs lean, straight and strong.

Head and skull: lean, light and wedge-shaped, ears erect.

Eyes
Not protruding, colour dark brown, lively with a fearless expression.

Ears
Placed high, erect, the height greater than the base; sharply pointed and very mobile.

Neck
Medium length, lean without loose skin, good carriage.

Forequarters
Legs lean, straight and strong, elbows tightly placed.

Body
Strong and short, but light; chest deep with good ribs; straight line of back, good loins, strong couplings, slightly drawn up.

Hindquarters
Only a little angulated, straight when seen from behind.

Feet
Rather small, oval in shape, with tightly closed toes.

Tail
Placed high on, short, thick and hairy, but without long hair tightly curled.

Coat
Close and harsh, but smooth; on head and front legs—short close and smooth; longer on chest, neck and shoulders and back of legs and inside of tail curl. The coat is made up of a harsh top hair, with soft wool undercoat.

Colour
Wheaten (biscuit), black, red (if the red is not too dark), wolf-sable. Preferably self-coloured but small symmetric markings such as white on chest and legs, blaize on head and narrow ring on neck, black masks and ears and black tips to the tail are permissible.

Size
Dogs not more than $17\frac{3}{4}$ inches (45 centimetres); bitches somewhat less.

Faults
White dogs. Light eyes. Light nose. Undershot or overshot mouth. Drop ear.

Note
Male animals should have two apparently normal testicles fully descended into the scrotum.

AKC VARIATION TO STANDARD
This dog is not granted championship status by the AKC.

OLD ENGLISH SHEEPDOG

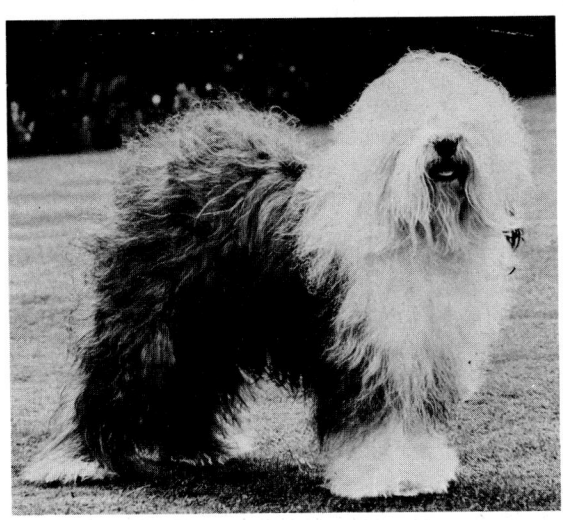

NATIONAL GROUPING		
	Name	Number
KC(GB)	Working	5
AKC	Working Dogs	III
FCI	Herding Dogs	I

There are a number of different reasons why certain breeds of dog attain popularity. At its best this is because of the qualities of the animal itself, but there are other and less admirable reasons. Connections with courts and noble families, or more recently with the stars of stage and screen, their inclusion in literature as characters in a story, their stardom in films such as Lassie and Rin Tin Tin, all have helped to popularise different breeds. More recently it has been the media, and particularly the advertising media that has had its effect. Two breeds of dog owe their enormous rise in popularity to worldwide use in connection with advertising, and one of these is the Old English Sheepdog. Early records show that a dog very much like the present Old English Sheepdog existed in 1771 when Gainsborough painted a portrait of the Third Duke of Buccleuch with what is palpably a specimen of the breed, and the engraving of Reinagle's painting of a Shepherd Dog in the Sportsman's Cabinet of 1803 is certainly of an unbobbed bobtail.

It is suggested that the Bearded Collie and the Old English Sheepdog share a common ancestry, and this may well be true, as there are certainly points of similarity, though overall they now differ fairly widely. The Old English Sheepdog as we now know it was developed from the older herder's dog into its present form in England rather than in Scotland, and throughout the 19th century the breed was fairly well established in Suffolk, Hampshire and Dorset as well as in Wales. By the beginning of this century the numbers had grown until at the Clerkenwell Show of 1905 there were over a hundred on exhibition. Since then growth was fairly steady until the early 1970s, when the numbers suddenly quadrupled almost certainly because of the considerable exposure of the breed.

As a show dog the Old English Sheepdog has always had an enthusiastic following, and as long ago as the turn of the century ringside applause for the breed was recorded. Today, his appearance is so striking that his entrance into the big ring at many shows is again greeted with applause. His striking coat, which varies in colour from grey, through grizzle to blue, (with duck-egg blue being considered by many to be the most desirable), the volume of coat that modern breeders and exhibitors have managed to encourage on the dog, and his peculiar ambling gait which is so different from that of any other breed, make him a great favourite with spectators. Although his preparation and presentation present some problems, as the heavy coat needs constant and expert attention, he is still a grand dog to show, being big, friendly and very tractable. A ring full of these large beautifully groomed dogs is always guaranteed a large audience.

Temperamentally the Old English Sheepdog is a lovely animal. He is playful and somewhat boisterous when young (even sometimes when quite mature) and he is very intelligent and friendly. He is reputed to be extremely good with children, making a good guard as well as a decorative addition to any household.

OFFICIAL STANDARD

General appearance
A strong, compact-looking dog of great symmetry; absolutely free of legginess; profusely coated all over; very elastic in a gallop but in walking or trotting has a characteristic ambling or pacing movement; and his bark should be loud, with a peculiar 'pot casse' ring in it. All round he is a thick-set, muscular, able-bodied dog, with a most intelligent expression, free of all Poodle or Deerhound character.

Head and skull
Skull capacious and rather squarely formed, giving plenty of room for brain power. The parts over the eyes should be well arched and the whole well-covered with hair. Jaw fairly long, strong, square, and truncated; the stop should be defined to avoid a Deerhound face. Nose always black, large, and capacious.

Coat: profuse and hard, showing fashionable grooming pattern.

Head and skull: nose large, black and capacious, head covered with hair.

Eyes
Dark or wall eyes are to be preferred.

Ears
Small and carried flat to side of head, coated moderately.

Mouth
Teeth strong and large, evenly placed and level.

Neck
The neck should be fairly long, arched gracefully, and well coated with hair.

Forequarters
The forelegs should be dead straight, with plenty of bone, holding the body well from the ground, without approaching legginess; well coated all round. The shoulders sloping and narrow at the points, the dog standing lower at the shoulders than at the loin.

Body
Rather short and very compact, ribs well sprung, and brisket deep and capacious. The loin should be very stout and gently arched.

Hindquarters
The hindquarters should be round and muscular, hocks well let down and the hams densely coated with a thick, long jacket in excess of that of any other part of the body.

Feet
Small, round; toes well arched, and pads thick and round.

Tail
Puppies requiring docking should have the operation performed within a week from birth, preferably within four days.

Coat
Profuse, and of good hard texture; not straight, but shaggy and free from curl. The undercoat should be a waterproof pile when not removed by grooming.

Colour
Any shade of grey, grizzle, blue or blue merle, with or without white markings; any shade of brown or sable to be considered distinctly objectionable and not to be encouraged.

Weight and size
22 inches and upwards for dogs, slightly less for bitches. Type, symmetry and character of the greatest importance, and on no account to be sacrificed to size alone.

Faults
A long, narrow head.

Note
Male animals should have two apparently normal testicles fully descended into the scrotum.

AKC VARIATION TO STANDARD
Tail: preferably none. Never in excess of $1\frac{1}{2}$ to $2\frac{1}{2}$ inches.

PYRENEAN MOUNTAIN DOG

Many of the large breeds used in Asia and Europe as guards and sheepdogs descended from the original Mastiff, and the Great Pyrenees Mountain Dog or Pyrenean is no exception. As the need for dogs to herd sheep decreased in Europe so those dogs used for the purpose declined in numbers. At the turn of the century it was estimated that no more than a dozen really typical Pyrenean Mountain Dogs remained in Europe. There is no doubt that the breed is of very ancient origin, based as it was on the Tibetan Mastiff. Used with sheep, its work was that of guard rather than herder, and like the Anatolian Karabash, which

NATIONAL GROUPING		
	Name	Number
KC(GB)	Working	5
AKC	Working Dogs	III
FCI	Herding Dogs	I

does similar work today in Turkey, its main purpose was to protect the flocks against wolves. This resulted in a very large tremendously strong and fierce dog not at all suited to being a family pet. The decline of the breed was halted by the efforts of a small number

229

of enthusiasts such as M. Dretzen, who scoured the Pyrenees at the beginning of the century and finally found half a dozen specimens which he considered typical of the breed at its best. At the same time the breed appeared in Britain, and one very good specimen was shown in 1900 which was said to be thirty inches high at the shoulder.

As with so many of the larger breeds, conditions during wartime prevented the development of these heavy feeders, and no progress was made until the 1920s. Even after that very few were kept and the breed was not officially recognised by the Kennel Club in Britain until 1944. Since that time, in spite of their enormous size and very large appetites, progress has been remarkable, and the numbers throughout the world have risen until he is now among the more popular dogs, something like a thousand a year being registered with the Kennel Club in Britain and the same sort of progress is being made in the United States.

He is among the biggest, and is probably one of the strongest dogs around today, though some of the sledge hauling dogs could match his pulling power. His limbs are huge, and he can be ridden by children who use him as a pony, though the practice is not advised. He is a tremendous guard, his sheer size and very loud voice causing anyone who wanted to

enter where he was not supposed to, to change his mind. He shares with some of the other herding dogs the double dew-claws on his hind legs. This gives a slight appearance of clumsiness, and although various reasons have been put forward for the practice of leaving them on, few are very convincing. It is probably just a tradition.

He is a noble looking animal in the show ring. Prepared as he invariably is to a state of snowy whiteness, he creates an impression that few other breeds can match. He carries his tail low when standing and curls it like a plume over his back when he moves, and this with his high head carriage and free ambling gait make him look even bigger than he really is. At one time there were temperament problems, and some of these dogs were far from trustworthy. Realising, however, that in a dog of this size this was a very dangerous trait, the breed club wrote into the standard that bad temperament should be considered a fault, and proceeded to breed from dogs selected for their steadiness as well as appearance, with the result that today's dogs are much more trustworthy and easy going than those of previous years. The fact that he is now a popular house pet in spite of his great size, his enormous appetite and that he tends to shed white hairs over the furniture, proves that he is now very acceptable in that capacity as well as being a fine show dog.

OFFICIAL STANDARD

Characteristics
The Pyrenean is a natural guard dog and was originally employed as a protector of the shepherd and of his flocks.

General appearance
The Pyrenean should possess great size, substance and power, giving an impression of an immensely strong yet well-balanced dog. These qualities should be accompanied by a certain elegance resulting from a combination of the attractive coat, the correct head and a general air of quiet confidence. It is of the utmost importance that nervousness or unprovoked aggression should be heavily penalised.

Head and skull
It is very important that the head should give an impression of strength with no sign of coarseness; it should not be too heavy in proportion to the size of the dog. The top of the skull, as viewed from front and side, should show a definite curve so as to give a somewhat domed effect and the breadth of the skull at its widest point should be about equal to the length from occiput to stop. The sides of the head should be nearly flat and of a good depth. There should be no obvious stop and only a slight furrow so that the skull and muzzle are joined by a gentle slope. The muzzle should be strong, of medium length and with a slight taper near its tip. The nose should be absolutely black. When viewed from above the head should have the general form of a blunt 'V' well filled in below the eyes.

Head and skull: strong but not coarse, skull curved.

Eyes
The eyes should be almond-shaped and of a dark amber-brown colour. The close-fitting eyelids should be set somewhat obliquely and should be bordered with black. Drooping lower eyelids should be penalised. The expression should be intelligent and contemplative.

Ears
The ears should be fairly small and triangular with rounded tips, the root of the ear being on a level with the

eyes. Normally the ears lie flat against the head, but may be slightly raised when the dog is alert.

Mouth
There should be a complete set of healthy strong even teeth, the incisors meeting in either a scissor or a pincer bite. The two central lower incisors may be set a little deeper than the others but this should not be regarded as a serious fault.

The lips should be close fitting, the upper ones extending downwards just sufficiently to cover the lower. They should be black or heavily marked with black in common with the roof of the mouth.

Neck
The neck should be fairly short, thick and muscular. Some dewlap is permitted.

Forequarters
The shoulders should be powerful and lie close to the body. There should be medium angulation between the shoulder-blade and the upper arm. The forelegs should be straight, heavily boned and well muscled. The elbows should not be too close to the chest nor should they stand off too far from it, so that a good width of stance and a free striding movement are obtained. Pasterns should show flexibility, but no weakness.

Body
The chest should be broad and of sufficient depth to reach just below the elbows. The sides should be slightly rounded and the rib cage should extend well to the rear. The back should be of a good length, broad, muscular, straight and level. Dogs usually have a more pronounced waist than bitches, giving a greater curve to the lower body line.

Hindquarters
The loins should be broad and muscular with fairly prominent haunches, the rump should be slightly sloping and the tail should be set on so that the topline curves smoothly onto it. Male animals should have two apparently normal testicles fully descended into the scrotum.

The thighs should have great strength and be heavily muscled, tapering gradually down to strong hocks. The stifle and hock joints should both have medium angulation as seen from the side.

The hindlegs should each carry strongly-made double dewclaws and lack of this identifying characteristic is a very serious fault.

The hind feet may turn out slightly, but the legs themselves when viewed from behind should be straight. Pronounced cow hocks should be heavily penalised.

Feet
The feet should be short and compact, the toes being slightly arched and equipped with strong nails.

Gait
It is very important that the gait should be unhurried, and one should gain the impression of a large dog propelled by powerful hindquarters moving steadily and smoothly well within its capacity, yet able to produce bursts of speed. At slow speeds the Pyrenean tends to pace.

Tail
The tail should be thick at the root and should taper gradually towards the tip, which for preference, should have a slight curl. It should be of sufficient length to reach below the hocks and the thick coating of fairly long hair should form an attractive plume. In repose, the tail should be carried low with the tip turned slightly to one side, but as the dog becomes interested the tail rises and when he is fully alert it should be curled high above the back in a circle.

Coat
The undercoat should be profuse and composed of very fine hairs whilst the longer outercoat should be of coarser texture, thick and straight or slightly wavy but never curly or fuzzy.

The coat should be longer around the neck and shoulders, where it forms a mane, and towards the tail. The forelegs should be fringed. The hair on the rear of the thighs should be long, very dense and more woolly in texture, giving a 'pantaloon' effect. Bitches tend to be smoother-coated than dogs and usually have a less developed mane.

Colour
(a) Mainly white with patches of badger, wolf-grey or pale yellow; and (b) White.

(a) and (b) are of equal merit and judges should show no preference for either. Areas of black hair, where the black goes straight down to the roots, are a serious fault.

The coloured markings can be on the head, the ears and at the base of the tail, but a few patches on the body are permitted.

The nose and eye rims should be black. The presence of liver pigmentation or pink is a serious fault.

Weight and size
The shoulder height of a bitch should be at least 26 inches (66 centimetres) and of a dog 28 inches (71 centimetres). Most specimens will exceed these heights by several inches and great size should be regarded as absolutely essential, provided that correct type and character are retained. The weight of a bitch should be at least 90 pounds (40 kilogrammes) and of a dog 110 pounds (50 kilogrammes). (These weights apply only to specimens of minimum height and taller ones should weigh considerably more). Weight should always be in proportion to height, giving a powerful dog of great strength. Excess weight due to fat should be penalised.

Note
Male animals should have two apparently normal testicles fully descended into the scrotum.

AKC VARIATION TO STANDARD
Feet: double dewclaws behind, single in front. *Weight and size:* average height at shoulder, dogs 27 to 32 inches, bitches 25 to 29 inches. Dogs 100 to 125 pounds, bitches 90 to 115 pounds.

ROTTWEILER

NATIONAL GROUPING		
	Name	Number
KC(GB)	Working	5
AKC	Working Dogs	III
FCI	Guard Dogs	2

One of the favourite sports in Germany over the centuries has been boar hunting. Though today it is not carried out in quite the same way as it once was, the advent of gunpowder making life easier for the hunter and more conclusive for the game, the race of dogs used then, or at least something very like it, exists still. At one time it was a question of chasing the boar, cornering him and then despatching him with a spear. The dogs used were the ancestors of the modern Great Dane, the Saufinder and the Hatzrüden, tough fierce dogs, strong and short in the leg and with powerful jaws. The Hatzrüden has disappeared, but the dog that most closely resembles the sort of dog that he probably was, is the Rottweiler. He originated in Rottweil in Southern Germany, and was used by butchers as a droving dog, being known as the Rottweiler Metzgerhund, helping to drive the cattle from the countryside to the market and acting as guards to the drovers when the cattle had been converted into cash.

In 1900 it was reported that the breed had declined to such an extent that it was likely to disappear, which undoubtedly it would have done had not a breed club been established to look after its interests. This proved to be the turning point in the history of the breed as from then on not only did it take its rightful place in the show rings of the world, but increasing interest in the breed was taken by those who wished to use it as a working and guard dog. Since the Second World War the breed has thrived, and is today one of the more popular dogs in Germany. The first Rottweilers came to Britain in 1936 and were exhibited at Crufts in the following year, though they were known in the United States of America some years earlier and the breed was recognised in 1935 by the American Kennel Club. A good deal of work has been done on the breed in Scandinavia, and a very flourishing club exists in Sweden where extensive trials are held to improve the working qualities and temperament of the breed.

For his size the Rottweiler must be one of the strongest dogs in the world, being very heavy for his height and standing four square on very powerful legs. He is powerful and compact and capable of great endurance, and when fit, is very muscular, carrying no excess weight and being remarkably agile for a large dog. His massive head and well-armed powerful jaws are those of the one time boar hunter, and there is no doubt that when roused he would be a formidable opponent.

Although he appears regularly in the show rings of many countries, he has never made quite the impression that perhaps he deserves, but the numbers are steadily increasing and the enthusiasm of the breed clubs will ensure that his popularity will certainly not decline. He is usually in competition in a group that includes breeds that more regularly win top honours, and they have perhaps stolen the limelight. He is not a difficult dog to show, as his descent from a long line of hunting dogs has given him a natural ability to learn obedience to commands, and though the occasional dog will object to the close attentions of another one in the ring, it is by no means rare to see one handled by a child.

He is a very intelligent dog, and can be taught simple tricks as well as the more usual exercises of the obedience ring. At one time he was not so settled temperamentally as he is now, but careful elimination of the bloodlines that carried too much temper has produced a dog that is friendly and a very good companion. As a guard he is first class, having a very strong sense of duty and well developed sense of territory. At night, when as a dark coloured dog he is difficult to see, his deep roar and obvious powerful presence is usually sufficient.

OFFICIAL STANDARD

General appearance
The Rottweiler is an above average sized stalwart dog. His correctly proportioned, compact and powerful form permits of great strength, manoeuverability and endurance. His bearing displays boldness and courage; his tranquil gaze manifests good nature and devotion.

Head and skull
The head is of medium length, the skull between the ears is broad. The forehead line is moderately arched as seen from the side. Occipital bone well developed but not conspicuous. Cheeks well muscled but not prominent, with the zygomatic arch well formed. The skin on the head should not be loose although it is allowed to form moderate wrinkle when the dog is attentive. Muzzle fairly deep with topline level and length not longer than the length from stop to occiput.

Nose
The nose is well developed with proportionately large nostrils and is always black.

Eyes
The eyes should be of medium size, almond shaped and dark brown in colour; eyelids close lying.

Ears
The ears are pendant, small in proportion rather than large, set high and wide apart on the head, lying flat and close to the cheek.

Body: chest roomy, broad and deep.

Mouth
The teeth are strong and the incisors of the lower jaw must touch rhe inner surface of the upper incisors. The flews are black and firm; they fall gradually away towards the corners of the mouth, which do not protrude excessively.

Neck
The neck should be of fair length, strong, round and very muscular. It should be slightly arched and free from throatiness.

Forequarters
The shoulders should be well placed on the body, long and sloping with the elbows well let down, but not loose. The legs should be muscular with plenty of bone and substance. The pasterns should be bent slightly forward and not be completely vertical. The front legs seen from all sides must be straight and not placed too closely to one another.

Body
The chest should be roomy, broad and deep with the ribs well sprung. The depth of brisket will not be more, and not much less than 50% of the shoulder height. The back should be straight, strong and not too long; ratio of shoulder height to length of body should be as 9 is to 10; the loins short strong and deep, the flanks should be tucked up. The croup should be broad, of proportionate length, and very slightly sloping.

Hindquarters
The upper thigh not too short, broad and strongly muscled. The lower thigh well muscled at the top and strong and sinewy lower down. Stifles fairly well bent. Hocks well angulated without exaggeration and not completely vertical.

Feet
The feet should be strong, round and compact with the toes well arched. The hind feet are somewhat longer than the front. The pads should be very hard and the toenails short, dark and strong. Rear dewclaws removed.

Gait
In movement the Rottweiler should convey an impression of supple strength, endurance and purpose. While the back remains firm and stable there is a powerful hind thrust and good stride. First and foremost, movement should be harmonious, positive and unrestricted.

Tail
Carried horizontally. It is short, strong and not set too low. It should be docked at the first joint.

Coat
The coat, which consists of top coat and undercoat, should be of medium length, coarse and flat. The undercoat, which is essential on the neck and thighs, should not show through the outer coat. The hair may also be a little longer on the back of the forelegs and breachings.

Colour
The colour is black with clearly defined markings on the cheeks, muzzle, chest and legs, as well as over both eyes and the area beneath the tail. Colour of markings ranges from rich tan to mahogany brown.

Size
For dogs the height at the shoulder should be between 25 to 27 inches and for bitches between 23 to 25 inches. However, height should always be considered in relation to the general appearance of the dog.

Faults
The following faults are noted for the clarification of the Standard.
1. Too lightly or too heavily built. 2. Sway backed or roach backed. 3. Cow hocked, bow hocked, or weak hocked. 4. Long or excessively wavy coat. 5. Any white markings. 6. Nervousness and viciousness are highly undesirable.

Note
Male animals should have two apparently normal testicles fully descended into the scrotum.

AKC VARIATION TO STANDARD
Head: stop well pronounced. *Body:* croup not sloping. *Height:* at shoulder dogs $23\frac{3}{4}$ to 27 inches, bitches $21\frac{1}{4}$ to $25\frac{3}{4}$ inches.

ST BERNARD

Legend has it that this great dog spent a good deal of its time ploughing through the deep snow surrounding the Hospice of St. Bernard with a small keg of brandy fastened to his collar, rescuing snowbound travellers. How much credence should be placed on this story it is difficult to estimate. The only thing that is known is that the Hospice sticks to the story and the dog is certainly large enough and powerful enough to perform the deeds that it is reputed to have done. They would be able to scent out travellers lost in the snow and act as guides in extreme weather, and the monks still keep these striking animals even though the pass is now completely negotiable and more modern methods of rescue are employed. There is some evidence that there were dogs at the Hospice in the 17th century, and these would probably have been the Alpine Mastiff or some similar dog used largely as a guard. It is known that the dogs at the Hospice virtually died out and that the monks had to recourse to using other breeds as an

NATIONAL GROUPING		
	Name	Number
KC(GB)	Working	5
AKC	Working Dogs	III
FCI	Guard Dogs	2

outcross, the Newfoundland and the Pyrenean Mountain Dog are suggested as possibilities.

1866 saw the first St. Bernards being shown in Britain, they had been imported from the Hospice of St. Bernard where reputedly only the worst specimens were allowed to leave by the monks. They in fact created an immediate sensation, and a club was formed shortly afterwards to look after the interests of the breed. The dogs at the Hospice are said to have been half-coated, neither rough nor smooth, but the outcross with other breeds resulted in two coats, and dogs that were brought into Britain produced stock that was both smooth or rough indiscrimately, something that still happens. The original Alpine Mastiff was a fairly smooth-coated dog and it is probable that the smooth coats of today are a reversion to this type. After considerable popularity around the turn of the century, when a great deal of breeding took place and dogs changed hands for very large sums of money (Sir Bedivere being sold to the United States of America for instance for £1,300 which was a fortune in those days) the breed went into a decline. The St. Bernard Club is one of the old established clubs in Britain, but even they could not prevent the fall in numbers that took place. But fashion is fickle, and now that one of the breed has won the Supreme Award at Crufts, there could easily be an upsurge in its fortunes.

He is still one of the heaviest dogs in the world, weights of two hundred pounds not being unknown, and his strength is enormous. It would be foolish to pretend that he is an easy dog to keep. To begin with he takes up a great deal of space, and needs a large amount of high quality food to maintain his immense bulk in condition. In the search for size, soundness was for a long time sacrificed, and even now in order to rear a St. Bernard, a great deal of correct exercising is needed to prevent weakness of the hindquarters. He has moreover the habit of drooling, and it is not unusual to see one of these dogs sitting in a car with a bib tied round his neck to prevent him soiling the upholstery.

Given those slight drawbacks, he makes a magnificent show dog. The rich mixture of colours and well-defined markings distinguishes him from all the other large breeds, and his sheer size makes his presence felt especially when a number of these dogs are grouped together. He has a very steady temperament as most of the large dogs have, and though he objects to the close attention of another dog, he is perfectly friendly with people and especially with those that he knows.

OFFICIAL STANDARD

General appearance
Expression should betoken benevolence, dignity, and intelligence. Movement is most important, and St. Bernards have often failed in this direction, the hind legs being especially faulty.

Head and skull: massive, dignified expression.

Head and skull
Large and massive, circumference of skull being rather more than double the length of the head from nose to occiput. Muzzle short, full in front of the eye, and square at nose end. Cheeks flat; great depth from eye to lower jaw. Lips deep, but not too pendulous. From nose to stop perfectly straight and broad. Stop somewhat abrupt and well defined. Skull broad, slightly rounded at the top, with somewhat prominent brow. Nose large and black, with well developed nostrils.

Eyes
Rather small and deep set, dark in colour, not too close together, the lower eyelid drooping so as to show a fair amount of haw at the inner corner, the upper eyelid falling well over the eye.

Ears
Of medium size lying close to the cheeks, and not heavily feathered.

Mouth
Level.

Neck
Lengthy, thick, muscular, and slightly arched, with dewlap well developed.

Forequarters
Shoulders broad and sloping, well up at the withers. Legs perfectly straight, strong in bone and of good length.

Body
Back broad and straight, ribs well rounded. Loin wide and very muscular. Chest wide and deep. The lower part should not project below the elbows.

Hindquarters
Legs heavy in bone, hocks well bent and thighs very muscular.

Feet
Large and compact with well-arched toes. Dew-claws should be removed.

Tail
Set on rather high, long, and in long-coated variety well

Hindquarters: heavy bone, hocks well bent.

feathered. Carried low when in repose, and when excited or in motion should not be curled over the back.

Coat

In Rough specimens, should be dense and flat, rather fuller round the neck; thighs well feathered. In Smooth specimens it should be close and hound-like, slightly feathered on thighs and tail.

Colour

Orange, mahogany-brindle, red-brindle; white with patches on body of any of the above-named colours. The markings should be as follows: white muzzle, white blaze up face, white collar round neck, white chest, white forelegs, feet, and end of tail; black shadings on face and ears.

Weight and size

The taller the better, provided that symmetry is maintained; thoroughly well proportioned, and of great substance. The general outline should suggest great power and capability of endurance.

Faults

Dudley, liver, flesh-coloured or split nose; over or undershot mouth; snipy muzzle; light or staring eyes; cheek bumps; wedge head; flat skull; badly set or carried, or heavily feathered ears; too much peak; short neck; curly coat; flat sides; hollow back; roach back; flat thighs; ring tail; open or hare feet; cow-hocks; fawn or self-coloured, straight hocks.

Note

Male animals should have two apparently normal testicles fully descended into the scrotum.

AKC VARIATION TO STANDARD

Head: deeply imbedded between eyes and starting at root of muzzle a furrow runs over whole skull. It is strongly marked in first half, gradually disappearing toward base of occiput. Skin of forehead above eyes forms rather noticeable wrinkles, more or less pronounced which converge toward furrow especially when dog is in action. *Mouth:* black roof. Scissors bite preferable. *Ears:* flap is tender and forms rounded triangle, slightly elongated toward point, front edge lying firmly to head, whereas back edge may stand somewhat away from head. *Body:* back gently sloping to rump. *Height:* at shoulder minimum should be dogs $27\frac{1}{2}$ inches, bitches $25\frac{1}{2}$ inches.

SAMOYED

NATIONAL GROUPING		
	Name	Number
KC(GB)	Working	5
AKC	Working Dogs	III
FCI	Guard Dogs	2

Many dogs in their early association with man, were put to work by him: they herded stock, guarded property or hunted game for food. Some, where conditions were suitable, were used as haulers and the Samoyed is a typical example of this. He is one of the sledge hauling dogs used under arctic conditions, where teams of dogs could be harnessed together to tow loads through snow. He is typical of the Spitz group of dogs with erect ears, curled tail and stand-off coat, and is one of a small group used for work in snow. Unlike the others, however, his somewhat more glamorous appearance attracted popular attention and he was soon drawn into the world of the show dog, becoming very popular all over the world whilst the others remained in comparative obscurity.

He is said to have originated in the north west of Siberia among the Samoyed tribe who were originally a nomadic people who herded reindeer and used their dogs for this purpose as well as for pulling their sledges. The tribe is now settled, but their dogs have spread their influence over the whole world, to such an extent that most people would know what a Samoyed was. Originally he was a multi-coloured dog,

and in the early days of importation into Britain there were many that were black, black and tan, or black and white, but the white specimens eventually predominated. In the United States racing with teams of Samoyeds is still popular, which means that the working propensities of the breed are preserved, but little is done in this direction in other countries and he is now primarily a show dog, and a very popular one. Having first arrived in Britain only at the turn of the century, registration figures are now running at nearly a thousand each year.

The Samoyed is a strong, well built dog, and sturdy though not as short and cobbily built as some of the Spitz breeds. His coat is one of his most striking features, the white being the glistening white of snow, and the fullness and density of the coat being reminiscent of the most expensive of furs. He is intelligent, alert and friendly, being almost affectionate towards his owners and never unfriendly even to strangers. He is tremendously hardy, and though it is not now the general practice, he will sleep out of doors in the coldest weather, burying himself in the snow and making a sort of igloo in which his body heat, retained by his heavy coat allows him to remain reasonably comfortable as it did his ancestors of long ago.

As a show dog he is a most attractive breed. Exhibitors vie with presentation, bathing their dogs until the white coat is pure glistening white, with the result that a ring full of these dogs is a brilliant sight at any large modern show. He is an easy dog to show, as he appears to enjoy the atmosphere of the ring as so many of the Spitz breeds do, and he is rarely overawed by the surroundings of the dog show. He enjoys a game, loves plenty of exercise, and even though he does from time to time tend to shed white hairs on the furniture, he makes a wonderful house pet.

OFFICIAL STANDARD

Characteristics
The Samoyed is intelligent, alert, full of action but above all displaying affection towards all mankind.

General appearance
The Samoyed being essentially a working dog should be

strong and active and graceful, and as his work lies in cold climates his coat should be heavy and weather-resisting. He should not be too long in back as a weak back would make him practically useless for his legitimate work; but at the same time a cobby body, such as a Chow's, would also place him at a great disadvantage as a draught dog. Breeders should aim for the happy medium, viz., a body not long, but muscular, allowing liberty, with a deep

Head and skull: powerful and wedge-shaped.

chest and well sprung ribs, strong neck proudly arched, straight front and exceptionally strong loins. Both dogs and bitches should give the appearance of being capable of great endurance but should be free from coarseness. A full grown dog should stand about 21 inches at the shoulder. On account of the depth of chest required the legs should be moderately long, a very short-legged dog is to be deprecated. Hindquarters should be particularly well developed, stifles well angulated, and any suggestion of unsound stifles or cow hocks severely penalised.

Head and skull
Head powerful and wedge-shaped with a broad, flat skull, muzzle of medium length, a tapering foreface not too sharply defined. Lips black. Hair short and smooth before the ears. Nose black for preference, but may be brown or flesh-coloured. Strong jaws.

Eyes
Almond shaped, medium to dark brown in colour, set well apart with alert and intelligent expression. Eyerims should be black and unbroken.

Ears
Thick, not too long and slightly rounded at the tips, set well apart and well covered inside with hair. The ears should be fully erect in the grown dog.

Mouth
Upper teeth should just overlap the underteeth in a scissor bite.

Neck
Proudly arched.

Forequarters
Legs straight and muscular with good bone.

Body
Back medium in length, broad and very muscular. Chest broad and deep ribs well sprung, giving plenty of heart and lung room.

Hindquarters
Very muscular, stifles well angulated; cow hocks or straight stifles very objectionable.

Feet
Long, flattish and slightly spread out. Soles well cushioned with hair.

Gait
Should move freely with a strong agile drive showing power and elegance.

Tail
Long and profuse, carried over the back when alert; sometimes dropped when at rest.

Coat
The body should be well covered with a thick, close, soft and short undercoat, with harsh hair growing through it, forming the outer coat, which should stand straight away from the body and be free from curl.

Colour
Pure white; white and biscuit; cream.

Weight and size
Dogs 20 to 22 inches at the shoulder. Bitches 18 to 20 inches at the shoulder. Weight in proportion to size.

Faults
Big ears with little feathering. Drop ears. Narrow width between ears. Long foreface. Blue or very light eyes. A bull neck. A long body. A soft coat; a wavy coat; absence of undercoat. Slack tail carriage; should be carried well over the back, though it may drop when the dog is at rest. Absence of feathering. Round, cat-like feet. Black or black spots. Severe unprovoked aggressiveness. Any sign of unsound movement.

Note
Male animals should have two apparently normal testicles fully descended into the scrotum.

AKC VARIATION TO STANDARD
Head: stop well defined. Lips slightly curved at corner of mouth giving 'Samoyed smile'. *Neck:* strong well muscled, carried proudly erect, set on sloping shoulders. *Body:* back straight. Loins strong and slightly arched. Belly tightly muscled, slightly tucked-up. Croup full and slightly sloping. *Colour:* includes plain biscuit. *Forelegs:* pasterns should be strong sturdy and straight but flexible with some spring. *Hindquarters:* hocks well developed. The hindlegs should be parallel when viewed from rear in a natural stance, strong well developed, turning neither in nor out. *Disqualifications:* blue eyes. Any colour other than specified.

SHETLAND SHEEPDOG

NATIONAL GROUPING		
	Name	Number
KC(GB)	Working	5
AKC	Working Dogs	III
FCI	Herding Dogs	I

It is notable that the islands off the north coast of Scotland have over the years produced much reduced versions of a number of domestic animals. They have a small hardy breed of sheep, the Shetland Ponies, and a small breed of sheepdog. It is probably not true that the severe climatic conditions have stunted the growth of these animals, but simply that with the lack of space the smaller animals have been more suitable. It was the habit, and indeed still is in some remote parts, to move the farm animals under cover in the same building as the family during the winter, with a separate space but a common roof, and clearly large animals would create some difficulties. The breed was at one time known as the Miniature Collie or the Shetland Collie, and the islanders were said to have used these little dogs as sheepherders, a task which they performed with considerable skill, being active, intelligent and as one writer put it, 'as hardy as Terriers'.

It was not until after 1908 that the first breed club was formed, and since that time the breed has never looked back, the original clubs settling their differences, deciding on a standard for the breed and encouraging shows to put on separate classes for them rather than scheduling them as Miniature Collies. The breed is now third in popularity in the Working Group after the German Shepherd Dog and the Rough-coated Collie, and boasts in Britain some six thousand registrations each year.

The Shetland Sheepdog still retains many of the characteristics of its working ancestors, being a sturdy and hardy little dog capable of withstanding a great deal of bad weather being well-protected by its soft undercoat and long harsh outer coat in spite of its somewhat delicate appearance. He is active and gay, enjoys exercise as most of the working breeds do, being virtually tireless.

It would be a mistake these days to look upon the Shetland Sheepdog as just a miniature of the Rough Collie, as there are distinct differences, especially about the head, where the proportions are quite distinctive to the breed. It must be remembered too that they are essentially a working breed, and a Shetland Sheepdog that looks weedy, or begins to look like a toy dog is not a typical Sheltie.

As a show dog he is very popular, and the numbers appearing at the major shows throughout the world are very high. His size helps, as where an exhibitor would take two Rough Collies, the same exhibitor could easily take half a dozen Shetland Sheepdogs to a show because of less time needed for preparation and less space occupied in transport. The colours are attractive too, and whilst sables in the range from gold to mahogany predominate, there is always a sprinkling of tricolours and blue merles which add colour to the ring. They repay attention to coat, as do most breeds, but the Shetland Sheepdog more than most, and when he has his coat really well sorted out, with his pronounced mane and abundant feathering prepared to full advantage, he is a very handsome little dog.

He is a happy dog, alert and friendly, not always prepared to accept strangers immediately, and a very good guard and housedog. He makes a very good companion, rapidly becoming part of the family and loving to join the children in their games. He is not difficult to train, and he is from time to time seen in the obedience ring where he acquits himself well in competition with the more usual breeds.

OFFICIAL STANDARD

Characteristics

To enable the Shetland Sheepdog to fulfil its natural bent for sheepdog work, its physical structure should be on the lines of strength and activity, free from cloddiness and without any trace of coarseness. Although the desired type is similar to that of the Rough Collie there are marked differences that must be noted. The expression, being one of the most marked characteristics of the breed, is obtained by the perfect balance and combination of skull and foreface, size, shape, colour and placement of eyes, correct position and carriage of ears, all harmoniously blended to produce that almost indefinable look of sweet, alert, gentle intelligence.

The Shetland Sheepdog should show affection and response to his owner, he may show reserve to strangers but not to the point of nervousness.

General appearance

The Shetland Sheepdog should instantly appeal as a dog of great beauty, intelligence and alertness. Action lithe and graceful with speed and jumping power great for its size. The outline should be symmetrical so that no part appears out of proportion to the whole. An abundance of coat, mane and frill, with shapeliness of head and sweetness of expression all combine to present the ideal Shetland Sheepdog that will inspire and secure admiration.

Head and skull

The head should be refined and its shape when viewed from the top or side is a long blunt wedge tapering from ear to nose. The width of skull necessarily depends upon the combined length of skull and muzzle and the whole

Head and skull: refined, wedge-shaped.

must be considered in connection with the size of the dog. The skull should be flat, moderately wide between the ears, showing no prominence of the occipital bone. Cheeks should be flat and merge smoothly into a well rounded muzzle. Skull and muzzle to be of equal length, central point to be the inner corner of the eye. In profile the topline of the skull should be parallel to the topline of the muzzle, but on a higher plane due to a slight but definite stop. The jaws should be clean and strong and with a well developed underjaw. Lips should be tight. Teeth should be sound and level, with an evenly spaced scissor bite.

Eyes

A very important feature giving expression to the dog. They should be of medium size obliquely set and of almond shape. Colour dark brown except in the case of merles, where blue is permissible.

Ears

Should be small and moderately wide at the base, placed fairly close together on the top of the skull. When in repose they should be thrown back, but when on the alert brought forward and carried semi-erect with tips dropping forward.

Neck

The neck should be muscular, well arched and of sufficient length to carry the head proudly.

Body and quarters

From the withers the shoulder blade should slope at a 45 degree angle, forward and downward to the shoulder joint. At the withers they are separated only by the vertebrae but they must slope outwards to accommodate the desired spring of ribs. The upper arm should join the shoulder blade at as nearly a right angle as possible. The elbow joint to be equi-distant from the ground and the withers. The forelegs should be straight when viewed from the front, muscular and clean, with strong bone. Pasterns strong and flexible. The body is slightly longer from the withers to the root of the tail than the height at the withers, but most of the length is due to the proper angulation of the shoulder and hind quarters. The chest should be deep reaching to the point of the elbow. The ribs well sprung but tapering at their lower half to allow free play of the forelegs and shoulders. The back should be level with a graceful sweep over the loins and the croup should slope gradually to the rear. The thigh should be broad and muscular, the thigh bones to be set into the pelvis at right angles, corresponding to the angle of the shoulder blade. The stifle joint where the femur bone joins the tibia bone must have a distinct angle, hock joint to be clean cut, angular and well let down with strong bone. The hock must be straight when viewed from behind.

Tail

Set on low, tapering bone must reach at least to the hock joint, with abundant hair and slight upward sweep, raised when the dog is moving, but never over the level of the back.

Feet
Oval in shape, soles well padded, toes arched and close together.

Gait
The action of the Shetland Sheepdog should denote speed and smoothness. There should be no pacing, plaiting, rolling or stiff stilted up and down movement.

Coat
Must be double, the outer coat of long hair of harsh texture and straight, the under coat soft (resembling fur) short and close. The mane and frill should be very abundant and forelegs well feathered. Hind legs above the hocks profusely covered with hair, but below the hocks fairly smooth. The mask or face smooth. What are commonly known as smooth coated specimens are barred.

Colour
Tricolours should be an intense black on the body with no signs of ticking, rich tan markings on a tricolour to be preferred. Sables may be clear or shaded, any colour from gold to deep mahogany but in its shade the colour should be rich in tones. Wolf sable and grey colours undesirable. Blue Merles, clear silvery blue is desired, splashed and marbled with black. Rich tan markings to be preferred, but the absence not to be counted as a fault. Heavy black markings, slate coloured or rusty tinge in either top or undercoat is highly undesirable. General effect should be blue. White markings may be shown in the blaze, collar, chest frill, legs, stifle and tip of tail. All or some tan markings may be shown on eyebrows, cheeks, legs, stifles and under tail. All or some of the white markings are to be preferred whatever the colour of the dog, but the absence of these markings shall not be considered a fault. Black and White and Black and Tan are also recognised colours. Over markings of patches of white on the body are highly undesirable. The nose black whatever the colour of the dog.

Size
Ideal height measured at the withers 14 inches for bitches, $14\frac{1}{2}$ inches for dogs, anything more than 1 inch above these heights to be considered a serious fault.

Faults
Domed or receding skull, lack of stop, large drooping or pricked ears, over-developed cheeks, weak jaw, snipy muzzle, not full complement of teeth, crooked forelegs, cow hocks, tail kinked, short or carried over the back, white or white colour predominating. Pink or flesh coloured nose, blue eyes in any other colour than merles. Nervousness. Full or light eye. Under or overshot mouth.

Note
Male animals should have two apparently normal testicles fully descended into the scrotum.

AKC VARIATION TO STANDARD
Feet: nails hard, strong. Dewclaws should be removed. *Height:* 13 to 16 inches at shoulder. *Disqualifications:* below or above size range. Brindle.

SIBERIAN HUSKY

There are several breeds that were originally used for sledge towing that have some similarities, the Siberian Husky, the Alaskan Malamute and the Eskimo Dog are the three most obvious ones. Their points of similarity lead some people to believe that they date back to the time when there was a land ridge between Alaska and Siberia. Even if this is not a fact, there is every possibility that arctic fishermen moved with their dogs from one continent to the other. The Siberian Husky was originally the sledge dog of the Chukchis of the far north-eastern part of Asia. The Chukchis are said to have maintained the breed in the 19th century as a pure breed, treasuring them for their speed and endurance, and this is the race of dogs that were the ancestors of today's Siberian Husky.

During the 19th century sledge dogs were in constant use in Alaska, as they were virtually the only way of carrying loads over snow and ice between stations. The people of Alaska had their own dog, the Malamute, but he was heavier, and proved slower, and the men who wished to travel further and faster turned their attention to the Siberian Husky whose reputation had spread from its native country. Early Russian explorers had made extensive journeys and charted the coastline of Siberia using these Huskies, realising the value of having a large number of lighter and faster dogs, and later both Peary and Nansen followed suit, using a mixed force of both East and

NATIONAL GROUPING		
	Name	Number
KC(GB)	—	–
AKC	Working Dogs	III
FCI	Guard Dogs	2

West Siberian dogs. The first team of Siberian Huskies appeared in a race on the North American Continent in the All Alaska Sweepstakes Race in 1909, and in the following year a number were imported, Fox Maule Ramsay won with a team which covered four hundred miles in the race.

One of the most dramatic stories of the Siberian Husky's prowess was when Nome in Alaska suffered an epidemic of diphtheria, and the serum was relayed to the stricken town by teams of Huskies. This event focussed attention on the breed, and it was taken up in a big way both for work and for competition. The breed became established in the United States and was granted recognition in 1930. The Siberian Husky is now seen in many countries, and is growing in popularity in Britain where at the moment it competes only in rare breed and variety classes. It is, however, making its mark, and wins such classes frequently. He makes a good show dog, being striking in appearance with his colour and marking, and unusual coat, which is more dense than anything seen in other dogs. He is quick on his feet, and very graceful when moving, his gait appearing completely effortless. He stands well in the ring, enjoying the experience, watching the other dogs, and from time to time breaking off to look into the distance as if he was expecting snow. He is a strong well-made dog with good bone, and the bitches manage to look feminine without losing anything in power and nobility.

He is a friendly dog, affectionate almost with those that he becomes attached to, makes a very good guard, and is adaptable to any conditions, living equally happily in a house or flat, and out of doors in any weather. He is hardy, suffers from few illnesses, and is a perfectly amiable dog despite the stories of team dogs fighting to the death.

OFFICIAL STANDARD

General appearance

The Siberian Husky is a medium-sized working dog, quick and light on his feet and free and graceful in action. His moderately compact and well-furred body, erect ears and brush tail suggest his Northern heritage. His characteristic gait is smooth and seemingly effortless. He performs his original function in harness most capably, carrying a light load at moderate speed over great distances. His body proportions and form reflect this basic balance of power, speed and endurance. The dogs of the Siberian Husky breed are masculine but never coarse; the bitches are feminine but without weakness of structure. In proper condition, with muscle firm and well-developed, the Siberian Husky does not carry excess weight.

Head: eyes almond-shaped, ears triangular, erect, well-furred.

Head

Skull: of medium size and in proportion to the body; slightly rounded on top and tapering gradually from the widest point to the eyes. *Faults:* head clumsy or heavy; head too finely chiseled. *Muzzle:* of medium length; that is, the distance from the tip of the nose to the stop is equal to the distance from the stop to the occiput. The stop is well-defined and the bridge of the nose is straight from the stop to the tip. The muzzle is of medium width, tapering gradually to the nose, with the tip neither pointed nor square. The lips are well-pigmented and close fitting; teeth closing in a scissors bite. *Faults:* muzzle either too snipy or too coarse; muzzle too short or too long; insufficient stop; any bite other than scissors. *Ears:* of medium size, triangular in shape, close fitting and set high on the head. They are thick, well-furred, slightly arched at the back, and strongly erect, with slightly rounded tips

pointing straight up. *Faults:* ears too large in proportion to the head; too wide-set; not strongly erect. *Eyes:* almond shaped, moderately spaced and set a trifle obliquely. The expression is keen, but friendly; interested and even mischievous. Eyes may be brown or blue in color; one of each or parti-coloured are acceptable. *Faults:* eyes set too obliquely; set too close together. *Nose:* black in gray, tan or black dogs; liver in copper dogs; may be flesh-colored in pure white dogs. The pink-streaked 'snow nose' is acceptable.

Body

Neck: medium in length, arched and carried proudly erect when dog is standing. When moving at a trot, the neck is extended so that the head is carried slightly forward. *Faults:* neck too short and thick; neck too long. *Shoulders:* the shoulder blade is well laid back at an approximate angle of 45 degrees to the ground. The upper arm angles slightly backward from point of shoulder to elbow, and is never perpendicular to the ground. The muscles and ligaments holding the shoulder to the rib cage are firm and well-developed. *Faults:* straight shoulders; loose shoulders. *Chest:* deep and strong, but not too broad, with the deepest point just behind and level with the elbows. The ribs are well-sprung from the spine but flattened on the sides to allow for freedom of action. *Faults:* chest too broad; 'barrel ribs'; ribs too flat or weak. *Back:* The back is straight and strong, with a level topline from withers to croup. It is of medium length, neither cobby nor slack from excessive length. The loin is taut and lean, narrower than the rib cage, and with a slight tuck-up. The croup slopes away from the spine at an angle, but never so steeply as to restrict the rearward thrust of the hind legs. In profile, the length of the body from the point of the shoulder to the rear point of the croup is slightly longer than the height of the body from the ground to the top of the withers. *Faults:* weak or slack back; roached back; sloping topline.

Legs and feet

Forelegs: when standing and viewed from the front, the legs are moderately spaced, parallel and straight, with elbows close to the body and turned neither in nor out. Viewed from the side, pasterns are slightly slanted, with pastern joint strong, but flexible. Bone is substantial but never heavy. Length of the leg from elbow to ground is slightly more than the distance from the elbow to the top of withers. Dewclaws or forelegs may be removed. *Faults:* weak pasterns, too heavy bone; too narrow or too wide in the front; out at the elbows. *Hindquarters:* when standing and viewed from the rear, the hind legs are moderately spaced and parallel. The upper thighs are well-muscled and powerful, the stifles well-bent, the hock joint well-defined and set low to the ground. Dewclaws, if any, are to be removed. *Faults:* straight stifles, cowhocks, too narrow or too wide in the rear. *Feet:* oval in shape, but not long. The paws are medium size, compact and well-furred between the toes and pads. The pads are tough and thickly cushioned. The paws neither turn in nor out when dog is in natural stance. *Faults:* soft or splayed toes; paws too large and clumsy; paws too small and delicate; toeing in or out.

Tail

The well-furred tail of fox-brush shape is set on just below the level of the topline, and is usually carried over the back in a graceful sickle curve when the dog is at attention. When carried up, the tail does not curl to either side of the body, nor does it snap flat against the back. A trailing tail is normal for the dog when working or in repose. Hair on the tail is of medium length and approximately the same length on top, sides and bottom, giving the appearance of a round brush. *Faults:* a snapped or tightly curled tail; highly plumed tail; tail set too low or too high.

Gait

The Siberian Husky's characteristic gait is smooth and seemingly effortless. He is quick and light on his feet, and when in the show ring should be gaited on a loose lead at a moderately fast trot, exhibiting good reach in the forequarters and good drive in the hindquarters. When viewed from the front to rear, while moving at a walk the Siberian Husky does not single-track, but as the speed increases the legs gradually angle inward until the pads are falling on a line directly under the longitudinal center of the body. As the pad marks converge, the forelegs and hind legs are carried straight forward, with neither elbows nor stifles turned in or out. Each hind leg moves in the path of the foreleg on the same side. While the dog is gaiting, the topline remains firm and level. *Faults:* short, prancing or choppy gait, lumbering or rolling gait; crossing; crabbing.

Coat

The coat of the Siberian Husky is double and medium in length, giving a well-furred appearance, but is never so long as to obscure the clean-cut outline of the dog. The undercoat is soft and dense and of sufficient length to support the outer coat. The guard hairs of the outer coat are straight and somewhat smooth-lying, never harsh nor standing straight off from the body. It should be noted that the absence of the undercoat during the shedding season is normal. Trimming of the whiskers and fur between the toes and around the feet to present a neater appearance is permissible. Trimming of the fur on any other part of the dog is not to be condoned and should be severely penalized. *Faults:* long, rough or shaggy coat; texture too harsh or too silky; trimming of the coat, except as permitted above.

Color

All colors from black to pure white are allowed. A variety of markings on the head is common, including many striking patterns not found in other breeds.

Temperament

The characteristic temperament of the Siberian Husky is friendly and gentle, but also alert and outgoing. He does not display the possessive qualities of the guard dog, nor is he overly suspicious of strangers or aggressive with other dogs. Some measure of reserve and dignity may be expected in the mature dog. His intelligence, tractability, and eager disposition make him an agreeable companion and willing worker.

Size

Height: dogs: 21 to 23½ inches at the withers. Bitches: 20 to 22 inches at the withers. *Weight:* dogs: 45 to 60 pounds. Bitches: 35 to 50 pounds. Weight is in proportion to height. The measurements mentioned above represent the extreme height and weight limits, with no preference given to either extreme. *Disqualification:* dogs over 23½ inches and bitches over 22 inches.

Summary

The most important breed characteristics of the Siberian Husky are medium size, moderate bone, well-balanced proportions, ease and freedom of movement, proper coat, pleasing head and ears, correct tail, and good disposition. Any appearance of excessive bone or weight, constricted or clumsy gait, or long, rough coat should be penalized. The Siberian Husky never appears so heavy or coarse as to suggest a freighting animal; nor is he so light and fragile as to suggest a sprint-racing animal. In both sexes the Siberian Husky gives the appearance of being capable of great endurance. In addition to the faults already noted, obvious structural faults common to all breeds are as undesirable in the Siberian Husky as in any other breed, even though they are not specifically mentioned herein.

DISQUALIFICATION
Dogs over 23½ inches and bitches over 22 inches.

AKC VARIATION TO STANDARD

This dog is not granted championship status by the KC(GB).

CARDIGAN WELSH CORGI

As long as Welshmen exist, the debate over the origin of the Corgi, and which variety came first, will continue. The protagonists of the Pembroke will insist that theirs was earlier, whilst those who favour the Cardigan will insist that their favourite breed not only existed before the Pembroke, but was probably responsible for all the other heelers and the Swedish Vallhund as well. Most opinion tends towards the Cardigan as being the more ancient of the two corgis, and there is little doubt that dogs used for rounding up and driving cattle were used in Wales centuries ago. These dogs were almost certainly short-legged, to enable them to move in quickly behind the cattle, give a sharp nip and escape before the resultant kick could reach them. It is odd, however, that many of the old books completely ignore the breed, and that it was not until the formation of the Welsh Corgi Club in 1926

NATIONAL GROUPING		
	Name	Number
KC(GB)	Working	5
AKC	Working Dogs	III
FCI	Herding Dogs	I

that attention was drawn to these attractive little dogs.

At first the two varieties were mixed, and were shown together, competing against one another for the challenge certificates offered by the Kennel Club, and it was only in 1934 that certificates were offered to both varieties. Fashion is unpredictable, and it is difficult to reason why it should be that the Pembroke variety should become one of the most popular dogs in the world, whilst the Cardigans remained very much in the background, with only a small number of enthusi-

246

asts keeping the breed alive. In recent years the Cardigan Corgi has had something of a revival and numbers crept slowly up, particularly in Australia.

The Cardigan is a sturdy little dog, heavy for its height, and with strong short legs that carry it over the ground at a remarkable speed and allow it to whip round quickly in its own length. He is a real all-weather dog, being just as happy in the pouring rain as basking in sunshine, and staunch enough to face up to exercise all day without undue tiring. His coat is hard and water-resistant and his very sharp hearing allows him to wander considerable distances and still retain contact with his owner.

As a show dog he is much admired for his steady character. He rarely shows nerves in the ring, and whilst suspicious of strangers, he allows himself to be handled rather than encouraging it.

Temperamentally he is somewhat stolid compared with many other breeds, tending to enjoy a romp with others of his kind rather than with people. With those to whom he becomes attached, however, he is remarkably companionable, affectionate without being over-fussy, and attentive without fawning. He is an even tempered dog, both with people and with other dogs, and will rarely enter a fight unless forced into it, preferring to retain his somewhat aloof exterior whilst other and lesser canines join battle. He does retain the working instinct, and can easily be trained to be quite obedient, obeying commands at quite long distances as he once needed to when working with cattle.

OFFICIAL STANDARD

General appearance
Expression to be as foxy as possible; alertness essential; the body to measure about 36 inches from point of nose to tip of tail.

Head and skull
Head to be foxy in shape and appearance. Skull to be fairly wide and flat between the ears, tapering towards the eyes, above which it should be slightly domed. Muzzle to measure about 3 inches in length (or in proportion to skull as three to five) and to taper towards the snout. Nose black (except in Blue Merles) slightly projecting and in no sense blunt, with nostrils of moderate size. Underjaw to be clean cut and strong but without prominence.

Eyes
To be of medium size, but giving a sharp and watchful expression, rather widely set with corners clearly defined; preferably dark in colour but clear. Silver eyes permissible in Blue Merles.

Ears
To be rather large (in proportion to size of dog) and prominent, moderately wide at the base, carried erect, set about 3½ inches apart and well back so that they can be laid flat along neck.

Mouth
Teeth strong, level and sound.

Neck
To be muscular, well developed and in proportion to the dog's build, fitting into well sloped shoulders.

Forequarters
Front to be slightly bowed, with strong bone. Legs short and strong. Shoulders strong and muscular.

Body
Chest to be moderately broad with prominent breast bone. Body to be fairly long and strong, with deep brisket, well sprung ribs and clearly defined waist.

Hindquarters
To be strong with muscular thighs. Legs short and strong.

Feet
Round and well padded. All dew claws removed. Rather large.

Tail
To be moderately long and set in line with body (not curled over back) and resembling that of a fox.

Coat
Short or medium, of hard texture.

Colour
Any colour except pure white.

Weight and size
Height to be as near as possible to 12 inches at shoulder.

Tail: set in line with body and resembling that of a fox.

Weight: dogs 22 to 26 pounds. Bitches 20 to 24 pounds.

Faults

Over or undershot mouth, high peaked occiput, prominent cheeks, low flat forehead, expressionless eyes, crooked forearms, splayed feet, tail curled over back. Silky coat.

Note

Male animals should have two apparently normal testicles fully descended into the scrotum.

AKC VARIATION TO STANDARD

Head: muzzle less fine than Pembroke. *Eyes:* blue eyes or one dark and one blue permissible in blue merles. *Ears:* slightly rounded at tips. *Forequarters:* elbows close to side. *Body:* topline level except for slight slope of spine above tail. *Size:* length usually 36 to 44 inches from nose to tip of tail. *Disqualifications:* a distinctly long coat. Pure white.

PEMBROKE WELSH CORGI

It is difficult to understand why when two breeds of dog are so close together in appearance, temperament and origin as the two varieties of Corgi, one should remain fairly rare whilst the other is to be seen on every street corner. The Cardigan is still a comparatively rare breed, whilst the Pembroke is one of the most popular breeds in the world. The origins of the two varieties are so closely interwoven that there can be no doubt that at one time they were one and the same

NATIONAL GROUPING		
	Name	Number
KC(GB)	Working	5
AKC	Working Dogs	III
FCI	Herding Dogs	I

breed, used for centuries in the Welsh hills for the herding of cattle. They were probably used for sheep

249

too, and almost certainly for the herds of small Welsh Ponies that run wild on the hills of some parts of Wales. It is interesting that although almost every book that deals with the breed mentions its antiquity, no book prior to the turn of the century mentions them at all.

It was in 1926 that the Welsh Corgi Club was formed, but its interests covered both varieties, the Pembroke and the Cardigan, and though challenge certificates were granted in 1928, they were for competition between both types. The division did not come about until 1934, and from that time the Pembroke Welsh Corgi has never looked back, increasing in popularity at a tremendous rate, and becoming one of the most popular pet dogs in the world. The enormous growth in recent years has undoubtedly been partly due to the fact that the breed became the favourite of the British Royal Family. The Queen owns a number, and is frequently seen, either being greeted by them on her return from overseas, or bidding them farewell before leaving the country. The registration figures of the breed reached a peak in the late sixties in Britain, since when they have shown some decline, but their popularity in other countries, particularly in Australia and South Africa does not appear to be on the wane.

The Pembroke Corgi is a slightly smaller dog than the Cardigan, the head is generally sharper and the ears smaller. He is a thoroughly sturdy little dog, and although his popularity as a pet may have generally softened him, a fit Pembroke is still very much the tough little working dog, very muscular, and still capable of considerable exercise without distress in spite of his short legs. He is a particularly clean, neat little dog and fits well into modern living conditions, being easily trained, intelligent and obedient, and not subject to some of the ailments to which other dogs are prone.

As a show dog he is a near perfect subject especially if he is shown as a hobby. He is easily fed and housed, small enough to transport in numbers, grooming is no problem, and he is so easily trained to behave well and comport himself with dignity in the ring, that even very young puppies can be trained to show like veterans. He is a dog that is anxious to please, and his reactions to people bred into him from generations of being a working dog housed under small-family conditions, are friendly and willing.

Temperamentally he is completely suited to the life of a pet dog. If he has a vice at all, and it is by no means certain that he has, it could be gluttony, and his appealing expression has such an effect on people, and especially children, that many that are kept as pets become overweight. He is one of the most friendly of dogs, being particularly attached to children with whom he loves to play, prefers a game to a fight at any time, and is great fun to have either in the house or on country walks. As a working dog he is not easily tired, and his enthusiasm for investigation and native inquisitiveness make him the ideal companion for the country life as he entertains himself. He has the additional advantage of being an excellent guard, being naturally suspicious of strangers and with a strongly developed sense of territory.

OFFICIAL STANDARD

General appearance
Low set, strong, sturdily built, alert and active giving an impression of substance and stamina in a small space, outlook bold, expression intelligent and workmanlike. The movement should be free and active, elbows fitting closely to the sides, neither loose nor tied. Forelegs should move well forward, without too much lift, in unison with thrusting action of hind legs.

Head and skull
Head to be foxy in shape and appearance, with alert and intelligent expression, skull to be fairly wide and flat between the ears; moderate amount of stop. Length of foreface to be in proportion to the skull as three is to five. Muzzle slightly tapering. Nose black.

Eyes
Well set, round, medium size, hazel in colour and blending with colour of coat.

Ears
Pricked, medium sized, slightly pointed. A line drawn from the tip of the nose through the eye should, if extended, pass through, or close to, the tip of the ear.

Mouth
Teeth level, or with the inner side of the upper front teeth resting closely on the front of the under ones.

Neck
Fairly long.

Forequarters
Legs short and as straight as possible. Ample bone carried right down to the feet. Elbows should fit closely to the sides, neither loose nor tied.

Body
Of medium length, with well sprung ribs. Not short coupled or terrier like. Level top line. Chest broad and deep, well let down between the forelegs.

Hindquarters
Strong and flexible, slightly tapering. Legs short. Ample bone carried right down to the feet. Hocks straight when viewed from behind.

Feet
Oval, the two centre toes slightly in advance of two outer ones, pads strong and well arched. Nails short.

Tail
Short, preferably natural.

Coat
Of medium length and dense; not wiry.

Colour
Self colours in red, sable, fawn, black and tan, or with white markings on legs, chest and neck. Some white on

Head and skull: foxy, alert, intelligent.

head and foreface is permissible.

Weight and size
Dogs 20 to 24 pounds; Bitches 18 to 22 pounds. Height from 10 to 12 inches at shoulder.

Faults
The following are serious faults:
White on the body giving a piebald or skewbald effect, or hound like markings. Long fluffy coat, accompanied with feathering on ears and feet. Overshot or undershot mouth.

Note
Male animals should have two apparently normal testicles fully descended into the scrotum.

AKC VARIATION TO STANDARD
Head: very slight rounding of cheek, and not filled in below the eyes. *Eyes:* oval, set somewhat obliquely. Eye rims dark. *Mouth:* lips should be black, tight with little or no fullness. *Forelegs:* pasterns firm and nearly straight when viewed from side. *Coat:* short thick, weather resistant undercoat with coarser longer outercoat. *Weight:* not to exceed 30 pounds for dogs and 28 pounds for bitches.

TERRIER GROUP: SPORTING BREEDS

Airedale Terrier

American Staffordshire Terrier

Australian Terrier

Bedlington Terrier

Border Terrier

Bull Terrier

Cairn Terrier

Dandie Dinmont Terrier

Miniature Bull Terrier

Fox Terrier (Wire)

Fox Terrier (Smooth)

Irish Terrier

Kerry Blue Terrier

Lakeland Terrier

Manchester Terrier

Norfolk Terrier

Norwich Terrier

Sealyham Terrier

Scottish Terrier

Skye Terrier

Soft-coated Wheaten Terrier

Staffordshire
Bull Terrier

Welsh Terrier

West Highland
White Terrier

TERRIER GROUP: SPORTING BREEDS

This Group is fairly recent in its development. The very name 'Terrier', which refers to the native inclination to dig into the ground, infers that most of the breeds included in the Group grew up with domestication and industry. They are largely vermin hunters, have little to do with the more ancient sports, and have never needed to take upon themselves the mantle of the sheep-herding dogs or the game hunters. For some reason which is difficult to explain, the majority of the Terriers originated in Britain. It is not logical to suppose, as some of the older writers did, that this resulted from their use by hunts, as the basic stock from which they descended must have existed long before fox-hunting became fashionable. They were certainly known in the 15th century as Dame Juliana Berners included them in her list of types.

They all have one thing in common, and that is that given the opportunity they will dig and attempt to go to ground after vermin. This has become difficult for some breeds as they have been evolved and perfected to be too long in the leg for the purpose, for example one cannot imagine an Airedale having much success attempting to dig out a rabbit. Nicholas Cox in 1677 divided the Terriers of his time into two groups, the short-haired and the crook-legged type which in his words 'will take earth well, and will lie very long at fox or badger' and the long-legged shaggy sort which will not only hunt above ground but will also enter the earth with much fury. At the time that Cox was writing this would probably have been the only general division, but since then things have changed considerably.

In the first instance a great deal of selective breeding has taken place to produce dogs of very differing types. This process was speeded up with the advent of the dog show, and whole new breeds have appeared. In addition, there were a number of Terriers which by accidents of geography were being bred along fairly rigid lines in Ireland and the islands off the coast of Scotland. These developments not only produced different breeds of dogs for different forms of fox-hunting with packs of hounds, but as fashions changed, even produced entirely different types for other purposes. The country sport of badger digging demanded a much stronger dog than the ordinary Terriers used for the fox, and crosses with Bulldogs were resorted to which produced formidable terriers with fighting instincts. These were encouraged and resulted in yet another sport, that of dog fighting.

Generally speaking the smaller Terriers were used by working men for a little weekend sport hunting rats around the industrial buildings that mushroomed as the result of the country's greatly increased dependence on coal and steel. The middle-sized Terriers with rather longer legs such as the Fox Terriers and the Border Terriers remained the favourites of the hunts and were used in conjunction with packs of hounds to drive the fox from his earth or hold him there until the huntsmen could dig him out. The more heavily built low-to-ground Terriers such as the Sealyham and the Dandie Dinmont proved to be the best badger dogs, their greater strength and stronger jaws dealing effectively with their much stronger and fiercer quarry, whilst the more recent developments from the Bulldog and Terrier crosses became the fighting dogs of the 18th century.

Dog fighting became illegal, the badger became a subject for preservation, and the number of hunts declined over the past hundred years. Fortunately, however, the Terriers prospered as show dogs and from the very early days of dog shows the Terriers held a very important position. In Britain dog shows first started as one of the pastimes of the working man, taking place in public houses, and being an increasingly important recreation towards the latter part of the 18th century. Many areas had produced their own breeds of Terrier in which the locals took a great deal of pride so that there was always considerable rivalry for instance between the men of Bedlington and those of Manchester. They tended to look down on such things as Spaniels as foreign dogs, and Terriers became very popular. Unfortunately the golden age did not last, and at shows today the Terrier breeds are on the whole the worst supported.

AIREDALE TERRIER

The word 'terrier' when applied to a dog, implies the ability to go to ground, and to call a dog as large as an Airedale a Terrier seems to many people to be a complete misuse of the word. Yet in fact he is the absolute essence of Terrier, and is known as the King of the Terriers, not just because of his size, but because he combines all the Terrier characteristics. He is a fairly recent dog, having been produced in the area of the valley of the river Aire in South Yorkshire around the middle of the 19th century, probably as the result of crossing the old fashioned black and tan hard-coated northern tyke with the Otterhound. The

NATIONAL GROUPING		
	Name	Number
KC(GB)	Terrier	3
AKC	Terriers	IV
FCI	Terriers	3

natives of Yorkshire have always been sportsmen, and have for centuries been interested in animals, dogs in particular, and the production of new varieties. They will redesign the canary, grow new varieties of chrysanthemums or produce a new strain of dog at the drop of a hat. Otter hunting was a favourite sport in the valleys of the Aire and the Wharfe where several packs were kept, and there were always at one time a number of hounds in private ownership. Ratting, and the casual sport of hunting vermin has been going on in the county for as long as people can remember, and when the sportsmen of the Otley district decided that they wanted a large game terrier-type dog, it was natural for them to take the two available types and cross them. The dog that resulted, having been perfected, is not only the largest of the true Terriers, but is a noble animal worthy of the county of the White Rose.

In the early years he was known as the Waterside Terrier or the Bingley Terrier, and he was not the smart dog that he is today, being bad in colour, shaggy in appearance and with rather large ears. But after about twenty years the breed had settled down and in 1883 three classes were scheduled at the Birmingham Show and by 1886 the breed was recognised and admitted to the stud book. From this time onwards the breed progressed both in numbers and in quality, the coat and colour improving and the hound type gradually disappearing in favour of a true Terrier. Just before the turn of the century the Airedale Terrier Club was formed and the success of the breed was assured.

He is one of the finest guards and protectors of property in the canine world, and many a successful show dog has first been discovered as a yard dog in South Yorkshire. He has proved his value in this respect in many countries, and especially in those places where protection against wild animals is needed, as he is completely fearless and willing to tackle anything. During the First World War he was trained as a messenger dog and sentry, and has even been trained for police work. In recent years, however, it has been as a show dog that he has proved supreme, winning major awards at the larger shows throughout the world.

As with most of the hard-coated Terriers, a considerable amount of work is involved in his preparation for show, as the coat has to be shaped and trimmed to make the most of his smart outline. This can be tedious work that goes on for a fairly lengthy period before a show, and it is for this reason that many of these dogs are in the hands of professional handlers who are experts at presentation and who know the short cuts to success. He is still, however, very much in demand as a guard and house dog, as his qualities of faithfulness and affection to the members of the family are well known.

OFFICIAL STANDARD

Characteristics
Keen of expression, quick of movement, on the tip-toe of expectation at any movement. Character is denoted and shown by the expression of the eyes, and by the carriage of the ears and tail.

General appearance
The various parts of the dog should be in proportion to each other giving a symmetrical appearance. In movement, the legs should be carried straight forward, the forelegs being perpendicular and parallel with the sides. The propulsive power is furnished by the hind legs, perfection of action being found in the Terrier possessing long thighs, and muscular second thighs well bent at the stifles, which admit of a strong forward thrust or snatch of the hocks. When approaching, the forelegs should form a continuation of the straight line of the front, the feet being the same distance apart as the elbows; when stationary it is often difficult to determine whether a dog is slightly out at shoulder, but directly he moves, the defect if it exists, becomes most apparent, the forefeet having a tendency to cross. When, on the contrary, the dog is tied at the shoulder, the tendency of the feet is to move wider apart. When the hocks are turned in (cow-hocks) the stifles and feet are turned outward, resulting in a serious loss of propulsive power. When the hocks are turned outward, the tendency of the hind feet is to cross.

Head and skull
The skull should be long and flat, not too broad between the ears, and narrowing slightly to the eyes. It should be

Head: stop hardly visible, cheeks level, foreface well filled.

well balanced, with only little apparent difference in length between skull and foreface. The skull to be free from wrinkles, with stop hardly visible, and cheeks level and free from fullness. Foreface must be well filled up before the eyes, not dish-faced or falling away quickly below eyes, but on the other hand a little delicate chiselling should keep appearance from wedginess and plainness. Upper and lower jaws should be deep, powerful, strong and muscular, as strength of foreface is a great desideratum of the Airedale, but there must be no excess development of the jaws to give a rounded or bulging appearance to the cheeks, as 'cheekiness' is not desired. Lips to be tight. The nose should be black.

Eyes
Should be dark in colour, small, not prominent, full of terrier expression, keenness and intelligence.

Ears
Should be 'V' shaped with a side carriage, small, but not out of proportion to the size of the dog. The top line of the folded ear should be above the level of the skull. A pendulous ear, hanging dead by the side of the head like a hound's, is a fault.

Mouth
Teeth strong and level being capable of closing together like a vice.

Neck
Should be clean, muscular, of moderate length and thickness, gradually widening towards the shoulders, and free from throatiness.

Forequarters
Shoulders should be long, well laid back, and sloping obliquely into the back, shoulder blades flat. Forelegs should be perfectly straight, with plenty of bone. Elbows should be perpendicular to the body, working free of the sides.

Body
Back should be short, strong, straight and level, with no appearance of slackness. Loins muscular. Ribs well sprung. In a well ribbed-up or short-coupled dog there is little space between ribs and hips. When the dog is long in couplings some slackness will be shown here. Chest to be deep but not broad.

Hindquarters
Should be long and muscular with no droop. Thighs long and powerful with muscular second thigh, stifles well bent, not turned either in or out. Hocks well let down, parallel with each other when viewed from behind.

Feet
Should be small, round and compact, with a good depth of pad, well cushioned, and the toes moderately arched, not turned either in or out.

Tail
Should be set on high and carried gaily, but not curled over the back. It should be of good strength and substance, and of fair length.

Coat
Should be hard, dense and wiry, and not too long as to appear ragged. It should also lie straight and close, covering the body and legs; the outer coat of hard, wiry, stiff hairs, the undercoat should be a shorter growth of softer hair. Some of the hardest coats are crinkling or just slightly waved; a curly coat is objectionable.

Colour
The head and ears, with the exception of dark markings on each side of the skull, should be tan, the ears being of a

Tail: set on high, carried gaily.

darker shade than the rest. The legs up to the thighs and elbows also should be tan. The body to be black or dark grizzle.

Weight and size
Height about 23 to 24 inches for dogs, taken from top of shoulder, and bitches about 22 to 23 inches. Weight to be commensurate with height and type.

Note
Male animals should have two apparently normal testicles fully descended into the scrotum.

AKC VARIATION TO STANDARD
Nose: not too small. *Colour:* small white blaze on chest is characteristic of certain strains of breed. *Faults:* yellow eyes. Round ears. White feet. Soft coat. Much over or under the size limit. Undershot or overshot. Poor movement.

AMERICAN STAFFORDSHIRE TERRIER

This breed is a typical example of a split in a breed resulting eventually in two distinct breeds. The division by ears of the Norwich and Norfolk Terriers is another. The American Staffordshire Terrier and the Staffordshire Bull Terrier were originally one and the same animal, resulting from a cross between the Bulldog and the old English Smooth Terrier. In Britain the result remained the Staffordshire Bull Terrier, and was recognised as such in 1935. He was not, however, recognised in the United States of America at that time, but the Staffordshire Terrier was, and the name was changed to the American Staffordshire Terrier in 1972. In the meantime the Staffordshire Bull Terrier had been growing in status and numbers in Britain, and in 1974 he too was recognised as a different breed by the American Kennel Club. This means that two breeds with a common ancestry and many similarities of appearance now exist in the United States.

In Britain the size of the breed was kept down, the height at the shoulder being fourteen to sixteen inches, and it was here that the major change took place. In America it was decided that a bigger dog was desirable, and the standard requires a male to be between eighteen and nineteen inches high with weight in

NATIONAL GROUPING		
	Name	Number
KC(GB)	—	—
AKC	Terriers	IV
FCI	Terriers	3

proportion. A quick look at other breeds shows that a fully grown dog could weigh around forty-five pounds.

It was in the late 19th century that the Staffordshire dog first arrived in America. He was known at that time as the Pit Dog because of his association with the rat pit and the dog fighting pit, as it was in this particular sphere that his considerable abilities as a fighting dog were usually employed. There is little doubt that this now illegal, so-called sport, was as much enjoyed in the early days in his new country as it was in the old.

It has really only been in this century that the qualities of the dog have been fully appreciated. His admission to register was held up in Britain by the fact that he was always associated with what were considered to be the rougher and less gentlemanly elements of society. In fact the 'gentry' as they were known, were frequenters of dog fights albeit often in disguise, and were certainly the heaviest betters. It was comparable with cock fighting, in that although it was frowned upon, a blind eye was turned upon it by the authorities for fear that the squire, the local doctor or even the mayor might be present!

Like his British cousin, the American Staffordshire Terrier is a remarkably strong dog for his size, built with tremendous power in both his sholders and his hindquarters, but with a gracefulness that reminds one of the well-trained boxer, always ready for anything, and always on his toes.

He will never turn tail on anything however large, looking around himself constantly in the ring or out of it, facing up to other and often considerably larger dogs with a positive though not threatening attitude. He will not pick a fight, but he will never run away from one, and his very attitude frequently deters potential opposition which usually discovers that it has a pressing engagement elsewhere. With people he is the essence of kindness and affection, and makes a wonderful companion for either children or the elderly, being very possessive and a good guard.

OFFICIAL STANDARD

General impression
The American Staffordshire Terrier should give the impression of great strength for his size, a well put-together dog, muscular, but agile and graceful, keenly alive to his surroundings. He should be stocky, not long-legged or racy in outline. His courage is proverbial.

Head
Medium length, deep through, broad skull, very pronounced cheek muscles, distinct stop; and ears are set high. *Ears:* cropped or uncropped, the latter preferred. Uncropped ears should be short and held half rose or prick. Full drop to be penalized. *Eyes:* dark and round, low down in skull and set far apart. No pink eyelids. *Muzzle:* medium length, rounded on upper side to fall away abruptly below eyes. Jaws well defined. Underjaw

Head: deep, broad skull, pronounced cheek muscles, distinct stop, cropped-eared version.

to be strong and have biting power. Lips close and even, no looseness. Upper teeth to meet tightly outside lower teeth in front. Nose definitely black.

Neck
Heavy, slightly arched, tapering from shoulders to back of skull. No looseness of skin. Medium length.

Shoulders
Strong and muscular with blades wide and sloping.

Back
Fairly short. Slight sloping from withers to rump with gentle short slope at rump to base of tail. Loins slightly tucked.

Body
Well-sprung ribs, deep in rear. All ribs close together. Forelegs set rather wide apart to permit of chest development. Chest deep and broad.

Tail
Short in comparison to size, low set, tapering to a fine point; not curled or held over back. Not docked.

Legs: front straight rather than bowed.

Legs
The front legs should be straight, large or round bones, pastern upright. No resemblance of bend in front. Hindquarters well-muscled, let down at hocks, turning neither in nor out. Feet of moderate size, well-arched and compact. Gait must be springy but without roll or pace.

Coat
Short, close, stiff to the touch, and glossy.

Color
Any color, solid, parti, or patched is permissible, but all white, more than 80 per cent white, black and tan, and liver not to be encouraged.

Size
Height and weight should be in proportion. A height of about 18 to 19 inches at shoulders for the dog and 17 to 18 inches for the bitch is to be considered preferable.

Faults
Faults to be penalized are: Dudley nose, light or pink eyes, tail too long or badly carried, undershot or overshot mouths.

Approved 10 June 1936

AKC VARIATION TO STANDARD
This dog is not granted championship status by the KC(GB). The above standards are those of the AKC.

AUSTRALIAN TERRIER

NATIONAL GROUPING		
	Name	Number
KC(GB)	Terrier	3
AKC	Terriers	IV
FCI	Terriers	3

The history of the Australian Terrier is comparatively recent, as it was not exhibited until 1872, when it was shown in Melbourne as a Broken-coated Terrier of blackish blue sheen. By 1880 it had become the Blue and Tan, by 1884 the Toy, in 1888 it was the Blue Terrier and finally in 1900 it was shown as the Rough-coated Terrier, Blue and Tan. It has been reported that early in the 19th century settlers in Tasmania were breeding broken-coated terriers that were blue and tan and were excellent guards and weighed around ten pounds. By 1906 this little dog was being shown in Britain, though he did not achieve breed status until 1933, and was even later in the United States of America where he arrived during the first quarter of the century and was finally recognised in 1960.

It is almost certain that the Australian Terrier and the Australian Silky Terrier shared a common ancestry, both descending from the old broken-coated terriers of Tasmania, New South Wales and Victoria. That dog in its turn probably resulted from crossing the Skye, the Dandie Dinmont and the Scottish Terrier, traces of all of these appearing in the present breed. From the Skye came the coat, from the Scottie the head and conformation and from the Dandie the tendency towards a soft topknot. From time to time Yorkshire Terrier blood was introduced to improve colour and even later the Manchester, to give the breed a better tan. At some stage the Australian Terrier and the Silky Terrier parted company, and whilst the Silky was bred down to a size to conform with the requirements of the Toy dog Group, the other became the hard-bitten tough little Terrier that we see today.

There is no question that he is tough, for his size he is a bundle of terrier characteristics, being sharp in his reactions, tough with other dogs, and a splendid little hunting dog. For some time he was essentially a blue and tan dog, but Mr. McPharlane of Adelaide introduced the red colour, probably by using a Cairn Terrier cross, so that now, whilst the blue and tans predominate, some reds are regularly seen. He is one of the smallest of the working Terriers, standing only ten inches at the withers and weighing a mere twelve to fourteen pounds, but his air of importance makes him appear a much larger dog. He was used as a guard in Australia for farms and mines, and even looked after flocks of sheep, where his keen eyesight and hearing permitted him to give early warning of danger and his native fierceness was sufficient to deter anything but the boldest predator.

He makes a smart little show dog, very little preparation being needed to keep him in show trim as he is not heavily coated, and his love of exercise and will to work, keeps him in fine muscular condition. He is an affectionate and generally quiet little dog for a Terrier, and makes a very pleasing housedog and pet, being well mannered and very good with children.

OFFICIAL STANDARD

General appearance
A rather low-set dog, compact and active.

Head and skull
Head long, skull flat, full between the eyes; with a soft hair top-knot; long powerful jaw, nose black.

Eyes
Small, keen, dark colour.

Ears
Small, set high on skull, pricked, or dropped towards the front, free from long hair.

Mouth
Teeth level.

Forequarters: straight, well set under.

Head and skull: long, skull flat, long powerful jaw.

Neck
Neck inclined to be long in proportion to body, with a decided frill of hair.

Forequarters
Legs, perfectly straight, well set under the body, slight feather to the knee.

Body
Rather long in proportion to height; well ribbed up; back straight.

Hindquarters
Good strong thighs, hocks slightly bent.

Feet
Clean, small and well padded with no tendency to spread. Black toe nails.

Tail
Docked.

Coat
Straight hair from 2 to $2\frac{1}{2}$ inches long, of hard texture.

Colour
First, blue or silver grey body, tan colour on legs and face (the richer the tan the better). Top-knot blue or silver. Second, clear sandy or red with soft top-knot.

Weight and size
Average weight about 10 or 11 pounds. Average height about 10 inches.

Faults
Flesh-coloured toe nails or nose; white on feet; white breast; curly or woolly coat, all black coat (puppies excepted). Overshot or undershot mouths.

Note
Male animals should have two apparently normal testicles fully descended into the scrotum.

AKC VARIATION TO STANDARD
Mouth: a level bite is acceptable. *Forequarters:* elbows close; pasterns strong. *Tail:* docked leaving 2/5. *Weight:* average weight 12 to 14 pounds.

BEDLINGTON TERRIER

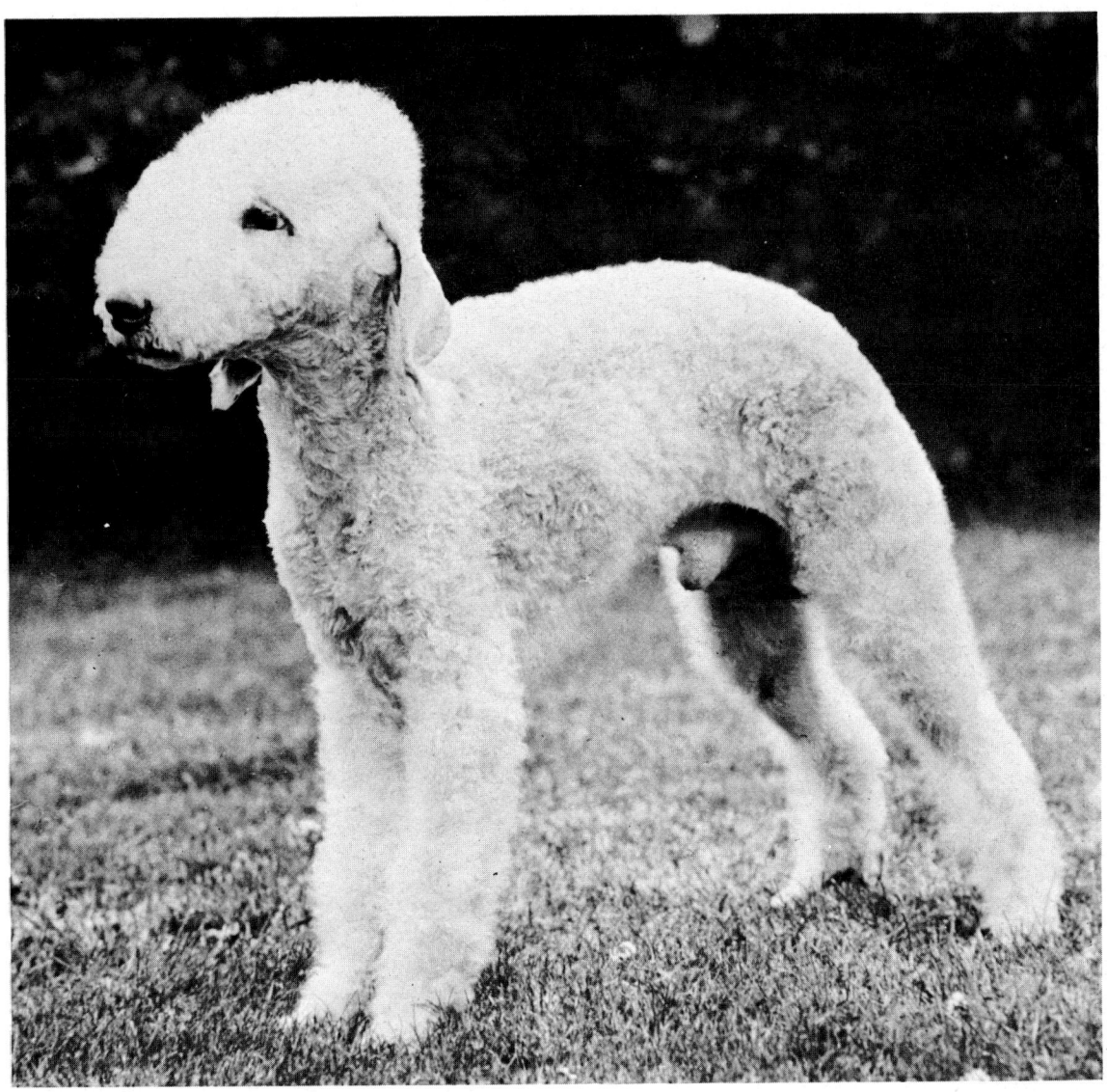

A mason named Joseph Aynsley can claim the credit for naming this delicate yet gamest of Terriers. It was previously known as the Rothbury Terrier or the Northern Counties Fox Terrier, but in 1825 Aynsley christened it the Bedlington Terrier and the name had a certain ring about it and it stuck. His bitch, called Phoebe came from a friend of his at Alnwick and was mated to a Rothbury dog and they produced the dogs that became the first of the Bedlington Terriers. The North country working man has always been involved in developing new varieties of almost everything and in the Newcastle area he set about producing a dog that

NATIONAL GROUPING		
	Name	Number
KC(GB)	Terrier	3
AKC	Terriers	IV
FCI	Terriers	3

was distinctive, particular to the area, and capable of helping him enjoy himself, and from time to time to assist in feeding the family. He took Aynsley's dog, and by the introduction of other blood, probably the Whippet to give some speed and the Dandie Dinmont to give the coat and the Terrier toughness that that breed has in abundance, he produced the sort of dog he wanted.

He was capable of joining the steelworker on a mornings ratting around the warehouse and factories of his native Northumberland and Durham, and, if the gamekeeper happened not to be on the lookout, would sneak off into the nearby fields and catch a rabbit which would help out the meagre rations of the family. In 1877 the National Bedlington Club was formed in England to further the interest of the breed and put him before the public. In this the club at first failed, and at the Crystal Palace show of 1895, only six dogs were shown which was certainly less than the number exhibited at the first show for the breed held in Bedlington in 1870. Since that time there has been a steady increase as the breed was taken up by fanciers outside its own area who realised the potential of this delightful little dog, that paid so well for care in presentation. It was this preparation, the trimming of the coat particularly, which prevented the breed from becoming very

popular, as there is considerable art in shaping the coat to make the most of the dog. It is more like the work of the sculptor than the dog handler, and the finished product often bears little relationship to the dog underneath. The result is that over the years the less expert have been completely overshadowed by those who could do the job well, and have ceased to exhibit even when they had a good dog. He is a delicate looking, mincing little dog whose appearance completely belies his actual nature, as he is tough, very willing to take part in a scrap at a moments notice, and whilst rarely seeking a fight, is quite capable of looking after himself.

He is hardy, not difficult to raise or feed, takes up very little space, and is quiet and unobtrusive in the house. Like most of the terriers he is very friendly, attaches himself to one particular place and family, and even to one individual. Provided he has enough exercise, hunting around anywhere where there is the smell of small game, he remains a very fit and happy dog.

OFFICIAL STANDARD

General appearance
A graceful, lithe, muscular dog, with no sign of either weakness or coarseness. The whole head should be pear or wedge-shaped, and expression in repose mild and gentle, though not shy or nervous. When roused, the eyes should sparkle and the dog look full of temper and courage. Bedlingtons are capable of galloping at great speed and should have the appearance of being able to do so. This action is very distinctive. Rather mincing, light and springy in the slower paces, could have slight roll when in full stride. When galloping must use the whole body.

Head and skull
Skull narrow, but deep and rounded; covered with profuse silky top-knot which should be nearly white. Jaw long and tapering. There must be no 'stop,' the line from occiput to nose end being straight and unbroken. Well filled up beneath the eye. Close fitting lips, without flew. The nostrils must be large and well-defined. Blues and blue-and-tans must have black noses; livers and sandies must have brown noses.

Eyes
Small, bright and well sunk. The ideal eye has the appearance of being triangular. Blues should have a dark eye; blue-and-tans have lighter eyes with amber lights, and livers and sandies have a light hazel eye.

Ears
Moderate sized, filbert shaped, set on low, and hanging flat to the cheek. They should be covered with short fine hair with a fringe of whiteish silky hair at the tip.

Mouth
Teeth, level or pincer-jawed. The teeth should be large and strong.

Head and skull: narrow, deep and rounded.

Neck
Long tapering neck, deep at the base; there should be no tendency to throatiness. The neck should spring well up from the shoulders, and the head should be carried rather high.

Forequarters
The forelegs should be straight, but wider apart at the chest than at the feet. Pasterns long and slightly sloping without weakness. Shoulders flat and sloping.

Body
Muscular, yet markedly flexible; flat-ribbed and deep through the brisket; well ribbed up. The chest should be deep and fairly broad. The back should be roached and

Neck: long and tapering. Shoulders: flat and sloping.

the loin markedly arched. Muscular galloping quarters which are also fine and graceful.

Hindquarters
Muscular and of moderate length. The hind legs, by reason of the roach back and arched loin, have the appearance of being longer than the forelegs. The hocks should be strong and well let down.

Feet
Long hare feet with thick and well closed up pads.

Tail
Of moderate length, thick at the root, tapering to a point and gracefully curved. Should be set on low, and must

never be carried over the back.

Coat
Very distinctive. Thick and linty, standing well out from the skin, but not wiry. There should be a distinct tendency to twist, particularly on the head and face.

Colour
Blue, blue and tan, liver, or sandy. Darker pigment to be encouraged.

Weight and size
Height should be about 16 inches at the shoulder. This allows of slight variation below in the case of a bitch and above in the case of a dog. Weight should be between 18 and 23 pounds.

Note
Male animals should have two apparently normal testicles fully descended into the scrotum.

AKC VARIATION TO STANDARD
Mouth: lower canines clasp outer surface of upper gum just in front of upper canines. Upper premolars and molars lie outside those of lower jaw. *Eyes:* almond shaped; no tendency to tear or water. Eye rims are black in the blue, and blue and tans, and brown in all other solid colours. *Ears:* triangular with rounded tips. *Feet:* dewclaws should be removed. *Coat:* when in show trim must not exceed 1 inch on body; hair on legs is slightly longer. *Colour:* in bi-colours the tan markings are found on legs, chest, under tail, inside hindquarters and over each eye. The topknots of all adults should be lighter than body colour. Patches of darker hair from injury are not objectionable as these are temporary. *Gait:* must not cross, weave or paddle. *Weight:* 17 to 23 pounds. *Serious Fault:* dogs under 16 inches or over $17\frac{1}{2}$ inches. Bitches under 15 inches or over $16\frac{1}{2}$ inches.

BORDER TERRIER

Some of the smaller Terriers were one of the trappings of fox-hunting. The Wire and Smooth Fox Terriers show this association in their name, but the Terrier that has by tradition been connected with the hunt, is the Border. There is evidence of tough hard-bitten small Terriers in the Border country between England and Scotland back in the 18th century, and it is probable that the Dandie Dinmont and the Bedlington came from these originally. He is said to have acquired his name from the Border Hunt whose master Mr. Jacob Robson did much to make the qualities of these little dogs more widely known. The work that he was required to do, dictated what sort of dog he should be. He had to be long in the leg to follow a horse, though in more sophisticated later years he was supplied with a

NATIONAL GROUPING		
	Name	Number
KC(GB)	Terrier	3
AKC	Terriers	IV
FCI	Terriers	3

saddle bag in which he rode when distances became too long for a small dog. He had to be small enough to go to ground after a fox, and hardy enough to look after himself when he got down an earth and found himself face to face with his quarry. For this purpose he needed an even more powerful jaw than the normal Terrier as he could quite easily find himself facing the much rougher badger. He had to be active, strong and tireless, have endless patience, and the sort of waterproof coat that would enable him to face up to a long day in the pouring rain without wilting, in fact he had to be a very remarkable dog.

It says much for the early breeders that they did in fact produce such a dog. Starting with the old rough Terrier they introduced other blood to develop the qualities that they needed, and by the turn of the century the breed was perfected and fixed. Soon after the First World War their fame began to spread, and enthusiasts in the south of England began to hear of the Terrier shows that were being held in the Border country. These events became so important a part of the northern dog scene that by 1921 a Border Terrier Club was formed and shortly afterwards the breed was recognised by the Kennel Club in England. From that time onwards they were not only taken up by exhibitors, but appeared as working terriers with hunts further south, and their future was assured.

The breed has become quite popular in Britain, and is one of the most generally adopted family pets among the terriers in recent years, many litters being bred purely for the pet market, and show quality puppies becoming very difficult to obtain. He has just begun to appear in the United States of America, and in a few other countries, though there are many places in the world that have not yet begun to appreciate his qualities. On the bench one or two very good specimens have begun to take Groups at major shows, with the result that there is increasing interest in him as a show dog, and registrations are rising.

He makes a very good housedog, being remarkably good with children and somewhat quieter than many of the Terriers. He is a fine guard and very possessive about property. He enjoys being in the company of people, and is never happier than when out for a country walk with the children or enjoying the warmth of the fireside in the evenings.

OFFICIAL STANDARD

Characteristics
The Border Terrier is essentially a working terrier. It should be able to follow a horse and must combine activity with gameness.

Head and skull
Head like that of an otter, moderately broad in skull, with a short strong muzzle; a black nose is preferable but a liver or flesh-coloured one is not a serious fault.

Ears: small v-shaped dropping to cheek.

Head: moderately broad with strong short muzzle.

Eyes
Dark, with keen expression.

Ears
Small, v-shaped, of moderate thickness and dropping forward close to the cheek.

Mouth
Teeth should have a scissor-like grip, with the top teeth slightly in front of the lower, but level mouth is quite acceptable. An undershot or overshot mouth is a major fault and highly undesirable.

Neck
Of moderate length.

Forequarters
Forelegs straight and not too heavy in bone.

Body
Deep and narrow and fairly long; ribs carried well back, but not oversprung, as a terrier should be capable of being spanned by both hands behind the shoulder.

Hindquarters
Racy. Loin strong.

Feet
Small with thick pads.

Coat
Harsh and dense with close undercoat. The skin must be thick.

Colour
Red, wheaten, grizzle and tan or blue and tan.

Weight and size
Weight: dogs, between 13 to $15\frac{1}{2}$ pounds; bitches, between $11\frac{1}{2}$ to 14 pounds.

Note
Male animals should have two apparently normal testicles fully descended into the scrotum.

Tail
Moderately short and fairly thick at the base, then tapering, set high and carried gaily but not curled over the back.

AKC VARIATION TO STANDARD
Head: plenty of width between eyes and between ears. A slight moderately broad curve at stop rather than a pronounced indentation. *Ears:* should not break above level of skull. *Eyes:* moderate in size. *Neck:* muscular, gradually widening into shoulder. *Hindquarters:* thighs long and nicely moulded. Stifles well bent and hocks well let down. *Colour:* small amount of white allowed on chest but white feet should be penalised.

BULL TERRIER

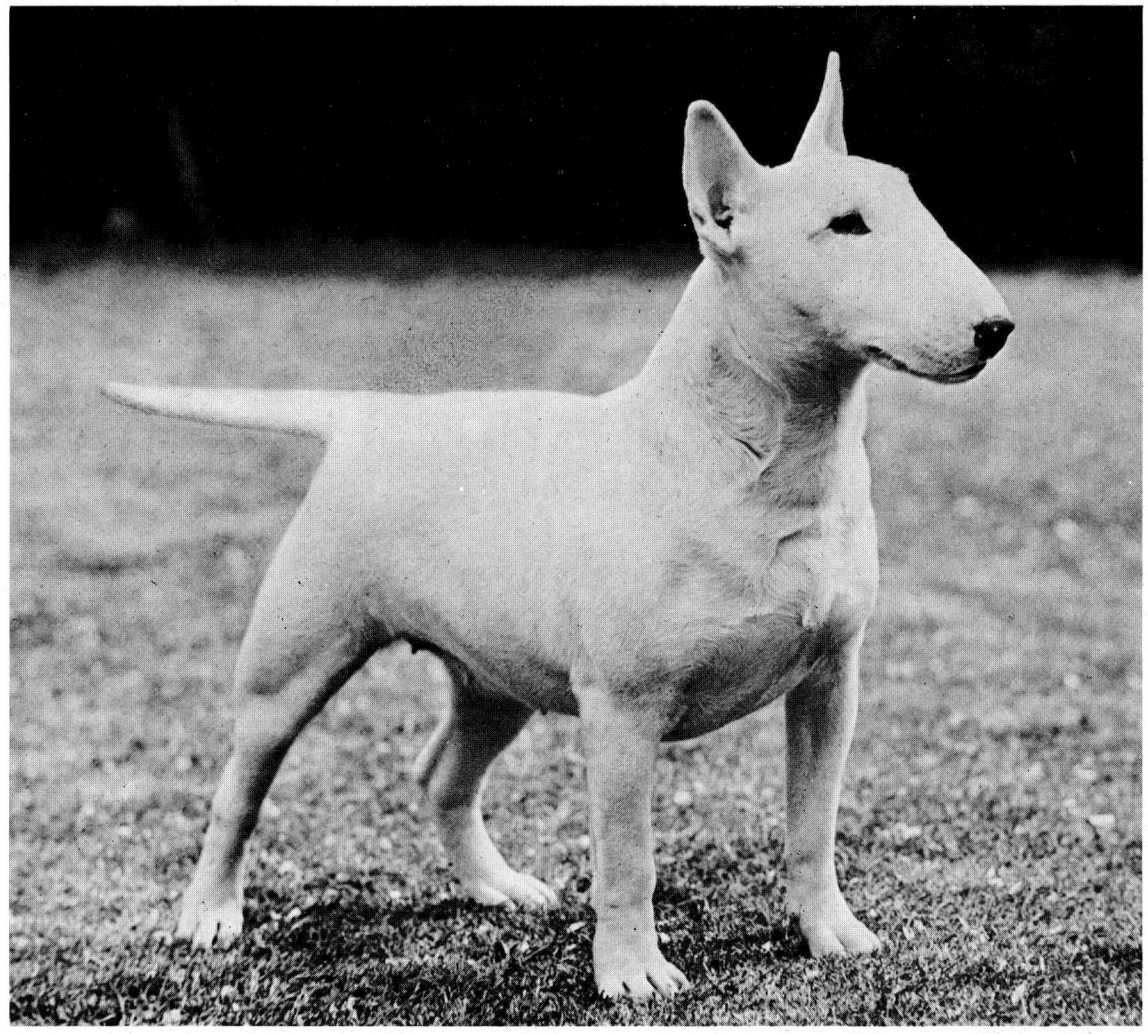

The Bull Terrier is by no means an ancient breed, though he is descended from the earliest Terriers in Britain and the now extinct Old English White Terrier. By a process of evolution, selective breeding and crossing with other breeds, notably the Bulldog, the Staffordshire Bull Terrier was produced, and around the middle of the 19th century, James Hinks, a well known dog dealer of Birmingham perfected a strain of pure white Bull Terriers based on these early dogs. He was originally nothing of the aristocrat that he is today, being essentially connected with ratting and fighting, and considered to be the associate of low fellows. He was bred and trained to fight, and

NATIONAL GROUPING		
	Name	Number
KC(GB)	Terrier	3
AKC	Terriers	IV
FCI	Terriers	3

contests took place on which considerable sums of money were wagered.

Mr. Hinks's strain of pure whites lifted the Bull Terrier out of his somewhat murky surroundings, and placed him alongside all the other pedigree dogs on the show bench. He became a popular dog with fashionable young men, and the all-white strain swept the board at shows in the 1860s. One of Mr. Hinks's better known bitches, Puss, was challenged by some of the adherents of the old type who maintained that in breeding for the show bench he had lost the fighting qualities of the breed. Mr. Hinks accepted the challenge, and backed his bitch against one of the old bull-faced types for a five pound note and a case of champagne. The fight took place at Tuppers in Long Acre, and Puss had killed her opponent in half an hour, and was so little injured herself that she took an award on the following morning at a dog show.

After this time the long-faced type became popular, and the more graceful dog with less of a pugilistic look about him, longer and straighter legs and the longer muzzle, completely ousted the older type. In recent years a good deal of attention has been paid to head qualities, the eyes have become smaller, the stop non-existent, and the whole head now has a filled in oval appearance from any aspect, being compared to an egg or a rugby football. Not only have his associates become more gentlemanly, but he himself has ceased to look a rough sort of dog. He is now refined, both in appearance and nature, though he is still capable of looking after himself. Whilst he will rarely pick a fight, he will never back away from one, and will generally continue the contest until either he or his opponent is exhausted. As he is usually a very fit strong dog, that can take a long time.

He has become one of the top show dogs of the world, winning major awards at all the large shows, on both sides of the Atlantic, in South Africa and Australia. He is noted in the ring for his gladiatorial attitude to competition, standing four square, scorning the opposition, and demanding that he should be not only looked at but considered seriously as the potential winner, which, should he escape from his lead he would undoubtedly be. He is, however, the kindest of dogs with people, even soft and affectionate, especially with children with whom he seems to have a particular rapport. Naturally enough he makes a magnificent guard, as he is completely fearless, and will tackle anything or anyone that he feels is threatening the property which he believes is his responsibility.

OFFICIAL STANDARD

General appearance
The Bull Terrier is the Gladiator of the canine race and must be strongly built, muscular, symmetrical and active, with a keen, determined and intelligent expression, full of fire and courageous but of even temperament and amenable to discipline. Irrespective of size, dogs should look masculine, and bitches feminine. Male animals should have two apparently normal testicles fully descended into the scrotum. The moving dog shall appear well-knit, smoothly covering the ground with free easy strides and with a typical jaunty air. Fore and hind legs should move parallel each to each when viewed from front or behind, the forelegs reaching out well and the hindlegs moving smoothly at the hip and flexing well at the stifle and hock with great thrust.

Head
The head should be long, strong and deep, right to the end of the muzzle, but not coarse. Viewed from the front it should be egg-shaped and completely filled, its surface being free from hollows or indentations. The top of the skull should be almost flat from ear to ear. The profile should curve gently downwards from the top of the skull to the tip of the nose, which should be black and bent downwards at the tip. The nostrils should be well developed. The underjaw should be strong.

Eyes
The eyes should appear narrow, obliquely placed, and triangular, well sunken, black, or as dark brown as possible, so as to appear almost black, and with a piercing glint. The distance from the tip of the nose to the eyes should be perceptibly greater than that from the eyes to the top of the skull.

Head: long, strong and deep but not coarse.

Ears
The ears should be small, thin and placed close together. The dog should be able to hold them stiffly erect, when they should point straight upwards.

Mouth
The teeth should be sound, clean, strong, of good size and perfectly regular. The upper front teeth should fit in front of and closely against the lower front teeth. The lips should be clean and tight.

Neck
The neck should be very muscular, long, arched, tapering from the shoulders to the head, and free from loose skin.

Forequarters

The shoulders should be strong and muscular but without loading. The shoulder blades should be wide, flat and attached closely to the chest wall, and should have a very pronounced backward slope of the front edge from bottom to top. The forelegs should have the strongest type of round quality bone and the dog should stand solidly upon them; they should be moderately long and perfectly parallel. The elbows should be held straight and the strong pasterns upright.

Body

The body should be well rounded with marked spring of rib, and great depth from withers to brisket, so that the latter is nearer the ground than the belly. The back should be short and strong with the top line level behind the withers and arching or roaching slightly over the loin. The underline from brisket to belly should form a graceful upward curve. The chest should be broad viewed from in front.

Hindquarters

The hind legs should be in parallel viewed from behind. The thighs must be muscular and the second thigh well developed. The stifle joint should be well bent and the hock well angulated, with the bone to the foot short and strong.

Feet

The feet should be round and compact with well arched toes.

Tail

The tail should be short, set on low, it should be carried horizontally. Thick at the root it should taper to a fine point.

Coat

The coat should be short, flat, even and harsh to the touch, with a fine gloss. The skin should fit the dog tightly.

Body: well-rounded, marked spring of rib.

Colour

For white, pure white coat. Skin pigmentation and markings on the head should not be penalised. For coloured, the colour should predominate; all other things equal, brindle to be preferred.

Weight and size

There are neither weight nor height limits but there should be the impression of the maximum of substance to the size of the dog.

Faults

Any departure from the foregoing points should be considered a fault and the seriousness of the fault should be in exact proportion to its degree.

Note

Under Kennel Club Show Regulations deafness is a disqualification.

AKC VARIATION TO STANDARD

Mouth: scissors bite. *Ears:* near together, high up on head. *Colour:* the coloured Bull Terrier is recognised as a separate variety. *Disqualifications:* blue eyes. In coloured class—any dog that is predominantly white.

BULL TERRIER (MINIATURE)

Everything that one can say about the Bull Terrier holds good for the Miniature Bull Terrier, as he is virtually the same breed. He has escaped the problems that are usually associated with miniaturisation, as there have always been many smaller Bull Terriers occurring in litters of the larger dog. This appears to be one of the peculiarities of the Bull breeds; the same thing happens in Bulldogs, where the weight differential has from time to time been as much as forty pounds. To produce the Miniature Bull Terrier all that has been necessary is to select the smaller Bull Terriers and to breed from them. This is not to say that the breed is a recent development, as many exhibitors, taking advantage of the standard which allowed weights between fifteen and fifty pounds at the beginning of this century, bred and continued to show

NATIONAL GROUPING		
	Name	Number
KC(GB)	Terrier	3
AKC	—	—
FCI	Terrier	3

the smallest specimens. They were often scheduled by size, and divided into the smaller and the larger dogs at shows and at the Islington Show of 1863 there were even classes for dogs under ten pounds.

They are now recognised as a separate variety, and although until recently interbreeding was permitted, that will shortly cease. These small but quite typical Bull Terriers will then exist as a breed in their own right throughout the world as they do in Britain.

OFFICIAL STANDARD

General appearance

The Bull Terrier is the Gladiator of the canine race and must be strongly built, muscular, symmetrical and active, with a keen, determined and intelligent expression, full of fire and courageous but of even temperament and amenable to discipline. Irrespective of size, dogs should look masculine, and bitches feminine. Male animals should have two apparently normal testicles fully descended into the scrotum. The moving dog shall appear well-knit, smoothly covering the ground with free easy strides and with a typical jaunty air. Fore and hind legs should move parallel each to each when viewed from in front or behind, the forelegs reaching out well and the hindlegs moving smoothly at the hip and flexing well at the stifle and hock with great thrust.

Head

The head should be long, strong and deep, right to the end of the muzzle, but not coarse. Viewed from the front it should be egg-shaped and completely filled, its surface being free from hollows or indentations. The top of the skull should be almost flat from ear to ear. The profile should curve gently downwards from the top of the skull to the tip of the nose, which should be black and bent downwards at the tip. The nostrils should be well developed. The underjaw should be strong.

Eyes

The eyes should appear narrow, obliquely placed, and triangular, well sunken, black, or as dark brown as possible, so as to appear almost black, and with a piercing glint. The distance from the tip of the nose to the eyes should be perceptibly greater than that from the eyes to the top of the skull.

Ears

The ears should be small, thin and placed close together. The dog should be able to hold them stiffly erect, when they should point straight upwards.

Mouth

The teeth should be sound, clean, strong, of good size and perfectly regular. The upper front teeth should fit in front of and closely against the lower front teeth. The lips should be clean and tight.

Neck

The neck should be very muscular, long, arched, tapering from the shoulders to the head, and free from loose skin.

Forequarters

The shoulders should be strong and muscular but without loading. The shoulder blades should be wide, flat and attached closely to the chest wall, and should have a very pronounced backward slope of the front edge from bottom to top. The forelegs should have the strongest type of round quality bone and the dog should stand solidly upon them; they should be moderately long and perfectly parallel. The elbows should be held straight and the strong pasterns upright.

Body

The body should be well rounded with marked spring of rib, and great depth from withers to brisket, so that the latter is nearer the ground than the belly. The back should be short and strong with the top line level behind the withers and arching or roaching slightly over the loin. The underline from brisket to belly should form a graceful upward curve. The chest should be broad viewed from in front.

Hindquarters

The hind legs should be in parallel viewed from behind. The thighs must be muscular and the second thigh well developed. The stifle joint should be well bent and the hock well angulated, with the bone to the foot short and strong.

Feet

The feet should be round and compact with well arched toes.

Tail

The tail should be short, set on low, it should be carried horizontally. Thick at the root it should taper to a fine point.

Coat

The coat should be short, flat, even and harsh to the touch, with a fine gloss. The skin should fit the dog tightly.

Colour

For white, pure white coat. Skin pigmentation and markings on the head should not be penalised. For coloured, the colour should predominate; all other things equal, brindle to be preferred.

Weight and size

Height should be not more than 14 inches. Weight should be not more than 20 pounds.

Faults

Any departure from the foregoing points should be considered a fault and the seriousness of the fault should be in exact proportion to its degree.

Note

Under Kennel Club Show Regulations deafness is a disqualification.

AKC VARIATION TO STANDARD
This dog is not granted championship status by the AKC.

CAIRN TERRIER

Although the Cairn Terrier has only existed as a show dog since the beginning of this century, and before that no book concerned with the exhibition of dogs even gives them a mention, there is no doubt at all that they existed as a separate breed many years before that time. The breed was developed on the Island of Skye, and this led to confusion with the Skye Terrier which became the show dog associated with that island and somewhat overshadowed his less glamorous cousin.

The Cairn was essentially a working dog, used to

NATIONAL GROUPING		
	Name	Number
KC(GB)	Terrier	3
AKC	Terriers	IV
FCI	Terriers	3

bolt foxes and otters from among the rocks, and it is from this skill that he draws his name. He was probably at that time not the standardised dog that he is today, but existed in different forms in different parts of Scotland as each breeder exercised his own choice of type and colour. He would, however, even in those days be a sturdy, hard-coated active dog with the temperament that was needed for him to face up to some fairly strong adversaries.

On its formation the Cairn Terrier Club of England had as its object the maintenance of the old working type of dog, an ambition that it shared with the Cairn Terrier Club of the United States of America. They have adopted the same standard and the same size of dog as the ideal, and in that the modern Cairn is still a hardy tough active dog, they have succeeded in their object.

He was first exhibited in Britain at the Inverness Show in 1909 by Mrs. Alastair Campbell and was described as a short-haired Skye Terrier. The colours varied from those that we know today, to black, but they were similar to the modern Terrier. They were unrecognised by the Kennel Club and the established Skye Terrier exhibitors raised considerable objection both to the dogs and to their name but by 1912 challenge certificates were on offer and the breed became recognised by the Kennel Club. Since that time the dog has become one of the most popular of the Terriers, second in registration numbers only to the West Highland White, and the Cairn Terrier Club is still looking after his interests, holding shows and very jealously maintaining the original type.

He differs physically from the other Terriers in a number of ways. His head is shorter and broader than most and his great activity demands that whilst he remains a short-legged Terrier to enable him to go to ground, he must be longer in the leg than say the modern Scottish Terrier. He is shown in the rough, in that he looks natural, though this is deceptive, as a great deal of skilful work goes into reducing what would otherwise be a very ragged dog indeed into something looking fairly smart in a very natural sort of way. His coat is one of his characteristics, as it is hard, double and weather-resistant with the typical somewhat softer hair on the skull.

He is popular with the public as a show dog who see in him their idea of a natural Terrier very much more appealing than some of the other Terrier breeds which some people look on as being overdressed. He is a great little sport, loves hunting, and is happy to spend the whole day out in the country just ferreting around. He does, however, make an excellent house dog as he is friendly, has no vices, and is a very good guard.

OFFICIAL STANDARD

Characteristics
This terrier should impress with his fearless and gay disposition.

Ears: small, pointed, erect, not too close.

General appearance
Active, game, hardy, and 'shaggy' in appearance; strong, though compactly built. Should stand well forward on forepaws. Strong quarters, deep in ribs. Very free in movement. Coat hard enough to resist rain. Head small, but in proportion to body, a general foxy appearance is the chief characteristic of this working terrier.

Head and skull
Skull broad in proportion; strong, but not too long or heavy jaw. A decided indentation between eyes; hair should be full on forehead. Muzzle powerful but not heavy. Very strong jaw, which should be neither undershot nor overshot.

Eyes
Set wide apart; medium in size; dark hazel, rather sunk, with shaggy eyebrows.

Ears
Small, pointed, well carried and erect, but not too closely set.

Mouth
Large teeth. Jaw strong and level.

Neck
Well set on, but not short.

Forequarters
Sloping shoulder and a medium length of leg; good, but not too large, bone. Forelegs should not be out at elbow.

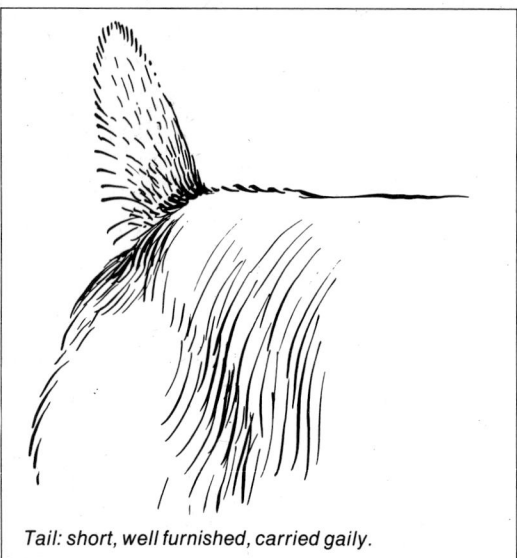
Tail: short, well furnished, carried gaily.

Note
Male animals should have two apparently normal testicles fully descended into the scrotum.

Legs must be covered with hard hair.

Body
Compact, straight back; well sprung deep ribs; strong sinews. Back medium in length and well-coupled.

Hindquarters
Very strong.

Feet
Forefeet, larger than hind, may be slightly turned out. Pads should be thick and strong. Thin and ferrety feet are objectionable.

Tail
Short, well furnished with hair, but not feathery; carried gaily, but should not turn down towards back.

Coat
Very important. Must be double-coated, with profuse, hard, but not coarse, outer coat, and undercoat which resembles fur, and is short, soft and close. Open coats are objectionable. Head should be well furnished.

Colour
Red, sandy, grey, brindled, or nearly black. Dark points such as ears and muzzle, very typical.

Weight and size
Ideal weight, 14 pounds.

Faults
Muzzle: undershot or overshot. *Eyes:* too prominent or too light. *Ears:* too large or round at points; they must not be heavily coated with hair. *Coat:* silkiness or curliness objectionable; a slight wave permissible. *Nose:* flesh or light coloured, most objectionable. In order to keep this breed to the best old working type, any resemblance to a Scottish Terrier will be considered objectionable.

AKC VARIATION TO STANDARD
Weight and size: dogs 14 pounds; bitches 13 pounds. Height at withers dogs 10 inches; bitches $9\frac{1}{2}$ inches. Length of body from $14\frac{1}{4}$ to 15 inches from front of chest to back of hindquarters. *Faults:* too narrow in skull. Too long and heavy foreface. Too short back and compact body, hampering quickness of movement and turning ability. Tail set on too low. Back not level. Open coats, blowsy coats, too short or dead coats, lack of sufficient undercoat; lack of head furnishings; lack of hard hair on legs. Silkiness or curliness. Slight wave permissible. White on chest, feet or other parts of the body.

DANDIE DINMONT TERRIER

This very distinctive little dog, with his individual outline, somewhat strange coat and soulful eyes, is one of the older breeds of Terrier. He first appeared in about 1700 and was probably bred from the rough native Terriers of the Border country by selective breeding. He was used for the hunting of the badger and the otter as well as the fox, and no-one should be misled by his large soulful eyes, as he is one of the fiercest of all the Terriers when he is roused. He was popularised, and indeed named by Sir Walter Scott, who, in his travels is said to have encountered Mr. James Davidson of Hawick with his dogs, and immediately made him the hero of his story called Guy

NATIONAL GROUPING		
	Name	Number
KC(GB)	Terrier	3
AKC	Terriers	IV
FCI	Terriers	3

Mannering published in 1814. The name of Scott's character in the novel, 'Dandie Dinmont' was seized upon as the name for the dog.

It is recorded that a letter existed at one time in the handwriting of James Davidson concerning his dogs in which he said 'Tarr, reddish and wire-haired, a bitch; Pepper, shaggy and light, from Dr. Brown, of Borjenwood. The race of Dandies are all bred from the two last.' If authentic, and there is no reason to suppose that it is not, we know from this letter the actual names of the two dogs from which the whole race of Dandie Dinmont Terriers descended. Since those early days of popularity the breed has never quite captured the public fancy which has meant that he has never become too numerous. This suits the enthusiasts who feel that by keeping it in the hands of a smaller number of people who are dedicated to retaining the original qualities and characteristics, the breed will not degenerate. His numbers in Britain remain fairly steady, though they are on the increase in Europe where quite large numbers of them are seen at the major shows.

He is no longer used for working, but has retained the working characteristics and temperament. He is not easily roused, but when he is he is completely fearless and will tackle anything, which makes him an excellent guard of property. He is stronger than his somewhat attenuated figure would suggest, extremely hardy and virtually impervious to adverse weather conditions. He has a rough double coat which looks a little sparse at times, and he boasts two colours only, called pepper and mustard, which describes the main part of the coat, but which in each instance is high-lighted by lighter points and topknot. His coat needs regular care and frequent plucking to improve the colour as otherwise it grows long and has a faded appearance.

He is intelligent, fond of children and makes an excellent guard and housedog. He is not the most obedient of dogs, having a will of his own and at times will go about his own business in a rather superior manner. As a show dog he is excellent, though he does not always appreciate the close attention of another dog and will react somewhat violently. He is on the whole, however, quiet and obedient in the ring, and whilst he rarely manages to gain major awards, is always popular with the spectators, largely because of his rather quaint appearance.

OFFICIAL STANDARD

Head and skull
Head strongly made and large, not out of proportion to the dog's size, the muscles showing extraordinary development, more especially the maxillary. Skull broad between the ears, getting gradually less towards the eye, and measuring about the same from the inner corner of the eye to back of skull as it does from ear to ear. The forehead well domed. The head is covered with very soft silky hair, which should not be confined to a mere top-knot, and the lighter in colour and silkier it is the better. The cheeks, starting from the ears proportionately with the skull, have a gradual taper towards the muzzle, which is deep and strongly made, and measures about three inches in length, or in proportion to skull as three is to five. The muzzle is covered with hair of a little darker shade than top-knot, and of the same texture as the feather of the forelegs. The top of the muzzle is generally bare for about an inch from the back of the nose, the bareness coming to a point towards the eye, and being about one inch broad at the nose. The nose black.

Eyes
Set wide apart, large, full, round but not protruding, bright, expressive of great determination, intelligence, and dignity, set low and prominent in front of the head, colour, a rich dark hazel.

Ears
Pendulous, set well back wide apart, and low on the skull, hanging close to the cheek, with a very slight projection at the base, broad at the junction of the head and tapering almost to a point, the forepart of the ear coming almost straight down from its junction with the head to the tip. They shall harmonise in colour with the body colour. In the case of a pepper dog they are covered with a soft, straight, dark hair (in some cases almost black). In the case of a mustard dog, the hair should be mustard in colour, a shade darker than the body, but not black. All should have a thin feather of light hair starting about two inches from the tip, and of nearly the same colour and texture as the top-knot, which gives the ear the appearance of a distinct point. The animal is often one or two years old before the feather is shown. The cartilage and skin of the ear should not be thick, but very thin. Length of ear, from three to four inches.

Mouth
The inside of the mouth should be black or dark coloured. The teeth very strong, especially the canine, which are of extraordinary size for such a small dog. The canines fit well into each other, so as to give the greatest available holding and punishing power, and the teeth are level in front, the upper ones very slightly overlapping the under ones. Undershot or overshot mouths are equally objectionable.

Neck
Very muscular, well developed, and strong, showing great power of resistance, being well set into the shoulders.

Head and skull: large, skull broad, forehead domed.

Forequarters: forelegs short, strong, straight.

Forequarters
The forelegs short, with immense muscular development and bone, set wide apart and chest, coming well down between them. Bandy legs are objectionable. The hair on the forelegs of a pepper dog should be tan, varying according to the body colour from a rich tan to a pale fawn; of a mustard dog they are of a darker shade than its head, which is a creamy white. In both colours there is a nice feather about two inches long, rather lighter in colour than the hair on the fore part of the leg.

Body: long, low at shoulders, arch over loin.

Body

Long, strong, and flexible; ribs well sprung and round, chest well developed and let well down between the fore-legs; the back rather low at the shoulders having a slight downward curve and a corresponding arch over the loins, with a very slight gradual drop from top of loin to root of tail; both sides of backbone well supplied with muscle.

Hindquarters

The hind legs are a little longer than the fore ones, and are set rather wide apart, but not spread out in an un-natural manner; the thighs are well developed, and the hair of the same colour and texture as the fore ones, but having no feather or dew claws.

Feet

Flat feet are objectionable. The whole claws should be dark, but the claws of all vary in shade according to the colour of the dog's body. The feet of a pepper dog should be tan, varying accordingly to the body colour from a rich tan to a pale fawn; of a mustard dog they are a darker shade than its head. Hind feet should be much smaller than the fore feet.

Tail

Rather short, say from eight to ten inches, and covered on the upper side with wiry hair of a darker colour than that of the body, the hair on the under side being lighter in colour, and not so wiry, with a nice feather about two inches long, getting shorter as it nears the tip; rather thick at the root, getting thicker for about four inches, then tapering off to a point. It should not be twisted or curled in any way, but should come up with a curve like a scimitar, the tip, when excited, being in a perpendicular line with the root of the tail. It should neither be set too high nor too low. When not excited it is carried gaily, and a little above the level of the body.

Coat

This is a very important point. The hair should be about two inches long; that from the skull to root of tail a mixture of hardish and soft hair, which gives a sort of crisp feel to the hand. The hard should not be wiry; the coat is what is termed pily or pencilled. The hair on the under part of the body is lighter in colour and softer than that on the top. The skin on the belly accords with the colour of the dog.

Colour

The colour is pepper or mustard. The pepper ranges from a dark bluish black to a light silvery grey, the intermediate shades being preferred, the body colour coming well down the shoulder and hips, gradually merging into the leg colour. The mustards vary from a reddish brown to a pale fawn, the head being a creamy white, the legs and feet of a shade darker than the head. The claws are dark as in other colours. (Nearly all Dandie Dinmont Terriers have some white on the chest, and some have white claws.) White feet are objectionable.

Weight and size

The height should be from eight to eleven inches at the top of shoulder. Length from top of shoulder to root of tail should not be more than twice the dog's height, but, preferably, one or two inches less. The ideal weight as near eighteen pounds as possible. This weight is for dogs in good working order.

Note

Male animals should have two apparently normal testicles fully descended into the scrotum.

AKC VARIATION TO STANDARD
Weight: 18 to 24 pounds.

SMOOTH FOX TERRIER

Few breeds of dog have retained their popularity as the Smooth Fox Terrier has. He was known at the beginning of the 19th century, and was popular before dog shows started. Arthur Wardle depicted the famous 'Totteridge Eleven' at the start of this century, and they are still being shown in fairly large numbers to this day. He has become one of the most widely known of all British dogs, and invariably when thinking about Terriers, and British Terriers in particular, most people think of one or other of the two Fox Terriers. He started life as the old English Terrier, the sort of dog mentioned by Dame Juliana Berners in 1486, and a century later by Dr. Caius when he speaks of 'Another sorte there is which hunteth the Fox and the Badger or Greye onely, whom we call Terrars'. This is the same sort of basic Terrier depicted in a Reinagle engraving in The Sportsman's Repository of 1820, though in that instance they are a slightly rougher type.

NATIONAL GROUPING		
	Name	Number
KC(GB)	Terrier	3
AKC	Terriers	IV
FCI	Terriers	3

The modern Smooth Fox Terrier starts from about 1860 from which time pedigrees can be traced, and with the advent of the Fox Terrier Club in 1876 and the care that was taken in the compiling of the stud books, the history of the breed since that time is clear. One of the first dogs of note was Old Jock who was first shown in 1862 at Birmingham and for the last time at Crystal Palace·in 1870. He was said to have been a smart, well-balanced Terrier, with perhaps too much daylight under him and wanting something in jaw power, but at least he was away from the Bull

Terrier type. Some idea of the value placed on these early dogs is shown by the fact that when Mr. Burbidge's kennel was sold in 1892, the dogs fetched up to £135 each, which was a vast sum of money in those days. That the breed has changed very little is shown by the fact that the standard devised by the Fox Terrier Club in the very early days, holds good today except for the question of size which has been reduced from twenty to eighteen pounds.

It would be a very bold enthusiast for the modern Smooth Fox Terrier who would claim that today's show dog would go to ground and work as his ancestors did, even though he retains all the old fire and hunting instinct. He has come a long way in appearance since the days of the Rev. John Russell and his stocky shorter-legged dogs. He is now a beautifully balanced little dog with a symmetrical outline, great refinement of head and a dignified movement, all qualities that make him a very popular show dog. His neat ears, straight bone and mostly all-white colour with interesting markings make him most attractive to look at in the ring, and the manner in which he sets off his fellow Terriers and appears to sparkle underlines the fact that he is still very much the Terrier. Although he was historically first in the ring, he has never quite attained the popularity numerically of his wire-coated brother, which is probably due to the fact that so many people have always associated the word 'terrier' with a dog that has a rough coat.

He is a dog of great charm, friendly, as most of the Terriers are, a pleasant companion with a love of exercise, never lazy, always ready for a game whether it is just a romp on the lawn or a more serious go at the local rabbits. He is clean and mannerly in the house, quiet except when he feels that intrusion of some sort is imminent, when he becomes one of the best guards.

OFFICIAL STANDARD

General appearance
The dog must present a general gay, lively, and active appearance; bone and strength in a small compass are essentials, but this must not be taken to mean that a Fox Terrier should be cloggy, or in any way coarse, speed and endurance must be looked to as well as power, and the symmetry of the Foxhound taken as a model. The Terrier, like the Hound, must on no account be leggy, nor must he be too short in the leg. He should stand like a cleverly made Hunter, covering a lot of ground, yet with a short back. He will then attain the highest degree of propelling power, together with the greatest length of stride that is compatible with the length of his body.

Head and skull
The skull should be flat and moderately narrow, and gradually decreasing in width to the eyes. Not much 'stop' should be apparent, but there should be more dip in the profile between the forehead and the top jaw than is seen in the case of the Greyhound. The cheeks must not be full. The jaw, upper and under, should be strong and muscular, should be of fair punishing strength, but not so in any way to resemble the Greyhound. There

Head:
not much stop, skull flat, tapering jaw, strong.

should not be much falling away below the eyes. This part of the head should, however, be moderately chiselled out, so as not to go down in a straight line like a wedge. The nose, towards which the muzzle must gradually taper, should be black.

Eyes
Should be dark in colour, small and rather deep set,

full of fire, life, and intelligence; as nearly as possible circular in shape.

Ears
Should be V-shaped and small, of moderate thickness, and dropping forward close to the cheek, not hanging by the side of the head like a Foxhound's.

Mouth
The teeth should be nearly as possible level, i.e. the upper teeth on the outside of the lower teeth.

Neck
Should be clean and muscular, without throatiness, of fair lengths, and gradually widening to the shoulders.

Forequarters
The shoulders should be long and sloping, well laid back, fine at the points, and clearly cut at the withers.

Body: chest deep, back short, loin powerful.

Body
Chest deep and not too broad. Back should be short, straight and strong, with no appearance of slackness. Loin should be powerful and very slightly arched. The fore ribs should be moderately arched, the back ribs deep; and the dog should be well ribbed up.

Hindquarters
Should be strong and muscular, quite free from droop or crouch; the thighs long and powerful; hocks near the ground, the dog standing well up on them like a Foxhound, and not straight in stifle.

Feet
Should be round, compact and not large. The soles hard and tough. The toes moderately arched, and turned neither in nor out.

Tail
Should be set on rather high, and carried gaily, but not over the back nor curled. It should be of good strength.

Coat
Should be straight, flat, smooth, hard, dense and abundant. The belly and under side of the thighs should not be bare.

Colour
White should predominate; brindle, red or liver markings are objectionable. Otherwise this point is of little or no importance.

Weight and size
Weight is not a certain criterion of a Terrier's fitness for his work—general shape, size and contour are the main points—and if a dog can gallop and stay, and follow his fox up a drain, it matters little what his weight is to a pound or so, though, roughly speaking, 15 to 17 pounds for a bitch and 16 to 18 pounds for a dog in Show condition are appropriate weights.

Faults
Nose, white, cherry, or spotted to a considerable extent with either of these colours. Ears, prick, tulip or rose. Mouth, much undershot or much overshot.

Note
Male animals should have two apparently normal testicles fully descended into the scrotum.

AKC VARIATION TO STANDARD
The AKC has one standard for both varieties, and that corresponds most directly to the KC standard for the Wire-haired variety. *Ears:* top line of folded ear should be well above level of skull. *Eyes:* dark rims. *Forelegs:* viewed from any direction they must be straight with bone strong right down to feet showing little or no appearance of ankle in front, and being short and straight in pasterns. *Weight and size:* according to present-day requirements, a full-sized well-balanced dog should not exceed $15\frac{1}{2}$ inches at withers; length of back from withers to root of tail should not exceed 12 inches; the head should not exceed $7\frac{1}{4}$ inches or be less than 7 inches. Bitches proportionately smaller. Dogs 18 pounds; bitches 2 pound less—with a margin of 1 pound either way.

WIRE FOX TERRIER

The original basic stock from which both the Smooth Fox Terrier and the Wire Fox Terrier descended was probably what one might call half-coated. He was neither rough nor smooth, and old paintings and engravings endorse this opinion. The Terriers in the Sportsman's Repository of 1820 are neither rough nor smooth, and a contemporary model of one of the dogs belonging to the Rev. John Russell, at present in the possession of the Kennel Club in London, shows a Terrier with a somewhat mixed coat, fairly short in places but with a certain amount of feathering and roughness around the neck and shoulders. It is generally accepted that the old black and tan, Wire-

NATIONAL GROUPING		
	Name	Number
KC(GB)	Terrier	3
AKC	Terriers	IV
FCI	Terriers	3

haired Terrier which was among the earliest terriers in Britain was used to produce the coat of the Wire Fox Terrier. At the same time, there existed the old English White Terrier which was smooth coated and which probably helped in the evolution of the Smooth Fox Terrier. It was probably by the judicious crossing of the two types that the white colour of the one and the hard coat of the other were retained.

In the early days of the breed there was considerable crossing between the smooth and wire-haired variety. This was probably with the intention of improving both, but certainly as far as the Wire is concerned, it was with the intention of retaining the large proportion of white as this was fashionable. It was also felt that the Smooth had the neater and smarter head, smaller ears and a better outline. There was also a determined effort at one time to reduce the size of both Terriers, and whilst one succeeded to a certain degree in that a miniature Fox Terrier with a smooth coat was evolved and enjoyed a vogue for a time as a Toy Fox Terrier, the eighteen pound dog is still the accepted version of the breed.

One of the problems with the Wire Fox Terrier is that in order to keep him looking neat and smart, his coat needs constant attention, having to be plucked and trimmed regularly, and from time to time taken right down so that the new coat will grow strong and hard. This has led to the breed being very much the province of the professional handler as far as showing is concerned, and the number of dogs shown by their owners is now very much in the minority. Even many of those that are handled in the ring by their proud proprietors are prepared professionally. The result is a very high degree of presentation in the breed, and any dog that enters the ring in a state of unpreparedness, has little chance of success. This has caused the criticism that the breed is artificial and wooden, and that it has lost its terrier character, but nothing could be further from the truth. The Wire Fox Terrier is still every bit as much a devil as he always was, full of fun and fire, always ready to have a go at anything, however large, and still one of the real sports of the race. It has also been claimed that the breeding for a long narrow head has resulted in a dog that has no

brains, but this is equally untrue. Accepted into the family and treated as a normal dog, he is as intelligent and responsive as he has always been, even if untrimmed he looks like a floor mop!

There are few breeds that have more consistently reached the top at dog shows all over the world. From America to Britain, from Australia to Scandinavia, he is constantly winning Groups and Best in Show, and these wins are always greeted with thunderous applause as he looks the part of the perfect show dog. His temperament is all Terrier, affectionate with those that he knows, suspicious of those that he does not, sharp, even fierce towards anything or anyone who offends him, but an excellent companion in the house, and a bright cheerful animal to have around.

OFFICIAL STANDARD

Characteristics
The Terrier should be alert, quick of movement, keen of expression, on the tip-toe of expectation at the slightest provocation. Character is imparted by the expression of the eyes and by the carriage of ears and tail.

General appearance
The dog should be balanced and this may be defined as the correct proportions of a certain point or points, when considered in relation to a certain other point or points. It is the keystone of the Terrier's anatomy. The chief points for consideration are the relative proportions of skull and foreface; head and back; height at withers; and length of body from shoulder-point to buttock—the ideal of proportion being reached when the last two measurements are the same. It should be added that, although the head measurements can be taken with

absolute accuracy, the height at withers and length of back are approximate, and are inserted for the information of breeders and exhibitors rather than as a hard-and-fast rule. The movement or action is the crucial test of conformation. The Terrier's legs should be carried straight forward while travelling, the forelegs hanging perpendicular and swinging parallel to the sides, like the pendulum of a clock. The principal propulsive power is furnished by the hind legs, perfection of action being found in the Terrier possessing long thighs and muscular second-thighs well bent at the stifles, which admit of a strong forward thrust or 'snatch' of the hocks. When approaching the forelegs should form a continuation of the straight of the front, the feet being the same distance apart as the elbows. When stationary it is often difficult to determine whether a dog is slightly out at shoulder but directly he moves the defect—if it exists—becomes more apparent, the fore-feet having a tendency to cross, 'weave' or 'dish'. When, on the contrary, the dog is tied at the shoulder, the tendency of the feet is to move wider apart, with a sort of padding action. When the hocks are turned in—cow hocks—the stifles and feet are turned outwards, resulting in a serious loss of propulsive power. When the hocks are turned outwards the tendency of the hind feet is to cross, resulting in an ungainly waddle.

Head and skull
The top line of the skull should be almost flat, sloping slightly and gradually decreasing in width towards the eyes. In a well-balanced head there should be little apparent difference in length between skull and foreface.

Head and skull: balanced, skull flat, well-developed jaw.

If, however, the foreface is noticeably shorter, it amounts to a fault, the head looking weak and 'unfinished'. On the other hand, when the eyes are set too high up in the skull, and too near the ears, it also amounts to a fault, the head being said to have a 'foreign appearance'. Although the foreface should gradually taper from eye to muzzle and should dip slightly at its juncture with the forehead, it should not 'dish' or fall away quickly below the eyes, where it should be full and well made up, but relieved from 'wedginess' by a little delicate chiselling. While well-developed jaw bones, armed with a set of strong white teeth, impart that appearance of strength to the foreface which is desirable. An excessive bony or muscular development of the jaws is both unnecessary and unsightly, as it is partly responsible for the full and rounded contour of the cheeks to which the term 'cheeky' is applied. Nose should be black.

Eyes
Should be dark in colour, moderately small and not prominent, full of fire, life, and intelligence; as nearly as possible, circular in shape and not too far apart. Anything approaching a yellow eye is most objectionable.

Ears
Should be small and V-shaped and of moderate thickness, the flaps neatly folded over and drooping forward close to the cheeks. The top line of the folded ear should be well above the level of the skull. A pendulous ear, hanging dead by the side of the head like a hound's is uncharacteristic of the Terrier, while an ear which is semi-erect is still more undesirable.

Mouth
Both upper and lower jaws should be strong and muscular, the teeth as nearly as possible level and capable of closing together like a vice—the lower canines locking in front of the upper and the points of the upper incisors slightly overlapping the lower.

Neck
Should be clean, muscular, of fair length, free from throatiness and presenting a graceful curve when viewed from the side.

Forequarters
Shoulders when viewed from the front, should slope steeply downwards from their juncture, with the neck towards the points, which should be fine. When viewed from the side they should be long, well laid back, and should slope obliquely backwards from points to withers, which should always be clean cut. A shoulder well laid back gives the long fore-hand, which, in combination with a short back, is so desirable in Terrier or Hunter. Chest deep and not broad, a too narrow chest being almost as undesirable as a very broad one. Excessive depth of chest and brisket is an impediment to a Terrier when going to ground. Viewed from any direction the legs should be straight, the bone of the forelegs strong right down to the feet. The elbows should hang perpendicular to the body, working free of the sides, carried straight through in travelling.

Body
The back should be short and level, with no appearance of slackness—the loins muscular and very slightly arched. The brisket should be deep, the front ribs moderately arched, and the back ribs deep, and well sprung. The term 'slackness' is applied both to the portion of the back immediately behind the withers when it shows any ten-

General appearance: relative proportions important, height and length the same.

dency to dip, and also the flanks when there is too much space between the back-ribs and hip-bone. When there is little space between the ribs and hips, the dog is said to be 'short in couplings', 'short-coupled', or 'well-ribbed up'. A Terrier can scarcely be too short in back, provided he has sufficient length of neck and liberty of movement. The bitch may be slightly longer in couplings than the dog.

Hindquarters

Should be strong and muscular, quite free from droop or crouch; the thighs long and powerful; the stifles well curved and turned neither in nor out; the hock-joints well bent and near the ground; the hocks perfectly upright and parallel with each other when viewed from behind. The worst possible form of hindquarters consists of a short second-thigh and a straight stifle, a combination which causes the hind-legs to act as props rather than instruments of propulsion. The hind-legs should be carried straight through in travelling.

Feet

Should be round, compact, and not large—the pads tough and well cushioned, and the toes moderately arched and turned neither in nor out. A Terrier with good-shaped fore-legs and feet will wear his nails down short by contact with the road surface, the weight of the body being evenly distributed between the toe-pads and the heels.

Tail

Should be set on rather high and carried gaily but not curled. It should be of good strength and substance and of fair length—a three-quarters dock is about right—since it affords the only safe grip when handling working Terriers. A very short tail is suitable neither for work nor show.

Coat

The principal difference between that of the Smooth and Wire variety is that, whereas the former is straight and flat, that of the latter appears to be broken—the hairs having a tendency to twist. The best coats are of a dense, wiry texture—like cocoa-nut matting—the hairs growing so closely and strongly together that when parted with the fingers the skin cannot be seen. At the base of these stiff hairs is a shorter growth of finer and softer hair—termed the under coat. The coat on the sides is never quite so hard as that on the back and quarters. Some of the hardest coats are 'crinkly' or slightly waved, but a curly coat is very objectionable. The hair on the upper and lower jaws should be crisp and only sufficiently long to impart an appearance of strength to the fore-face, thus effectually differentiating them from the Smooth variety. The hair on the fore-legs should also be dense and crisp. The coat should average in length from $\frac{3}{4}$ to 1 inch on shoulders and neck, lengthening to $1\frac{1}{2}$ inches on withers, backs, ribs and quarters. These measurements are given rather as a guide to exhibitors than as an infallible rule, since the length of coat varies in different specimens and seasons. The judge must form his own opinion as to what constitutes a 'sufficient' coat.

Colour

White should predominate: brindle, red, liver, or slaty blue are objectionable. Otherwise, colour is of little or no importance.

Weight and size

Bone and strength in a small compass are essential, but this must not be taken to mean that a Terrier should be 'cloddy', or in any way coarse—speed and endurance being requisite as well as power. The Terrier must on no account be leggy, nor must he be too short on the leg. He should stand like a cleverly-made, short-backed Hunter, covering a lot of ground. According to present-day requirements, a full-sized, well-balanced dog should not exceed $15\frac{1}{2}$ inches at the withers—the bitch being proportionately lower—nor should the length of back from withers to root of tail exceed 12 inches, while to maintain the relative proportions, the head—as before mentioned—should not exceed $7\frac{1}{4}$ inches or be less than 7 inches. A dog with these measurements should scale 18 pounds in show condition—a bitch weighing some 2 pounds less—with a margin of 1 pound either way.

Faults

Nose: white, cherry, or spotted to a considerable extent with either of these colours. Ears: prick, tulip, or rose. Mouth: much undershot or much overshot.

Note

Old scars or injuries, the result of work or accident, should not be allowed to prejudice a Terrier's chance in the show-ring, unless they interfere with its movement or with its utility for work or stud.

Note

Male animals should have two apparently normal testicles fully descended into the scrotum.

IRISH TERRIER

Ireland has produced three or four native Terriers, and they are all very different from anything else that we know in the Group. Whether for size, colour, or even shape, they cannot easily be traced back to either a combination of any of the old established breeds or to any of the basic Terrier types. This is probably due to the relative isolation of the island which resulted in breeds being kept fairly free from dilution from other quarters in the days before transport improved and freedom of movement between Ireland and the mainland became as quick and easy as it is now. Certainly

NATIONAL GROUPING		
	Name	Number
KC(GB)	Terrier	3
AKC	Terriers	IV
FCI	Terriers	3

the Irish Terrier developed as a very individual dog, with a colour of its own, from wheaten to bright red, a size between the Lakeland and the Airedale, and a temperament which has earned him the reputation for fearlessness and devilishness second to none in the Terrier group. Though classes for the breed were staged in Lisburn in 1875 and in Dublin during the previous year, he was virtually unknown in England and it was not until some time later that he became generally known outside his native country.

Prior to the end of the 19th century the colour of the Irish Terrier was by no means fixed, black and tan, grey, and brindle being quite common colours, and it was from a bitch called Poppy who was a rich red colour and who threw puppies of the same hue, that the breed probably owes its present distinctive colouration. The black and grey, as well as the brindle was rigidly bred out of the breed, until by this century all the members of the breed were self-coloured and of the colours accepted today. The conformation of the modern Irish Terrier is very different from most of the other members of the group. His body is longer for one thing and his lines much more racy. He is leggier than many of the other Terriers, showing a good deal more daylight under his body than say the Airedale or his own fellow Irishman, the Kerry Blue Terrier.

He has never become very popular, and registration figures have fallen steadily in recent years so that he is now in something of a decline. This may in part be due to his reputation, as he is definitely included among the dogs that are not easy to handle in the show ring. It has been the habit in the Irish Terrier ring to set off one dog against another to smarten him up and make him show. The skirmishes that resulted never meant a great deal, as they were more in the nature of skirmishes than serious warfare, but unfortunately in the eyes of the public who witnessed them the breed was seen as a fierce and intractable dog. In fact he is nothing of the sort, and whilst full of spirit and always prepared to look after himself, he can be very obedient and trains easily. This was proved during the First World War, when he was used successfully as a messenger dog.

He is tremendously staunch and loyal, a wonderful protector of property and persons, and is most adaptable, living happily enough out in the country where he can roam at will, or in a town house or flat where he settles down in complete harmony with his surroundings. He remains however very much a sporting dog, and as the dog man will say, he is all Terrier.

OFFICIAL STANDARD

Characteristics

Dogs that are very game are usually surly or snappish. The Irish Terrier as a breed is an exception, being remarkably good tempered, notably so with humans, it being admitted, however, that he is perhaps a little too ready to resent interference on the part of other dogs. There is a heedless, reckless pluck about the Irish Terrier which is characteristic, and coupled with the head-long dash, blind to all consequences, with which he rushes at his adversary, has earned for the breed the proud epithet of 'The Dare Devils'. When 'off duty' they are characterised by a quiet caress-inviting appearance, and when one sees them endearingly, timidly pushing their heads into their master's hands, it is difficult to realise that on occasions, at the 'set on', they can prove that they have the courage of a lion, and will fight unto the last breath in their bodies. They develop an extraordinary devotion for, and have been known to track their masters almost incredible distances.

General appearance

The dog must present an active, lively, lithe and wiry appearance; with lots of substance, at the same time free of clumsiness, as speed and endurance, as well as power, are very essential. They must be neither 'cloddy' nor 'cobby', but should be framed on the 'lines of speeds', showing a graceful 'racing outline'.

Head and skull

Head long; skull flat, and rather narrow between ears, getting slightly narrower towards the eye; free from wrinkles; stop hardly visible except in profile. The jaw must be strong and muscular, but not too full in the cheek, and of a good punishing length. The foreface should not 'dish' or fall away quickly between or below the eyes, where it should be well made up, being relieved of 'wedginess' by delicate chiselling. The hair should be crisp and only sufficiently long to impart an appearance of additional strength to the foreface. Lips should be well fitting and externally almost black in colour. The nose must be black.

Eyes

A dark colour, small, not prominent, and full of life, fire and intelligence. A light or yellow eye is a fault.

Head: long flat skull, narrow between ears.

Ears

Small and V-shaped, of moderate thickness, set well on the head, and dropping forward closely to the cheek. The top of the folded ear should be well above the level of the skull. The ear must be free of fringe, and the hair thereon shorter and darker in colour than the body.

Mouth

The teeth should be even, strong and free from discoloration, the top teeth slightly overlapping the lower.

Neck

Should be of a fair length and gradually widening towards the shoulders, well carried, and free of throatiness. There is generally a slight frill at each side of the neck, running nearly to the corner of the ear.

Forequarters

The shoulders must be fine, long, and sloping well into the back. The legs moderately long, well set from the shoulders, perfectly straight, with plenty of bone and muscle; the elbows working freely clear of the sides; pasterns short and straight, hardly noticeable. The forelegs should be moved straight forward when travelling. The hair on the legs should be dense and crisp.

Body

Chest deep and muscular, but neither full nor wide. Body moderately long; back should be strong and straight, with no appearance of slackness behind the shoulders; the loin muscular and slightly arched; ribs fairly sprung, rather deep than round, and well-ribbed back.

Hindquarters

Should be strong and muscular, the thighs powerful, hocks near the ground, stifles moderately bent. The hind legs should be moved straight forward when travelling, the stifles not turned outwards. The hair on the legs should be dense and crisp.

Feet

Should be strong, tolerably round, and moderately small, toes arched, and neither turned out nor in; black toe nails most desirable. Pads must be sound and free from cracks or horny excrescences.

Tail

Generally docked to about three quarters; should be free of fringe or feather, but well covered with rough hair, set on pretty high, carried gaily, but not over the back or curled.

Coat

Hard and wiry, having a broken appearance, free of softness or silkiness, not so long as to hide the outline of the body, particularly in the hindquarters, straight and flat, no shagginess and free of lock or curl. At the base of these stiff hairs is a growth of finer and softer hair, usually termed the undercoat.

Colour

Should be 'whole-coloured', the most preferable colours

Hindquarters: strong and muscular, powerful, hocks low.

being a bright red, red wheaten, or yellow red. White sometimes appears on chest and feet and is more objectionable on the latter than on the former, as a speck of white on chest is frequently to be seen in all self-coloured breeds.

Weight and size

The most desirable weight in Show condition is, for a dog, 27 pounds, and for a bitch, 25 pounds. Height at shoulders, approximately 18 inches.

Note

Male animals should have two apparently normal testicles fully descended into the scrotum.

AKC VARIATION TO STANDARD

Head: foreface and skull from occiput to stop should be approximately equal in length. *Faults:* excessive muscular development of cheeks, or bony development of temples. Two lumps of bony structure above eyes. Profuse, goat-like beard, or absence of beard.

KERRY BLUE TERRIER

This is another of the purely Irish dogs. He was first found in the fabulous piece of country known as the Ring of Kerry; an area, which, until tourism became one of the major industries of Ireland, remained very much a backwater of hills and valleys, small subsistence farms and tiny fishing ports. He had been known in Kerry for at least a century, and was another breed that had benefitted by the comparative isolation of his native country, until he was discovered by the English around the turn of the century. It is in fact quite remarkable that a breed of such distinction should remain unknown in a neighbouring dog-conscious country such as England for so long, but he gets no mention in any dog book prior to this century and it was not until 1922 in England and 1926 in the United States of America that breed clubs were formed.

Since that time he has become increasingly popular as a show dog, winning major awards in a great many countries, especially on the continent and in Australasia. He remains very much a sporting dog and the Irish Blue Terrier Club of Ireland has established the preservation of that side of the dog's character as one of its aims. For some time the Irish club discouraged the trimming of the dog's coat though some cleaning up has not been declared undesirable in other countries. In the rough he carries too much coat, and the quality of it, which is soft and wavy, makes it difficult to deal with when it grows too long, which meant that a good deal of surreptitious trimming has always gone on. All puppies are born black, which creates yet another slight difficulty, as the colour change takes place at any time between nine months and two years, generally the ones that change too early eventually become too pale in colour and those that change late grow the desired and fashionable deeper blue. At any stage the coat may go through stages of showing patches of black and even a brownish tinge, all of which makes the selection of puppies a gamble. Many breeders run on a litter until the colour change has started which is an expensive and time-consuming business in which there is very little profit.

He is a real all-round Terrier, making an excellent guard, being easily trained to the gun and will retrieve like a gundog. He loves the water and with his farming background it is not surprising that he has even proved successful as a herder. He has a good many advantages as a house dog, not the least of which being that his coat, although it needs attention to keep it tidy, does not shed like some breeds.

As a show dog he often reigns in the Group, and from time to time takes Best in Show All-breeds at some of the large shows. Being somewhat larger than others in the group, and having his distinctive colour, he is always spectacular in the ring. Being a positive dog, something of an extrovert and a flashy mover, he usually looks like a potential winner. His temperament is excellent, although like the other Irish Terriers, and indeed like many in the Group he does not take kindly to what he considers interference by other dogs, when a scrap usually results. He is very kind with people, is not snappy or nasty tempered, and fits in well with the average household.

OFFICIAL STANDARD

Characteristics

Disciplined gameness. The Kerry Blue Terrier is a compact, powerful terrier, showing gracefulness and an attitude of alert determination, with definite terrier style and character throughout.

General appearance

The typical Kerry Blue Terrier should be upstanding, well knit and well proportioned, showing a well-developed and muscular body.

Head and skull

Well balanced, long, proportionately lean, with slight stop and flat over the skull. Foreface and jaw very strong, deep and punishing; nose black; nostrils of due proportion.

Eyes

Dark as possible. Small to medium with keen Terrier expression.

Ears

Small to medium and V-shaped, carried forward but not as high as in some terrier breeds.

Mouth

Teeth level with upper teeth just closing over the lower; dark gums and roof.

Neck

Strong and reachy, running into sloping shoulders.

Forequarters

Shoulders flat as possible with elbows carried close to the body while the dog is standing or in action. Legs straight, bone powerful. Front straight, neither too wide nor too narrow.

Body

Short coupled with good depth of brisket and well sprung ribs. Chest to be deep. Topline level.

Hindquarters

Large and well developed, stifle bent and hocks close to the ground giving perfect freedom of hind action.

Feet

Round and small. Toe nails black.

Tail

Set on high to complete a perfectly straight back and carried erect.

Coat

Soft and silky, plentiful and wavy.

Colour

Any shade of blue, with or without black points. A shade of tan is permissible in puppies, as is also a dark colour up to the age of 18 months. A small white patch on chest should not be penalised.

Weight and size

The most desirable weight for a fully-developed dog is from 33 to 37 pounds, and bitches should weigh proportionately less, but 35 pounds is the most desirable weight to aim for. Ideal height: dogs 18 to 19 inches at shoulder; bitches slightly less.

Faults

Hard or woolly coat. Solid black after 18 months. In excess of 19 inches in height. Bumpy cheek bones, teeth undershot or very overshot. Rose ears. Snipy foreface. Light-coloured or full eyes. Roach or hollowback. Close, stilted or cow-hocked hind action.

Note

Male animals should have two apparently normal testicles fully descended into the scrotum.

AKC VARIATION TO STANDARD

Head: skull narrowing very slightly to eyes. Cheeks clean and level and free from bumpiness. Nostrils large and wide. *Body:* loin short and powerful with a slight tuck up. *Legs:* moderately long. Forelegs should be straight from both front and side view, with elbows hanging perpendicularly to body and working clear of sides in movement. Pasterns short, straight and hardly noticeable. Both forelegs and hind legs should move straight forward when travelling, stifles turning neither in nor out. *Feet:* toes arched, turned neither in nor out. *Weight and size:* dogs 33 to 40 pounds; bitches proportionately less. Dogs $17\frac{1}{2}$ to 20 inches. Bitches 17 to 19 inches. *Disqualifications:* solid black. Dewclaws on hind legs.

Head and skull: long, lean, flat skull. Ears: small v-shaped.

LAKELAND TERRIER

It was only during the 19th century that the Terriers of Britain began to sort themselves out. The breeds peculiar to Scotland kept themselves very much to themselves as did those in Ireland, but with the growth of fox hunting with packs of hounds, each area of the rest of Britain seemed to develop a strain of its own that suited the terrain over which the pack worked, that is the conditions under which the fox went to ground. At one time it was even the fashion of the day for visiting sportsmen to bring their own personal Terriers to the hunt. The English Lake District was a very strong hunting area, and in addition to the regular packs, there were always a considerable number of irregular hunts organised to keep down the number of foxes, something that was always important in a sheep-rearing area. The origins of the Lakeland Terrier are linked, as are those of many other Terriers with the Old English Black and Tan rough-coated Terrier, but as time went by the different strains became known by names which denoted the area of their origin, so we had the Patterdale Terrier, the Elterwater Terrier and the Fell Terrier.

They were all in fact Lakeland Terriers in that they belonged to that district, but they were not known as such until a club was formed in 1912. The advent of the First World War put a stop to further progress and it was 1921 before the breed was formally recognised and a standard drawn up. Cumberland was the county of origin of the breed and is still one of its strongholds, the large agricultural shows of the county usually having a good display of the breed, often alongside classes of hunt Terriers, shown under different rules and mostly composed of his nearest rival, the Border Terrier. By 1931 the breed was well established and was granted challenge certificates in Britain though there was still considerable discussion about which was the correct type. The colour range that is acceptable in the United States of America and in Britain gives some indication of the broad Terrier basis on which the breed was built, and whilst at one time the mixed colours were the most popular in Britain, there is a growing tendency for more self-coloureds to be shown.

In a very few years he has made his mark on the show scene all over the world, having taken many group wins and Best in Shows and his handy size, attractive personality and pleasing colour range has made him one of the popular Terriers. In recent years the number of registrations has steadied down around the same figure as for Bedlingtons and Welsh Terriers and there is little doubt that after a shaky and rather late start, he is very much here to stay. He is one of those Terriers that pays for trimming and attention to coat, though his critics will claim that perhaps at times there is too much attention, and that there is a wide gap between the appearance of a Lakeland in the ring and a pet one at home. He is however very smart, bright and sparkling in the ring, and a great little showman.

Temperamentally he is ideal as a house dog, being an excellent guard, small and easily accommodated, yet very happy and sporting, enjoying a game as all the Terriers seem to, and being very much on his toes when exploring the countryside. He is not a quarrelsome dog, but is well able to look after himself if attacked, being agile, very muscular with powerful jaws for his size.

OFFICIAL STANDARD

General appearance
Smart and workman-like, with gay fearless demeanour.

Head and skull
Well balanced. Skull flat and refined. The jaws powerful and the muzzle should be broad but not too long. The length of the head from the stop to the tip of the nose should not exceed that from the occiput to the stop. Nose black.

Eyes
Should be dark or hazel.

Ears
Moderately small, V-shaped and carried alertly. They should not be placed too high or too low on the head.

Mouth
Teeth even, closing scissor fashion, i.e., top teeth fitting closely over lower.

Neck
Reachy.

Forequarters
Shoulders well laid back. Forelegs straight, well boned.

Forequarters: shoulders well laid back, forelegs straight.

Body
Chest reasonably narrow. Back strong, moderately short, well coupled.

Hindquarters
Strong and muscular, thighs long and powerful, well turned stifles, hocks low to ground and straight.

Feet
Small, compact, round and well padded.

Tail
Well set on, carried gaily but not to curl over the back.

Coat
Dense and weather resisting, harsh with good undercoat.

Colour
Black and tan, blue and tan, red, wheaten, red grizzle, liver, blue or black. Small tips of white on feet and chest not to debar. Mahogany or deep tan is not typical.

Weight and size
The average weight of dogs is 17 pounds, bitches 15 pounds. The height should not exceed $14\frac{1}{2}$ inches at the shoulder.

Faults
A true Lakeland Terrier expression is determined by head, ears and eyes. Too long a head, ears set on the top of the head, and slanting eyes are faults.

Note
Male animals should have two apparently normal testicles fully descended into the scrotum.

AKC VARIATION TO STANDARD
Head: cheeks almost straight sided, stop barely perceptible. *Eyes:* moderately small, somewhat oval in outline, set squarely in skull, fairly wide apart. *Ears:* fold just above top of skull, inner edge close to cheeks, flap pointed down. *Neck:* good length, refined but strong, clean at throat, slightly arched, widening gradually into shoulders. Withers noticeably higher than level of back. *Body:* overall length to height proportion is approx. square. Narrow chest is deep, it extends to elbows which are held close to body. Ribs well sprung, moderately rounded. Back level in topline. Loins are taut and short, although they may be a trifle longer in bitches. *Feet:* Nails strong. Dewclaws removed. *Disqualifications:* front teeth over or undershot.

MANCHESTER TERRIER

NATIONAL GROUPING		
	Name	Number
KC(GB)	Terrier	3
AKC	Terriers	IV
FCI	Terriers	3

Tough, somewhat cloddy smooth-coated black-and-tan Terriers have existed in Britain for centuries. They were often more tan than black, and did not follow the fashion for the carefully placed areas of this colour that is so much a feature of the breed today. The black-and-tan colour is remarkable in that the general pattern of the patches of the two colours is very much the same in a number of breeds all over the world, the Rottweiler, the Dobermann and the Afghan Hound for example all display the same basic pattern. The old Black-and-Tan Terrier in Britain was marked in roughly the same way. He was, however, a bull-headed dog often with cropped ears, and was used as a fighter and vermin killer. In the mining areas of Britain the rat pit was an accepted sport, and matches were regularly held to find which dog could kill the most rats in a given time. The dog most generally used for the purpose was the Black-and-Tan Terrier and a very famous dog named Billy is said to have dispatched one hundred rats in eight and a half minutes, and to have then capped this performance by destroying the same number in six minutes and thirteen seconds. Needless to say, apart from the thrill of the fight, a great deal of wagering on the result took place.

One of the early dogs, famed for his prowess in the rat pit was also a very good rabbiting dog and as the coursing of the rabbit was also very popular, the experiment of crossing this dog with a Whippet was made. The result was a strain of dogs in the Man-chester area which were faster and more refined than the old Black-and-Tan, and were known as Manchester Terriers. In those early days there were few dog shows, and those that were held were casual affairs usually held in a public house. In the Manchester area these meetings became a regular feature of the weekend life of the working man, and soon his favourite dog, the Manchester, was playing an important part in the proceedings with classes of his own. By the end of the 19th century the breed was widespread. It had lost some of its original association with Manchester and was called the Black-and-Tan Terrier. It had reached the United States of America, and in 1923 when the Manchester Terrier Club of America was formed, the name reverted to the original.

Since those early days he has had his ups and downs, as many breeds have, and the Terriers in particular. It seems that once the original purpose of a breed has disappeared either through fashion or because of legislation against it, the breed tends to go into a decline, and though no-one would wish to see the rat pit back again, it would be a fillip for many of the Terrier breeds if their usefulness could be proved in some way. As a show dog he has always had his adherents in many countries, but particularly in the United States and in his country of origin. He has not been an easy dog to maintain in his original form, as with the emphasis on colour and markings, some of the structural requirements were lost sight of and he went through a bad patch. Now, however, he is being shown as a very sound and showy dog with a lean attractive head, neat ears and a close-fitting glossy coat.

He makes a very good pet and house dog, as although his background is in some respects not a salubrious one, he has always been associated with people and families, living as one of the household and being kept in small numbers rather than in large kennels. The result is that he is very domesticated, friendly with people and especially with children, and clean and mannerly around the house.

OFFICIAL STANDARD

General appearance
The dog shall be compact in appearance with good bone and free from any resemblance to the Whippet.

Head and skull
Long, flat in skull and narrow, level and wedge-shaped, without showing cheek muscles; well-filled up under the eyes, with tapering, tight lipped jaws.

Eyes
Small, dark and sparkling, oblong in shape, set close in head, not prominent.

Ears
Small and V-shaped, carried well above the top line of the head and hanging close to the head above, the eyes.

Mouth
Should be level.

Neck
The neck should be fairly long and tapering from the shoulder to the head and slightly arched at the crest, free from throatiness.

Forequarters
The shoulders should be clean and well sloped. The chest narrow and deep. The forelegs must be quite straight, set on well under the dog; and of proportionate length to the body.

Body
Short with well-sprung ribs, slightly roached and well cut up behind the ribs.

Hindquarters
The hind legs should be neither cow-hocked nor with the feet turned in and well bent at the stifle.

Feet
Small, semi-harefooted, and strong with well-arched toes.

Tail
Short and set on where the arch of the back ends, thick where it joins the body and tapering to a point, carried not higher than the level of the back.

Coat
Close, smooth, short and glossy, of a firm texture.

Colour
Jet black and rich mahogany tan distributed as follows: on the head, the muzzle to be tanned to the nose, the nose and nasal bone to be jet black. There shall be a small tan spot on each cheek and above each eye, the under-jaw and throat to be tanned with a distinct tan 'v'. The legs from the knee downward to be tanned with the exception of the toes which shall be pencilled with black, and a distinct black mark (thumb mark) immediately above the feet. Inside the hind legs tanned but divided with black

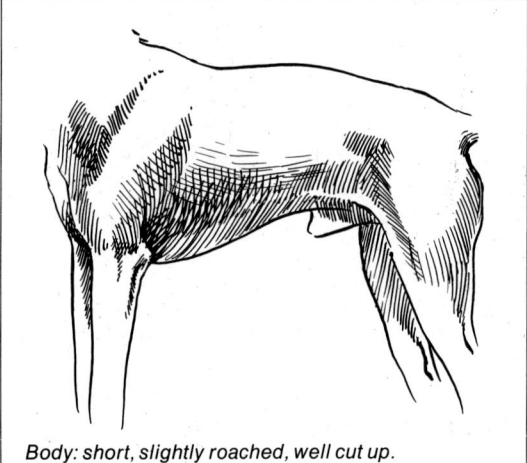

Body: short, slightly roached, well cut up.

at the stifle joint. Under the tail tanned, the vent tanned but as narrow as possible so that it is covered by the tail. A slight tan mark on each side of the chest. Tan outside the hind legs, commonly called breeching, a defect. In all cases the black should not run into the tan or vice versa, but the division between the colours shall be clearly defined.

Weight and size
Desired height at shoulders: 16 inches long; 15 inches bitches.

Note
Male animals should have two apparently normal testicles fully descended into the scrotum.

AKC VARIATION TO STANDARD
Eyes: slanting upwards on outside, should neither protrude nor sink in skull. *Ears:* erect or button, smaller at root, set as close together as possible to top of head. If cropped, to a point, long, carried erect. *Feet:* compact, jet black nails, middle toes in front feet rather longer than others; hind feet cat-like. *Weight:* over 12 and not to exceed 22 pounds. *Disqualifications:* white in any part of coat forming a patch as much as $\frac{1}{2}$ inch in its longest dimension. Dogs over 22 pounds.

NORFOLK TERRIER

Dr. Caius, writing in 1576, said 'Another sort there is that hunteth the fox and the badger only, whom we call Terrars, they creep into the ground, and by that means make afraid, nip and bite the fox and badger in such sort that either they tear them in pieces with their teeth being in the earth, or else hail and pull them out perforce out of their lurking angles, dark dungeons, and close caves'. This paints a very graphic picture of what a Terrier is supposed to do, and making allowances for the somewhat picturesque language, gives a very good idea of the conditions under which he is supposed to work. The protagonists of the short-legged Terriers will say that the long-legged ones are incapable of doing this sort of work, and will point to other breeds and even to other Groups, for examples

NATIONAL GROUPING		
	Name	Number
KC(GB)	Terrier	3
AKC	Terriers	IV
FCI	Terriers	3

of the build of the dogs that go to ground. The ideal dog for the purpose is obviously a strong one, low to the ground with powerful legs and hind-quarters to push and probe, and with the sort of jaw power that will allow it to deal with a fairly fierce trapped adversary whilst taking care of itself. Those who produced the two Terriers from East Anglia will say that they solved the problem.

OFFICIAL STANDARD

Characteristics
The Norfolk Terrier is one of the smallest of the terriers, but a 'demon' for its size. Of a lovable disposition, not quarrelsome, with a hardy constitution. Temperament: Alert and fearless.

General appearance
A small low keen dog, compact and strong with short back, good substance and bone.

Head and skull
Skull wide and slightly rounded with good width between the ears. Muzzle wedge-shaped and strong; length of

Forequarters: short, powerful, straight legs.

Ears: medium-sized, V-shaped, drooping to cheek.

muzzle slightly less than half the length of skull. Stop should be well defined.

Eyes
Oval shaped and deep set, in colour dark brown or black. Expression alert, keen and intelligent.

Ears
Size medium v-shaped but slightly rounded at tip, dropping forward close to the cheek.

Mouth
Tight lipped, jaw strong; teeth strong and rather large; scissor bite.

Neck
Medium length and strong.

Forequarters
Clean and powerful shoulders with short powerful and straight legs.

Body
Compact with short back and well sprung ribs.

Hindquarters
Well muscled, good turn of stifle, hocks well let down and straight when viewed from rear; with great powers of propulsion.

Feet
Round with thick pads.

Tail
Medium docked, not excessively gay.

Coat
Hard, wiry and straight, lying close to the body. It is longer and rougher on the neck and shoulders. Hair on the head, ears and muzzle short and smooth.

Colour
All shades of red, red wheaten, black and tan or grizzle. White marks or patches are undesirable but shall not disqualify.

Size
Ideal height 10 inches at withers.

Faults
Excessive trimming is not desirable. Honourable scars from fair wear and tear shall not count against.

Note
Male animals should have two apparently normal testicles fully descended into the scrotum.

AKC VARIATION TO STANDARD
This dog is known as the Norwich Terrier (Drop ear) in the US. *Ears:* neat, small with break just above skull line, front edge close to cheek, not falling lower than outer corner of eye. *Body:* level topline. *Disqualification:* cropped ears.

NORWICH TERRIER

This is the longer established of the two East Anglian Terriers, having been accepted to the KC (GB) register as a recognised breed in 1932. At that time there was just the one breed, with either erect or drop-ears as breeding and rearing dictated. He is an old-established native Terrier of Norfolk, a county of wide areas under cultivation, large tracts of grassland and countless woods, lakes and rivers, an area rich in game and in the history of the hunt. He was first known of in the middle of the 19th century, when a small, short-legged dog was used for hunting fox and badger, and was later said to have been taken up by the young gentlemen of Cambridge who, as a break from their studies

NATIONAL GROUPING		
	Name	Number
KC(GB)	Terrier	3
AKC	Terriers	IV
FCI	Terriers	3

enjoyed a little vermin hunting with a dog small enough and unobtrusive enough to join them in their lodgings.

After the First World War, a number of specimens of the breed were imported into the United States of America where for a time they were known as Jones

Terriers after the man who bred them in Britain. They proved very successful as hunt Terriers, and were maintained by hunt kennels to continue the work that they enjoyed at home. For the major part of their history, and indeed right up to the 1960s the erect-eared and the drop-eared were freely kept together as one breed and interbred, and only the persistence of those who preferred and bred continuously the drop-eared variety eventually persuaded the Kennel Club to grant them a separate register as the Norfolk Terrier. Interbreeding has now ceased in Britain, and the two strains are being carefully maintained. It is interesting that this question of ears becomes so much a matter of national as well as personal preference and fashion. For instance the drop-eared Papillon is considered a separate breed in Europe and is even given a different name, whilst the Manchester Terrier has tipped ears in Britain but they are optional in the United States of America.

He has made very steady progress towards popularity over the years since 1935, and now matches the Scottish and the Dandie Dinmont in numbers. A few very good specimens are making their mark in the show world owing to the efforts of a small number of enthusiastic and dedicated breeders and exhibitors. He is in fact a very good show dog, being easy to keep in trim, as though his coat needs the same sort of care and attention as that of the other hard-coated terriers, he is much smaller and he merely needs tidying up rather than sculpting. He is small, easily transported, and his appetite is moderate, which makes him an ideal house dog and pet. His temperament is attractive, as he has all the spirit of a Terrier, but is more stolid and easy-going than many of them. He is loyal, quite affectionate, and is an extremely good house guard, having sharp hearing and a strong sense of territory.

The Norfolk Terrier is the drop-eared version of this type of dog, distinguished from the Norwich only by this feature. At one time, not many years ago the two breeds were indistinguishable and interbred, and it was only in 1932 that the Norwich was accepted as a separate breed in Britain, and 1936 in the United States of America. The separation into the two varieties only took place when challenge certificates were offered for the first time to the Norfolk Terrier in 1965. His origins are obscure, and no terrier that resembles him is mentioned in any early work. One can only presume that he is that rarity these days, a thoroughly basic Terrier that evolved in a particular area for a specific purpose by selective breeding from one or two short-legged examples of the indigenous English Terrier that was widespread and very varied. It has been suggested that he was developed from a short-legged version of the Irish Terrier, but this is probably more of a bow to his colour than anything based on fact. With the Scottish Terrier being occasionally wheaten or brindle, and the Cairn often being red or sandy, it would be more realistic to conjecture that those two breeds in their early form had something to do with his ancestry.

He is a remarkably strong and sturdy little dog for his size, being very compact, muscular and well-boned. He is very active, moves much more rapidly than his short legs would indicate, and enjoys the benefit of an almost weatherproof coat. He is very game, enjoys hunting every bit as much now as his forebears must have done.

He is just beginning to make his mark as a show dog, and one or two outstanding specimens are now appearing in the ring. Numerically he is still a long way behind the Norwich, but as he has only been in existence officially for ten years as against the forty years of his near relative, this is not surprising. He is not the spanking little extrovert showman that some of the other Terriers are, but he is confident enough, very steady in the ring and responsive to command. His size, amiable temperament and loyalty to the family make him an excellent housedog.

OFFICIAL STANDARD

Characteristics
The Norwich Terrier is one of the smallest of the terriers. Of a lovable disposition, not quarrelsome, tremendously active and with a hardy constitution. Temperament gay and fearless.

General appearance
A small, low, keen dog, compact and strong with good substance and bone. Honourable scars from fair wear and tear should not be penalised unduly.

Head and skull
Muzzle wedge shaped and strong; length about one third less than a measurement from the occiput to the bottom of the stop, which should be well defined. Skull wide, good width between the ears, and slightly rounded.

Eyes
Small and oval shaped, dark, full of expression, bright and keen.

Ears
Erect, set well apart on top of skull. Of medium size with pointed tips. Held perfectly erect when aroused. Can be laid back when not at attention.

Mouth
Tight lipped, jaws clean and strong. Teeth strong, rather large. Scissor bite.

Neck
Neck strong of good length, commensurate with correct overall balance, flowing into well laid back shoulders.

Ears: medium-sized, erect, pointed tips

Feet

Round, well padded and catlike. The point straight forward standing and moving.

Tail

Medium docked. Set on high to complete a perfectly level topline. Carried erect.

Coat

Hard, wiry and straight, lying close to the body with a thick undercoat. Longer and rougher on the neck forming a ruff to frame the face. Hair on head and ears short and smooth, except for slight whiskers and eyebrows.

Colour

All shades of red, wheaten, black and tan, or grizzle. White marks or patches are undesirable.

Size

Ideal height 10 inches (25.4 centimetres) at withers. This ideal height should not be attained by excessive length of leg.

Faults

Any departure from the foregoing points should be considered a fault and the seriousness of the fault should be in exact proportion to its degree.

Note

Male animals should have two apparently normal testicles fully descended into the scrotum.

Forequarters

Legs short, powerful and straight; elbows close to body. Pasterns firm and upright. Legs should be moving straight forward when travelling.

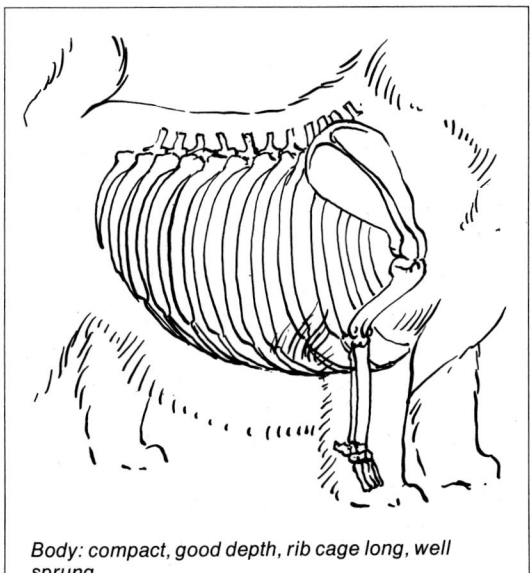

Body: compact, good depth, rib cage long, well sprung.

Body

Short back, compact body with good depth. Rib cage should be long and well sprung with short loin. Level topline.

Hindquarters

Broad, strong and muscular, with well turned stifle. Low set hock with great powers of propulsion. Hind legs should follow in the track of the forelegs when moving, showing the pads and with hocks parallel.

AKC VARIATION TO STANDARD

No variations with the Norwich Terrier (Prick ear).

SCOTTISH TERRIER

NATIONAL GROUPING		
	Name	Number
KC(GB)	Terrier	3
AKC	Terriers	IV
FCI	Terriers	3

There are few dogs about which as much controversy has raged as about the origin of the Scottish Terrier. In the early days a number of different breeds existed in Scotland, almost all of which, being Terriers from Scotland, were known or wished to be known as Scottish Terriers—which indeed but for the capital letters they were, as they were all 'terriers' from Scotland. Add to that the confusion that was caused when early Terriers of the type that we now know as the Scottish Terrier were bred on the Isle of Skye, and were first exhibited as Skye Terriers though they were nothing like the dog that we now know by that name. There have always been Terriers of different sorts in Scotland, and on the islands particularly, isolation led to fairly close inter-breeding and the early establishment of fixed types. Although he had been in existence for a long time, he was superseded into the ring by some of the other Scottish Terrier breeds such as the Dandie and the Skye, which were known and recognised, with the result that a number of somewhat odd looking dogs were exhibited as Scottish Terriers in the second half of the 19th century.

In 1877 so mixed up had the situation become, that the editor of the Live Stock Journal having endured a lengthy and sometimes scurrilous correspondence on what in fact constituted a Scottish Terrier, finally put a stop to the flood of letters with the comment, 'We see no use in prolonging this discussion except each correspondent describes the dog he is talking about and holds to be the true type'. Capt. Gordon Murray eventually in 1879 described what he felt the Scottish Terrier should look like, deplored the exhibiting of what he called mongrels with hair ten and a half inches long, and thus started a movement towards the breed as we know it today. S. E. Shirley supported him, and arranged for two classes of the type of dog that he described to be staged at the Kennel Club show at Alexandra Palace, and the breed was on its way to present day popularity. The Scottish Terrier often went by the name of Aberdeen Terrier, and still does to this day in some parts of Britain.

The Scottish Terrier Club was formed in 1882 and in that year a joint committee of representatives from Scotland and South of the Border drew up a standard for the breed which has varied very little from that time. The American standard was adopted in 1925 by a small committee, the only real difference between that and the British standard being in the matter of weight, the American standard allowing a slightly lighter dog.

To many people, the Scottish Terrier is a black dog, largely because many of them were at one time black and this colour featured in a well-known publicity campaign for a famous Scottish product. He may, however, be any one of several colours, and some of the lighter dogs are very striking. He is a strong heavily built little dog, short on the leg and with strong bone and very good muscle. His head has for many years been one of his important features, with its square well-furnished muzzle and long skull. His ears are neat and carried high, his neck long and his body strong, and in total he presents a picture of one of the smartest show dogs possible. His temperament is keen, as might be expected of a dog that is very much the Terrier, but he is kindly with those he knows, and he makes an excellent pet and house dog.

OFFICIAL STANDARD

General appearance

A Scottish Terrier is a sturdy thick-set dog of a suitable size to go to ground, placed on short legs, alert in carriage, and suggestive of great power and activity in small compass. The head gives the impression of being long for a dog of its size. The body is covered with a close-lying, broken, rough-textured coat; with its keen intelligent eyes and sharp prick ears, the dog looks willing to go anywhere and do anything. In spite of its short legs, the construction is such that it is a very agile and active dog. The movement of the dog is smooth, easy, and straight forward, with free action at shoulder, stifle and hock.

Head and skull: skull flat, slight stop.

Head and skull

Without being out of proportion to the size of the dog, it should be long, the length of skull enabling it to be fairly wide and yet retain a narrow appearance. The skull is nearly flat and the cheek-bones do not protrude. There is a slight, but distinct stop between skull and foreface just in front of the eye. The nose is large, and in profile the line from the nose towards the chin appears to slope backwards.

Eyes

Should be almond-shaped, dark brown, fairly wide apart and set deeply under the eyebrows.

Ears

Neat, of fine texture, pointed and erect.

Mouth

The teeth large, the upper incisors closely overlapping the lower.

Neck

Muscular, of moderate length.

Forequarters

The head is carried on a muscular neck of moderate length, showing quality, set into a long sloping shoulder; the brisket well in front of the forelegs, which are straight and well-boned to straight pasterns. The chest fairly broad and hung between the forelegs, which must not be out at elbows nor placed under the body.

Body

The body has well-rounded ribs, which flatten to a deep chest and are carried well back. The back is proportionately short and very muscular. In general the top line of the body should be straight and level; the loin muscular and deep, thus powerfully coupling the ribs to the hindquarters.

Hindquarters

Remarkably powerful for the size of the dog. Big and wide buttocks. Thighs deep and muscular, well bent at stifle. Hocks strong and well bent and turned neither inwards nor outwards.

Feet

Of good size and well padded, toes well arched and close-knit.

Tail

Of moderate length to give a general balance to the dog, thick at the root and tapering towards the tip, set on with an upright carriage or with a slight bend.

Coat

The dog has two coats, the undercoat short, dense, and soft; the outer coat harsh, dense, and wiry; the two making a weather-resisting covering to the dog.

Colour

Black, wheaten, or brindle of any colour.

Weight and size

The ideally-made dog in hard show condition should weigh from 19 to 23 pounds. Height, 10 to 11 inches.

Note

Male animals should have two apparently normal testicles fully descended into the scrotum.

AKC VARIATION TO STANDARD

Head: nose black. *Feet:* strong nails, forefeet larger than hindfeet. *Faults:* soft coat; round or very light eye; overshot or undershot: obviously oversize or undersize; shyness, timidity; tail and head not up when shown.

SEALYHAM TERRIER

NATIONAL GROUPING		
	Name	Number
KC(GB)	Terrier	3
AKC	Terriers	IV
FCI	Terriers	3

The evolution of the Sealyham Terrier began in the second half of the 19th century when Capt. John Edwardes of Sealyham, Haverfordwest in Pembrokeshire developed from some obscure Terrier strains a dog to use on badger and fox, one small enough to go to ground and game enough to tackle such large and fierce quarry. It is suggested that he imported Dandie Dinmont blood into his kennels to shorten the legs whilst maintaining the pluck of his Terriers, as there are few Terriers as persistent in attack on vermin as the Dandie. It is possible, too, that Bull Terriers were used to increase jaw power, but whatever went into the make-up of the Sealyham, one thing remains clear and that is that the end result was a very game and very smart Terrier. The breed was first shown in 1903 in Haverfordwest, and in 1908 the Sealyham Terrier Club of Haverfordwest was founded. The Great Joint Terrier Show was the first show in Britain to have challenge certificates on offer in 1911, and in March of that year the breed attained recognition for the first time. By that year too the breed had been recognised in the United States of America and made its debut at the San Mateo Show in California.

The breed went ahead very quickly after those early days, even though for a while many of the dogs shown were indifferent in type and little like the classy dog of today. After the First World War the breed really came into its own and a great deal of careful selective breeding for type took place so that by the 1920s he was a breed that not only looked really smart, but was still capable of doing the work for which he was first intended. He is one of the few Terriers that happily hunts in a pack, and one very well-known English gentleman, Sir Jocelyn Lucas, was to be seen at one time with a large number of these dogs that ran together. By the mid-twenties the demand was very great, many being exported to the United States and becoming a very popular show dog in that country, taking Group and Best in Show awards at major All-breed shows.

The sporting side of the breed had not been ignored, and the Sealyham Terrier Badger Digging Association was formed to preserve the dogs' working qualities. Winnie Barber writing in 1948 said that contrary to gloomy predictions that the breeders of show Sealyhams were ruining the breed, in spite of the interruption of the Second World War, the Sealyham has not only retained his beauty and brains, but his pluck and sporting proclivities as well. It will be interesting to see what happens in future years with the badger becoming a protected animal.

The Sealyham has been a tremendously successful show dog in many parts of the world and though the registration figures in Britain show a steady decline he is in no danger of becoming rare. He is one of those dogs that pays for most careful preparation work, and whilst he retains his basic shape when put down in the ring rather more than some breeds do, he does look so much better for a certain amount of clever shaping. He is bold and carefree in the ring, outward looking, almost invariably interested in what is going on around him, and moves with the commanding presence of one who knows that he looks well and has an admiring public.

Those who have owned one say that they never wish to own any other breed, as temperamentally he is quite captivating. He has an entertaining sense of humour, thoroughly enjoys a game or a romp, and tends to invent tricks and games of his own. He makes a grand companion and house pet, is a very good guard and child minder, and his voice sounds like that of a much larger dog to any intending intruder.

OFFICIAL STANDARD

General appearance
Should be that of a freely moving and active dog.

Head and skull
The skull slightly domed and wide between the ears. Jaw powerful and long, with a punishing and square jaw. Nose black.

Head and skull: skull slightly domed, jaw powerful and long.

Eyes
Dark, well set, round and of medium size.

Ears
Size medium, slightly rounded at tip, and carried at side of cheek.

Mouth
Teeth level and square, strong, with canine teeth fitting well into each other, and long for the size of the dog.

Neck
Fairly long, thick and muscular, strongly set on sloping shoulders.

Forequarters: forelegs short, strong and straight.

Forequarters
Forelegs short, strong, and straight.

Body
Medium length, level, and ribs well sprung. Body very flexible. Chest broad and deep, well let down between forelegs.

Hindquarters
Remarkably powerful for size of dog. Thighs deep and muscular, well bent at stifle. Hocks strong, well bent and neither turned inwards nor outwards.

Feet
Round and cat-like with thick pads.

Tail
Carried erect.

Coat
Long, hard and wiry.

Colour
Mostly all white, or white with lemon, brown, or badger pied markings on head and ears.

Weight and size
Weight: dogs should not exceed 20 pounds; bitches should not exceed 18 pounds. Height should not exceed 12 inches at the shoulder.

Faults
Eyes, light in colour or small. Nose, white, cherry, or spotted to a considerable extent with either of these colours. Ears, prick, tulip or rose. Colour, much black objectionable. Teeth, defective, much undershot or overshot. Coat soft and woolly.

Note
Male animals should have two apparently normal testicles fully descended into the scrotum.

AKC VARIATION TO STANDARD
Head: long, broad and powerful without coarseness. Length of head roughly $\frac{3}{4}$ height at withers. Breadth between ears little less than one half length of head. Moderate stop. Large nostrils. *Eyes:* fairly wide apart and oval in shape. *Hindquarters:* hindlegs longer than forelegs and not so heavily boned. *Feet:* toes well arched. Forefeet larger, though not quite so long as hind feet. *Tail:* docked, set on far enough forward so that spine does not slope down to it. *Weight and size:* $10\frac{1}{2}$ inches at withers. Dogs 23 to 25 pounds, bitches slightly less.

SKYE TERRIER

The appearance of the Skye Terrier completely belies his character. He looks like what one might call the 'fancy pants' of the Terriers, but in the words of one Scot, he is a 'terrible fetcher'. If two get to grips their steel-trap jaws are extremely difficult to prise apart, and they will attempt to fight to the death. He is one of the oldest of all the Terrier breeds, and Dr. Caius, writing at the time of Queen Elizabeth I, describes a dog from the north which he said came from Iceland, which almost completely fits the description of the breed as we know it today. He came, as his name suggests from the Island of Skye, which is so far north that to Dr. Caius it could well have appeared to be Iceland, and is one of two of today's breeds that emanated from that island. There is a tradition sometimes referred to, that he was evolved from dogs that swam from the ships of the Armada wrecked off the Isle of Skye, but Dr. Caius's description predates the Armada by some twenty years.

He was very much a working dog, and his low-to-the-

NATIONAL GROUPING		
	Name	Number
KC(GB)	Terrier	3
AKC	Terriers	IV
FCI	Terriers	3

ground build enabled him to go to ground to fox or badger, whilst his long hard outer coat and short close undercoat protected him from the undergrowth and from the teeth of the animals with which he often found himself engaged. He has always been a great hunter, and his apparently soft appearance completely disappears when he joins some of his fellows in a cross-country hunt. That is not to say that he becomes a ravening beast, but that his strength and fitness prove him to be the able hunter that he always has been. He has been used to produce several other breeds as exhibitors envied his lovely coat, and there is little doubt that he was ancestor to the Yorkshire Terrier in Britain and the Australian Silky. He had become one of the pre-eminent show breeds in the United States of America before the turn of the century, and though since that time his popularity has declined he is still regularly seen in top competition.

In Britain too his popularity is on the wane, though he has been readily accepted in many other countries who see in him one of the glamour dogs of the Terrier Group and a potential Group and Best in Show winner. He is not a difficult dog to prepare for show as his coat repays for regular brushing and combing, and does not soften with the occasional bath as does that of some of the hard-coated Terriers. There is no trimming, and all that is needed is to keep him in a fit condition and to encourage his coat to grow. His coat is clearly one of his most striking features, and not only are the colours themselves striking but there is also some very subtle shading, and the black fringes on his ears complete a very pleasing picture.

He is game, staunch and courageous with great stamina and agility and is generally good tempered. With those whom he knows he is friendly, gay and loyal, but with strangers he is somewhat cautious and wary. His coat is not the sort that sheds easily which means that he can be kept as a house dog, a situation which he makes quite clear that he prefers. His appearance certainly gives any owner a feeling of one-upmanship when the dog is compared with the more prosaic animals usually kept by the neighbours.

OFFICIAL STANDARD

Characteristics
A one-man dog, distrustful of strangers but not vicious.

Head and skull
Head long with powerful jaws. Nose black.

Eyes
Hazel, preferably dark brown, medium size, close set and full of expression.

Ears
Prick or drop. When prick, gracefully feathered, not large, erect at outer edges and slanting towards each other at inner edge, from peak to skull. When drop, larger, hanging straight, lying flat and close at front.

Mouth
Teeth closing level.

Neck
Long and slightly crested.

Ears: gracefully feathered.

Forequarters
Shoulders broad and close to body, chest deep. Legs short and muscular.

Body
Long and low. Back level. Ribs well sprung, giving flattish appearance to sides.

Hindquarters
The hindquarters and flanks full and well developed. Legs short and muscular, no dew claws.

Feet
Large and pointing forward.

Tail
When hanging, upper part pendulous and lower half thrown back in a curve. When raised, a prolongation of the incline of the back, not raising higher nor curling up.

Coat
Double. Under-coat short, close, soft and woolly. Over-coat long, hard, straight, flat and free from crisp and curl. Hair on head shorter, softer, veiling forehead and eyes. On ears overhanging inside, falling down and mingling with side locks, surrounding the ears like a fringe and allowing their shape to appear. Tail gracefully feathered.

Colour
Dark or light grey, fawn, cream, black, with black points. In fact, any self colour allowing shading of the same colour and lighter undercoat, so long as the nose and ears are black. A small white spot on the chest is permissible.

Weight and size
Height 10 inches, total length 41½ inches, weight 25 pounds. Bitch, slightly smaller in same proportions.

Faults
Yellow eyes, tail curled over back or any deformity.

Note
Male animals should have two apparently normal testicles fully descended into the scrotum.

SOFT-COATED WHEATEN TERRIER

This is one of the three large Terriers native to Ireland, and in most countries the least known of the three though its origins are ancient and it has a very active breed club looking after its interests. In spite of a long tradition the people of Ireland have not been great record keepers, and although it is suspected that this breed goes back hundreds of years, there is nothing written down which has yet been discovered to confirm the fact. Agriculturally Ireland is a fascinating country in that there are a few fairly large estates but very few large farms. In fact most are what is called subsistence farms where the work is carried out by members of the family over a small acreage surrounding an enclosed farm consisting of dwellings and buildings for the stock and its winter feed, and peat for the family fire. In these surroundings a good all-round dog was an essential, the sort that would deal with vermin, of which there would usually be an ample supply around the buildings, would help to round up the stock, and could even at a pinch be trained as a gundog. He needed too to be a good guard, as although there are no longer any dangerous wild beasts in Ireland, many farms are very isolated and it was not the habit to lock, bolt and bar doors as constantly as it is in some other countries.

He is believed to have played a part in the evolution of the Kerry Blue Terrier, and apart from the colour,

everything else about him would confirm that belief. Originally a good deal of cross-breeding took place, and there is little doubt that prior to some form of control, the Irish farmer would breed from those dogs around him irrespective of their blood lines in order to produce the sort of working dog that he wanted. In 1934 a breed club was formed and although application was made for the breed to be recognised, it was not until 1937 that the Irish Kennel Club granted this. In that year, fittingly enough on St. Patrick's Day, the breed made its debut at the IKC Championship Show in Dublin. Dr. G. J. Pierse was a great campaigner for the breed in those early days of its acceptance into the show world, and it is largely due to his efforts that early difficulties were overcome. For many years the breed was required to prove itself in the field, and even now the working qualities are considered to be important.

Considerable controversy has centred around the question of whether he should be left in the rough, or trimmed as is the Kerry Blue Terrier. There are two quite definite schools of thought on this, but a compromise seems now to have been reached and in the future a certain amount of tidying up will probably be the policy, leaving it largely to the judges to decide how far this should be allowed.

The first dogs of the breed arrived in the United States of America in 1946 and were shown at Westminster in 1947, though recognition was not granted at that time. On St. Patrick's Day in 1962 the Soft-Coated Wheaten Terrier Club of America was formed, and since then the breed has made steady progress. In Britain the first were registered in 1971 and numbers have since increased sufficiently for the breed to be awarded championship status.

He is a straightforward Terrier to show, having spirit, but being quite obedient, and apart from the tidying up process his preparation is a simple matter. He is affectionate, and devoted to his owner, can easily be trained to be obedient, and is fond of children. He is game, full of fun, extremely hardy, and makes an excellent house dog.

OFFICIAL STANDARD

Characteristics

The Soft-Coated Wheaten Terrier should be good tempered, spirited and game. Full of confidence and humour; a delightful, affectionate, intelligent companion. A natural terrier with strong sporting instincts, hardy and of strong constitution.

General appearance

A medium-sized, compact, upstanding terrier well covered with a soft, wheaten coloured, natural coat that falls in loose curls or waves. An active, short-coupled dog, strong and well built; well balanced in structure and movement, not exaggerated in any way. Standing four square with head and tail up, giving the appearance of a happy dog, full of character.

Head: well-balanced, moderately long, profusely covered with coat.

Head

Head moderately long and profusely covered with coat which should fall forward over the eyes. The skull, while not being coarse, should not be narrow. Skull flat and not too wide between the ears. The stop should be well defined and the cheek bones not prominent. The distance from the eyes to nose not longer, and preferably shorter, than the distance from the eye to the occiput. Jaws strong and punishing, muzzle square with no suggestion of snipiness. The top-line of the muzzle absolutely straight and parallel with skull. The nose should be black and large for the size of dog. Head in general, powerful without being coarse.

Eyes

A clear bright dark hazel. Squarely set under a strong brow and of medium size. Eye rims black.

Ears

V-shaped and folded at level of skull. The forward edge should drop down and slightly forward to lie closely along the cheek, the back edge standing slightly away from the side of the head. Thin, small to medium in size, covered with coat and with a fringe.

Mouth
Teeth large. Bite scissors (the tips of the upper incisors should lie tightly in front of the lower incisors). Overshot and undershot are equally objectionable. Lips tight and black.

Neck
Moderately long, strong, muscular and slightly arched. Without throatiness. Gradually widening toward, and running cleanly into, the shoulders.

Forequarters
Shoulders long, well laid back, and slope inwards from points to withers. Well knit in, fine, but muscular. Viewed from any angle, the forelegs perfectly straight. Good bone and muscle. Pasterns strong and springy. Chest moderately wide. Dew claws on the front legs may be removed.

Body
Compact, with powerful short loins. Back strong and level. Ribs well sprung, without roundness, providing a deep chest with relatively short coupling. Length of back from point of withers to base of tail should measure about the same as, or slightly less than, from point of withers to ground. Male animals should have two apparently normal testicles fully descended into the scrotum.

Hindquarters
Thighs strong and muscular. Hindlegs well developed with powerful muscle and well bent stifles. Hocks well let down and turning neither in nor out. Dew claws on the hind legs should be removed.

Feet
Strong and compact, turned neither in nor out. Good depth of pad. Toenails black.

Gait
Movement free, graceful and lively. Well co-ordinated with long, low strides. Having reach in front and good drive behind; straight action fore and aft. The head and tail should be carried high, the backline remaining level.

Tail
Docked. The tail of the fully grown dog should be about 4 to 5 inches long. Set on high, carried gaily, but never over the back. Not curled and not too thick.

Coat
Soft and silky. Neither woolly nor wiry. Loosely waved or curly, but if curly, the curls should be large, light and loose. The coat should not stand off but should flow and fall naturally. The coat should be abundant all over the body and especially profuse on the head and legs. The length of the leg coat should be sufficient to give good balance to the length of coat on the head and body. There is no seasonal change in the length or texture of the mature coat. The Soft-Coated Wheaten Terrier is a natural dog and should so appear. Dogs that appear to be over trimmed or stylized should be penalised. For show purposes the coat may be tidied up to present a neat outline. Coat colour and texture do not stabilize until about 18 months and should be given some latitude in young dogs.

Colour
A good clear wheaten. A shade of ripening wheat. A white coat and a red coat are equally objectionable. Dark shading on the ears is not untypical. There is often a slight fluctuation in the intensity of colour in the mature coat, but the overall effect should be light wheaten. Dark overall colour and the even darker markings often present in the immature coat clear by about 18 months, if not before.

Weight and size
Height: dogs approximately 18 to 19½ inches measured at the withers. Bitches slightly less. Weight: dogs approximately 35 to 45 pounds. Bitches somewhat less.

Faults
Any departure from the foregoing points should be considered a fault and the seriousness of the fault should be in exact proportion to its degree.

Body: compact, back strong and level, deep chest.

AKC VARIATION TO STANDARD
Major Faults: over or undershot. Coat texture deviation. Any colour save wheaten.

STAFFORDSHIRE BULL TERRIER

NATIONAL GROUPING		
	Name	Number
KC(GB)	Terrier	3
AKC	Terriers	IV
FCI	Terriers	3

The origins of the Staffordshire Bull Terrier are far from attractive. In the first quarter of the 19th century, attempts were being made to improve the types of Terrier existing in Britain, and fanciers were seeking new breeds. At that time rat killing was a favourite pastime among the working classes and the young bloods with time on their hands, and the dogs used were tough and agile. Stories of the prowess of these dogs are probably on the whole apocryphal, but it is recorded that Jimmy Shaw's Jacko could finish off a thousand rats in one and a half hours. The young sportsmen who frequented these rat-pit meetings wanted something more exciting and thought up the idea of organised dog fights as an alternative. They wanted a dog with all the gameness of the Terrier and the courage and fighting instinct of the Bulldog so they proceeded to mate the two. The result was·an agile dog with tremendous strength of jaw and an insatiable desire to fight.

These early dogs were indisputably ugly, and one that Lord Camelford presented to Belcher the pugilist is described as a short-legged, thick set fawn coloured individual with closely amputated ears, a broad blunt muzzle and considerable lay-back. For some reason this type of dog became popular among undergraduates and was considered a very manly possession for a young man to have. The dog fight of those early days was quite ritualistic, and no hit-or-miss affair. Meets were arranged, often in public house yards, some of which sported these pits as objects of curiosity long after the so-called sport was declared illegal. Naturally enough a great deal of money often depended on the result of a match, which led to a considerable amount of unsportsmanlike behaviour.

The rules were simple enough, and it was not so much an attempt to kill the other dog, as to be game enough to try. The arena was a boarded-in rectangle over which the spectators watched. There were such tricks as rubbing a contestant with pepper or other distasteful substance, and dogs were frequently washed to remove this. Each owner was permitted to lick or 'taste' the opposing dog as an additional precaution. Each dog was released in turn to cross a 'scratch' line drawn across the centre of the ring, being encouraged to do so by his 'setter'. The battle was lost by the first dog that failed 'to come up to scratch'. The result of all this was a race of remarkably fit and game dogs that would tackle anything that looked like a dog, and would fight to the death.

Attempts to show a dog of this type were doomed, as by 1863 Mr. Hinks had perfected his long-faced all-white smart Bull Terrier proper, and the Bull and Terrier, which is virtually what the fighting dog was, was being completely outshone.

The RSPCA eventually succeeded in a campaign to have the sport of dog fighting banned, and the breed that had been evolved for this purpose found itself with no future as a fighter. Fortunately he had developed other qualities, descending as he had done partly from the Bulldog, which in spite of appearance is one of the kindest dogs in the world, and there was a future for him as a pet and a show dog. He was finally recognised as such by the Kennel Club in England in 1935 and in the United States of America in 1974, and has made his mark in both these countries as well as throughout the world.

He is one of the kindest and most friendly dogs around, though he still has the inherent tendency to dispute with other dogs, and particularly with other Bull Terriers. With humans, however, he is faithful, affectionate and tremendously loyal, and his love of children is well known.

OFFICIAL STANDARD

Characteristics
From the past history of the Staffordshire Bull Terrier, the modern dog draws his character of indomitable courage, high intelligence and tenacity. This coupled with his affection for his friends, and children in particular; his off-duty quietness and trustworthy stability, makes him the foremost all-purpose dog.

General appearance
The Staffordshire Bull Terrier is a smooth coated dog. He should be of great strength for his size and although muscular, should be active and agile.

Head and skull
Short, deep through, broad skull, very pronounced cheek muscles, distinct stop, short foreface, black nose.

Head and skull: short, deep, broad, pronounced cheek muscles.

Eyes
Dark preferable but may bear some relation to coat colour. Round, of medium size, and set to look straight ahead.

Ears
Rose or half-pricked and not large. Full drop or prick to be penalised.

Mouth
The mouth should be level, i.e., the incisors of the bottom jaw should fit closely inside the incisors of the top jaw, and the lips should be tight and clean. The badly undershot or overshot mouth to be heavily penalised.

Neck
Muscular, rather short, clean in outline and gradually widening towards the shoulders.

Forequarters
Legs straight and well-boned, set rather wide apart, without looseness at the shoulders, and showing no weakness at the pasterns, from which point the feet turn out a little.

Body
The body should be close-coupled, with a level topline, wide front, deep brisket, well-sprung ribs and rather light in the loins.

Hindquarters
The hindquarters should be well muscled, hocks let down with stifles well bent. Legs should be parallel when viewed from behind.

Feet
The feet should be well padded, strong and of medium size.

Tail
The tail should be of medium length, low set, tapering to a point and carried rather low. It should not curl much and may be likened to an old-fashioned pump handle.

Coat
Smooth, short and close to the skin.

Colour
Red, fawn, white, black or blue, or any of these colours with white. Any shade of brindle or any shade of brindle with white. Black-and-Tan or liver-colour not to be encouraged.

Weight and size
Weight: dogs, 28 to 38 pounds. Bitches, 24 to 34 pounds. Height (at shoulder), 14 to 16 inches, these heights being related to the weights.

Faults
To be penalised in accordance with the severity of the fault: light eyes or pink eye-rims. Tail too long or badly curled. Non-conformation to the limits of weight or height. Full drop and prick ears. Undershot or overshot mouths. *The following faults should debar a dog from winning any prize:* pink (Dudley) nose. Badly undershot or overshot mouth. Badly undershot—where the lower jaw protrudes to such an extent that the incisors of the lower jaw do not touch those of the upper jaw. Badly overshot—where the upper jaw protrudes to such an extent that the incisors of the upper jaw do not touch those of the lower jaw.

Note
Male animals should have two apparently normal testicles fully descended into the scrotum.

AKC VARIATION TO STANDARD
Disqualification: black-and-tan or liver colour.

WELSH TERRIER

This long-legged Terrier is one of the two that are claimed as native to Wales, and there is little doubt that they have been known in the Principality for a considerable time. Like so many of the medium-sized Terriers, he almost certainly descended from the old rough Black-and-Tan Terrier that was fairly common in Britain in the 18th and 19th centuries. Old prints and paintings depict a Terrier of that time which was not far removed from the Welsh Terrier of today. It was, however, towards the end of the 18th century that he was first seen as a distinct breed in North Wales, and they were running with a pack of hounds at that time under the name Ynysfor. They were definitely working dogs as all Terriers were, and it was not until towards the end of the 19th century that anyone thought of them as a show breed.

In 1885 the Welsh Terrier Club was formed, and in the following year the breed was recognised by the Kennel Club in England. It was not until 1901 that classes were staged at the Westminster Show, but since that time their popularity has grown. The club did a great deal to improve and refine the breed, as the Old English Black-and-Tan was a roughish little dog with a head that lacked the square-cut character

NATIONAL GROUPING		
	Name	Number
KC(GB)	Terrier	3
AKC	Terriers	IV
FCI	Terriers	3

that has become desirable in most Terriers, and the coat, though strong and wiry, did not have the desired quality. Many of the old working Terriers were bowed in front too, but selective breeding from good specimens has produced a straight-fronted dog with an attractice head and a pleasing coat.

He has often been confused with the Lakeland Terrier, but the differences are quite marked, especially around the head. He has been described too as a miniature Airedale, but he differs in proportion as well as in detail from the king of the Terriers. He is in fact an individual dog with a great many admirers, particularly in his own country still, where he is looked upon as something of a mascot. There are few shows, however small, where one or two specimens of the breed do not appear. In Britain registration figures remain remarkably steady around the three hundred per year mark, and he is beginning to spread to other countries where he has been seen as a possible addition to the Terrier list.

As a show dog he has been remarkably successful without hitting the high spots. He is no more difficult to prepare than any other Terrier, and indeed because of his darker colour is easier than some. He is somewhat steadier than some of the others in the Group and is very easy to handle. His long tradition of obedience to command which comes from his working background results in a willingness to please, and although he retains all the gameness of the other Terriers, he lacks some of their independent spirit. He is a gay yet not over-exuberant companion, very good with children, and compact enough in size to fit in with modern living conditions. Although many are kept as kennel dogs, a way of life that they fit into naturally enough, they are excellent house dogs.

OFFICIAL STANDARD

Head and skull: flat and wider than wire-haired fox terrier.

Characteristics

The Welsh Terrier is of a gay, volatile disposition and is rarely of a shy nature. He is affectionate, obedient and easily controlled, thus making him an eminently suitable dog for town life. His size and colour render him ideal as a house dog, as the former point is in his favour where accommodation is limited, whilst the latter feature precludes the necessity for frequent washing as in the case of a white terrier. He is game and fearless, but definitely not of a pugnacious disposition, although at all times able to hold his own when necessary. He is ideally constituted to be a perfect town or country companion. Welsh Terriers are normally hardy and of robust constitution, and need no pampering, whilst as working terriers they are second to none, being easily trained to all sorts of game and vermin to work with gun or ferrets, and are generally found to be capital water dogs.

Head and skull

The skull should be flat and rather wider between the ears than the Wire-Haired Fox Terrier. The jaw should be powerful, clean cut, rather deeper, and more punishing— giving the head a more masculine appearance than that usually seen on a Fox Terrier. Stop not too defined, fair length from stop to end of nose, the latter being of a black colour.

Eyes

Should be small, well set in, of a dark colour, expressive and indicating abundant keenness. A round full eye is undesirable.

Ears

Should be V-shaped, small, not too thin, set on fairly high, carried forward and close to the cheek.

Mouth

Should be level with strong teeth.

Neck

The neck should be of moderate length and thickness, slightly arched and sloping gracefully into the shoulders.

Forequarters

The shoulders should be long, sloping and well set back. The legs should be straight and muscular, possessing ample bone, with upright and powerful pasterns.

Body

The back should be short, and well ribbed up, the loin strong, good depth, and moderate width of chest.

Hindquarters

Should be strong, thighs muscular, and of good length, with the hocks well bent, well let down and with ample bone.

Feet

The feet should be small, round and catlike.

Tail

The tail should be well set on, but not too gaily carried.

Coat

Should be wiry, hard, very close and abundant. A single coat is undesirable.

Colour

The colour should be black and tan for preference, or black grizzle and tan, free from black pencilling on toes. Black below the hocks is a fault.

Weight and size

The height at shoulder should not exceed $15\frac{1}{2}$ inches. 20 to 21 pounds shall be considered a fair average weight in working condition.

Faults

A white, cherry or spotted nose. Prick, tulip or rose ears. An appreciable amount of black below the hocks.

Note

Male animals should have two apparently normal testicles fully descended into the scrotum.

AKC VARIATION TO STANDARD

Eyes: not too deeply set in nor protruding out of skull. *Hindquarters:* hocks moderately straight. *Disqualifications:* nose white, cherry or spotted. Ears, prick tulip or rose. Undershot jaw or pig-jawed. Black below hocks or white to an appreciable extent.

WEST HIGHLAND WHITE TERRIER

It is very likely that all the Terriers of Scotland came originally from the same root stock, and that it was only by selective breeding from those that displayed difference of size, type and colour, that we now have such diverse breeds as the Dandie Dinmont Terrier and the Scottish Terrier, or the Skye and the Cairn. The relative isolation of various parts of the country and of its islands made the maintenance of pure lines a simple matter once a type had been established, as even the most ardent of dogs would find some trouble in trying to swim some of the lochs and seaways. Col. E. D. Malcolm of Poltalloch first drew attention to these little short-legged white Terriers, which in 1907 he had been breeding for sixty years, and which were first shown as Poltalloch Terriers. Though he confessed to being no dog man, he got together with one or two other interested gentlemen and formed the first club to further the interest of the breed. Early photographs show his dogs as being rather longer in the leg than is now fashionable but all-white, and with the same keen expression and smartly pricked ears that have become such a feature of the breed.

The original Poltalloch Terriers were built along foxy lines, tremendously hard and flexible, and fitted to the work of hunting the fox in a rocky terrain. In that sort of country a fox's earth is not a hole dug in

NATIONAL GROUPING		
	Name	Number
KC(GB)	Terrier	3
AKC	Terriers	IV
FCI	Terriers	3

soft ground, but a passageway scraped between huge immovable rocks, often very narrow and always impossible to dig through. The Terrier had to be prepared to force his way through narrow openings, often against stiff opposition, and frequently with no opportunity of turning round to get out again. He had to be prepared to fight his way through, and struggle out backwards if he was able, which meant that he had to be an extremely fit, agile and active little animal. Fortunately the early fears of enthusiasts that the West Highland White would develop into merely a white Scottish Terrier have not been realised, and the modern respresentatives of the breed have all the sporting characteristics of their ancestors.

It is true that they have been taken in hand for show purposes, often by professional handlers, and have been given an external appearance which is very different from that of the old Poltalloch dogs, but underneath this they are still sporting, flexible and agile. He is now recognised as one of the top winning Terriers in the Group, with many Best in Shows to his credit including Crufts, and his reputation is high in most countries. He has the sort of character that makes him an ideal show dog, cocky, full of fun, and enjoying the admiration that comes to those that win. His coat is such that expert attention brings out the best in him, and he can be shaped to give a delightfully smart outline, extending his neck, giving his legs the desirable sturdy appearance, and accentuating the whiskers of his head until his face looks like three little black spots in a white circle.

He is an affectionate character, hardy, loving to romp and play under any conditions, rolling in the sunshine or digging in the snow, it all comes alike to him. He is a fine house dog, being very alert and protective about his family, and having the acute hearing of all the prick-eared Terriers. He is a wonderful companion and pet, and a tremendous dog to have around the house.

OFFICIAL STANDARD

General appearance
The general appearance of the West Highland White Terrier is that of a small, game, hardy-looking Terrier, possessed of no small amount of self-esteem; with a varminty appearance; strongly built, deep in chest and back ribs; level back and powerful quarters on muscular legs, and exhibiting in a marked degree a great combination of strength and activity. Movement should be free, straight and easy all round. In the front the legs should be freely extended forward by the shoulder. The hind movement should be free, strong and close. The hocks should be freely flexed and drawn close in under the body, so that when moving off the foot, the body is pushed forward with some force. Stiff, stilted movement behind is very objectionable.

Head and skull
The skull should be slightly domed and when gripped across the forehead, should present a smoother contour. There should only be a very slight tapering from the skull at the level of the ears to the eyes. The distance from the occiput to the eyes should be slightly greater than the length of the foreface. The head should be thickly coated with hair, and carried at a right-angle or less, to the axis of the neck. On no account should the head be carried in the extended position. The foreface should gradually taper from the eye to the muzzle. There should be a distinct stop formed by heavy, bony ridges, immediately above and slightly overhanging the eye, and a slight indentation between the eyes. The foreface should not dish or fall away quickly below the eyes where it should be well made up. The jaws should be strong and level. The nose must be black. Should be fairly large, and forming a smooth contour with the rest of the muzzle. The nose must not project forward giving rise to a snipy appearance.

Eyes
Should be widely set apart, medium in size, as dark as possible in colour. Slightly sunk in head, sharp and intelligent, which, looking from under the heavy eyebrows, imparts a piercing look. Full or light-coloured eyes are objectionable.

Ears
Small, erect and carried firmly, terminating in a sharp point. The hair on them should be short, smooth (velvety) and should not be cut. The ears should be free from any fringe at the top. Round pointed, broad, large or thick ears are very objectionable, also ears too heavily coated with hair.

Mouth
Should be as broad between the canine teeth as is consistent with the sharp varminty expression required. The teeth should be large for the size of the dog, and should articulate in the following manner: the lower canines should lock in front of the upper and lower incisors. The upper incisors should slightly overlap the lower incisors, the inner side of the upper incisors being in contact with the outer side of the lower incisors. There should be no

Head and skull: slightly domed, thickly coated with hair.

appreciable space between the incisors when the mouth is closed ensuring a keen bite; a dead level mouth is not a fault.

Neck
Should be sufficiently long to allow the proper set on of head required, muscular and gradually thickening towards the base allowing the neck to merge into nicely sloping shoulders, thus giving freedom of movement.

Forequarters
The shoulders should be sloped backwards. The shoulder blades should be broad and lie close to the chest wall. The joint formed by the shoulder blade and the upper arm should be placed forward, on account of the obliquity of the shoulder blades, bringing the elbows well in, and allowing the foreleg to move freely, parallel to the axis of the body, like the pendulum of a clock. Forelegs should be short and muscular, straight and thickly covered with short hard hair.

Body
Compact. Back level, loins broad and strong. The chest should be deep and the ribs well arched in the upper half presenting a flattish side appearance. The back ribs should be of a considerable depth and the distance from the last rib of the quarters as short as is compatible with free movement of the body.

Hindquarters
Strong, muscular and wide across the top. Legs should be short, muscular and sinewy. The thighs very muscular and not too wide apart. The hocks bent and well set in under the body so as to be fairly close to each other when standing, walking or trotting. Cow-hocks detract from the general appearance. Straight or weak hocks are undesirable and are a fault.

Feet
The forefeet are larger than the hind ones, are round, proportionate in size, strong, thickly padded and covered

Body: compact, back level, distance from last rib short.

over the back. A long tail is objectionable and on no account should tails be docked.

Coat
Colour pure white, must be doublecoated. The outer coat consists of hard hair, about 2 inches long, free from any curl. The under coat, which resembles fur, is short, soft and close. Open coats are objectionable.

Colour
Pure white.

Weight and size
Size about 11 inches at the withers.

Note
Male animals should have two apparently normal testicles fully descended into the scrotum.

with short hard hair. The hind feet are smaller and thickly padded. The under-surface of the pads of feet and all nails should be preferably black.

Tail
5 to 6 inches long, covered with hard hair, no feather, as straight as possible, carried jauntily, not gay nor carried

AKC VARIATION TO STANDARD
Tail: should be set on high enough so that spine does not slope down to it.

TOY GROUP: NON-SPORTING BREEDS

Affenpinscher

Australian Silky Terrier

Bichon Frise

Cavalier King Charles Spaniel

Chihuahua

Italian Greyhound

English Toy Terrier (Black and Tan)

Griffon Bruxellois

Japanese Chin

King Charles Spaniel

Lowchen

Maltese

Miniature Pinscher

Papillon

Pekingese

Pomeranian

Pug

Yorkshire Terrier

TOY GROUP: NON-SPORTING BREEDS

This Group contains some of the dogs claiming the greatest antiquity as specific breeds. Whilst the working dogs certainly were part of the early life of mankind, they were not so clearly developed into breeds, and were bred for performance as were the early Hounds, rather than for appearance. The toy dogs, however, carefully bred for appearance for centuries (some claim even for thousands of years), and as small lap dogs and companion dogs; have been favourites of the courts and noble families for as long as records have been kept. They are recognised by their size, though some of the recent additions to the group do not entirely conform in this aspect. They have without exception been produced by a process of selective miniaturisation, as none of the wild stock from which all dogs descended is as small as they are, and in most cases their ancestry can be traced back to other and larger breeds.

The members of the Group can be split up roughly into dogs related to the other Groups. There is a Spaniel sub-group, consisting of such breeds as the Toy Spaniels and the Japanese. The running group is represented by the Italian Greyhound, the Spitz group by the Pomeranian and the Terrier Group by the Yorkshire Terrier and the English Toy Terrier. In addition to these, the foreign Terriers are represented by the Miniature Pinscher and the Griffon, whilst in the United States the Toy Poodle is included by reason of its lack of size, as is the Shih Tzu, though both appear elsewhere in other countries.

We are fortunate in that we have better visual records of the breeds in the Toy Group than in almost any of the others. Down through the centuries it has been the habit of ladies of the courts, and gentlemen too for that matter, to include their favourite dog, usually a lap dog, when having their portrait painted. As a result of this we have a very clear picture of what the early Toy Spaniels looked like in the time of Charles II; we know with some certainty that the Italian Greyhound has changed very little since the time of Anne of Denmark; and that Hogarth's pet Pug painted in 1745 was a fair representative of the breed even by today's standards.

The early civilisations of the Far East have preserved for us some of the best ancient records of many of the toy breeds, as several of them originated in that part of the world, the Pekingese for example occupying a very important place in the history of Imperial China. In Tibet too the smaller dogs were revered and the pure breeding of some of the older types of toy dogs was practised by the monasteries of that country where they were used in religious ceremonies. Some of the smaller dogs in other parts of the world have been said to have an association with religion, the Chihuahua from South America for example, and myth and legend play a formidable part in the history of the members of the Group.

Some of the early writers were extremely scornful about the toy breeds, steeped as they were in the world of the coursing and shooting dog. Dr. Caius for instance describes them as 'These dogges are little, pretty, and proper, and fyne, and sought for to satisfie the delicatenesse of daintie dames and wanton women's wiles, instruments of folly for them to play and dally withall, to tryfle away the treasure of time, to withdraw their mindes from their commendable exercises'. In fact, many of the toy dogs are very sporting indeed, and it has been placed on record that at the beginning of this century one gentleman regularly shot over his team of Toy Spaniels.

In more recent times Europe has been the centre of the breeding of the toy dogs, and breeds that have their origin in the Far East, found their way into Europe as world trade grew during the last two hundred years. The Papillon for instance, looked upon as a French breed and even carrying a French name, almost certainly came from the Orient. Similarly, the Pug, known at one time as the Dutch Pug, is an ancient Chinese breed that was developed in Europe. Some of the newcomers to the Group, the Chihuahua, the Bichon and the Lowchen are making tremendous strides in popularity, evidence of the fact that there always was and always will be an interest in the toy dogs.

AFFENPINSCHER

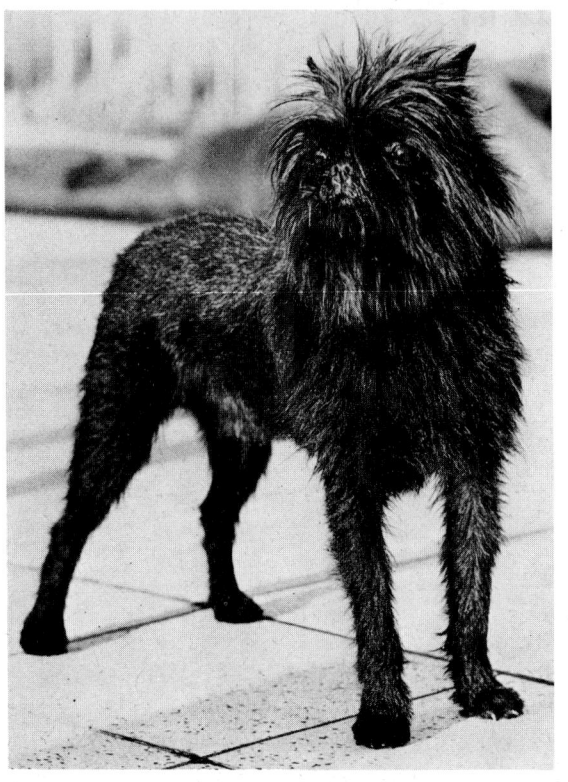

NATIONAL GROUPING		
	Name	Number
KC(GB)	—	–
AKC	Toys	v
FCI	Companion Dogs	9

sed by the American Kennel Club in 1936, but the Second World War slowed down his progress. After the cessation of hostilities, however, his numbers began to grow steadily and the toy dog people became interested in him. He is still hardly known outside the United States of America and in his home country, and has made no impression in Britain at all.

He is a small—under ten inches—dog with a sturdy build, strong straight-backed terrier-like body and straight legs. He is covered with a short dense coat that develops on the legs and around the eyes, nose and chin into a shaggy, hard wiry and much longer coat which gives the square appearance and the monkey expression. He is game, alert and intelligent, and though he can be quite aggressive for his size, and makes a good guard, he is an affectionate little dog that makes a fine pet and house dog. Although overshadowed by the Griffon Bruxellois as a show dog in numbers, he is rapidly gaining ground.

This quaint little dog is one of the oldest toy dogs of Europe, having been known for at least the past three centuries and in his early days, with the delightful title of Monkey Pinscher. The word 'pinscher' means simply 'terrier' in the German language and the prefix 'Affe' can be freely translated as 'monkey'. He is believed to have been one of the ancestors of two other well-known breeds, the Griffon Bruxellois and Miniature Schnauzer, in both of which similarities about the head and expression can be seen. His origin is obscure. All that is known for certain is that there were originally two sizes and that it is the smaller version that has survived and which is now accepted worldwide.

At the turn of the century there existed a dog known as the Wire-haired Pinscher 'Deuthscher Rauhhaariger Pinscher' that could have been the larger type. He was described as being from twelve to eighteen inches high and having a short beard and whiskers. He was known familiarly as the Rattler, and appeared mostly as a black dog, though other colours were seen. As the Schnauzer gets no mention at that time, this dog could well have been that breed and it is likely that in fact the breeds were so intermingled that a considerable amount of confusion existed. He was recogni-

OFFICIAL STANDARD

General appearance
Small, but rather sturdy in build and not delicate in any way. He carries himself with comical seriousness and he is generally quiet and a very devoted pal. He can get vehemently excited, however, when attacked and is fearless toward any aggressor.

Coat
A very important factor. It is short and dense in certain parts and shaggy and longer in others, but should be hard and wiry. It is longer and more loose and shaggy on the legs and around the eyes, nose and chin, giving the typical monkey-like appearance from whence comes his name. The best color is black, matching his eyes and fiery temperament. However, black with tan markings, red, gray and other mixtures are permissible. Very light colors and white markings are a fault.

Body: proportions square, chest deep.

Legs
Front legs should be straight as possible. Hind legs without much bend at the hocks and set well under the body. *Feet:* should be round, small and compact. Turned neither in nor out, with preferably black pads and nails.

Head: showing arrangement of facial hair.

Hindquarters: little bend.

Head
Should be round and not too heavy, with well-domed forehead. *Eyes:* should be round, of good size, black and very brilliant. *Ears:* rather small, set high, pointed and erect, usually clipped to a point. *Muzzle:* must be short and rather pointed with a black nose. The upper jaw is a trifle shorter than the lower jaw, while the teeth should close together; a slight undershot condition is not material. The teeth, however, should not show.

Neck
Short and straight.

Body
The back should be straight with its length about equal to the height at the shoulder. Chest should be reasonably deep and the body should show only a slight tuck-up at the loin.

Tail
Cut short, set and carried high.

Size
The smaller dog, if of characteristic type, is more valuable, and the shoulder height should not exceed $10\frac{1}{4}$ inches in any case.

Approved 15 September 1936

This dog is not granted championship status by the KC(GB) therefore the above standards are those of the AKC.

AUSTRALIAN SILKY TERRIER

NATIONAL GROUPING		
	Name	Number
KC(GB)	Toy	6
AKC	Toys	V
FCI	Terriers	3

This interesting little dog has been established as a breed in fairly recent years. Prior to the Second World War it was virtually unknown outside Australia, but afterwards became quite popular in the United States of America though there are still none in Britain. The two main ancestors of the breed were the Yorkshire Terrier and the Australian Terrier. The first was developed from crossing the Skye, the Black and Tan and the Maltese, and the second from the Skye, the Dandie Dinmont and the indigenous broken-coated Terrier of Australia. The result is a well set up dog, somewhat larger than the Yorkshire Terrier but with a silky coat. At first in Australia the two breeds were closely involved, the Yorkshire Terrier and the Australian Silky, the two breeds sharing a breed club in 1900. The first record of a small dog resembling the Australian Silky Terrier is of Broken-coated Terriers being shown at the second Royal Melbourne Show in Victoria in 1872. Later in 1884 they were shown as Broken-coated Toy Terriers and later still in 1900 the Victorian Silky and Yorkshire Terrier Club drew up standards for the two breeds as obviously there was

danger of confusion, and indeed perhaps even fusion of the two breeds.

Soon after the turn of the century breeders in Sydney commenced the Sydney Silky Club and the breed became widely known as the Sydney Silky. It was not until 1959 that the Australian National Kennel Council adopted a standard for the breed and changed its name to the Australian Silky Terrier. Breeders in Australia are still anxious lest there should be any confusion between the Yorkshire Terrier and the Australian Silky. They prefer a dog that is around nine inches high and that weighs about eight to ten pounds, and they are quite firm that the coat should be only some five or six inches long and should not trail on the ground as does that of the Yorkshire Terrier. They prefer too that the coat should be a real blue colour rather than the steely colour of the Yorkie.

The Silky Terrier is a compact low set dog with enough substance to look as though he can hunt, which indeed he can, being very much the vermin killer. He is much more the Terrier than the Toy, being very alert, and extremely active. He now appears in quite large numbers at the Australian dog shows, and having had challenge certificates awarded since 1924, is well-established in his home country. His popularity extends to New Zealand and he is still quite familiar to showgoers in the United States where it is called simply the Silky Terrier. He looks at his best at the outdoor championship shows of Australia, where the brilliant sunshine shows off his silky coat to the fullest advantage. He is a very attractive pet dog, and whilst he is included among the Toys, has more fire and sparkle than some, being just as much at home sniffing at a rat hole as he is lying around on the furniture. He is a very picturesque dog, decorative and handsome, and looks well in a modern apartment. He is a good guard, making a noise out of all proportion to his size, and being very possessive about his family and their property.

OFFICIAL STANDARD

General appearance

The dog is compact, moderately low set, of medium length with a refined structure, but of sufficient substance to suggest the ability to hunt and kill domestic rodents. It should display Terrier characteristics, embodying keen alertness, activity and soundness; the parted, straight silky hair presenting a well-groomed appearance.

Head and skull

Of moderate length, slightly shorter in length from the tip of the nose to between the eyes than from the same position to the top rear of the occiput. It must be strong and of Terrier character, being moderately broad between the ears; the skull flat, without fullness between the eyes. Long fall of hair on foreface and cheeks very objectionable. Fine silky top-knot, not falling over the eyes. Nose black.

Eyes

Should be small, round, dark as possible in colour with a keen intelligent expression.

Ears

Should be small, V-shaped, leather fine, high on skull and pricked; entirely free from long hair.

Mouth

Strong jaws, teeth even and not cramped, the upper incisors fitting closely over the lower, lips tight and clean.

Neck

Medium length, refined and slightly crested. Well covered with long silky hair.

Forequarters

Shoulders fine and well laid back, fitting with well angulated upper arms snugly to ribs, elbows turned neither in nor out, forelegs refined round bone, straight and set well under body with no weakness in pasterns.

Body

Should be moderately long in proportion to the dog's height. Level topline, well sprung ribs extending back to strong loins. Chest of moderate depth and breadth.

Hindquarters

Thighs well developed. The stifles should be well turned and the hocks well bent. When viewed from behind the hocks should be well let down and parallel with each other.

Feet

Small, well padded, cat-like, closely knit toes with black or very dark toenails.

Gait

The movement should be free and straight-forward without slackness at shoulders or elbows. There should be no turning of feet or pasterns. The hindquarters should have strong propelling power with ample flexibility at stifles and hocks. Viewed from behind the movement should be neither too close nor too wide.

Tail

Should be docked and carried erect, but not over-gay.

Coat

Must be fine and glossy and of a silky texture; a length of coat of from 5 to 6 inches from behind the ears to the set-on of the tail is desirable. Legs from knees and hocks to feet free from long hair.

Colour

Blue and tan or grey-blue and tan, the richer of these colours the better. Blue on tail to be very dark. The distribution of the blue and tan is as follows: silver-blue or fawn top-knot desirable, tan around the base of ears, muzzle and on side of cheeks, blue from the base of skull to tip of tail running down the forelegs to near the knees and down the thighs to the hocks, tan line showing down the stifles and tan from the knees and hocks to the toes and around the vent.

Weight and size

The most desirable weights are from 8 to 10 pounds. Height approximately 9 inches at the withers.

Faults

Nose: any colour other than black. *Coat:* curly, woolly, wavy, short or harsh. *Colour:* any colour other than blue and tan or grey-blue and tan (puppies excepted). *Mouth:* undershot or overshot. *Weight:* over or underweight. White toenails. Ewe neck. Weediness, coarseness, unsoundness. The blue body coat must be free from tan or bronze, and the tan markings free from smut or dark shadings.

Note

Male animals should have two apparently normal testicles fully descended into the scrotum.

Although this dog has been given an interim standard it has not been granted championship status by the KC(GB).

AKC VARIATION TO STANDARD
This dog is known as the Silky Terrier in the USA.

BICHON FRISE

This little dog is recorded back into history more faithfully than most, as having been a favourite with court families he appears in portraits and genre paintings of many centuries ago. The portrait dog is not immediately recognisable as the Bichon Frise we know today, but he is so similar that there is little doubt that small curly-coated dogs existed that must have been his ancestors. He is said to have originated in the Mediterranean area around the 18th century, discovered by Italian sailors who brought him back to the mainland from the Canary Islands. He was certainly known in France in the 16th century and in the courts of Spain, figuring frequently in the paintings by Murillo. His 'The Holy Family and the Little Bird' is a typical example, in which a small white dog which can hardly have been anything else but a Bichon is a central figure. In later paintings by Goya similar dogs appear.

Like the Poodle and many of the other curly-coated dogs of Europe, the Bichon descended from the Water Spaniel or Barbet, a much larger sporting dog, by a process of selective breeding and miniaturisation. He existed at first in four forms, the Maltais which probably became the Maltese or dogs of Melita, the Bolognais, which seems to have disappeared (but which is depicted somewhat wildly in a porcelain by Kirchner in the Metropolitan Museum of Art in New York), the Havanais and the Tenerife. Another porcelain of 1750, said to represent a dog belonging to the

NATIONAL GROUPING		
	Name	Number
KC(GB)	Toy	6
AKC	Non-Sporting Dogs	VI
FCI	Companion Dogs	9

Marquise de Pompadour depicts a typical Bichon Frise. During the late 19th century the breed lost its aristocratic connections and became the plaything of stage and circus, running the streets, acting as a catchpenny for beggars and generally going into something of a decline as a pedigree dog as the bloodlines became diluted.

At the end of the First World War the breed had virtually disappeared, and it was only the interest of a small number of enthusiasts that kept it alive. In 1933 an official standard was adopted and the breed became established under two names, the 'Bichon' and the 'Tenerife', and it was Madame de Leemans who proposed the name Bichon Frise as describing both the antiquity of the breed and its appearance. The breed is now recognised and is becoming popular in most countries. The first entered the United States of America in 1956 and further imports took place during the following years. Recognition was granted by the American Kennel Club in 1972 and the breed then enjoyed a rapid climb to popularity. Britain was much later in the field, when a few specimens came into the country in the mid-seventies. Their climb to popularity has been one of the phenomena of the modern show scene in Britain and there is no doubt that the Bichon Frise will be one of the popular dogs of the next decade.

The Bichon is a most attractive little dog, full of charm, and very appealing. He is sturdy, very stylish and full of confidence, attracting great attention wherever he appears. His coat, which consists of a mass of loose silky curls is trimmed to show the eyes and to give a full rounded appearance to the head and the body, with the result that he looks like a well-made, snow-white fluffy child's toy when he appears in the show ring. He is intelligent and attentive, shows really well, with great mobility for so small a dog. His generations of dependence on human beings gives him a sense of belonging to the family which comes out in his enjoyment of comfort and company, and his love of people.

OFFICIAL STANDARD

General appearance
Gay, happy, lively little dog, the coat falling in soft, corkscrew curls. The head carriage is proud and high; the eyes alert and full of expression.

Head and skull
The skull longer than the muzzle, the whole head in balance with the body. The muzzle should not be thick or heavy; nor should it be snipy; the cheeks flat and not very strongly muscled; the stop should be slight and the hollow between the eyebrows just visible. Skull flat when touched, although the hair tends to make it look round. The nose should be round, black, soft and shiny.

Head: skull flat, covered with hair.

Eyes
Dark, with dark eye-rims, fairly round, never almond shaped nor obliquely set; lively, not too big; never showing any white. Neither large nor prominent. The socket should not be pronounced.

Ears
Narrow and delicate. Hanging close to the head and well covered with tightly curled, long hair. Carried forward when the dog is alert but in such manner that the forward edge touches the skull and not carried obliquely away from the head. The leather should reach halfway along the muzzle.

Mouth
Scissor bite, that is to say, the incisors of the lower jaw should be placed immediately behind and in contact with those of the upper jaw. The lips should be fine, fairly tight and completely black, drooping just sufficient for the lower lips to be covered by the upper, but never heavy nor hanging. The lower lip should be neither heavy, protruding nor flabby and should never show the mucous membrane when the mouth is closed.

Neck
Fairly long, carried high and proudly. Round and slim near the head, gradually broadening to fit smoothly into the shoulders. Length about one third the length of the body (proportions of 33 centimetres to 11 centimetres for a dog of 27 centimetres high at the withers).

Forequarters
Shoulders oblique, not prominent, and equal in length to the upper arm (approximately 10 centimetres). The upper arm should fit close to the body. Legs straight when seen from the front, perpendicular and finely boned. The pastern should be short and straight when viewed from the front, very slightly sloping when viewed from the side.

Body
Chest well developed, with deep brisket. The floating ribs well rounded and not terminating abruptly. Loin broad, well-muscled, slightly arched and well tucked-up. The pelvis broad, the croup slightly rounded.

Hindquarters
Thighs broad and well-muscled, oblique. Stifles well-bent and hocks well let down.

Feet
Small, rounded and well knuckled-up. Nails preferably black.

Tail
Normally carried raised and curled gracefully over the back but never tightly curled. It should not be docked and should not touch the backbone but the hair should always fall on to the back. Slightly low set.

Coat
Fine, silky, with soft corkscrew curls. Neither flat nor corded, and measuring 7 to 10 centimetres in length. The dog may be presented untrimmed or have muzzle and feet slightly tidied up.

Coat: profuse, silky, loosely-curled.

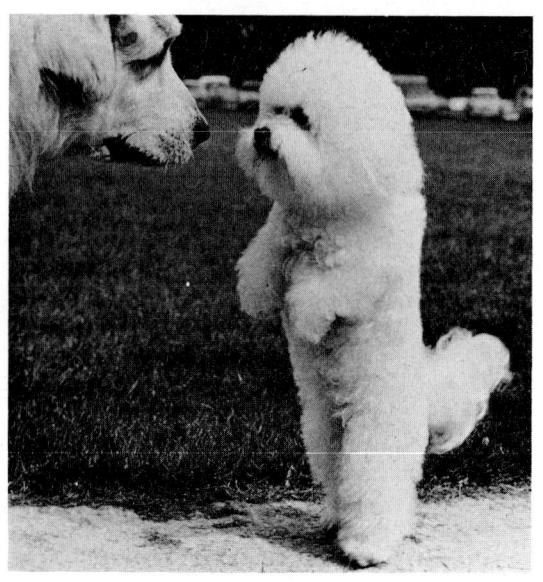

Faults
Any departure from the foregoing points should be considered a fault and the seriousness of the fault should be in exact proportion to its degree.

Note
Male animals should have two apparently normal testicles fully descended into the scrotum.

Although this dog has been given an interim standard it has not been granted championship status by the KC(GB).

Colour
Pure white. Under the white coat dark pigment is preferred. Black, blue or beige markings are often found on the skin.

Height
Less than 30 centimetres, smallness being highly desirable.

AKC VARIATION TO STANDARD
Faults: cowhocks, snipy muzzle, poor pigmentation, protruding eyes, yellow eyes, undershot or overshot bite.
Serious faults: corkscrew tail, black hair in coat.

CAVALIER KING CHARLES SPANIEL

NATIONAL GROUPING		
	Name	Number
KC(GB)	Toy	6
AKC	—	–
FCI	Companion Dogs	9

A good deal of confusion existed in the various breeds of toy Spaniels up to the early part of this century, old paintings depicting dogs that were either Cavaliers or King Charles Spaniels or something produced from oriental Spaniels arriving by way of France. The Cavalier King Charles Spaniel really owes its existence to an enthusiast in the United States of America who was so impressed with the differences shown in old paintings that he decided to resurrect the longer tailed and longer nosed variety as a separate breed. The main distinctive features of the Cavalier that the others did not have were the longer face, flat skull, less stop and the much-prized spot in the middle of the skull of the Blenheims. The King Charles Spaniel was known at one time as the 'Comforter' and according to chroniclers of the time, Charles II enjoyed the company of his dogs more than he did that of the members of his court. He kept a number of these little dogs around him, and according to Pepys 'he often suffered the bitches to puppy and give suck, which rendered it very offensive and indeed made the whole court nasty and stinking'. The dog that was the favourite of Charles II was almost certainly the King Charles, the black and tan version. The others were the Prince Charles, which was a tricolour, the Blenheim, which was red and white and first bred by the Duke of Marlborough at Blenheim, and the Ruby, which was a solid rich red.

The colours have remained, but the division took place in the early 1920s, when Mr. Eldridge of Long Island, New York, gave special prizes for those Toy Spaniels which most nearly fitted the description that he preferred from among those that he had studied on old paintings. A club was formed in 1928 to promote the Cavalier King Charles Spaniel, and since that time the breed has gone from strength to strength. Whilst it is not numerically the strongest breed in the Toy Group, that distinction going to the Yorkshire Terrier, it is easily the most popular at shows, and the entries in the breed constantly top all the others.

Apart from the detailed differences between the Cavalier and the King Charles Spaniel, the Cavalier is much the larger of the two, the standard allowing from twelve to eighteen pounds as against the eight to fourteen of the King Charles. In fact fashion has decreed that the King Charles and Cavaliers should be at opposite ends of the popularity scale so that the difference in size is even more acute than the standard would suggest. In recent years in Britain, and probably in other countries too, the breed has suffered as many breeds do when their popularity takes a sharp upward turn. The award of Best in Show All-breeds at Crufts to a Cavalier King Charles Spaniel in 1973 led to a great deal of indiscriminate breeding and the standard of the breed has suffered as a result. He is one of the heavy-weights of the Toy dog Group, and when one of the larger specimens manages to win Best of Breed and appears in the Group, it can look somewhat out of place alongside some of the much smaller breeds.

The Cavalier King Charles is sturdy for a toy dog, having a short strong body and straight bone, and retains something of the characteristic Spaniel quality of his ancestors. He will enjoy a good deal of exercise, being very active and not tiring easily, and is a good companion on a country walk. As a show dog he presents few problems. Some are a little shy or reserved, but few are really nervous, and the coat needs no special preparation, the only problem being keeping coat rather than trimming off excess. He is an enjoyable dog to own, as he is kindly and affectionate, with no vices at all, and with centuries of domestication behind him, he takes naturally to living indoors.

333

OFFICIAL STANDARD

General appearance
An active, graceful and well-balanced dog. Absolutely fearless and sporting in character and very gay and free in action.

Head and skull
Head almost flat between the ears, without dome. Stop shallow. Length from base of stop to tip about 1½ inches. Nostrils should be well developed and the pigment black. Muzzle well tapered. Lips well-covering but not hound like. Face should be well filled out underneath the eyes. Any tendency to appear 'snipy' is undesirable.

Forequarters: shoulders well laid back.

Ears
Long and set high with plenty of feather.

Mouth
Level; scissor-bite preferred.

Neck
Moderate length—slightly arched.

Eyes
Large, dark and round but not prominent. The eyes should be spaced well apart.

Ears: long, set high, plenty of feather.

Body: short with plenty of spring of rib.

Forequarters
Shoulders well laid back; legs moderate bone and straight.

Body
Short-coupled with plenty of spring of rib. Back level. Chest moderate leaving ample heart room.

Hindquarters
Legs with moderate bone; well-turned stifle—no tend-

Colour: black and tan (shading shows position of tan markings).

ency to cow or sickle hocks.

Feet
Compact, cushioned and well-feathered.

Tail
The docking of tails is optional. No more than one-third to be removed. The length of the tail should be in balance with the body.

Coat
Long, silky and free from curl. A slight wave is permissible. There should be plenty of feather.

Colour
The only recognised colours are: Black and tan: Raven black with tan markings above the eyes, on cheeks, inside ears, on chest and legs and underside of tail. The tan should be bright. Ruby: Whole coloured rich red. Blenheim: Rich chestnut marking well broken up on a pearly white ground. The markings should be evenly divided on the head, leaving room between the ears for the much valued lozenge mark or spot (a unique characteristic of the breed). Tricolour: Black and white well spaced and broken up, with tan markings over the eyes, on cheeks, inside ears, inside legs, and on underside of tail. Any other colour or combination of colours is most undesirable.

Weight and size
Weight: 12 to 18 pounds. A small well-balanced dog well within these weights is desirable.

Faults
Light eyes. Undershot and crooked mouths and pig jaws. White marks on whole-coloured specimens. Coarseness of type. Putty noses. Flesh marks. Nervousness.

Note
Male animals should have two apparently normal testicles fully descended into the scrotum.

AKC VARIATION TO STANDARD
This dog is recognised by the AKC in the Miscellaneous Class.

CHIHUAHUA (LONG AND SMOOTH COAT)

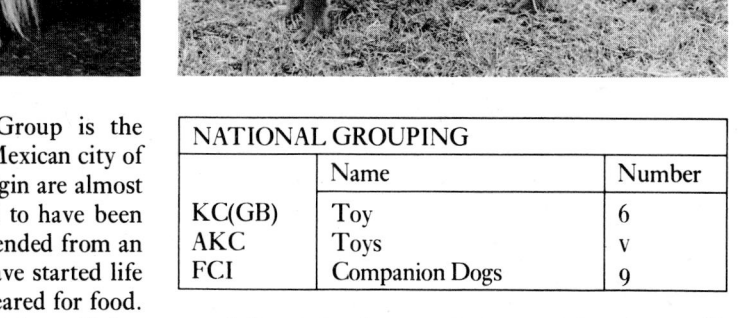

One of the real tinies of the Toy Group is the Chihuahua. It takes its name from the Mexican city of the same name, and the stories of its origin are almost as numerous as the dog itself. It is said to have been the sacred dog of the Aztecs, to be descended from an early mute dog of South America, to have started life with the Incas, and even to have been reared for food. Whatever the real truth is, there is no doubt at all that it is a real South American product. The first record of the breed is of the purchase of a litter of three in 1888, all black and white and with mixed coats. It has been established that he existed as a separate breed as early as the 9th century called the Techichi and kept by the Toltecs. Carvings in the monastery of Huejotzingo depict a dog very like the present day Chihuahua, and this building dates in part to the pyramids of the Toltecs. It is, however, by no means certain that this original Mexican dog was the sole ancestor of the Chihuahua of today, and it is suspected that a small hairless dog such as the Chinese Crested came across from Asia and was used to produce the modern dog.

Columbus in writing to the King of Spain reported that he found small barkless domesticated dogs. Archaeologists have found remains of these little dogs in Mexico and the United States of America. He is said to have played a part in the religious ceremonies of the Aztecs, perhaps even being sacrificed. According to Aztec mythology the souls of the dead had to be

NATIONAL GROUPING		
	Name	Number
KC(GB)	Toy	6
AKC	Toys	v
FCI	Companion Dogs	9

guarded over the rivers on their way to the other world, and payment had to be made by means of slips of paper to the dogs that performed this duty. This possibility led to the practice of sacrificing dogs and burning the corpses as part of the funeral rite. Whatever the truth of the ancestry of the Chihuahua there is no doubt at all that the modern dog that has resulted from selective breeding from the original imports from Mexico has become not only the smallest, but one of the most popular dogs in the world. From the two dozen or so dogs imported into the United States between 1850 and the end of the century almost all the Chihuahuas of today are descended. The breeders worked hard on their dogs and in 1904 the American Kennel Club recognised the breed, and accepted the registration of the Chihuahua Club of America in 1923.

He was certainly known in Britain in the early part of this century, and probably before, but it was not until considerably later, in 1934 that a breeding pair was imported into the country, and not until after the Second World War that the breed became in any way popular. Since that time its rise has been phenomenal and something over four thousand registrations in both coats are now recorded annually at the Kennel Club. For some time the two coats were exhibited together, but in recent years, in 1952 in the United States and 1965 in Britain, the varieties were separated.

The Chihuahua is a wonderful show dog as he completely forgets his lack of size, and refuses to be intimated by any other dog in the ring, however large it may happen to be. He is of course remarkably portable, and it is not unusual for one exhibitor to take as many as twenty to one show at a time. In the ring he is completely fearless, accepting being handled by a stranger, not disturbed by extraneous noises, and in the Group is always very competitive. As a pet he is delightful, being a real toy, a mere handful of a dog but at the same time an excellent guard, being most alert and noisy at the approach of strangers. Oddly enough he prefers the company of his own kind, and whilst he will suffer the company of any number of other Chihuahuas, he objects strongly to any other breed of dog.

OFFICIAL STANDARD

Characteristics
An alert and swift moving little dog with a saucy expression.

General appearance
Small, dainty and compact with a brisk forceful action.

Head and skull
A well rounded 'Apple Dome' skull with or without Molero, cheeks and jaws lean, nose moderately short, slightly pointed. Definite stop.

Eyes
Full, round but not protruding, set well apart, dark or ruby. (Light eyes in light colours permissible).

Ears
Large, set on at an angle of about 45 degrees; this gives breadth between the ears.

Mouth
Level, scissor bite.

Ears: large, set at 45 degrees.

Neck
Slightly arched, of medium length.

Forequarters
Shoulders should be well up, lean, sloping into a slightly

Forequarters: shoulders lean and sloping, straight forelegs.

Tail: should be long, and full as a plume.

broadening support above straight forelegs that are set well under, giving free play at the elbows.

Body
Level back, slightly longer than the height at shoulder. Well sprung ribs with deep brisket.

Hindquarters
Muscular with hocks well apart, neither out nor in, well let down.

Feet
Small with toes well split up, but not spread, pads cushioned. Fine pasterns (neither 'Hare' nor 'Cat' foot). A dainty foot with nails moderately long.

Tail
Medium length carried up or over the back. Preferred furry, flattish in appearance, broadening slightly in the centre and tapering to a point.

Coat
Smooth, of soft texture, close and glossy.

Colour
Any colour or mixture of colours.

Body: level back, slightly longer than height at shoulder.

Feet: small, fine, dainty.

Coat: a large ruff on the neck is desired.

Note
Male animals should have two apparently normal testicles fully descended into the scrotum.

LONG COAT
The Standard of the Chihuahua (Long Coat) is the same as the Standard of the Chihuahua (Smooth Coat) with the exception of the following:

Coat
Long, of soft texture (never coarse or harsh to the touch) either flat or slightly wavy. No tight curly coat. There should be feathering on the feet and legs, pants on the hind legs, a large ruff on the neck is desired and preferred, the tail should be long and full as a plume.

Weight
Up to six pounds, with 2 or 4 pounds preferable. If two dogs are equally good in type, the more diminutive preferred.

Faults
Cropped tail, brokendown ears.

AKC VARIATION TO STANDARD
The long and smooth-coated varieties are shown as one class in the USA. *Tail:* tip just touching back, never tucked under.

ENGLISH TOY TERRIER (BLACK AND TAN)

NATIONAL GROUPING		
	Name	Number
KC(GB)	Toy	6
AKC	Toys	v
FCI	Companion Dogs	9

Most of the toy dogs have an ancestry that is based on one or more of the dogs that form the other Groups, so that we have toy Spaniels, toy Greyhounds and of course toy Terriers. As most of the Terriers originated from Britain it is natural enough that the typical example in the Toy Group should be called the English Toy Terrier. Towards the end of the 19th century one of the most popular of Terriers in England was the Black and Tan Terrier, known as the Manchester Terrier, a breed which exists to this day, and in the United States the English Toy Terrier is known as The Manchester Terrier (Toy). They were vermin killers and one of the favourite dogs for use in the rat pits, a popular form of sport among the working classes, and indeed among the gentry too at that time. The common practice of miniaturisation produced the Black and Tan Toy Terrier, and this was done either by selecting smaller specimens to breed from, or as has been suggested by crossing with the Italian Greyhound. The second method is likely as the English Toy Terrier (Black and Tan), to give it its full name, is a much more delicate animal than the Manchester or the old-fashioned Black and Tan Terrier from which he is supposed to have descended, which looked rather like a Staffordshire Bull Terrier. An early standard of the Black and Tan of 1881 reveals that miniatures existed at a very early stage, as the weight permitted is from seven to twenty pounds indicating that small and normal Terrier sized specimens were exhibited together.

The pattern of the colouring of the breed has been considered so important that the breed club and the Kennel Club have laid down strict standards that must be adhered to. The black parts of the coat must be jet black, the tan a rich mahogany and this must appear on the muzzle, the underjaw and the throat with a small spot on each cheek. The tan on the forelegs must reach up to the knee in front and the elbow behind with a thin black line called the 'pencilling' up each toe and with a black thumb mark on each pastern. The colour requirements are just as strict on other parts of the body and this very carefully devised pattern is an attempt to retain the original black and tan markings of the parent stock, which dates back centuries.

In recent years, the breed, along with its larger cousin the Manchester Terrier, has gone into something of a decline. It seems that fewer and fewer people are interested in the traditional and tend to become involved in things that are more modern and exotic. Whilst the registration figures in the country of origin of this attractive little dog have dropped to below fifty each year and the Manchester likewise, breeds that only a comparative short time ago were being exhibited among the foreign dogs at our major shows boast ten times as many. One reason for this is probably that breeders in recent years have failed to produce a sound dog, sacrificing construction to the more specialist features such as the colour and markings, and many of the dogs entered at shows nowadays are rather weak and weedy specimens with none of the staunch terrier character of their forebears.

He has never made much of a mark in the show ring, being overshadowed by the more picturesque 'comforter' breeds in the Toy Group, and many people prefer a breed of dog that has been associated with man—or more particularly in some cases with woman—down through the centuries. He suffers from the disadvantage of being considered by some to have a rather plebeian background rather than to have descended from the pets of kings and princes. A good one is, however, very attractive in the ring, and judges who have studied the dog's past history and who understand him, will sometimes look with favour on a good specimen in strong competition. There is always the feeling with a breed such as the English Toy Terrier that he is part of our heritage and should be looked upon with certain sympathy.

OFFICIAL STANDARD

General appearance
A well balanced, elegant and compact Toy with Terrier temperament and characteristics. It must be borne in mind that in the past the breed was required frequently to be able to acquit itself satisfactorily in the rat pit. Therefore present day specimens should be sleek and cleanly built giving an appearance of alertness combined with speed of movement but not of whippet type.
In realization of the fact that this is a Toy Dog with Terrier characteristics unduly nervous specimens cannot rank as wholly typical representatives of the breed. Judges, when officiating, should bear this in mind.

Head and skull
The head should be long and narrow with a flat skull, wedge-shaped without emphasis of cheek muscles and well filled up under the eyes. The top and bottom jaws should be held tightly together within compressed lips. Upon close inspection of the foreface one finds indications of a slight 'stop'. The foreface then tapers gently to provide a wedge-shaped impression in profile similarly corresponding to that given when it is viewed direct. Although an illusion of being 'overshot' can result, any suggestion

Ears: candle-flame shape.

of a snipy appearance is undesirable. Nose—Black.

Eyes
These should be very dark to black without light shading from the iris. They should be small, almond shaped, obliquely set and sparkling.
Note: Light, large and round, protruding or disproportionately wide or narrow set eyes should be regarded as faults.

Ears
These should be of 'candle-flame' shape, slightly pointed at the tips, placed high upon the back of the skull and proportionately close together. A guide to the size can be obtained by bending the ear forward. It should not reach the eye. From nine months of age the ear carriage must be erect. The entire inside of the ear should face the front. The leather of the ear should be thin. A cat ear appearance is wrong.
Note: Large or 'flapping' ears should be regarded as faults.

Mouth
Teeth should be level and strong. The upper front teeth should close slightly over the lower front teeth, the latter to lean forward fractionally thus establishing the correct level bite.

Head: long, wedge-shaped.

Neck

The neck should be long, graceful, and slightly arched. The shoulders should be well laid back not straight. The pattern of the neck line flowing into the shoulders, and sloping off elegantly. Throatiness is undesirable.

Forequarters

The chest narrow and deep. Legs falling straight from the shoulders, with the elbows close to the chest providing a straight front. Loose elbows and wide fronts are faults. Fine bone is eminently desirable. The ideal fore-movement is that akin to the 'extended trot', hackney action is not desirable; equally to be discouraged is a 'shuffling' gait.

Body

The body is compact, head and legs proportionate thus producing correct balance. The back very slightly curving from behind the shoulder to the loin falling again to the root of the tail. The chest should be narrow and deep with the ribs well sprung to a well cut up loin. The buttocks should be gently rounded.

Faults

A roached, dipped or dead flat back, hindquarters higher than the shoulders.

Hindquarters

A well-rounded loin leading to a good turn of stifle is required, hocks well let down, a 'tucked under' appearance is undesirable. Hind-action should be smooth and suggest ease and precision combined with drive. There should be a 'flowing quality' to give true soundness.

Feet

Dainty compact, split up between the toes, and well arched, with jet black nails; the two middle toes of the front feet rather longer than the others and the hind feet shaped like those of a cat. Hare feet are not desirable, and should be regarded as a fault.

Tail

The tail should be thick at the root, tapering to a point. Set low and not reaching below the hock. A 'gay' tail carriage is undesirable if displayed to excess.

Coat

The texture should be thick, close, smooth and of glossy appearance. A density of short hair is required.

Note: Sparse, weak coats should be regarded as faults.

Colour

Black and tan. The black should be ebony and the tan can be likened to a new chestnut, deeply rich. These colours should not run, or blend into each other, but should meet abruptly, forming clear and well defined lines of colour division. Forelegs tanned to the knee in front. The tan then continuing inside and at the back of the foreleg to a point just below the elbow. A thin black line up each toe (Pencilling) and a clearly defined black mark 'thumb mark' on the centre of each pastern, and under the chin.

The hind legs should be well tanned in front and the inside, with a black 'bar' dividing the tan at the centre of the lower thigh. Each toe 'pencilled'. Heavy tan on the outside of the hindquarters, 'breeching', is a fault. On the head the muzzle is well tanned, nose black, the black continuing along the top of the muzzle, curving below the eyes to the base of the throat. A tan spot above each eye and a small tan spot on each cheek. The under jaw and throat are tanned, the lip line black. The hair inside the ears tanned (tan behind the ears a fault). Each side of the chest is slightly tanned. The vent and under root of the tail tanned. White hairs forming a patch anywhere are a serious fault.

Weight and size

The ideal weight is between that of 6 to 8 pounds and a height of 10 to 12 inches at the shoulders is most desirable. Judges are encouraged to use scales, as it is hoped this will help to establish uniformity.

Note

Male animals should have two apparently normal testicles fully descended into the scrotum.

AKC VARIATION TO STANDARD

This dog is granted championship status by the AKC, as the Manchester Terrier (Toy) in Group V: Toys.

GRIFFON BRUXELLOIS

This little dog started life as a guard on the front seats of cabs in Brussels, where his wonderful spirit in spite of lack of size, endeared him to a great number of people. Something of a street urchin still, the 'gamin' of the dog world, his quaint appearance and cockiness make him one of the personality dogs if not one of the beauties of the Toy Group. His ancestry is a little confused, but he probably descended from the German Affenpinscher and a mixture of street curs that frequented the less fashionable areas of Brussels during the last century and earlier. There were a number of breeds in Belgium and Northern France at one time that had the rough coat and moustachioed appearance of the Griffon Bruxellois, but most of them were considerably larger and were hunting dogs. It is not difficult, however, to picture a situation in which smaller specimens unsuitable for chasing game would find their way into the hands of pet owners who used them as a basis for a particular breed of their own.

Later this little rough-coated dog was crossed with the Pug and produced the smooth-coated variety known as the Brabançon. By 1880 the breed was established and was being shown, and some authorities suggest that at around that time Schnauzer and Yorkshire Terrier blood was introduced to improve the coat and reduce the size of the breed. It has also been suggested that the King Charles Spaniel was used to give the breed the characteristic very short

NATIONAL GROUPING		
	Name	Number
KC(GB)	Toy	6
AKC	Toys	V
FCI	Companion Dogs	9

nose. The Griffon Bruxellois first began to appear at shows in Europe in the late 19th century, and was soon adopted in other countries, his quaint assurance endearing him to exhibitors in Britain and the United States.

Those who own a Griffon become addicted to the breed, finding them extremely intelligent and very good guards and companions. Compared with others in the Toy Group he lacks any hint of aristocratic background, but in any case he lays no claim to this, and is prepared to be accepted at face value. He is certainly no beauty, but his facial expression and the peculiar whiskered foreface give him a charm all of his own. He is very much the man-in-the-street's toy dog as far as appearance goes, but he has now outlived his lowly background and has become accepted as something of a society pet among the few who own the breed. He is still something of the Terrier, will hunt if he is given the opportunity, and he is among the strongest and sturdiest built of any in the Toy Group.

The Griffon has never made a great impact as a show dog, one or two kennels only showing the breed at the highest level. Registrations have hardly varied over the years from their fairly low figure which compares with the Maltese or the Lakeland Terrier in Britain, and is considerably lower in some countries. He has the sort of coat that does not need a great deal of attention, having something of the quality of the Irish Terrier's and not requiring the excessive trimming that many of the Terriers do. Some tend to be rather nervous in the ring, the Brabançon version perhaps more so than the Bruxellois, but the ones that have confidence show remarkably well.

In the home he is a fearless little dog, having a strongly developed territorial sense, and being very possessive about the family to which he belongs. To them he is most affectionate, and having no vices, he makes a splendid pet and companion. He needs to be appreciated as the intelligent dog that he is, and when trained he becomes very obedient and easily managed.

OFFICIAL STANDARD

Characteristics
The Griffon is a smart little dog with the disposition of a terrier. There are two varieties, the rough coated, the Griffon Bruxellois and the smooth coated, the Petit Brabancon. Both with the pert monkey-like expression but heavy for their size.

General appearance
A well-balanced square little dog, lively and alert, giving the appearance of measuring the same from withers to tail root as from withers to ground. Its action should be free, well bent hocks giving the correct drive from behind and moving true coming and going. High stepping front movement should be discouraged.

Head and skull
The head should be large and rounded but in no way domed and should be wide between the ears. Hair on the skull, in the rough variety, should be rather coarse. Nose always black, as short as possible, with large open

Head and skull: large, rounded, furnished with beard.

nostrils, high set sloping back to the skull with a deep stop between nose and skull. Wide muzzle, neat lips and with good turn-up. Chin prominent and slightly undershot without showing teeth and (in the rough variety) furnished with a beard.

Eyes
Black rimmed, very dark, large and round, clear and alert.

Ears
Semi-erect, high set, the smaller the better.

Mouth
Mouth slightly undershot with regular teeth.

Neck
Of medium length, slightly arched, springing from well laid-back shoulders.

Forequarters
Chest rather wide and deep, legs straight of medium length and bone.

Body
Short back, level from withers to tail root, neither roaching nor dipping, deep well-sprung ribs, short strong loin.

Hindquarters
Well muscled thighs of good length, short hocks, carried well bent and turning neither in nor out.

Feet
Small, thick cat-like feet with black toenails.

Tail
Short docked, carried high, emerging at right angles from a level top-line.

Coat
Roughs: harsh wiry and free from curl, preferably with an undercoat. Smooths: short and tight.

Colour
Clear red, black or black and rich tan. In the clear red, a darker shade on the mask and ears is desirable. Ideally each hair should be an even red from tip to root. Frosting on the muzzles of mature smooths should not be penalised.

Weight and size
From 5 to 11 pounds, most desirable 6 to 10 pounds.

Faults
Showing teeth or tongue, overshot or wry mouths, light eyes, brown nose, eyerims or toenails, curly coat, white patches. Roaching or dipping the back should be penalised.

Note
Male animals should have two apparently normal testicles fully described into the scrotum.

AKC VARIATION TO STANDARD
Rough coated variety called 'Brussels Griffon'. Smooth coated variety called 'Brabancon'. *Head:* domed forehead. *Ears:* cropped or natural. *Eyes:* eyelashes long, black. *Jaws:* incisors of lower jaw should protrude over upper incisors; lower jaw rather broad. *Weight:* usually 8 to 10 pounds; should not exceed 12 pounds; a small sturdy, well proportioned dog should not be penalised. *Disqualifications:* dudley or butterfly nose.

ITALIAN GREYHOUND

There can be few dogs with the ancient history of the Italian Greyhound, and even if there are those which compete, few have been recorded as well as he has. He has been a favourite of royalty and the noble families as we know from portraits, and there is even evidence that he existed in that capacity as far back as the glorious days of Pompeii. He is one of the few breeds that has not changed in appearance over the centuries, and the little dogs portrayed in paintings of court favourites by the Spanish and Italian painters of three or four hundred years ago vary hardly at all from those seen in the showrings of today. His actual origin is obvious from his appearance, as he is simply a Greyhound in miniature, and there is little doubt that he was the product of miniaturisation by careful selective breeding. This process, which must have taken many years was itself quite a remarkable achievement as the Greyhound proper can weigh as much as eighty

pounds whilst the toy has been bred down to as little as five pounds.

The first specimens were brought over to Britain in the 17th century during the reign of Charles I, and they quickly became the court favourites they had been in their own country. In later years, the Sportsman's Repository published in 1820, mentions the Italian Greyhound, one of only two toy breeds included in the book, which indicates that he predates most of the Group. He was the favourite of the Court in Britain for many years, and reached the peak of his popularity

345

during the reign of Queen Victoria. Since that time enthusiasm for the breed has declined and in the years immediately following World War II it had almost disappeared from Britain. There is now an upward trend once more, and though it is still one of the minority breeds, numbers are slowly increasing.

One of the problems with the breed was the result of the very miniaturisation that produced it. In the first instance, its sturdiness decreased in proportion to the reduction in size, and some difficulty was experienced in producing really sound specimens of the tiny size that was fashionable. In the early days, when the breed was purely decorative, and when it was expected to do little more than grace a silken cushion, this was not important, but in more recent years, when everyone, and not the least of all, judges, preferred a sound dog even in the tiniest of breeds, this lack of good conformation was a distinct handicap. Fortunately in some countries, and particularly in Scandinavia, the ability to course has been encouraged, and as a result, whilst some of the Scandinavian dogs are a little larger than was at one time fashionable, they can at least perform as a running dog.

In fact the Italian Greyhound is not nearly so tender a dog as has been made out. There are old stories that his bones were not strong enough to stand any sort of rough and tumble, and one writer even gave instructions on how to pick up an Italian Greyhound without breaking it. The same writer would have been surprised to see one belonging to the author jump from a bedroom window at a height of fifteen feet, shake on landing and run off across the lawn. He will still chase small game, and he has a leaping ability that even permits him to capture small and unsuspecting birds in flight. He does, however, need rather more shelter and warmth than many breeds as his coat is fine and silky, and he does not enjoy either cold or strong winds.

As a show dog he has suffered from the fault, already mentioned, of lack of good conformation, but he is still a delightful dog to exhibit. He has the natural good manners of his ancestral cousin the Greyhound, and the ability of the Whippet to stand still. He is not an easy dog to condition as his appetite is small and unless he is given a great deal of exercise to build up muscle and encourage eating, he tends to look rather frail. Temperamentally he is quite delightful, and those who have owned one can readily understand the reason for him becoming a Court favourite. He is a little reserved, becomes very attached to one person only, and occupies so little space that he can, and does, accompany his owner everywhere.

OFFICIAL STANDARD

Characteristics
High stepping and free action.

General appearance
A miniature Greyhound, more slender in all proportions, and of ideal elegance and grace in shape, symmetry and action.

Head and skull
Skull long, flat and narrow. Muzzle very fine. Nose dark in colour.

Eyes
Rather large, bright, and full of expression.

Ears
Rose-shaped, placed well back, soft and delicate.

Mouth
Teeth level.

Neck
Should be long and gracefully arched.

Forequarters
Shoulders long and sloping. Legs straight, well set under the shoulders; fine pasterns; small delicate bones.

Body
Chest deep and narrow. Back curved, and drooping at the hindquarters.

Head: muzzle very fine.

Hindquarters
Hocks well let down. Thighs muscular.

Feet
Long, hare-feet.

Tail
Rather long, fine, with low carriage.

Coat
Skin fine and supple. Hair, thin and glossy, like satin.

Colour
Recognised colours, all shades of fawn, white cream, blue,

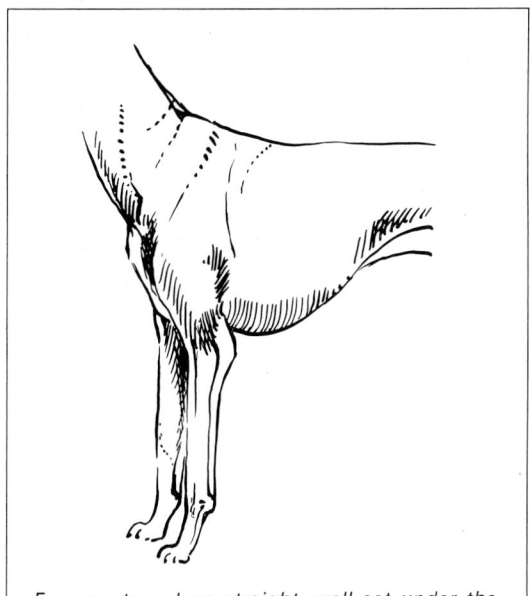

Forequarters: legs straight, well set under the shoulders.

Note
Male animals should have two apparently normal testicles fully descended into the scrotum.

black and fawn and white pied.

Weight and size
The most desirable weight is from 6 to 8 pounds, and not exceeding 10 pounds.

Faults
Black or blue with tan markings, brindle.

AKC VARIATION TO STANDARD
Eyes: medium size. *Feet:* well arched toes. *Size:* height at withers ideally 13 to 15 inches.

JAPANESE CHIN

NATIONAL GROUPING		
	Name	Number
KC(GB)	Toy	6
AKC	Toys	V
FCI	Companion Dogs	9

Several of the small dogs that have become part of the everyday dog show scene in the modern Western World, started off as breeds that were favoured by the courts of the Orient. The Japanese, Japanese Spaniel, or Chin is one of them. Although its name infers that it owes its origins to Japan, it almost certainly in fact originated in China and it has been reported that a pair was presented by the emperor of China to the emperor of Japan some thousand years ago. The similarity between this little dog and the Pekingese is no accident, and there is little doubt that the one is the result of changes brought about by the selective breeding from the other, though which came first it is impossible to say.

In 1853 Commodore Perry was presented with a pair of these dogs which he brought back to Britain and presented to Queen Victoria whose interest in dogs is well known. Later others were brought out of the Orient by sailors who realised the potential profit in taking these tiny dogs back to Europe and the United States. In 1894 the breed was recognised by the Kennel Club in Britain and soon afterwards their influence on the toy dog world was felt in many other countries. The early specimens brought into the Western World were larger than the dogs seen today, and some miniaturisation was resorted to. This was probably done by selection, but possibly by the introduction of the King Charles Spaniel blood already available, and

individuals were eventually bred which weighed as little as two and a half pounds as adults. The efforts of the Japanese Chin Club did much to settle the standard of the breed and it is largely due to them that we now have a very sound little dog of around seven pounds in weight.

Numbers in recent years have remained very steady and the breed is firmly established as a show dog. At one time he was said to be a dog that was constitutionally delicate and needed special care in feeding. Opinion has changed, however, and there is now no reason why because his origin was oriental that he should be considered incapable of standing up to western climate or that his diet should largely consist of rice. Most of the breed are black and white, but other colours such as red, or lemon or even brindle markings are acceptable. He has one breed characteristic which differentiates him from many other breeds in that his eyes are placed wide apart on his skull which, in his effort to look straight ahead give him a perpetual astonished and even apparently cross-eyed look.

He makes a delightful little show dog, as he is something of an extrovert and enjoys being in the public eye, but it is probably as a puppy that he is at his most attractive, being just a tiny ball of black and white fluff which children find adorable. He has never been among the top winners at major shows in Britain, but is always much admired for his aristocratic and stylish appearance. Many carry profuse coats of great quality and his sparkling colours in contrast with his white coat make him an attraction whenever he appears in the ring. His manners are impeccable and he is a bright, intelligent and alert companion. He is sensitive and responsive to human companionship becoming very much part of the family that adopts him, and his diminutive size makes him an ideal pet for the small house or flat.

OFFICIAL STANDARD

Characteristics
The Japanese Chin is a lively little dog of dainty appearance, smart compact carriage and profuse coat. These dogs should be essentially stylish in movement, lifting the feet high when in motion, carrying the tail, which is heavily feathered, closely curved or plumed over the back.

Head
Large but in proportion to size of dog, broad skull rounded in front, rounded between ears but in no way domed.

Head and skull: broad skull rounded in front. Muzzle short and wide. Eyes large, dark, set wide apart.

Nostrils
Should be large and black, except in the case of the red and white, where the colour can be the same as the markings.

Eyes
Should be large, dark, set far apart. It is desirable that the white shows in the inner corners, this gives the Japanese Chin that characteristic look of astonishment (wrongly called squint) which should on no account be lost.

Muzzle
Muzzle very short and wide and well cushioned, i.e. upper lips rounded on each side of nostrils and mouth level.

Ears
Small, set wide apart and high on the head, carried slightly forward, v-shaped and well feathered.

Neck
Moderate length held up proudly.

Body
Should be squarely and compactly built, wide in chest, 'cobby' in shape. The length of the dog's body should be equal to its height at the withers.

Forequarters
Legs straight, and bone fine, giving them a slender appearance, well feathered to the feet.

Hindquarters
Straight viewed from behind, good turn of stifle, profusely feathered from the back of the thighs.

Feet
Should be slender and hare shaped, feathered at tips.

Tail
Set high on a straight back, profusely feathered, closely curved or plumed over the back.

Coat
Profuse coat, long soft and straight of silky texture. Absolutely free from curl or wave, not too flat, having a tendency to stand out especially at the frill of the neck.

Colour
Black and white or red and white. Red includes all shades, sable, brindle, lemon or orange. The brighter and clearer the red the better. Colour evenly distributed on the cheeks and ears, and as patches on the body. Not too heavily marked desirable. White should be clear, not flecked.

Size
The daintier they are the better, providing type, quality and soundness are not sacrificed. As a guide suggested size 4 to 7 pounds.

Faults
Flying ears, wry mouth, tongue showing, tri-colour.

Note
Male animals should have two apparently normal testicles fully descended into the scrotum.

AKC VARIATION TO STANDARD
Nose: nostrils must be colour of dog's markings. *Neck:* should be short and moderately thick. *Tail:* must be well twisted to either right or left from root or carried up over back and flow on opposite side. *Disqualification:* in black and whites, a nose any other colour than black.

KING CHARLES SPANIEL

NATIONAL GROUPING		
	Name	Number
KC(GB)	Toy	6
AKC	Toys	V
FCI	Companion Dogs	9

Many of the toy dogs have their origin in breeds that still exist in other Groups, for example the Italian Greyhound is descended from the gazelle hounds and probably from the Greyhound proper. The English Toy Spaniel, or the King Charles Spaniel as he is known in Britain, is another example. The word 'spaniel' itself suggests Spain as the origin of the race, and there is little doubt that although variations on the spaniel theme have occurred in many countries the whole family originated on the Iberian peninsula. At one time the present differences were not so clearly defined and it is unlikely that the King Charles Spaniel and the Cavalier King Charles existed as different breeds; they were all toy Spaniels. This particular little dog descended from a breed that was a great favourite of King Charles II, and Macauley writes of the King that he could be seen before the dew was off the grass in St. James's Park, striding among the trees and playing with his Spaniels.

It is claimed by some sources that the Spaniel originated in the Far East, and that it was in Spain that larger specimens were developed as gundogs and sporting dogs, the smaller ones remaining as toy dogs. The fact, however, that Dr. Caius, physician to Queen Elizabeth described Spaniels, and toy Spaniels at that, indicates that the breed has been around for many centuries. Ellis's letters recording the execution of Mary Queen of Scots describes how her toy Spaniel refused to leave her body after her beheading. The dogs so beloved by King Charles II were of the black and tan variety and were later called King Charles in Britain, but the division into the two breeds did not take place until fairly recent times. A good deal of confusion over the name exists even now in the minds of those who do not have the two breeds clearly defined. This has probably led to the situation in which the Cavalier, having completely outstripped the numbers of English Toy Spaniels in Britain, still remains in the Miscellaneous Class in the United States.

The breed still varies a good deal in size and length of leg, and one of the problems is to produce a dog of the desirable weight that retains the soundness of its Spaniel ancestors. The standard describes a compact strong little dog with a wide and deep chest and short straight legs, but in fact the attempts to breed down to a fashionable size have produced a dog that rarely measures up to this. It is probably this as much as anything which has kept him very much a minority breed in recent years and the numbers appearing at major shows in Britain are now comparatively small. He does in fact make a delightful little show dog, having a very appealing look, with his very large dark eyes and low hanging ears, and he needs very little preparation to get him ready for the ring. The dog tends to grow a little rough or woolly coat in patches which needs tidying up, but otherwise it is largely a matter of washing and grooming and maintaining the long silky coat. He makes a most attractive pet, being very affectionate and friendly, somewhat reserved towards strangers, but once he has made friends, is very welcoming. His small size, clean habits and quietness endear him to those who own the breed, and those who become attached to him, rarely look for another breed of dog.

OFFICIAL STANDARD

General appearance
Compact and cobby, on refined lines, chest wide and deep, legs short and straight, back short and level. Tail well flagged, and not carried over the level of the back. Movement free active and elegant.

Head and skull
Skull massive in comparison to size, well domed, and full over the eyes. Nose black with large wide open nostrils, very short and turned up to meet the skull. The stop between skull and nose should be well defined. Jaw; muzzle square, wide, and deep and well turned up, lower jaw wide, lips exactly meeting, giving a nice finish.

Eyes: large, dark, set wide apart.

The cheeks should not fall away under the eyes, but be well cushioned up. A protruding tongue is objectionable, but does not disqualify.

Eyes
Very large and dark, set wide apart, with eyelids block square to face line, and with pleasing expression.

Ears
Set on low, and to hang quite flat to cheeks, very long and well feathered.

Coat
Long, silky and straight, a slight wave allowed, not curly. The legs, ears and tail should be profusely feathered.

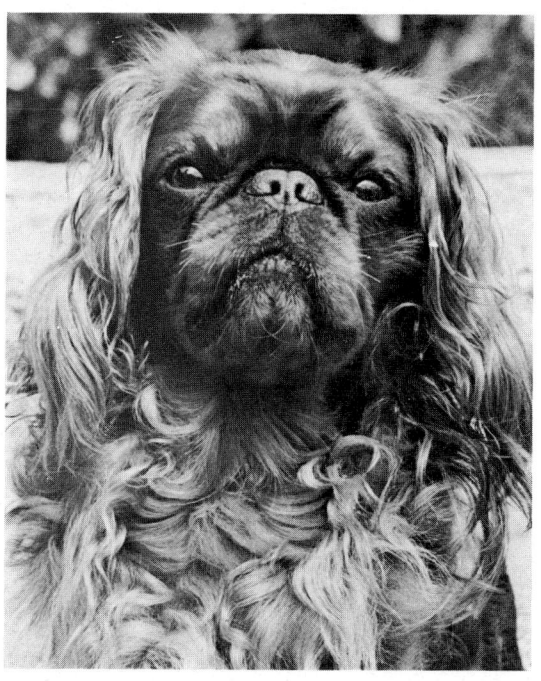

Colour
Black and tan: A rich glossy black, with bright, mahogany tan markings, on muzzle, legs, chest, linings of ears, under tail, and spots over eyes. Tri-colour; Ground pearly white and well distributed black patches, brilliant tan markings on cheeks, linings of ears, under tail, and spots over the eyes. A wide white blaze between the eyes, and up the forehead. Blenheim: A ground of pearly white with well distributed chestnut red patches. A wide clear blaze with the 'spot' in centre of skull. The 'spot' should be a clear chestnut red mark about the size of a sixpence in centre of skull. Ruby: Whole coloured, a rich chestnut red.

Weight and size
The most desirable size is 8 to 14 pounds.

Faults
The presence of a few white hairs on the chest of a black and tan or ruby is undesirable, but a white patch is a major fault.

Note
Male animals should have two apparently normal testicles fully descended into the scrotum.

AKC VARIATION TO STANDARD
Shown as the English Toy Spaniel in the USA. *Colour:* two show varieties. 1 solid colour: King Charles—Black and Tan or Ruby. 2 broken colour: Blenheim and Prince Charles—Tricolour. *Disqualification:* King Charles and Ruby: A white patch on the chest, or white on any other part.

LOWCHEN

NATIONAL GROUPING		
	Name	Number
KC(GB)	Toy	6
AKC	—	–
FCI	Companion Dogs	9

Although this is one of the latest breeds to be admitted to championship level in Britain it is a very ancient type of dog that has been known and exhibited in Europe for a considerable time. It is said variously to have originated in Russia, the Mediterranean and France, and in addition to its two more usual names is also known as the Petit Chien Lion. It was known in Britain at the beginning of this century, but was not imported, and was often said to be found in Germany and Holland. Like many of the small European companion dogs, its origins are fairly obscure. It is clearly related to the Bichon and Barbet, which were themselves connected with the Miniature and Toy Poodles, and there is a certain resemblance though a superficial one, with those breeds.

It would be a mistake to connect the breed with the Lion Dogs of the Far East, which gained their name from the myths connected with their courage rather than with their appearance. The name of the Lowchen, the Little Lion Dog came from the manner in which it was trimmed, giving it the look of a well-maned male lion in miniature. Vero Shaw in 1881 wrote of the Poodle being trimmed to imitate the Lion Dog (*Canis Leoninus*), of which a degenerate scion still exists in Malta; whilst Richard Cope even earlier in 1840

described an animal very like today's Lowchen which he too attributed to Malta but said that it was extremely timid, feeble and inactive, which is completely unlike the dog that we now know. One or two breeders in Europe kept the breed alive during its depressed period in the early part of the present century, Madame M. de Conninck of Dieghem showing them prior to the First World War with some success. It was not, however, until after the Second World War that there was a real revival of interest, principally in Germany.

None were registered in Britain until 1971, but since that time their growth in popularity has been one of the phenomena of the British dog scene, and by 1976 their numbers had risen to such an extent that they were granted championship status, the first challenge certificates being on offer at Crufts of that year. The popularity of the breed continues to grow and they are now being exported to many countries.

He is a sturdy little dog, with a remarkably strong body and stouter construction than the average Poodle of a similar size. His general appearance on casual acquaintance is reminiscent of the Poodle but he differs in many respects, principally in the head, where he is broader and stronger in muzzle, and in proportionately greater strength of body and hindquarters. His coat too is softer and more silky in texture, with a slight wave. He makes a very good show dog, being quite striking in appearance, with considerable variation in colour, and remarkably steady in the ring.

His temperament is quite delightful. He is not the timid, feeble dog that was described a century or so ago, but is bold and very active. He is friendly with everyone, becomes very attached to his owner, and though gay and boisterous, is kind and playful with no vices. He makes an admirable house pet and friend of the family and is very good with children.

OFFICIAL STANDARD

General appearance
Small intelligent dog, affectionate and lively disposition combining all the good qualities of a companion dog. The body is clipped in the traditional lion clip and the tail, also clipped, is topped with a pom pom, thus giving the dog the appearance of a little lion.

Head
Short. Skull wide in proportion.

Nose
Black.

Head: short, broad, well furnished.

Eyes
Round, large and intelligent, dark in colour.

Ears
Pendant, long and well fringed.

Forequarters
Forelegs straight and fine boned.

Body
Short and well proportioned.

Hindquarters
Hindlegs straight when viewed from the rear, with good turn of stifle.

Feet
Small and round.

Tail
Of medium length, clipped with a tuft of hair left to form a pom pom.

Tail: medium length, clipped leaving tuft.

Coat
Fairly long and wavy but not curly.

Colour
Any colour permissible, be it self colour or parti-colour. The most sought after colours are white, black and lemon.

Weight and size
Height 8 to 14 inches (20 to 35 centimetres) at the withers. Weight 4 to 9 pounds.

Faults
Any departure from the foregoing points should be considered a fault and the seriousness of the fault should be in exact proportion to its degree.

Note
Male animals should have two apparently normal testicles fully descended into the scrotum.

AKC VARIATION TO STANDARD
This dog is not granted championship status by the AKC.

MALTESE

Malta as an island has a very ancient and noble history. Its geographical position has always made it an important place in the Mediterranean since it was settled by the Phoenicians some four thousand years ago. It developed a culture and a race of people with distinctive characteristics, and a race of dogs in the little Maltese which differs from almost every other breed. Malta's situation gave it an ecology which remained undiluted by outside influences much as in a very large way did that of Australia, and the Maltese was bred as a pure breed for centuries as a result. Dr. Caius referred to the breed in 1576 when he wrote 'the dogges of this kind doth Callimachus call Melitaers of the Iseland Melita in the sea of Sicily'. They were favourites in the time of Phidias and of the Imperial Court of Rome and Theoprastus wrote 'When his favourite dog dies he deposits the remains in a tomb and erects a monument over the grave with the inscription "Offspring of the stock of Malta"'. Early Italian painters often depicted the breed, or something very like it in court paintings, and though there may

NATIONAL GROUPING		
	Name	Number
KC(GB)	Toy	6
AKC	Toys	V
FCI	Companion Dogs	9

be some confusion with the Shock Dog and the Bichon, many of the early works depict these little dogs so clearly that there is no doubt at all that they are indeed Maltese.

Maltese were first imported into Britain during the reign of Henry VIII and were certainly favourites in the time of Queen Elizabeth I to whose physician we owe our early reference. By the middle of the 19th century the breed was well established as a pet dog in Britain, and when dog shows began, the Maltese featured among the early exhibits. In the period 1860 to 1870 Mr. Mandeville had a brace of dogs that were winning at all the big shows and later other breeders took the Maltese up seriously, giving the breed greater prominence. Later still, by the turn of the century there was some decline and the Maltese was being overtaken by some of the newer Toy breeds being imported into the country. At that time specimens were being exported from Britain into the United States of America, where the splendid coat and sheer showmanship of these beautiful dogs made a rapid impression.

The fact that the Maltese has for centuries been the pampered pet of house and court must to a certain extent account for his refinement and fastidiousness, though it would be a mistake to consider him as just a soft little dog needing special care and attention. He was at one time known as the Maltese Terrier, and there is a good deal of the Terrier in his makeup. He is strong, very active and muscular, and thoroughly enjoys a good deal of exercise. His long silky coat does need, however, a great deal of attention if it is to retain its length and tidiness. He needs considerable bathing to keep the coat white and clean, and only a dog in perfect health will carry the coat of the desired length and quality.

As a show dog he is supreme, having all those qualities which serve a dog so well. He is easily trained to stand still and to move with spirit, he is amenable to discipline and is not easily scared by strangers which means that he will allow himself to be handled in the ring without shrinking away from the judge. His snowy whiteness makes him very attractive in the ring, and he is one of those dogs that looks at his best at an indoor show under powerful artificial light. He makes a very good pet dog and companion, being friendly and attentive to his owner, and enjoying the warmth and comfort of a house, being very much a furniture and fireside dog.

OFFICIAL STANDARD

Characteristics
Sweet tempered and very intelligent.

General appearance
Should be smart, lively and alert. The action must be free, without extended weaving.

Head and skull
From stop to centre of skull (centre between forepart of ears) and stop to tip of nose should be equally balanced. Stop should be defined. Nose should be pure black.

Eyes
Should be dark brown, with black eyerims, set in centre

Body: balanced, short, cobby.

cheeks and not bulging.

Ears
Should be long and well feathered and hanging close to the side of the head, the hair to be mingled with the coat at the shoulders.

Mouth
Level or scissor bite with teeth even.

Neck
Of medium length—set on well sloped shoulders.

Forequarters
Legs should be short and straight. Shoulders well sloped.

Body
Should be in every way well balanced and essentially short and cobby, with good rib spring and the back should be straight from the tip of the shoulders to the tail.

Hindquarters
Legs should be short and nicely angulated.

Head and skull: equally balanced, stop defined.

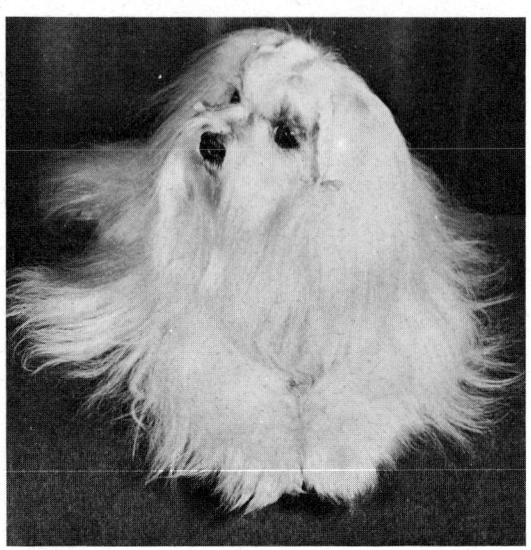

Colour
Pure white, but slight lemon markings should not penalise.

Size
Not over 10 inches from ground to top of shoulder.

Faults
Bad mouth, over or undershot; gay tail; curly or woolly coat; brown nose; pink eye rims; unsound in any way.

Note
Male animals should have two apparently normal testicles fully descended into the scrotum.

Feet
Should be round and the pads of the feet should be black.

Tail
Should be well arched over the back and feathered.

Coat
Should be good length, but not impeding action, of silky texture, not in any way woolly and should be straight. It should not be crimped and there should be no woolly undercoat.

AKC VARIATION TO STANDARD
Tail: long-haired plume carried gracefully over back, its tip lying to side over quarter. *Size:* weight under 7 pounds, 4 to 6 pounds preferred.

MINIATURE PINSCHER

The Miniature Pinscher is an ancient breed, though probably not in the style that we know it today. He is a German dog descended from Terrier types indigenous in Germany for centuries, the word 'pinscher' meaning 'terrier' in the German language. The fact that the Doberman is known as the Doberman Pinscher was a miniaturisation of this breed, a belief heightened by the fact that there is a superficial resemblance. In fact the two are not related and the Miniature Pinscher is probably the older breed. There was at one time a large Pinscher in Germany that existed in two coats, wire and smooth, and it was probably from the latter that the Miniature Pinscher was developed. He was a strong active dog about the size of an Irish Terrier and seems to have had a fondness for stables where he was employed keeping down the rat population. He probably still exists in Germany in his original form, but since the late 19th century, when there was a medley of types, things

NATIONAL GROUPING		
	Name	Number
KC(GB)	Toy	4
AKC	Toys	V
FCI	Companion Dogs	9

have been sorted out and the rough-coated version has been developed into the Schnauzer.

The German *Pinscher Klub* was formed in 1895 and it was this club which gave the breed its standard and improved it prior to the First World War, but it was after the War that the breed really began to make progress. Prior to 1928 and until the breed club was formed in the United States there were few Miniature Pinschers seen in the show rings there. Since that time the breed has developed steadily on both sides of the Atlantic, and whilst the numbers in

Britain remain fairly steady at around the same figure as the Japanese, specimens are now finding their way into a great many countries.

The Miniature Pinscher is a tremendously sturdy and active little dog, hard as nails, so muscular that he can outjump many dogs far larger than he is, and is built in a square and stylish fashion. He is sporting, will hunt all day given the opportunity, and likes nothing better than a scramble through the woods in search of small game, and for that matter not-so-small game too, as he is fearless and will tackle anything several times his size. He is one of the most soundly constructed dogs in the Toy Group, having straight limbs, an excellent conformation, and many of the physical attributes of the working and hunting dogs.

As a show dog there is hardly anything in the Toy Group that can approach him for smartness, style and spirit. He stands like a rock in the ring, and yet is always fully prepared to whip round at the too-near approach of another dog, being continually on guard against intrusion into what he feels is his territory. His outline has the smart clean-cut look of the trotting pony, an illusion which is increased by his straight legs and close, hard and lustrous coat. He is a dog that always has the appearance of supreme fitness, and it is this look, combined with his snappy appearance in the ring which always makes him a very keen competitor at the major shows.

He is very much the house dog these days, as the need for vermin hunters in modern society has declined, but he makes a very good one, being an extremely keen guard, with an alert sense of hearing and well-developed quick reactions to anything unusual. He is friendly though somewhat reserved at first approach, and until he has ascertained that a visitor is welcome, he is somewhat guarded in his approach. Once he has made friends, however, he is pleasant and sociable, and towards his own household he is free from vice and amenable to discipline.

OFFICIAL STANDARD

General appearance
The Miniature Pinscher is structurally a well balanced, sturdy, compact, elegant, short-coupled, smooth-coated toy dog. He is naturally well groomed, proud, vigorous and alert. The natural characteristic traits which identify him from other toy dogs are his precise Hackney gait, his fearless animation, complete self-possession and his spirited presence.

Head and skull
Rather more elongated than short and round. Narrow and without conspicuous cheek formation. In correct proportion to the body. The skull should appear flat when viewed from the front. The muzzle must be rather strong and proportionate to the skull. The nose well formed, black only with the exception of livers and blues, which may have a self-coloured nose.

Head and skull: rather elongated, skull flat from front, drop-ear version.

Eyes
Fitting well into the face. Neither too full nor round, neither too little nor slanting. Black or nearly black.

Ears
Must be set on high, as small as possible, erect or dropped.

Mouth
Scissors bite.

Neck
Strong yet graceful. Slightly arched. Well fitted into the shoulders. Free from throatiness.

Ears: Set on high erect version.

Forequarters

Forechest well developed and full, moderately broad, shoulders clean, sloping with moderate angulation. Co-ordinated to permit the true action of the Hackney pony.

Body

To be square, back line straight, sloping slightly towards the rear. Belly moderately tucked up. Ribs well sprung, deep rather than barrelled. Viewed from the top slightly wedge shaped.

Hindquarters

Should be parallel to each other and wide enough apart to fit in with a properly built body. The hindquarters should be well developed and muscular with a good sweep of stifle and their hocks turning neither in or out.

Feet

Legs straight, medium bone. Feet cat-like, elbows close to body. Nails dark.

Tail

A continuation of the top-line carried a little high and docked short.

Coat

Smooth, hard and short. Straight and lustrous. Closely adhering to and uniformly covering the body.

Colour

Black, blue, chocolate with sharply defined tan markings on cheeks, lips, lower jaw, throat, twin spots above eyes and chest, lower half of fore-legs, inside of hindlegs and vent region, lower portion of hocks and feet. All the above colours should have black pencilling on toes with no thumb marks. Solid red of various shades. Slight white on chest is permissible but undesirable.

Height

The height is to range from 10 to 12 inches at the withers.

Note

Male animals should have two apparently normal testicles fully descended into the scrotum.

AKC VARIATION TO STANDARD

Eyes: full, slightly oval, almost round. *Teeth:* perfect alignment and apposition. *Ears:* upstanding. *Nose:* black only with exception of chocolates which may have self-coloured nose. *Faults:* structurally lacking in balance, too long- or short-coupled, too coarse or too refined (lacking in bone development causing poor feet and legs), too large or too small, lethargic, timid or dull, shy or vicious, low in tail placement and poor in action (action not typical of the breed requirements). Knotty over-developed muscles. *Head:* too large or too small for the body, too coarse or too refined, pinched and weak in foreface, domed in skull, too flat and lacking in chiselling, giving a vapid expression. *Neck:* too straight or too curved; too thick or too thin; too long or short; knotty muscles; loose, flabby or wrinkled skin. *Body:* from top—too long, too short, too barreled, lacking in body development. From side—too long, too short, too thin or too fat, hips higher or considerably lower than withers, lacking depth of chest, too full in loin, sway back, roach back or wry back. From rear—quarters too wide or too close to each other, overdeveloped, barreled vent, underdeveloped vent, too sloping croup, tail set low. Forequarters—forechest and spring of rib too narrow (or too shallow and underdeveloped), shoulders too straight, too loose, or too short and overloaded with muscles. Hindquarters—too narrow, undermuscled or overmuscled, too steep in croup. Too thick or thin bone development, large joints, spreading flat feet. *Forelegs and Feet:* bowed or crooked, weak pasterns, feet turning in or out, loose elbows. Hind legs—thin underdeveloped stifles, large or crooked hocks, loose stifle joints. *Tail:* set too low, too thin, drooping, hanging or poorly docked. *Coat:* thin, too long, dull; upstanding; curly; dry; area of various thickness or bald spots. Any colour other than listed; very dark or sooty spots. *Faults:* oversize; undersize; too fat; too lean. *Disqualifications:* colour: thumb marks or any area of white on feet or forechest exceeding $\frac{1}{2}$ inch in its longest dimension. *Size:* a dog of either sex measuring under 10 or over $12\frac{1}{2}$ inches.

PAPILLON

This little dog is another of the dwarf Spaniels evolved in Europe from the root stock which was either Oriental or Spanish in origin, and opinions differ on that point. He was known centuries ago, as there is a record of one having been sold as early as 1545, and certainly Madame de Pompadour and Marie Antoinette were both owners and admirers of the breed. The dog first became popular in Spain, where it was the pet of the courts, and it soon spread as fashion decreed that it should, through Italy where it became very popular and to France where it gained its name. The overall appearance of the head, with its large upstanding fringed ears and clearly defined blaze down the face was said to resemble the butterfly, hence the name

NATIONAL GROUPING		
	Name	Number
KC(GB)	Toy	6
AKC	Toys	V
FCI	Companion Dogs	9

Papillon. They were at one time known as Squirrel Spaniels because they carried their heavily plumed tail over their back as does the squirrel, and the version with the folded down ears, accepted as a separate breed in some continental countries, was called the Phalene as the head was then said to resemble a moth.

By the turn of the century the breed was being shown

at dog shows in France, and soon afterwards it found its way across the Channel and appeared in the show rings in Britain and the United States. When he first came into Britain he was a much larger dog than is fashionable at the present time, and only careful selective breeding produced the sound very small dog that can be seen today, though even now from time to time larger specimens are produced which are unsuitable for the show ring but which make very attractive pets. In the early days too, they were often self-coloured, red-mahogany, ruby, reddish chestnut or dark yellow, lending weight to the argument that they were closely related to some of the other small Spaniels. It became fashionable, however, to breed the white dogs with patches of these colours, and this is the type that has survived and the standard now states that he should always be a parti-coloured dog.

The Papillon is a hardy little dog, not nearly so delicate as his appearance might suggest, and certainly not needing as much coddling as some people give him. He has a fairly long fine coat which is weather resistant and neither winter cold nor summer heat appears to worry him. He is a refined and not a cobby dog, but his

bone though slender is straight and this, together with his well-developed hindquarters make him one of the more active members of the Group. He is still something of a hunter, enjoys pursuing vermin, and will kill a rat if given the opportunity.

He makes a fine show dog, being smart, active in the ring and very amenable to discipline. The variation in the colours, and the snowy whiteness of the white parts of his coat make an attractive picture when a number of them are gathered in the ring together. He is steady, and when trained to the ring, carries his head with great pride and his tail curled over giving a picture of a very alert little dog doing his best to please. Preparation is no problem, as keeping the coat in condition is largely a matter of physical fitness and of washing and brushing to get the best out of the fine long silky coat. The fringes on the ears are a desirable feature, and exhibitors spend considerable time and ingenuity in growing and keeping these as long as possible. As a pet he is delightful, being merry and sociable and liking nothing better than being in the company of those to whom he becomes firmly attached.

OFFICIAL STANDARD

General appearance
This dainty, balanced little toy dog should have an attractive head, an alert bearing and an intelligent and lively expression. Movement should be sound, light and free and not cramped or restricted in any way.

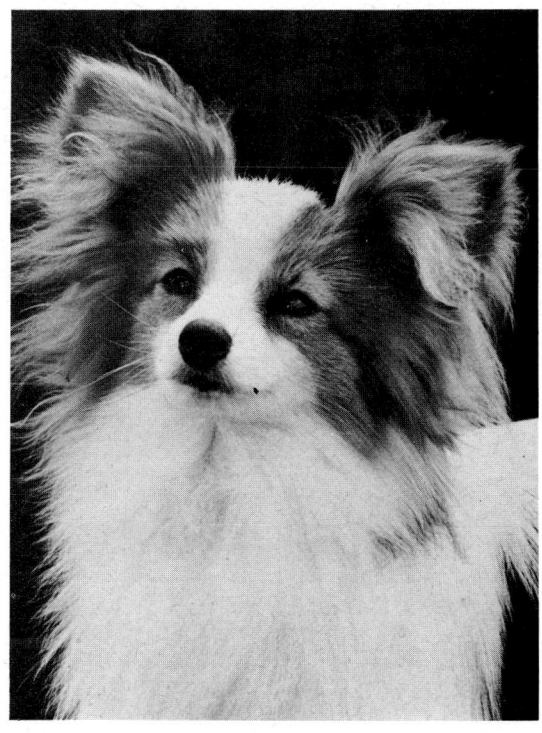

Head and skull
The skull slightly rounded between the ears, the muzzle finely pointed and abruptly thinner than the skull accentuating the stop which should be well defined. Length from tip of the nose to the stop approximately a third length of the head. Nose should be black.

Faults
Muzzle over long or coarse. Skull flat or apple shaped. Nose other than black.

Eyes
Of medium size, rounded, dark in colour, placed rather low in the head and should not bulge.

Faults
Eyes light in colour, too small or too large or protruding.

Ears
The ears should be large with rounded tips, heavily fringed, set towards the back of the head far enough apart to show the slightly rounded shape of the skull. The ears must be completely erect or dropped. When the ears are erect they must be carried obliquely like the spread wings of a butterfly, therefore the name, Papillon. When the ears are dropped they must be completely dropped, and this type is known as the Phalene (moth).

Faults
Semi-erect or not fully dropped, small, sharply pointed or set too close together.

Mouth
Scissor bite, upper teeth fitting close over lower. The lips thin and tight.

Ears: large, rounded tips, heavily fringed.

Ears: dropped ear version or phalene.

Faults
Over or undershot to the extent that the incisors do not touch at all. Wry mouth.

Neck
Of medium length.

Forequarters
Shoulders well developed and sloping back. Chest rather deep. Forelegs straight and slender and fine boned.

Faults
Shoulders straight. Out at elbow.

Body
Level topline. The body should have plenty of length, well formed with well sprung ribs, good length of loin which must not be weak, with slightly arched belly.

Faults
Topline roached, dipped or cobby. Legs malformed and crooked, cow-hocked, too long or too short. Stifles straight, coupled with weak hindquarters.

Hindquarters
Well developed, good turn of stifle. Legs when viewed from behind, should be parallel. Dew claws on the hind legs must be removed.

Feet
Fine and fairly long as in the hare. The tufts of hair between the toes extending far beyond them.

Tail
Long and well fringed, set on high, arched over the back with the fringes falling to the side to form the plume.

Faults
Tail unduly short, too low set.

Coat
Should be abundant, (flowing) but without undercoat, long, fine, silky, falling flat on back and sides forming a profuse frill on the chest, short and close on the skull, muzzle and front part of the legs. Back part of the front legs to pasterns, tail and thighs covered with long hair.

Faults
Harsh, curly or stand-off coat.

Colour
White with patches which may be any colour except liver. A tricolour must be black and white with tan spots over the eyes, tan inside ears and under root of tail and on cheeks. The head marking should be symmetrical about a white, narrow, clearly defined blaze.

Size
The ideal height at the withers from 8 to 11 inches. The dog will appear to be slightly longer than high when properly furnished with ruff and hind fringes.

Faults
Muzzle over long or coarse. Skull flat or apple shaped. Nose other than black. Eyes light in colour, too small or too large or protruding. Ears semi-erect or not fully dropped, small, sharply pointed or set too close together. Mouth over or undershot to the extent that the incisors do not touch at all. Wry mouth. Shoulders straight. Out at elbow. Topline roached, dipped or cobby. Legs malformed and crooked, cow hocked, too long or too short. Stifles straight, coupled with weak hindquarters. Tail unduly short, too low set. Harsh, curly or stand-off coat.

Note
Male animals should have two apparently normal testicles fully descended into the scrotum.

AKC VARIATION TO STANDARD
Colour: ears must not be white. *Disqualification:* height over 12 inches. All white dog or a dog with no white.

PEKINGESE

NATIONAL GROUPING		
	Name	Number
KC(GB)	Toy	6
AKC	Toys	V
FCI	Companion Dogs	9

The ancient oriental background of this dog makes him one of the most fascinating as well as one of the most popular of all the Toy dogs. His origins are well documented as the country that produced him was one with a long history of keeping written and illustrated records of everything including its animal life. We know therefore more about what the Pekingese looked like centuries ago than we do about almost any other breed. They were the Royal Dogs of China and their history goes back to at least the Tang dynasty. They were held as sacred, and the theft of a dog from the Imperial Palace was punishable by death. The bloodlines were kept pure by breeding them only within the walls of the palace, and staff were kept whose sole duty it was to look after the imperial dogs. Emperors had dog portraits painted in books kept for the purpose, and which formed a pictorial standard of the breed. The staff of eunuchs who looked after the dogs vied with one another as to who should produce the best dogs to present to the Emperor, and remarkable lengths were gone to to encourage desirable features of stunted growth, short nose and exaggerated width of front.

The Emperor's favourites were given rank and were treated as people rather than as dogs, visitors even being expected to pay homage to them. Legend has it that the Pekingese was produced by crossing a marmoset with a lion and that he has had the heart of a lion ever since. Certainly he was a good little fighter, and the eunuchs often staged fights for entertainment. He came into the Western World as the result of the looting of the Imperial Palace at Peking in 1860, when a number of these little dogs were found by the British troops, in spite of the fact that many of them had been killed to prevent them falling into the hands of the enemy. Admiral Lord John who was present at the overrunning of the palace brought five back to Britain on his return, one being presented to Queen Victoria and the other two pairs being kept by the officers concerned. Two of these, that spent the rest of their days at Goodwood were the ancestors of the modern Pekingese.

The Pekingese was first exhibited in Britain in 1893 when the breed appeared at Chester and from that time on, their appearance and their remarkable history captured the public imagination so thoroughly that they quickly became very popular. By 1909 the Pekingese Club of America was in being and since that time this appealing little dog has spread all over the world. His sporting character as well as his somewhat quaint appearance has endeared him to a great number of people. Despite the fact that for centuries he was a pampered pet, he is nothing of the 'softie' being quite fierce when aroused, and by no means averse to having a scrap, something that often leads to trouble as his eyes are particularly vulnerable. He is a strong dog for his size, and when picking one up the impression should be that he is surprisingly heavy for so small a dog.

He makes a wonderful show dog, being very picturesque with his enormous coat, strong colouring and distinctive shape. His head, which is one of his major features, is full of character and to see as one often does, a line of these little dogs being held up for the judge to examine their heads, or being lined up on a table for the same purpose is one of the sights of the show rings of the world. Temperamentally he is very positive and opinionated, wilful even and with fixed ideas about what constitutes his own affairs. He is at the same time extremely friendly. He can be pompous as indeed he has every right to be with his history, and he almost always remains calm and good-tempered. Although rarely aggressive, he remembers that he is supposed to have the heart of a lion and will never turn tail if attacked; and he remains one of the greatest of all the pet dogs.

363

OFFICIAL STANDARD

General appearance
Should be small, well-balanced, thickset dog of great dignity and quality. He should carry himself fearlessly in the ring with an alert, intelligent expression.

Head and skull
Head massive, skull broad, wide and flat between the ears, not domed; wide between eyes. Nose very short and broad, nostrils large, open, and black; muzzle wide, well wrinkled, with firm underjaw. Profile should look quite flat with nose well up between the eyes. Deep stop.

Head: skull broad, wide, flat.

Eyes
Large, clear, dark and lustrous. Prominent but not bolting.

Ears
Heart-shaped, set level with the skull and carried close to the head. Long profuse feathering on ears. Leather not to come below the muzzle.

Mouth
Level lips, must not show teeth or tongue.

Neck
Very short and thick.

Forequarters
Short, thick, heavily-boned forelegs; bones of forelegs bowed but firm at shoulder. Absolute soundness essential.

Body
Short but with broad chest and good spring of rib, falling away lighter behind; lion-like with distinct waist, level back; well slung between the legs, not on top of them.

Hindquarters
Hind legs lighter but firm and well shaped. Close behind but not cow-hocked. Absolute soundness essential.

Feet
Large and flat, not round. The dog should stand well up on feet, not on pasterns. Front feet turned slightly out. Absolute soundness essential.

Gait
A slow dignified rolling gait in front, with a close gait behind, this typical movement not to be confused with a roll caused by slackness of shoulders.

Tail
Set high, carried tightly, slightly curved over back to either side. Long feathering.

Coat
Long and straight with profuse mane extending beyond the shoulders forming a cape or frill round the neck; top coat rather coarse, with thick undercoat. Profuse feathering on ears, legs, thighs, tail and toes.

Colour
All colours and markings are permissible and equally good, except albino or liver. Parti-colours should be evenly broken.

Weight and size
The ideal weight of the Pekingese should not exceed 11 pounds for dogs and 12 pounds for bitches. The dog should look small but be surprisingly heavy when picked up; heavy bone and a sturdy well-built body are essentials of the breed.

Note
Male animals should have two apparently normal testicles fully descended into the scrotum.

AKC VARIATION TO STANDARD
Colour: all colours are acceptable. *Faults:* protruding tongue, badly blemished eye, overshot, wry mouth. *Disqualification:* weight over 14 pounds. Dudley nose.

POMERANIAN

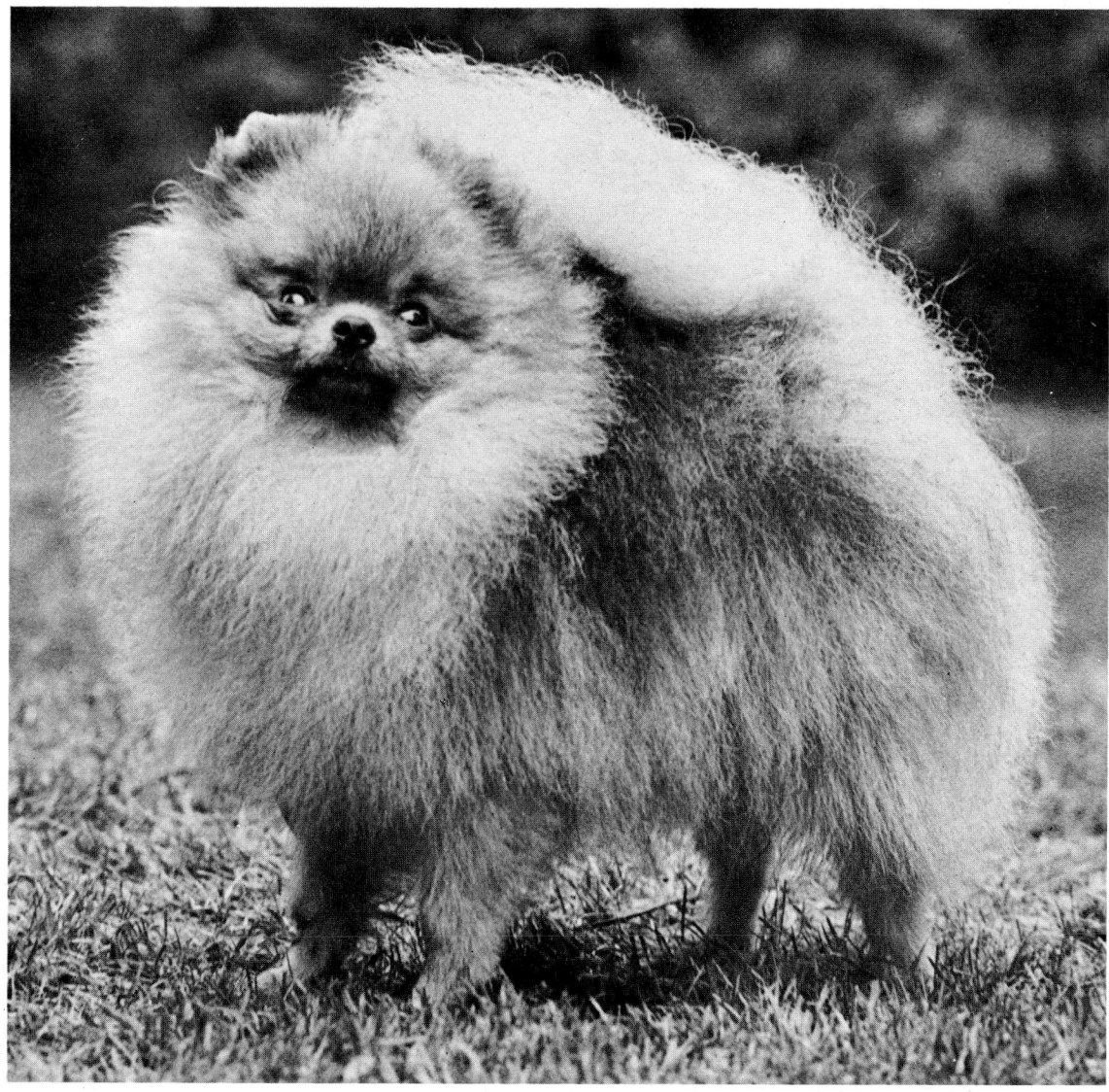

The smallest of the Spitz group of dogs, the Pomeranian is a descendent of the much larger sledge hauling dogs of the Arctic countries. He came to the modern show ring via Germany and more particularly Pomerania, where he was bred down in size from the Deutscher Spitz to the Deutscher Kleinspitz, and from where he took his name once he left his country of origin. In the early stages he was a fairly large dog with herding capabilities, and was often white. This version still survives in some countries where it is known as the Japanese Spitz, but is almost certainly a descendant of the original Pomeranian. In the early years of the breed in the United States of America and Britain white was the fashionable colour and it is only recently that this

NATIONAL GROUPING		
	Name	Number
KC(GB)	Toy	6
AKC	Toys	V
FCI	Companion Dogs	9

has been superseded by the now more popular sables and oranges. Some books on the breed prefer to consider that the origin of the breed goes back to much earlier days, and quote Greek and Roman sources for their theories, but the evidence is vague and the sledgedog theory is much more realistic.

The Pomeranian was hardly known in Britain until

365

1870 when the Kennel Club in Britain recognised the Spitz dog, but the interest shown in the breed by Queen Victoria in 1890 when a number entered her kennels soon popularised the breed, though her large greyish specimens were very different from the much smaller and more colourful ones that soon became fashionable. The formation of the Pomeranian Club in 1891 and the establishment of a standard for the breed was to ensure the future popularity of the smaller dogs. In the United States the first classes for the breed were staged at Westminster in 1900 and it is interesting to note that at that time blues and chocolates were being shown. In the same year the American Pomeranian Club was formed, and the admission of that club to the American Kennel Club brought about an immediate increased interest in the breed and began its rise to present popularity.

In the early days white was a very popular colour, but there is no doubt that the bloodline for this colour was too near the origins of the breed, and dogs that were white were almost always far too big, some of them weighing upwards of thirty pounds. In their efforts to produce smaller and smaller dogs, breeders concentrated on the other colours, and the browns and sables together with the blacks formed the bulk of the show stock. The first clear orange dog, Mrs. Parker's Ch. Mars, created a sensation when he first appeared and there were many theories as to where the colour came from. In fact it probably confirmed the origins of the breed among the northern Spitz dogs, as bright red regularly appears in both the Finnish Spitz and the Chow Chow, members of the northern Spitz group.

The Pomeranian is one of the great little show dogs of the world. In recent years more and more emphasis has been placed on coat length and quality until now the top specimens are just tiny balls of beautifully prepared stand-off coat in glowing colour. Careful control of the shape of the coat has been developed to a fine art and the Spitz outline with tail well over the back and head carried well back has been encouraged until he stands in the ring like a beautifully sculptured little statue. The ideal show size is now around four or five pounds, and to see these tiny dogs battling for Best in Show awards against enormous dogs, and defying them, is one of the exciting sights of the modern dog show world. This tremendous spirit and vivacity is one of the characteristics of the breed, and that, with his normally docile temper and great affection makes him an ideal family pet.

OFFICIAL STANDARD

General appearance
The Pomeranian in build and appearance should be a compact, short-coupled dog, well knit in frame. He should exhibit great intelligence in his expression, activity and bouyancy in his deportment.

Head and skull
The head and nose should be foxy in outline, or wedge-shaped. The skull being slightly flat, large in proportion to the muzzle, which should finish rather fine and be free from lippiness. The hair on the head and face should be smooth and short-coated. The nose should be black in white, orange, and shaded sable dogs; brown in chocolate tipped sable dogs, but in other colours may be 'self-coloured', but never parti-coloured or white.

Eyes
Should be medium in size, slightly oval in shape, not full, not set too wide apart, bright and dark in colour, and showing great intelligence. In white, orange, shaded-sable and cream dogs the rims round the eyes should be black.

Ears
Should be small, not set too far apart, not too low down, but carried perfectly erect like those of a fox.

Mouth
Teeth should be level, and should on no account be undershot, or overshot.

Neck
Should be rather short and well set in.

Forequarters
The shoulders should be clean and well laid back. The legs must be well feathered and perfectly straight, of medium length and not such as would be termed 'leggy' or 'low on leg', but in length and strength in due proportion to a well-balanced frame.

Body
The back must be short and the body compact, being well ribbed up and the barrel well rounded. The chest must be

Ears: small, erect.

Body: short, compact, well-rounded, deep.

fairly deep and not too wide but in proportion to the size of the dog.

Hindquarters
The legs and thighs must be well feathered down to the hocks and must be neither cow-hocked nor wide behind. They must be fine in bone and free in action.

Feet
The feet should be small and compact in shape.

Tail
The tail is one of the characteristics of the breed, and should be turned over the back and carried flat and straight, being profusely covered with long, harsh, spreading hair.

Coat
There should be two coats, an undercoat and an overcoat, the one a soft, fluffy undercoat, the other a long, perfectly straight coat, harsh in texture and covering the whole of the body, being very abundant round the neck and forepart of the shoulders and chest, where it shall form a frill of profuse off-standing straight hair, extending over the shoulders. The hindquarters should be clad with long hair or feathering from the top of the rump to the hocks.

Colour
All whole colours are admissible, but they should be free from black or white shadings. At present the whole-coloured dogs are: white, black, brown, light or dark, blue, as pale as possible. Orange, which should be as self-coloured and bright as possible. Beaver. Cream dogs should have black noses and black rims around the eyes. Whites must be quite free from lemon or any other colour. A few white hairs, in any of the self-coloured dogs, shall not heavily penalise. Dogs (other than white) with white or tan markings, are decidedly objectionable and should be discouraged. They cannot compete as whole coloured specimens. In parti-coloured dogs, the colours

should be evenly distributed on the body in patches; a dog with white or tan feet or chest would not be a parti-coloured dog. Shaded-sables should be shaded throughout with three or more colours, the hair to be as uniformly shaded as possible, and with no patches of self-colour. In mixed classes, where whole-coloured and parti-coloured Pomeranians compete together, the preference should, if in other points they are equal, be given to the whole-coloured specimens.

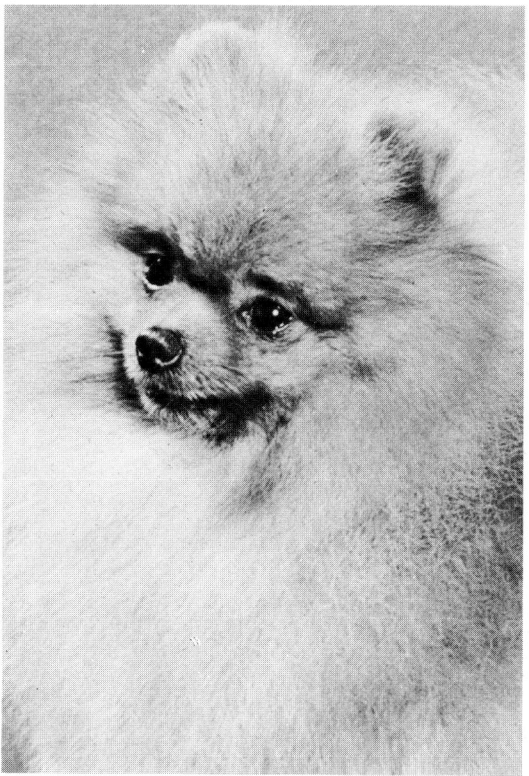

Weight and size
4 to $4\frac{1}{2}$ pounds for a dog and $4\frac{1}{2}$ to $5\frac{1}{2}$ pounds for bitches.

Faults
Undershot or overshot mouths; double jointed; light eyes; off-coloured nose; a tail carried to the side; 'hare' feet.

Note
Male animals should have two apparently normal testicles fully descended into the scrotum.

AKC VARIATION TO STANDARD
Teeth: scissors bite. *Colour:* all colours to be judged on an equal basis.

PUG

This member of the Toy dog Group, originating in the Orient, is something of an oddity in the Group, as whilst most of the others descend from the Spaniels or the Terriers, this one is undoubtedly a very tiny Mastiff type. He has the large head, the wrinkled face and the heavy-weight body of that group, which numbers among its members some of the largest dogs in the world. He was known at one time as the Dutch Pug and it was rather taken for granted that he was of Dutch origin, but the trade carried on between Holland and the Far East during the time of the Dutch East India Company gave every opportunity for him to have been brought into Holland from China. The name is said by some to have originated from the latin word 'pugnus'—a fist, as the head was said to have borne some resemblance to the human clenched fist. Others maintain that the name means 'monkey-faced'. In China the wrinkles on the head of the Pug were considered extremely important and the so-called 'prince mark' the vertical wrinkle on the forehead which was similar to the Chinese character for 'prince', was a very much sought after feature.

The pug was first brought to Britain during Victorian times, and like so many other breeds, particularly toys, found favour with the Monarch who quickly added some to her kennels. At that time his ears were cropped very short to give a smart appearance and to emphasize the wrinkles, and it is in this form that so many of them were depicted in early ceramic sculpture at such factories as Meissen where they were called Mopser, a name still used for the breed in some parts of Europe. The breed became a great favourite with sculptors and painters and one of the most famous of all, a dog named Trump which was owned by Hogarth, was not only painted by the artist, but used as a model by sculptors of the time. Lady Willoughby de Eresby of Lincoln and Mr. Morrison of Waltham Green established early kennels in Britain and during their time fawn Pugs were known as Willoughby or Morrison Pugs. The two types were later interbred and the early colour differences vanished.

The black Pug came some time later, in about 1886 when some were exhibited at the Maidstone show, and there was considerable difference of opinion as to how he originated. It was suggested that he resulted from an infusion of blood from Japan, or that some nondescript small black dog was used to start off the strain. The most likely answer is that an occasional black dog cropped up as happens sometimes in the self-coloured darker dogs and by using these more and more blacks eventually resulted. The modern Pug varies very little from his ancestors, and photographs of Pugs taken seventy years ago show dogs that have all the characteristics of today's breed and which would conform to the modern standard. Though numbers have declined a little in recent years, in Britain for example from the near one-and-a-half thousand per year to something like half that number, he still remains one of the more popular of the toy dogs. The esteem with which he was held in Victorian Britain can be seen from the fact that there are still in existence stuffed remains of family pets set up in glass cases, dating back to the time when the family could not bear to be parted from their companion and kept him on the sideboard.

As a show dog he is simple to transport and prepare.

He travels happily enough in a box and his short coat needs the minimum of grooming, a quick rub down with a hound glove or chamois leather is all that is required. He normally stands very quietly in the ring and moves off with his characteristic rolling gait. His temperament is near perfect, and he is extremely friendly, attaches himself to a household and the family with complete acceptance of the fact that he is an essential part of their lifestyle, and in his old age becomes very much the rather wheezy old relation sitting in the most comfortable chair in front of the fire.

OFFICIAL STANDARD

General appearance
A decidedly square and cobby dog. The Pug should be 'multum in parvo', but this condensation should be shown by compactness of form, well-knit proportions, and hardness of developed muscle.

Head and skull
Head large, massive, round—not apple-headed, with no indentation of the skull. Muzzle short, blunt, square but not upfaced. Wrinkles large and deep.

Eyes
Dark in colour, very large, bold and prominent, globular in shape, soft and solicitous in expression, very lustrous, and when excited, full of fire.

Ears
Thin, small, soft, like black velvet. There are two kinds—the 'rose' and the 'button'. Preference should be given to the latter.

Tail: curled tightly over hip.

Head and skull: large, massive, round.

Forequarters
Legs very strong, straight, of moderate length, and well under the body.

Body
Short and cobby, wide in chest and well-ribbed.

Hindquarters
Legs very strong, straight, of moderate length, and well under.

Feet
Neither so long as the foot of the hare, nor so round as that of the cat; well-split-up toes; the nails black.

Tail
(Twist.) Curled tightly as possible over the hip. The double curl is perfection.

Coat
Fine, smooth, soft, short and glossy, neither hard nor woolly.

Colour
Silver, apricot fawn or black. Each should be clearly decided, to make the contrast complete between the colour, the trace and the mask. Markings: Clearly defined. The muzzle or mask, ears, moles on cheeks, thumbmark or diamond on forehead and the trace should be as black as possible. Mask: The mask should be black, the more intense and well defined, the better. Trace: A black line extending from the occiput to the twist.

Weight and size
Desirable weight from 14 to 18 pounds (dog or bitch).

Faults
Lean, leggy. Short legs and long body.

Note
Male animals should have two apparently normal testicles fully descended into the scrotum.

YORKSHIRE TERRIER

This little dog has no claim at all to being an ancient breed. It is well known that he has been produced in comparatively recent years, and it is not difficult to conjecture which of the other breeds went to his make-up. As Robert Leighton said, Bradford and not Babylon was his ancestral home. Yorkshire, however, is not only England's largest county, it is also the county that is steeped in the breeding and development of livestock of all kinds from cats to canaries, and certainly of dogs. One needs only to remember that not only has it given its name to a breed of dog, but even one of its very small areas, Airedale, produced and gave its name to Britain's largest Terrier. It is obvious from the result that no haphazard mixture produced this little dog, but that wise livestock breeders knew exactly what they wanted and set out to get it. There have apparently always been Terriers in York-

NATIONAL GROUPING		
	Name	Number
KC(GB)	Toy	6
AKC	Toys	V
FCI	Companion Dogs	9

shire. Since the time of the industrial revolution they have been the companions of the working man who spent his days in the pits or mills of the county and found in vermin hunting his relaxation at weekends. Before that time when the county was purely agricultural and arboreal it was rich in wildlife such as rabbits and foxes and the Terriers were used in hunting these.

The designers of the breed, and they could hardly be called anything else, probably took the Clydesdale

Terrier as the starting point. He himself was the progenitor of the Skye Terrier, was described as rare in 1900 and has now disappeared. He had many of the characteristics of the Skye but was a smaller dog, his weight rarely exceeding eighteen pounds which is the minimum weight for a Skye, which meant that he was a good start towards miniaturisation.

At first the Yorkshire Terrier was exhibited as a Scotch Terrier and was broken-coated. The introduction of the old English Black and Tan Terrier would give the desired colour and markings, especially as at that time there was a blue and tan version of this dog. Skye blood and probably the Maltese would give the length and silkiness of coat, and possibly even the Dandie Dinmont Terrier was used. At first the Yorkshire Terrier was not a particularly small dog and show classes divided them into over and under five pounds. Fashion decreed, however, that the smaller ones were preferable, and at the same time also decided that the longer the coat the better, and in 1900 a dog that was five and a half pounds in weight had a coat of a uniform length of twenty-four inches. Continued attempts to produce smaller dogs have resulted in a strange state of affairs now, when the larger bitches are often retained by breeders for breeding purposes and mated to considerably smaller dogs. Whelps from the resulting litters can grow into dogs with considerable variation in size. This has meant that there have always been large numbers of dogs unwanted for show and available to the pet market. More Yorkshire Terriers are now being bred and exported from Britain than any other breed, yet the entries at shows in no way reflect this fact.

As a show dog he is a wonderful proposition, as his tiny size makes transportation a simple matter (the writer having seen two being taken to a show in a shopping bag on one occasion) and their coat repaying the tremendous amount of care and attention that is paid to it. In between shows the coat of the dog is tied up in small ribbons or papers to prevent it becoming damaged and in this way a great length of fine silky coat is encouraged. When brushed out, and standing in the ring shining in the sun or artificial lights, there is hardly a breed that is more striking. He appears to enjoy being shown and will stand still for considerable periods of time with his ears erect and having a jaunty appearance. Although very much a pampered pet, he is at the same time still a Terrier, enjoying games and walks, and reverting to his ancestral hunting background at every opportunity.

OFFICIAL STANDARD

General appearance
Should be that of a long-coated toy terrier, the coat hanging quite straight and evenly down each side, a parting extending from the nose to the end of the tail. The animal should be very compact and neat, the carriage being very upright and conveying an 'important' air. The general outline should convey the impression of a vigorous and well-proportioned body.

Head and skull
Head should be rather small and flat, not too prominent or round in the skull, nor too long in the muzzle, with a perfect black nose. The fall on the head to be long, of a rich golden tan, deeper in colour at the sides of the head about the ear roots, and on the muzzle where it should be very long. On no account must the tan on the head extend on to the neck, nor must there be any sooty or dark hair intermingled with any of the tan.

Eyes
Medium, dark and sparkling, having a sharp intelligent expression, and placed so as to look directly forward. They should not be prominent and the edge of the eyelids should be of a dark colour.

Ears
Small V-shaped, and carried erect or semi-erect, and not far apart, covered with short hair, colour to be of a very deep rich tan.

Mouth
Perfectly even, with teeth as sound as possible. An animal having lost any teeth through accident not to be faulted providing the jaws are even.

Forequarters
Legs quite straight, well covered with hair of a rich golden tan a few shades lighter at the ends than at the roots, not extending higher on the forelegs than the elbow.

Ears: small, 'v'-shaped, erect.

Body: compact, level back.

Body
Very compact with a good loin. Level on the top of the back.

Hindquarters
Legs quite straight, well covered with hair of a rich golden tan, a few shades lighter at the ends than at the roots, not extending higher on the hind legs than the stifle.

Feet
As round as possible; the toe-nails black.

Tail
Cut to medium length; with plenty of hair, darker blue in colour than the rest of the body, especially at the end of the tail, and carried a little higher than the level of the back.

Coat
The hair on the body moderately long and perfectly straight (not wavy), glossy like silk, and of a fine silky texture.

Colour
A dark steel blue (not silver blue), extending from the occiput (or back of skull) to the root of tail, and on no account mingled with fawn, bronze or dark hairs. The hair on the chest a rich bright tan. All tan hair should be darker at the roots than in the middle, shading to a still lighter tan at the tips.

Weight and size
Weight up to 7 pounds.

Note
Male animals should have two apparently normal testicles fully descended into the scrotum.

Pattern of blue and tan.

AKC VARIATION TO STANDARD
Head: either scissors or level bite is acceptable.

UTILITY GROUP: NON-SPORTING BREEDS

Bulldog

Boston Terrier

Chow Chow

Dalmatian

French Bulldog

Keeshond

Giant Schnauzer

Lhasa Apso

Standard Poodle

Miniature Poodle

Toy Poodle

Schipperke

Schnauzer

Shih Tzu

Miniature Schnauzer

Tibetan Terrier

Tibetan Spaniel

UTILITY GROUP: NON-SPORTING BREEDS

When dog shows first started in Britain in the middle of the 19th century, all the dogs were lumped together, so that the Boston Terriers, the Maltese, the Bulldogs and the Spaniels all appeared in the local public house at the same time. The first division into Sporting and Non-Sporting was fairly straightforward, as breeds identified themselves by purpose. The next division within the Non-Sporting Group by extracting the Toy Dogs and giving them a Group of their own was a simple matter, but it was in recent years in Britain when the remainder of the Non-Sporting Group became so large as to be unwieldy that problems were encountered. There was a great deal of discussion concerning which breeds should go into the Working Group and which should go into the new Group and what it should be called. There are still those who find it difficult to understand why the Dobermann for instance which is a guard dog should be in the Working Group, whilst the Schnauzer, which is also a guard dog and is in the Working Group in the United States of America is placed in the Utility Group in Britain.

A more or less parallel Group now exists, however, on each side of the Atlantic, and unless some system such as the Scandinavian one of dividing into yet more Groups is adopted, there will always be anomalies. The Group consists of those dogs which were not developed for any specific purpose, or those whose purpose if it once existed, has now disappeared. They are the larger dogs bred for appearance rather than for performance, such as the Dalmatian and the Poodle which are decorative rather than useful. This does not mean in fact that they were not originally bred as working dogs. The Poodles for instance are descended from the Old Water Dog which was very much a sporting dog, and a case could even be made out for the Bulldog, which for no fault of its own is now out of work, whilst the Boxer, which is also descended from a race of bull-baiting dogs is included everywhere as a working dog.

The breeds within this Group are a very mixed bag indeed, originating as they did in a number of countries as wide apart as America and Tibet, and it is interesting that they include a number of breeds which are recognised as national dogs. The Boston Terrier is as American as any dog could be, whilst the Bulldog typifies everything that is British. The Poodle is immediately associated with France even though it was not originally a French dog. The Chow Chow is Chinese to everyone, the Keeshond even takes its name from national upheavals in Holland and is the national dog of that country, whilst nothing could be more redolent of Tibet than the Tibetan Terrier.

The one thing that is noticeable about the Group when it is seen in the ring with all the breeds represented, is that it is full of interest. The dogs are of no particular size, as they are in the Toy Group, nor are they roughly of the same shape, as they are in the Working Group, which gives them great spectator appeal. The breeds within the Group are very much talking points. The Bulldog with his squat formidable conformation, the decorative quality of the Dalmatian with all its association with tradition, elegance and the silver screen, and the quaint appearance of the dogs from the roof of the world in Tibet, give additional flavour to what might otherwise be just a collection of dogs. It so happens, too, that just about every type and colour of coat is also seen in the Group.

It is possible that at some future date world agreement will be reached concerning the placing of breeds within groups, and possibly the international acceptance of names for those groups. It could then well be that those breeds which have ceased for one reason or another to practice the purpose for which they were evolved, will be placed in a group known by a name which best describes their reason for existing in a modern world. The title 'Large Companion Dogs' is already in use in some countries and might be adopted.

BOSTON TERRIER

There are many breeds in the world that have a history stretching so far back that their origins are obscure, but there are others whose development has been well recorded and whose origins are so recent that they can easily be traced. Such a breed is the Boston Terrier. He is very much an American dog, and is recognised in many countries as the national dog of America, though in fact his ancestors came from Britain. The very first was a dog called Hooper's Judge, a cross between a Bulldog and an English Terrier, and he was purchased by a Mr. Robert C. Hooper of Boston, and was a dark brindle with a white blaze and throat, cropped ears and a screw tail. From this original dog the Boston Terrier as it is known today descended and by careful breeding for colour, markings and type, the breed was fixed. It is suggested that the careful introduction of French Bulldog blood helped in perfecting the breed.

Several were exhibited at the Boston Show in 1878, and in 1891 the American Bull Terrier Club of Boston applied for registration and was refused until the name Bull Terrier was removed, and the club became

NATIONAL GROUPING		
	Name	Number
KC(GB)	Utility	4
AKC	Non-Sporting Dogs	V
FCI	Companion Dogs	9

the Boston Terrier Club, being given full recognition in 1893. The Bostonians persevered with their efforts to produce a strain of dogs removed from the old Bull Terrier image and their dogs gradually became recognised outside Massachusetts until they were one of the most popular breeds in the United States. Soon after the First World War the breed appeared in Europe, and a number came to Britain in the mid-twenties. Whilst they have not achieved the popularity that they have in the United States, they have steady registration figures of some hundreds per year, and are shown fairly extensively in Britain.

The first Bostons were tough, as would be expected from a cross between a Bulldog and a Terrier proper, both of which are noted for their pugnacious qualities, and there is some suggestion that the early ones were encouraged to fight. There was some diversity of opinion as to the correct size, and for a time they were exhibited in weight classes. Eventually, however, the weight was standardised at something more generally acceptable to a dog with a fighting background.

He is a dapper little dog these days with a settled temperament, a certain ruggedness and the ability to take care of himself. He still has something of the jaw power of the Bulldog, the agility and sharpness of a Terrier and the quickness of reaction of the Bull Terrier that was his ancestor.

As a show dog the Boston Terrier is supreme, being smart to look at, gay and classy in ring behaviour, and easily trained to stand imperturbably among a collection of much larger dogs. He is easily cared for, having a short shiny coat that needs very little more than a brisk rub down to bring out its natural shine. He is easily transported, being small, and will allow himself to be boxed with little protest. His temperament is first class, and he is claimed by those who own one to be the most affectionate dog on earth. Certainly as a house dog there are few breeds with his qualities. He rapidly becomes one of the family, will occupy his favourite—and usually the most comfortable—chair, and will not be offended if a human expresses a desire to join him on it. He loves company, has remarkable understanding, and whilst remaining soft and sweet-tempered, is a very good guard, being very possessive about his own territory.

OFFICIAL STANDARD

Characteristics
A proportionate combination of 'Colour' and 'Ideal Markings' is a particularly distinctive feature of a representative specimen. A dog with a preponderance of white on body or without the proper proportion of brindle and white on head is at a disadvantage. The ideal 'Boston Terrier Expression' as indicating 'a high degree of intelligence' is also an important characteristic of the breed. 'Colour and Markings' and 'Expression' should be given particular consideration in determining the relative value of 'General Appearance' to other points.

General appearance
The general appearance of the Boston Terrier should be that of a lively, highly intelligent, smooth-coated, short-headed, compactly built, short-tailed, well balanced dog of medium size, of brindle colour and evenly marked with white. The head should indicate a high degree of intelligence and should be in proportion to the size of the dog; the body rather short and well knit; the limbs strong and neatly turned; tail short and no feature to be so prominent that the dog appears badly proportioned. The dog should convey an impression of determination, strength and activity, with style of a high order; carriage easy and graceful. The gait of the Boston Terrier is that of a sure-footed straight-gaited dog, forelegs and hindlegs moving straight ahead in time with perfect rhythm, each step indicating grace and power.

Head and skull
Skull square, flat on top, free from wrinkles; cheeks flat; brow abrupt, stop well defined. Muzzle short, square, wide and deep, and in proportion to the skull; free from wrinkles; shorter in length than in width and depth, not exceeding in length approximately one-third of length of skull; width and depth carried out well to end; the muzzle from stop to end of nose on a line parallel to the top of the skull; nose black and wide with well-defined line between nostrils. The jaws broad and square. The chops of good depth but not pendulous, completely covering the teeth when mouth is closed.

Head and skull: square, free from wrinkles, muzzle short, square, wide, and deep.

Eyes
Wide apart, large and round, dark in colour, expression alert but kind and intelligent. The eyes should set square in the skull, and the outside corners should be on a line with the cheeks as viewed from the front.

Ears
Carried erect; small and thin; situated as near corner of skull as possible.

Mouth
Teeth short and regular, bite even, or sufficiently undershot to square muzzle.

Neck
Of fair length, slightly arched and carrying the head gracefully; neatly set into the shoulders.

Forequarters
Legs set moderately wide apart and on a line with the

Colour: ideal white.

Ideal markings: white muzzle, even white blaze over head, collar, breast, part or whole of forelegs, and hind legs below hocks.

Weight and size
Weight should not exceed 25 pounds, divided by classes as follows: lightweight, under 15 pounds; middleweight, 15 and under 20 pounds; heavy weight, 20 and under 25 pounds.

Faults
Solid black, black and tan; liver or mouse colour; dudley nose; docked tail. Skull 'domed' or inclined; furrowed by a medial line; skull too long for breadth, or vice versa; stop too shallow; brow and skull too slanting. Eyes small or sunken; too prominent; light colour or wall eye; showing too much white or haw. Muzzle wedge-shaped or lacking depth; down faced; too much cut out below the eyes; pinched or wide nostrils; butterfly nose; protruding teeth; weak lower jaw; showing 'turn-up'. Ears poorly carried or in size out of proportion to the head. *Neck:* ewe-necked; throaty, short or thick. *Body:* flat sides; narrow chest; long or slack loins; roach back; sway back; too much cut-up in flank. Loose shoulders or elbows; hind legs too straight at stifles; hocks too prominent; long or weak pasterns; splay feet. A long or gaily carried tail; extremely gnarled or curled against body. (Note: the preferred tail should not exceed in length approximately half the distance from the set-on to hock). *Colour and markings:* all white; absence of white markings; preponderance of white on body; without the proper proportion of brindle and white on head; or any variations detracting from the general appearance. *Coat:* long or coarse; lacking lustre.

Note
Dog animals should have two apparently normal testicles fully descended into the scrotum.

AKC VARIATION TO STANDARD
Ears: either cropped to conform to shape of head, or natural bat.

point of the shoulders; straight in bone and well muscled; pasterns short and strong. Elbows standing neither in nor out.

Body
Deep with good width of chest; shoulders sloping, back short; ribs deep and well sprung, carried well back to loins; loins short and muscular; rump curving slightly to set-on of tail; flank very slightly cut up. The body should appear short but not chunky.

Hindquarters
Legs set true, bent at stifles, short from hocks to feet; hocks turning neither in nor out; thighs strong and well muscled.

Feet
Round, small and compact, and turned neither in nor out; toes well arched.

Tail
Set-on low; short, fine and tapering; straight or screw; devoid of fringes or coarse hair, and not carried above horizontal.

Coat
Short, smooth, bright and fine in texture.

Colour
Brindle with white markings; brindle must show throughout the body distinctly; black and white markings are permissible, but brindles with white markings are preferred. (Ideal colour shall be one in which the brindle colouring is evenly distributed throughout the body).

BULLDOG

It sometimes happens that countries adopt as their national symbol an animal which is native to their country, but which has no special significance apart from that, the kangaroo of Australia for instance or the bear of Russia. There is one animal, however, which has been accepted as a symbol of something more, of the character of a nation, and that is the Bulldog of Britain. Whether it is a true reflection or a hopeful one is a matter for some argument, but the fact remains that throughout the world the Bulldog is recognised as something peculiarly British. The origins of the breed lie certainly in the Mastiff which is one of the oldest of British breeds, and there is no doubt that by continuous selective breeding for shorter and shorter legs the Bulldog was produced. The so-called sport of bull-baiting was a regular scene in Britain prior to 1835, when it became illegal, and the Bulldog was produced for this sport alone. The practice was for the bull to be tied to a stake usually on a village green or similar space in an urban area, and the dogs were encouraged by handlers to attack and lay hold on the bulls by what was called pinning him by nose. The bull defended himself by keeping his nose close to the ground, and even sometimes digging a hole for the purpose, tossing the indiscreet dogs, which the handlers attempted to catch to break their fall. Considerable betting took place and large sums of money changed hands on the performance of an individual dog or bull.

After the banning of bull-baiting the Bulldog was still bred as a fighting dog but the Bull Terrier proved a much better breed for this purpose, and it needed the formation of the Bulldog Club Incorporated in 1864 to ensure the continuance of the breed. Since that time a certain amount of exaggeration of characteristics has taken place, and the opponents of the pedigree dog usually use the Bulldog as a typical example of how selective breeding can ruin the appearance and health of a breed of dog. In fact a fit modern Bulldog has all the power and agility of its forebears, is capable of running at considerable speed and has still the quick reaction that would be the envy of many of its ancestors. The modern dog has become something of a cult, and there are now probably more Bulldog clubs than those of any other breed, each with its specialist shows.

At his best the Bulldog is a powerful superbly muscled fighting machine of a dog with tremendous weight for his height, with enormous chest and shoulders and the look of an animal planted firmly on the ground and difficult to upset. His head is his great feature, and much store is placed on the head details, the standard for which occupies a large part of the standard for the whole dog. His head is massive, and out of proportion by the standards of a more normal dog, and the jaw is enormously powerful. At his worst, overweight and underexercised he loses attraction more quickly than most breeds, which gives rise to some of the criticism levelled at him.

He is something of a specialist's problem as a show dog, being by no means the easiest of dogs to show to best advantage, as he rarely adopts his best stance in the ring, and needs a considerable amount of attention. This is not for any reason of temperament, as he is an easy dog to handle, but fashion has dictated that he should stand in a certain way. In fact, temperamentally he is quite delightful, being most affectionate and friendly towards people, and not overprone towards being aggressive to other dogs. The puppies in the breed are most attractive, and so irresistible that many people who do not understand the later problems of the breed enter into owning one and sometimes regret it later. Those who become addicted to the breed never want any other sort of dog.

OFFICIAL STANDARD

General appearance

In forming a judgment on any specimen of the breed, the general appearance, which is the first impression the dog makes as a whole on the eye of the judge, should be first considered. Secondly should be noticed its size, shape and make, or rather its proportions in the relation they bear to each other. No point should be so much in excess of the others as to destroy the general symmetry, or make the dog appear deformed, or interfere with its powers of motion, etc. Thirdly its style, carriage, gait, temper and its several points should be considered separately in detail, due allowance being made for the bitch, which is not so grand or as well developed as the dog.

The general appearance of the Bulldog is that of a smooth-coated, thick-set dog, rather low in stature, but broad, powerful and compact. The head strikingly massive and large in proportion to the dog's size. The face extremely short. The muzzle very broad, blunt, and inclined upwards. The body short and well knit; the limbs stout and muscular. The hindquarters high and strong but rather lightly made in comparison with its heavily made foreparts. The dog should convey an impression of determination, strength, and activity, similar to that suggested by the appearance of a thick-set Ayrshire Bull.

From its formation the dog has a peculiar heavy and constrained gait, appearing to walk with short, quick steps on the tips of its toes, its hind-feet not being lifted high, but appearing to skim the ground, and running with the right shoulder rather advanced, similar to the manner of a horse in cantering.

Head and skull

The skull should be very large—the larger the better—and in circumference should measure (round in front of the ears) at least the height of the dog at the shoulders. Viewed from the front it should appear very high from the corner of the lower jaw to the apex of the skull, and also very broad and square. The cheeks should be well rounded and extended sideways beyond the eyes. Viewed at the side, the head should appear very high, and very short from its back to the point of the nose. The forehead should be flat, neither prominent nor overhanging the face; the skin upon it and about the head very loose and well wrinkled. The projections of the frontal bones should be very prominent, broad, square, and high, causing a deep and wide indention between the eyes termed the 'stop'. From the 'stop' a furrow both broad and deep should extend up to the middle of the skull, being traceable to the apex. The face, measured from the front of the cheek-bone to the nose, should be as short as possible, and its skin should be deeply and closely wrinkled. The muzzle should be short, broad, turned upwards and very deep from the corner of the eye to the corner of the mouth. The nose should be large, broad and black, and under no circumstances should it be liver coloured or brown; its top should be deeply set back almost between the eyes. The distance from the inner corner of the eye (or from the centre of the stop between the eyes) to the extreme tip of the nose should not exceed the length from the tip of the nose to

Head and skull: large, broad, square, skin loose and well-wrinkled.

the edge of the under lip. The nostrils should be large, wide, and black, with a well-defined vertical straight line between them. The flews, called the 'chop' should be thick, broad, pendant, and very deep, hanging completely over the lower jaw at the sides (not in front). They should join the under lip in front and quite cover the teeth. The jaws should be broad, massive and square, the lower jaw should project considerably in front of the upper and turn up. Viewed from the front, the various properties of the face must be equally balanced on either side of an imaginary line down the centre of the face.

Eyes

The eyes seen from the front, should be situated low down in the skull, as far from the ears as possible. The eyes and 'stop' should be in the same straight line, which should be at right angles to the furrow. They should be as wide apart as possible, provided their outer corners are within the outline of the cheeks. They should be quite round in shape, of moderate size, neither sunken nor prominent, and in colour should be very dark—almost, if not quite, black, showing no white when looking directly forward.

Ears

The ears should be set high on the head—i.e., the front inner edge of each ear should (as viewed from the front) join the outline of the skull at the top corner of such outline, so as to place them as wide apart, and as high and as far from the eyes as possible. In size they should be small and thin. The shape termed 'rose ear' is correct, and folds inwards at its back, the upper or front edge curving over outwards and backwards, showing part of the inside of the burr.

Mouth

The jaw should be broad and square and have the six

small front teeth between the canines in an even row. The canine teeth or tusks wide apart. The teeth should not be seen when the mouth is closed. The teeth should be large and strong. When viewed from the front, the underjaw should be centrally under the upper jaw to which it should also be parallel.

Neck
Should be moderate in length (rather short than long) very thick, deep and strong. It should be well arched at the back, with much loose, thick and wrinkled skin about the throat, forming a dewlap on each side, from the lower jaw to the chest.

Forequarters
The shoulders should be broad, sloping and deep, very powerful and muscular, and giving the appearance of having been 'tacked on' to the body. The brisket should be capacious, round and very deep from the top of the shoulders to the lowest part where it joins the chest, and be well let down between forelegs. It should be large in diameter and round behind the forelegs (not flat-sided, the ribs being well rounded). The forelegs should be very stout and strong, set wide apart, thick, muscular, and straight, with well-developed forearms, presenting a rather bowed outline, but the bones of the legs should be large and straight, not bandy or curved. They should be rather short in proportion to the hind-legs, but not so short as to make the back appear long, or detract from the dog's activity, and so cripple him. The elbows should be low, and stand well away from the ribs. The pasterns should be short, straight and strong.

Body
The chest should be very wide, laterally round, prominent, and deep, making the dog appear very broad and short-legged in front. The body should be well ribbed up behind, with the belly tucked up and not pendulous. The back should be short and strong, very broad at the shoulders, and comparatively narrow at the loins. There should be a slight fall to the back close behind the shoulders (its lowest part), whence the spine should rise to the loins (the top of which should be higher than the top of the shoulders), thence curving again more suddenly to the tail, forming an arch—a distinctive characteristic of the breed—termed 'roach back'.

Hindquarters
The legs should be large and muscular, and longer in proportion than the forelegs, so as to elevate the loins. The hocks should be slightly bent and well let down, so as to be long and muscular from the loins to the point of the hock. The lower part of the leg should be short, straight and strong. The stifles should be round and turned slightly outwards away from the body. The hocks are thereby made to approach each other, and the hind feet to turn outwards.

Feet
The hind feet, like the fore feet, should be round and compact, with the toes well split up and the knuckles prominent. The fore feet should be straight and turn very slightly outward, of medium size and moderately round. The toes compact and thick, being well split up, making the knuckles prominent and high.

Tail
The tail, termed the 'stern', should be set on low, jut out rather straight, then turn downwards. It should be round, smooth and devoid of fringe or coarse hair. It should be moderate in length—rather short than long—thick at the root, and tapering quickly to a fine point. It should have a downward carriage (not having a decided upward curve at the end), and the dog should not be able to raise it over its back.

Coat
Should be fine in texture, short, close and smooth (hard only from the shortness and closeness, not wiry).

Colour
The colour should be whole or smut (that is, a whole colour with a black mask or muzzle). The only colours (which should be brilliant and pure of their sort) are whole colours—viz., brindles, reds, with their varieties, fawns, fallows, etc., white and also pied (i.e., a combination of white with any other of the foregoing colours). Dudley, black and black with tan are extremely undesirable colours.

Weight and size
The most desirable weight for the Bulldog is 55 pounds for a dog and 50 pounds for a bitch.

Note
Male animals should have two apparently normal testicles fully descended into the scrotum.

AKC VARIATION TO STANDARD
Tail: if screwed bends or kinks should be well defined, they may be abrupt or even knotty, but no portion of the member should be elevated above base or root. *Size:* mature dogs 50 pounds; mature bitches 40 pounds. *Gait:* style and carriage are peculiar, gait being a loose-jointed shuffling, sidewise motion, giving characteristic 'roll'. Action must be unrestrained, free, vigorous.

CHOW CHOW

NATIONAL GROUPING		
	Name	Number
KC(GB)	Utility	4
AKC	Non-Sporting Dogs	VI
FCI	Companion Dogs	9

When man first took the dog as his companion, he almost certainly saw him as a guard, as an assistant on a hunt, and later as a herder. It is most unlikely, however, that he saw him as a potential source of food. Wild game was so plentiful that in most parts of the world there was no need to look upon dogs as part of the diet, but in China things were rather different. The Chow Chow has existed in China for at least the past two thousand years, in the north the rough-coated variety and in the south the smooth, indeed the smooth-coated Chow Chow, or at least a dog very like it still exists in fair numbers in southern China and Hong Kong. It is longer in the leg and looks something like an Akita, but it is basically a Chow. The coat of the northern rough-coated Chow Chow was so rich and warm, that in that very cold country the skins were looked upon as a useful article of clothing, and dog skins were sold in the markets of Manchuria and Mongolia. Not only was the skin used, but in a thickly populated country such as China, nothing that was edible could be wasted, and the flesh of the Chow Chow was an acceptable adjunct to the normal diet. Dog ranches were by no means unusual, and the breeding of these dogs on a commercial basis was quite common.

He is one of the Spitz types, allied to the other rough-coated prick-eared curled-tailed breeds, and his history in China goes back to very early days even in that country where time is measured in tens of centuries. The first report of the breed in Britain is in the letters of Gilbert White the naturalist, who in the 18th century wrote that he had seen a pair belonging to a neighbour who had brought them from Canton, the description of which is clearly that of a Chow Chow. He was certainly in Britain by the 19th century, and began to appear at shows, and by the turn of the century he was well-established. There was some interest before the First World War, but it was not until the 1920s that they began to hit the headlines, a number being shown at Crufts in 1925, and one particularly outstanding dog being exported to Mrs. Earl Hoover of Chicago.

Since that time the breed has made steady progress and registrations in Britain are now running at around one-and-a-half thousand each year. He is a massive short-backed heavily boned dog with one peculiarity of hind movement, having little or no angulation of stifle. His coat is a very important feature, and whilst the short-coat crops up from time to time, some breeders even deliberately breeding for that characteristic, it is the rough-coated variety which has captured the public interest. He has another peculiarity in that the inside of his mouth should always be black.

The Chow Chow has always been a great performer and very popular at shows, his colourful character, his very showy coat, and his strange gait endearing him to spectators. Chows have been among the biggest winners in the show rings of the world since the First World War, and one alive at present in Britain holds the all-time record for winning challenge certificates over every other breed. As puppies Chow Chows are quite delightful, looking more like woolly toys than dogs, and children find them irresistible. His temperament is very different from many dogs. He is somewhat aloof and distant at times, gazing away from those who speak to him and appearing very haughty, but with people that he likes he is most affectionate. He has no vice, though he is not easily trained in the normal way, and is seldom if ever seen in say the obedience ring, as he has a will of his own. He is fairly obedient without being servile, and well-behaved without being selfconscious about it.

OFFICIAL STANDARD

Characteristics
A well-balanced dog, leonine in appearance, with proud dignified bearing; loyal yet aloof; unique in its stilted gait and bluish-black tongue.

General appearance
An active, compact, short-coupled and well-balanced dog, well knit in frame, with tail carried well over the back.

Head and skull
Skull flat and broad, with little stop, well filled out under the eyes. Muzzle moderate in length, broad from the eyes to the point (not pointed at the end like a fox). Nose black, large and wide in all cases (with the exception of cream and white in which case a light-coloured nose is permissible and in blues and fawns a self-coloured nose); but in all colours a black nose is preferable.

Eyes
Dark and small, preferably almond-shaped (in blue or fawn dog a light colour is permissible).

Ears
Small, thick, slightly rounded at the tip, carried stiffly erect but placed well forward over the eyes and wide apart, which gives the dog the peculiar characteristic expression of the breed, viz., a scowl.

Mouth
Teeth strong and level, giving scissor bite. Tongue bluish black. Flews and roof of mouth black. Gums preferably black.

Head and skull: flat, broad well filled out.

Neck
Strong, full, set well on the shoulders and slightly arched.

Forequarters
Shoulders muscular and sloping. Forelegs perfectly straight, of moderate length and with good bone.

Body
Chest broad and deep. Back short, straight and strong. Loins powerful.

Hindquarters
Hindlegs muscular and hocks well let down and perfectly straight which are essential in order to produce the Chow's characteristic stilted gait.

Feet
Small, round and catlike, standing well on the toes.

Tail
Set high and carried well over the back.

Coat
Abundant, dense, straight and stand-off. Outer coat rather coarse in texture and with a soft woolly undercoat. The Chow Chow is a profusely coated dog and balance should therefore be assessed when the coat is at its natural length.

Colour
Whole coloured black, red, blue, fawn, cream or white, frequently shaded but not in patches or parti-coloured (the underpart of tail and back of thighs frequently of a light colour).

Weight and size
Minimum height for Chows to be 18 inches, but in every case balance should be the outstanding feature and height left to the discretion of the judges.

Faults
Drop ears, tongue splashed or patchy, tail not carried over the back, parti-coloured, off black noses except in the colours specified, viz., creams, whites, blues or fawns. Any artificial shortening of the coat which alters the natural outline or expression of the dog should be penalised (The standard of the smooth variety is identical with the above except that the coat is smooth).

Note
Male animals should have two apparently normal testicles fully descended into the scrotum.

AKC VARIATION TO STANDARD
Mouth: lips somewhat full, overhanging. *Disqualifications:* nose spotted or distinctly other than black except in blues, which may have solid blue or slate noses. Tongue red, pink or obviously spotted with red or pink. Drop ears.

DALMATIAN

NATIONAL GROUPING		
	Name	Number
KC(GB)	Utility	4
AKC	Non-Sporting Dogs	VI
FCI	Companion Dogs	9

The decorative value of a dog has been recognised by the ladies, and for that matter the gentlemen, of court circles at least since the Imperial Court of Rome. The pampered pet of the gentlewomen of the Italian and the Spanish courts was depicted as a foil to the lady's beauty, almost as part of her personality. The Dalmatian is a typical example of a dog that has been evolved for just that purpose. He is not a working dog, nor does he hunt or course. He was developed simply as an adjunct to the fashionable person's equipage. The breed is quite an ancient one, and it has been suggested that it was originally a guard dog, and even a war dog in Dalmatia or Croatia, though there is a possibility that here it was being confused with the spotted German Mastiff known at one time as the Tiger Dog, which was a hunting and fighting dog. In the middle of the 19th century it was considered to be fashionable to have one of these spotted dogs trotting along with one's carriage. In Dalmatia where these dogs are said to have originated they were probably a small version of the spotted or harlequin Great Dane, and probably these were later crossed with Pointers to reduce the size and improve the markings.

In Victorian England the Dalmatian was certainly a carriage dog, often living in the stables, not normally entering the house, and appearing only when the horses were being prepared, when they would join the carriage, and either trot alongside, even in front, or what was considered the height of fashion, beneath the rear axle. For a while, with the advent of the motorcar, the Dalmatian went into something of a decline, but a dog with all the qualities that he has could not be kept down for long, and he has climbed up once more into a very strong position in the popularity poll. As happened with some other breeds, it needed a book and Walt Disney to give him the boost that he needed.

He is a very intelligent dog, as his ancestry would suggest, as both the Great Dane and the Pointer which are supposed to have been used to produce the breed are very intelligent dogs. In order to accomplish the feats of running that he did during his carriage dog days, he had to be a very muscular well-built dog with great powers of endurance and persistence, and these qualities he has to this day, never appearing to tire, and being one of the most symmetrically built dogs in the world. As a showdog he has proved remarkably successful, and there is little at any of today's shows that attracts more attention than a ring full of these beautifully spotted animals. Being always willing to please, and attentive to his handler, he is easily trained to stand perfectly still in the ring, and his excellent conformation makes him a pleasure to see as he moves freely up and down the ring. He has no vices, and a ring full of Dalmatians is one of the quietest and the best behaved rings at any show.

Temperamentally he is the perfect companion dog. Years of association with man have given him a natural sense of what is correct behaviour, and whilst he enjoys life as much as any dog, he is amenable to discipline and makes a wonderful pet and housedog. He still enjoys a hunt as his forebears undoubtedly did, and he is at his happiest on a walk through the country, but enjoys the fireside in the winter too, and he is remarkably well-behaved and troublefree in the house. His intelligence and good manners have endeared him to circus and stage folk and in the United States he has been associated with the Fire Service, for which he has been used as a badge for many years.

OFFICIAL STANDARD

General appearance

The Dalmatian should be a balanced, strong, muscular, active dog of good demeanour. Symmetrical in outline, free from coarseness and lumber, capable of great endurance with a fair amount of speed.

Head and skull

The head should be of fair length, the skull flat, reasonably broad between the ears but refined, moderately well defined at the temples, i.e. exhibiting a moderate amount of stop; not in one straight line from nose to occiput bone. Entire free from wrinkle. The muzzle should be long and powerful, never snipy, the lips clean, fitting the jaw moderately close. The nose in the black spotted variety should always be black, in the liver spotted variety always brown.

Eyes

The eyes, set moderately well apart should be of medium size, round, bright and sparkling, with an intelligent expression, their colour, depending on the marking of the dog; dark in the black spotted, amber in the liver spotted. The rim round the eyes should be complete; black in the black spotted and liver brown in the liver spotted.

Ears

The ears should be set on rather high, of moderate size, rather wide at the base, gradually tapering to a rounded point. Fine in texture, carried close to the head. The marking should be well broken up, preferably spotted.

Mouth

The teeth should meet. The upper slightly overlapping the lower. (Scissor bite.)

Neck

The neck should be fairly long, nicely arched, light and tapering. Entirely free from throatiness.

Forequarters

The shoulders should be moderately oblique, clean and muscular. Elbows close to the body. The forelegs perfectly straight with strong round bone down to the feet, with a slight spring at the pastern joint.

Body

The chest should not be too wide but deep and capacious with plenty of lung and heart room. The ribs well sprung, well defined wither, powerful level back, loins strong, clean and muscular, and slightly arched.

Hindquarters

Rounded, muscles clean with well developed second thigh, good turn of stifle and hocks well defined.

Tail

In length reaching approximately to the hocks. Strong at the insertion gradually tapering towards the end, it should not be inserted too low or too high, be free from coarseness and carried with a slight upward curve, never curled. Preferably spotted.

Feet

Round, compact, with well arched toes (cat feet) and round tough elastic pads. Nails black or white in the black spotted variety, in the liver spotted—brown or white.

Gait

The Dalmatian should have great freedom of movement. A smooth, powerful rhythmic action with a long stride. Viewed from behind, the legs should move in parallel the hindlegs tracking the fore. A short stride and paddling action is incorrect.

Coat

The coat should be short, hard and dense, sleek and glossy in appearance. The ground colour should be pure white. Black spotted dogs should have dense black spots and liver spotted dogs liver-brown spots. They should not run together but be round and well defined the size of sixpence to a half crown, as well distributed as possible. Spots on the extremities should be smaller than those on the body.

Size

Overall balance of prime importance, but the ideal height to be aimed at is dogs 23 to 24 inches, bitches 22 to 23 inches.

Faults

Patches, black and liver spots on the same dog (tri colours). Lemon spots. Blue eyes. Bronzing and other faults of pigmentation.

Note

Male animals should have two apparently normal testicles fully descended into the scrotum.

AKC VARIATION TO STANDARD

Eyes: in liver-spotted variety they should be golden or light brown or blue. *Major faults:* butterfly or flesh coloured nose. Lack of pigment in eye rims. Cowhocks. *Disqualifications:* patches, tri-colours and any colour markings other than black or liver. Any dog or bitch over 24 inches.

FRENCH BULLDOG

NATIONAL GROUPING		
	Name	Number
KC(GB)	Utility	4
AKC	Non-Sporting Dogs	VI
FCI	Companion Dogs	9

From time to time there have cropped up in some lines of British Bulldogs, specimens much smaller than average. Indeed, whilst there have been Bulldogs that weighed nearer to eighty than the fifty pounds which is the average, there have been many which have weighed as little as twenty pounds. At one time around the middle of the 19th century, a Toy Bulldog existed, and was shown as such until the Kennel Club at the turn of the century decided that this was a contradiction in terms and insisted on the use of the name 'Miniature Bulldog'. There is little doubt that the French Bulldog is descended from some of these very small Bulldogs. The French authorities claim that the breed was in fact native to their country. Some claim that the breed originated with the Dogue de Bordeaux which still exists as a very large Mastiff type of up to twenty-six inches at the shoulder, but which was miniaturised to produce both the Bulldog and the French Bulldog. All will agree, however, that the miniature version of the Bulldog had something to do with the ancestry of the French Bulldog.

The breed in some form has been known since the 17th century, and in its early days in Paris was bred by the Lutetian bootmakers and other artisans, and became popular as a fighting dog. One stalwart breeder, Mr. George Krehl brought dogs over from France to exhibit them in Britain around the turn of the century, and at that time an attempt was made to reintroduce the miniature or toy Bulldog. This failed, however, and in 1902 the French Bulldog Club of England was formed against considerable opposition from the established Bulldog clubs and the Toy Bull-dog Club which was still in existence. The first show was held shortly afterwards in Britain, and the breed was recognised by the Kennel Club. In the United States of America the adoption of the breed took place somewhat earlier, and by 1898 the first breed show had already been held, the breed soon becoming very popular.

The attempt to revive the toy Bulldog in Britain persisted until the First World War, and for a while the very small Bulldog of under fifteen pounds was recognised, and whilst some breeders still prefer the smaller type, the fifty pound average is now accepted generally as the norm. The real parting of the ways between the two breeds came with the acceptance of the bat-ears, which are a feature of the French Bulldog, but abhorrent to those who breed the Bulldog proper.

He is a heavy little dog with a large chest and a wide front, and apart from the head is just like a smaller version of the Bulldog with a roach, a dip towards the withers and an impression of great strength in a small compass. He is tremendously active, keeping remarkably fit by virtue of the great deal of exercise that he takes normally in play and adventure. He makes a wonderful show dog, as he reacts so well to human companionship. He can be trained to stand perfectly still without losing his natural alertness and looking cowed, and he enjoys himself so obviously in the ring that his spirit is infectious. When he moves, providing he is a fit and healthy dog, he moves with freedom and with the sort of assurance that the earlier Bulldogs had.

His temperament is delightful, and it is in this respect that it is so easy to visualise that he had the Bulldog as an ancestor. He has the same sort of personality, being very charming and quaint on the one hand and extremely positive on the other. There are few half-measures about a French Bulldog, when he plays he does so wholeheartedly, but if he sulks it takes a great deal to console him. He is intelligent enough to make the most of the comfortable surroundings with which most people indulge him, and he soon becomes very much a part of the family.

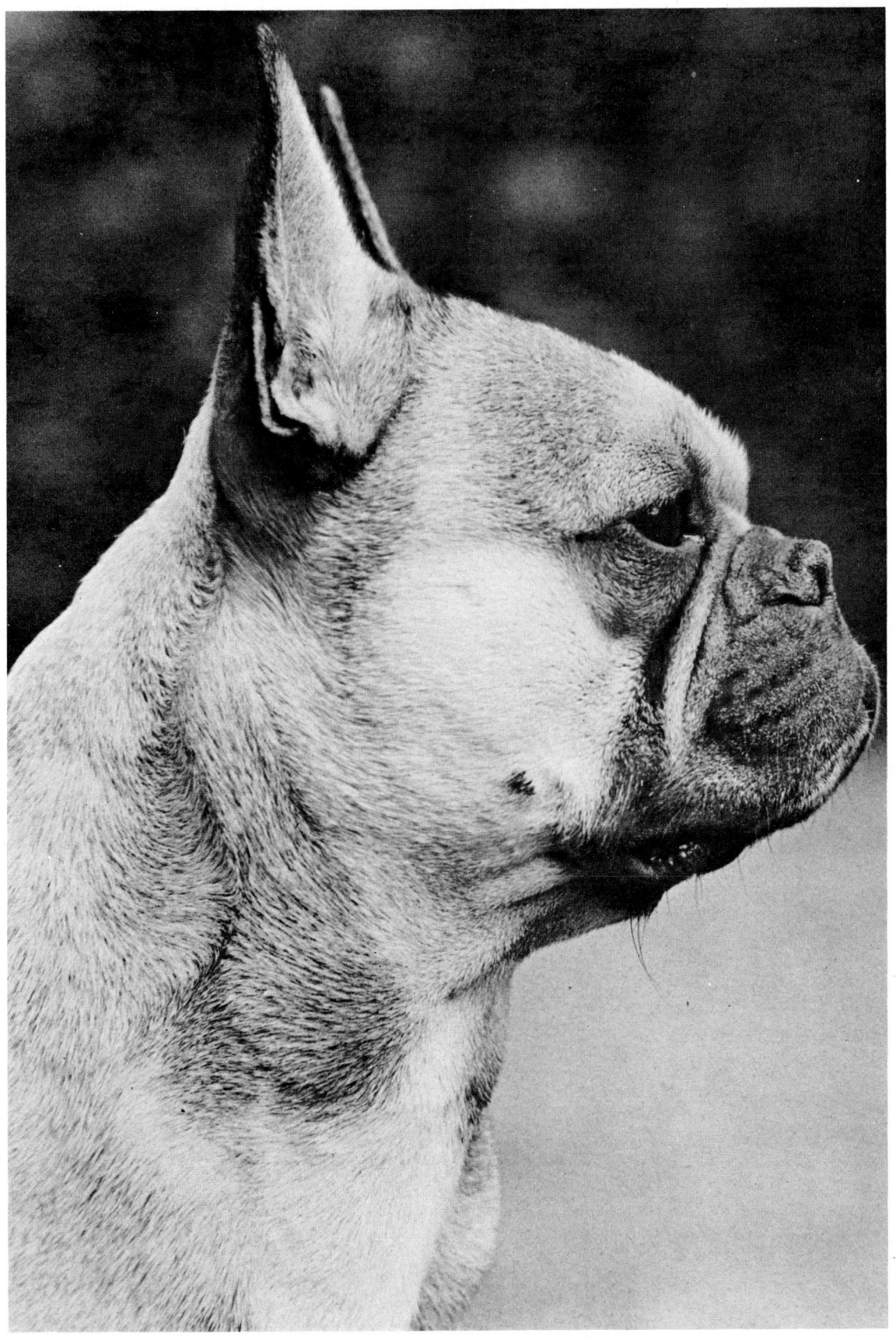

OFFICIAL STANDARD

General appearance
A French Bulldog should be sound, active and intelligent, of compact build, medium or small sized, with good bone, a short smooth coat, and the various points so evenly balanced that the dog does not look ill-proportioned.

Head and skull
Head massive, square and broad. Skull nearly flat between the ears, with a domed forehead, the loose skin forming symmetrical wrinkles. Muzzle broad, deep and laid back with the muscles of the cheek well developed; nose and lips black. Stop well defined. Lower jaw should be deep square, broad, slightly undershot and well turned up. Nose extremely short, black and wide, with open nostrils and the line between well defined. Lips thick, the lower meeting the upper in the middle, completely hiding the teeth. The upper lip should cover the lower on each side with plenty of cushion, but not so exaggerated as to hang too much below the level of the lower jaw.

Eyes
Should be dark, of moderate size, round, neither sunken nor prominent showing no white when looking straight, set wide apart and low down in the skull.

Ears
'Bat ears' of medium size, wide at the base, rounded at the top, set high, carried upright and parallel, a sufficient width of skull preventing them being too close together; the skin soft and fine and the orifice, as seen from the front, showing entirely.

Mouth
Teeth sound and regular, but not visible when the mouth is closed. Tongue must not protrude.

Neck
Should be powerful, with loose skin at the throat, but not exaggerated. Well arched and thick, but not too short.

Forequarters
Legs set wide apart, straight boned, strong, muscular and short.

Body
Should be short, cobby, muscular and well rounded, with deep wide brisket, roach back, strong, wide at the shoulders and narrowing at the loins, good 'cut up' and well sprung.

Hindquarters
Legs strong, muscular and longer than the forelegs so as to raise the loins above the shoulders. Hocks well let down and with very fine movement.

Feet
Should be small, compact and placed in continuation of the line of the leg, with absolutely sound pasterns. The hind rather longer than the fore-feet. Toes compact, knuckle high, nails short, thick and preferably black.

Head and skull: massive, square, broad, domed forehead with loose skin.

Tail
Very short, set low, thick at the root, and tapering quickly towards the tip, either straight or kinked, but never curling over the back. A good tail is placed so that it cannot be carried gaily.

Coat
Texture fine, smooth, lustrous, short and close.

Colour
The colours allowed are brindle, pied and fawn.
(1) The brindle is a mixture of black and coloured hairs. This variety may contain white on condition that brindle predominates.
(2) The pied is a dog in which the white predominates over the brindle. White dogs are classified with the pieds, but their eyelashes and eyerims should be black. In pieds the white should be clear with definite brindle patches and no ticking or black spots.
(3) The fawn dog may contain brindle hairs but must have black eyerims and eyelashes.

Weight and size
The ideal weight is 28 pounds for dogs and 24 pounds for bitches but soundness must not be sacrificed to smallness.

Faults
Nose other than black. Eyes of different colours. Ears not erect. Hare lip. Tail docked. Colour: tan, mouse grey (blue).

Note
Male animals should have two apparently normal testicles fully descended into the scrotum.

AKC VARIATION TO STANDARD
Weight: lightweight class under 22 pounds. Heavyweight class 22 pounds and not over 28 pounds. *Disqualifications:* nose other than black except in case of lighter coloured dogs where lighter coloured nose is acceptable. Black and white, black and tan, liver, solid black.

GIANT SCHNAUZER

NATIONAL GROUPING		
	Name	Number
KC(GB)	Utility	4
AKC	Working Dogs	III
FCI	Guard Dogs	2

The largest of the three Schnauzers, the Giant Schnauzer or Riesenschnauzer is the most recent of the three to arrive on the dog show scene outside Germany. Known for some time in European countries, it is only in recent years that it has appeared in the United States of America and Britain. The origin of the breed is somewhat obscure, but he is certainly a manufactured dog as were the Boxer and the Doberman. He was probably produced from some of the Belgian breeds such as the Bouvier Des Flandres and the Briard, both of which have his colours and something of his square look, though the strong wiry coat must have come from some other source.

He is a big, square, strong dog, built to combine strength and agility as he is in many ways the typical Terrier, having something of the look of a large strangely coloured Airedale. He can be trained to obedience work to a certain extent, which means that although he has a quickness of temper, he is normally very much under control, and he shows extremely well. His coat, like that of the two smaller Schnauzers, needs a great deal of preparation for the ring. The coat is hard and strong, and a good deal of trimming is needed which involves considerable hard work. In the rough he is still an attractive dog, but it is unlikely that he will ever become popular as a house pet, though his guarding instincts are well-developed.

OFFICIAL STANDARD

General appearance
The Schnauzer is a powerfully built, robust, sinewy, nearly square dog (length of body equal to height at shoulders). His temperament combines high spirits, reliability, strength, endurance and vigour. Expression keen and attitude alert. Correct conformation is of more importance than colour or other purely 'beauty' points.

Head and skull
Head strong and elongated, gradually narrowing from the ears to the eyes and thence forward toward the tip of the nose. Upper part of the head (occiput to the base of the forehead) moderately broad between the ears—with flat, creaseless forehead and well muscled, but not too strongly developed cheeks. The powerful muzzle formed by the upper and lower jaws (base of forehead to the tip of nose) should end in a moderately blunt line, with bristly, stubby moustache and chin whiskers. Ridge of the nose straight and running almost parallel to the extension of the forehead. The nose is black and full. Lips tight and not overlapping. Medium stop to accentuate eyebrows.

Head and skull: strong and elongated muzzle powerful.

Eyes
Medium sized, dark, oval, set forward, with arched bushy eyebrows.

Ears
Neat and V shaped, set high and dropping forward to temple.

Mouth
Scissor teeth, slightly overlapping from the top; with strongly developed fangs; healthy and pure white.

Neck
Moderately long, nape strong and slightly arched, skin close to throat, neck set cleanly on shoulders.

Forequarters
Shoulders flat and sloping. Forelegs straight viewed from any position. Muscles smooth and lithe rather than prominent; bones strong, straight and carried well down to the feet, elbows set close to the body and pointing directly backward.

Body
Chest moderately broad, deep, with visible strong breast bone reaching down to at least the height of elbow and slightly rising backward to loins. Back strong and straight, slightly higher at the shoulder than at the hindquarters, with short well developed loins. Ribs well sprung. Length of body equal to height from top of withers to ground.

Hindquarters
Thighs slanting and flat, but strongly muscled. Hindlegs (upper and lower thighs) at first vertical to the stifle, from stifle to hock in line with the extension of the upper neck line, from hock vertical to ground.

Hindquarters: vertical to stifle and in hock, flat and strongly muscled.

Feet
Short, round, extremely compact with close-arched toes (cat's paws) dark nails and hard soles. The feet also deep or thickly padded, pointing forward.

Tail
Set on and carried high, cut down to three joints.

Coat
Hard and wiry and just short enough for smartness, clean on neck, shoulder, ears and skull, plenty of good hard hair on front legs. Good undercoat is essential.

Colour
All pepper and salt colours in even proportions, or pure black.

Height
The ideal height for bitches shall be between $23\frac{1}{2}$ and $25\frac{1}{2}$ inches (60 and 65 centimetres) and for dogs between $25\frac{1}{2}$ and $27\frac{1}{2}$ inches (65 and 70 centimetres). Any variation of more than 1 inch (3 centimetres) in these heights should be penalised.

Faults
Too heavy or too light; too low or high on the leg. Head too heavy or round; creased forehead; sticking out or badly carried ears; light eye, with yellow or light grey rings; strongly protruding cheek-bones; flabby throat skin; undershot or overshot jaw. Muzzle too pointed or too small. Back too long, sunken or roached; barrel-shaped ribs; slanting crupper; elbows turned out; heels turned in, hindpart overbuilt (too steep). Toes spread open; paws long and flat (hare). Coat too short and sleek, or too long, soft or curled. All white, spotty, tigered or red colours. Small white breast spot or marking is not a fault. Among other serious faults are cow-hocks, sunken pasterns, or any weakness of joint, bone or muscular development.

Note
Male animals should have two apparently normal testicles fully descended into the scrotum.

KEESHOND

NATIONAL GROUPING		
	Name	Number
KC(GB)	Utility	4
AKC	Non-Sporting Dogs	VI
FCI	Companion Dogs	9

One of the most typical of the Spitz group of dogs after the Finnish Spitz, is the Keeshond. He is rather like a very large Pomeranian of a different colour. He is really the product of the Netherlands, and when first imported into Britain was known as the Dutch Barge Dog. He is by no means a recently developed dog, and probably descended from the Wolf Spitz of Germany and has been known in Europe in one form or another for the past two hundred years or more. The dog probably takes his name from the two patriots Kees de Witt and Kees de Gyselaer, and he became the mascot of Keezen, an 18th century peoples' party which opposed the House of Orange. He was best known, however, as a dog used as a companion and guard by the barge people of Holland.

The modern Keeshond has been known in Britain from the turn of the century since when it has made steady progress both there and in the United States. More recently it has achieved a degree of worldwide popularity and is seen more frequently almost everywhere than it is in its country of origin. The first one shown outside its native country was probably a dog called simply Kees which was exhibited around 1900 and was described as a Wolf Spitz though undoubtedly from its description it was in fact a Keeshond. It was shown in the foreign dog class, and was immediately objected to by another exhibitor who claimed that it should have been shown in the class for Pomeranians, which is not so odd as it may sound, as many Pomeranians at that time were as large as the modern Keeshond.

He is a strong and active dog with a very distinctive and clear bark, and the typical stand-off coat, prick ears and curled tail of the Spitz dogs. He has one particular mark of difference which distinguishes him from other breeds in the pencilling of dark marks around and behind the eyes known as the spectacles, which are a feature of the breed and very desirable.

As a show dog he has the one attribute of all the Spitz group, the ability to adopt a completely statuesque attitude in the ring and to hold it for a considerable time. This takes some training, and is usually done by food attraction, but it is not unusual to see a whole line of these dogs standing almost head to tail in the ring and completely motionless, watching every move of the handler's free hand which is usually somewhere near his mouth. He has no vice in the ring, or for that matter out of it, and will rarely interfere with any of the other dogs. His coat, when well-prepared is quite spectacular, with its distinctive wolf-grey colour, profuse feathering and well-developed ruff. An occasional dog will get into the habit of barking in the ring, when his loud bell-like tones will tell anyone in the vicinity which breed is being judged.

Long years of association with man have produced a dog ideally suited to life in a house. Although he is a fairly large dog, he curls himself up into a corner much as his close cousins in the group, the arctic dogs, curl themselves up in the snow, and he occupies the minimum of space. He is friendly, even affectionate, becomes very attached to those that he knows well, but still remains very much the guard dog, in which role his acute hearing and strong voice prove extremely valuable.

OFFICIAL STANDARD

General appearance

A short, compact body; alert carriage, foxlike head; small pointed ears; a well-feathered, curling tail, carried over the back; hair very thick on the neck, forming a large ruff; head, ears and legs covered with short thick hair. Dogs should move cleanly and briskly (not lope like an Alsatian) but movement should be straight and sharp. Dogs should show boldly.

Head and skull

Head well proportioned to the body, wedge-shaped when seen from above; from the side showing definite stop. Muzzle should be of medium length, neither coarse nor snipy.

Eyes

Dark with well-defined spectacles.

Ears

Small and well set on head, not wide and yet not meeting.

Mouth

Should be neither over nor undershot, upper teeth should just overlap under teeth and should be white, sound and strong (but discoloration from distemper not to penalize severely).

Forequarters

Forelegs feathered, straight, with good bone and cream in colour.

Hindquarters

Hind legs should be straight, showing very little hock and not feathering below the hock. Cream in colour.

Feet

Round and cat-like with black nails.

Tail

Tightly curled, a double curl at the end is desirable. Plume to be white on the top where curled, with black tip.

Coat

Dense, and harsh (off-standing), dense ruff and well feathered, profuse trousers; a soft, thick, light-coloured undercoat. Coat should not be silky, wavy or woolly, nor should it form a parting on the back.

Colour

Should be wolf, ash-grey; not all black or all white, and markings should be definite.

Weight and size

The ideal height is 18 inches for dogs and 17 inches for bitches, but type is of more importance.

Faults

Light eyes, prominent eyes. Curly or wavy tendency in coat. Silky coat. Absence of spectacles. Nervous demeanor. Drop ears. Whole white foot or feet. Black marks below the knee, pencilling excepted. White chest. Apple head or absence of stop.

Note

Male animals should have two apparently normal testicles fully descended into the scrotum.

AKC VARIATION TO STANDARD

Mouth: lips should be black and closely meeting not thick coarse or sagging, with no wrinkle at corner of mouth. *Eyes:* should be dark brown in colour, medium size, rather oblique in shape and not set too wide apart. *Ears:* triangular in shape, dark in colour, covered with thick velvety short hair. *Body:* neck should be moderately long, well shaped and well set on shoulders; covered with a profuse mane, sweeping from under the jaw and covering whole of front part of shoulders and chest, as well as top part of shoulders. Body should be compact with a short straight back sloping slightly downward toward hindquarters; well ribbed, barrel well rounded, belly moderately tucked up, deep and strong of chest. *Feet:* cream in colour, toes are nicely arched. *Tail:* should be set on high, moderately long. It should lie close to body. Tail should form part of silhouette of dog's body.

LHASA APSO

The history of the dogs of Tibet is closely connected with the history of the monasteries of that country. Many of the dogs were kept in monasteries and were considered to be holy animals, and some, particularly the Tibetan Spaniels are said to have turned prayer wheels as part of their duty. Of these sacred dogs, the Apso is the most recent one to have become popular in the Western World. His name is believed to have evolved from a corruption of the Tibetan word for goat, 'rapso', as his coat resembles that of this animal. It was said that the souls of lamas entered the bodies of Apsos on death, and the dogs were therefore treated with considerable respect. The ancient Chinese myth of the Lion Dog complements the beliefs concerning the dog in Tibet, and although the story is more generally applied to the history of the Pekingese, the lamas of Tibet had a very similar story. This supposed transfer of the soul leaving a body and entering a dog was accepted at one time so completely that it became a rite, and dogs were used to identify the presence of evil in a corpse.

Tibetan dogs were known to the rest of the world more than fifty years ago, the first to become well-known being the Tibetan Spaniel, and it was some time after that that the Lhasa Apso first made its mark. The first came into the possession of Colonel Kennedy, a medical officer who was given a couple in 1921. They were brought to this country and were exhibited at a show in London in 1929. A breed club was formed in 1933 and from that time the breed has never looked

NATIONAL GROUPING		
	Name	Number
KC(GB)	Utility	4
AKC	Non-Sporting Dogs	VI
FCI	Companion Dogs	9

back, the number of registrations rapidly overtaking those of the other Tibetan breeds.

He is a very sturdy little dog, strongly made and with a coat that protects him from the most rigorous weather conditions. In spite of his lack of size he is a forceful character and very much a guard dog and it would be unfortunate if because of his lack of size he became considered as a toy dog. In recent films emanating from Tibet this little dog can still be seen running around the monasteries, apparently little changed over the centuries by the influx of foreign blood, the comparative inaccessability of the country probably accounting for this. Seen thus they are fairly rough, with a comparatively short, hard and somewhat neglected coat. As we see them today in the rest of the world they are very different.

The Lhasa Apso is one of those dogs that really repays attention to his coat. The hair is long, and easily separated, with the result that today's exhibitors spend considerable time preparing their dogs for exhibition. His coat now normally reaches the ground, giving him a very glamorous appearance which makes him attractive to spectators and constantly encourages more people to own one. In the ring he is well-behaved, being steady, ignoring in an amusingly pompous manner the presence of other dogs, however large, and when asked to move, strides out with all the drive and presence of a very much larger dog.

He is an amusing little character, giving the impression all the time that inside his small frame there is a much larger dog trying to express himself. He is always full of confidence, even cheeky, and behaves in a playful, gay and attractive manner. He is very active, needs a great deal of exercise, which he fortunately gets with the endless games that he will play with anything or anyone, and he makes one of the most entertaining companions. He looks at his best when kept in the company of his fellows, and there are few more attractive sights in the canine world than a number of these little dogs enjoying the games that they invent for themselves on a sunny day in the garden.

OFFICIAL STANDARD

Body: length greater than height.

Characteristics
The Apso should give the appearance of a well-balanced, solid dog. Gay and assertive, but chary of strangers. Free and jaunty in movement.

Head and skull
Heavy head furnishings with good fall over the eyes, good whiskers and beard. Skull moderately narrow, falling away behind the eyes in a marked degree; not quite flat, but not domed or apple shaped. Straight foreface, with medium stop. Nose black. Muzzle about $1\frac{1}{2}$ inches long, but not square; the length from tip of nose to be roughly one-third the total length from nose to back of skull.

Eyes
Dark. Medium sized eyes to be frontally placed, not large or full, or small and sunk. No white showing at base or top of eye.

Ears
Pendant, heavily feathered. Dark tips an asset.

Mouth
Upper incisors should close just inside the lower, i.e., a reverse scissor bite. Incisors should be nearly in a straight line. Full dentition is desirable.

Neck
Strong, well covered with a dense mane which is more pronounced in dogs than in bitches.

Forequarters
Shoulders should be well laid back. Forelegs straight, heavily furnished with hair.

Body
The length from point of shoulders to point of buttocks greater than height at withers. Well ribbed up. Level topline. Strong loin. Well balanced and compact.

Hindquarters
Well developed with good muscle. Good angulation. Heavily furnished. The hocks when viewed from behind should be parallel and not too close together.

Feet
Round and cat-like, with good pads. Well-feathered.

Tail
High set, carried well over back and not like a pot-hook. There is often a kink at the end. Well feathered.

Coat
Top coat heavy, straight and hard, not woolly or silky, of good length. Dense under-coat.

Colours
Golden, sandy, honey, dark grizzle, slate, smoke, parti-colour, black, white or brown.

Size
Ideal height: 10 inches at shoulder for dogs; bitches slightly smaller.

Note
Male animals should have two apparently normal testicles fully descended into the scrotum.

STANDARD POODLE

NATIONAL GROUPING		
	Name	Number
KC(GB)	Utility	4
AKC	Non-Sporting Dogs	VI
FCI	Companion Dogs	9

The Poodle family is divided into three varieties by size in most countries, but the history of the breed is the same for all of them. The Poodle is the most entertaining of dogs and has a long association with the stage as a performer. He is a wonderful companion as one is never quite certain what he will do next, and he is full of fun and inventiveness. He will constantly surprise by his actions, and although he can be trained to repeat actions easily enough, he will indulge in activities which are the result of spur-of-the-moment decisions. His history is complicated somewhat by the fact that for many years France laid claim to him as the country of origin of the breed, whereas in fact it was almost certainly Germany that can claim the honour. He started off life as the Water Dog or Pudel of Germany, and old engravings of this dog look almost exactly like a somewhat neglected poodle.

The Standard Poodle was almost certainly originally a large gundog, though the uses to which he was subsequently put changed his appearance to some extent. In Russia the same dog became almost invariably large and black, in Germany the dogs were used as load pullers and became heavier and stronger, being used for pulling milk carts, whilst in France they became smaller and were almost exclusively companions. Many other breeds were probably used to produce the dog as we know him today, and it would not be simply a case of selective breeding. There were a

number of long-coated breeds of sheepdog in Hungary and Germany whose coats corded as the Poodle's will, and the very ancient Little Lion Dog has something of the look of a Poodle.

For a great number of years the Poodle was a regular part of the French circus, as he can be trained to perform apparently most difficult tricks with ease, and at the same time can be trimmed and clipped into patterns which themselves are entertaining. In more modern times his history has been less lowly, as he has become one of the finest of show dogs. Many of the early Poodles shown had what is called a corded coat which means that the coat was oiled and persuaded to mat into long separate cords which in a good specimen reached to the ground. This went out of fashion largely because of the difficulty encountered in keeping the coat in that condition, but the Puli exhibitors do the same thing successfully with the coat of their dogs today and it would be interesting to see what the modern Standard Poodle would look like with cords down to the ground.

He is a big fine dog, very elegant yet at the same time having great strength. His height has not caused him to sacrifice anything in the way of robustness, and his love of exercise and play means that he can be kept in excellent muscular condition with little difficulty. His coat needs constant attention to keep it in mat-free condition, but as it is quite acceptable that a dog not intended for exhibition may be clipped all over and still look very presentable, this is what most owners do.

He is one of the most striking and noble of all show dogs. His sheer height, and he can now be as much as twenty-five or more inches at the shoulder makes him very spectacular. Add to that the fact that at least four colours are often seen in the ring together, and that each in its way is a lovely clear colour and the whole picture becomes a very attractive one. To keep him in show trim means a considerable amount of work, and he will need a daily brushing as well as hours of trimming and clipping to put him into the ring looking his best. That it is worth while is proved by the fact that Standard Poodles have won major awards at every big show in the world including Westminster and Crufts.

He is a joyous animal to own, being very playful and full of high spirits, friendly and completely without vice. One never hears of a Poodle attacking anyone or biting at a show, or indeed anywhere else, but he is a natural guard with a very strong sense of territory.

OFFICIAL STANDARD

Characteristics and general appearance
That of a very active, intelligent, well balanced and elegant looking dog with good temperament, carrying himself very proudly.

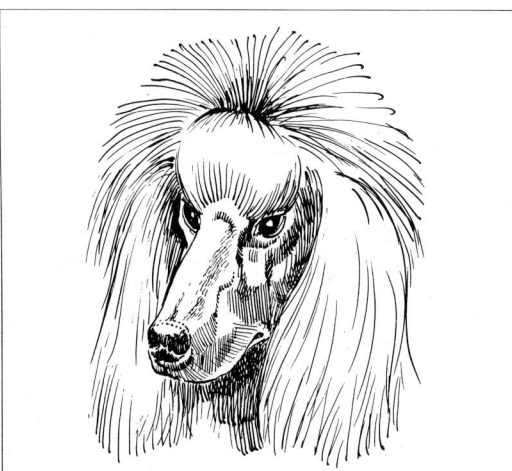

Head and skull: long and fine, foreface strong, lips tight-fitting.

Gait
Sound, free movement and light gait are essential.

Head and skull
Long and fine with slight peak at the back. The skull not broad and with a moderate stop. Foreface strong and well chiselled, not falling away under the eyes; bones and muscle flat. Lips tight fitting. Chin well defined, but not protruding. The whole head must be in proportion to the size of the dog.

Eyes
Almond shaped, dark, not set too close together, full of fire and intelligence.

Ears
The leather long and wide, low set on, hanging close to the face.

Mouth
Teeth: white, strong, even, with scissor bite. A full set of 42 teeth is desirable.

Neck
Well proportioned, of good length and strong to admit of the head being carried high and with dignity. Skin fitting tightly at the throat.

Hindquarters: well-developed and muscular, hocks well let down.

Faults

Heavy build, clumsiness, long back, snipy in foreface, light or round or prominent eyes, lippiness, bad carriage, heavy gait, coarse head, over or undershot or pincer mouth, flesh coloured nose, coarse legs and feet, long flat toes, open soft coats with no curl, particolours—white markings on black or coloured poodles, lemon or other markings on white poodles, vicious temperament.

Note

Male animals should have two apparently normal testicles fully descended into the scrotum.

Forequarters

Shoulders: strong and muscular, sloping well to the back, legs set straight from the shoulders, well muscled.

Body

Chest: deep and moderately wide. Ribs: well sprung and rounded. Back: short, strong, slightly hollowed, loins broad and muscular.

Hindquarters

Thighs well developed and muscular, well bent stifles, well let down hocks, hind legs turning neither in nor out.

Feet

Pasterns strong, tight feet proportionately small, oval in shape, turning neither in nor out, toes arched, pads thick and hard, well cushioned.

Tail

Set on rather high, well carried at a slight angle away from the body, never curled or carried over the back, thick at the root.

Coat

Very profuse and dense of good harsh texture without knots or tangles. All short hair close, thick and curly. It is strongly recommended that the traditional lion clip be adhered to.

Colour

All solid colours. White and cream poodles to have black nose, lips and eyerims, black toenails desirable, brown poodles to have dark amber eyes, dark liver nose, lips, eyerims and toenails. Apricot poodles to have dark eyes with black points or deep amber eyes with liver points. Black, silver and blue poodles to have black nose, lips, eyerims and toenails. Cream, apricot, brown, silver and blue poodles may show varying shades of the same colour up to eighteen months. Clear colours preferred.

Size

15 inches and over.

AKC VARIATION TO STANDARD

Head: moderately rounded, with a slight but definite stop. *Tail:* docked but sufficient in length to insure a balanced outline. *Coat:* a poodle may be shown in the 'Puppy' or 'English Saddle' (Lion) clip, or traditional 'Continental' clip. Poodles shown in any other clips shall be disqualified. Poodles under a year old may be shown in Puppy clip with coat long. Face, throat, feet and base of tail are shaved. Entire shaven foot is visible. There is pompon on end of tail. In order to give neat appearance, slight shaving of coat is permissible; however, a poodle in puppy clip that is excessively scissored shall be dismissed. *Disqualifications:* parti-colours. The coat of a parti-coloured dog is not an even solid colour at the skin but is of two or more colours. Dogs in any type of clip other than those listed under 'coat'. Dogs over or under height limits specified.

MINIATURE POODLE

NATIONAL GROUPING		
	Name	Number
KC(GB)	Utility	4
AKC	Non-Sporting Dogs	VI
FCI	Companion Dogs	9

It is almost certain that the Miniature Poodle as we now know it, was developed from the normal sized Pudel of Germany. The Standard Poodle of today is much taller than his ancestors would have been, and the Toy Poodle much smaller. It is the Miniature Poodle which is probably nearer in height to the original, though these days he is much more slender and refined and does not have the strength that the Pudel had. Some authorities state that the original was the Standard Poodle, but the dog shown in Europe today, where the sizes are not so clearly defined as they are in the United States and Britain, is not nearly as tall as the modern Standard Poodle. This would lead one to believe that the original Pudel was not a particularly tall dog, and an engraving of German Poodles dated around 1880 shows them as a medium sized dog, incidentally, with long tails.

In 1907 the Miniature Poodle was described as the Toy Poodle, and had to be less than fifteen inches at the shoulder, and it was not until later, when in the United States they required a Toy Poodle to be under ten inches and Britain under eleven, that the position was finally cleared up. Descended from the larger dog, which was often used as a gundog, the Miniature Poodle still retains the instinct to work. Though many of today's dogs are far from steady enough to work satisfactorily, the fact that they can easily be trained to take part in obedience tests proves that they still retain the ability. The rise of the Miniature Poodle was meteoric in the years after World War II, and by the 1960s he was one of the most popular dogs in the world. As a result of this puppies fetched very high prices and a great deal of indiscriminate breeding took place, puppies being produced with little regard for quality, and the standard of the breed declined. Fortunately, the position improved as the numbers decreased, and most of today's stock is most carefully bred.

It is impossible to lose sight of the fact that the Poodle was once a performing dog, and indeed still is in many parts of the world, particularly in France, where he is used extensively on the stage. He can be taught to perform a multitude of tricks, many of them apparently completely outside the natural habits of a dog. The result is that he is a very popular pet, having the sort of personality that endears him to elderly people particularly, as he has certain childlike qualities. He is still, however, a sporty little dog, needing a good deal of exercise, and in spite of his somewhat quaint appearance when clipped he is more of the sportsman than the dandy.

Few breeds of dog have had the success in the show ring of the Poodle, and particularly the Miniature Poodle. In Britain where variety classes are a feature at shows, the scene is frequently stolen by the beautifully presented Miniature Poodle. He appears to enjoy showing off, seems to appreciate the fact that he is being admired, and usually storms round the ring behaving like a dog twice his size. Coat preparation is vital, and nothing looks worse than a badly prepared Miniature Poodle. This preparation starts weeks before the show and continues right up until the dog enters the ring, and often beyond.

He is a lovely dog to own, or, as some suggest, to be owned by. He has to be accepted as part of the household, does not take kindly to being shut in kennels, and probably only reveals his true and complete personality when he is kept as a member of the family. Under these conditions he becomes a complete extrovert, and gains such confidence that he is clearly of the opinion that he is quite indispensable. He makes a good guard, as all the Poodles do, being very noisy at the approach of any intruder on to what he believes is his property, and putting up a show of fierceness remarkable in so small a dog.

OFFICIAL STANDARD

The Poodle (Miniature) should be in every respect a replica, in miniature, of the Poodle (Standard). Height at shoulder should be under 15 inches but not under 11 inches.

AKC VARIATION TO STANDARD
Height: 10 to 15 inches.

TOY POODLE

NATIONAL GROUPING		
	Name	Number
KC(GB)	Utility	4
AKC	Toys	V
FCI	Companion Dogs	9

One of the results of more and more people living closer together and in smaller houses has been the increased popularity of the smaller dogs. Miniaturisation was either an accident seized upon and developed by someone who wanted something different, or it was done for a purpose, as in the case of the smaller Dachshunds. More recently small breeds have been evolved to suit modern conditions, and the Toy Poodle is one of these. He was virtually unknown as a breed until this century. It is true that small long-coated dogs existed in France, such as the Bichon, and in Germany the Lowchen, though they were not the typical, but tiny Poodle that we know today. Perhaps the Barbet was nearest, though even this was often much larger than the modern Toy Poodle.

In the early days of the attempt to produce a very small version of the Poodle, small, and often rather weak Miniature Poodle offspring were selected, and by continually breeding from these, animals were produced which were certainly small enough, but in many cases were rather grotesque as well. Bent fore-legs would bring the shoulders under the ten inch or eleven inch measure, and short legs on long bodies would do the same thing, so that when the variety first began to appear in the show rings they were somewhat ludicrous compared with the miniatures and the standards. They were very much objects of scorn among those who owned what they called real dogs. Fortunately some of the more serious breeders continued with a careful programme and eventually succeeded in evolving a tiny dog that was a replica of his larger cousins, and with all their smartness and temperament. This success was finally crowned when one of these tiny dogs was Best in Show All-breeds at Crufts in 1966.

Progress continues in the breed, and where at one time only the blacks had pleasing heads, now all the other colours have caught up, and equally attractive whites and apricots as well as silvers are regularly seen. The rigid standard for height laid down in the early days of the breed has now been relaxed in Britain, and whereas at one time those that would not go under the measure were disqualified and required to leave the ring, now they may in fact remain and may win provided that in the opinion of the judge the degree of their oversize is a lesser fault than those of other exhibits and that the oversize dog is of better quality.

Now that the breeding of the Toy Poodle has settled down, there is no longer the fear of a litter of puppies all growing to be oversize. He is a sturdy little dog, solid and well-made, and remarkably hardy. Although by size he is included in the Toy Group in some countries, he remains in the Utility Group in Britain alongside the other two varieties. It is believed that he earns that place by virtue of his ancestry, which is not comparable with the small companion dogs that form most of the Toy Group, and because of his sturdy independence. In the ring he is certainly not overshadowed by either of the other two, or for that matter any breed for spirit and game performance, as he will continue to stride out in the ring at the end of a long hard day, full of confidence and independence. For his size he sparkles, moving with very rapid long strides, and covering the ground at a speed which many people find remarkable until they recall that he is in fact just a small version of what was once a hunting dog.

His temperament is quite delightful, and like his larger relatives he has no vice, being easy going and cheerful at all times, welcoming family and visitors alike with effusion, standing on his hind legs and bouncing up and down in his excitement. It is this gay spirit that endears him to everyone, and though he is not a toy, children love him for his small size and playfulness.

OFFICIAL STANDARD

The standard of the Poodle (Toy) is the same as that of the Poodle (Standard) and Poodle (Miniature) except that the height at shoulder should be under 11 inches.

AKC VARIATION TO STANDARD
Height: 10 inches or less.

SCHIPPERKE

NATIONAL GROUPING		
	Name	Number
KC(GB)	Utility	4
AKC	Non-Sporting Dogs	VI
FCI	Companion Dogs	9

It is virtually impossible to write an extended history of the Schipperke, as the background to the breed is so simple. With some of the characteristics of the Spitz group, insofar as the body shape is typical and the ears are erect, he is so much smaller than the remainder of the Group that he does not seem to belong. This diminutive size does not appear to have been a matter of miniaturisation, as he has always been small. He was in use for many years as a barge dog in Belgium and Holland, living on board, guarding property and probably from time to time encouraging the lazier towing horses to move a little faster. His name comes from a corruption of the word for little skipper, and his somewhat pompous attitude as he made his way around the canals, probably led to the description.

He first appeared in Britain and the United States at about the same time, probably because the Queen of the Belgians purchased a specimen in 1888 and three came into Britain in about the same year. They immediately became popular, and it was this popularity which may have persuaded the dog people of Belgium that their little dog had a future, and led to the formation of a breed club there which devised the standard of the breed. The first burst of enthusiasm soon lost its impetus, and after a time during the 1920s when he was seen at almost every show, numbers declined and the Schipperke is now one of the minority breeds in Britain, though in some countries, and particularly in South Africa he is still very popular.

Although described in the early days as a tailless dog, this was not entirely correct, as some were born with them. An early meeting of representatives of the Schipperke Club with a sub-committee of the Kennel Club in Britain agreed that the tail if present, could be docked, and modern examples always appear in the ring without a tail. The question of colour was a much-vexed one too, as by tradition the Schipperke had always been looked upon as a black dog though from time to time specimens were born which were of other colours. By the early 1900s it had been agreed that other colours could be permitted so long as they were whole colours, and some very attractive dogs have now been bred in cream and fawn.

He is an extremely active little dog, always on the alert, very much the guard dog, and very suspicious of strangers. One of the characteristics of the breed is his extreme inquisitiveness, and encouraged, he makes a very effective vermin dog, though there is little of the Terrier in his make-up. He is a sturdy, strong-bodied little dog, wiry and very strong for his size. His coat is virtually waterproof, and the distinctive mane is a feature of the breed. He is not a heavy-boned dog, his tendency being towards activity and agility rather than towards the miniature cart-horse type.

As a show dog he has always had adherents, as he is something of the natural showman that all the Spitz types are. He stands rock-steady in the ring, ignores other dogs and pays attention only to his handler. His size makes transport a simple matter as he can be boxed in comfort and will travel long distances in the back of a car without being a nuisance to passengers. Preparation is no problem, simply a matter of the glow of good health, the removal of a few white hairs which are almost always present in whole coloured dogs, and some nail trimming.

The Schipperke does not make friends easily with strangers and is something of a one-man dog, defending his territory and his family with a fearlessness that belies his lack of size. At the same time he is affectionate with children and has few vices, and his generations of association with families make him one of the best of house dogs.

OFFICIAL STANDARD

General appearance
A small cobby animal, with sharp expression, intensely lively, presenting the appearance of being always on the alert.

Head and skull
Head foxy in type, skull not round, but fairly broad, flat and with little stop. The muzzle should be moderate in length, fine but not weak, should be well filled out under the eyes. Nose black and small.

Eyes
Dark brown, small, more oval than round and not full; bright and full of expression.

Ears
Sharp, of moderate length, not too broad at the base, tapering to a point. Carried stiffly erect and strong enough not to be bent other than lengthways.

Mouth
Teeth strong and level.

Neck
Strong and full, rather short set, broad on the shoulders, and slightly arched.

Body: chest deep, back short, loins powerful.

Coat
Abundant, dense and harsh, smooth on the head, ears and legs, lying close on the back and sides, but erect and thick round the neck, forming a mane and frill and with a good culotte on the back of the thighs.

Colour
Should be black but other whole colours are permissible.

Weight and size
Weight about 12 to 16 pounds.

Faults
Drop or semi-erect ears, Dudley noses in the coloured variety. A light-coloured eye. Head narrow and elongated, or too short. Coat sparse, wavy or silky. Absence of the mane and 'culotte'. Coat too long, and white spots. Undershot or overshot mouth.

Note
Male animals should have two apparently normal testicles fully descended into the scrotum.

Head and skull: foxy, skull fairly broad.

Forequarters
Shoulders muscular and sloping. Legs perfectly straight, well under the body, with bone in proportion to the body.

Body
Chest broad and deep in brisket. Back short, straight and strong. Loins powerful, well drawn up from brisket.

Hindquarters
Fine compared to the foreparts, muscular and well-developed thighs; tailless rump well rounded. Legs strong, muscular, hocks well let down.

Feet
Should be small, cat-like, and standing well on the toes.

AKC VARIATION TO STANDARD
Coat: undercoat dense and short on body. *Weight:* up to 18 pounds. *Faults:* large prominent eyes. Ears too long or too rounded. Domed skull. Bull Terrier shaped head, straight hocks. Straight stifles and shoulders, cowhocks, feet turning in or out, legs not straight when viewed from front. *Disqualifications:* any colour other than solid black. Drop or semi-erect ears. Badly overshot or undershot.

SCHNAUZER

NATIONAL GROUPING		
	Name	Number
KC(GB)	Utility	4
AKC	Working Dogs	III
FCI	Guard Dogs	2

Britain is the home of the Terriers, by far the majority of the breeds in the Group originating in that country, but there are Terriers in other countries, and particularly in Germany, Terriers which have existed in one form or another for centuries. The best known of these is the Schnauzer. He exists in three forms, the Schnauzer proper, known in some countries as the Standard Schnauzer or Medium Schnauzer, the Miniature Schnauzer or Zwergschnauzer and the Giant or Riesenschnauzer, all of which stem from a common stock dating back to around 1500. Central Europe has always had its Terriers, and it was from a mixture of several of these, probably the Schafer Pudel and the Wire-haired German Pinscher that this now very distinctive breed of dog was produced. The result of using one breed that was essentially a working dog and crossing it with another which was a Terrier, was a dog that combined most of the admirable characteristics of both, a strong, staunch positive sort of dog that was capable of doing most things likely to be required of it.

The breed first appeared in the show ring in the late part of the 19th century and gained such immediate popularity that a club was formed, a standard drawn up, and speciality shows soon held. Soon after the turn of the century the first was imported into the United States and was considered to be a Terrier and shown as such. There had been a certain amount of confusion concerning the naming of the breed, and both Schnauzers and Dobermans were being called Pinschers which for all practical purposes means Terrier. Later the breed was moved in the AKC from the Terrier Group to the Working Group whilst in Britain it was classified as one of the Utility dogs. The Schnauzer was introduced much later into Britain and it was not until 1928 that the first one appeared in the foreign dog class at Crufts.

He has never achieved the popularity that the Miniature Schnauzer has, and registration numbers are running at only about one tenth of the more popular little version. In Germany, with the change from agriculture to industry, the Schnauzer found a new role as a guard dog rather than the herder that he had undoubtedly been formerly, and in this he has proved very successful. He is a strong dog, very stout in limb, and a particularly active and ferocious guard. He is not vicious and will not normally persist in an attack, but his aspect is sufficient usually to deter intruders.

He has in recent years become reasonably popular as a show dog, especially in the Scandinavian countries, and a few very enthusiastic breeders have kept him in front of the public eye and he is regularly seen at most of the major shows. He is not a particularly easy dog to show as he has a good deal of the Terrier temperament and his coat needs considerable attention. Left in the rough he is a fairly ragged sort of individual, and it is only when an expert has spent some hours on his coat, trimming and shaping him, and brushing up on the legs and muzzle that he begins to look the picture of the smart Terrier type dog. He makes a very good guard indeed, and those who own a Schnauzer will say that there is not a better house dog and watchdog in the world.

OFFICIAL STANDARD

General appearance
The Schnauzer is a powerfully built, robust, sinewy, nearly square, dog (length of body equal to height at shoulders). His temperament combines high spirits, reliability, strength, endurance and vigour. Expression keen and attitude alert. Correct conformation is of more importance than colour or other purely 'beauty' points.

Head and skull
Head strong and elongated, gradually narrowing from the ears to the eyes and thence forward toward the tip of the nose. Upper part of the head (occiput to the base of the forehead) moderately broad between the ears—with flat, creaseless, forehead and well muscled, but not too

strongly developed cheeks. Medium stop to accentuate prominent eyebrows. The powerful muzzle formed by the upper and lower jaws (base of forehead to the tip of the nose) should end in a moderately blunt line, with bristly, stubby moustache and chin whiskers. Ridge of the nose straight and running almost parallel to the extension of the forehead. The nose is black and full. Lips tight and not overlapping.

Eyes
Medium sized, dark, oval, set forward, with arched bushy eyebrows.

Ears
Neat and V shaped, set high and dropping forward to temple.

Mouth
Scissor teeth, slightly overlapping from the top; with strongly developed fangs; healthy and pure white.

Body: chest deep, strong breast bone, back strong and straight.

Neck
Moderately long, nape strong and slightly arched, skin close to throat, neck set cleanly on shoulders.

Forequarters
Shoulders flat and sloping. Forelegs straight viewed from any position. Muscles smooth and lithe rather than prominent; bone strong, straight and carried well down to the feet; elbows set close to the body and pointing directly backward.

Body
Chest moderately broad, deep, with visible strong breast bone reaching down to at least the height of elbow and slightly rising backward to loins. Back strong and straight, slightly higher at the shoulder than at the hindquarters, with short, well developed loins. Ribs well sprung. Length of body equal to height from top of withers to ground.

Hindquarters
Thighs slanting and flat, but strongly muscled. Hindlegs (upper and lower thighs) at first vertical to the stifle, from stifle to hock, in line with the extension of the upper neck line, from hock, vertical to ground.

Feet
Short, round, extremely compact with close-arched toes, (cat's paws) dark nails and hard soles. The feet also deep or thickly padded, pointing forward.

Tail
Set on and carried high, cut down to three joints.

Coat
Hard and wiry and just short enough for smartness, clean on neck, shoulder, ears and skull, plenty of good hard hair on front legs. Good undercoat is essential.

Colour
All pepper and salt colours in even proportions, or pure black.

Height
The ideal height for bitches shall be 18 inches and for dogs 19 inches. Any variation of more than 1 inch in these heights should be penalised.

Faults
Too heavy or too light; too low or high on the leg. Head too heavy or round, creased forehead, sticking-out, or badly carried, ears; light eye, with yellow or light grey rings; strongly protruding cheek-bones; flabby throat skin; undershot or overshot jaw. Muzzle too pointed or too small. Back too long, sunken or roached; barrel-shaped ribs; slanting crupper; elbows turned out; heels turned in, hindpart overbuilt (too steep). Toes spread open; paws long and flat (hare). Coat too short and sleek, or too long, soft or curled. All white, spotty, tigered or red colours. Small white breast spot or marking is not a fault. Among other serious faults are cow-hocks, sunken pasterns, or any weakness of joint, bones or muscular development.

Note
Male animals should have two apparently normal testicles fully descended into the scrotum.

AKC VARIATION TO STANDARD
This dog is granted championship status by the AKC in Group III: Working Dogs. *Head:* total length of head is about ½ length of back. *Ears:* when cropped, pointed tips, carried perpendicular at inner edges with as little bell as possible along other edge. *Body:* shoulders slope well forward where they join upper arm at nearly a right angle. Such angulation permits maximum forward extension of forelegs without binding or effort. Croup full, slightly rounded. *Feet:* dewclaws should be removed on hindlegs. *Disqualifications:* over or undershot. Shyness or viciousness.

MINIATURE SCHNAUZER

By breeding from the smaller dogs in a litter and probably by introducing new blood from other breeds, a steady process of miniaturisation produced the smallest of the three Schnauzers, the Miniature. Compared with the other two he is quite a tiny dog in his modern form, and whilst the standard suggests that an ideal height of thirteen to fourteen inches should be aimed at, there are many fine specimens that are smaller even than this. He came from the same root stock as the Schnauzer, but it is suggested

NATIONAL GROUPING		
	Name	Number
KC(GB)	Utility	4
AKC	Terriers	IV
FCI	Companion Dogs	9

that the Affenpinscher was used to help reduce the size whilst at the same time retaining the Terrier characteristics. He became a very popular dog in the

United States of America, and has been bred in that country successfully for the past half century or so, though they decided at an early date that he was a Terrier, something with which many countries disagree, not the least Britain where he is firmly established in the Utility group.

The breed has steadily increased throughout the world, and there is no sign that numbers are decreasing. His handy size, pleasant temperament and delightful showmanship constantly gaining new admirers for him. He is a square dog, and this is exaggerated by his presentation, the head having very pronounced hair on the eyebrows, the body coat being kept very short with the leg hair encouraged as much as possible. The total appearance is that of a very sharp, smart little dog. He is still a great vermin hunter, and likes nothing better than a good rat hunt, but his small size and cleanliness suit him admirably to life in a small apartment with a nearby park for exercise.

As a show dog he is ideal, few dogs repaying care and attention to presentation as he does. He can be shaped and trimmed to make the most of his characteristics, and whilst he always looks the epitome of smartness in show trim there is never anything artificial about him. When released from the tension of being shown his exuberance is infectious. He can be trained to stand absolutely still in the ring with just a little temptation by his handler, and in competition with other breeds usually scores on sheer ring performance. As a pet he is completely reliable, with no vice, great good spirits, and very friendly with everyone including children.

OFFICIAL STANDARD

General appearance
The Miniature Schnauzer is a powerfully built, robust, sinewy, nearly square, dog (length of body equal to height at shoulders). His temperament combines high spirits, reliability, strength, endurance and vigour. Expression keen and attitude alert. Correct conformation is of more importance than colour or other purely 'beauty' points.

Head and skull
Head strong and elongated, gradually narrowing from the

ears to the eyes and thence forward toward the tip of the nose. Upper part of the head (occiput to the base of the forehead) moderately broad between the ears—with flat, creaseless, forehead and well muscled, but not too strongly developed cheeks. Medium stop to accentuate prominent eyebrows. The powerful muzzle formed by the upper and lower jaws (base of forehead to the tip of the nose) should end in a moderately blunt line, with bristly, stubby moustache and chin whiskers. Ridge of the nose straight and running almost parallel to the extension of the forehead. The nose is black and full. Lips tight and not overlapping.

Eyes
Medium sized, dark, oval, set forward, with arched bushy eyebrows.

Ears
Neat and V shaped, set high and dropping forward to temple.

Mouth
Scissor teeth, slightly overlapping from the top; with strongly developed fangs; healthy and pure white.

Neck
Moderately long, nape strong and slightly arched, skin close to throat, neck set cleanly on shoulders.

Forequarters
Shoulders flat and sloping. Forelegs straight viewed from any position. Muscles smooth and lithe rather than prominent; bone strong, straight and carried well down to the feet; elbows set close to the body and pointing directly backward.

Body
Chest moderately broad, deep, with visible strong breast bone reaching down to at least the height of elbow and slightly rising backward to loins. Back strong and straight, slightly higher at the shoulder than at the hindquarters, with short, well developed loins. Ribs well sprung. Length of body equal to height from top of withers to ground.

Neck: moderately long, nape strong, slightly arched, skin close.

long and flat (hare). Coat too short and sleek, or too long, soft or curled. All white, spotty, tigered or red colours. Small white breast spot or marking is not a fault. Among other serious faults are cow-hocks, sunken pasterns, or any weakness of joint, bones or muscular development.

Note
Male animals should have two apparently normal testicles fully descended into the scrotum.

Hindquarters
Thighs slanting and flat, but strongly muscled. Hindlegs (upper and lower thighs) at first vertical to the stifle, from stifle to hock, in line with the extension of the upper neck line, from hock, vertical to ground.

Feet
Short, extremely compact with close-arched toes, (cat's paws), dark nails and hard soles. The feet also deep or thickly padded, pointing forward.

Tail
Set on and carried high, cut down to three joints.

Coat
Hard and wiry and just short enough for smartness, clean on neck, shoulder, ears and skull, plenty of good hard hair on front legs. Good undercoat is essential.

Colour
All pepper and salt colours in even proportions, or pure black.

Height
The ideal height for bitches shall be 13 inches and for dogs 14 inches. Too small, toyish-appearing dogs are not typical and should be penalised.

Faults
Too heavy or too light; too low or high on the leg. Head too heavy or round, creased forehead, sticking-out, or badly carried, ears; light eye, with yellow or light grey rings; strongly protruding cheek-bones; flabby throat skin; undershot or overshot jaw. Muzzle too pointed or too small. Back too long, sunken or roached; barrel-shaped ribs; slanting crupper; elbows turned out; heels turned in, hindpart overbuilt (too steep). Toes spread open; paws

AKC VARIATION TO STANDARD
This dog is granted championship status by the AKC in Group III: Working Dogs. *Head:* moderately broad between ears with width of skull not exceeding $\frac{2}{3}$ length. *Mouth:* lips black. *Ears:* carried erect when cropped. *Tail:* not less than 1 inch and not more than 2 inches. *Coat:* outer coat proper Show length is approximately $1\frac{1}{2}$ inches except that it may be closely trimmed on ears, head, neck, chest and belly. *Size:* ideal at shoulder blades: dogs $18\frac{1}{2}$ to $19\frac{1}{4}$ inches, bitches $17\frac{1}{2}$ to $18\frac{1}{2}$ inches. *Disqualifications:* vicious dogs. Dogs under 18 inches or over 20 inches. Bitches under 17 inches or over 19 inches.

SHIH TZU

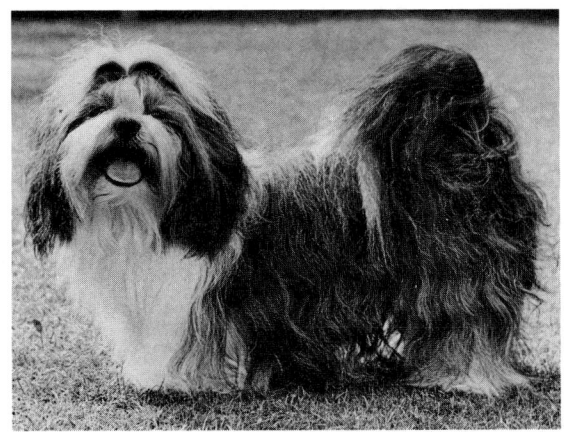

Several dogs have their origin in the Far East, and one or two in China. The Shih Tzu is undoubtedly one of these though a good deal of confusion exists because of the resemblance between a number of the small dogs that began life in that country. The Tibetan Spaniel, the Lhasa Apso and the Pekingese all bear a superficial resemblance to the Shih Tzu. The ancient myths and legends woven around the Lion Dog of China, half lion and half dog, playing with his ball, could refer to any one of these tiny dogs. In Tibet the small Lion Dogs were kept as house pets and for indeterminate duties round the temples. They were treated with considerable reverence, and their supposed relationship to the lion which is an animal that is much respected in the Buddhist religion, added to the esteem in which they were held. It is possible that these dogs were bred in the temples of Tibet and taken to China as tributes, as gifts of dogs were considered a great honour, largely because there were always dogs at the Imperial Courts of China. Much of the early history of these small companion dogs in China depends on the written word which tells of small short-nosed dogs which could have been anything from a Pug to a Pekingese, which makes the distinguishing of the Shih Tzu as a separate breed extremely difficult.

It was not until the 1930s that the breed really began to be recognised as a separate one outside China. At a dog show held in Peking in 1936 a European with an interest in these little dogs, recognised them as something other than a Pekingese or an Apso. The first recorded importation into Britain was of a bitch which entered the country in 1931, and when first shown in 1933 the dogs were classified with the Apsos,

NATIONAL GROUPING		
	Name	Number
KC(GB)	Utility	4
AKC	Toys	V
FCI	Companion Dogs	9

and it was not until the Tibetan Breed Association sorted things out in 1934 that they were recognised as a separate breed. They arrived in the United States of America in 1938 and were reregistered as Apsos. In 1940 the breed was granted a separate register in Britain, and from that time it has never looked back. Something like two thousand are registered in Britain every year, and the breed now draws very large classes at all the major championship shows. It is rapidly gaining in popularity in most countries of the world, and has outstripped all the other Tibetan breeds.

The Shih Tzu is a very sturdy little dog with few of the toy dog characteristics being heavy for his size, and with strong limbs and great stamina. He is bold and sporty without being belligerent, and happy to hunt with other dogs, thoroughly enjoying being one of the pack. As a show dog he has achieved real prominence in the short time since he first arrived on the scene in the Western World, and he now features regularly as a Group or Best in Show winner at many of the major shows. He is a pleasant dog to show, being very amenable to the discipline of the ring, and almost always the complete extrovert, enjoying putting on a performance in front of admirers, and never disturbed by other dogs or the big occasion. His preparation is not a hardship as his coat is strong and fairly straight, and if kept constantly groomed, show preparation is reduced to a simple matter of a bath and brushing and combing.

Temperamentally he is one of the most delightful dogs in the world, being almost human in his response to the companionship of the human race, settling into living in a house as if it were his natural right, which it probably is as he has lived thus for centuries. He is gay, forthcoming and resilient, bouncing back from a reprimand with an entertaining charm that is irresistible, and joins in the games of the children with an enthusiasm that is infectious. There is no doubt that he appreciates that as a dog he is something special, and he probably dreams of the times when he was the revered inmate of a Tibetan temple.

OFFICIAL STANDARD

General appearance
Very active, lively and alert, with a distinctly arrogant carriage. The Shih Tzu is neither a terrier nor a toy dog.

Head and skull
Head broad and round; wide between the eyes. Shock-headed with hair falling well over the eyes. Good beard and whiskers; the hair growing upwards on the nose gives a distinctly chrysanthemum-like effect. Muzzle square and short, but not wrinkled like a Pekingese; flat and hairy. Nose black for preference and about one inch from tip to stop.

Eyes
Large, dark and round but not prominent.

Ears
Large, with long leathers, and carried drooping. Set slightly below the crown of the skull; so heavily coated that they appear to blend with the hair of the neck.

Mouth
Level or slightly underhung.

Forequarters
Legs short and muscular with ample bone. The legs should look massive on account of the wealth of hair.

Body: longer than height, well coupled, sturdy.

Body
Body between withers and root of tail should be longer than height at withers; well-coupled and sturdy; chest broad and deep, shoulders firm, back level.

Hindquarters
Legs short and muscular with ample bone. They should look straight when viewed from the rear. Thighs well-round and muscular. Legs should look massive on account of the wealth of hair.

Feet
Firm and well-padded. They should look big on account of the wealth of hair.

Tail
Heavily plumed and curled well over back; carried gaily, set on high.

Coat
Long and dense, but not curly, with good undercoat.

Colour
All colours permissible, but a white blaze on the forehead and a white tip to the tail are highly prized. Dogs with liver markings may have dark liver noses and slightly lighter eyes. Pigmentation on muzzle as unbroken as possible.

Weight and size
10 to 18 pounds. Ideal weight 10 to 16 pounds. Height at withers not more than $10\frac{1}{2}$ inches; type and breed characteristics of the utmost importance and on no account to be sacrificed to size alone.

Faults
Narrow heads, pig-jaws, snipyness, pale pink noses and eye-rims, small or light eyes, legginess, sparse coats.

Note
Male animals should have two apparently normal testicles fully descended into the scrotum.

AKC VARIATION TO STANDARD
This dog is granted championship status by the AKC in Group V: Toys. *Head:* definite stop. *Eyes:* placed well apart. *Feet:* hair between pads. Dewclaws generally removed on hind feet. *Weight and size:* at withers 9 to 10 inches—no more than 11 inches and not less than 8 inches. Weight of mature dogs should be no more than 18 pounds, not less than 9 pounds.

TIBETAN SPANIEL

NATIONAL GROUPING		
	Name	Number
KC(GB)	Utility	4
AKC	—	–
FCI	Companion Dogs	9

This delightful little dog was one of the first of the Tibetan breeds to arrive in Britain. It had been used for centuries by the monks of Tibet as a Prayer Dog being trained to turn the prayer wheels by means of a small treadmill. Each turn of the wheel which contained rolled up parchment scrolls is believed to give the prayers the necessary push to bring them nearer to heaven. He was highly prized and was often given as a special gift to the Emperors of China, where it is claimed that he could easily have been one of the ancestors of the Pekingese. Certainly when the breed first arrived in Britain in around 1900 they were considered to resemble the Pekingese very closely and it was only the efforts of early breeders to eliminate the short-nosed specimens that resulted in the present clear distinction. Even so to this day they are often mistaken for Pekingese by the general public.

As with the other small dogs from the Far East, the origins are obscured by time and lack of information, and it is probable that in the very early days of its development, when trade between China and Tibet was a feature of the daily life of those countries, the breeds were very interbred. It is only in recent years—recent that is in the context of development of a breed of dog—that the distinct separation has taken place. Even since the introduction of the Tibetan Spaniel to the Western World it has been hinted that some out-crossing took place to improve certain characteristics of the breed, and from time to time even now certain specimens have too much of the Pekingese look about them. Early Chinese drawings depict dogs that look different yet have a good deal in common, and allowing for a certain amount of artistic licence, could be any one of three or four different breeds in their early stages of development.

He is a very positive little dog, outgoing temperamentally and strong physically, and though his size—or rather lack of it—persuades some people that he is really a Toy dog, his manner and his conviction that he is as big as a Great Dane places him, at least in his own opinion, very firmly outside that Group. Since his early days as a show dog he has made tremendous strides, very enthusiastic and efficient clubs have watched carefully over the progress of the breed, and the Tibetan Breeds Association included the breed among its interests from 1934 onwards. He is still invading new countries and the first specimens have just arrived in South Africa. The number of registrations have climbed steadily and although one writer stated as recently as 1948 that in his opinion it was the Tibetan Terrier that was most likely to succeed as a fancy, the Tibetan Spaniel has completely outstripped its rival and now numbers something like three times that of the Terrier.

He is an enjoyable little dog to show, as when part of a team he travels happily boxed up with the rest, waits his turn patiently, watching his kennelmates and all that is going on around him with keen interest, and then when it is his turn, enjoys the experience to the full. There are few problems with preparation, some removal of excess soft woolly coat being all that is needed.

The temperament of this little dog is delightful. He is full of fun, enjoys life to the full, and is every bit as happy racing through the woods after a rabbit, real or imaginary, as he is sitting on a silk cushion on the most comfortable chair in the house. It is perhaps in the latter environment that his sense of superiority shows most clearly. There is little doubt that he is subconsciously aware that his ancestors were part of the ritual of the monasteries.

OFFICIAL STANDARD

Characteristics
Gay and assertive, highly intelligent, aloof with strangers.

General appearance
Should be small, active and alert. The outline should give a well balanced appearance, slightly longer in body than height at withers.

Head and skull
Small in proportion to body and proudly carried giving an impression of quality. Masculine in dogs but free from coarseness. Skull slightly domed, moderate width and length. Stop slight, but defined. Medium length of muzzle, blunt with cushioning, free from wrinkle. The chin should show some depth and width. Nose black preferred.

Head and skull: skull slightly domed, stop slight but defined.

Eyes
Dark brown in colour, oval in shape, bright and expressive, of medium size set fairly well apart but forward looking giving an ape-like expression. Eye rims black.

Ears
Medium size, pendant, well feathered in the adult and set fairly high. They may have a slight lift from the skull, but should not fly. Large heavy low set ears are not typical.

Mouth
Ideally slightly undershot, the upper incisors fitting neatly inside and touching the lower incisors. Teeth should be evenly placed and the lower jaw wide between the canine tusks. Full dentition desired. A level mouth is permissible providing there is sufficient width and depth of chin to preserve the blunt appearance of muzzle. Teeth must not show when mouth is closed.

Neck
Moderately short, strong and well set on. Covered with a mane or 'shawl' of longer hair which is more pronounced in dogs than bitches.

Forequarters
The bones of the forelegs slightly bowed but firm at shoulder. Moderate bone. Shoulder well placed.

Body
Slightly longer from point of shoulder to root of tail than the height at withers, well ribbed with good depth, level back.

Hindquarters
Well made and strong, hocks well let down and straight when viewed from behind. Stifle well developed, showing moderate angulation.

Feet
Harefooted, small and neat with feathering between toes often extending beyond the feet. White markings allowed.

Gait
Quick moving, straight, free, positive.

Tail
Set high, richly plumed and carried in a gay curl over the back when moving. Should not be penalised for dropping tail when standing.

Coat
Double coat, silky in texture, smooth on face and front of legs, of moderate length on body, but lying rather flat. Ears and back of forelegs nicely feathered, tail and buttocks well furnished with longer hair. Should not be over-coated and bitches tend to carry less coat and mane than dogs.

Colour
All colours and mixture of colours allowed.

Weight and size
Weight 9 to 15 pounds being ideal. Height about 10 inches.

Faults
Large full eyes, broad flat muzzle, very domed or flat wide skull, accentuated stop, pointed weak or wrinkled muzzle, overshot mouth, long plain down face without stop, very bowed or loose front, straight stifle, cow hocks, nervousness, cat feet, coarseness of type, mean expression, liver or putty coloured pigmentation, light eyes, protruding tongue.

Note
Male animals should have two apparently normal testicles fully descended into the scrotum.

AKC VARIATION TO STANDARD
This dog is not granted championship status by the AKC.

TIBETAN TERRIER

NATIONAL GROUPING		
	Name	Number
KC(GB)	Utility	4
AKC	Non-Sporting Dogs	VI
FCI	Companion Dogs	9

Whilst the other Tibetan breeds were largely the urban dogs of their native country, the Tibetan Terrier was the rural one. Whilst the others spent most of their time being cossetted to a certain extent in and around the villages and monasteries, this dog was working for his living as a herding dog and as a guard. He is supposed to have been the original 'holy dog' of Tibet, and when that country was subjected to paying tribute in the form of goods and treasures to China, this little dog was the one that guarded the caravans. It was in fact the awe in which the dog was held rather than his size or ferocity that prevented the caravans from being raided, as he is a small and fairly quiet animal.

The confusion that affected all the small Tibetan breeds in the early days of their introduction to the Western World, was seen in the Tibetan Terrier as much as in the others. An early photograph of what is described as the best Lhasa Terrier imported into Britain around 1900, shows a dog that is very little like the Tibetan Terrier that we know today, and was clearly more of an Apso or a Shih Tzu than the breed that it purported to be. Fortunately for the breed Mrs. Greig and her daughter, Dr. A. R. H. Greig took the breed to their hearts, and almost all the dogs being shown today have, way back in their pedigrees the names 'Ladkok' or 'Lamleh'. Dr. Greig showed her dogs fearlessly all over Britain, and survived to see the breed well-established as a show dog, and would have been very happy to see the great wins of recent speci-

mens. The first Best in Show All-breeds was recorded at an Open show in Britain in August 1963 when the author was the judge.

Registrations have quadrupled since that time, and the rings at most important shows are well-filled when the breed is scheduled. He is a strong dog of considerable activity, and at first sight conveys the impression of a miniature Old English Sheepdog as he is square, has considerable hair over his eyes, and his tail curved well over his back gives the same appearance as the upward lift over the hindquarters of the Bobtail. He is the only dog with a standard that states that he should stand well down on his pads. This was a point that Dr. Greig always felt was very important, maintaining that the large flat feet gave the breed the ability to perform well over very rough mountainous country which by tradition it had to do, and over which small terrier type feet would prove a handicap.

The breed now appears in the show rings in a great variety of colours, which makes a parade of them a very attractive spectacle. The only colour that is barred in the standard is chocolate. In recent years a great deal of attention has been paid to grooming and presentation as was necessary to compete an equal terms with such glamorous animals as Afghan Hounds and Poodles, and a Tibetan Terrier shown now in the rough, as once was the practice, would look very out of place. The coat still retains its strong weatherproof qualities, however, and though the breed has been glamorised, it has lost none of its original character.

He is as delightful temperamentally as all the other Tibetan breeds, and though somewhat sharper than the others as would be expected of a dog that needs to live up to the title of Terrier, he has no vice, and is an amenable and affectionate companion. He makes a good house dog, is small enough to fit into a modern flat and modern transport, and makes a very good guard.

413

OFFICIAL STANDARD

Characteristics
Alert, intelligent and game, not fierce nor pugnacious. Chary of strangers.

General appearance
A well muscled medium sized dog, in general appearance not unlike an Old English Sheepdog in miniature.

Head and skull
Skull of medium length, not broad or coarse, narrowing slightly from ear to eye, not domed but not absolutely flat between the ears. The malar bones are curved, but should not be over developed so as to bulge. There should be a marked stop in front of the eyes, but this must not be exaggerated. The head should be well furnished with long hair, falling forward over the eyes. The lower jaw should carry a small, but not exaggerated amount of beard. The length from eye to tip of nose equal to length from eye to base of skull; not broad nor massive. Nose black.

Eyes
Large, dark, neither prominent nor sunken: should be set fairly wide apart. Eyelids dark.

Ears
Pendent, not too close to head, V shaped, not too large, heavily feathered.

Mouth
Level by preference but if slightly undershot not to be penalised.

Forequarters
Legs parallel and heavily furnished. Pasterns slightly sloping.

Body: compact, length equals height.

Body
Compact and powerful. Length from point of shoulder to root of tail equal to height at withers. Well ribbed up. Loin slightly arched.

Hindquarters
Heavily furnished, should be slightly longer than forelegs with well bent stifles and low set hocks giving a level back.

Feet
The feet should be large, round, heavily furnished with hair between the toes and pads. The dog should stand well down on its pads. There should be no arch in the feet.

Gait
When walking or trotting the hind legs should neither go inside nor outside the front ones but run on the same track.

Tail
Medium length, set on fairly high and carried in a gay curl over the back. Very well feathered. There is often a kink near the tip.

Coat
Double coated. The undercoat fine wool, the top coat profuse, fine but not silky or woolly; long; either straight or waved.

Colour
White, golden, cream, grey or smoke, black, particolour, and tricolours; in fact any colour except chocolate or liver colour.

Size
Height at shoulders, dogs should be from 14 to 16 inches, bitches slightly smaller.

Faults
A weak snipy foreface should be penalised. Lack of double coat. Cat feet.

Note
Male animals should have two apparently normal testicles fully descended into the scrotum.

AKC VARIATION TO STANDARD
Weight: 22 to 23 pounds. *Disqualification:* nose not black.

PART TWO:
Breeds recognised by the Fédération Cynologique Internationale (FCI)

In every country in the world in which the breeding of pedigree dogs, their preservation, exhibition, and their welfare, are considered important, there is an organisation to govern canine affairs. In some countries where the world of the pedigree dog is under the control of separate states there is more than one organisation. There is, however, one international body whose sphere of influence is wider than any one country. It began in Europe and has spread to many other countries including South America, and is known to everyone connected with dogs, as the *FCI*.

Most countries, and the United States of America and Britain are typical examples, have their show dogs organised on a two-tier basis. The upper tier is composed of those breeds which are considered important enough and which are numerically strong enough within that country to warrant the award of champion status, and a second tier which is made up of those breeds which are recognised, but because they are at the moment few in number, are shown but not granted champion status.

The *Fédération Cynologique Internationale*, with its headquarters in Belgium, recognises a great many more breeds than any individual country and awards champion status to them even though they are often very few in number, or indeed have not been shown outside their own country. Thirty-one countries are federated within the *FCI*, and all the breeds recognised by those countries are accepted by the *FCI*, and are eligible for the award of the title International Champion. A further fifteen countries are associated with the *FCI* though not federated, and in those countries the title of International Champion is not available. The *FCI* recognises nearly three hundred breeds of dogs, which is something like twice as many as any other individual country.

The standards of the breeds from each member country are submitted to the *FCI* council for approval, and only when this has been given is the breed then admitted to the *FCI* list. The standards are then kept on register by the *FCI* and may only be altered by the country of origin in consultation with the council. The *FCI* then publishes the standard in several languages. In addition to this rather detailed involvement in the canine affairs of many of the countries of the world, the *FCI* holds an annual international congress in a different centre each year at which many important topics are discussed concerning canine affairs internationally. There has been a move in recent years towards the acceptance of standardised forms of breed standards throughout the world, and the *FCI* has been one of the principal advocates of this. At present standards, even of the same breed, vary from country to country though in the main these variations are minor ones only, and in many cases countries adopt the standards of the country of origin.

In the subsequent chapters of this book the breeds which are recognised by the *FCI* (other than those granted championship status by the United States of America and Britain) are described, and are arranged in *FCI* groups which are ten in number.

FCI GROUP I:

Herding dogs, guard dogs, sheepdogs and dogs that are useful

Australian Cattle Dog

In the early days the Australian settlers were faced with the problem of controlling vast herds of cattle and flocks of sheep grazing over huge tracts of land, and the answer lay in using dogs. They started with a dog known as the Smithfield the origin of which is itself obscure, but it was a large and somewhat cumbersome beast that was too noisy and disturbed the herds. A man named Timmins of New South Wales, and a drover by trade, crossed the Smithfield with the native Dingo around 1830 and produced a litter of red, bob-tailed pups which were known as Timmins Biters. In 1840 a landowner named Hall imported a couple of smooth blue merle Collies from Scotland and these, in turn crossed with the Dingo and the Timmins dogs, produced what were known as Hall Heelers.

From that time onwards there were continued efforts to improve the breed, and the present-day blue and red mottled Cattle Dogs are the result. A standard was drawn up in 1897 for what was then

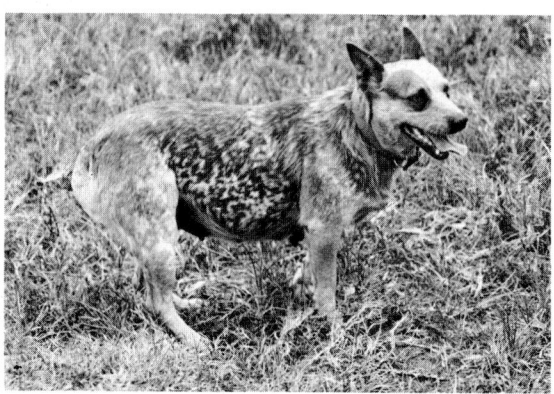

known as the Australian Heeler and the name has since been changed to Australian Cattle Dog, the standard being updated and adopted in 1963. He is a fantastic working dog with tremendous powers of endurance and courage. He will work in the exhausting conditions of the Australian climate all day, and rarely flags. As a show dog he has proved an immediate success, as he is most impressive for his appearance of sheer strength and absolute doggedness. He still works, however, and that side of his character has not been neglected.

Australian Kelpie

In 1870 a grazier named Allen imported into Australia a pair of so-called Fox Collies from Scotland, they

were black and tan with prick ears. They mated on board ship and whelped a litter, one red, and the others black and tan. They proved to be good workers, fast and quiet and capable of working over wide areas. At about the same time a smooth black and tan bitch named 'Kelpie' appeared in New South Wales and was mated to one of the original litter and produced a famous winning dog also named 'Kelpie'. She was the foundation of the breed as all her progeny turned out to be good workers with sheep, and more or less in her honour they were all called Kelpies.

The breed was first exhibited at Melbourne in 1908. From the same line there descended a black strain which for a while were known as Barbs, a name which has now died out, but which still sometimes crops up when sheep men are talking about a black Kelpie, which they will refer to as a 'Barb'. They were shown for a time as a separate breed, but now appear together. The Kelpie is one of the cleverest and certainly one of the hardest working sheep dogs in the world, being famed for the use of what is called 'eye', which is the almost mesmeric manner in which they control the sheep by just gazing at them. They are fine show dogs, being easily prepared, almost always in good muscular condition, and obedient in the ring. Their guarding qualities have become a legend.

Beauceron (Berger de Beauce)

There are a number of French sheep-herding dogs probably developed from common stock, somewhat similar in size and type, but varying in some details from one area to another, and having been bred true to type in those areas. The Beauceron, comes oddly enough from the region of Brie rather than from Beauce, and was probably given the name to differentiate him from the Briard which originated in more or less the same area. He looks something like a short-coated German Shepherd Dog though with rather more elegance. He was bred originally to herd the large flocks of sheep which at one time were common in France, and he is still a farmer's dog as well as one recognised as a specific breed by the FCI.

Like many of the other breeds which were used for guarding the flocks as well as working them, he has a certain aggressiveness allied to his tractability, which,

when controlled gives him a positive quality. He is highly intelligent, easily trained and very obedient. He is not seen a great deal outside his own country, and has not achieved the popularity of his countryman the Briard.

Belgian Shepherd Dog (Laekenois)

This is the one variety of Belgian Shepherd Dog which so far has not become known outside his own country as have the Groenendael, the Malinois and the Tervuren. His origins are in a small area of Belgium near Antwerp where one of his duties was to guard the fields in which linen was put out to bleach in the rain and sun, known in Britain as 'bleachcrofts'. Like the

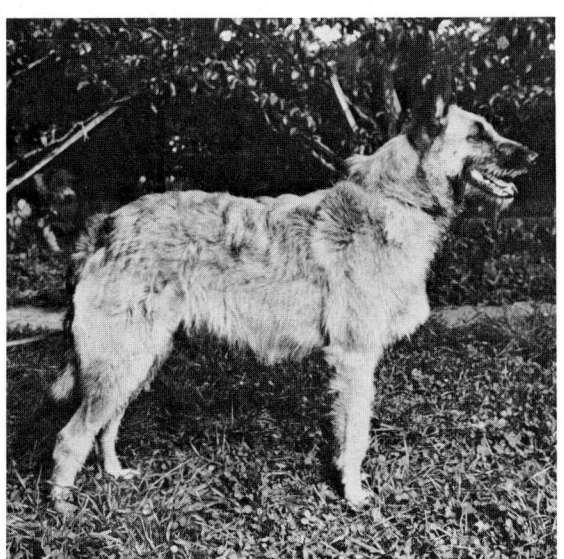

others of the family he is every bit as much a guard dog as a herder, and it is in this capacity that in recent years he has found a place in society. The breed appears in small numbers at the larger dog shows in Belgium and other European countries.

He is very like the Groenendael in some ways, but is fawn in colour with some black on the muzzle, and his coat is quite different. In the main it is rough and shaggy with a certain hardness of texture, long on the body and shorter on the head. He is an intelligent dog, easily trained and a very good guard and companion. He stands about twenty-five inches high at the shoulder with long neck and the general outline of an active working dog.

Berger Polonais de Vallée (Owczarek Nizinny)

This is an old breed of herding dog native to Poland, to which country it was probably taken by the Huns. In order to work on the terrain of its native country, a smaller and more active dog than some of the large Mastiff type guard and herding mountain dogs of other countries was needed, and yet because of the climate a dog with a protective coat was essential. For this reason the Nizinny was developed. He is a medium-sized dog up to twenty inches at the shoulder and is well-proportioned and strongly built. He is resistant to bad weather conditions, is lively and intelligent and capable of feats of memory.

He is somewhat like a small Old English Sheepdog with his long shaggy coat which covers his eyes, and his lack of tail, which is either rudimentary or docked soon after birth. His coat is long, very thick and shaggy, and though with a tendency to wave, does not cord as does that of some of the other European sheepdogs. All colours and markings are acceptable, but he is usually self-coloured or marked with very large patches of colour on white. He is very intelligent, alert and friendly, an excellent guard and has an inbuilt tendency to herd.

Cane da Pastore Bergamasco

This breed is one of the herding dogs traditionally used in the mountains of Northern Italy. His appearance suggests some connection with the Briard, but at the same time he also has something of the look of the herding dogs of Eastern Europe. He is a large dog, up to twenty-five inches at the shoulder with a short back, and is flexible and agile rather than heavy and slow. He is descended from the herding dogs described at least two thousand years ago, and until such time as modern transport methods opened up the mountainous districts he was probably bred fairly true to type.

He has a long, somewhat wavy coat, which when brushed out has something of the quality of that of the Briard, but with a thick undercoat which allows a certain amount of cording on the sides of the body similar to that of the Puli. He is a trustworthy and courageous dog that makes a very good guard.

Catalan Sheepdog (Gos d'Atura)

Though dogs of definite types have existed in Spain for centuries, and the use of dogs for sport, particularly hunting, has been popular in that country for a considerable length of time, the organisation of dog shows and the recognition of the importance of native breeds has been a comparatively recent development.

This little herding dog with his great character and individual appearance originated in Catalonia, and probably descended from some of the original mastiff types indigenous to the Iberian peninsula. He has now spread throughout Spain and has to a certain extent lost his original name being known as the Catalan Sheepdog. He was one of the dogs brought into military service during the Spanish Civil War, and there earned

himself a reputation as a guard and messenger.

He exists in two forms, the short-haired, which has gained favour as a companion and show dog, and the long-haired which is the one more commonly used as a sheep dog. He has great courage and tenacity and will drive the most stubborn and obstinate cattle single-handed, appearing to understand what is required with the minimum of instruction. He seems to have developed the same sort of 'eye' as the Australian herding dogs and can hold a herd merely by imposing his will upon them. He is a small dog, somewhat smaller than a Springer Spaniel and very strong and flexible. His size and temperament suit him perfectly to life as a companion or house dog.

Croatian Sheepdog (Kraski and Hrvatski Ovčar)

This is one of the oldest established and individual working dogs of Yugoslavia originating in Croatia, where it was used as a herder in mountainous country, but has now become much more widespread. He exists in two sizes, listed by the FCI as the Kraski Ovčar and the Hrvatski Ovčar, the Kraski standing up to twenty-four inches at the shoulder whilst the Hrvatski stands only up to twenty. The breed is one of the old indigenous breeds peculiar to a limited part of Yugoslavia and was used as a herding dog and watch dog.

He is a long-coated dog with erect, or sometimes pendant ears, and is reminiscent of the working sheepdog seen in many other parts of the world. He is strongly built with a wide chest and a strong loin with some curve towards the hindquarters and a bushy tail which he carries low but curls up when he becomes excited. His coat is quite long, three or four inches, soft and strong with a slight wave or curl on the body and shorter on the head and legs. He has considerable feathering and the long hair over the shoulders gives the effect of a soft mane. He is normally black in colour with some grey hairs, and white on the legs, feet and chest is not objected to. He is extremely hardy, virtually weatherproof, and is a fast and active worker.

Dutch Sheepdog

This very old sheep-herding dog from the Netherlands exists in three coat forms. The smooth and the rough, which look something like the Belgian sheep-dogs, and the long-coated which has something of the appearance of the long-coated shepherd dogs of the southern European countries. The breed had been in existence for a good many years before the breeders got together in the late 19th century to form a club to look after the interests of the breed and ensure its survival.

Most of these dogs come from the area of North Brabant but are very much working dogs and until recently were not seen very frequently at shows. This is, however, changing and the breed is being exhibited.

The wire-haired variety is particularly attractive looking rather like a small Bouvier Des Flandres, and has a very pleasing temperament. He is extremely hardy, very faithful and attached to places and people and can be trained very easily not only as a herder, but in what is called 'man work', as a police dog, for example. He is in fact capable of doing most of the work that a German Shepherd Dog does, but unfortunately the rapid growth of popularity of that breed has ousted the Dutch from public favour.

Iceland Dog

This small dog, only some twelve to sixteen inches at the shoulder has existed for centuries in Iceland, though he is rarely seen outside his own country. He is rather like a small Elkhound, though with less coat, and of mixed as well as plain colours. In the early years of this century he was known in Britain, several specimens being imported and recognised by the Kennel

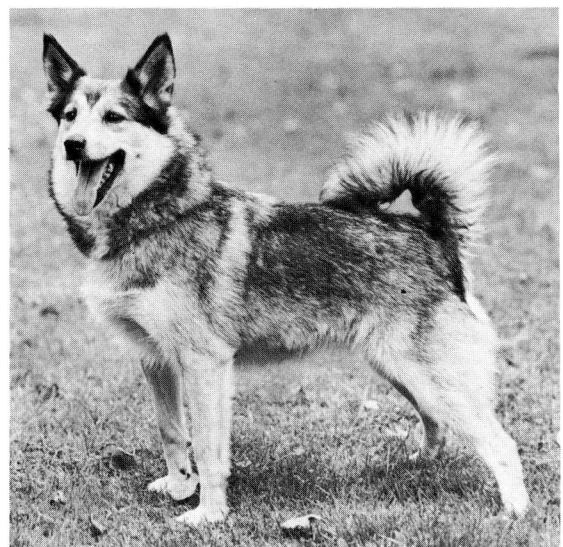

Club, but he did not gain favour. Unlike so many of the other Spitz types he does not have a very highly developed hunting instinct, but he is an excellent herder and guard dog, being used for driving both sheep and horses. A standard for the breed was accepted by the Danish authorities in 1898.

Lapinporokoira (Lapponian Vallhund)

This breed was produced in southern Finland by crossing the existing Lapphund, which is better known and seen more frequently in other countries, with such breeds as the German Shepherd Dog and the Collie. A dog was needed that had the highly developed herding instincts of the Collie and the German Shepherd Dog allied to the hardiness and guarding instincts of the indigenous Lappland Spitz.

He is a medium-sized dog with many of the Spitz characteristics, but somewhat longer in the back than most of the family. He has an alert-looking head with

tapering muzzle and erect ears, though tipped ears are permitted. He is strongly made with muscular hindquarters and loin and tail curled over his back, though this may droop at times. He has a double coat, the outer coat long, hard and glossy, and fitting fairly close to the body, and a soft woolly undercoat as protection against the weather which in his country can be fairly rigorous. His colour varies from white with darker shading, through brown to black, with some white markings. He is an extremely hardy dog and will work in all weathers, with tremendous stamina and willingness. His hunting instincts have virtually disappeared which has improved his performance as a herder. He was approved as a separate breed by the FCI in 1946 but is not seen outside Scandinavia.

Lapphund (Lapinkoira, Swedish Lapp Spitz)

This is one of the oldest Spitz breeds in Scandinavia, having been used originally as a herding dog for reindeer in Lappland. It was more or less adopted by

Sweden and a standard was written for the breed by the Svenska Kennelklubben. The breed has been taken up by the Swedish army who are breeding these dogs with the intention of using them as guard dogs, a task which they undoubtedly have always doubled with their herding activities from very early days. The breed is very much the Spitz type with the pricked ears, the dense coat and the curled tail of all the members of the group, though in the case of this breed the coat is rather longer and more glossy than some of the others.

He is a fairly small dog standing around eighteen inches which is about the size of a Whippet, but he is a strong square dog with roomy body and very stout, not too long legs. He is not a hunter, which makes him

for a time two forms of the breed were recognised by the farmers, and it was not until well into the present century that it was finally agreed that they were one and the same dog.

He is a large dog with a certain independence of spirit, and being naturally very intelligent he almost scorns training. He becomes attached to people, but only in the capacity of a guard and not as a house-pet, retaining his freedom of spirit and not allowing himself to fawn on anyone. He is a wonderful guard of anything, flocks, property and children, and can be very fierce when these responsibilities are challenged by animal or human. He first appeared in the show ring in Britain before the end of the 19th century, but disappeared again, to be seen once more from the early 1930s, when a number were introduced and have steadily increased. Upwards of a hundred are now registered with the Kennel Club in Britain and they are seen regularly at some of the major shows, where classes for the breed are staged.

more valuable as a guard and herder than some of the other Scandinavian Spitz breeds which would sooner chase game than stay at home. He is, however, courageous in protecting his home, intelligent and faithful, and makes a very affectionate companion. He is as yet not recognised by the American or British Kennel Clubs, but enjoys a reasonable vogue in Scandinavian countries where he is regularly seen among the native breeds at the important shows.

Maremma Sheepdog (Cane da Pastore Maremano-Abruzzese)

This very ancient breed of herding dog probably descended from the old white working dogs of the Magyars. Large white dogs of this type have been described in manuscripts and paintings for several hundreds of years. The area of Maremma from which the breed takes its name is the stretch of open rolling country down the coast as far as Rome and has been a grazing as well as a hunting area for centuries. The flocks were moved from plains to mountains as the weather dictated, and whilst some of the dogs stayed behind to guard the farms, others went with the flocks to act both as herders and guards. The result was that

Mudi

This breed originated in Hungary as a natural development of the ancient sheep-herding dogs of that country. It was unknown at the end of the 19th century, the role of the herder and guard being filled by the Komondor and the Puli which are much older breeds. There was, however, a need for an active dog with the build that would allow it to work over difficult territory, and without the coat problems of the corded breeds. He is a taller and heavier animal than the Puli, and is very much a guard as well as a herder, being capable of tackling large predators and is even used for the hunting of wild boar. He is a very useful animal around the farm or household, being a keen and watchful guard and an enthusiastic rodent hunter.

His coat, like Jacob's, is of many colours. Although black predominates, white or parti-colours are permitted and one colour, the so called 'pepita' which is an evenly distributed mixture of colours, is a peculiarity of the breed. He has a wavy and shiny coat which is shorter and smoother on the muzzle and legs, and which needs considerably less attention than that of the corded Hungarian dogs. He is docile and affectionate and very easily trained, but is brave in the face of danger. He is virtually unknown outside his own country.

Berger Picard

The Picard is one of the oldest of the French sheepdogs, originating in the North of France and believed

to have been brought to that country in the time of the Celts, in the 9th century. He is not only one of the most ancient breeds, but one of the biggest, standing as high as twenty-six inches at the shoulder, which makes him the size of a German Shepherd Dog. He is a medium-coated dog with a strong rough outer coat and a thick weatherproof undercoat.

He is very intelligent, easily trained, and affectionate, particularly with children. He is not known outside his own country, and not frequently seen inside France, as he remains very much a working dog and has not

been taken up by the show fraternity. He is a somewhat pugnacious guard and makes a very good housedog.

Polish Tatra Herd dog (Owczarek Podhalanski)

This large white herding dog is one of the ancient breeds of Poland, where it has been used by the mountain people as a sheepdog and guard against the attacks of wolves and bears. The interest in these fine dogs began during the middle of the 19th century

when mountain exploration became popular, and between the two World Wars a standard for the breed was approved. During the Second World War the breed almost ceased to exist and breeders needed to make a fresh start. The FCI recognised the breed in 1967 and its future is now secure. Dog shows incorporating trials for sheep herding dogs are regularly staged.

He is a large dog, standing up to twenty-six inches at the shoulder, and is very strong and muscular with it, with a massive body and well-boned legs. One of the characteristics of the breed is that the dogs are shorter in the body than the bitches. His general appearance is that of the Kuvasz, or the Maremma. His coat is close and fairly short on the head, and longer and dense on the body with a distinct feather on the tail and some feathering on the hindquarters. He is almost always white, though at times this is a creamy white rather than pure white. He is a fine worker, intelligent and alert and an excellent guard. His temperament is steady and friendly though reserved with strangers.

Portuguese Sheepdog (Cao da Serra de Aires)

This is one of the old-established breeds of Portuguese Sheepdogs, descending from the early indigenous types. He is unrelated to the other sheepdog, the

Laboreiro, and is different in appearance, being considerably smaller, up to nineteen inches at the shoulder only, and having a long coat. He looks rather like a smallish Bearded Collie though with less coat and minus the beard, and it could be that the origins were the same as small hairy herding dogs have been native to the whole of Europe, and as far east as Hungary, for centuries.

He is a deep-chested dog with strong limbs and a long, smooth or rather wavy coat which is waterproof but without the tendency to cord as in some of the Hungarian dogs. His colours vary between fawn and black through the greys and chestnut and though a few white marks are permitted, parti-coloured or white dogs are not. He is tough and reliable, quick and a very good worker with sheep. He is not normally seen outside his own country.

Pyrenean Sheepdog (Berger des Pyrénées)

The rapid rise to popularity throughout the world of the other herding dog from the Pyrenees, the Pyrenean Mountain Dog, has overshadowed this very attractive working dog, due partly to the fact that there is some variation in type from one district to another. There are in fact at least five recognisable varieties, different from one another mostly in colour, though most of them look like small Collies or Bearded Collies, and a short-coated version also exists. His general description is of a handy-sized, up to twenty inches high, fairly heavily coated dog of the working type, strong and flexible, very active and intelligent.

He is very much the working dog, tough, hardy and lively. He is rather reserved and shy of strangers, but easily trained and an eager worker. He is rarely seen outside his own country, and is unlikely to become a popular show dog.

Pumi

This little terrier type dog evolved in Hungary during the 17th and 18th centuries, by the crossing of the ancient Puli with the drovers' dogs from France and Germany that entered the country. From the Puli came its tendency to a long and somewhat unruly coat and from the visiting droving dogs came the semi-erect ears and volatile temperament. The crossing with different breeds to produce a keen droving dog went on for a considerable number of years, and it was not until the beginning of this century that he finally became accepted as a fixed breed of dog with a recognised pedigree. It is remarkable in the light of this that a dog evolved so like the Tibetan Terrier in many ways.

He is an extremely lively dog, quite incapable of remaining quiet except when at rest. He has developed into a very forceful and audacious drover of cattle, and in spite of his lack of size, as he is only about the same size as a Fox Terrier, he is quite capable of driving the most obstinate of cattle. He has good scenting powers too, and is a very good exterminator of pests and even of predators. He is a strongly built square little dog with strong jaws. The favourite colours are silver, dove grey or slate, though other colours frequently occur. Mixed colours and marking are not allowed. He makes a good house pet, though he is a noisy and volatile guard.

Schapendoes

This is the smaller very ancient breed of sheep-herding dog from the Netherlands. His origins are obscure, but his appearance is very like that of many of the other European working dogs, being shaggy-coated like the Bearded Collie and with the proportions of the Puli. He was at his peak as a breed in Holland when there were large flocks of sheep in that country, but with the changes that have taken place in the agricultural economy of the country, he has declined in numbers. Fortunately there is now a club which preserves an interest in the breed, and he is seen from time to time at shows.

He is a very lively, gay and active dog, courageous and yet friendly, has a very good intellect, is easily trained to perform most of the duties of a herder and guard. He makes a good housedog, and there is little doubt that with his coat, which repays attention, he could easily become a fairly popular show dog.

Swedish Vallhund (Väsgötaspets)

This is the most recent dog to invade the British show scene from Sweden, recent importations already making their mark and winning regularly, largely owing to the efforts of one British judge who brought in the first ones. The breed is an ancient one, though their close resemblance to the Corgi results in a constant discussion as to which is ancestor and which descendant. It has been suggested that the Vikings either took Corgis back with them, or brought the Väsgötaspets over with them, and this discussion will probably never end. In Sweden he has been known for a great number of years as a cattle-herding dog as well as a vermin catcher and a watch dog, but although he had been bred true for a considerable length of time, he was so much a part of the agricultural scene that few people paid him much attention.

It was only in the beginning of the present century that one or two breeders began to make serious attempts to popularise the breed as a show dog, and in 1943 it

was recognised by the Svenska Kennelklubben. Throughout the world, those accustomed to the bright colours of the Pembroke Corgis will find it strange at first that there is another breed of the same type but of considerably duller colours, as this little dog is often grey, brownish yellow or brindle. He has, however, a most attractive temperament, being very intelligent, friendly and affectionate with those whom he knows, but is a sharp and active guard when needed.

Yugoslavian Herder (Jugoslovenski Ovcarski Pas Sarplaninas)

This large grey herding dog has been in existence in Yugoslavia for centuries in the mountainous areas of the South East, and has recently become fairly widespread throughout the whole of the country. The breed was registered with the FCI in 1939 as the Ilirski Ovčar, but approaches from the Yugoslavian Kennel Authority in 1957 resulted in the name being changed to Chein De Berger Yougoslave de Charplanina. The origins of the breed are obscure, but there is little doubt that it shared ancestry with the other large Mastiff type breeds common in Southern Europe. Though the breed is essentially a herding dog, it doubles up as a flock guard, protecting domesticated animals against the attacks of wolves and other predators.

He is a big dog, at least twenty-five inches at the shoulder, and this is considered so important that smaller specimens are not allowed to be used for breeding. His head, ears and front of his legs are covered with short dense hair whilst the rest of the body carries a long fairly hard coat which is longer still on the neck and shoulders and on the feathering. He is uniformly coloured in various shades of grey with some white on the chest and legs. He has a good steady temperament, is easily trained, and whilst a staunch guard, is well-mannered towards people.

FCI GROUP 2:
Guard dogs, dogs that are useful and hauling dogs

Aidi (Chien de l'Atlas)

The flocks of Morocco are not comparable in size or behaviour with those of Europe, with the result that sheep-herding as it is practised elsewhere is unknown in that country. The herds consist of goats and native sheep which are more domesticated than those of other countries, and more accustomed to being moved about quietly by young shepherds. Sheepdogs as such are not needed, but at the same time there is a need for flock-guarding dogs, and it is for this purpose that the Aidi has been developed. He is a big strong dog standing up to twenty-five inches at the shoulder and very solidly built, but quick and active.

He is a mountain dog with a protective coat which is very thick and rough, and he is quite capable of protecting his charges against the possible attack of wild beasts. He can be almost any colour from fawn, through red to black and white. In some parts of the country it is the habit to crop the ears and dock the tail of the working dogs though the practice is not a desirable one. He is not known outside his own country.

Ainu (Hokkaido-Ken)

This is one of the older Japanese native breeds, having been bred by the Ainu on the island of Hokkaido for centuries as a hunting and watch dog. He is essentially one of the Spitz type, but nearer to the Scandinavian Spitz dogs than the other Japanese breeds such as the Akita, being rather more stockily built. He is a small dog, around sixteen inches at the shoulder, and has the prick ears and curled tail of the family. His coat is fairly short and dense with a thick undercoat. In colour he is red, white or black, and can be grizzle or black and tan. He is an excellent guard, having plenty of courage for a small dog, is intelligent and easily trained, and is lively and active.

Appenzell Mountain Dog (Appenzeller-Sennenhund)

This is one of the four breeds known as the Swiss mountain dogs, the most generally popular of which is the Bernese. This is one of the smaller members of the family and in its native country one of the more popular. Starting off as a farmer's dog and a worker, it is now gaining popularity among townspeople. He is one of a number of ancient working dogs used as a herder and drover of cattle in and around the canton of Appenzell, and is still used for those purposes. Like many of the working dogs of the world, he suffered the effects of mechanisation on farming, and became reduced in numbers during the second half of the 19th century. Fortunately, around the turn of the century a breed club was formed to protect his interests, and since that time preservation has been assured.

The first example of the breed was imported into Britain in the 1930s, but he has never gained the popularity of his larger cousin the Bernese. He is fairly well known in Germany and some other European countries where he is seen from time to time

at shows. He is a kindly and friendly dog, very attached to his owners, and an excellent guard. He is intelligent and easily trained, and small enough to be suitable as a house dog.

Austrian Pinscher (Oesterreichische Kurzhaarige Pinscher)

This is one of the old indigenous breeds of Austria which has existed as a working terrier-type for a considerable length of time without becoming known elsewhere. He is a smallish dog, only up to about twenty inches at the shoulder and often much smaller. He is short-haired, with small neat ears which may be pendant, but are preferred when tight and 'button'. In build he is very much like the other Pinschers, having a short deep body with good spring of rib and standing on shortish, strong straight legs and neat terrier feet.

His coat is short and strong rather like that of the Smooth Fox Terrier, and he is usually fawn, red, black or brown with white markings on cheeks, neck and legs. His tail, which is high-set is either docked, or left on, when it is short and curled. He is a lively little dog, a typical terrier and is seen only at shows in his own country.

Canaan Dog

This breed is accepted as almost the national breed of Israel though its origins are obscure. It has been suggested that it was developed by selective breeding from the Pariah dogs of the Middle East, though these vary considerably in type, and it is generally accepted that they themselves are descended from various domesticated types which have become feral. The Pariah dog varies according to the area in which it lives, and indiscriminate breeding eventually results in a similarity of character which is sometimes mistaken for type. The Canaan Dog is a fixed type, looking rather like a heavy-weight Smooth Collie, but with a curled tail.

He is a medium-sized dog standing up to twenty-four inches at the shoulder, has a short deep strong body and prick ears. He is sturdy and well-boned and has neat round feet. His coat is medium length straight and hard, and though longer coat is permissible it is not considered desirable. He is parti-coloured in white, tan or black. He is a good watch-dog, being alert and courageous, is intelligent and easily trained and becomes attached to one family. Only recently is he being seen outside Israel, when shown in small numbers in other countries.

Dogue de Bordeaux

This French breed like many other ancient breeds is said to have descended from the Molossus of Rome, and he certainly appears the very essence of the ancient Mastiff type, being very heavily built and with a massive head. The influence of the forces of England on the

Bordeaux area centuries ago probably resulted in the mixing of Mastiff blood from the other side of the Channel, as these dogs frequently travelled with the armies and courts of England. It is possible too that there was an influx of blood from Spain in the form of the ancient Alaunt. They were at one time used for fighting bears and wolves in Southern France and later became the butchers' dogs of the Bordeaux area.

He is rarely seen outside European countries as he is not recognised by either the American or the British Kennel Clubs, and is unlikely to become popular in either of these countries where in his particular field the Mastiff is already established. He is a real heavy-weight, being massively built and standing up to twenty-six inches at the shoulder. He was used both to fight and guard, and these elements seem to have remained to some extent in his character, as he is very independent and can be somewhat short-tempered. One of the popular colours is a very distinctive pale

golden yellow which certainly gives him the appeal of looking very different from the ordinary run of dogs.

Entlebuch Mountain Dog (Entlebucher Sennenhund)

This dog is one of the closely related group which originated in Switzerland as drovers and general purpose dogs. Centuries ago there was a good deal of

trading carried on through the mountain passes of Switzerland, and travellers took with them not only goods, but their cattle and flocks. They also needed largely to live off the land, so that a dog which could drive cattle, guard them at night, and do a little hunting when needed, was invaluable. This dog is the medium-sized member of the family and is shorter in the leg and lower to the ground than the others.

The various breeds were established mainly by the efforts of a Mr. Heim who, working with the Swiss Kennel Club established the differences and the standards for each variety during the early years of the present century. The Entlebuch was the latest of the family to gain any popularity, but is now well established and in no danger of becoming extinct. He is rarely seen outside his native country and has not yet appeared in British and American show rings as has his larger cousin the Bernese Mountain Dog. He is a very quiet dog, completely trustworthy and easily trained, and makes an excellent watchdog and guard.

Eskimo Dog

The Eskimo Dog is one of the most famous working dogs in the world, but unfortunately has suffered from confusion as the result of other, smaller and less popular sledge dogs being credited with his name. The Eskimo Dog proper originated in Greenland and is the most generally useful of the hauling dogs of all the Arctic countries. He is very much part of the heritage of northern Canada, and known to the Inuit people as the 'Kingmik', he was the only breed of domestic animal known to the early Arctic peoples. He hauled sledges, carried packs and was used for hunting. He guarded the camps and property, was the plaything of the children when he was young, and whilst working hard he lived frugally and made little inroad into the limited resources of the people with whom he lived.

These dogs were first encountered by explorers who immediately found them the only answer to their

transport problems. He was first written about one hundred and fifty years ago and was accepted as a separate breed by the Canadian Kennel Club before the turn of the century. Although mechanisation has restricted the absolute need for these magnificent dogs, they are still used competitively. There was at one time danger that the breed would disappear, but recent efforts to ensure its continuance are proving entirely successful. He is a large strong dog of rugged build with a weatherproof coat, and the more attractively marked ones that are appearing in the show rings of the world are gaining the breed new friends all the time. He is a very intelligent and good-natured dog.

Estrela Mountain Dog (Cao Serra da Estrela)

When the first specimens of this breed entered Britain they were called Portuguese Mountain Dogs, but it was decided that to avoid possible confusion later they should be named after the location from which they originated and the name Estrela Mountain Dog was adopted. The breed is certainly an ancient one, though the conditions under which it evolved were not conducive to the keeping of accurate records, and it is impossible to be certain about which breeds were its ancestors. He is large enough and heavy enough to be considered one of the Mastiff family and is more of a watchdog and guard than he is a herder of stock, so it is more than likely that he has a close relationship with the Spanish Mastiffs and even the similar dogs of France and Italy.

He is very much a farmer's dog, and in a country and

at a time when predators were common, he acted as a day and night guard for property and stock and was strong enough and staunch enough to tackle anything. During this century he has grown in stature as a show dog and is seen regularly at major shows both in his own and in neighbouring countries. His coat varies from the short and rather harsh to the long and wavy. He is an extremely strong dog that can be difficult to handle unless he is trained to obey from an early age.

Eurasier

This is one of the newest breeds of dog to be evolved as the result of the whims and efforts of virtually one man, within the past two or three decades. In the 1950s a gentleman named Wipfel, living in Bergstrasse in the German town of Weinheim decided to create, or perhaps recreate would be more accurate, a dog which resembled the ancient German Wolfspitz. He used the Chow Chow and the Samoyed type of sledge dog of Asia which he originally called the Wolf-Chow. The development of the breed reached its peak in the 1960s, and it was recognised by the German Kennel Club and the FCI and the name Eurasier was adopted in deference to its origins in Europe and Asia.

The Eurasier Club was formed, to look after the interests of the breed, and the development has been carefully controlled by a small number of enthusiasts centred on Weinheim, the town of its origin. He is a medium-sized Spitz type of dog with a stand-off coat short enough to allow the body contours to remain visible, and varies in colour from red in various shades, wolf-grey to black or black with well-defined markings.

Fila Brasileiro (Cão de Fila)

During the conquest of Central America in the 16th century the Portuguese and the Spaniards took with them some of the native Mastiff type dogs indigenous to the Iberian peninsula at that time. A good example of the type of dog is seen in Velasquez's painting of the 'Family of Philip IV' in the middle of the following century. These mastiffs, crossed with the indigenous dogs of the natives produced the Filo Brasileiro. They are still used as guards and drovers on the large estates, and are also used as hunters.

He is a big dog, standing twenty-seven inches at the shoulder and has many of the characteristics of his Spanish and Portuguese ancestors, a large and heavy head, pendant ears, heavy bone and a short dense coat. He varies in colour from any solid colour except white, and is often brindle. He is extremely strong with long stout bone and great musculation. He is a forceful dog with a strong personality, tremendous courage, (as he has to have in a country where there are still large wild cats) and very active. He is friendly with those whom he knows, but is suspicious of strangers which makes him a valuable watch-dog. He is unknown outside his own country.

Great Swiss Mountain Dog (Grosser Schweizer Sennenhund)

This is the larger, smooth-coated version of the much better known Bernese Mountain Dog, standing a couple of inches higher at the shoulder, but in many ways similar. He was almost certainly descended from the Alpine Mastiff and was known at least two hundred years ago.

He was once popular throughout Switzerland, where he was used for hauling small carts, and after almost disappearing at the beginning of this century, has since that time made a steady comeback. At one time he was lumped together, under the one general name of Sennenhunden, with the other similar dogs, but it was realised that there were in fact at least four different types, and these have now been sorted out and established.

In colour he is really what we now call a tricolour, being mainly black, with red markings on cheeks, over the eyes and on the legs, with white flashes on chest, tail and feet. He is a large strongly made dog with a very short dense and shiny coat which is virtually weatherproof. He is easily trained and most obedient, being used from time to time as a rescue dog. He is a natural watchdog, very faithful to the family that he serves, and is well known for his attachment to children. He was recognised in 1908 by the Swiss Kennel Club, but is not seen outside his own country to any extent, and remains unrecognised by either the American or the British Kennel Clubs.

Greenland Dog (Grønlandshund)

Considerable difference of opinion still exists concerning the names of the arctic sledge-hauling dogs. The Alaskan Malamute and the Siberian Husky have been successfully separated in name, classification and recognition by the major canine authorities, but there is still some confusion concerning the Grønslandshund and the Eskimo Dog, some authorities still dividing the two. The FCI however recognises the Grønslandshund, whilst the Canadian Kennel Club recognise the Eskimo Dog. He is big, up to twenty-five inches at the shoulder and strong and well-built with it, his stand-off coat making him look even more massive.

As a sledge-hauling dog he played his part in the exploration of the Arctic regions, and is still used competitively in sledge races. The Eskimoes used dogs for work for centuries before mechanisation took over, and in addition to the actual hauling that he did, the Greenland dog proved to be an excellent guard, and watchdog. His coat is long and hard, and he has a thick soft undercoat which affords him protection from the weather. He is extremely hardy, capable of existing on the minimum of sustenance and out of doors in the worst weather. His colour is not considered to be an important feature, but white, grey, black and a little

tan in almost any proportions are acceptable. He is reserved with strangers but becomes attached to those with whom he lives.

Hovawart

This is a very old breed of guard dog, known as long ago as the 15th century as the Hofewart, or 'warden of the estate and farmyard'. He went out of fashion, and apparently disappeared during the 19th century, but was revived by a group of German breeders in the early part of this century. They took several breeds of local guard dogs, from the Harz and Black Forest regions, and by careful selective breeding reproduced a dog which closely resembled the original. Their work and patience was rewarded when the German Kennel Club recognised the breed in 1936 with the name Hovawart.

He is a big dog of roughly the same size and with

something of the general appearance of the Flat-Coated Retriever. He is usually black, black and gold, or deep gold in colour, and whilst used principally as a guard dog as his ancestors were, he has a good nose and can be used for hunting. He is very intelligent, and is easily trained. He makes a particularly good dog to have as a companion either in or around the house as he becomes attached to the members of a family and can be quite affectionate.

Japanese Middle Size Dog (Sanshu)

This is another of the Spitz type dogs from Japan, and is a smaller version of the Akita, only up to twenty-one inches at the shoulder. He has the same reputation for complete faithfulness as his larger relative, and stories of his attachment to families are legion. It is interesting that a dog which looks very like him is seen

frequently on the waterfront at Hong Kong, being bred there and being used as a guard dog among the boats and wharves. There he tends to be called a smooth Chow Chow, but he is far too tall to qualify as a member of that breed.

He has the typical prick ears and curled over tail of the Spitz race and is a beautifully constructed dog with a strong body and stout straight limbs. He has an intelligent-looking head with a calm and even kindly expression, a medium-to-short coat with dense soft warm undercoat. His colour varies considerably from almost white to black through brown, grey and tan. He could well be the same dog that was imported into Europe at the turn of this century and was known as the Phu Quoc Dog having been brought from Cambodia.

Landseer

In most countries the Newfoundland is accepted in all its normal colours including black-and-white, which is known as the Landseer variety because the artist of that name in 1838 painted a work entitled 'A distinguished member of the Humane Society'. As his subject he took a black-and-white Newfoundland, a colour which was particularly popular at the end of the 18th century, and became even more so as a result of the painting. History of the breed shows that in the 18th century Newfoundlands were varicoloured, some being liver and white.

European countries, and those others which have associated themselves with the FCI, have decided, however, that the black-and-white variety is a separate breed, and it is this which is known as the Landseer. At present those specimens which are exhibited appear to differ from the Newfoundland as he is known in other countries by being rather less heavily built and without the same strength of bone as the majority of the breed. Beauty of marking is very important, and the head should be black with a white muzzle and blaze and the body and legs should be white with large patches of black on the saddle and quarters with some other smaller spots on both body and legs permitted but not desirable. He is an affectionate and very intelligent guard, kindly with those whom he knows, and supreme in water, where he is almost certainly the strongest swimmer of all the canine race.

Leonberger

It is amusing that in 1907 the Leonberger was dismissed as a cross between a Newfoundland and a St. Bernard when it was first introduced into Britain. One writer of the time stating that its merits were only recognised by the enterprising gentleman who had presented it as a 'new breed'. In fact it was such a cross, but that is how many of today's recognised breeds made their start. Herr Essig of Leonberg returned a couple of St. Bernards to the hospice of St. Bernard to help replace the stock lost when an avalanche and an outbreak of distemper decimated the kennels there. Before returning the bitch she was mated to a Newfoundland and the resultant litter were the first Leonbergers.

By 1907 a few were being shown in the Chiens de Montagne classes in Paris, and since that time the breed has made rapid progress. He is now shown regularly at most European championship shows, and at the 1976 Winners Show in Amsterdam there were fifty-six on exhibition. He is one of those breeds developed for no particular purpose except to look attractive, and Herr Essig in taking as his model the heraldic lions on the coat of arms of Leonberg was ambitious, but successful, as he produced a very handsome dog that is rapidly becoming admired in many countries outside his own. Leonberg is still inordinately proud of the dog that carries the name of the city. At one time he is said to have been used for herding flocks of sheep and cattle, but that side of his character, even if it ever existed has not been developed. He is an intelligent strong dog that makes an excellent watchdog, and could well be one of the popular large show-dogs of the future.

Neapolitan Mastiff (Mastino Napoletano)

This very ancient breed of dog, peculiar to Southern Italy, is, like many ancient breeds, a descendant of the Roman Mollossus. He has been bred with considerable care and in small numbers in his home country and the type frequently seen today varies very little from the dogs seen in ancient paintings and manuscripts. He is a somewhat terrifying dog as he is very large and heavy with a particularly forbidding head, an appearance which is increased by the fact that in Italy the ears are frequently so closely cropped as almost to disappear. In fact his appearance is deceptive, as, with one or two exceptions, in which the hereditary fierceness of the original fighting dog comes uppermost, the dog is a comparatively gentle and kindly creature.

He is a guard dog almost without peer, as not only is his appearance alone usually sufficient to deter intruders, he is also immensely strong and will attack,

usually only on command. There is a small number of breeders in Italy who keep the breed alive, but outside his home country he is rarely seen. One or two specimens have recently been imported into Britain but have not yet appeared in the show rings there. In Italy he is regularly exhibited, and has a staunch following.

Norbottenspets

This small Spitz dog from the North of Sweden is typical of the family, having prick ears, curly tail and the thick stand-off coat of the race. His origins are obscure, though there is a family resemblance to the even smaller Lundehund from the same area. It is

probable that he descended from the German Spitz and the Arctic Spitz types, but that can only be conjecture. He almost became extinct in the early part of the present century before the value of native breeds was fully appreciated, and the breed has increased since its recognition in 1960.

He is a medium sized dog, not more than fifteen inches at the shoulder with a short strong body and pointed muzzle. His coat is hard and stand-off with a soft dense undercoat, and he is white with black, red or cream patches. Like most of the Spitz breeds he was undoubtedly bred formerly as a hunting dog, but has now become more of a housedog and watchdog. He is cheerful, active and lively, and becomes attached to a family. He is rarely seen outside his own country.

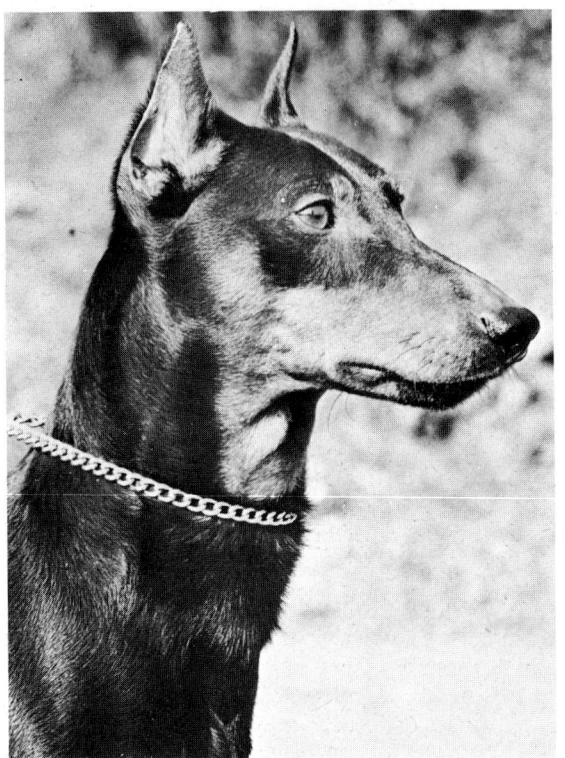

Pinscher

This is a very old established German breed of terrier-type dog developed centuries ago and probably descending from a medieval hunting dog. As a basic type he has been produced along very specific lines and is now a medium-sized short-coated dog shown only in the one size in his home country, but he was used to produce other breeds including the Doberman and the Miniature Pinscher both of which are popular throughout the world. He was officially recognised in 1879, and during the present century his interests have been looked after by the parent Pinscher-Schnauzer Club.

He is a sporting dog, a great vermin killer and a first-class watchdog. His coat is smooth and glossy and although he appears in a variety of colours, black and tan or brown seem to be the most popular. He makes a very good show dog as he is responsive and obedient, and is seen regularly at the larger shows in Europe. So far he has made no headway in other countries though a few have been imported into Britain from time to time. He makes a friendly and lively companion, and is an adventurous hunter.

Perro de Presa Mallorquin

This is a very ancient breed of Mastiff type dog from the Azores. He is a hunting dog capable of dealing with big game, and is descended from the Spanish Mastiffs and the Portuguese dogs carried by early explorers. In appearance he is rather like the Alano, but his leonine look is increased by the fact that at one time his ears were trimmed short and round like those of the big cats. The Perro de Presa is a big, heavy dog, some twenty-three inches at the shoulder; weighing up to one hundred and fifty pounds, and has a massive head and strong bone. His coat is very short and smooth and he is almost invariably a shade of yellow in colour with some white or darker patches. Little has been heard of him lately and numbers could well be on the decline. He is unknown outside his own country.

Portuguese Cattle Dog (Cão de Castro Laboreiro)

This very old breed of Portuguese dog was used exclusively for the herding of cattle. Principally found in the north of the country, in those parts where sheep were less plentiful, a smaller more active but even harder type of dog was needed. The area being fairly isolated for many years, the breed was fixed by using local dogs with the right temperament and physical properties rather than importing other breeds. Although as a breed he was always fairly popular, he was not seen at shows until comparatively recently. A standard has now been drawn up, however, and the breed has been considerably encouraged by the efforts of the Portuguese canine authorities.

He is a particularly tough and well-built dog as his height to weight ratio of twenty-three inches and sixty-five pounds would suggest. (Oddly enough this suggests a dog of the build of the Australian Cattle Dog.) He is a well-muscled dog but very flexible and quick-moving despite this. He has a short coat with a certain harshness on the body which renders it waterproof, and he is usually grey to dark grey with a darker mask. He is not a particularly friendly dog, is suspicious of strangers and makes a very good guard and watch dog.

Portuguese Shepherd Dog (Cão Rafeiro do Alentejo)

This very ancient Portuguese herding dog is one of the largest and most imposing of the country. He comes originally from the Alentejo province south of Lisbon and is descended from the early Mastiff types. Years of responsibility for guarding flocks and herds at night have given him the habit of being particularly alert at that time, when he becomes a keen guard and even aggressive. He is a strong dog that can weigh over one hundred pounds when adult and has a short and dense coat with weather-resisting properties. His appearance is striking as he is strongly marked with large white patches on a dark coloured or black ground.

He is not normally a show dog, and is rarely seen outside Portugal.

Portuguese Water Dog (Cão de Agua)

This is an ancient breed that has always been associated with the fishermen of the coasts of Portugal. His ancestry is obviously closely linked with the old

Water Dog of other European countries, the dog that produced the modern poodle and even the Irish Water Spaniel. Over the centuries he has accompanied the fishermen on their boats and has been used to retrieve equipment washed overboard and even to recover lost fish. On shore they were used to guard boards and nets. Numbers shrank around the beginning of this century and the breed was virtually restricted to the Algarve coast, but efforts in the period between the two World Wars encouraged a revival of interest in the breed, and examples were seen at the major Portuguese shows.

He is a very fit and hardy dog that will spend a considerable time in the water under trying conditions. His coat is usually clipped, but not in the extreme fashion of some other breeds, and he retains his essential working dog appearance. He is strongly built, very active, and an excellent guard. In temperament he is somewhat forceful, and though he has over the centuries been the companion of fishermen, it is unlikely that he will ever become very popular as a house pet. The earliest known animal portrait in English art, that of Sir John Harington's dog Bungy, painted nearly four hundred years ago, is undoubtedly a portrait of a Portuguese Water Dog.

Pyrenean Mastiff (Mastin de los Pirineos)

This breed, along with the Pyrenean Mountain Dog, descended from the ancient Tibetan Mastiff, and thus probably originally from the even more ancient Molossus. The Mountain Dog and the Mastiff were almost certainly originally one breed. Selective breeding for two types, however, produced some differences which were due to some extent to the the dog evolved in Spain and France. A large guard dog which would tackle the fierce predators of the mountain regions was needed, and yet at the same time a general purpose animal that could do some herding and act as a companion was preferred. The Pyrenean Mastiff filled all these roles, and though there is some divergence of type, he exists as a separate breed.

He is a large dog, up to thirty-two inches at the shoulder, massive, though not quite as large as the Pyrenean Mountain Dog, and is white with grey, dark grey or yellow patches on the head, and some are allowed on the body. He is intelligent, obedient and friendly with people he knows.

Spanish Mastiff (Mastin Español)

This is another descendant of the ancient Mastiffs of Europe which probably themselves descended from the Roman Molossus. Unlike the Italian version which has a very short coat, this breed has a dense medium length coat and greater refinement of head. He was used originally as a guard dog, but has a well-developed hunting instinct and will tackle large game. He is also

strong enough to be used as a military guard and all-purpose dog. He was at one time known as the Spanish Bulldog though he is much longer in the leg than the British Bulldog.

Several examples of the breed were imported into Britain in the late 18th century and were exhibited. Like the Italian Mastiff he had his ears cropped and was used for fighting, but was certainly one of the heavyweights of the arena, as a good specimen even in hard fighting condition could weigh as much as a hundred pounds. He is now not seen outside his own country and it is likely that he has degenerated from the original type by crossing with other breeds, particularly the British Bulldog. He is courageous, obedient and responsive to training, and is a great protector of both stock and property.

Tibetan Mastiff

This large guard dog, originating in the foothills of the Himalayas and Central Asia is considered by many not to be a true Mastiff. He is fairly large and has a head which resembles some of the other so-called Mastiffs, but there the likeness ends, as he is not particularly heavy for his size, nor does he have the typical heavy jowl and furrowed brows of the other members of the family. In their native country they were used as guards, to herd sheep and cattle, and as hunting dogs from time to time, but they have little of the native ferocity of the other Mastiffs. He is, however, a big handsome dog with a well-developed sense of belonging to the tribe or family, and whilst he will not normally persist in an attack, he puts on a brave show that deters any intruder.

He was well-known in Britain in the latter part of the 19th century, two good examples of the breed having been imported by King George IV. At the end of the century a dozen were imported into Britain by a

Mr. Jamrach but were said to be not typical of the breed. Though they were shown, and one specimen, said to be an exceedingly good one of which photographs exist was shown at the Crystal Palace in 1906, they never became popular, and are now unknown in Britain. He is said to be a docile dog, and though attached to his owner, very suspicious of strangers.

Tosa Fighting Dog

This large Mastiff type dog was bred from the middle of the 19th century onwards when dog-fighting was popular in Japan. The biggest and toughest breeds were used to produce him, including the Mastiff, the Bull Terrier and the Bulldog, which were crossed with the original fighting dogs bred in the area of Kochi. It is interesting that the smaller tougher type of Mastiff was spread over so large an area, appearing in countries as far apart as South America and Tibet,

and it is probably from the ancient Molossus that the Tibetan and thus the Japanese Mastiff type was evolved.

The Tosa is described as deep, broad and massive with a short, hard and dense coat. His ears are small and his eyes hard and tiny as befits a fighting dog. He has some loose protective skin around the neck and throat, and is said to be gentle but full of courage. In the light of this it is noteworthy that some specimens recently exhibited were shown on double leads and with two handlers.

FCI GROUP 3:
The working Terriers

Cesky Terrier

This short-legged terrier from the Bohemia district of what is now Czechoslovakia is a fairly modern creation. The sportsmen of the country, looking for a dog that would go to ground and yet would be strong enough and sufficiently courageous to tackle fox and badger underground, crossed the Scottish and Sealyham Terriers. The German Jagdterriers which were available to them were longer in the leg, and though they are great hunting Terriers they were not quite suitable for the purpose.

He is a dog that is slightly larger than either of his fashionable ancestors, being up to fourteen inches at the shoulder and with a build that is commensurate with that height. He has a long punishing head, strong body and short well-boned legs. His coat is not so hard as that of many of the Terriers, and is wavy with some sheen. He is an excellent working terrier, and is becoming increasingly popular as a show dog, appearing at many of the large shows in Europe. He has most of the Terrier qualities and characteristics and makes an excellent companion and house dog.

German Hunting Terrier (Deutscher Jagdterrier)

This breed did not exist at the beginning of this century, and is another product of man looking for certain qualities in existing breeds, failing to find what he wanted and setting out to produce it by selective breeding and crossing. The sportsmen of Bavaria wanted a tough working terrier that combined the keen qualities of the Fox Terriers with the strength of some of the old original Terriers which they thought had largely disappeared as the result of breeding for show purposes. Starting with a Welsh Terrier bitch, and a dog who descended from the old-fashioned Broken Coated Terrier of Britain, they crossed with both wire and smooth Fox Terriers and produced a very tough fierce hunting dog.

He is capable of going to ground to most game, with a very good nose and tremendous terrier pluck, and yet a dog that can double-up as a Retriever if need be.

He is a small dog, very slightly larger than a Wire Fox Terrier but considerably more robust with a strong body, well-muscled legs and larger feet than would be acceptable in a Fox Terrier. He has moreover a wide head, very strong jaws and a dense smooth close-lying coat. In colour he is a dark dog, black, brown or dark grey with tan markings, and is reminiscent of a stout rather tough-looking Welsh Terrier. He is somewhat fierce, and distrustful of strangers.

Japanese Terrier (Nihon Terrier)

This is a small Terrier, bred in Japan by crossing the indigenous dogs of Japan with Short-haired Terriers from other countries, probably the Smooth Fox Terrier from Britain or the small Toy Terrier, the Amertoy of America. He is a small dog, up to fifteen inches at the shoulder though often smaller, has a smooth coat and prick ears and is white with black or tan markings. He is not known outside Japan.

FCI GROUP 4:

Dachshunds. See Hound Group pages 93-160

FCI GROUP 5:

Hounds for hunting large game

Billy

The larger pack Hounds of France were used for hunting the stag which was restricted to the forests of the north and the west as well as to some areas of Burgundy. A good many packs existed, and the hunt was carried out with a considerable amount of ritual with a method and a language of its own. The Billy was bred by M. G. Hublot du Rivault and takes its name from his home in Poitou. It is a descendant of some of the ancient pack Hounds of the time of Louis XII, which were themselves probably evolved from the old Southern Hound and the St. Hubert Hound.

In later years many of the Hounds of France were crossed with Foxhounds from Britain to produce

what were known as Batards, and combined the best qualities of the French forest Hounds and those more accustomed to working open country. The Billy is distinguished as many of the French Hounds are by his colour. He is large, up to twenty-six inches at the shoulder and is white with markings of lemon or orange. He is used for hunting deer and wild boar and is a scent hunting dog that hunts in packs.

Black Elkhound

This variety of Elkhound was once much more wide-spread than it now is, being fairly well-known in Norway and seen from time to time in other parts of Scandinavia. It is now less popular, however, and has been superseded by the more common grey Elkhound which has been accepted by all other countries as the more typical variety. The Black Elkhound is a smaller and lighter dog and carries considerably less coat than the more generally accepted form, and completes the trio of Elkhound types known to Scandinavia which includes the much larger Jämthund. He is a Spitz dog with all the characteristics of that group, the pricked ears, curled tail and dense coat, and has the independence of temperament common to most of them.

He is now rarely seen at shows in his own country, and never outside it, and can really be numbered among those breeds in danger of extinction. He is a hunting dog used for big game in the difficult terrain and intense cold of his native country. He is tough, active and hardy, somewhat quarrelsome with other dogs but friendly enough with people. He makes an excellent guard as he has the distinctive bell-like voice of his near relatives and has considerable territorial conscientiousness. His colour is a jet black, but white marks on feet and chest are permitted.

Chambray

This is another of the very large family of French hunting dogs. When one remembers that in France at the turn of the century, hunting was so popular a pastime that there were three hundred packs of Hounds, and rememberining too that the average hunt has a very partisan attitude towards its own Hounds, it is hardly surprising that so many different breeds of Hounds have survived in that country. He is a large dog, and somewhat less elegant than many of the other French breeds. He stands up to twenty-eight inches high at the shoulder and is wide, muscular and deep-chested.

He has a short fine close coat, and a white and yellow parti-coloured pattern which tends to disappear with age until he is almost white. Occasionally he has ticking of yellow and even grey, and has the yellow spot on the skull which is seen in many other breeds of dogs. He is not fast, but has great stamina and is a steady but enthusiastic hunter.

Chien de Trait (Matin Belge)

As the name implies, this was a Mastiff type dog, used as a leash dog or *limier*, which suggests that it was in fact comparable with the St. Hubert Hound or Bloodhound. He is reputed in fact to be the darker coloured form of the French large Hound which can still be seen as an influence on the British Bloodhound. It is probable that the French and the Belgian versions of this dog were indistinguishable, but in any case the Societe Royale Saint Hubert of Belgium state that the breed is now extinct.

Chien Français Blanc et Noir

The number of packs of Hounds in France was severely reduced when the great estates and courts ceased to occupy the important position that they once did in the social life of the country. For centuries the descendants of the old Celtic Hound had flourished, and it is unlikely that any other country could have competed at one time with France in the number and

variety of dogs for the chase which were once kept. Many of the varieties have disappeared, but the Blanc et Noir has survived.

He is one of the bigger Hounds standing up to nearly thirty inches at the shoulder and is a survivor of the Hounds that hunted deer, wild boar and other big game when these existed in large numbers in the country. When the authorities held a survey in 1957 of the hounds still extant in France, sufficient numbers of the Blanc et Noir remained for them to be listed as a separate breed. He is a big handsome well-balanced hound with long neck and straight bone. His coat is short and hard and his colour is important. His ground colour is white, and he has large black patches including a mantle and some ticking. Some red is permitted on the legs, and pale russet marks on head, under the ears and root of tail are allowed. He is friendly, and a forceful hunter. He is not known outside France.

Chien Français Tricolore

This is yet another of the large hunting dogs of France, a breed that survived the disturbances of the end of the

18th century. He is another of the tall Hounds used for the hunting of big game and especially deer. Prior to the reign of Louis XV these Hounds were bred true to type, but after that time the English Foxhound cross was used to improve speed with the result that many of the older breeds disappeared. When the French authorities carried out a survey of the remaining Hounds however in 1957, there were enough of these Hounds for acceptance as a separate breed.

He is a tall Hound, up to twenty-eight inches at the shoulder, and has the soft, long slightly folded ears that denote his ancient lineage. He has a long neck and very elegant body and limbs, and soft expression denoting intelligence and friendliness. His coat is short, fine and smooth, and he is always tricolour, black, white and tan. He is an excellent hunter with great stamina, is intelligent and friendly and though he has many friends in his own country, is hardly known outside it.

Grahund

A number of the stockily built Spitz type dogs were developed in Scandinavia as hunting dogs to cope with the extreme conditions of snow and ice in Norway and Sweden. The more commonly known of these are of course the Elkhound and in Sweden the Jämthund, but these are both larger dogs. The Grahund, which translates simply enough into grey dog, is one of the varieties that has evolved from the original Scandinavian dogs as a separate breed. He first appeared and was recognised by the Svenska Kennelklubben under the name 'Nørsk Elghund' in 1891, which makes the present use of the name Norwegian when added to the Elkhound, somewhat confusing.

He is a medium sized dog, up to twenty inches, powerfully built and with the typical stand-off coat, pricked ears and curled tail of the Spitz group. He is rather less bulky in appearance than the Elkhound, but is similar in colour, with various shades of grey, black tips to the ends of the outer coat and a soft paler undercoat. The pale colour shows on the chest, hindquarters and throat. He is a hunting dog and is lively and enthusiastic, but remains friendly with those that he knows. He is seen frequently in Sweden, but is not known elsewhere.

Grand Blue de Gasgogne

This is one of the old breeds of French Hounds descending from the Grands Chiens Courants of the early days of hunting in France. He has something of the St. Hubert Hound in his ancestry as can be seen from his head qualities and his long folded ears. He is distinguished from the Hounds by his colour, and is more lightly built than some of the Hounds, weighing up to around sixty pounds, but is very strong and has great stamina. Henry IV of France owned a famous pack of these Hounds.

He is always white with black patches, and so ticked with the same colour that the overall effect is that of a blue dog. He has very distinctive head markings, with a black patch on either side of the head and a small patch on the skull. The head, legs and rump are marked with red or tan. Like so many of the pack-hunting Hounds, he is friendly and calm in temperament. A smaller version exists known as the Petit Bleu de Gascogne which must not exceed twenty-two inches at the shoulder.

Grand Gascon-Saintongeois

This French Hound is very unlike any Hound that is commonly seen in other countries, being larger, up to twenty-eight inches at the shoulder, and leggy, and having a considerable amount of loose skin around the head and neck. He was produced by crossing the Saintongeois with the Gascon, and is used for hunting

the roe deer. He is white, with black mantle or patches and a considerable amount of ticking, and has the distinctive feature of a small fawn spot on the hind legs above the hock known as the 'marque de chevreuil.'

He is not seen outside France, but remains well known in his own country as a pack dog. He is said to be gentle, quiet and affectionate. A smaller version known as the Gascon Saintongeois Petit which is identical in all other respects to the 'Grand' version has been produced exclusively for hare hunting.

Grand Griffon Vendéen

This is one of the more famous of the French hunting breeds, being well-known by name if not in fact in in the show world, but at present he is unknown outside his own country.

Hungarian Hound (Erdélyi Kopo)

This very ancient breed of Hungarian Foxhound, originated in the heavily wooded districts of Eastern Hungary, a district rich in game. Early writings report that there were at one time two forms of Hound, a larger black variety used for hunting big game, and a smaller red version which hunted the hare and the fox. The smaller type can now be considered extinct, but the larger one has been carefully preserved. During the process of conservation some cross-breeding with other Hounds has taken place, but this was eventually abandoned in favour of trying to retain the original characteristics of the breed.

In appearance he is something akin to the Swedish Hounds, but with the longer ears of some of the French dogs, though he lacks the skin folds of those breeds which descended from the St. Hubert Hound. He is usually black in colour with tan legs and head markings and some white marks on chest and paws. He has a smooth but hard coat, and is rather longer in the body than some Hounds. He is not a pack hunter, but something of a loner, becoming very attached to one master who usually finds that he can be trained as a retriever as well as a hunter.

Karelian Bear Dog (Karelsk Björnhund)

Around the area between Russia and Finland there have been tough bear hunting dogs for centuries. They have served two purposes, as guard dogs they were fierce enough to drive off dangerous predators, and the step from that task to actually going out and hunting these animals was a natural and simple one. They have always been of the Spitz type, hardy, dense-coated with pricked ears and stubborn temperament. In Russia they were accepted as a variety of Laika

many countries among dog people. He is shorter and higher on the leg than some of the other Griffons, and is constructed in such a way that he exemplifies the tough hunting dog accustomed to working under arduous conditions and even in water. Many packs of these Hounds, often mixed with the Nivernais, were at one time in existence in France.

His prevailing colour is white or wheaten, with vari-coloured markings, and his coat is rough and hard with a thick undercoat. He is a remarkably friendly dog, even jolly and appears to enjoy a joke, an appearance which is added to by his somewhat large and quizzical head with its long furry ears and heavy furnishing of hair. He is rarely seen outside France in the long-legged form though the Basset variety is rapidly gaining favour in some countries. There is a smaller version known as the Briquet Griffon Vendéen.

It is his quaint appearance, resulting from his heavily whiskered face, that is endearing him to so many people who are acquainted with the rather more popular smooth-coated dogs, and who are seeking something a little out of the ordinary.

Hanoverian Schweisshund

This old breed of tracking Hounds from Hanover was produced by crossing the heavier type of Bracke, a dog rather like the St. Hubert Hound, with the lighter breed from the Harz mountains. The connection with the St. Hubert type is shown by his larger head and loose folds of skin, whilst the colour recalls the old Haidbracke from the lighter form of Hound. He was originally used by huntsmen on a long lead to track the game in the first instance before laying on lighter Hounds. Other breeds were similarly used in France and Britain, where the Bloodhound performed the same duties.

He dates back to around 1800 and has remained fairly true to type since that time. He is a patient and persistent tracker and is still used by huntsmen. He is, like the Bloodhound, a quiet and dignified Hound, and completely trustworthy. Being smaller and handier than his larger relatives, he might well have a future but in recent years the Russians have decreed otherwise and now claim all the varieties of that breed as their own.

The Bear Dog was at one time used exclusively for bear hunting, but more recently it has been used for other game and particularly for elk. He is noted for his courage and persistence, but it is those very qualities that have led him into some trouble, as he is notoriously quarrelsome and fierce, and over the years every attempt has been made to moderate those qualities without losing any of his tenacity as a hunting dog. Since 1935 he has been pure bred in Finland where he is frequently seen in shows, and is now growing in popularity in other Scandinavian countries. He is an interesting dog, and there is little doubt that he will soon be taken up by other countries where his striking black and white appearance will soon gain him adherents.

Levesque

Lord Ribblesdale who had had experience with the French packs of Hounds, once said 'There can be little doubt that a good Batard is a better hound for forest hunting than a draft hound from the Holdernesse or the Tedworth'. The Batard to which he referred was in fact a cross between the traditional French Hound and the English Foxhound. One of the most popular of these for some time was the Levesque which was a mixture of the Gascon, the Saintongeois and the English Foxhound.

He is a big fine dog with a smooth coat, and is invariably black and white, the black, which at times appears almost blue-black is in the form of a saddle and patches and some irregular ticking of black in other parts of the body, and there may be some small tan markings especially on the hocks. He is, like so many of the pack hounds, very friendly.

Podengo

Many of the native dogs of Portugal remain little known outside their own country, and the Podengo is no exception. The breed is an old one, though a fair amount of crossing with other breeds has taken place at various times in order to improve the hunting qualities. There are three sizes, the largest being around twenty-five inches and being used mainly for the hunting of hare, the medium of about eighteen inches and the small which is fourteen inches, the two latter being used mostly for hunting rabbits. For the most part the larger dogs are hunted in pairs or singly and course in the manner of a Greyhound, whilst the smaller dogs are hunted in packs.

Many of the countrymen and farmers of Portugal have one or even a small pack of these dogs, and they have never lost their popularity outside the towns and cities. They are regularly shown at the Portuguese shows and it is surprising that their size and sporting

inclinations have not found them a wider public in other countries. He is a strong little dog with great flexibility, and a short hard coat which appears in many colours, though fawn or tan predominate. He is intelligent, has something of the alertness of the Terriers, and is affectionate and faithful. He makes an excellent house pet and companion and is a good guard.

Poitevin

This is one of the older varieties of French Hound, dating back at least to the 18th century, when packs were well-established in the Haut-Poitou region. These were decimated by rabies in 1842, leaving just a few

specimens from which all the present dogs are descended. English Foxhound blood was introduced to help preserve the breed, with the result that of all the French hounds, this one resembles more closely the common conception of a Foxhound.

He is a fairly big hound, up to twenty-eight inches at the shoulder, is more symmetrical than many of the traditional French hounds, and has less loose skin. His colour too is reminiscent of many of the English packs, being what is usually referred to as hound-marked, in other words, tricolor, with a black mantle on a red and white background. He is a lively and intelligent hound and very friendly, but is rarely seen outside his own country.

Polish Hound (Ogar Polski)

This is a traditional breed, known for centuries as both a hunting dog and a guard. During the troubled times of the early part of the present century and during the two World Wars the breed, in common with many of the other native dogs went into a decline. It was only after the Second World War that attempts were made to regenerate the breed and to evolve it

437

along uniform lines. The standard was eventually accepted by the FCI and the breed is now no longer in danger of becoming extinct. He is a dog with a remarkable inborn ability for orientation, a great hunter and tracker with well-developed tendencies to quarter ground thoroughly.

He is used extensively for the hunting of the wild boar, and the natural toughness that assists him in this work has to be controlled at an early age, when he needs fairly rigorous training. He is a medium-sized dog up to twenty-four inches at the shoulder but very strongly made and well-muscled, so much so that he can be used for bear hunting. He is an enthusiastic and somewhat noisy hunter and will follow a track for hours with great persistence. He has a strong hard short coat which is slightly longer on the neck and tail, and he is black in colour with tan markings on head and feet. Like most of the hounds he is friendly with people.

Rastreador Brasileiro

This little-known breed was produced in Brazil by crossing the Foxhound with other breeds in order to produce a race of dogs capable of hunting the large wild cat of that country, the Jaguar. Leander J. McCormick describes in his stories of fishing round the world, published in 1937, a visit to an *estancia* where just such experimental breeding was going on. The rancher in this case was crossing the Foxhound with such breeds as the German Shepherd Dog, and was producing animals with the combined qualities of both breeds.

He is a big strong and rather coarse Foxhound with a short coat, great strength and courage and the pendant ears of his ancestors.

St Hubert Hound

The greatest of all patron saints of the chase was St. Hubert who spent his youth hunting, even on Holy days. On one Good Friday when he was hunting in the forests of the Ardennes, he had a vision of a white stag with a crucifix between its horns. According to the legend Our Lord spoke to him and as a result he changed his ways, withdrawing to an abbey. Later he is said to have received a message instructing him to go to Rome and he finally became the bishop of Liege. The abbots in the Ardennes monastery developed the St. Hubert Hound after their saint. The breed was renowned for its scenting and hunting qualities throughout the whole of Europe, and his fame spread to such an extent that assisted by the legend, a cult grew up around the dog. A mass known as the 'Mass of St. Hubert' was celebrated, and as the dog became a legend, so the legend became a dog.

The St. Hubert Hound is virtually the same dog as the Bloodhound, and there is no doubt that the breed now shown in most countries by that name is a direct

descendant of dogs imported into Britain from France. He is a dog that has proved his value as a hunter over centuries, being used in most parts of the world to track criminals, and slaves, and for competition work. His powers of tracking are very highly developed, and under ideal conditions has been known to follow a trail that is days old. In spite of his reputation in some quarters he is the kindest and most tractable animal imaginable.

Slovakian Hound (Slovensky Kopov)

This early breed of hound was evolved in Czechoslovakia and is something of a national breed. There is a close and obvious relationship with the Polish Hound and the two breeds probably descended from the same stock. He is an excellent tracking dog, capable of following a trail for a considerable length of time and of picking up lost trails easily. He is smaller than the Polish Hound, standing only up to twenty inches at the shoulder but is capable of hunting the wild boar which still abounds in parts of his country. A number of devoted breeders are persevering with the breed, and his future is assured so long as boar hunting continues.

His coat is short, strong and thick with a dense undercoat, and in colour he is always black and tan, the tan markings occurring on the head, legs and feet and on the hindquarters. He is affectionate, gentle, and has well-developed guarding instincts. As dog shows increase in Czechoslovakia, his popularity in this, for him, new sphere, is almost certain.

Swedish Elkhound (Jämthund)

This is the largest and the strongest of the Elkhound types of dog native to Sweden. He can be up to twenty-five inches high at the shoulder and proportionately heavy. He is closely related to the well-known Norwegian Elkhound, but unlike that breed, he is hardly known outside Scandinavia. The hunting of the elk has been a pastime and indeed a necessity in Scandinavia for centuries, and the people of the Jamtland bred their own large version of the Elkhound which was recognised as a separate breed by the Svenska Kennelklub in 1946.

Since that time he has become a popular dog in Sweden being used as a guard as well as a hunting dog, and becoming quite popular as a show dog. He is seen in fairly large numbers at the major Swedish shows, where his admirers from overseas will undoubtedly eventually import examples into their own countries. He will make a spectacular addition to the show scene wherever he goes as he is the biggest dog of his type, has the same distinctive grey colour as his more popular and widely known cousin, and has the additional attraction of large cream marks on the jaws. He has proved a successful show dog in his own country, and is sufficiently positive in temperament to be steady and to stand with some defiance in the ring. He is in fact very friendly and intelligent with no vice and few handling problems.

FCI GROUP 6:

Hounds for hunting small game

Ariègeois

This is one of the smaller French hounds, comparable in size with the Harrier, up to twenty-four inches at the shoulder. He originated in the Ariège region of south-west France and was produced by crossing the Briquet with the Grand Gascon Saintongeous. He is a finely built and rather slender hound with long ears and a gaily carried tail. He is an ardent hunter and intelligent. His short coat is mostly white in colour with black patches or mottling and some tan markings. He is quiet and affectionate.

Austrian Hound (Carinthian Brandlbracke)

There are two very old native hound breeds in Austria which are descended from the once very widespread Black and Tan Hounds which were common to France and many other European countries. The Austrian Hound is one of them. He is a medium-sized dog standing up to twenty inches at the shoulder with a fairly long and deep chested body and pendant flat ears. He is smooth-coated, with a thick flat coat which is glossy and flexible, and is invariably black and tan in colour with some white markings on the chest. He is a good working dog, lively and active, and has an attractive quiet and calm temperament. He is not known outside his own country.

Balkan Hound (Balkanski Gonic)

The whole of the Eastern Mediterranean was for centuries an area in which empires rose and fell, nation conquered nation and new nations who spent their time either conquering other countries and trade routes opened up. As these trade routes spread into Europe and Asia, dogs, which were a form of merchandise also spread, with the result that the hounds which had been used for hunting in Egypt, found their way into many other countries. The Balkan states formed one of the routes through from the Mediterranean to eastern European countries and the hounds that traders took with them on their travels formed the basis for a number of indigenous types of hound in the Balkans.

The Balkanski Gonici is a typical example of the sort of hound that evolved from these early types, being a reliable hunter for a variety of game, hardy and a good tracker, and obedient and a hard worker. All these qualities were essential in a country in which hunting was as much a necessity as a sport. He is a medium-sized hound up to tweny-one inches in height, and is red with a black saddle and with black marks over his eyes. He is quiet and gentle and very obedient as well as being a hard worker. He is not known outside his own country.

Barbet

This is one of the most ancient of all the French breeds, reputed to have been the ancestor of the Bichon, the Poodle and some of the Sheepdogs. By the early part of the present century the breed had virtually disappeared, just a few specimens remaining in existence, and even those not definite in type. Efforts were made to preserve the breed, and in recent years they have again begun to appear in some numbers. He was originally one of the water dogs, if not even the Water Dog of Europe, and at the turn of the century is described as an excellent dog for waterfowlers, apparently working happily in ice-covered water and being impervious to the worst weather. He was at that sime said to be identical with the old English Water Dog, and certainly Reinagle's engraving in the Sportsman's Repository bears this out.

He is a medium-sized dog, up to twenty-two inches at the shoulder, strong and well-boned with large round feet. His coat is long and woolly and with a tendency to cord. He is usually mixed in colour, white or grey predominating, with brown or black markings.

Basset Artésien Normand

This is probably the most popular of the short-legged hunting dogs from France, being seen regularly at both French shows and those of many other countries in Europe. A number of the ancient French hunting dogs were developed in the short-legged form in order to slow them down as the need arose for them to work in more restricted areas during the 18th century. The story that they were developed in order to allow the overweight members of the French court to follow them is probably a fallacy.

This particular little dog is a powerfully built long-bodied hound with the long folded ears of the St.

Hubert Hound and the short smooth coat of so many of the pack hounds. He is not as heavy or as powerfully built as the Basset Hound proper which now has

world-wide acceptance and probably descended from him and the differences become very clear when they appear alongside one another in the show ring as they do from time to time. The Basset Artésien Normand is a much lighter built and more slender dog with a smaller head and muzzle and lighter bone. He is a friendly but rather wilful hound with strong hunting instincts.

Basset Bleu de Gascogne

This dog is probably somewhat misnamed as he did not originate in Gascogny, but is descended from the long-legged Petit Bleu de Gascon by a process of selective breeding to produce a short-legged and slower Hound which is more fitting for modern conditions. He is very like the Artésien Normand, but not so deep in the body, often shorter in the legs and more heavily boned. This gives him a more balanced outline. He has little in common with the Bassets of

centuries ago, which were more like short-legged Terriers, but is a rather elegant animal.

His distinctive feature, like that of his taller relatives, is his colour as he is white with blue and black marks and spotting and with distinctive tan markings on muzzle, head and feet. He has a short dense coat, and like the other Bassets has a well-developed hunting instinct allied with a friendly but somewhat stubborn nature. He is seen regularly in his own country, but remains virtually unknown in the rest of the world.

Basset Fauve de Bretagne

When the Bassets were first introduced into Britain from France, there were three main strains. This was around the late part of the 19th century. British enthusiasts had seen these varieties at the Paris show held in 1863 for the first time, and had decided which type was to be the one on which their own breeding experiments were to be based. The Basset Fauve de Bretagne was the one that did not enter into their plans, partly because of geography as he was centred in Brittany which was some way from the centre of affairs, and partly because of his very different appearance. He was certainly connected with the Basset Griffon Vendéen, but had none of the glamour of colour or coat of that or the other varieties.

He is a Short-coated dog, but it is not the smooth coat of the Basset Bleu or the Artésien Normand. It is rather the hard rough coat of the Cardigan Corgi, indeed it has even been suggested that there was some early connection. He is self-coloured from wheaten to red and white marks are undesirable. He is a friendly and lively little dog, a good and enthusiastic hunter but remains practically unknown outside his own country.

Basset Griffon Vendéen

When the Basset was first introduced into Britain at about the middle of the 19th century, they were bred and shown as the one breed, but with either smooth or rough coats. They were known as Griffon Bassets but

were not considered a separate breed. When they were further imported in the middle of this century they were given their correct name, and achieved immediate popularity, appearing in the variety classes at most of the major shows in Britain. In France they vary in size to some extent, the larger dog being one of the biggest of the Bassets with a shoulder height of up to sixteen inches and corresponding weight.

He is mostly white in colour with markings of tan, grey or black, and has the typical Griffon hard stand-off coat with extra furnishing around the head and muzzle. His legs tend to be stronger and straighter than many of the other Bassets and he is remarkably active for his size and build. He is rather wilful as many of the Pack Hounds tend to be, but at the same time he is a very friendly and affectionate dog with great charm of manner and makes an excellent showdog and family pet.

Bavarian Schweisshund (Bayerischer Gebirgs-Schweisshund)

The Hanoverian Schweisshund proved too heavy and clumsy for the task of hunting the red deer in the mountains of Bavaria. This breed was therefore crossed with the old Bavarian Hound to produce a lighter and smaller dog. The Hanoverian was itself a cross between the heavy Leitbracke and the lighter Haidbracke, whilst the Bavarian was related to the much smaller and lighter Tyrolean Hound. The combination of all these foundation breeds produced a very agile and active Hound with excellent scenting powers.

He is a fairly small dog, up to twenty inches, with a rather light and long body and strong shortish legs. His coat is dense and hard and his colour varies from wheaten through fawn to red, red-grizzle or brindle. He is particularly suited to working in the mountains, either as a *limier* or free, is extremely adept at hunting down wounded game, and is owned almost exclusively by those who hunt deer. He is lively and responsive, but is unknown outside his own country.

Beagle Harrier

This small French Hunting dog fills the gap in size between the Beagle and the Harrier as his name suggests. He is normally between fifteen and seventeen inches in height at the shoulder. He was produced by selective breeding as a well-built and compact Hound which was at the same time energetic and active, for the hunting of hare, and it is interesting that for hundreds of years the Beagle and the Harrier were considered to be one breed. It could be that the French sportsmen in perpetuating this breed have gone full circle.

He is a distinctive dog, with certain elegance and yet substance. His head is typical of that of the larger Hounds and he has a lively and intelligent expression. His coat is fairly short and flat and he is generally tricoloured though greys are not frowned upon. He is not known outside France.

Berner Laufhund

In a small country such as Switzerland, in which there were a large number of different Hounds, many of which had developed along separate lines in different geographical locations, it would have been a simple matter for them all to have interbred until there were no individual types. Fortunately the Swiss Hound Club which was formed in 1931, has most carefully defined the different types of Hound in the country and has encouraged the breeding of the individual varieties.

The Bernese is a typical example of this individuality. He is very like the other Laufhunds in type, with a narrow head and pendant folded ears. His body is long and not heavy and his legs, though well-boned are not heavy. His coat in the smooth variety is dense, hard and close, and in the rough version is wiry and stand-off with a fairly long outer coat and a short dense and softer undercoat. In colour he is white with black patches and some ticking and some tan markings. He can also be tricolour. The medium version is around twenty inches at the shoulder and the short-legged version up to fifteen inches. He is gentle and affectionate.

Chien Courant de Bosnie à Poil Dur

This is a medium-sized hunting dog from Yugoslavia, and only recently recognised internationally although probably an old breed. He was previously known as the 'Chien Courant d'Illyria' or Illyrian Hound, and is used for hunting the hare, fox, and even wild boar. He is a medium-sized powerfully built running Hound with a strong body, pendant ears that reveal the part that the Celtic Hound played in his ancestry, and a rather long head. He stands up to twenty-two inches at the shoulder with the bitches slightly smaller.

His undercoat is soft and dense, and his outer coat long and stand-off with extra long guard hairs. In colour he is white, fawn or greyish with spots of other colours and some ticking, and tends to be paler under the throat, body and on the legs. He is an excellent hunting dog, a good tracker and has great stamina. His temperament is lively but friendly. He is not seen outside his own country.

Chien Courant de la Vallée de la Save

This is another of the smaller Hounds from Yugoslavia, used in the hunting of hare and small game. He was first registered in 1955 by the FCI under the name 'Chien Courant du Bassin du Kras'. He is a medium-sized strongly built dog around twenty-three inches in height at the shoulder and slightly long in the body. He is a strong working dog, with great stamina and a loud bell-like voice. His coat is short, up to an inch long and strong and dense with a little feathering on the legs and the tail. He is wheaten or reddish in colour with some white marks on the head and neck, the latter forming a collar. There are also white marks on his chest, stomach and lower part of his legs, but these must not cover the major part of the body. He is a lively dog with a good temperament, quiet and obedient when trained. He is not known outside his own country.

Chien d'Artois

This is one of the old forms of French hunting dogs, numbered along with the Vendéen, the Poitou and the Normand as one of the original types from which many of the others have descended. He himself originated in northern France as a descendant of the St. Hubert Hound, and at the beginning of this century there were still a number of packs of these Hounds being used for hare hunting. He is one of the smaller Hounds and more nearly approaches the Foxhound in general appearance and colour than many of the French Hounds. He is usually tricolour with a distinct saddle or large patches of fawn or grey, and his coat is smooth and dense. He is affectionate with people and courageous in the chase. He is not known outside his own country.

Drever

This little hunting dog, developed from the Dachsbracke of Westphalia, has become one of the more popular breeds in Sweden. He originated at the beginning of the present century and was used for the hunting of the fox, hare and wild boar. His mixture of blood from the hounds of Sweden and the hunting Dachshund type dog from Germany imprinted firmly on him the sheer hunting instinct as one of his more typical characteristics. He is a tracking and driving hound, particularly useful in hunting deer, which are nervous if driven too fast and break wildly. The slower moving Drever is more adept at keeping the game moving gently towards the guns without exciting it too much.

He was recognised in Sweden in 1949, and since that time has become a popular show dog as well as a sporting hound, numbers of them appearing at most Swedish shows. He is a small dog and long in the body, but has many of the typical pack hound features, being very deep in the brisket and with a hound's head. Though it has ancestral connections with the Dachshund types in Germany it is not a great deal like a Dachshund, but has the lines of a lightly built short-legged Foxhound. The flashy white markings are a feature of the breed as they are said to make him more easily visible when hunting through the thick forests of Sweden, which are his normal environment.

Dunker

This is essentially a Norwegian dog, started by Wilhelm Dunker who crossed the Harlequin Hound from Russia with other hound types. He is a hunting dog used particularly to hunt the hare by scent rather than by sight, and though very much a tracking dog, can be used as a retriever. His one individual characteristic is his colour, as he is marbled black or blue on white, with brown patches, and in common with other dogs of this colour wall eyes are permitted. Herr Dunker started with one dog which happened not only to look like the breed that he was trying to develop, but also had the ability in the field which he as a hunting man desired. To that dog he mated others which were as near as possible to his foundation sire, in an attempt to fix the tracking ability and the distinctive appearance.

There was a later attempt to cross the breed with the Hygenhund, another Norwegian hunting dog developed from the Holsteiner Hound, and a notable scent hunting dog, but it was finally decided that in attempting to produce a hound that combined the best of two very good ones, some of the individual characteristics of both might be lost, and they remained two separate breeds. He is a strong dog and a typical

hunting hound in conformation, with deep chest and fairly long strong legs. He is rarely seen in the show ring, and is virtually unknown outside his own country. He is said to be affectionate, very trustworthy, and extremely confident.

Erz Mountains Dachsbracke

This breed, which looks rather like a cross between the Foxhound and the Dachshund, is in fact nothing of the kind, but is an entirely separate breed which originated in the Erz Mountains region of Bohemia. He was used for hare hunting and eventually spread

over a large area of Austria as his qualities became appreciated. Carinthia is now the area where the breed is most frequently met. He is distinguished from the German version, the Westphalian Dachsbracke by his colour as he is always either red, or black and tan.

He is a clever and versatile hound, useful in hunting hare and fox, and makes a good line dog or *limier*. He is affectionate and makes a good house pet, but is rarely seen at shows, and is virtually unknown outside his own country.

Finnish Hound (Finsk Stövare)

This is yet another of the fairly large number of hunting dogs from Scandinavia. It is a breed that has been developed from English Foxhounds, French and German Hounds and some of the Stövare types in Sweden. These dogs have been known for about the last hundred years and were originally shown in Finland in the late 1870s. Since that time, by further careful outcrosses the present type of hound has been fixed, appearance never being considered more important than hunting ability in a country in which that sport remains very popular. Consequently his numbers are now on the increase in Finland.

He is a big strong dog, taller than the other Scandinavian hounds, and about the size of the American Foxhound. He is very much the hunting dog, and has most of the characteristics of that family, being friendly, and even affectionate, but with the streak of independence common to most of the scent hunting hounds. Like many of the bigger hounds, however, he is very generous and good-natured.

German Spaniel (Wachtelhund)

A type of Spaniel very like the Wachtelhund existed in Britain centuries ago, as it did in Europe, and was almost certainly the result of selective breeding from the old Water Dog from which so many of the European sporting dogs descended. Like the Wachtelhund of today he was a fairly small dog with typical spaniel features and a wavy coat. He disappeared, as did the miniature Trawler Spaniel, but played a large part in the evolution of the whole family of spaniels. He almost disappeared in Germany, but a group of enthusiastic spaniel breeders got together in 1897 with the aim of reviving the breed, which they did so successfully that he is now one of the popular German gun dogs.

He is noted for his working qualities, and German spaniel breeders maintain that he should not become a show dog for fear that he may lose some of his working qualities. He is especially useful in heavy woodland where his remarkable scenting powers make him a very good game hunter. He can also be trained as a retriever and is a good water dog. He is a strong dog half way in size between a Cocker and a Springer and has a fairly long slightly wavy coat which makes him attractive when well groomed. His temperament is excellent and he makes a very good companion in the country and a good house dog and guard.

Grand Griffon Nivernais

The race of dogs known as the Griffons are peculiar to France in the large hunting form. They should not be confused with the Griffon Bruxellois which is a toy and is probably not related. They more closely resemble the old Otter Hound of Britain than anything else, and they do the same sort of work. The Griffon

Vendéen is probably the best known of the group, but the Nivernais variety, which is on the whole darker in colour and longer in the body than the Vendéen, was at one time equally well-known. Packs of these hounds were kept for the rougher sort of hunting in the forests of the Nivernais province.

He was developed specifically for hunting the boar, and though not very tall, only up to twenty-four inches at the shoulder, he is courageous, active and strong, and is well-protected by his strong hard and shaggy coat. He is usually grey in colour of various shades, though he can be black and tan or fawn. He

is an affectionate and lively animal but is rarely seen outside his own country. A smaller version known as the Griffon Nivernais de Petit Taille also exists.

Greek Greyhound (Albanian Greyhound, Ellenikos Ichnilatis)

This is a large running dog from Greece, used extensively for coursing small game, particularly hare and small deer. In general appearance he is very like the Saluki, having a similar head and outline and roughly the same coat. He is a tall dog, up to twenty-seven inches at the shoulder with long slender well-muscled legs. He is a quick, lively dog with great stamina and is clearly related to the eastern Greyhound types. He works equally well in rocky mountainous country as on the plains.

He has the long head of the Saluki with similar soft pendant ears. His coat is short and close and a little hard and he is generally black and tan in colour though a white blaze on the chest is permissible. He hunts with a melodious voice, enjoys human company and the comforts of the home, and is an intelligent and pleasing companion.

Griffon Bleu de Gascogne de Petite Taille

This is one of the rough-coated hounds from France, similar in many ways to the Grand Bleu, but smaller, up to twenty inches at the shoulder only and distinguished by a rough hard coat. He has a rather slender neck which makes him more elegant than some of the other hounds, fairly long ears which lie flat and do not fold, and he is rather long-backed. His coat is harsh and flat-lying, is shorter on the head and ears but with prominent brow hair like the other Griffons, and rather wavy on the legs.

His colour is similar to the larger smooth-coated Grand Bleu, being a dark blue grey on white with small ticking in black to give an overall blue appearance. He has red marks on head and feet. He is an active friendly dog and affectionate with people. He is not seen outside his own country.

Griffon Fauve de Bretagne

This rough-coated hound was evolved in the Brittany area for the hunting of fox and wild boar and as a general purpose game hunting dog. He is medium-sized, up to twenty-two inches at the shoulder and is

strongly built with stout legs. His coat is his distinguishing feature, as it is very harsh but not overlong. He has a long tail covered with strong hair, and medium length supple ears hanging low on a fairly narrow head. His colour is always fawn of various shades from pale fawn to red, and black is not allowed.

He is a fairly strong-willed hound, not noted for his friendliness, but he is a great hunter as a pack hound, being very fast, tough and musical. He is virtually unknown outside France.

Haldenstövare

This hunting dog from Norway is named after the town of Halden in the South East corner of Norway near to the Swedish border, an area in which hunting has been a popular pastime for centuries. There are four recognised Stövare types and this is the largest of the family, standing around twenty-six inches at the shoulder. He was developed from the native hounds of the area by selective breeding and by crossing with imported hounds from Sweden, Germany and Russia, with possibly later crosses with French and British hounds. He is, however, very much a native hound, and is different from any other recognised type.

His most distinctive feature is his colour, as he is mostly white with large black patches often surrounded by brown shadings, and with brown markings on the head. Like the other Norwegian hounds he is not a pack dog, but hunts individually by his powers of scent. He is a big strong dog with deep chest and strong legs, possessed of great stamina to permit him to hunt through deep snow in the sometimes bleak winters of his native country. Like the other members of the family he is affectionate and completely trustworthy, and makes a very good family companion. He is not so frequently seen in the show rings of Scandinavia as some of the other hounds, and rarely outside his native country, though he clearly has visual qualities that would prove him popular.

Hamiltonstövare

This is a Swedish breed of general purpose hound, developed from the extinct Hölsteiner Hound and the Heiderbracke with the introduction of Curlandish Hound blood. He was developed by a Swedish sportsman named Hamilton who was interested more in the working quality of the breed than in its appearance. He did, however, manage to produce a very attractive dog that has made its mark in the show rings of Scandinavia. This is exemplified by the fact that since the turn of the century he has been the most popular of all the hound breeds of this type in Sweden, having classes of his own since 1886, and today frequently outnumbering the other scent hunting hounds at shows in his native country.

The breed is now appearing in other countries, and

after the first imports into Britain were mistakenly registered as Swedish Foxhounds, it was realised that there was a variety of such hounds in Sweden and the error has been corrected. He is not a pack dog, but hunts on his own through the deep snow-laden forests of Sweden, where he has proved popular as a show dog. He is a neat and stylish dog with attractive markings and colour, and a rather longer and more elegant head than some of the other scent hounds. He is very steady in the show ring, but an affectionate and cheerful character outside it, having a lively personality and being very active.

Hygenhound (Hygenstövare)

This is another of the Scandinavian hounds, separated one from the other almost entirely by size and colour, as in type they are very similar, and in many cases descended from the same basic stock. The Hygenhound originated in the middle of the 19th century in the kennel of the Norwegian breeder F. Hygen who crossed the old Hölsteiner Hounds with other Scandinavian breeds. For a time the breed was intermixed with the Dunker and was shown as one breed, but in 1934 they were divided and the Hygenhound was again recognised as a separate breed. The breed is not recognised by other kennel clubs, and is by no means one of the popular hounds at shows in its native country.

He is about the same size as the Dunker, and a good deal smaller than the Haldenstövare. He has a more pointed muzzle than the other Scandinavian hounds and a somewhat longer body, and he is mostly yellow in colour with white markings though other colours are permitted. He is a strong active dog with good bone and a deep chest, and makes a good individual hunting dog for smaller game. He is affectionate and very trustworthy, and like most of the type makes an excellent companion. In the ring he is steady and shows well, and his short, dense coat needs no preparation other than a good brush down.

Istrian Hound (Istarski Gonica)

This ancient breed of Yugoslavian hound exists in two forms, the short-coated or Kratkodiaki and the rough-coated or Resati, the latter undoubtedly playing a part in the ancestry of the Styrian Mountain Hound. He is used for hunting the hare and the fox, and is generally useful as a tracking dog. He is a medium-sized, twenty-inch dog with the long narrow head, prominent occiput and pendant ears of the French hounds. In the short-coated variety the coat is smooth and dense with a glossy finish whilst in the rough-coat it is long, hard and stand-off, with an abundance of protective hair on the body.

He is a white dog with yellow or orange markings on the body and rather heavier colouration on the head and ears. He is a tough and active hound with a good voice, and capable of long spells of work under strenuous conditions. In temperament he is friendly and lively but trainable. He is not seen outside his own country.

Italian Hound (Segugio)

This is the only remaining true Italian hound that is recognised as a separate breed. The breed descended from the ancient Celtic Hound, and more nearly approaches the description of the mythical black 'Dogs of Hell' than any of the other breeds. He has great endurance and will work either in a pack or as a single gundog, and exists in two varieties, smooth and rough. He is unusual in that he often occurs as a self-coloured dull black dog which must be one of the very old colour forms, unspoiled by crossing with other breeds. He also has the long fine pendant ears of the early hounds which fall into folds as do those of the St. Hubert Hound. He can be brown or tricolour. The Segugio has the reputation of being quiet and gentle in his dealings with people and a good house dog.

Jura Laufhund

This hound from Switzerland differs from the other native hounds in that he is nearer in appearance to the St. Hubert Hound. His head is larger and heavier with a broader skull and prominent occiput and his forehead is much more wrinkled than that of the other breeds. His ears are longer and heavier and very low-set, and he himself is heavier, longer and lower, a height of eighteen inches being ideal. He originates from the Jura mountains which Switzerland shares with France, and it was probably this close proximity which led to the French influence on the breed.

He is a very keen hound with an excellent nose and a resonant clear voice which he uses when on a trail. He exists in the one variety of coat only, a short, dense hard one, and in colour he is either tan with occasionally a black saddle, or black and tan, a white spot on the chest being permissible. The short-legged version is below fifteen inches at the shoulder and is a heavy, long-cast hound, reminiscent of the Basset Artésien Normand. Both types are used for hunting hare, fox and small deer.

Lundehund

This smaller member of the Spitz group has been bred for many years in Northern Norway for hunting the Puffin, the fat carcasses of which have been staple diet for centuries among the islanders. The breed originated in Vaerog, an island off the coast of Norway, and were trained to hunt on their own in the inaccessible rocky areas that are the habitual home of these little birds. The dogs caught the birds and carried them back to the hunters, and in season were trained to search for nests full of eggs.

He needed to be a small and very active dog with

the same manner of working as the Cairn or West Highland White Terrier of the Scottish islands. He needed to be capable of climbing like a cat, of forcing his way into narrow and confined spaces, and of doubling up as a retriever. The people of Vaerog produced such a dog in the Lundehund which proved very successful. Since that time he has been bred true, and is recognised by the Scandinavian countries though not elsewhere. He is quite small, only some nine to ten inches in height, and for his size is remarkably robust, having a strong deep body, well-boned legs and tough feet with double dew claws. He is intelligent, lively and boisterous, and the danger to

his future lies in the fact that if he becomes popular outside his native country he will be looked upon as a toy dog because of his lack of size.

Luzerner Laufhund

Hunting in Switzerland posed the dog breeder different problems from those that faced the sportsman whose country contained a greater proportion of flatter more heavily cultivated land. The result was a race of small fairly light hunting dogs divided into two sizes, the larger ones being only medium-sized animals and the shorter-legged versions developed by crossing with such breeds as the Dachsbracke or the Dachshund. The Luzerner Laufhund is a typical

example of the results of this careful selective interbreeding. He has the head qualities of the St. Hubert Hound, the colour of the Grand Bleu de Gascogne and the short legs in the Niederlaufhund version of the Teckel or Dachshund.

He is a lightly built, active and fast hound, not too heavily boned and with a fairly long body. His head is that of the St. Hubert Hound with long folded ears and narrow skull. In the medium-sized hound a height of twenty inches is aimed at, and in the shortlegged dogs a maximum of fifteen inches is allowed. Unlike the other two varieties, he is a short-coated dog only, with a dense hard and close coat, which is heavily ticked and marked with blue and black spots and patches on a white ground, with some tan marks. His temperament is like that of the other Swiss hounds, quiet and even affectionate.

Porcelaine

One of the most decorative and delightfully named of the French hounds, the Porçelaine is a very ancient breed that has been bred true to type for centuries. It was used originally for the hunting of the hare and small deer and may have at one time been related to some of the Swiss breeds. He is one of the most elegant of hounds with long neck and finer bone than others, and looks more of the running dog. He is fairly tall, up to twenty-three inches at the shoulder, and is principally white with fairly round orange patches and small orange markings on the ears, which are fine, long and folded. He is not known outside France, which is perhaps unfortunate, as he could well become quite popular. He is friendly, very active and a good hunter.

Sabueso (Espanöl de Monte)

This breed can be traced back to the old Celtic hound, though it is much more hound-like than many that have so descended. His name comes from some of the early inhabitants of France, though he is now essentially a Spanish dog. He exists in two sizes, but the smaller one, which is under twenty and a half inches in height is the one more frequently seen at the Spanish dog shows. He is a versatile dog, being very good in a pack, as a line or tracking hound and even as a police dog. He makes a good show dog and many excellent specimens are seen at the major Spanish shows.

He is a forceful hunter and not the easiest of dogs to train, being somewhat temperamental and wilful. For this reason he does not make the best of house-dogs or pets, but retains a considerable degree of popularity among sportsmen in a country devoted to the chase. He has a short, hard and dense coat, and is usually white with large orange or black patches.

Schillerstövare

This is yet another of the Scandinavian hunting dogs, and in this case a lighter-built and smaller hound, which whilst popular in some parts of Sweden as a hunting dog, does not rival the more popular Hamilton-stövare in the show ring. The breed descends from German, Austrian and Swiss hounds, and was perfected by a certain Mr. Schiller who used his dogs for hunting his more open country. The breed was evolved earlier than the Hamiltonstövare and was breeding true before that breed appeared. He is used for hunting the snow hare and fox, and as a tracking dog, and is claimed by his admirers to be a much faster dog than the other Scandinavian hounds.

He is a short-bodied and long-legged hound with more of the look of the running dog about him than the stockier scent hounds. Scandinavian sportsmen prefer the lighter type of dog that will cover the ground more quickly in those areas which are not so heavily wooded. He makes a good show dog as most of the hounds do, being steady and obedient, and essentially willing. He is friendly and cheerful and makes a devoted companion, and his short dense smooth coat makes him a clean dog to have around the house as well as an easy dog to prepare for the show ring. It is doubtful whether he will ever become popular outside his own country as he is recognised by no other Kennel Club, and his admirers are quite happy with him as a hunting dog working in the field.

Schweizer Laufhund

This is one of the three principal types of hounds native to Switzerland, all of which exist in two forms, the long-legged and the short-legged version. They originated from the same sources as the ancient French hounds, but the terrain of Switzerland dictated that they should develop along different lines, and they are generally smaller and lighter than the surviving French hounds.

The Schweizer Laufhund is a medium-sized dog, up to twenty inches at the shoulder and has a fairly long head with a narrow skull on the lines of the Bloodhound but smaller. He is rather lightly built with a long body which is flexible and stands on long well-boned but not heavy legs. His coat is dense and short and close-fitting in the smooth variety, and a hard and stand-off outer coat with softer dense undercoat, in the rough-haired dogs. In colour he is white with varying sized pale to deep red patches and often a red mantle. He is a good hunter, and calm and quiet in behaviour when kept under domestic conditions. The Schweizer Niederlaufhund is similar to the larger version, but is below fifteen inches at the shoulder.

Sicilian Hound (Cirneco dell'Etna)

This breed of running dog from the island of Sicily would seem to be an ancient type of dog. It has a good

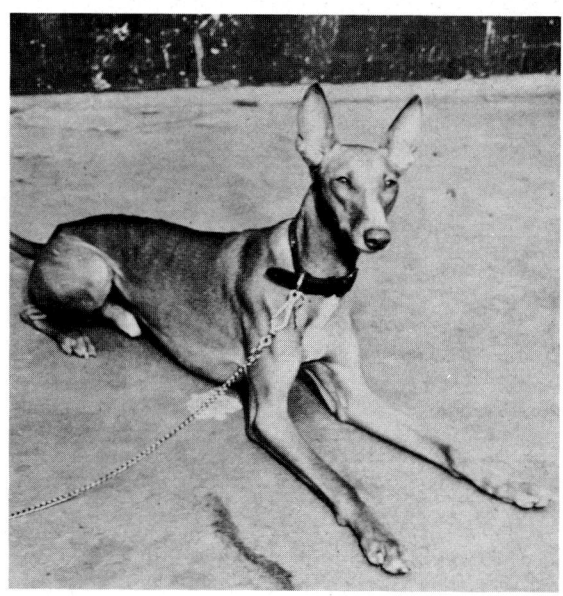

deal in common with the Pharaoh Hound and the Podenco, both of which probably had an older form of Mediterranean coursing dog as ancestor. In Sicily he has been bred true to type and with little influence from outside breeds and he is now accepted as a pure breed, being carefully preserved by a few enthusiasts. He is very active, finely built and extremely fast in the pursuit of rabbits which are his favourite quarry.

He is smooth-coated, red in colour with some white markings, and has a pleasing temperament, being friendly towards people and yet gay and forceful when hunting. He is virtually unknown outside Sicily.

Smalandsstövare

This is the oldest of the Stövare breeds of Scandinavia, originating in the dense forests of Smaland in southern Sweden. The breed differs from the others of the family in that some of them are born with a short tail, so that whilst docking is not permitted, many are seen with a tail that is unusually short for a hound. One of the earlier breeders, Baron von Essen had a preference for the short-tailed specimens, and it was his interest that preserved this characteristic despite the crossing with other of the stovares in order to improve the quality of the breed.

He is the smallest and the more heavily built of the family as might be expected in a dog bred to hunt the forests rather than the more open country. He is distinctive in colour, always black, with tan markings on muzzle and eyebrows and on the lower parts of the legs, with white flashes on tail end and feet, which makes him a very showy dog in the ring. His coat is particularly smooth and glossy and needs merely a good brushing and hand finish, as with the Whippet, to bring out the best in it. He was recognised by the Swedish Kennel Club in 1921, and is seen in fair numbers at most of the Swedish major shows. He is a quiet and steady dog with no vice, and makes a very affectionate and devoted companion.

Steinbracke

This medium-sized German running hunting hound is very like many of the other breeds used for the hunting of small game in Europe. He bears a close resemblance to some of the French hounds, and to the Swedish Stövare, in both shape and colour. There were at one time many different types of closely related hounds of this type in Germany, but in 1955 the German Hound Club issued a standard which was accepted by the FCI, in an effort to produce a line of dogs more easily recognised as a separate breed.

He is an excellent tracking dog, enthusiastic and with a very good nose and melodious voice, but is almost entirely in the hands of huntsmen and not seen at shows. He is elegant but with strong bone and the depth of brisket of the typical hound, and the long head of many of the French scent-hunting dogs. His

coat is short, hard and dense with some brush on the tail. His colour is always yellow to reddish-tan, with a black saddle and typical white markings on the head, chest, legs and tail tip. He is a friendly dog with a lively personality.

Styrian Mountain Hound (Peintinger)

This is a fairly modern breed of hound from the Austrian province of Styria. The breed was evolved towards the late 19th century by crossing some of the German hounds, the indigenous Austrian hounds and the rough-coated Istrian Hound. What was wanted was a hound which would work well in rough mountain country, with great stamina and a good voice, and the Styrian Mountain Hound was the result. He is a medium-sized hound up to twenty inches at the shoulder, rather long in the body and flexible. His head is typical of the hounds and his ears are medium-sized and flat.

He is a rough-coated hound to withstand extremes of weather, the coat being rough and hard, coarse but not as shaggy as some of the herding dogs, and with an inclination towards feathering on legs and chest. His colour varies from wheaten to red and a white patch on the chest is permissible. His hunting instinct is well-developed, so much so that he is not normally used for any other purpose, though he is quiet and becomes attached to his owner. He has a particularly loud and melodious voice.

Tyrolese Hound

This variety is very similar to the Austrian hound but differs in both size and colour, and can vary in coat. The breed is an ancient one, originating centuries ago with the old French hounds and the mountain hounds of Switzerland. His close resemblance to some of the Swedish hounds would also suggest the influence of some of the old German dogs. He is smaller than the

Austrian Hound, up to eighteen inches only, and a smaller version still, under fifteen inches also exists. He comes originally from the Tyrol and is used as a hunting dog, being used for both tracking and beating coverts.

He is black and tan or red, with some white marking on the chest, and his coat varies between the smooth, hard, and rough. In the rough variety there is some fringing and the tail is in the form of a brush. He is a vigorous and active hound with a good steady temperament.

Westphalian Dachsbracke

As distinct from the Erz Mountain Dachsbracke of Austria, which is an old and original breed, this dog was produced by crossing the Dachshund with the long-legged German hounds. German hunting men, looking for a dog which combined the best hunting qualities of the Dachshund and the greater speed of the Foxhound type, created this pack-hunting dog. He is taller than the Dachshund, being up to fourteen inches at the shoulder, which is the height of the small Shetland Sheepdog.

He is smooth coated and is usually hound-marked in any combination of hound colours with white. He has an attractive head and expression and a calm and obedient manner. As a hunting dog he is keen and has great persistence and stamina. He is not known outside his own country.

Yugoslavian Hound (Planinski Gonic)

This distinctive breed of running hound has descended from ancient indigenous Yugoslavian hounds. He is a medium-sized strong dog with a fairly broad head, low-slung medium-length ears and a muzzle which is slightly shorter than the length of the skull. He is used for hunting the hare, fox and other small game and is a persistent and enthusiastic scent hound. He has strong straight bone and feet which are a little longer than those of some of the hounds.

His coat is short and dense and very close-fitting but slightly longer on the throat and shorter on the head and ears. He is a black and tan hound with the classical markings of that colour, on the cheeks, over the eyes and on the feet, and a small white spot on the chest is not objected to. He is a quiet and affectionate dog that enjoys the company of people, but at the same time enjoys equally the work of the chase. The Yugoslavian Tricolour hound is a similar dog that differs principally in his colour.

FCI GROUP 7:
Gundogs, except the British and American gundogs see page 457

Auvergne Pointer (Braque d'Auvergne)

This French pointer from the Auvergne, in the mountainous central part of the country, is one of the heavier early types of Pointer that shows less influence from English Pointer blood than most. He is said to have been brought originally from the south, and to have been crossed with pointers brought over later from Britain. At one time he existed in two forms, the Braque Bleu which is said to have had better proportions and more elegance, and the Grand Braque which was more of a heavy-weight.

He is an extremely good bird dog and an active worker with a good nose, slower than some of the other Pointers, but steady and certain. He has a short, hard glossy coat, and is mostly white, though with a great number of black speckles which gives him a somewhat grey overall appearance. The head has a good deal of black, which should be well-balanced around the eyes. He is very intelligent, quiet and easily trained, but is not known outside his own country.

Bourbonnais Pointer (Braque de Bourbonnais)

This is one of the older forms of French Pointer which shows less of the influence of the English Pointer blood. The breed became a separate one around the turn of the century in Bourbonnais in central France. He has never become very popular outside his home region, is not seen at shows and is unknown outside France. The indications are that he is on the decline and may well disappear. One of the reasons for this is that he is a rather unattractive looking dog, being cloddy, short and rather compact and lacking the elegance of many of the other Pointers. His muzzle is heavy and pendulous and his ears small and his back is humpy and rounded which gives him a clumsy outline. His tail is docked to around two inches in length.

He is however a very good working dog, much esteemed in his own area, and slow, careful and faultless when standing his game. He can in addition be taught to retrieve which makes him more useful to the one-dog man. He is a medium-sized dog, up to twenty-two inches at the shoulder. His coat is short, dense and waterproof, and he is always white with widespread ticking of fawn or pale brown. He is very docile and gentle.

Dupuy Pointer (Braque Dupuy)

The family of French Pointers have a good deal in common, they are all similar in size and conformation, and vary only in colour, length of tail and by their names, which are usually based on either the place where they were developed or the name of the person who did the early work on perfecting the variety. The Old Braque of France was a rather coarse animal with short neck and a head reminiscent of a hound rather than a gundog. The introduction of a great deal of English Pointer blood improved the appearance of the French Pointers and at the same time improved their speed of work, and to a certain extent their powers of scent.

The breed which shows the English influence more than most is the Braque Dupuy which was said at the beginning of this century to more nearly approach the English Pointer in appearance than any of the other Braques. He is a tall and elegant dog, so elegant in fact that the suggestion that he had Greyhound blood is not unreasonable. He has a long narrow and rather fine head, long ears that are rather thin and tend to hang in folds, and gentle expressive eyes. His short coat is hard and smooth and he is white with large patches of brown and some ticking. He is a good worker, useful in water, and is very much the sportsman's dog, rarely shown and unknown outside France.

French Pointer (Braque Français)

This breed of French Pointer is among the oldest of all the French breeds, having originated with the Spanish Pointer, described in detail in the Sportsman's Repository of 1826 and illustrated with a Reinagle engraving which looks remarkably like the present-day dog. He is described at that time as looking something like the old Southern Hound and having 'the tenderest nose and most exquisite scenting, joined with true game and steadiness in pursuit, and proportionate want of speed.' This, in a volume not much given to praise, is praise indeed. He has himself become the ancestor of many of the French gundogs, and it is somewhat surprising that he has survived so little changed.

He exists in two sizes, the Braque Français proper

which stands up to twenty-six inches at the shoulder, and the Braque Français Petite Taille, which does not exceed twenty-two. He is a tall looking dog as his body, whilst deep is not so far through as some of the other Pointers. His head is broader than the English Pointer, and in the smaller version differs in that the muzzle is shorter and that the ears are smaller and hang flat. He has a short dense coat and is invariably white with chestnut speckles and patches. The smaller version has more extensive chestnut marking. He is intelligent, easily trained and is kind and friendly.

Italian Pointer (Bracco Italiano)

This is one of the oldest Italian sporting dogs, based on the indigenous hounds, which were crossed with gundogs; the breed came into existence as a separate

one at the beginning of the 18th century. Since that time he has altered very little and remains one of the characteristic dogs of Italy. He is still both in appearance and temperament a mixture of the two types of dog, having the large heavy head of the early hounds but the body and limbs of a heavy-weight gundog. His temperament is also a mixture of typical houndlike independence and gundog enthusiasm.

He is fairly large, up to twenty-six inches in height which is about the same as a Pointer, but his tail is docked to roughly the same length as that of the German Short-haired Pointer. His coat is short, dense and glossy, which, allied with his striking white and orange or white and brown, makes him a very attractive looking dog. He is quiet, friendly and obedient, has remained fairly popular in his own country, but is rarely seen outside it.

St Germain Pointer (Braque Saint-Germain)

The French Pointers have existed for centuries in several different forms and it is probable that they, like

Dutch Partridge Dog (Drentse Patrijshond)

Although the name of this dog appears to indicate a degree of specialisation as far as work is concerned, he is famed in his country of origin as an all-purpose gun dog that will work well with any sort of game and is strong enough to retrieve pheasant or hare. He has been known in Holland for at least three hundred years and appears in old paintings, depicted almost exactly as he is today. The very fine head study by Henrick Goltzius (1558–1617) is a typical example. He originated in the province of Drenthe, in North East Holland bordering West Germany.

One of the more interesting things about the Drentse Partrijshond is that he represents the very early type of half Spaniel, half Setter that could well have been the ancestor of many of the modern gun dogs, and his origins could be much more ancient than the three hundred years with which he is normally

the English Pointer, owe their origin to the Spanish Pointer. The Braque St. Germain is one of the older varieties and was evolved towards the early part of the 19th century by crossing the early Pointer with other old breeds of French gundogs. The breed was concentrated for a while in the area around St. Germain en Laye, which led to his name, and was used for hunting fairly large game.

He is a fine upstanding dog, rather more leggy than is fashionable with the English Pointer, and is invariably white with clear orange marking and spots, which result from his early ancestry which is known to have started from an orange and white bitch. His coat is short, soft and dense and he carries his full tail which is long and tapering. He is rather reserved with strangers, but gentle and quiet, and a willing worker.

Czechoslovakian Pointer (Cesky Fousek, Böhmisch Rauhbart)

This Czechoslovakian pointing dog which has an obvious resemblance to many of the old gundog breeds, is also fairly closely related to the German Rough-haired Pointer. During the period preceding the First World War he was one of the more popular of the rough-haired gundogs of Czechoslovakia, but during that war he almost disappeared. Between the wars the breed was resurrected by careful selection and encouragement and is now the second most popular gundog of his country.

He is a fairly tall dog with a distinctive coat which consists of a dense undercoat which disappears in the summer, and a fairly flat outer coat, itself overlaid with longer hairs up to about three inches in length. These tend to stick out from the coat giving the dog a rather shaggy or bristly appearance. He is either brown, or white with brown ticking, or with larger brown markings.

credited. He is a biggish strong dog with a fairly broad head full of character. He is very intelligent, easily trained, and an easy-going sort of dog. His popularity as a farmer's dog and as a pet has not declined although he has never become a particularly well-known show dog. As importations to other countries, particularly the United States of America and Britain are now taking place, this situation could well change.

Epagneul Français

This is one of the old French breeds of Spaniel, though, in common with other French breeds, it is longer in the leg than some people associate with the title, looking rather like a heavy-weight Setter. In fact, in the first few years of the present century it was said that he was actually a Setter in all essential respects, but that was at a time when English writers were stating that because of the success of British Setters in Europe, there was little point in encouraging the native breeds. The Epagneul Français in fact looks more like a somewhat lanky English Springer than anything else, and is the same colour.

He is a fairly tall dog, up to twenty-five inches at the shoulder, and is strongly boned. He has the typical head of a Spaniel with long flat ears and a broad muzzle. His coat is thick, slightly wavy and he has some feathering on legs, ears and the tail, which is long. He is white with large brown patches and some speckles. There was a possibility at one time that the breed would disappear, partly because of the importation of British gundogs, and partly because of the increasing popularity of rival breeds of Spaniel. He has now, however, re-established himself in the favour of French sportsmen as he has proved himself to be very versatile. He is intelligent and obedient and very friendly.

Epagneul Pont Audemer

This breed originated towards the end of the 18th century as the result of crossing some of the old French

Spaniels with other gundog breeds. It was concentrated around the area of Pont-Audemer in Normandy but is now few in number. He is a fairly heavy medium-sized dog that looks rather like a woolly Springer Spaniel. He is adept at working in water and is used principally for wild duck and other marsh dwellers. His head, rather longer than that of the other Spaniels, is his distinguishing feature, being surmounted by a definite top-knot of longer hair. This crest together with the thick curly coat indicates the Water Dog or Irish Water Spaniel as one of his ancestors.

He is a medium-sized dog, twenty-three inches at the shoulder, with a sturdy body and strong legs. His coat is rather soft and curly and is either chestnut or grey with white markings, or self coloured chestnut. He is a very energetic worker, intelligent and easily trained, and makes an excellent companion. He is rarely seen in the show ring at the present time, and is unknown outside his own country.

German Long-haired Pointer (Deutsch Langhaar Vorstehund)

There are three types of German Pointer, the Short-haired, the Wirehaired and the Longhaired, and whilst the first two are almost certainly closely related, the last is the product of crosses between other ancestors. He was used in earlier years for hawking and falconry and was produced by crossing the old Water Spaniel, a breed which has featured in the evolution of so many European breeds, with the Spaniels from France. As a result of these experiments a whole family of hunting pointing dogs with fairly long coat and many other characteristics in common, was produced. Since the early days, other blood has been introduced, including probably that of the Gordon Setter, and the resultant dog looks rather like a somewhat coarser version of the Irish Setter but liver, or liver and white in colour.

He is an excellent gundog, with a particular aptitude for working with feathered game, but versatile, useful in water and a very good dog in close coverts. He is a powerful dog with a feathered tail which may be shortened by docking. He is intelligent, very obedient and faithful, lively and a good companion. Unlike the Shorthaired version, he is virtually unknown outside his own country.

German Rough-haired Pointer (Deutsch Stichelhaar Vorstehund)

This is one of the oldest of the German gundogs used for feathered game. He is very like the Pointing Griffon though less massive and with a smaller head. He has not achieved the popularity of the other varieties of German Pointer, but was revived in 1865 by a German breeder and saved from extinction. He is a tough rough-coated dog of about the same size and weight as the German Shorthaired Pointer, and is usually brown and white or a mixture of brown and grizzle with darker markings. He is obviously fairly closely related to the other rough pointers and to the French Griffons, but he is unknown outside his own country.

Griffon à Poil Laineux

This is the long-coated version of the Wire-haired Pointing Griffon of France, but has not achieved the international recognition of that breed. He is very like the Korthals Griffon, but was in fact developed by a M. Boulet in France at the beginning of the 19th century, probably by crossing the Wire-haired variety with the Barbet. He was known at one time as the Griffon Boulet after the gentleman who perfected the breed. He is fractionally smaller than the Korthals Griffon and differs from that breed in coat and colour.

His coat is long, soft and silky, lies fairly flat and is sometimes wavy but never curled. He is brown in colour with some small white markings at times, but never large areas of white. He is an intelligent and industrious gundog of considerable versatility, and is easily trained and quiet.

Old Danish Pointer (Gammal Dansk Honsehund)

This is a very old form of Danish gundog which was developed in the 17th century from the even older Spanish Pointer. He went into disfavour at one time and there was a risk of him becoming extinct, but a drive for revival took place and he was finally recognised by the Danish Kennel Club in 1962. In many ways he is as much like his Spanish ancestor as any of the other Pointers, having the same colouration and markings and the rather heavy and broad head of the Spanish dog. He is rather small for a Pointer, only twenty-two inches at the shoulder and is heavy around the neck. His coat is short and dense and in colour he is white with brown patches and some flecking. He is a good worker, easily trained and a general purpose

gundog suited to the flat terrain of his home country. He is quiet and intelligent but is rarely seen outside Denmark.

Perdigeiro Portugues

This is one of the native gundogs of Portugal, being related to early importations of gundogs from Spain as were most of the early Portuguese breeds. He is a bird dog, and indeed the name 'perdigueiro' means partridge. He is a smallish dog, around twenty-two inches in height, usually cream to red in colour with a dark mask and with or without white or black patches and with a short, rough coat. He is virtually unknown outside his own country, but in Portugal is a popular house dog as well as being used for hunting. He is friendly, easily trained, and a very lively companion.

Picardy Spaniel (Epagneul Picard, Epagneul Bleu de Picardie)

By the standards that have become accepted in most parts of the world, the Picardy Spaniels are not Spaniels at all, as in size, proportions and head qualities they are comparable with the Setters. The breed is an old

one, and has been popular in Picardy for many years where he has proved particularly suited to hunting the marshes and woodlands. His overall appearance recalls the engravings of early Springers and Setters, and is something like the early Gordon Setter.

He is a fairly tall dog, up to twenty-five inches at the shoulder and is strongly built on good legs and rather large feet. His coat is fairly long, rather dense and hard, but finer and longer on the ears and the tail. He exists in two colours, the Picardy proper being dark blue roan with flecks of red and some patches, and more red on the legs and feet. The Blue roan version without the red marking, but with red on head and feet is known as the Epagneul Bleu de Picardie. He is very intelligent, easily trained, and becomes attached to one owner.

Poodle Pointer (Pudel Pointer)

This dog completely gives the lie to those who say that the Poodle is a stupid beast not fit for anything but pampering and shows. He was produced by crossing the Pointer with the Poodle towards the end of the 19th century by those sportsmen who wanted all the excellent gun dog qualities of the Pointer with the dash and bright intelligence of the Poodle, and at the same time a dog that had the Poodle's protective coat. They remembered that the Poodle was itself descended from the old race of Water Dogs which were exceptional retrievers in water. It took some considerable time as there was a fair amount of divergence of type and it was not easy to fix, but well into this century it was accomplished and the Poodle Pointer became an established sporting dog in his native country.

In recent years he has been imported into the United States of America though he has not yet appeared in Britain, but in the former he is being found as superb a gun dog as his German originators originally intended him to be. He is a big strong dog with a hard and dense coat, and very little of the original Poodle about his appearance, looking very akin to the German Wirehaired Pointer apart from his colour, as he is always brown or the colour of dead leaves. He is an important sporting dog in Germany where he may only be entered into the stud book when he has succeeded in the field.

Rough-haired Vizsla (The Drótszörü Magyar Vizsla)

This variation on the normal smooth-coated and more popular Vizsla was obtained by crossing that breed with the Roughcoated German Pointer. The breed is of recent origin, being developed during the 1930s. The Vizsla himself is so outstanding a gundog that he has become accepted as something of a mascot by the sportsmen of Hungary who are extremely proud of their fine national dog. He has a great reputation, possessing a wonderful nose, fine ability as a tracker and can be trained to retrieve. The short-haired version had but one shortcoming, his very fine smooth coat was not entirely suitable for long hard days in the field under extreme conditions.

The Drótszörü version is said to have all the excellent qualities of his contemporary, and has in addition the ability to work under the most arduous conditions for considerable lengths of time. He is a great water dog, and will work in frozen marshland and icy water all day. In appearance he is almost exactly the same as the Vizsla proper, but he carries a rough hard coat of up to two inches in length with a soft undercoat. His tendency towards a beard and face whiskers is considered desirable. He is a very active and willing dog, easy-going and friendly.

Small Munsterlander (Kleiner Münsterländer)

This is yet another of the large number of sporting dogs descended from the old Spaniel types indigenous to Western Europe. They probably started life in Spain like the others, but variations resulted from crosses with other native dogs such as the Water Dog and the smaller rough-coated hounds popular in France centuries ago. With no natural boundaries a great deal of interbreeding would have taken place which resulted in numerous slightly different types. Bird dogs went out of fashion as the gun superseded the falcon, and smaller, slower breeds that would hunt and spring game became more popular. The Kliener Münsterländer was developed in Westphalia in Germany from small gun dogs related to the Drentse Patrijshond and some of the French spaniels.

At the beginning of the present century he became quite popular as he proved to be a very hard-working all-round gun dog, but after a while he almost disappeared. Vigorous attempts to preserve the breed resulted in a revival after the First World War and the breed was eventually recognised by the German Kennel Club. He is now increasing in parts of Germany and is becoming known in other European countries though he has not yet been accepted outside Europe. He is smaller by about three inches than his larger cousin, and differs in that he is brown and white instead of black and white.

Spanish Pointer (Perdiguero Burgalés)

Pointers have existed in Spain for at least three hundred years, and although Alonzo de Espinar in his 'Arte de Ballesteria' mentions them in 1644, the Spanish Pointer as he is known today is a fairly modern breed. Espinar wrote that there were two types, the one that tracked and the one that hunted with the nose held high in the true Pointer fashion. The original dog was a fairly heavily built animal with little of the elegance and refinement of the British Pointer, but the introduction of blood from that breed has brought about changes.

He remains a larger dog, up to thirty inches at the shoulder and is more heavily built than his British counterpart, and is liver and white in colour with patches or ticking. He is an excellent gundog, being a good pointer, an eager worker and extremely active. Temperamently he is very quiet and trustworthy with the affection of the average gundog for his owner, and an easy-going nature which endears him to the family. He is often seen at the major championship shows in Spain where he is frequently placed high in the breeders and family groups as his well-matched size and colour make him very attractive. He is rarely seen outside his own country.

Spinone

This is one of the more popular native show dogs of Italy, appearing in fairly large numbers at the major Italian championship shows. He was produced by crossing a number of the ancient breeds of France, from where he is said to have originated. The Barbet,

the Griffon and some of the hounds may be among his ancestors. He is an ancient breed of dog, evolved as a hunter, and used successfully over the years, specialising in work through rough woodland and marshes. he bears some resemblance to the other native hunting dog of Italy, the Bracco, in that he has a heavy head and low-slung ears, which indicate the hound side of his ancestry.

He makes a very good show dog as he is calm and easily trained for exhibition purposes, is quiet in the ring and has a very attractive personality. His coat is his particularly distinguishing feature, being harsh and rugged like that of the French Griffons and he is mainly white with orange or chestnut patches and spots. He has the long eyebrow and jaw hair of the Griffon type which gives him a somewhat massive

appearance. He is a big friendly dog that can be trustworthy and staunch, and he makes a very good guard.

Stabyhoun

This small gun dog of the Spaniel type, originated in the Friedland province of Holland, where he is still seen though often in a bigger form than the standard requires. This confirms the conjecture that he was descended from the larger Drentse Patrijshond probably by crossing with the German or French Spaniels. He is a well-established breed that goes back many years and was developed as a gun dog to work in the flat country of Friesland where control and obedience are more important than speed or drive. It has never been a numerous breed, a dozen appearing at the Winner Show in Amsterdam in 1976, but its supporters are very faithful.

He is a first rate all-round gundog, makes an excellent retriever which is an important feature in Friesland where fairly small fields are divided by deep drainage ditches not easy for the sportsman to cross. He is good through water, and is strong, hardy and has great stamina.

He comes in four different colour patterns which makes a very attractive sight when several are running together, and he makes an excellent housedog and guard and is particularly patient with children.

Wetterhoun

This gun dog from the province of Friesland in Holland is one of the strongest of the Spaniel types of dog. He is very robust with a strong head, very short, broad and deep in the body and stands four square on stout legs. It is not surprising therefore to learn that he was developed largely for hunting the otter rather than as a normal gun dog. He was not used as part of a pack, but hunted singly, and is staunch enough to face his courageous opponent. He has a good deal in common in appearance with the old Water Dog, having a curly coat, a curled tail and the same sort of pattern and colours, and it is likely that he is a fairly direct descendant of that now extinct breed.

In recent years the modern gundogs have become more fashionable and the Wetterhoun has been ousted from popularity as a wildfowling dog. He is however still used for the hunting of the otter, and will face up to a polecat. He is a popular guard and farm dog, remains an all-purpose gundog, and is impervious to the most severe weather conditions. He is intelligent and fairly easily trained though he has a streak of wilfulness and is a fairly tough character when aroused. Those who support the breed will admit that he needs a fairly firm hand, but when trained he makes an excellent watch dog. He is not seen a great deal at shows, rarely appears outside Holland and Germany, and has not yet reached the United States of America or Britain.

FCI GROUP 8:

American and British Gundogs
See Sporting Dogs pages 25–92

FCI GROUP 9:

Companion dogs including the toy dogs

Bolognese

This is one of the family of Bichons, the small hairy dogs that have existed in Europe for centuries. The Bolognese is a small toy dog, under twelve inches in height and is covered with a mass of curls. There is an early example of the breed depicted in Kirchner's model of around 1730 for the Meissen factory, described oddly enough as a Bolognese Hound. He is probably related to the very early Shock Dog which was one of the European Water Dogs, and small enough to be developed as a lap dog.

He appears to have been in existence in Northern Italy in the 15th century and reached Britain via the Canary Islands some two hundred years ago. He is pure white in colour with often a few fawn or light yellow marks. His coat is very long and shaggy and consists of a mass of curls on most parts of the body with a shorter coat on the muzzle. He is still recognised in Italy, but is rarely seen outside that country.

Coton de Tulear

This little toy dog which is clearly related very closely to the Bichon family, originated in Southern Madagascar. His ancestors were probably brought into the country by the troops of the Indian Company who settled on the island of Bourbon from the year 1665. On the island of Reunion there is a very similar little dog known as the Chien Coton, and both this variety and the Coton de Tulear closely resemble the Maltese and the Teneriffe Dog. By successive cross-breeding over the past half century breeders in Madagascar have produced a delightful little dog, and by the later introduction of bloodlines from the Maltese, the breed has been strengthened and firmly established. A fairly large number of these little dogs were exported from the island, either to 'La Reunion' or to France as their owners finally left, and the breed is now thinly distributed throughout Madagascar.

He is a small dog, the males not more than twelve inches high, and the females considerably less, and weighing not more than nine pounds. His principal characteristic as his name suggests, is his coat, which is white, long and fluffy rather than silky. Some yellow markings are permitted. He has a lively and intelligent look underneath a dense crest of long white hair. His eyes are deep-seated and dark, and he makes an elegant and attractive pet.

German Spitz (Wolf Spitz)

The German Spitz has been in existence since around the beginning of the 17th century, and had two forms. The small white variety which was bred largely in Pomerania, and which, when exported to Britain, changed its colour, became smaller still and is known as the Pomeranian. The larger version, a dog with a minimum height of seventeen inches and closely resembling the Keeshond remained a German breed with his interests looked after by the German Spitz club formed in 1899 who issued standards for the breed. There was a smaller black version which was bred in Württemberg to guard the vineyards.

The Wolf Spitz is a strongly made dog with a stand-off coat and a distinct mane, and from the colour of the coat, which is wolf grey, comes his name. Like many of the Spitz breeds he is an all-purpose dog, being sporting by nature, and yet an excellent guard and watchdog. The Small German Spitz is similar to the larger dog, but must be less than eleven inches in height, and varies considerably in colour. This leads to some confusion in shows in those countries that recognise both the British Pomeranian and the Small German Spitz, as the two are indistinguishable in the ring.

Harlequin Pinscher (Harlekinpinscher)

This is the most recent of the German Pinschers to be recognised, having been accepted as a separate breed by the FCI as recently as 1958. In size he comes between the Pinscher proper and the Miniature Pinscher and is the typical German short-haired terrier type of dog with short body and prick ears. His most distinctive feature, from which he gets his name is his colour, as he is patched with dark or black on a white ground. There was clearly at one time a basic form of dog in central Europe which had the harlequin colouration, as the Great Dane, and to a certain extent the Dalmation, both of which emanated from Germany have a similar pattern.

He is a typical Terrier, a great hunter of vermin and small game, very sporting and full of fun, and is particularly suited to the duties of a guard and a house-dog. He is lively, attentive to humans, whose company he enjoys, and very faithful. He is very little seen outside his native country.

Japanese Small Size Dog (Shiba Inu)

This is the smallest of the ancient dogs of Japan. The breed has been traced through ancient remains to very primitive times, when it is believed that it was brought over from the Southern Seas. For a long time these little dogs have been used for hunting small wild animals in the mountains. At one time there was some confusion and he was included in with the larger version as one breed, but is now considered to be a separate variety under the name Shiba Inu which means 'small dog'.

He is a cheerful and active little dog, keen and rather highly strung, very watchful and both faithful and obedient. He has the typical head of the Spitz breeds, with broad skull, sharp muzzle and erect ears which are carried slightly forward. He is strong and very muscular for a small dog with straight bone and compact feet. His coat is hard and straight with a soft warm undercoat and some feathering on his tail. In colour he varies from white through red and brown to black with an occasional brindle. His height is

described in Japanese very picturesquely as '1 shaku 3 sun' which translates into thirty-nine centimetres or fifteen inches.

Japanese Spitz

Although the name Japanese Spitz has become accepted as almost the family name of the small group of dogs from Japan known as the Inu, and including the Akita, the Shiba and the Nippon, there is a small white Samoyed type of dog which has achieved some popularity in other countries than Japan which is known as the Japanese Spitz. They are seen in Ceylon, and one or two specimens have appeared in Britain though the breed is not recognised there. It could well be that this breed is a rather long-coated version of the family which is known sometimes by its familiar names of Japanese Large Size Dog, Japanese Middle Size Dog and Japanese Small Size Dog.

There is a possibility that the charming white dogs that are now seen in countries outside Japan have been produced from a cross between the Japanese dogs and the small white German Spitz that produced the Pomeranian. He is certainly a dog of considerable charm, makes a delightful show dog, being quite dramatic in appearance, smart in outline and repays grooming. He could easily become very popular in other countries as he is an excellent house dog and family pet.

Kromfohrländer

This is one of the newest breeds to be accepted by the German Kennel Club, being recognised in 1953, and is a typical example of an individual setting out to produce a new breed from an accidental mating and the resultant discovery of something attractive. Frau Schliefenbaum in the Krumme Furche area of Siegen in Germany owned a Wire-haired Terrier bitch and was presented with a nondescript little dog by some American troops at the end of the Second World War. These two when mated, produced a litter of puppies which so delighted Frau Schliefenbaum that she decided to attempt to fix the breed, an attempt which was successful when the German Kennel Club accepted it. Though the original sire is a matter of some conjecture, it is believed to have been a Griffon Fauve de Bretagne, a belief that is borne out by the similarity, apart from colour, between the two breeds.

He is a small dog, around sixteen to seventeen inches in height with the rough coat of his ancestors and a distinctive preferred white saddle. He is rapidly gaining in popularity in Germany, and since his acceptance by the FCI is becoming known in other countries. He is very intelligent, faithful and friendly, and makes an excellent watchdog.

Mexican Hairless Dog (Xoloizcuintli)

There are a number of hairless or partly hairless dogs, which are claimed by many experts to have originated in Africa and to have travelled by various means through China to America. It has been stated that the ancestors of the Chihuahua and the Mexican Hairless were brought to South America by traders as long ago as the 17th century, and there is an obvious similarity between this breed and the Chinese Crested Dog. They were imported into Britain during the early years of this century and created something of a sensation, though there was some confusion at that time as to whether they were actually Mexican Hairless or Chinese Crested.

Interest in the breed was maintained around the port of Acapulco and there is said to have been a con-

nection with an ancient religious cult, which led to the name. Despite his strange appearance, he is quite a sporting little dog, full of character and fun, and some of the early importations proved themselves adept at hunting rabbits and rats. He obviously is not suited to an outdoor life in a country subject to wintry conditions, but with care can adapt to a normal temperate climate. He has lost ground in popularity to the Chinese Crested Dog which is making some progress in Britain and other countries at present.

Volpino

The early history of the modern Pomeranian is often confused by those who claim that the small Spitz type of dog depicted on wall paintings, Roman drawings and carvings is in fact that breed. It is much more reasonable to suppose that it was in fact the Volpino that was being recorded, as this little dog has existed in Italy for as long as records have been kept. It could be of course that the Volpino went to Germany, from which country the Pomeranian originated, as many of the early Deutscher Kleinspitz were white. Further confusion is caused by the existence of a tiny white dog called the Seidenspitz in Germany at one time, and the continued existence of the Japanese Spitz which is merely a slightly larger version.

The Volpino is a small dog, no higher than eleven inches at the shoulder and not weighing more than nine pounds. The head is not so sharp and well-defined as the Kleinspitz. The coat, which is long and stand-off with a dense undercoat, is always white. Like so many of the smaller Spitz type, the noise that he can make is out of all proportion to his size, and he therefore makes an excellent watchdog.

FCI GROUP 10:
The coursing dogs

Magyar Agár

This is an ancient breed of Hungarian Greyhound, evidence on tombstones dating back to the conquest of Hungary in the 9th century pointing to the existence of a coursing dog very like the present day one at that time. In the 13th century Greyhounds were imported from other countries with the result that the modern dog looks very like the Greyhound proper of the United States and Britain. Between the two world wars the numbers of the older type of dog were much reduced and further importations took place. It is probable that the early Magyar dog was similar, and probably connected with the Sloughi and the other Eastern Greyhound types.

He is used as a coursing dog, principally for hare, though in earlier times he was used also for chasing and killing the fox. It is said in Hungary that he is better hunting by sight and in not having a 'nose', and in fact this can be detrimental. He is extremely fast and clever, generations of coursing ancestors with no track-running blood having produced an animal more like the coursing Greyhound than the show dog. He is friendly, devoted to his owners, and is an excellent housedog and guard. He is not known outside his own country and is not seen at shows.

Sloughi

There has been considerable discussion about the claim of this breed to be distinct and separate, many experts stating that it is merely a smooth-coated Saluki which has degenerated in type by crossing with other running dogs. It is however recognised by the FCI and acknowledged as a separate breed by the Kennel Club in Britain. He originated basically in North Africa, though in an early form he was probably brought into that country from elsewhere. A type of Wolfhound existed in North Africa many centuries ago, and ancient drawings and carvings depict a strong running dog which could well have been one of the ancestors of the Sloughi. These dogs were probably brought back from places further east such as

Saudi Arabia, which leads to the suggestion by some authorities that they are descended from the ancient Eastern Greyhound from which came the Saluki and the Afghan Hound.

The name Sloughi appeared during the Middle Ages and followed the dog that we now know as the Saluki when that was first imported into Britain. At that time the name used was 'slughi' which led to even further confusion as they were undoubtedly not the Sloughi of Northern Africa which was well known at the same time. He is a strong fast running hound used for hunting hare and small deer, and has appeared at shows in Europe for a number of years. The early specimens that arrived in Britain were not completely typical and the European examples are better. He is a good watchdog, aloof with strangers but affectionate with those that he knows.

Spanish Greyhound (Galgo Español)

This breed is a typical Greyhound, though smaller than the one normally seen as the Greyhound in shows throughout the world. There has been considerable discussion concerning the position the breed occupies in relationship to the Ibizan Hound and the Greyhound proper, and whether in fact he descended from

the Pharaoh Hound. The fact that he is frequently fawn and white in colour lends credence to the latter theory. There has been some crossing with the British Greyhound, and there was an attempt to establish a breed known as the Anglo-Spanish Greyhound.

He is used as a coursing dog, frequently for hunting on horseback, and is an intelligent, fast and hardy running dog with excellent stamina. His coat varies, though for the most part it is short and strong. He is seen frequently at Spanish shows.

PART THREE:
Other Pedigree Breeds

GROUP A

Recognised in their native country, some at championship status

There are many breeds of dog which can be considered to be pedigree dogs, in that they exist as separate breeds, and have records of their breeding carefully kept, which are not recognised by any one of the major authorities. They are often, though not always, working dogs, and have been used for specific purposes in limited areas.

It is possible that in some cases the numbers are so small that the breed has almost ceased to exist, whilst in other cases, and the Jack Russell Terrier is a typical example, they exist in large numbers and have only failed to achieve recognition because their type remains unsettled. Many of them are shown at dog shows, as although they are not approved for the award of championship status, they are accepted as a distinct breed, whilst others appear at shows not under the authority of the Kennel Club concerned, as working dogs of one sort or another. They all, however, have their place in a book of this sort, the popular ones because they earn their place by virtue of that popularity, and the less common ones in the hope that their inclusion will draw attention to the need for preserving them.

Alano

This breed is a descendant of the old Celtic hound, which was crossed with the Mastiff to produce a powerful heavy-weight hunting dog. It was suggested at one time that it was the same breed as the so-called Spanish Bulldog which was imported into Britain at the turn of the century, but there is probably no basis in fact for this suggestion. He was said too at one time to have taken part in bullfights, but in fact he is more of a hunting than a fighting dog. He is used for the hunting of the wild boar, being used as a pack dog, cornering and holding the quarry at bay until the arrival of the huntsmen.

He is a massive dog with a large head, powerful body and a short harsh coat. He is red in colour with a dark mask, all of which gives him a Mastiff like appearance, though he is in fact a hunting dog. He is an ardent hunter, vigorous in the chase, but with the calm temperament of the larger hunting hounds.

American Toy Terrier (Amertoy)

Attempts have been made in recent years in the United States to produce a Toy Terrier. By selective breeding from small Smooth Fox Terriers a line of very small dogs which weigh only a few pounds has been developed and there have been moves to popularise them. The American Kennel Club has not recognised them as a separate breed. Earlier unsuccessful attempts were made in Britain to produce toy Bulldogs and Toy Bull Terriers, and they suffered from the normal disadvantages of poor bone quality and weak physique generally that accompanies such experiments. The Toy Terrier has the advantage of a foundation in an already fairly small dog which does from time to time produce an extra small specimen, and these experiments could well produce a tiny dog of great charm and all the Terrier characteristics.

Further crossing with the Chihuahua and the English Toy Terrier has resulted in a smooth-coated tiny dog with prick ears, a somewhat domed skull, generally white with some black and orange markings.

Anatolian Karabash

This Mastiff type herding dog from Turkey has a history which probably goes back to the time when animal husbandry first began there. The breed clearly has a close relationship with the rough-coated Mastiffs of Spain and Southern Europe, and was almost certainly at one time as important as a guard as it was as a herder of sheep. The climate in which it was developed and worked is not one that would be suitable for a lesser dog, and the flocks that it guarded, as they moved from one area to another needed protecting against wolves and other predators.

He does not herd in the normal way as they are fairly constantly moving slowly feeding as they go, and he normally patrols rather than herds. He works with his family in this duty and has evolved a technique of very effective ambush. He is an active, rather long-legged dog with great agility and stamina, and is hardy and capable of living under conditions which other dogs would find very trying. His coat is medium length, very dense, rather soft, and though pale colours such as fawn, with a black mask are most common, entirely black specimens do occur. In Turkey his ears are cropped and he wears a heavy spiked collar as extra protection.

Argentinian Mastiff (Dogue d'Argentine)

The origins of this dog are obscure, as although Mastiffs would certainly have been taken over to South America by the Spanish and Portuguese during the period of the exploitation of that country, they would hardly have been the type that is now accepted as the Dogue D'Argentine. The Spanish Mastiff is a large coloured dog with a fairly long coat whilst the Portuguese equivalent is also coloured and has longish hair. The Argentinian Mastiff, today, however, is an all-white dog with a short hard coat, and is little like the Fila Brasileiro which is descended from the early Mastiff types. The Argentine Mastiff is like a rather oversize white Boxer. He is used for hunting the puma and other big game and is a very strong and courageous animal with the loose skin around the neck of the fighting dogs. He is seen in other countries, but has not yet appeared in Britain.

Egyptian Sheepdog (Armant)

This is an ancient working dog used by Egyptian shepherds for hundreds of years. He is named after the village of Armant in Upper Egypt and is said to be descended from the French dogs which were taken there with the armies of Napoleon during the 18th century. Formerly he was purely a droving dog, but he later becme a guard and a fairly aggressive one. The breed first appeared in Europe when specimens were brought to Berlin by Professor Nachat Pascha whilst he was Ambassador. He is a medium sized dog somewhat smaller than a Collie, has a long, rough, shaggy coat, and is found in all shades of grey with a dark mask and some white marking, as well as in many other colours. He is somewhat suspicious of strangers, and makes an excellent guard. He is rarely seen outside his own country, and is not a show dog.

Artésien Normand

The old Norman Hound which appears to have been evolved during the time of Louis XIV was a heavy, strong dog, more along the lines of the Bloodhound than the Foxhound. He was developed to hunt many types of games in the French forests and is a fairly big and heavy dog. His head is rather like that of the Bloodhound, with loose skin on the cheeks, long in the skull and with a pronounced occiput, his ears are long and pendant with a definite twist. He has a longer body than some of the other hounds, and his general appearance lacks refinement. He is usually tricolour or white with darker patches and his coat is smooth and fine to the touch.

Australian Greyhound

Many of the dogs imported into Australia by the early settlers proved too slow to catch the faster game of that country, and the bone-hard and often extremely tough conditions under which they had to work did not suit the English Greyhound. A variety of Greyhound was produced, therefore, which was around the same size but very sturdy and stout in build with great musculation and very good feet. They were used for catching small game on the cattle and sheep stations. This type, smaller than the English show Greyhound, still appear at Australian dog shows, but the breed is not recognised by the Australian Kennel Council and is not mentioned in modern works on Australian dogs.

Barb

The two original dogs that produced all the present Kelpie bloodlines are known, they were a dog named Brutus and a bitch called Jennie. This was in 1870, and at around the same time, another line was being produced from a bitch named Sally which produced an outstanding working dog, named Barb after a well-known racehorse of the time. He was a black, prick-eared and a tremendous worker, and became so prepotent a stud force that a whole line of black dogs was produced which became known as Barbs. He was noted as a forceful worker with sheep and became expert at the special type of work required around the stockyards. The breed was shown with Kelpies though as recently as the 1940s classes as a separate variety were staged. The name now seems to have ceased though old herders will still refer to a black Kelpie as a Barb.

Basset d'Artois

This is the short-legged version of the Chien d'Artois, a hound that originated in the North of France from the St. Hubert Hound. He is described as one of the most beautiful of the Bassets, being powerful and vigorous rather than elegant, and having great length. It could well be that this particular variety of Basset played some part in the evolution of the Basset in Britain, as that too is on the whole a heavier and stronger dog than the popular forms of French Bassets.

The Basset d'Artois is what is known as a half-crook fronted dog with very strong bone and a large rib cage. His coat is short and dense, and he is usually tricolour, or, less frequently has orange or grey markings on a white or speckled ground. He is noted for his hunting ability and voice. He is not so well-known as some of the other French Bassets and is not seen outside his own country.

Belgian Pointer (Braque Belge)

Many of the gundogs of Northern Europe, like the hounds, differ from one another in very few details and frequently only in the matter of colour. The large family of pointers and hounds in France spread its influence into other neighbouring countries, and by the selection of the desired type in the first instance and by careful selective breeding, dogs were produced which bred true to type and were eventually accepted as a separate breed. The Braque Belge is typical of these. For the countryside over which he was to hunt, a fast showy dog was not required, but something that was steady and certain, and perhaps more thoughtful than some of the light Pointers.

He is most distinctive for his colour, as he is slate-grey with patches and spots of brown, a colour which probably came from a mixture of the Grand Bleu of France and the Old Danish Pointer. He is a fairly tall dog, standing around twenty-five inches at the shoulders, and is strongly built with good ribs and a broad loin. He is a smart dog, as his ears are rather small and his tail is normally docked. His coat is hard and dense, but close, and his head is rather broader, and with less stop than some of the traditional pointers. He is a good, steady and reliable worker, but is not a popular show dog and is practically unknown outside his own country.

Berger de Languedoc

This is a group of breeds rather than one variety of dog, originating in the area of Languedoc, in the country bordering the Golfe du Lion. There are five types, each taking its name from the district in which it evolved. They are the Camargue, the Grau, the Farou, the Carrigues and the Larzac. Although they differ in some details, in height for instance, where they vary between sixteen and twenty inches, and in coat, where they vary from smooth and short, to rough and long, they are all more or less the same colour. The colour ranges from fawn to reddish-fawn and black. They are all excellent working sheepdogs that have lived on the farms of the plains and flat lands of the Languedoc area, and have always doubled up as guards and farm-yard dogs, protecting not only flocks and herds, but the property of their owners.

Border Collie

This breed is the most recent one to be recognised for show purposes in Britain, though it has been in exist-ence for hundreds of years, and has been exhibited in other countries for some time. The breed was developed from a mixture of working sheepdogs which were carefully controlled and registered as such by the International Sheepdog Society whose registers pre-date those of the Kennel Club. The intelligence, and capacity for work and training, of the breed, is a legend wherever sheep are kept, and it is the top competitor in many countries where international sheepdog trials are held. Though its numbers do not at present warrant the status of championship competition in the show ring, there is little doubt that these will rapidly increase as the popularity of the breed is very high indeed.

He is a typical Collie type dog, strong, flexible and active with a keen head and expression, and though black and white is the most popular colour, many others are acceptable. He exists in two coat forms, the rough, which is a medium length tough but shiny outer coat, with thick undercoat, and the smooth which is sleek and glossy. He has been shown extensively in Australia where the standard for the breed was approved in 1963 and where individual states were issuing their own challenge certificates even earlier. He is rapidly becoming popular as a show dog in other countries and his remarkable obedience, loyalty and quiet temperament, suit him particularly well to beauty competition.

Braco Navarro (Braco Carlos VIII)

In the extreme South West of Spain there exists a variety of gundog known as the Braco Navarro, which is similar to some of the smaller and lighter gundogs of central France. Braques have been mentioned in works on dogs since the middle of the 17th century, and the Navarro is one of the older breeds. He is reported as having been exhibited before the First World War and to have been popular in the early part of the 19th century.

He is a medium-sized short-coated dog, powerfully built and is usually white with dark brown spots or ticking and often with tan markings. At one time he is said to have been seen sometimes with wall eyes which could indicate an early relationship with some of the herding dogs. He is, however, essentially a hunting dog and is used as such, not appearing in the show ring, and being virtually unknown outside his own country.

Bouvier des Ardennes

As with many other countries, the farmers of Belgium, where incidentally the farming of sheep has always been very successful, produced a variety of sheepdogs. For many years they remained somewhat mixed and unclassified, but recently they have been divided into their separated breeds, based largely upon the area in which they evolved. The wire-haired herder of the

Ardennes has been known for many years, and though not achieving the world-wide popularity of his contemporary the Bouvier des Flandres, he has always had a following in his own country.

He is a tall dog, some twenty-four inches in height at the shoulder, very strong, and with erect ears. His tail is docked very short and he is covered with a shaggy harsh coat of medium length, with pronounced whiskers and beard of slightly longer hair. He can be any colour, though at one time many of them were grizzle. He is a guard dog as well as a herder, and accustomed to defend his farm against intruders. The result is that he is suspicious and rather ill-tempered with those that he does not know, whilst at the same time he is obedient and easily trained by his owners. There may be small pockets of the breed still in existence, but according to the Société Royale Saint Hubert, of Belgium, the breed is now extinct.

Chinese Crested Dog

This breed, the Mexican Hairless and the African Hairless have a great deal in common, in fact at one time at the beginning of this century they were looked upon in Britain as all belonging to the same breed. At that time there were two distinct types in Britain, the one rather leggy and whippet-like and the other described as short and rather cloddy. It was the latter type which had hair between the toes, a distinct hairy mane, and a tuft on the tail, and this was undoubtedly the Chinese Crested as we know it today. They failed to become popular, and disappeared from the dog scene for a good many years.

Recently there have been a number of importations into Britain and the breed is achieving a degree of notoriety once more, if not popularity, as his strange appearance and distinctive characteristics have endeared him to the media. The breed is now seen in some numbers at British shows, and always creates something of a sensation, particularly among the less experienced. The number of registrations is approaching the hundred mark, and there is no doubt that they will eventually reach championship status. They are friendly and attractive little dogs, full of fun and very attached to their owners.

Chinese Hound

There existed at one time in China a breed of dog described as a hound, and carrying the name Ma-Chu-Gou. This could well have been the dog described at the turn of the century as the Phu-Quoc, specimens of which were brought to France but did not survive. He is described as having the appearance of a heavy Greyhound with pricked or semi-pricked ears, and is said to have descended from a long-coated dog native to Kashmir. He is a dark brown shaded dog with a very dense short coat, with a tendency towards a ridge in the fashion of the Rhodesian Ridgeback.

It is by no means certain that the breed still exists as it was said some fifty years ago to be disappearing. He is an excellent hunter with a very good nose and a high degree of intelligence. He is keen and persistent in the pursuit of game, strong enough to handle boar and deer, and hunts in packs to bay his quarry until the approach of the huntsmen.

Chortaj

This is one of the running dogs from Eastern Europe. He is a large hard-coated dog of the Greyhound type with long neck and arched body, but is more heavily built and coarser than the Greyhound that is seen in dog shows in most countries of the world. The Cynological Congress held in Moscow in 1952 accepted this breed as one of the pure Russian breeds and one to be preserved. He is an extremely keen hunting dog, is used exclusively for coursing and is not seen outside his native country.

German Sheep Pudel

Although the modern Poodle is thought by many people to have originated in France, the breed almost certainly began life in Germany as the Pudel, a breed which itself evolved from the Water Dog and the Barbet. Vero Shaw states 'There is also a "sheep" Poodle in Germany . . . presenting altogether a heavy and uncouth appearance'. The Schafpudel is still very much admired by German shepherds for his intelligence and working ability, and though he does not appear in the show ring, is still preserved as a separate variety. He is a fairly large dog, up to twenty-four inches at the shoulder, and is covered with a long, shaggy coat with a dense undercoat. His colour is white, with some coloured marks or shading allowed. He is intelligent and gentle, but an excellent guard.

Dutch Hound (Steenbrak)

In the 17th century there was a race of farm dogs mainly kept in the Brabant region of Holland, which were of the hound type. They were crossed with some of the other European hounds, particularly those from Germany, and a small hound, under eighteen inches, was produced which survives. He is very like the German hound, being lightly built, small and rather leggy and with long ears. He has a short thick and hard coat and in colour is typically hound-marked, white, yellow to red, and black patches principally over the saddle. He is a handsome little dog with white blaze and feet, and whilst still a hunting dog, is affectionate and friendly.

Estonian Hound

During the time of the Tzars, hunting was a favourite pastime in Russia and some fine breeds of hounds were developed there. The Borzoi is a typical example. There were, however, a number of scent hunting hounds which were used either as pack hounds, or singly by individual huntsmen. The Estonian Hound is one of the few that have remained since the Russian Revolution brought about the cessation of hunting as a fashionable pursuit, the others disappearing in the confusion that existed immediately after the upheaval. He is a medium-sized dog, twenty inches at the shoulder, and is rather long cast in body.

He has a short, hard and dense coat, the long folded ears of those dogs that have the St. Hubert Hound in their ancestry, and a broad, deep and fairly rounded chest. His colour is the typical tricolour hound marking of yellow, white and black, the black sometimes covering almost the whole body and extending to the head. He is a fast hard-working hound with a good nose and excellent temperament.

Flemish Draught Dog (Vlaamsche Trekhond)

This large heavy-weight dog which descended from the old droving dogs of Belgium was used extensively as a draught dog to pull small carts for tradesmen. In the more remote areas he is still probably used to some extent for the purpose as he is capable of pulling quite heavy loads, is remarkably obedient and easily trained, and serves the double purpose of hauling as well as guarding property. He is a large dog up to thirty inches at the shoulder and tremendously strong. His coat is short, very hard and weather-resistant and he is usually ash-grey in colour with a dark mask.

German Hound (Deutsche Bracke)

In every respect other than size, this dog is very like many of the Foxhounds throughout the world. He is of the usual hound colours and markings, has the same type of head and is built along the same lines. In size he more nearly approaches the Harrier, however, and looks very like his geographical near neighbours, the Scandinavian Stövare. There were at one time many breeds of pack hounds in Germany, but they are now virtually extinct, and only the Deutsche Bracke remains as a separate breed. The standard was compiled by the Deutscher Bracken Club in 1955 in Olpe, with the result that he is sometimes known as the Olpe Hound.

He is a fine pack-hunting dog with a very good nose and an excellent voice, and like most of the scent hounds, is affectionate and friendly. He is not a show dog and is in the hands largely of huntsmen.

Glen of Imaal Terrier

As long as people in eastern Eire can remember there have been tough little dogs used for going to ground to badger. The centre of their activities has been in County Wicklow and especially in the Glen of Imaal. Primarily a hunting dog he developed such gameness that he was frequently used for staged dog fights, in which his toughness and protective coat gave him tremendous advantage.

He is not a common dog even in his native country, and was virtually ignored as a potential show dog until in 1933 the Irish Kennel Club staged classes for the breed. Since then he has gained a few supporters in other countries as well as his own, and is seen from time to time at the principal shows. He is a tough little dog, but with the delight in games that most of the Terriers have. He is a great hunter, likes nothing better than a walk in the country or a scramble over rough going, scenting out anything that smells catchable, and makes a wonderful companion.

Happa Dog

This is a little-known oriental breed from China, and in appearance is something like a Pekingese but without the long coat of that breed. The first were seen in England around 1907 when one was imported and exhibited by the Hon. Mrs. Lancelot Carnegie at the first show of the Pekingese Club. To complete the oriental picture it was led into the ring by a Chinese lady in native costume. The dog was said to have looked rather like a very tiny miniature Bulldog and was black and tan. Little is known about the present state of the breed, and it is certainly not known outside China.

Havanese

This is another of the Bichon family, being the typical small woolly toy dog. His origin is said to have been in Cuba or the Philipines, both of which claim him as a native. He is undoubtedly descended from the other Bichons, and probably the Maltese, which found their way to those countries from the Mediterranean. At the turn of the century there were several exhibited at shows in France, but they seem to have disappeared· from the scene in recent years.

He is a small dog, between eleven and thirteen inches at the shoulder, white, with large and small patches of biege, grey, or black, and can be solid chestnut. His coat is long, soft and curled and is silky rather than wiry. He is a gay little toy dog, very affectionate and an excellent house dog and pet.

Jack Russell Terrier

This breed originated as the result of many people deciding that the modern form of Fox Terrier had become far removed from the original English Terriers, and was a somewhat artificial animal bred solely for show purposes. They decided that a smaller, shorter-legged dog was more elemental, and proceeded to develop a Terrier along these lines. Considerable controversy resulted, and a number of unsuccessful attempts were made to persuade the Kennel Club in Britain to recognise the breed. These failed largely because of the number of different types that were being bred and sold as Jack Russell Terriers. The enormous popularity of these little dogs added to the problem, as they are not an obscure breed existing in small pockets in tiny numbers, but one of the most commonly seen breeds, not only in England, where they originated, but in many countries of the world.

They gain their name from a very famous Fox Terrier breeder, the Rev. John Russell, of Devonshire who had a great deal to do with the early development of the Fox Terrier. A model of one of his dogs is to be seen in the headquarters of the Kennel Club in London. A club has now been formed, and there is little doubt that when the breed has settled down it will achieve recognition. He is one of the spunkiest little dogs in the world, with tremendous spirit, a great hunter and one of the most persistent chasers of small game in the whole canine race.

Kangaroo Hound

In the early days, and indeed until quite recently the kangaroo was recognised as a pest in Australia, and its numbers needed to be reduced. Both the kangaroo and the wallaby are now however protected as part of Australia's policy of conservation, and the need to hunt them is reduced. For hunting, the Greyhound proved insufficiently tough, and a Greyhound/Deerhound cross was evolved which, by selection, has produced a very large and extremely tough running dog that can both catch and hold a kangaroo.

Although the need for such a dog has now ceased to exist, there are still some remote stations where he will be found. He is not shown, and is unknown outside his own country, and is probably now a dying breed.

Kerry Beagle

This hound, once fairly popular in Southern Ireland, but now limited to one pack, and a small number of individual animals, is one of the most attractive of the smaller hunting dogs. His history is obscure, but he is probably an offshoot of a much larger hound used at one time for deer hunting. The Scarteen pack was composed entirely of this type of hound in the second half of the 19th century and specimens can still be found in that part of the country. Though smaller than he was, he is still a much larger dog than the Beagle.

He is a dashing, close-coated hound, deeper in the muzzle and longer in the ears than the Foxhound, and is now mostly black and tan in colour. He is strong, melodious and spirited, and though essentially a pack hound, he obviously makes a reasonable companion, as specimens are still to be seen in that part of Ireland known as the Ring of Kerry. He is a handsome

hound, with something of the French hounds about him, but the colour of the Swedish Hamiltonstövare. He is quiet and affectionate, and though he has the innate wilfulness of most of the pack-hunting hounds, he makes a friendly house pet.

Laika

The Laikas are really a family of dogs rather than an individual breed. Primarily a sporting dog he has been used for a number of purposes including herding and draught work. The members of the family were bird dogs and the name comes from the habit of giving tongue in the chase. The smallest is the one that comes from that area of Russia nearest to Finland, and is related to the Finnish Spitz. The European type is larger and stronger, is black, grey or fawn, but still a typical Spitz dog. The type that comes from Eastern Siberia is larger still, and tends to resemble the oriental breeds, but because of its weight and strength is used for sleigh work as well as sport. The dog that comes from the north of Russia varies considerably, but tends towards the Samoyed rather than to any other well-known breed. He is an intelligent dog, easily trained and used for military and guard duties. It was a Laika which was first used in Russian space experiments.

Lurcher

This breed, or really crossbreed, has been known of for centuries. It is the breed of the Romanies or Tinkers of Ireland, and has been produced by crossing the Greyhound with the Collie to produce a running hunting dog with particular characteristics. His history has been passed on by word of mouth from generation to generation of these wandering people. He has been produced for the purpose of poaching, and will run down rabbit or hare silently so as not to give away his presence, and will return to his master, game in mouth, as he is one of the best retrievers in the world.

He is trained to avoid humans whilst hunting, and will disappear from the scene if a stranger shows, only to continue the hunt when he has gone. If, on return to his owner, with or without game, a stranger is in conversation with him, the dog will remain hidden until the stranger disappears, even if they have moved a considerable distance. He is a tall dog, often rough-coated, and usually fawn or grey in colour, and is very quiet and affectionate. Attempts are now being made by a small number of enthusiasts to stabilise the breed and fix a type.

Macellaio Herding Dog (Cane di Macellaio)

This is a small to medium-sized herding dog peculiar to Sicily and differing from his Italian neighbour in that he has a short coat. He is usually around twenty inches in height, with a strong head on the lines of a

Rottweiler and a massive body, with deep chest and strong loins. His tail is normally cropped fairly short and his ears cropped to a neat erect appearance. His coat is hard and short and he is either black and tan, black, or fawn in colour though brindles also occur. He is active, forceful but obedient, and makes an excellent guard.

North Eastern Sleigh Dog

This sledge-hauling dog is fairly widespread throughout the regions of Manchuria and the far North East of Siberia. He is clearly related to the other arctic dog used for this work, and in appearance looks very like a smaller version of the Eskimo Dog. He is fairly large, standing twenty-three inches at the shoulder with a massive head, strong muzzle and erect ears. He has a very powerful robust body and long well-muscled legs, and large strong feet. His coat is fairly long, thick and stand-off, and he has a thick soft dense undercoat which makes him virtually weatherproof. He exists in several colours and mixtures of colours, is sometimes all white or black, but commonly black and white. He is a tough hard-working sleigh dog.

Nova Scotia Duck Tolling Retriever

This strangely named dog from Canada is at present enjoying something of a revival. He is something like a light Golden Retriever. He originated in the *Maritimes* where he was developed as a house pet and gundog. He is characterised by a quiet and apparently disinterested attitude, until such time as he is asked to work, when he becomes the alert and active sporting dog.

His head resembles that of the Golden Retriever and he is well-boned down to strong webbed feet. His coat is fairly long, sleek and soft and with a dense soft waterproof undercoat. He is red or fawn, rather lighter than the Irish Setter and with some lighter shading. White blazes are not objected to, though efforts are being made to eliminate them. He is a quiet dog, and easy to train. He is a swimmer with outstanding endurance, as well as an excellent house dog and guard. He is not known outside his own country at present.

Owtscharka

The Russian herding dogs exist as a family group of four. They are partly herders and partly guards, as there are still predators in the USSR where the sheep graze. The Transcaucasian is a large and shaggy dog of over twenty-five inches, usually with a docked tail. He is found in various colours and is a vigorous protector of herds. The North Caucasian is smaller and has a shorter coat. The Mid-Asiatic version is a big strong and rather coarser dog, with a strong coat of medium length and of any colour except self-black. The Owtscharka of Southern Russia is a smaller dog,

only around twenty inches, with some resemblance to the Gos d'Atura.

None of them is known outside Russia though there was an attempt to introduce them into Germany in the mid 1930s. The smaller southern variety has an attractive coat which repays grooming, and if any of the family are to make an impression on the Western show world, it could be this smaller variety. They are all said to be intelligent and to have a good temperament, and the variety from Southern Russia is said to be easily trained.

Rampur Hound

At the turn of the century a number of hounds were brought from North West India to Britain, and some were exhibited at Dublin. They were large, rather clumsy looking running dogs employed principally for hunting jackal, and were either mouse-grey or black. He has a roman nose and yellow eyes and his tail is carried slightly curled up at the end, in the fashion of many of the eastern running dogs. He is said to have been bred to withstand the hard ground better than the English Greyhound. He is of uncertain temper, being inclined to bite without warning, though friendly enough with those that he knows. There has been little record of this dog in recent years.

Rumanian Sheepdog

This is an indigenous breed of herding dog still found in Rumania, though not in large numbers. In the early years of this century there were a number of herding dogs in the country though there was no settled type. Since that time there has undoubtedly been some crossing with other sheep-herding dogs, such as the German Shepherd Dog.

He is a large, heavy, strong dog, and a very enthusiastic guard of both the herd and herders' encampment. He is by nature suspicious and curious, and does not take kindly to strangers. Herders need a dog that is easily distinguished from the wolf, and this breed is so by his colour which is usually pied or brown.

Russian Hound

Three types of hound are recognised in Russia, the Estonian Hound, the Russian Hound and the Black-and-fawn Russian Hound. Since the days of the revolution many of the distinctive hounds of Russia such as the Gontschaga Sobaka which were kept in large packs by the Czar and the Grand Dukes have disappeared and no longer exist as separate breeds. The Estonian Hound is a medium sized twenty inch dog which is very fast and is mostly black with some fawn markings. The Russian Hound is a larger version up to twenty-five inches and is red or grizzle and white. This dog is used for the hunting of hare, fox, and badger and usually hunts singly.

The Black-and-fawn Russian Hound is again one of the larger types, about the same size as the Russian Hound proper, but is always black and fawn in colour. He is sometimes known as the Drab Yellow version, and has been recognised as a separate breed for the past fifty years. All of them are good hunters, and none of them is known outside its own country.

Smoushond

This little hard-coated dog varies little from the Terriers of Britain, being about the size and weight of a Fox Terrier, and having the same sort of temperament. He is by tradition the stable-yard dog of the Dutch farm, and is much more the working dog than a house pet. The Dutch Smoushond Club which was founded in 1905, drew up a standard of points, which was based to some extent on the older form known as the Smous-bart, and ensured the preservation of the breed. The standard lays emphasis on the rough and hard quality of the coat, with its strong and often black beard, moustaches and eyebrows, and it is from these qualities that the name of the breed originates. He is a guard dog and vermin killer, being hardy and extremely quick in reaction. He is a lively companion, and a keen guard. Although they are certain of being preserved in their own country, they have rarely been seen outside Holland.

Staghound

As a separate breed the Staghound has probably now ceased to exist, but as the hunting of the stag still takes place, even though with packs of large Foxhounds, it is worth recalling that the breed did have a part to play in the sporting life of the country gentleman in quite recent years. There was an old line of Staghounds in the Royal kennels at Windsor in the early part of the 19th century, described as large thirty inch dogs mostly white in colour. The whole pack was purchased and transported to France, where they undoubtedly played a part in the production of the many varieties of large hounds now in existence in that country.

He was a very tall strong hound, fast and persistent, and had so selective a nose that he was capable of tracking one individual deer through a herd. He hunted as a pack, and had all the friendliness of the pack-hunting dogs.

Stumpy-tailed Cattle Dog

This breed still exists as a separate breed in Australia though its numbers are small. They descended from the same line as the Cattle Dog, being produced from a cross between the Smithfield Collie and the Dingo, and were a tail-less offshoot from that breeding. The originated with a drover named Timmins and became known as Timmins' Biters and occurred as both red and blue or blue mottled dogs. The bob tail became fixed by selective breeding and is natural. He looks very like the Cattle Dog, apart from the fact that he is squarer. He has great courage, is very loyal, and an invaluable worker. There are few breeders in Australia at present and the survival of the breed is largely due to the efforts of Mrs Heale of Brisbane.

Tahl-Tan Bear Dog

This breed of hunting dog was originally used by the Tahl-Tan Indians of Canada. To them he was a personal dog having become by centuries of breeding part of their tribal heritage. It was the custom of the Indians to make an annual hunting excursion into the hills and on these occasions the Bear Dog was an invaluable help in feeding the tribe. In hunting the bear the dogs cornered him and kept him busy, whilst the hunter approached virtually unnoticed and dispatched him. The decline in the demand for bearskin led to a reduction in the numbers of the Tahl-Tan Dog, and there was danger of extinction.

The breed was recognised by the Canadian Kennel Club in 1941. He is a surprisingly small dog for one used on such ferocious game as the bear, standing only up to sixteen inches at the shoulder. He is, however, remarkably agile and alert, darting in and nipping the quarry and getting out of the way before the bear can retaliate. He is usually patched in grey or black and white, and has a mostly black head. His expression is foxy with erect ears. He has a short to medium coat with a distinctive tail, usually black with a white tip, is extremely thick and carried erect. He is unknown outside his own country.

Tasy

This breed, also known as the Mid-Asiatic Greyhound is another of the Russian running dogs. He is rather like the coursing Greyhound though less graceful in build. The breed is an ancient one but in more recent times has been crossed with the Chortaj and has probably had an influx of western Greyhound blood as well. He is strong and fast and is used for hunting hare, small deer, and even wolves. He is independent in temperament and has great stamina. Another variety known as the Tajgan exists locally, but is not recognised as a separate breed. He is unknown outside Russia.

Tenerife Dog

The Bichons are a small family of tiny pet dogs which began life as descendants of the Barbet and the Water Dog. It is probable that the Bichon Frise is descended in a direct line from the Tenerife Dog, in fact it could well be the same dog. The breed first made its appearance in France in the 16th century, and became very popular as the toy dog of the courts of France, Italy and Spain.

The other forms that exist, the Havanese and the

Bolognese, may have had a little to do with the ancestry of the modern Bichon Frise, though the fourth member of the family, the Maltese is rather different. In earlier times the Havanese was frequently brown, which leaves the Bolognese and the Tenerife as possible contenders. In 1933 the standard of the Bichon was adopted in France under two names, but later the name Bichon Frise was adopted.

Trailhound

The pedigrees of this dog are carefully controlled by its own association, and in that respect it is a pedigree dog. The normal form of hunting with horses and packs of hounds, is not suitable in the country towards the western side of Cumberland, and the local farmers have developed a sport of their own racing fast scent hunting hounds against one another over a man-laid trail.

The trail layers race over a measured course up into the hills and by a round-about route back to the start. They lay a trail by dragging along a small container loaded with a liquid, usually aniseed, and at a given signal the hounds are loosed to race over the trail. He is a hound of the Foxhound type, but over the years by judicious introduction of other blood, a very fast long-legged running dog has been evolved. He is a handsome friendly dog that spends his days with the family, and at the same time intelligent and lively.

Working Sheepdog

These dogs are known throughout the world for their remarkable ability to herd sheep, and to be trained to a phenomenal degree of expertise in competition work, as well as for normal work around the farm. This has been largely due to the efforts of the International Sheepdog Society which has kept a register of the finest working bloodlines. They are of no particular breed, and vary considerably in type, but must be included in this book as their omission would pander to the idea that only national kennel authorities keep records and pedigrees. Special demonstrations by these dogs, held in London, have attracted as many as 150,000 spectators in one day, and the famous Longshaw trials have been held since 1894. The interest in sheepdog trials has spread and international championships are held annually.

The dogs used are collies, but not the collie of the show bench. They are frequently black and white, and from them has sprung the breed which is now fixed and recognised in many countries as the Border Collie, but other colours are found. There is in fact no restriction as to type, colour size, or indeed any other characteristic, placed on entry into the stud book of the ISDS, whose records are based purely on working ability.

GROUP B

Not recognised in their native country.

There are a great many breeds of dogs which exist, or which were known to exist until recently, about which information is restricted. Some are bred for very special purposes and whilst records are kept, these are used specifically for the preservation of the best bloodlines for that purpose and are not generally available. Others, whilst existing as separate breeds, do so in remote areas where records are not kept, and the type is preserved purely as a matter of preference and largely by chance. These latter are listed below in alphabetical order.

Austrian Pinschner. (Medium-sized terrier.) *Austria.*
Abyssinian Sand Terrier. (Small companion and hunting dog.) *Africa.*
Baganda Hunting Dog. (Medium-sized hunting dog.) *Africa.*
Bagirmi Dog. (Medium-sized watchdog.) *Africa.*
Bantu Dog. (Small hunting dog.) *Africa.*
Batak Spitz. (Medium-sized hunting and watchdog.) *Africa.*
Brazilian Greyhound. (Large coursing dog.) *Brazil.*
Cameroons Dog. (Medium-sized hunting dog.) *Africa.*
Chinese Greyhound. (Large and small coursing dog.) *China.*

Congo Pygmies' Bush Dog. (Medium-sized hunting dog.) *Africa.*
Dingo. (Wild dog.) *Australia.*
East African Dog. (Medium-sized hunting dog.) *Africa.*
Fila da Terceiro. (Medium-sized guard dog.) *Portugal.*
Greek Herder. (Medium-sized herding dog.) *Greece.*
Hutespitz. (Medium-sized sheepdog.) *Germany.*
Javanese Dingo. (Medium-sized native dog.) *Indonesia.*
Kabyle Dog. (Large guard and herding dog.) *Africa.*
Kaffir Dog. (Spitz type.) *Africa.*
Koikerhond. (Small spaniel.) *Holland.*
Kuri Dog. (Small guard dog.) *Africa.*
Labrit. (Medium-sized sheepdog.) *South of France.*
Liberian Dog. (Small terrier.) *West Africa.*
New Ireland Dog. (Medium-sized guard.) *New Guinea.*
Pachon de Vitoria. (Medium-sized gundog.) *Spain.*
Papuan Dog. (Small tribal dog.) *New Guinea.*
Poligar Hound. (Large coursing hound.) *India.*
Plott Hound. (Medium-sized hunting dog.) *United States.*
Pocket Beagle. (Very small beagle.) *United States/Britain.*

Pommerscher Hutehund. (Medium-sized sheepdog.) *Germany*.
Redbone Hound. (Medium-sized hunting dog.) *United States*.
Sealydale Terrier. (Large short-legged terrier.) *Africa*.
South Russian Greyhound. (Large coursing dog.) *Russia*.
Steenbrak. (Small farm dog.) *Holland*.
Tajgan (Variety of greyhound.) *Russia*.

Treeing Walker Hound. (Medium-sized hunting dog.) *United States*.
Trigg Hound. (Medium-sized hunting dog.) *United States*.
Walker Hound. (Medium-sized hunting dog.) *United States*.
Zanzibar Dog. (Medium-sized hunting dog.) *East Africa*.
Zulu Dog. (Small hunting and guard dog.) *Africa*.

PART FOUR:
Old and Extinct Breeds

There are many breeds of dogs which at one time enjoyed a certain popularity but which have now ceased to exist. Some of them disappeared because there was no longer any need for their retention as their use vanished as civilisation advanced. Others changed type as they were absorbed as other breeds were evolved, so that their ancestral form has disappeared, and with it the name. One or two have unfortunately become extinct in fairly recent years as fashion dictated changes with little thought for conservation. It is, however, important that their names at least should be preserved.

Alaunt. (Ancient mastiff.) *Britain*.
Albanian Wolfhound. (Large hunting dog.) *Greece*.
Ban Dog. (Ancient guard dog.) *Britain*.
Barukhzy Hound. (Early form of Afghan Hound.) *India*.
Black Spaniel. (Ancestral spaniel type.) *Britain*.
Blue Paul. (Ancient smooth terrier.) *Scotland*.
Blue and Tan Manchester Terrier. (Small terrier.) *England*.
Bruno. (Heavy hound.) *Switzerland*.
Carlin a Poil Longue. (Long-haired Pug.) *France*.
Charnique. (Large coursing dog.) *Spain*.
Clydesdale Terrier. (Medium terrier.) *Scotland*.
Congo Terrier. (Small hunting dog.) *Africa*.
Cowley Terrier. (Small terrier.) *England*.
Elterwater Terrier. (Small terrier.) *England*.
English Water Spaniel. (Medium spaniel.) *England*.
Epagneul Ecossais. (Small setter.) *France*.
Fox Collie. (Medium-sized sheepdog.) *Scotland*.
Hare Indian Dog. (Sledge dog.) *Canada*.
Indian Tailless Dog. (Medium companion dog.) *India*.
Kirghiz Greyhound. (Large coursing dog.) *Southern Siberia*.
Lancashire Heeler. (Small herding dog.) *England*.

Mackenzie River Dog. (Sledge dog.) *Canada*.
Manilla Spaniel. (Small toydog.) *Philippines*.
Medelan. (Bear-hunting dog.) *Russia*.
Mongolian Dog. (Small pet dog.) *France*.
Norfolk Retriever. (Medium retriever.) *England*.
Norman Hound. (Large hunting dog.) *France*.
Old Braque. (Large pointer.) *France*.
Old English White Terrier. (Small terrier.) *England*.
Persian Greyhound. (Ancestor of the Saluki.) *Persia*.
Phu Quoc Dog. (Guard dog.) *Indo-China*.
Pittenweem Terrier. (Small terrier.) *Scotland*.
Polish Water Dog. (Medium gundog.) *Poland*.
Potsdam Greyhound. (Small coursing dog.) *Italy*.
Roseneath Terrier. (Small terrier.) *Scotland*.
Rough Beagle. (Small hunting dog.) *England*.
Russian Retriever. (Large gundog.) *Russia*.
Rough Pintsch. (Medium terrier.) *Germany*.
Seidenspitz. (Small toydog.) *Germany*.
Shropshire Terrier. (Ancestral terrier.) *England*.
Smithfield Collie. (Medium-sized herding dog.) *England*.
Snap Dog. (Ancestor of Whippet and terriers.) *England*.
Southern Hound. (Large hunting dog.) *England*.
Sudan Greyhound. (Small coursing dog.) *Sudan*.
Talbot. (Large hunting dog.) *Britain*.
Tie Dog. (Ancient Mastiff.) *Britain*.
Toy Bulldog. (Small companion dog.) *Britain*.
Toy Bull Terrier. (Small pet dog.) *Britain*.
Trawler Spaniel. (Miniature spaniel.) *England*.
Truffle Dog. (Rough variety of poodle.) *France*.
Ulmer Dog. (Early form of Great Dane.) *Germany*.
Welsh Hound. (Large hunting dog.) *Wales*.
Welsh Setter. (Medium black and tan setter.) *Wales*.
Wire-Haired Black and Tan Terrier. (Small terrier.) *England*.
Wurtemburg Pointer. (Large heavy gundog.) *Germany*.

INDEX